THE ANNOTATED
JULES VERNE

Twenty Thousand Leagues under the Sea

. . . This water which surrounded me was but another air. . . . Above me was the calm surface of the sea. Engraving from the original edition (1870).

THE ANNOTATED
JULES VERNE

Twenty Thousand Leagues under the Sea

The Only Completely Restored and Annotated Edition

WALTER JAMES MILLER

THOMAS Y. CROWELL COMPANY
New York   Established 1834

ACKNOWLEDGMENTS

Bonnie E. Nelson hunted down all the period illustrations and helped with the research. The New York Public Library photographed twenty three engravings from their copy of the original French edition. *The New York Times* supplied a map of the Red Sea area (permission to use this copyright material is acknowledged on page 203). Luigi Pelletieri and his Educational Photo Service prepared all the other prints. The Library of Congress supplied photostats of the original French text. Burt Britton of the Strand Book Store in Manhattan gave generous help in locating rare books. The basic idea of an *Annotated Jules Verne* is the brainchild of the editorial staff of Thomas Y. Crowell Company. My editor there, Hugh Rawson, has presided fondly but permissively over its development.

WJM

DESIGNED BY ABIGAIL MOSELEY

Manufactured in the United States of America

Library of Congress Cataloging in Publication Data

Miller, Walter James, date
   The annotated Jules Verne, Twenty thousand leagues under the sea.

   Bibliography: p.
   Includes index.
      1. Verne, Jules, 1828–1905. Vingt mille lieues sous les mers. I. Verne, Jules, 1828–1905. Vingt mille lieues sous les mers. 1976. II. Title.
PQ2469.V43M5 1976   843'.8   76–10968

ISBN 0–690–01151–2

1 2 3 4 5 6 7 8 9 10

CONTENTS

FOREWORD

A New Look at Jules Verne

Why There Are Two Jules Vernes

Verne experts agree: Verne's books are wasted on young people. "It's just as monstrous to give them to children to read," exclaims Raymond Roussel, "as it is to give them the Fables of Fontaine which are so profound that few adults can appreciate them." Another French critic, Jean Chesneaux, thinks that calling Verne a writer for children is an "alibi" used by people who cannot face the full force of Verne's ideology. There are passages in *Twenty Thousand Leagues under the Sea,* he notes, in which Verne's "technical considerations and strange assonances . . . have absolutely nothing to do with children."

Apparently millions of Continental Europeans agree: Jules Verne is essentially an author for adults. Year after year, Frenchmen, Germans, Italians buy millions and millions of copies of Verne's novels in adult editions. And Continental critics and cultural historians of all persuasions—"pop," psychoanalytic, sociological, structuralist—find that Verne has the self-renewing mythic power to challenge every generation anew.

Yet in America and England, readers and critics alike seem unaware that Verne can be read with profit by minds of all ages. Rather uneasily, for reasons we'll discover later, the British science-fiction writer Brian W. Aldiss sums it up this way: Verne's "books are regarded as fit merely for boys."

But how can there be a mature, "profound," challenging Verne for Europeans, and a juvenile Verne for us? What is it in Verne that can so excite Roussel, Chesneaux, and millions of other Europeans, and that we know nothing about? What are we missing? And how come?

This book—which is a combination nostalgia trip and exposé—is dedicated to finding the answers. We can get our first clues by taking a closer look at these two Vernes.

For more than a century now, Continental readers have taken it for granted that one of Verne's outstanding talents is his ability to appeal to all levels of intellect at once. Originally a Verne novel might run serially in a children's review, a "family" magazine, or an adult journal. But by the time it appeared in book form, it was being discussed by everyone from schoolboys and the ironworkers of Indret to the scientist Joseph Bertrand and the feminist author George Sand. Then as now, children would so thrill to Verne's basic story that they could wade right through his advanced mathematics and political satire looking for the next passage of "adventure." Meanwhile, European grown-ups have always soaked up Verne as painless "adult education" in matters scientific. Many laymen owe to Verne their first lessons in the mathematics of "escape velocity" in space travel and the problems of classifying marine life. And if working scientists have read Verne "with great respect"—as the European-born scientist Wernher von Braun tells us—it's because Verne always did his scientific homework "so carefully." Science-fiction buffs on the Continent cherish stories of how Verne so fanatically checked his mathematics with his cousin, a *lycée* professor; his hydrographics with his brother, a naval officer; and his applied physics with a friendly mining engineer.

Today European adults appreciate Verne for his political and social prophecies as well as for his scientific forecasts. For Verne not only foresaw the ecology crisis and the possibility of sailing under the polar ice caps. He also predicted the renascence of the African peoples, the industrialization of "backward" China, the smoldering of French separatism in Canada, the rise of the American Goliath. He warned about the prostitution of science by new power elites: by brutal State dictatorships, by subtle private financiers, and by the military-industrial complex.

Europeans are now hotly debating Verne's "real" politics because he gave major roles in his books to every shade of political and social opinion, from communism and utopian socialism to anti-Semitism and proto-fascism. They find him "relevant" today because he explored "alternatives," all varieties of nonconformism, from vagabondism to guerrilla warfare to philosophical anarchism. Indeed, Chesneaux ranks Verne with H. G. Wells as a major writer of political fiction.

Continental intellectuals enjoy, too, the fact that Verne stands up well against each new wave of literary criticism. Sociological critics see Verne as one of the first modern novelists to promote the anticolonialist and the dropout to the rank of Hero. Psychoanalytic critics explain Verne's perennial appeal by saying that everyone can identify with Verne's basic concerns: the restless search for the perfect father, the need of brothers to unite in adversity. Writers closer to the Jungian school stress Verne's "instinctive" ability to conjure up archetypes like the vulcanian powers, the journey of initiation, the blessed city. They judge some Verne characters, of course, not as personalities expected to "develop" but as mythic types. Leading structuralists delight in Verne's "oneiric [dream] mathematics." And Europe's new psychohistorians seem concerned with how fiercely Verne guarded the wells of his creative energy from everyone's scrutiny—including his own.

In short, sophisticated Continentals act as though they still have a lot to learn from Jules Verne.

But in today's Anglo-American world, strange to say, adults usually regard Verne as an author they have outgrown. They fondly recall him as a great "prophet of science" as they buy him, for their children, in editions illustrated for ten-year-olds. No, English-speaking adults don't remember being much impressed by any systematic social or political explorations in Verne. But then, they might tell you, Verne's specific content isn't that memorable: his characters are so thin, his narration so jerky.

Surprisingly, even those Anglo-American adults who stoutly defend science fiction as "mature" reading still tend to disparage Verne. He makes childish errors in mathematics, they recall, and he's lazy, pretentious, superficial in treating even the basic science of his own day. Some adult science fiction aficionados will tell you that *Galaxy* magazine once charged—and "proved" —that "Verne can get away with anything, and he does." And when Aldiss came to give us our first mature history of science fiction—his *Billion Year Spree* (1973)—he said, with that same uneasiness, "Verne seems fusty now."

Obviously the American *Galaxy* and the German-born von Braun are not talking about the same author. And by now you have surmised the simple truth. The English-speaking world has never had a fair chance to know the real Jules Verne. After you finish this book, you might even agree with me that some of Verne has in effect been suppressed in English-speaking countries. In any event, these are the objective facts:

> Some of Verne's best books are crudely abridged in English. Others are simply not yet available in our language. What is available is often badly translated, full of literary and technical errors that are not Verne's.
>
> Passages omitted from these "standard translations" are often Verne's most heavily political, philosophical, and scientific passages. They include some of Verne's finest literary efforts, too. These cuts—often subtracting 30 percent to 40 percent of Verne's text from the English editions—naturally weaken his story line, his characterization, his humor, and the integrity of his ideas.

You see the ironic consequences. First, the English version of Verne has been fumigated of much of his intellectual, adult message. And Verne's oeuvre has been damaged immeasurably as art. Second, almost all serious criticism of Verne to appear in English—from the famous *Galaxy* attack to Aldiss's uneasy conclusions—has been based on these mangled, incomplete "standard translations." And so, while Europe enjoys all of Verne either in the original or in complete translations fit for adult consumption, the English-language world has a Verne "fit merely for boys."

That strange disparity doubtless accounts for Aldiss's discomfort in his judgment of Verne. On the one hand, Aldiss obviously reviewed the "English" Verne before he came to the inevitable conclusions: Verne's "negative qualities" make him unsuitable for adult readers. On the other hand, shortly before he went to press (1973), Aldiss surely read the English version of Chesneaux's *The Political and Social Ideas of Jules Verne* (1972). That alone would have tipped Aldiss off to the fact that Europeans know a better Verne than we do. Perhaps Aldiss also perused my essay "Jules Verne in America" which prefaced a 1965 edition of *Twenty Thousand Leagues*. That essay was intended to blow the whistle on the "standard translations," but I was sure nobody had heard. No matter. The important thing now is that Aldiss, using a far more widely read medium—a history of science fiction—has been able to blow a louder whistle and he certainly is being heard. He says:

> The poverty of English translations of Verne . . . has . . . diminished his chance of better critical appraisal. . . . A good translation of his best novels might effect a revaluation of his vast *oeuvre*.

In other words, it's time to take a new look at Jules Verne.

And that's what our present book is all about. I can promise you, this new look will surely increase Verne's "chance of better critical appraisal." It will surely "effect a revaluation."

I called this venture a nostalgia trip and an exposé. It's also a casebook and a do-it-yourself kit.

It's a nostalgia trip because we'll revisit the wide-open world of Jules Verne. We'll travel back to a romantic age that saw in science a guarantee of man's fulfillment on earth. Indeed, this is a voyage to those days when technology still had a chance to deliver what it was promising to man, in return for what he was paying. Nostalgia will help us see where—maybe why—something went wrong.

It's an exposé with a happy ending. True, it will be a sad thing for you— as it was for me—to discover how something like character assassination was committed against a great man a century ago. And covered up ever since. But we shall have the pleasure of clearing his name.

It's a do-it-yourself kit because you can sort out and examine any or all of the evidence to your own satisfaction. You might even find some evidence I have not yet seen myself.

This is how I plan this trip. Since I hope I have created a new curiosity about Verne, I'll begin with a new biographical sketch of him, the first in English to take psychohistorical liberties. Then, since we are going—in the main part of the book—to investigate their handiwork, I'll tell you what I know about the men and women who produced the "standard" English version of Verne: the people who created a Verne fit only for juvenile readers. Then I'll present, as Exhibit A, the standard version of *Twenty Thousand Leagues under the Sea*—but in a new context.

That is, I shall restore, in my own new translation [and in brackets like these], all the many passages omitted from the "standard" version. These restorations will range from an important phrase all the way up to several scenes thousands of words in length. All together, they constitute about 23 percent of Verne's text.

Second, I shall offer you a smorgasbord of marginal comments. Some of these memos to you invite you to consider the effect those omissions have had on Anglo-American opinion of Verne. A few notes will suggest that Verne's translator was ideologically—maybe even politically—motivated when he cut Verne's text. In other notes I shall point out how the translator's mistakes in rendering Verne's science, mathematics, and even story line and dialogue have also damaged Verne's critical reputation. I delight in calling your attention to autobiographical and psychohistorical elements in Verne's story: for example, how his description of New York was based on his own visit there, why he was so obsessed with "floating islands." Such notes show how Verne drew equally well on both his objective experience and his fantasy life, maybe even on his repressed, unconscious memory.

Many annotations supply background information on matters well known in Verne's day but maybe obscure today. For example, Verne's readers in the 1870s had read repeated reports of sea monsters sighted in the Atlantic; they were convinced that physiognomists and chirognomists could detect character at a glance; they followed with avid interest the career of Virginia scientist Matthew Maury. My notes on such topical matters may help readers to appreciate Verne's method as a science-fiction writer. Indeed, I hope some of these marginal glosses will anticipate and answer questions that occur to you as you read the text itself: Why didn't Captain Nemo use a periscope? What's the secret behind the "artificial language" spoken on board the *Nautilus*? How could such a careful writer as Verne make such a blooper in the use of his underwater breathing apparatus? And I provide recent information on problems the novel deals with: Was Darwin right in his theory of atoll formation? Did the Israelites really cross the Red Sea? Which of Verne's predictions have come true?

At crucial points, my notes will evaluate Verne's literary maneuvers, his literary relations with Walter Scott and Edgar Allan Poe, his talent for social and political as well as scientific prophecy.

Third, throughout the book, keyed to both Verne's text and the annotations, are scattered some 150 illustrations from the period of Verne's adult life: roughly from 1850 to 1905. There are twenty-three engravings from the original 1870 edition of *Twenty Thousand Leagues*. These were rendered by "Hildibrand" from drawings by Alphonse de Neuville and Edouard Riou. Some of them Verne himself posed for. Many of them are nowhere else available to English readers today. I also include three engravings from other Verne novels discussed in the annotations, and a reproduction of Félix Nadar's famous 1853 photograph of Verne. The bulk of the illustrations are engravings from scientific treatises, periodicals, textbooks, a popular 1873 encyclopedia, all such as Verne's original readers themselves might have consulted.

Once we have taken this long, luxurious "new look" at Verne's masterpiece and at his world in general, I shall offer, in the afterword, the first critical analysis in English of *Twenty Thousand Leagues* to be based on the complete, reconstructed novel.

By then, we should have taken a big step toward rehabilitating Verne's reputation in America. By then we should have come much closer to seeing the real Jules Verne. And maybe as a consequence soon there will be only one Verne.

A Psychobiographical Sketch of Jules Verne

"I feel I am the least known of men," Verne wrote to a tactless journalist who persisted in grilling the novelist about his personal life. "A writer interests . . . the world only as a writer."

Verne, I believe I can show, had well-established reasons for maintaining fanatic privacy and leading a double life. Apparently he came to feel that his artistic productivity was linked to the Unknown in his makeup. He wanted to keep it that way. He destroyed most of his private papers and left no serious autobiographical writings. His official biographer, a niece by marriage, Marguerite Allotte de la Fuÿe, had sole access to his papers that survived. In *Jules Verne, sa vie, son oeuvre* (1928),* still our main source of information, she tries to tell his life story while protecting the family secrets. She does not, for example, commit to print the identity of "a wretched youth" who tried to assassinate Verne in 1886—he was a relative—and she is coy and peek-a-boo about "a unique siren" in Verne's life.

Nevertheless, from her slight study we still get the unmistakable impression of a sensitive man who wore a mask in social and even family life, and saved his feelings, opinions, hopes, fears for his writing. For much of the subject matter of his sixty-five volumes of fiction, he drew on events in his own past, often his recent past. That actually makes a psychohistorian's task easier than we might at first imagine. If Verne deliberately channeled himself almost entirely into his art, then the art, where it can be linked to known facts of his life, could serve us like a diary. So Verne was actually giving the journalist the truest directions possible.

Without attempting anything like the full psychohistory that needs to be written, we can approximate such an approach here in limited ways that serve our purpose. First we should outline the crucial situations in Verne's life. Then we might interpret those situations as they relate to his fictional content and method.

In 1825 Pierre Verne, son of a judge, bought a legal practice in Nantes, a seaport town on the Loire River some forty miles from the open sea. On the nearby Ile Feydeau, he met Sophie Allotte de la Fuÿe. Married in 1827, they lived with the bride's parents and had five children: Jules on February 8, 1828, another son a year later, then three girls. Jules's closest relations were to be with brother Paul.

Their father was known as "a lawyer with the soul of a classical poet," possibly because he dabbled in translation and read Walter Scott and James Fenimore Cooper to his family. But the word "classical," I think, must be taken to emphasize Reason: Pierre Verne sternly believed in the logic of clocks, of statute books, and of puritanical piety. When his growing practice allowed him to buy a summer house in nearby Chantenay, he trained a marine telescope on a distant monastery clock, and checked his strict household schedule against it. People said he knew exactly how many steps he had to take from home to office, where he dealt mainly in maritime law and insurance. Pierre decreed that Jules would go to law school and take over his father's practice.

Jules's mother was descended from merchants who had settled the Ile Feydeau in 1723. In her attic stood sea chests packed with West Indies bills of lading and other maritime documents. Jules's maternal relations and ancestors included a portrait artist, a seafarer who claimed to have discovered a Northwest Passage, Norman fishermen, and a quixotic grandfather whose

---

* *Jules Verne, His Life, His Work.* Translated by Erik de Mauny (1954) and now out of print.

whereabouts were often unknown. Jules thought of his mother as imagination, his father as rationality.

The brothers discovered early that their Ile Feydeau was naturally shaped like a ship, pointing downstream; original settlers had emphasized the similarity by rounding out the "stern." Here the boys lived in constant reminder of the nautical world. Fishermen brought in their catch and dried their nets. Fishwives cut open the cod, displayed them flat, shouted their wares. Nutbrown sailors came ashore with purple parrots on their shoulders and exotic tales to tell to gaping boys. Paul at least was free to dream of going to sea. When the Loire flooded in March, the brothers stared out their window at an island that seemed awash and even adrift.

When Jules was six, he went to a boarding school run by "Widow" Sambain. One lesson Jules never forgot was that the lady's sea-captain husband had sailed away after their marriage never to return: She believed he was stranded Crusoelike on a tropic isle. Later Jules and Paul boarded at a Latin secondary school. Jules became "king of the playground." In the classroom, when the teacher stepped out, he demonstrated ability to put familiar facts into new combinations. There was a horse-carriage service in Nantes; a steamboat with a tall smokestack plied the Loire. On the blackboard Jules designed a carriage powered by steam.

Early one summer morning in 1839, Jules stole out of the Chantenay cottage, walked to a sailors' inn in Nantes whence he was rowed out to the three-masted *Coralie*. The captain studied the narrow-waisted but strong-shouldered boy distinguished by beautiful teeth, a shock of hair like red-gold flame, and a penetrating gaze. The captain accepted Jules as cabin boy. The ship upped anchor and headed for the Atlantic.

His father was already piecing together reports from townspeople. Pierre knew that the *Coralie,* en route to the West Indies, would be on the Loire for hours before she reached the open sea. He knew the steamboat would get to Paimboeuf before the *Coralie.* And there the captain surrendered his cabin boy to the maritime lawyer. At home, Pierre caned Jules and sentenced him to bread and water. Sophie made her son take a vow: "Henceforth, I'll travel only in my imagination."

Skimping on his Latin lessons at the Nantes *lycée,* Jules devoured the works of Victor Hugo and Alexandre Dumas. Secretly, often writing in a bookstore, he composed poems and verse drama. At sixteen he became a full-time clerk in his father's office, copying wills and contracts, studying codes civil and criminal, while thinking of new libretti. These he would read to the town's appreciative literary *cercle.* Once he read a verse tragedy to a select group of cousins, including his peer, the sixteen-year-old Caroline, whom he loved. But she laughed just like the others. His family had assigned him the role of clown: They assumed his tragedy to be a parody. When Caroline and Jules were eighteen, she a graceful woman, he an awkward boy, he proposed. She treated it as another joke. When she became engaged to a rival, Jules fell into Byronic melancholy and cynicism.

Alarmed, Pierre and Sophie contrived to have him miss the next family reunion, planned for Caroline's wedding. Jules was sent to Paris to take the preliminary law examination; he managed to cram in a lot of time in the theatrical district. When he heard that the "execrable marriage" had indeed taken place, he wrote home: "I'll get my revenge by killing her . . . cat."

In October 1848 Paul, launched on the career of his own choice, was shipping out to the West Indies as a naval apprentice. Back home, Jules became erratic, elusive, the subject of local gossip. His parents decided he had better pursue his legal studies in Paris. He wrote ahead to composer Aristide Hignard: "I'm finally leaving, since I wasn't wanted here. But some day they will all see what stuff he was made of, the poor young man they knew as Jules Verne." The pronoun "they" obviously referred to others besides Caroline; again revenge seems indicated.

In November he settled on the Left Bank. Dutifully he attended law lectures but spent every spare moment either with literary people or with characters of his own creation. He was one of those young artists-to-be who dined at Monte Cristo on dishes prepared by Dumas himself. And Jules was in Dumas's box in the Théâtre-Historique when *The Three Musketeers* premiered. Soon Verne had three plays of his own to show Dumas. In 1850 Verne's verse comedy *Broken Straws* enjoyed a twelve-night run. It was good enough to start a rumor that Dumas himself had collaborated on it, and to be subsidized in book form by a rich friend. When it was staged later in Nantes, one critic called it risqué. Pierre agreed. Reflecting bitterness toward Caroline, it was at least misogynist. Jules submitted his thesis, passed his final examinations, but, waiting for conferral of his degree, continued to write songs, revues, operettas, short stories, essays. Not until his father summoned him home to join the Verne law firm did Jules let his family know the truth: He was going to stay in Paris to become a writer.

Jules's epistolary maneuvers seem to me significant at this point. Ostensibly protesting to his mother that of course he was managing to live on his writer's earnings, he would then supply comic descriptions of his food and apparel that would elicit from her secret packages of both. He wrote to pious Pierre about the death of a friend; himself protesting those conventional beliefs most calculated to interest his father, Jules still made the friend's impious way of life the main subject of the matter.

Among Jules's early stories is one about a clock-maker who comes to grief because he believes the escapement mechanism can take the place of the human soul. Oddly, Pierre enjoyed this story; it convinced him that after all his son had a mission as a writer. Still, while publishing fiction and enjoying a mild success in comic opera, Verne was forced to work for low pay for three years as secretary of the Théâtre-Lyrique. On a visit home he mounted an all-out campaign to win a Nantes beauty, Laurence Janmar. He wrote and starred in a skit produced at a costume ball she attended. Having won her obvious admiration, he was betrayed by his comic genius. Overhearing her complain that her whalebone corset was killing her, he ejaculated: "If only I could fish for whales on that coast!" (In French, the word for *coast, côte,* is also the word for *rib.*) Indignant, her father forbade her to dance with Jules. Next day, Pierre's formal proposal on behalf of his son was rejected.

Twice humiliated in love, sexually lonely, Verne was now willing to make compromises and take long detours. Verne attended a friend's wedding in

Amiens and fell in love with the bride's sister, a widow with two girls. Honorine Anne Hébé Morel née du Fraysne de Viane had dainty dancing feet, laughing eyes, a good soprano voice, and a clear complexion. Her brother made easy money on the stock exchange. This shocked Pierre, especially when Jules decided to borrow money from Pierre to buy himself a seat on the *Bourse* (Stock Exchange) to support a family of four. In 1857 Verne married Honorine and began a frantic gamble on being able to write in the early hours before going to work as a stockbroker.

His romantic love withered fast. He was soon spending his spare time in artistic circles again, taking long trips to Scotland and Scandinavia with Hignard. Verne returned from Norway just in time for the birth of his son Michel on August 3, 1861.

But his romantic composition suddenly flowered. Three of his plays were produced, and he sold a novel to the publisher Pierre Hetzel, a liberal democrat just returned from political exile. They signed a twenty-year contract calling for a minimum of forty novels. Jules quit the Exchange with a speech on the floor: "I have written a novel in a new genre, one all my own."

Five Weeks in a Balloon, published in 1863, established the ideal Verne formula. It combines the kind of scientific invention and the area of exploration most in the news at the time: in this case, aerial travel and Africa. And it established Verne's audience and their expectations. He proved to be predicting developments they themselves would live to see in a matter of years. And so he earned their confidence even when he was extrapolating far into the future. By the time all sixty-five *Voyages Extraordinary* (as the series was supertitled) were in print, Verne had predicted virtually every major technical development of the twentieth century. He had also explored every area of the globe not only for its exotic geography but also for its political dynamite.

By 1866 Verne's spectacular successes were supporting a fashionable town house in Paris, a cottage at Le Crotoy on the Somme, a small yacht with a crew of two. The *Saint Michel*—as he would call each of his three successive yachts—became his "floating study" and his male retreat. In 1867 he and Paul journeyed to America on the *Great Eastern.* He returned ready to invent its submarine equivalent. Most of *Twenty Thousand Leagues under the Sea* was written on board his yacht as Jules tirelessly crisscrossed the English Channel. Honorine would complain, fruitlessly, that he was hardly home but planning to sail on the next tide. As soon as he finished his submarine epic, he mined more of his notes on his *Great Eastern* trip for the story of *A Floating City* (1871).

When *Twenty Thousand Leagues* appeared in January 1870, Ferdinand de Lesseps, builder of the Suez Canal, nominated Verne for the Legion of Honor. Soon after Verne received the decoration, Emperor Louis Napoleon declared war on Germany. Verne was mustered into the coast guards as commander of the *Saint Michel* with rotating crews totaling twelve men. While they patrolled the Bay of the Somme, Verne finished four novels, including *Measuring a Meridian* (1872) in which he depicts the absurdity of war and nationalism. Exactly as he had predicted in his letters, France was forced to pay huge indemnities to Germany and then suffer civil war. When it was over, he learned that his cousin, Henri Garcet, the professor who had checked his mathematics, had died in the siege of Paris. Then, just before Verne was awarded a major prize by the prestigious French Academy, Pierre died of a stroke. Verne moved his family to Amiens, roughly midway between Paris and Le Crotoy.

There he finished *Around the World in Eighty Days* (1873), which became internationally famous even as it appeared in *Le Temps,* one of several adult journals in which he serialized. Foreign correspondents in Paris cabled home summaries of each installment. Adults all over the world placed bets on the outcome of the next chapter. Cunard and White Star tried to bribe Verne to have his hero finish his trip on one of their liners. In 1874 a stage version ran for eight hundred performances in Paris and then set out for record runs in other theater capitals. This was the first of several Verne novels to succeed in stage adaptation.

By 1876 he could buy a magnificent yacht from the Marquis de Préaulx; he engaged a crew of ten. Usually with Paul, Michel, Hetzel's son, and other men, sometimes with his wife and daughters, Verne sailed to all the ports of Europe and North Africa. Everywhere he was honored: by garrison commanders, diplomats, heads of state, royalty, the Pope. He became so tired of royal invitations he once upped anchor fast to escape the Prince of Wales. In Amiens he gave costume balls with elaborate entertainment for up to eight hundred guests. And then one night, as he was returning from his daily research stint in the library to the house where he had composed twenty novels in fourteen years, he saw a young man, standing near the garden gate, aiming a revolver. The first shot hit the stone lintel, the second struck Verne in the left leg. A servant came out to find the novelist walking up to Gaston Verne, Paul's son, to disarm him. The "wretched youth," a former diplomatic attaché, was suffering from persecution mania.

While Verne lay abed with a bullet in his shin that could not be removed, both his mother and Hetzel died. He limped to Nantes to settle his mother's estate, discovered his wound made it impossible for him to be active on deck, and sold *Saint Michel III* to the Prince of Montenegro. From Chantenay he wrote: "The air, once full of perfume of flowers and fruit trees, is now vitiated with a pall of black smoke."

He startled his conservative wife, and some neighbors cold-shouldered him, when in 1888 he ran for the Amiens Town Council on a progressive ticket. He won and was returned to office for sixteen years. He took a decent humanitarian stand on some issues but was otherwise most conventional in public office: He championed the rights of traveling performers but told female graduates to beware the pitfalls of feminism.

His 1894 letters to Paul reveal the nature of his literary and personal life. "Help me finish *Propeller Island*. . . . correct the hydrographic errors." Were there any mistakes in displacement, tonnage, calculation of motive power? Apologizing for not showing up for the launching of the yacht *Jules Verne,* at which Paul was left to represent him, Jules explained: "I bear too much sorrow to take part in these family festivities. All gaiety has become intolerable to me, my character has changed radically, I have suffered blows from which I shall not recover." It is assumed, on the basis of veiled hints given by his family biographer, that Verne was suffering the loss—by death or desertion?—of a mistress. That and other matters outlined here can be better developed when we reach certain points in our annotations.

In 1897 the now-famous Georges Méliès made an experimental film version of Verne's *From the Earth to the Moon* (1865). In 1898 Simon Lake, cruising off Florida in his experimental submarine, ran into a hurricane. While two hundred ships in the area took a terrible drubbing, Lake simply submerged to a calm depth. He notified Verne that this advantage of submarine travel, predicted in *Twenty Thousand Leagues,* had become a reality. But while Verne's ideas were achieving technological immortality, the prophet himself, always hard at work, was pressing the limits of personal mortality. After 1900 he suffered cataracts and deafness. Diabetes killed him at the age of seventy-seven on March 24, 1905. Five thousand people went to the funeral. He left nine volumes of *Voyages Extraordinary* for posthumous publication.

How had Verne's life circumstances influenced the method and content of his fiction? How did his art supply intimate details of his life and his true feelings? Verne himself ridiculed direct dissection of character in *The Day of an American Journalist in 2889* (1889). But my point here is that he revealed himself by indirect means whenever he sought expression in analogy, metaphor, pun, and the parable of plot.

His main concerns as a novelist, conscious and unconscious, first took shape on the Ile Feydeau. His mother's home and family represented outward romantic expansion into the unknown; his father's aim in the maritime world was to impose on it the home-based notions of classical law and order. Verne's series of novels and short stories would be called: *Voyages Extraordinary: Worlds Known and Unknown.*

Two examples suffice to show how the boy's Feydeau years provided theme and quality for the man's books. Mistress Sambain's pertinacious hope in her husband's Crusoelike survival prefigures Verne's own Crusoe obsession in such works as *The Mysterious Island* (1875), *School for Robinsons* (1882), *Mistress Branican* (1891). The boy's fascination with Feydeau awash produced such works as *The Fur Country* (1873) and *Propeller Island* (1895). It figures so prominently in *Twenty Thousand Leagues* that we can use our annotations to show in detail how Verne was able productively to tap the child in himself.

The *Coralie* day is of course traumatic and central. It shows that the eleven-year-old already knew that secret planning was the only answer to the cold patriarchal logic of Pierre. When Jules promised his mother, "Henceforth I will travel only in my imagination," he apparently meant "secret imagination." And henceforth, whenever he had to express himself, he might still hide his real feelings behind his mask of humor. That would work against him with Caroline and Laurence. It would seduce him into the long detour of musical comedy, that genre that both affects and denies the real. And even in the most serious scenes in his novels, characters would suddenly line up like a chorus and shout three cheers. Look for something like that when the gray old gunner fires a shot in *Twenty Thousand Leagues*. Notice how the narrator, even in serious predicaments, will mock himself.

After the *Coralie* crisis, then, Jules outwardly followed his father's plans for Jules-the-barrister while inwardly he was bending those plans to his own secret purposes. Thus from the age of sixteen to twenty-two he contrived to be supported by his father apparently as a candidate for law practice but in reality as an apprentice to literature. When the shock of deception hit Nantes, Pierre did not (so far as Mme. Allotte allows us to know) act as one deceived. But neither did well-to-do barrister support threadbare author.

During these difficult years, Verne reported in a letter home that to reach his attic room he had to climb 120 steps. Knowing his father's reputation for reducing life to arithmetic, and Verne's love of double meaning, we realize that Jules was joking about the Pierre in himself. In another letter to Nantes he asked that his copy of Garcet's *Elements of Mechanics* be mailed to him. Jules had rejected his father's profession of law but not his father's penchant for logic; Jules simply transferred this talent from law to science. In a third letter, he admired his mother's imagination, "faster than a tropical waterspout, . . . very curious when I compare it with the way my own mind works." He was grappling with the fact that to find himself as an artist, he had to combine Pierrelike reason with Sophielike fantasy. But even after such intuitions, he needed a decade to tune up the proper tension between these forces in his makeup. Then he would marry the objective strictures of science to the subjective liberties allowed the arts, and produce a new genre: science fiction.

Verne's letters home also show how those years of tactful deception and/or humorous concealment were helping to shape his literary style. He was becoming a master of irony, saying one thing and meaning another. On the glinting surface he would run a current of conventional sentiments; but the main force of his message was in the dark undertow. How patriarchal logic can survive such an undertow is indicated in Pierre's response to "Master Zacharius." There the clock worshipper is characterized as a shallow, mechanical person; but Pierre saw only the overt, pious message: Zacharius was a Faust defying God, and Jules's conventional punishment for a Faust reassured Pierre. And apparently Pierre also missed the point when Jules punned in the title of another story on the words *père* (father) and *pierre* (stone): "Père qui roule n'amasse pas mousse" ("A Rolling Father Gathers No Moss").

All his creative life Jules would play with variations on his father's clocklike regularity. Phileas Fogg, in *Around the World in Eighty Days* (1873), lives by the clock, triumphs, but remains a mechanical marvel. Captain Nemo, in *Twenty Thousand Leagues* (1870), is a much fuller person. He can foretell precisely that minute when the moon will lift his submarine off the coral reef where it is stranded. But he also can defy "civilization," play music rapturously, dream passionately of new breeds of men. Indeed, Captain Nemo reflects Verne's search for "the perfect father." In real life, according to the French psychoanalytic critic Marcel Moré, Verne found such a father-figure in Pierre Hetzel, his publisher. Since Verne's feelings toward this second Pierre in his life are revealed in a major scene in *Twenty Thousand Leagues*— where they mingle with echoes of the *Coralie* episode—we shall explore them in our annotations.

If we consider Jules's three failures in sexual romance we have the final elements necessary for understanding the relationships between his life and art. His father's choice of Cooper and Scott as family reading had predisposed Jules for asexual preferences in literature at least. Caroline's scorn for him, linked to his first gauche literary efforts, embittered him toward women. In his courtship of Laurence, the vengeance that "respectable" father and daughter took on him for his Rabelaisian pun—which expressed a still healthy interest in sex—further embittered him. Maybe it helped predispose him for the sexual double standard. For when his marriage failed, he took the conventional way out: Honorine now stood for "respectability" and the "unique siren" (whom we shall return to in the annotations) stood for uninhibited Rabelaisian love of life. One of Verne's few remarks as Councilman to be preserved expresses this perfectly. He was opposed to letting women as well as men vote on the actors to be engaged by the civic theater. Reason: It would force both kinds of ladies to rub shoulders around the ballot box—*"les dames comme il faut, et les dames comme il en faut."* Without benefit of Verne's pun, this translates: "ladies we must respect and ladies we cannot do without."

We can put this all together for a new overview of Jules Verne's life and work. Verne learned early to express dutiful conformity in his personal, civic, and social life and to express his passionate nonconformity only in his art. Whatever rebelling he seemed to permit himself in real life was quite conventionalized: It was "understood" that an affluent middle-class male was entitled to enjoy a mistress so long as he maintained the pretense of monogamy. In his home as in his political speeches, Verne sanctimoniously fostered domestic careers and supportive roles for women. But in his life as an artist, he read, corresponded and socialized with, and wrote about the feminist and "adulteress" George Sand. In his Councillor's pronouncements, Verne stood for law and order. But his books—for example, *The Steam House* (1880), *Keraban the Inflexible* (1883), *Islands on Fire* (1884), *Family without a Name* (1889), *Foundling Mick* (1893), *The Survivors of the "Jonathan"* (1909)—simply throng with rebels and dissidents.

Most interesting of all is the way Verne developed those ironic letter-writing techniques into a major fictional maneuver. In *The Survivors of the "Jonathan,"* Djer, a libertarian rebel and social outcast, seems at the end to have failed in his political experiments. Conventional beliefs ostensibly prevail, as the resolution of the plot seems to indicate. Yet in the course of Djer's struggles, he achieves nobility and respect, and his philosophy has been seriously expounded and illustrated in detail. Or, as you will see in the (reconstructed) *Twenty Thousand Leagues,* Captain Nemo takes an aggressive anticolonialist position and demonstrates systematically the principles of philosophical anarchism. Of course, he must suffer the conventional remorse at the end. Yet for the main course of the action, he is the most heroic and principled figure, and he remains the most memorable character.

In fiction, then, as in correspondence, Verne contrived always to give alternative views a thorough airing between his respectful salutation and his complimentary close.

This is not exactly akin to Milton's unconscious glorification of Satan. For the great mass of *Paradise Lost* still leaves us with the impression that the Establishment is in firm and rightful control. In Verne the proportions tip well over the other way.

A full psychobiography of Verne, our sketch here suggests, might demonstrate that repression of freedom by Father World logic intensifies the use of imagination; that the Mother World imagination reacts, through metaphor and parable, by exploring alternatives to the Father World. It might suggest, too, that the literary maneuver known as irony is born of a need to attack patriarchal logic while pretending to honor it. In any event, our sketch surely promises that *Twenty Thousand Leagues* is a richly psychobiographical novel, charged with Verne's feelings toward "Feydeau awash," the *Coralie* episode, his eleventh-hour rescue by Hetzel, and women.

Some Notes for Purists on Verne's Translators

A strange document was brewing in the Broad Street Academy in Philadelphia in April 1874. Mr. Edward Roth was writing a "Preface" to his translation of Verne's moon novels. First Mr. Roth explained how he had waited for five or six years while "not a single work of Jules Verne issued from the American press, except *Five Weeks in a Balloon.*" That lone translation contained "so many . . . mistakes . . . it must have been done in a hurry." Why had American publishers been so indifferent to the "Daniel Defoe of the nineteenth century"? Was it that his science was "too profound"?

Then, to Mr. Roth's further astonishment, American publishers suddenly chose to issue "hasty translations of Verne's work by English hands." These "spread like wild fire last year [1873] over the country and were everywhere hailed with the greatest delight by both young and old."

What astonished this Philadelphia teacher was not Verne's popularity— he had expected that, once Verne became available. No, what appalled Mr. Roth was that these British versions had been reprinted at all. ". . . through ignorance, incapacity, or prejudice," they, too, were full of errors and omitted "some of [Verne's] best passages."

And so Mr. Roth, as he explained at length, had decided that he would prepare truly accurate versions. And he would even "improve" on Verne— the word is his. (For example, he actually added situations to Verne's moon novels which are just pure Roth.)

Alas for America that Roth didn't simply publish a detailed exposé of those "hasty translations" while there was still time to prevent their becoming "standard." Even as Roth was posting the manuscript of his Verne-Roth moon stories, those "English hands" were at work on their version of the same books. These would prove Mr. Roth's suspicions beyond any doubt. Those British translators, "through ignorance, incapacity, or prejudice," were perfectly willing to foist incomplete and inaccurate versions of Verne on an unsuspecting public.

Hence today we have, ironically, at least two kinds of translations of Verne—some that give us less than Verne wrote and some that give us more.

To prepare for the main portion of this present book, we zoom in on just two pairs of "English hands." Main causes of Roth's indignation were Lewis Page Mercier and his sometime assistant, Eleanor E. King. Born in 1820, Lewis Mercier took his master's degree at Oxford and entered the Church. His first two publications reflect his inevitable (Oxonian) concern with classical literature: *A Manual of Greek Prosody* (1843) and *Selections from Aesop, Xenophon, and Anacreon* (1851). For the next two decades he wrote mainly on religious matters. We ought to keep his theological background in mind as we review later his handling of Verne's text. And so it might be interesting to consider the subjects of his religious publications. His tracts include *The Present European Crisis Viewed in its Relation to Prophecy* (1853), *The Principles of Christian Charity* (1855), *The Eucharistic Feast* (1868), and *Outlines of the Life of the Lord Jesus Christ* (1871, 1872). He also published some of his sermons, including *The Mystery of God's Providence,* preached on the occasion of the death of Prince Albert in 1861. In the 1870s he turned to translating current bestsellers from the Continent. His versions of Verne's *From the Earth to the Moon* and *A Trip Around It* appeared with this by-line: "Translated by Louis Mercier, M.A., (Oxon,), and Eleanor E. King." His versions of *Twenty Thousand Leagues* and *Around the World in Eighty Days* bore a different by-line: "Translated by Mercier Lewis." His last published work seems to have been the English edition of Carl Koldewey's *German Arctic Expedition of 1869–70,* "Translated and abridged by Louis Mercier."

His use of three versions of his name is interesting and maybe even significant. He chose to confer his real name, LEWIS PAGE MERCIER, only on his classical and religious works. Clearly those were closest to both his public image and his self-image. And just as clearly, his translations were not central to that image; he rather half-acknowledged them. But notice his two names for himself as translator—LOUIS MERCIER and MERCIER LEWIS. I sometimes feel that he put the stamp of LOUIS MERCIER on translations he himself had worked on directly, and the stamp of MERCIER LEWIS on translations he had farmed out, wholly or in part, to others. My annotations will show the reasons I have for thinking that *Twenty Thousand Leagues,* issued as a MERCIER LEWIS work, was done in collaboration: moreover, a collaboration very poorly coordinated.

For a century, Louis Mercier's, Mercier Lewis's, Edward Roth's, and other bad versions have constituted the "Verne" that American readers find in libraries, bookstores, and gift shops. Since these versions helped make Verne "fit merely for boys," it's appropriate that in hardcover they are available only with juvenile illustrations. Most popular among teachers for class use are certain inexpensive "abridged" editions—abridged by educational publishers apparently unaware that some Lewis and other versions were cut to begin with. Thus teachers inadvertently help perpetuate what Chesneaux called the "alibi" that Verne is only a juvenile author. Meanwhile, many Verne books once available in English are out of print. Some good libraries have only half a dozen titles.

Hopes for Verne's rehabilitation were raised in the 1960s, prematurely. Three paperback publishers issued new translations of one or two familiar titles. Here are some ironic results. The translator of the first new version of

Twenty Thousand Leagues apparently consulted Mercier Lewis whenever he was in doubt. Hence many of Lewis's worst errors were perpetuated. A second new version, while it corrected most of the traditional errors, was admittedly designed for young people and this obviously determined its tone and language. But it could boast a preface which, as I have said, did discuss the reasons America does not know the real Verne. A third translation came the closest yet to the "adult" Verne, in content at least. But like the others, it was issued only in paperback. This meant it was ignored by the critics. It is not available in typical libraries or regular bookshops. There is nothing in or on the book to explain how it differs from the standard version, or even to indicate that there is a Verne problem.

Such gestures have posed little threat to the Mercier Lewis monopoly. There are fifteen editions of the Mercier Lewis version of *Twenty Thousand Leagues* now in print in the United States alone.

The overall situation has not changed much, as Aldiss's 1973 conclusions indicated.

All of which meant that some more dramatic way of making a case for Verne's rehabilitation had yet to be devised. Sole credit for that belongs to the editors of Thomas Y. Crowell. They suggested an *Annotated Jules Verne* with adult illustrations, in permanent format, as the way to make our "case" heard and to meet the reader's needs. So here we have an edition of *Twenty Thousand Leagues under the Sea* that exposes typical crimes committed against Verne's reputation but, most of all, provides plenty of background and commentary for new appreciation of his talents.

WALTER JAMES MILLER

PART 1: CHAPTER I

A Shifting Reef[1]

The year 1866 was signalised by a remarkable incident, a mysterious and inexplicable phenomenon, which doubtless no one has yet forgotten. Not to mention rumours [2] which agitated the maritime population, and excited the public mind, even in the interior of continents, seafaring men were particularly excited. Merchants, common sailors, captains of vessels, skippers, both of Europe and America, naval officers of all countries, and the Governments of several states on the two continents, were deeply interested in the matter.

For some time past, vessels had been met by "an enormous thing," a long object, spindle-shaped, occasionally phosphorescent, and infinitely larger and more rapid in its movements than a whale.

The facts relating to this apparition (entered in various log-books) agreed in most respects as to the shape of the object or creature in question, the untiring rapidity of its movements, its surprising power of locomotion, and the peculiar life with which it seemed endowed. If it was a cetacean,[3] it surpassed in size all those hitherto classified in science.

[Neither Cuvier nor Lacépède, neither Duméril nor Quatrefages [4] would have admitted that such a monster could exist unless they themselves had seen it with their own eyes: the trained eyes of the scientist.]

Taking into consideration the mean of observations made at divers times,—rejecting the timid estimate of those who assigned to this object a length of two hundred feet, equally with the exaggerated opinions which set it down as a mile in width and three in length,—we might fairly conclude that this mysterious being surpassed greatly all dimensions admitted by the ichthyologists of the day, if it existed at all. And that it

1. *A Shifting Reef* The very words *Shifting Reef* were charged with excitement for both Verne and his original audience. Since 1861 they had been reading news accounts of sightings of giant squid in the Atlantic. These reports revived earlier speculations, mainly by Scandinavians, about sea monsters large enough to be mistaken for islands or reefs. Throughout this novel, Verne will play on his readers' interest in these developments. Besides, for Verne himself the notion of a *shifting reef* or a *floating island* had profound personal implications. Just notice how often he dwells on the idea in the opening chapters. This leads us, in Chapter VII, to a curious bit of psychohistory.

2. *signalised . . . rumours* The nineteenth-century British spellings used by Mercier Lewis, the translator, have been preserved in most American editions. For consistency's sake, we shall use them in the restored text as well. Our annotations, however, follow current American spelling practice, except when we quote directly from the translation.

3. *If it was a cetacean* That is, a whale, dolphin, porpoise, or other fishlike mammal. The term becomes important for our enjoyment of the action. Several species of cetacea will figure prominently in the narrative.

Baron Georges Cuvier as pictured on a medallion struck in his honor after his death in 1832. This illustration appeared on the title page of a memorial edition of his classic, *Le Règne Animal* (*The Animal Kingdom*).

4. *Cuvier . . . Quatrefages* Verne strives in all his fiction to educate us painlessly in the history of science. This first casual mention of Cuvier and Lacépède is typical of Verne's method: he will return to them later. They were leaders in man's effort to set up systems of classification true to nature. Bernard Germain Etienne de la Ville, comte de Lacépède (1756–1825) published his *History of Cetaceans* in 1804. Baron Georges Léopold Cuvier (1769–1832) laid the broad foundations for comparative anatomy and paleontology. The other two scientists were engaged in completing and correcting Cuvier's work.

Difficulties these men faced can be illustrated by a trap Cuvier fell into. It was not so easy in his day to observe sea life. He had to work largely from preserved specimens and published reports. Hence he occasionally overlooked the fact that fishes and cetaceans—like other animals—develop secondary sexual characteristics. They undergo dramatic changes during their growth. Cuvier actually described many such changes of development as different species, sometimes even as different genera.

As we shall see, Verne's characters are aware of some of these errors which had been discovered in Verne's lifetime. But the trap is still there today. For example, Professor J. Z. Young of the University of London wrote in 1975 that the "so-called pygmy blue whales . . . are probably

did exist was an undeniable fact; and, with that tendency which disposes the human mind in favour of the marvellous, we can understand the excitement produced in the entire world by this supernatural apparition. As to classing it in the list of fables, the idea was out of the question.

On the 20th of July, 1866, the steamer *Governor Higginson,* of the Calcutta and Burnach Steam Navigation Company, had met this moving mass five miles off the east coast of Australia. Captain Baker thought at first that he was in the presence of an unknown sandbank;[5] he even prepared to determine its exact position, when two columns of water, projected by the inexplicable object, shot with a hissing noise a hundred and fifty feet up into the air. Now, unless the sandbank had been submitted to the intermittent eruption of a geyser, the *Governor Higginson* had to do neither more nor less than with an aquatic mammal, unknown till then, which threw up from its blowholes columns of water mixed with air and vapour.

Similar facts were observed on the 23d of July in the same year, in the Pacific Ocean, by the *Columbus,* of the West India and Pacific Steam Navigation Company. But this extraordinary cetaceous creature could transport itself from one place to another with surprising velocity; as, in an interval of three days, the *Governor Higginson* and the *Columbus* had observed it at two different points of the chart, separated by a distance of more than seven hundred nautical leagues.[6]

Fifteen days later, two thousand miles farther off,[7] the *Helvetia,* of the Compagnie-Nationale, and the *Shannon,* of the Royal Mail Steamship Company, sailing to windward in that portion of the Atlantic lying between the United States and Europe, respectively signalled the monster to each other in 42° 15′ N. lat. and 60° 35′ W. long.[8] In these simultaneous observations, they thought themselves justified in estimating the minimum length of the mammal at more than three hundred and fifty feet, as the *Shannon* and *Helvetia* were of smaller dimensions than it, though they measured three hundred feet over all.

Now the largest whales, those which frequent those parts of the sea round the Aleutian, Kulammak, and Umgullich islands, have never exceeded the length of sixty yards, if they attain that.

These reports arriving one after the other, with fresh observations made on board the transatlantic ship *Pereire,* a collision which occurred between the *Etna* of the Inman line and the monster, a *procès verbal* [9] directed by the officers of the French frigate *Normandie,* a very accurate survey made by the staff of Commodore Fitz-James on board the *Lord Clyde,* greatly influenced public opinion. Light-thinking people jested upon the phenomenon, but grave practical countries, such as England, America, and Germany, treated the matter more seriously.

In every place of great resort the monster was the fashion. They sang of it in the cafés, ridiculed it in the papers, and represented it on the stage. All kinds of stories were circulated regarding it. There appeared in the papers caricatures of every gigantic and imaginary creature, from the white whale, the terrible "Moby Dick" of hyperborean regions, to the immense kraken **10** whose tentacles could entangle a ship of five hundred tons, and hurry it into the abyss of the ocean. The legends of ancient times were even resuscitated, and the opinions of Aristotle and Pliny **11** revived, who admitted the existence of these monsters, as well as the Norwegian tales of Bishop Pontoppidan,**12** the accounts of Paul Heggede, and, last of all, the reports of Mr. Harrington (whose good faith no one could suspect), who affirmed that, being on board the *Castillan,* in 1857, he had seen this enormous serpent, which had never until that time frequented any other seas but those of the ancient *"Constitutionnel."* **13**

Then burst forth the interminable controversy between the credulous and the incredulous in the societies of savants and scientific journals. "The question of the monster" inflamed all minds. Editors of scientific journals, quarrelling with believers in the supernatural, spilled seas of ink during this memorable campaign, some even drawing blood; for, from the sea-serpent, they came to direct personalities.

For six months war was waged with various fortune in the leading articles of the Geographical Institution of Brazil, the Royal Academy of Science of Berlin, the British Association, the Smithsonian Institution of Washington, in the discussions of the "Indian Archipelago," of the Cosmos of the Abbé Moigno, in the Mittheilungen of Petermann, in the scientific chronicles of the great journals of France and other countries. The cheaper journals replied keenly and with inexhaustible zest. These satirical writers parodied a remark of Linnaeus, quoted by the adversaries of the monster, maintaining "that nature did not make fools," and adjured their contemporaries not to give the lie to nature, by admitting the existence of krakens, sea-serpents, "Moby Dicks," and other lucubrations of delirious sailors. At length an article in a well-known satirical journal by a favourite contributor, the chief of the staff, settled the monster, like Hippolytus, giving it the death-blow

really not a separate species, but simply young ones."

5. *an unknown sandbank* In this passage, wherever the "standard translation" says *sandbank* read *reef.* Verne himself uses here the same word *écueil* that he uses in the chapter title, *Un Ecueil Fuyant (A Shifting Reef).* The inconsistency in the English version is typical of the translator, Mercier Lewis.

6. *nautical leagues* The league as a unit of distance has varied with time and place and only recently has it been standardized. In the nineteenth century seamen were apt to use the league as a rough unit of measure meaning somewhere between two and three miles. From later passages in this novel we can infer that Verne reckoned the nautical league as 2.16 nautical miles. Hence the *extraordinary creature* has traveled more than 1500 miles in three days. And Verne's title, *Twenty Thousand Leagues . . . ,* could be read as *Forty-Three Thousand Two Hundred Miles. . . .*

Today a nautical league is three nautical miles or 5.556 kilometers. A nautical mile is about 6080 feet. This is the length of one minute (1′) of arc of a great circle on the earth's surface.

7. *two thousand miles farther off* The English text is wrong. Verne says *deux mille lieues,* that is, *two thousand leagues* or 4320 miles.

The French *mille* can mean either *one thousand* or *one mile.* Apparently, here Mercier Lewis quickly read the word both ways to get *thousand miles!* And this error could be a complex free association, for in the ancient Roman army *one mile* was literally *mille passum* or *one thousand paces.* A pace was one left plus one right step, approximately five feet, and a mile was thus 5000 feet. Of course the French meanings of *mille* derive from the Latin.

8. *60° 35′ W. long.* In the original, Verne says *west of the meridian of*

Greenwich. He is not being pedantic. Rather he is preparing us for the fact that—as a major character will soon demonstrate—it is possible to reckon longitude east or west of *any* spot on the globe.

There's no point in missing Verne's romantic virtuosity in such matters. And so readers who have forgotten whatever they once knew about latitude and longitude may appreciate this brief reminder:

Latitude is distance north or south of the equator, and *longitude* is distance east or west of some imaginary line running through the poles. Usually the line used is the Greenwich meridian, linking both poles through Greenwich, England.

Latitude and longitude are expressed in degrees (°) and minutes ('). Thus, if a mariner is one-quarter around the globe west of Greenwich, he's at the 90th meridian or 90° west longitude. If he's halfway around, on the exact opposite side of the world from Greenwich, he's at 180° . . . unless of course he's using some other point of reference, as will soon happen in this novel.

By omitting Verne's mention of the Greenwich meridian, our "standard translation" has failed to prepare us for one of Verne's curiosities. As a romanticist, he always emphasizes that the choice of a point of reference is an arbitrary choice, a human choice, and not an absolute.

9. *procès verbal* An official memorandum, as we would say today, drawn up by the officers.

10. *the immense kraken* Kraken was the Norwegian name given to a sea monster reportedly big enough to be mistaken for an island.

11. *Aristotle and Pliny* In his *Natural History,* Pliny (A.D. 23–79) described a 700-pound monster, with arms 30 feet long, that came out of the sea at night to steal food at Rocadillo, Spain. Probably Pliny was confusing accounts of two very real sea animals: the octopus, renowned for its ability to travel short distances

amidst an universal burst of laughter. Wit had conquered science.

During the first months of the year 1867, the question seemed buried, never to revive, when new facts were brought before the public. It was then no longer a scientific problem to be solved, but a real danger seriously to be avoided. The question took quite another shape. The monster became a small island, a rock, a reef, but a reef of indefinite and shifting proportions.

On the 5th of March, 1867, the *Moravian,* of the Montreal Ocean Company, finding herself during the night in 27° 30′ lat. and 72° 15′ long., struck on her starboard quarter a rock, marked in no chart for that part of the sea. Under the combined efforts of the wind and its four hundred horse-power, it was going at the rate of thirteen knots. Had it not been for the superior strength of the hull of the *Moravian,* she would have been broken by the shock and gone down with the 237 passengers she was bringing home from Canada.

The accident happened about five o'clock in the morning, as the day was breaking. The officers of the quarter-deck hurried to the after-part of the vessel. They examined the sea with the most scrupulous attention. They saw nothing but a strong eddy about three cables' length **14** distant, as if the surface had been violently agitated. The bearings of the place were taken exactly, and the *Moravian* continued its route without apparent damage. Had it struck on a submerged rock, or on an enormous wreck? They could not tell; but on examination of the ship's bottom when undergoing repairs, it was found that part of her keel was broken.

This fact, so grave in itself, might perhaps have been forgotten like many others, if, three weeks after, it had not been re-enacted under similar circumstances. But, thanks to the nationality of the victim of the shock, thanks to the reputation of the company to which the vessel belonged, the circumstance became extensively circulated.

[There is no one alive who has not heard of the celebrated English shipowner Cunard.**15** In 1840, this shrewd industrialist started a postal service between Liverpool and Halifax with three wooden paddle-wheel steamers, each displacing 1162 tons and driven by 400-horse-power engines. In 1848, the Cunard fleet was increased by four ships of 1820 tons each with 650-horse-power engines, and, two years later, by two more vessels of even greater tonnage and power. In 1853, after Cunard's mail franchise had been renewed, they added to their fleet the *Arabia,* the *Persia,* the *China,* the *Scotia,* the *Java,*

There is no one alive who has not heard of the celebrated English shipowner Cunard. Photograph of Sir Samuel, taken shortly before his death, from the archives of W. C. North, vice president, Cunard Line, New York.

on land, and the giant squid, which was often cast up on the Spanish coast in ancient times.

12. *Bishop Pontoppidan* In his *Natural History of Norway* (1755), Erik Pontoppidan described the kraken as the "largest and most surprising of all the animal creation." Some specimens, he said, measured a mile and a half in circumference. From other more credible details that he supplied, it seems the kraken belonged to that natural division known as the Cephalopoda ("head-feet"); it was probably a giant squid.

13. *the ancient "Constitionnel"* A Parisian newspaper that had suspended publication.

14. *three cables' length* A *cable,* or *cable's length,* was roughly understood, in nautical usage of the past, to be equal to 100 fathoms or 600 feet. Officially, a cable is 608 feet in Great Britain, 720 feet in the United States.

15. *the celebrated . . . Cunard* Samuel Cunard was one of the heroes of nineteenth-century technology. One historian explains Cunard's success by saying "he thought in services when other people thought in ships."

The Cunard family had emigrated from Wales to Philadephia, but when the colonies declared their independence, the Cunards moved to Canada. There Samuel was born in Halifax, Nova Scotia in 1788. As a young man he became an agent for the East India Company. Stationed in Boston, he contracted to carry the British mail from Newfoundland and Boston to Bermuda.

Often he saw his mail ships, under full sail, passed by local steamships. He became an early advocate of conversion to steam in intercontinental shipping. But there were powerful forces arrayed against such a simple plan. Most experts were convinced that no ship could carry enough coal to complete a long voyage. And even if she could, they insisted that the coal bills would kill the profits. We

and the *Russia,* all top-notch ships and the biggest—except for the *Great Eastern*—that ever sailed the seas. By 1867, the company had twelve ships afloat, eight driven by paddle-wheel and four by propeller.

If I rehearse these details, it is to remind everyone of the importance of this shipping line, famous for its scientific management. No oceangoing line had ever been better organized, none rewarded with such success. In the past twenty-six years, Cunard ships have made 2000 Atlantic crossings without so much as a voyage cancelled, a delay recorded, a letter, man, or ship lost. This must be the reason why—according to a recent survey of official records—passengers continue to prefer Cunard, in spite of very solid competition offered by France. So, as we might expect, it caused quite a stir when an accident befell one of Cunard's best ships.**16]**

The 13th of April, 1867, the sea being beautiful, the breeze favourable, the *Scotia,* of the Cunard Company's line, found herself in 15° 12′ long. and 45° 37′ lat. She was going at the speed of thirteen knots and a half. [She was propelled by her 1000-horse-power engines. Her paddles treaded the water with perfect regularity. She drew twenty-two feet and displaced 6624 cubic meters.]

must remember that when the *Savannah* made her celebrated crossing from New York to Cork in twenty-six days in mid-1818, she actually used up all her coal in eighty hours of running her engines and did the rest on sailpower.

What was on Cunard's side was the growing demand for both speed and regularity of service. By 1830 Cunard was working out detailed plans for a steamship line that would make twenty trips a year between Liverpool, Halifax, and Boston. Hence he was perfectly prepared when, in the late 1830s, the Admiralty proposed to substitute steamships for sailing vessels in the transatlantic mail service. Cunard won the contract.

Part of his success surely was that he thought in terms of *classes* of ships, that is, fleets of sister ships that could offer identical services and if need be take each other's place. He had planned to start service with a three-ship fleet, as Verne indicates, but actually the line was launched with four vessels rated at 740 horsepower. The *Britannia* made the first run from Liverpool to Halifax to Boston in 14 days, 8 hours. The excitement caused by this historic event is clear from one fact alone: Cunard had to face 2000 invitations to dinner with Boston families! By 1848 the Cunard line extended its service to New York.

For his systematic improvement of transatlantic travel and communication, Cunard was made a baronet in 1859. Sir Samuel died in 1866, unaware that his line was soon to run afoul of the "enormous thing."

From our restoration of Verne's two paragraphs, we can see why he chose a Cunard vessel for *the climactic event* of his opening chapter. But why did Mercier Lewis omit these paragraphs so essential to Verne's *suspense?* As we shall see repeatedly, Lewis is indifferent if not hostile to Verne's admiration for science and technology.

16. *one of Cunard's best ships* Indeed, at the very moment that the story is taking place, the *Scotia* holds

The *Britannia* on February 3, 1844, after the people of Boston had cut a seven-mile channel in the ice to free the trapped ship. A crowd of Bostonians followed, cheering for the first mile or so, as the Cunarder headed for the open seas and Liverpool. The British Post Office later offered to reimburse Boston for its expenses in this operation, which had been financed by popular subscription. Proud Boston, eager to keep the Cunard mail service from shifting to New York, declined the offer. This illustration, from an old print issued in Boston to commemorate the event, appeared in *The Atlantic Ferry* (1893), by Arthur J. Maginnis, British naval architect.

At seventeen minutes past four in the afternoon, whilst the passengers were assembled at lunch in the great saloon, a slight shock was felt on the hull of the *Scotia,* on her quarter, a little aft of the port-paddle.

The *Scotia* had not struck, but she had been struck, and seemingly by something rather sharp and penetrating than blunt. The shock had been so slight that no one had been alarmed, had it not been for the shouts of the carpenter's watch, who rushed on to the bridge, exclaiming, "We are sinking! we are sinking!" At first the passengers were much frightened, but Captain Anderson hastened to reassure them. The danger could not be imminent. The *Scotia,* divided into seven compartments by strong partitions, could brave with impunity any leak. Captain Anderson went down immediately into the hold. He found that the sea was pouring into the fifth compartment; and the rapidity of the influx proved that the force of the water was considerable. Fortunately this compartment did not hold the boilers, or the fires would have been immediately extinguished. Captain Anderson ordered the engines to be stopped at once, and one of the men went down to ascertain the extent of the injury. Some minutes afterwards they discovered the existence of a large hole, of two yards in diameter, in the ship's bottom. Such a leak could not be stopped; and the *Scotia,* her paddles half submerged, was obliged to continue her course. She was then three hundred miles from Cape Clear, and after three days' delay, which caused great uneasiness in Liverpool, she entered the basin of the company.

The engineers visited the *Scotia,* which was put in dry dock. They could scarcely believe it possible; at two yards and a half below water-mark was a regular rent, in the form of an isosceles triangle. The broken place in the iron plates was so perfectly defined, that it could not have been more neatly done by a punch. It was clear, then, that the instrument producing the perforation was not of a common stamp; and after having been driven with prodigious strength, and piercing an iron plate 1⅜ inches thick, had withdrawn itself by a retrograde motion truly inexplicable.

Such was the last fact, which resulted in exciting once more the torrent of public opinion. From this moment all unlucky casualties which could not be otherwise accounted for were put down to the monster. Upon this imaginary creature rested the responsibility of all these shipwrecks, which unfortunately were considerable; for of three thousand ships whose loss was annually recorded at Lloyds',**17** the number of sailing and steam ships supposed to be totally lost, from the absence of all news, amounted to not less than two hundred!

Now, it was the "monster" who, justly or unjustly, was accused of their disappearance, and, thanks to it, communication between the different continents became more and more dangerous. The public demanded peremptorily that the seas should at any price be relieved from this formidable cetacean.

the record for running from New York to Liverpool in 8 days, 22 hours. She will lose the Blue Riband of the Atlantic to the Inman Line's *City of Brussels* in 1869. The *Scotia* had actually reached a record speed of 16½ knots on her trial run. Displacing 4000 tons, powered by 5000-horse-power engines, she was so big Cunard decided that with her he would begin to carry immigrants as well as first- and second-class passengers.

17. *recorded at Lloyds'* Verne says *Bureau Veritas,* the French equivalent of Lloyd's of London. Verne's statistics here came out of his personal experience. As a teen-ager, he clerked in his father's law office which was concerned largely with marine insurance. Young Verne had often to refer to data supplied by the Bureau and its prototype, Lloyd's.

Named after Edward Lloyd's Coffee House in London, the favorite gathering place of English marine underwriters, Lloyd's was founded in 1688 to regulate the safe issuance of sound insurance. *Lloyd's Register* is an annual compilation of data on oceangoing vessels of all nations. While other large countries have set up their own "bureaus," Lloyd's remains the central international authority on shipping data and standards.

The *Scotia, divided into seven compartments by strong partitions, could brave with impunity any leak.* This picture appeared in *The Atlantic Ferry* (1893) by Arthur J. Maginnis.

PART 1: CHAPTER II
Pro and Con

1. *disagreeable territory of Nebraska* This quaint mistranslation distorts the professor's character and does injustice to Verne's knowledge of geography, geology, and current events.

In the original French, Verne's professor says he has returned from a scientific expedition *dans les mauvaises terres du Nébraska,* that is to say, *in the badlands of Nebraska!* He is not expressing a personal opinion of that state; he is simply referring to an area by its common name.

In Verne's day as in our own, *the badlands* meant an extensive, barren, deeply eroded region of southwestern South Dakota and northwestern Nebraska. French-Canadian trappers had dubbed that area *les mauvaises terres à traverser,* bad (rough) lands to cross. Translated, the name caught on for another reason: this is obviously bad land *to farm.* For Professor Aronnax, a scientist, *les mauvaises terres* is an objective term denoting a heavily cut-up topography. And for him, this territory is *far from disagreeable—it's a paradise!*

Comprising thousands of square miles of deep tortuous gullies, jagged spires, sawtooth divides, staircase rock formations, abrupt buttes, large freestanding mesas, the badlands are the ideal grounds for fossil hunting. All this rough erosion had exposed stratum on stratum to provide perfect

At the period when these events took place, I had just returned from a scientific research in the disagreeable territory of Nebraska,[1] in the United States. In virtue of my office as Assistant Professor in the Museum of Natural History in Paris, the French Government had attached me to that expedition. After six months in Nebraska, I arrived in New York towards the end of March, laden with a precious collection. My departure for France was fixed for the first days in May. Meanwhile, I was occupying myself in classifying my mineralogical, botanical, and zoological riches, when the accident happened to the *Scotia.*

I was perfectly up in the subject which was the question of the day. How could I be otherwise? I had read and re-read all the American and European papers without being any nearer a conclusion. This mystery puzzled me. Under the impossibility of forming an opinion, I jumped from one extreme to the other. That there really was something could not be doubted, and the incredulous were invited to put their finger on the wound of the *Scotia.*

On my arrival at New York, the question was at its height. The hypothesis of the floating island, and the unapproachable sandbank,[2] supported by minds little competent to form a judgement, was abandoned. And, indeed, unless this shoal had a machine in its stomach, how could it change its position with such astonishing rapidity?

From the same cause, the idea of a floating hull of an enormous wreck was given up.

There remained then only two possible solutions of the question, which created two distinct parties: on one side, those who

were for a monster of colossal strength; on the other, those who were for a submarine vessel of enormous motive power.

But this last hypothesis, plausible as it was, could not stand against inquiries made in both worlds. That a private gentleman should have such a machine at his command was not likely. Where, when, and how was it built? And how could its construction have been kept secret? Certainly a Government might possess such a destructive machine. And in these disastrous times, when the ingenuity of man has multiplied the power of weapons of war, it was possible that, without the knowledge of others, a state might try to work such a formidable engine. After the chassepots came the torpedoes,[3] after the torpedoes the submarine rams, then—the reaction. At least, I hope so.

But the hypothesis of a war machine fell before the declaration of Governments. As public interest was in question, and transatlantic communications suffered, their veracity could not be doubted. But, how admit that the construction of this submarine boat had escaped the public eye? For a private gentleman to keep the secret under such circumstances would be very difficult, and for a state whose every act is persistently watched by powerful rivals, certainly impossible.

After inquiries made in England, France, Russia, Prussia, Spain, Italy, and America, even in Turkey, the hypothesis of a submarine monitor [4] was definitely rejected. [And so, once again the hypothesis of a monster had to be taken seriously, in spite of the endless jokes heaped on it by the popular press. Everyone began to wonder what such a fantastic creature could be like.]

Upon my arrival in New York several persons did me the honour of consulting me on the phenomenon in question. I had published in France a work in quarto, in two volumes, entitled, "Mysteries of the Great Submarine Grounds." This book, highly approved of in the learned world, gained for me a special reputation in this rather obscure branch of Natural History. My advice was asked. As long as I could deny the reality of the fact, I confined myself to a decided negative. But soon finding myself driven into a corner, I was obliged to explain myself categorically. And even "the Honourable Pierre Aronnax, Professor in the Museum of Paris," was called upon by the *New York Herald* to express a definite opinion of some sort. I did something. I spoke, for want of power to hold my tongue. I discussed the question in all its forms, politically and scientifically; and I give here an extract from a carefully-

cross sections of several geological periods. Scientists and amateur collectors converged on the badlands in the 1850s and 1860s and some made their reputations there. They discovered many vertebrate fossils, including the hitherto unknown oreodont, an extinct piglike cud-chewing mammal that has still not been found on any other continent. It developed that the oreodont had roamed North America from the late Eocene through the Pliocene epochs, from forty to one million years ago. Another spectacular find in the badlands was the titanothere, an herbivorous rhinoceroslike creature even older than the oreodont but not unique to America.

Now it is easy to see why Verne, always on top of the latest scientific developments, would choose the badlands as the reason Aronnax would be in America. As we shall see later, the professor has indeed returned with his share of badland fossils—including some oreodonts.

2. *unapproachable sandbank* Again, read *reef*.

The Whitehead "automatic fish" was pictured and described in *The American Cyclopaedia* (1873) as "a small cigar-shaped boat *a*, . . . carrying a contact torpedo in the bow, and containing an engine driven by some powerful agent, like compressed air, which, acting on the propeller *b*, gives it an effective range of about 300 yards.

3. *chassepots . . . torpedoes* The chassepot was a breech-loading rifle adopted by the French army in 1866. It was named after its inventor, Antoine Chassepot.

The torpedo Aronnax has in mind could be the new self-propelling or "automobile" torpedo invented by Robert Whitehead in 1866. He was an English engineer working for an Austrian firm in Fiume. His first model, driven by compressed air, could attain a speed of 6 knots and reach a target 600 feet away.

But Aronnax, digging in the badlands in 1866, might not have heard of the Whitehead torpedo. In that case he is using the word "torpedoes" in its older sense, to designate the underwater mines developed in the American Civil War. (When Admiral David Farragut said, "Damn the torpedoes! Full speed ahead!" he was looking at a minefield.)

Breech-loaders, minefields, "automobile" torpedoes, and the heavy artillery developed by the Union Army all saddened Verne, since they increased the efficiency of war-makers and the terror of their victims.

John Ericsson (above) and a scale drawing of his *Monitor* as it appeared in *The American Cyclopaedia* (1873).

4. *submarine monitor* Verne actually says "a submarine *Monitor*." Thus he specifically reminds the reader of John Ericsson's famous Union ironclad, with a low, flat deck and a revolving gun turret, which fought the Confederate ironclad *Merrimack* on March 9, 1862. All later warships modeled on the *Monitor*— even those with more than one turret —came to be known as *monitors*.

Until recent years, all Civil War monitors were lost to history. Then, in January 1967, engineers located the *Tecumseh.* Sunk in the Battle of Mobile Bay on August 5, 1864, she was found lying on her side, in deep mud, under 30 feet of water.

This discovery revived interest in

studied article which I published in the number of the 30th of April. It ran as follows:—

"After examining one by one the different hypotheses, rejecting all other suggestions, it becomes necessary to admit the existence of a marine animal of enormous power.

"The great depths of the ocean are entirely unknown to us. Soundings cannot reach them. What passes in those remote depths—what beings live, or can live, twelve or fifteen miles beneath the surface of the waters—what is the organisation of these animals, we can scarcely conjecture. However, the solution of the problem submitted to me may modify the form of the dilemma. Either we do know all the varieties of beings which people our planet, or we do not. If we do *not* know them all—if Nature has still secrets in ichthyology [5] for us, nothing is more conformable to reason than to admit the existence of fishes, or cetaceans of other kinds,[6] or even of new species, of an organisation formed to inhabit the strata inaccessible to soundings, and which an accident of some sort, either fantastical or capricious, has brought at long intervals to the upper level of the ocean.

"If, on the contrary, we *do* know all living kinds, we must necessarily seek for the animal in question amongst those marine beings already classed; and, in that case, I should be disposed to admit the existence of a gigantic narwhal.

"The common narwhal, or unicorn of the sea, often attains a length of sixty feet. Increase its size fivefold or tenfold, give it strength proportionate to its size,[7] lengthen its destructive weapons, and you obtain the animal required. It will have the proportions determined by the officers of the *Shannon,* the instrument required by the perforation of the *Scotia,* and the power necessary to pierce the hull of the steamer.

"Indeed the narwhal is armed with a sort of ivory sword, a halberd, according to the expression of certain naturalists.[8] The principal tusk [9] has the hardness of steel. Some of these tusks have been found buried in the bodies of whales,[10] which the unicorn always attacks with success. Others have been drawn out, not without trouble, from the bottoms of ships, which they have pierced through and through, as a gimlet pierces a barrel. The Museum of the Faculty of Medicine of Paris possesses one of these defensive weapons,[11] two yards and a quarter in length, and fifteen inches in diameter at the base.

"Very well! Suppose this weapon to be six times stronger,[12] and the animal ten times more powerful; launch it at the rate of twenty miles an hour, [multiply its mass by the square of its

"The common narwhal. . . . is armed with a sort of ivory sword, . . . [with] the hardness of steel. Some of these tusks have been. . . . drawn out . . . from the bottoms of ships, which they have pierced through and through, as a gimlet pierces a barrel. . . ." Narwhals as pictured in *The American Cyclopaedia* (1873).

speed,] and you obtain a shock capable of producing the catastrophe required. Until further information, therefore, I shall maintain it to be a sea-unicorn of colossal dimensions, armed, not with a halberd, but with a real spur, as the armoured frigates, or the 'rams' of war, whose massiveness and motive power it would possess at the same time. Thus may this inexplicable phenomenon be explained, unless there be something over and above all that one has ever conjectured, seen, perceived, or experienced; which is just within the bounds of possibility."

These last words were cowardly on my part; but, up to a certain point, I wished to shelter my dignity as Professor, and not give too much cause for laughter to the Americans, who laugh well when they do laugh.

I reserved for myself a way of escape. In effect, however, I admitted the existence of the "monster." My article was warmly discussed, which procured it a high reputation. It rallied round it a certain number of partisans. The solution it proposed gave, at least, full liberty to the imagination. The human mind delights in grand conceptions of supernatural beings. And the sea is precisely their best vehicle, the only medium through which these giants (against which terrestrial animals, such as elephants or rhinoceroses, are as nothing) can be produced or developed.

[The liquid masses **13** support the largest known species of

the final resting place of the original *Monitor*, which had gone down with all hands off Cape Hatteras in December 1862. Edward Jaeckel of *Industrial Research* magazine and Dr. Harold E. Edgerton of M.I.T. conducted detailed preliminary studies. Meanwhile the Duke University Marine Laboratory at Beaufort, North Carolina, had already begun its own search for the historic "cheesebox on a raft." The two teams joined forces. More than 60 specialists, including personnel from the Army, the Navy, several foundations, and other research organizations, were involved before they could announce in November 1974, that they had located the *Monitor*, bottom up, in 220 feet of water. Using deep-sea grappling apparatus, they even recovered the rudder, which had broken off when the ironclad had hit bottom.

The complexity of the scientific detective work would have fascinated Verne. Doubtless he would have extrapolated the procedures into future miracles of marine archaeology. For example, using undersea still and video cameras, the researchers had to shoot almost 6000 pictures and compose a "photo mosaic" before they could identify the wreck beyond any doubt.

5. *secrets in ichthyology* A typical textbook in Verne's day defined ichthyology as that "branch of zoology which treats of the internal and external structure of fishes, their mode of life, and their distribution in space and time."

6. *fishes, or cetaceans of other kinds* Verne says simply *the existence of fishes or of cetaceans.* Lewis's ambiguous phrasing could make it sound as if Verne thought fish were a kind of cetacean. In any event, it's a good place to remind ourselves of the main distinctions. *Fishes* are cold-blooded and water-breathing: they have gills. They are usually oviparous: that is, the female produces eggs that develop and hatch outside her body. *Cetaceans*, however, are aquatic mammals. They are warm-blooded and air-breathing; they have lungs. They are viviparous: that is, they produce their young alive, and they nourish them with milk.

This last statement is more dramatic than those simple words suggest. A nursing mother blue whale produces a ton of milk per day. Her baby, twenty-five feet long and weighing two tons at birth, gains two hundred pounds a day and grows about one inch every twenty-four hours before it is weaned at the age of seven months.

7. *give it strength* Verne says *give this cetacean the strength,* thus reminding the reader that the narwhal is related to the sperm whale, the dolphin, the bottlenose whale, the dugong, and the porpoise. Cetologists today recognize one hundred kinds of cetacea.

8. *expression of certain naturalists* As Aronnax takes us further into the field of natural history, notice how appreciative he is of its metaphoric language.

9. *principal tusk* The adult narwhal has two teeth. In the male, only one, usually the left, erupts to become what Aronnax calls *the principal tusk.* In some males, both teeth will emerge to provide them with double *halberds.* No teeth erupt in the female.

10. *buried in the bodies of whales* The narwhal is itself a whale. Verne says *dans les corps des baleines.* A sympathetic rendering would be *in the bodies of baleen* [or *whalebone*] *whales.*

11. *defensive weapons* Today's naturalists are not so certain that these *halberds* are *defensive weapons.* They simply do not yet know exactly what the function of these tusks is.

12. *six times stronger* Verne says *ten times stronger.* Lewis often confuses the French *dix* (ten) with *six* (*six*).

13. *The liquid masses* Our restora-

mammals. Maybe the oceans also conceal molluscs of unimaginable size, crustaceans too fearful to contemplate, like 300-foot lobsters, crabs weighing 200 tons. Why not? After all, in distant geological epochs, the land produced quadrupeds, quadrumanas, reptiles, and birds of enormous dimensions. The Creator cast them in a colossal mould which time has reduced. Now, why should not the seas, in their unknown depths, have conserved some of these gigantic specimens of earth life? For apparently the seas never change, while the earth undergoes continual mutation. Why could not the bosom of the ocean conceal the last of these titans, for whom centuries are but years?

But I have been carried away. Enough of the fantasies that time has now transformed into terrible realities for me. To repeat: opinion had crystallized as to the nature of the phenomenon, the public now accepted the existence of a prodigious creature distinct from the sea-serpents of myth and fable. While some persisted in seeing this as a purely scientific problem, more practical people—especially in America and England—felt strongly that the ocean must be purged of this redoubtable monster, to guarantee the safety of transoceanic communications.]

The industrial and commercial papers treated the question chiefly from this point of view. The *Shipping and Mercantile Gazette,* the *Lloyds' List,* the *Packet-Boat,* and the *Maritime and Colonial Review,* all papers devoted to insurance companies which threatened to raise their rates of premium, were unanimous on this point. Public opinion had been pronounced. The United States were the first in the field; and in New York they made preparations for an expedition destined to pursue this narwhal. A frigate of great speed, the *Abraham Lincoln,* was put in commission as soon as possible. The arsenals were opened to Commander Farragut,**14** who hastened the arming of his frigate; but, as it always happens, the moment it was decided to pursue the monster, the monster did not appear. For two months no one heard it spoken of. No ship met with it. It seemed as if this unicorn knew of the plots weaving around it. It had been so much talked of, even through the Atlantic cable, that jesters pretended that this slender fly had stopped a telegram on its passage, and was making the most of it.

So when the frigate had been armed for a long campaign, and provided with formidable fishing apparatus, no one could tell what course to pursue. Impatience grew apace, when, on the 2d of July,**15** they learned that a steamer of the line of San Francisco, from California to Shanghai, had seen the animal three weeks before in the North Pacific Ocean. The excitement caused by this news was extreme. The ship was revictualled and well stocked with coal. [Commander Farragut was given less than twenty-four hours to prepare for departure. Every man was ready at his post: to kindle the furnaces, or stoke up, or weigh anchor. Half a day's delay seemed inexcusable. But it was clear that Commander Farragut demanded nothing better than to get going.]

Three hours before the *Abraham Lincoln* left Brooklyn pier, I received a letter worded as follows:—

"To M. ARONNAX, Professor in the Museum of Paris,
"Fifth Avenue Hotel, New York. **16**

"SIR,—If you will consent to join the *Abraham Lincoln* in this expedition, the Government of the United States will with pleasure see France represented in the enterprise. Commander Farragut has a cabin at your disposal.

"Very cordially yours,
"J. B. HOBSON,
"Secretary of Marine." **17**

Cerithium (*Bellardia*) as represented in *Journal de Conchyliologie,* 1870.

tion of Verne's expansion of this idea makes it clear that he wanted to establish, early in the book, the *dynamics* of Aronnax's character. The professor can risk wild flights of fancy precisely because he can count on his ability to return to earth. Aronnax's love of hypothesizing not only makes him a restless scientist, it also creates suspense throughout the story.

14. *Lincoln. . . . Farragut* Verne uses many names for their echo value. Here he names the frigate after the martyred Civil War president, and her captain after the great naval hero of the 1861–1865 conflict, Admiral David Glasgow Farragut. The admiral was especially well known in Europe after his ceremonial visit in 1867 to the seaports of England and France.

15. *2d of July* The French edition from which Lewis worked confused some dates in Chapters II and IV. The overall chronology makes it clear that the action involved must have occurred in May or June. And so it seems best here to follow the redating adopted by some early editors of the Lewis version; read *2nd of June.*

16. *Fifth Avenue Hotel, New York* The original Fifth Avenue Hotel was second only to the Astor in world renown. Finished in 1859, it stood on the northwest corner of Fifth Avenue and Twenty-Third Street. When Paul and Jules Verne arrived in New York on the *Great Eastern* on April 9, 1867, that's where they checked in. They ate at Delmonico's, saw *New York Streets* at Barnum's Theatre (in Barnum's American Museum), and slept that night at the Fifth Avenue.

Verne's autobiographical delight in his writing is manifest in the passages devoted to New York. In the next chapter, notice that his detailed memory of the hotel will add to the verisimilitude of his story.

17. *Secretary of Marine* The American equivalent of Verne's language is, of course, *Secretary of the Navy.* In 1867 the actual Secretary was Gideon Welles.

PART 1: CHAPTER III

I Form My Resolution[1]

1. *I Form My Resolution* Verne's title for this chapter is *Comme il plaira à monsieur*, or *Whatever Pleases Monsieur*. One possible reason why Lewis changed the title will be suggested later in the chapter.

2. *the passage of the North Sea* It was no particular feat to navigate the North Sea in Aronnax's day, a thousand years after the Vikings had mastered its every current. But in 1867 no one had yet found *the North-west Passage* and that's exactly the feat Aronnax refers to in the original: *le passage du Nord-Ouest*.

For three centuries European mariners had sought a quick route from the Atlantic to the Pacific across the top of the world—through the Arctic Archipelago of Canada and Alaska—to India. Those who failed included some of the great explorers, like Henry Hudson and James Cook. In 1845 Sir John Franklin's expedition vanished without a trace. A ten-year search for Franklin's party helped stimulate both arctic exploration and public interest in the area. In 1850–1853, Sir Robert McClure did prove the existence of a Northwest Passage but part of his own trip was made over the ice.

One of Verne's earliest tales, "A Winter Amid the Ice," published in 1855, was inspired by the heroism of the arctic explorers. But neither Verne, who died in 1905, nor Aron-

Three seconds before the arrival of J. B. Hobson's letter, I no more thought of pursuing the unicorn than of attempting the passage of the North Sea.[2] Three seconds after reading the letter of the honourable Secretary of Marine, I felt that my true vocation, the sole end of my life, was to chase this disturbing monster, and purge it from the world.

But I had just returned from a fatiguing journey, weary and longing for repose. I aspired to nothing more than again seeing my country, my friends, my little lodging by the Jardin des Plantes,[3] my dear and precious collections. But nothing could keep me back! I forgot all—fatigue, friends, and collections—and accepted without hesitation the offer of the American Government.

"Besides," thought I, "all roads lead back to Europe (for my particular benefit), and I will not hurry me towards the coast of France. This worthy animal may allow itself to be caught in the seas of Europe (for my particular benefit) and I will not bring back less than half a yard of his ivory halberd to the Museum of Natural History." But in the meanwhile I must seek this narwhal in the North Pacific Ocean, which, to return to France, was taking the road to the antipodes.

"Conseil," I called, in an impatient voice.

Conseil was my servant, a true, devoted Flemish boy, who had accompanied me in all my travels. I liked him, and he returned the liking well. He was phlegmatic by nature, regular from principle, zealous from habit, evincing little disturbance at the different surprises of life, very quick with his hands, and apt at any service required of him; and, despite his name,[4] never giving advice—even when asked for it.

[Rubbing shoulders with learned men [5] in our little world at the Jardin des Plantes, Conseil had come to know a thing or two. In him I had a well-versed specialist in natural history classification. With an acrobat's agility he could run up and down the ladder of branches, groups, classes, subclasses, orders, families, genera, subgenera, species, and varieties. But his knowledge stopped there. To classify in the abstract was his whole life, he was helpless on the practical side. I do not think he could tell the difference, in real life, between a spermaceti whale and a baleen whale. But still, what a fine, decent chap he was.]

Conseil had followed me for the last ten years wherever science led. Never once did he complain of the length or fatigue of a journey, never made an objection to pack his portmanteau for whatever country it might be, or however far away, whether China or Congo. Besides all this, he had good health, which defied all sickness, and solid muscles, but no nerves; good morals are understood. This boy was thirty years old, and his age to that of his master as fifteen to twenty. May I be excused for saying that I was forty years old? **6**

But Conseil had one fault, he was ceremonious to a degree, and would never speak to me but in the third person,**7** which was sometimes provoking.

"Conseil," said I again, beginning with feverish hands to make preparations for my departure.

Certainly I was sure of this devoted boy. As a rule, I never asked him if it were convenient for him or not to follow me in my travels; but this time the expedition in question might be prolonged, and the enterprise might be hazardous in pursuit of an animal capable of sinking a frigate as easily as a nutshell. Here there was matter for reflection even to the most impassive man in the world. What would Conseil say?

"Conseil," I called a third time.

Conseil appeared.

"Did you call, sir?" said he, entering.

"Yes, my boy; make preparations for me and yourself too. We leave in two hours."

"As you please, sir," replied Conseil, quietly.

"Not an instant to lose;—lock in my trunk all travelling utensils, coats, shirts, and stockings—without counting, as many as you can, and make haste."

"And your collections, sir?" observed Conseil.

"We will think of them by and by."

"What! The archiotherium, the hyracotherium, the oreodons, the cheropotamus, and the other skins?" **8**

"They will keep them at the hotel."

nax, presumably, lived to see the day that Roald Amundsen finally made it entirely by sea, landing in Nome in 1906.

In 1958 the United States nuclear submarines *Nautilus* and *Skate* negotiated the passage by going under the ice. In 1969 the icebreaking tanker S.S. *Manhattan* established the commercial value of the passage when it demonstrated that ships could bring oil out from northern Alaska.

3. *Jardin des Plantes* Another name —corresponding to our "Botanical Gardens"—for the Paris Museum of Natural History.

4. *despite his name* The word *conseil* means *counsel* or *advice*.

5. *Rubbing shoulders with learned men* This passage, omitted in the "standard translation," is important in the characterization of both Conseil and the professor. For example, this description of Conseil's lopsided knowledge of biology prepares us for a comic scene later, a scene Verne uses to brief us on the classification of fishes.

6. *May I be excused for saying that I was forty years old* Our translator almost always kills Verne's jokes. In the original the professor says: *May I be excused for this roundabout way of admitting that I was forty?*

7. *would never speak to me but in the third person* Verne plants this observation at this point because (1) he wants us to observe closely how Conseil acts on his first entrance, and (2) Verne is preparing us for a scene later in the book when Conseil's grammar—and his character—will undergo a sudden, tragicomic change.

The idea is that Conseil (in the original) always addresses Aronnax like this: "Did monsieur call?" or "The professor should take better care of himself." And the professor secretly wishes that Conseil would say "Did *you* call?" or *"You* should take better care of *yourself."* Since Conseil's keeping himself at third-person distance is "provoking" to the professor, this helps characterize the phlegmatic Conseil as more interested in formality, and the sensitive Aronnax as lonely for a human relationship.

Alas, our translator kills the joke right after it's hatched. Even though Verne has just alerted us to Conseil's unfailing penchant for the third person, Lewis has him walk in and use the second! Conseil's speeches here should sound more like this:

"Did monsieur call?"

"Just as monsieur wishes."

"But what about monsieur's collections?"

And so on, until page 315, when Verne's joke should pay off. In deference to Verne's rights as the real author, we shall reconstruct his joke in Note 12, page 314.

Verne considered this a major clue to Conseil's characterization. We can see this from the title that Verne gave this chapter: *Comme il plaira à monsieur,* or *Whatever Pleases Monsieur.* Notice that Lewis has changed the chapter title to *I Form My Resolution.*

8. *and the other skins* A more sympathetic rendering in this context would be *and the other skeletons* or even better, *and all the other specimens.*

Verne's phrase is *et autres carcasses.* These are *badlands fossil remains,* hardly likely to include *skins* after millions of years. The hyracotherium, for example, a fox-sized mammal regarded as one of the earliest known ancestors of the horse, lived in the Eocene epoch, forty or more million years ago.

9. *by making a curve* Verne says *un crochet,* that is, *a detour.*

10. *a captain who is pretty wideawake* . . . Unlike our translator, who misses about 275 words in this passage. The first omission weakens the characterization of both Aronnax and Conseil; it cheats us of a few bread-and-butter details about the

"And your live Babiroussa, sir?"

"They will feed it during our absence; besides, I will give orders to forward our menagerie to France."

"We are not returning to Paris, then?" said Conseil.

"Oh! certainly," I answered, evasively, "by making a curve." **9**

"Will the curve please you, sir?"

"Oh! it will be nothing; not quite so direct a road, that is all. We take our passage in the *Abraham Lincoln.*"

"As you think proper, sir," coolly replied Conseil.

"You see, my friend, it has to do with the monster—the famous narwhal. We are going to purge it from the seas. The author of a work in quarto in two volumes, on the 'Mysteries of the Great Submarine Grounds' cannot forbear embarking with Commander Farragut. A glorious mission, but a dangerous one! We cannot tell where we may go; these animals can be very capricious. But we will go whether or no; we have got a captain who is pretty wideawake." **10**

["Wherever monsieur goes, there go I," Conseil replied.

"But think it over! I don't want to keep anything from you. This is one of those trips from which not everybody returns!"

"Whatever pleases monsieur."

Fifteen minutes later our bags were packed. Conseil had done everything in a jiffy. I knew nothing was missing, for that boy could classify shirts and suits as well as birds and mammals.

The hotel elevator took us down to the mezzanine, and we walked the few steps to the ground floor. I settled my bill at the desk, which as usual was besieged by a large crowd. I gave instructions for sending my cartons of straw-wrapped animals and dried plants to Paris.]

I opened a credit account for Babiroussa, and, Conseil following, I jumped into a cab. [Available at a fixed price of four dollars, the carriage went down Broadway to Union Square, followed Fourth Avenue to its junction with the Bowery, turned into Katrin Street and stopped at Pier 34. From there the Katrin Ferry took us all—people, horses, carriages—to Brooklyn, that great annex of New York, situated on the left bank of the East River. In a few minutes we arrived at the pier where the *Abraham Lincoln* was belching clouds of black smoke from her two smokestacks.]

Our luggage was transported to the deck of the frigate immediately. I hastened on board and asked for Commander Farragut. One of the sailors conducted me to the poop, where

I found myself in the presence of a good-looking officer, who held out his hand to me.

"Monsieur Pierre Aronnax?" said he.

"Himself," replied I: "Commander Farragut?"

"You are welcome, Professor; your cabin is ready for you."

I bowed and desired to be conducted to the cabin destined for me.

The *Abraham Lincoln* had been well chosen and equipped for her new destination. She was a frigate of great speed, fitted with high-pressure engines which admitted a pressure of seven atmospheres. Under this the *Abraham Lincoln* attained the mean speed of nearly eighteen knots and a third an hour—a considerable speed, but, nevertheless, insufficient to grapple with this gigantic cetacean.

The interior arrangements of the frigate corresponded to its nautical qualities. I was well satisfied with my cabin, which was in the after part, opening upon the gunroom.

"We shall be well off here," said I to Conseil.

"As well, by your honour's leave, as a hermit-crab in the shell of a whelk," [said] Conseil.

I left Conseil to stow our trunks conveniently away, and remounted the poop in order to survey the preparations for departure.

At that moment Commander Farragut was ordering the last moorings to be cast loose which held the *Abraham Lincoln* to the pier of Brooklyn. So in a quarter of an hour, perhaps less, the frigate would have sailed without me. I should have missed this extraordinary, supernatural, and incredible expedition, the recital of which may well meet with some scepticism.

But Commander Farragut would not lose a day nor an hour in scouring the seas in which the animal had been sighted. He sent for an engineer.

"Is the steam full on?" asked he.

"Yes, sir," replied the engineer.

"Go ahead," cried Commander Farragut.

[By means of a compressed-air signal, his order was relayed to the engine room where the engineers turned the starter-wheel. Steam whistled into the half-open slide valves. Long horizontal pistons groaned and pushed the rods and the drive-shaft. The blades of the propeller struck the water faster and faster. The *Abraham Lincoln* moved out majestically to meet an escort of a hundred ferry boats and tenders, all jammed with well-wishers.]

The quay of Brooklyn, and all that part of New York

professor's work. The second omission destroys Verne's smooth continuity. It cheats us of a good example of one of Verne's basic tricks: he makes science *fiction* more credible by mixing it with undeniable *facts* like the names of real streets or the actual fixed price of a cab ride.

Notice that our restorations here show how much material Verne could get out of a flying trip through a city. Need we add, he kept notebooks?

American boatswain (bo's'n), petty officer in charge of a deck crew. His whistle is his badge of office. Engraving from the 1864 edition of *The Kedge Anchor; or Young Sailors' Assistant* by William N. Brady, Sailing Master, U.S.N.

11. . . . *whose thirty-nine stars* Verne's own error. There were only thirty-seven stars in the American flag in 1867. Nebraska had been admitted to the Union as the thirty-seventh state on March 1, when Aronnax was probably en route from Nebraska to New York. The thirty-eighth state, Colorado, would not be admitted until 1876. The flag would not have thirty-nine stars until North Dakota joined the Union in 1889.

12. *mizzenpeak* The *mizzenmast* is the third mast aft. As Riou's engraving (p. 18) makes clear, the *Abraham Lincoln* is flying the colors from the peak, or outermost end, of a spar extended from the mizzenmast.

13. *abreast of the lightship* The last of these famous lightships can now be seen in the South Street Seaport Museum in Manhattan.

14. *Six bells struck* Time is sounded on the ship's bell every half hour on a four-hour system. Reckoning begins after the watch changes at 12 or 4 or 8 o'clock, A.M. or P.M. Thus *six bells,* in the watch that began at noon, corresponds to 3 P.M. And *eight bells,* in the succeeding watch that began at 4 P.M., signals 8 o'clock. Actually, in the French Verne gives these signals in clock hours.

bordering on the East River, was crowded with spectators. Three cheers burst successively from five hundred thousand throats; thousands of handkerchiefs were waved above the heads of the compact mass, saluting the *Abraham Lincoln,* until she reached the waters of the Hudson, at the point of that elongated peninsula which forms the town of New York. Then the frigate, following the coast of New Jersey along the right bank of the beautiful river, covered with villas, passed between the forts, which saluted her with their heaviest guns. The *Abraham Lincoln* answered by hoisting the American colours three times, whose thirty-nine stars **11** shone resplendent from the mizzenpeak; **12** then modifying its speed to take the narrow channel marked by buoys placed in the inner bay formed by Sandy Hook Point, it coasted the long sandy beach, where some thousands of spectators gave it one final cheer. The escort of boats and tenders still followed the frigate, and did not leave her until they came abreast of the lightship, **13** whose two lights marked the entrance of New York Channel.

Six bells struck, **14** the pilot got into his boat, and rejoined the little schooner which was waiting under our lee, the fires were made up, the screw beat the waves more rapidly, the frigate skirted the low yellow coast of Long Island; and at eight bells, after having lost sight in the north-west of the lights of Fire Island, she ran at full steam on to the dark waters of the Atlantic.

The frigate . . . Abraham Lincoln . . . ran at full steam on to the dark waters of the Atlantic. Engraving from the original (French) edition (1870).

PART 1: CHAPTER IV
Ned Land

Captain Farragut was a good seaman, worthy of the frigate he commanded. His vessel and he were one. He was the soul of it. On the question of the cetacean there was no doubt in his mind, and he would not allow the existence of the animal to be disputed on board. He believed in it, as certain good women believe in the leviathan,—by faith, not by reason. The monster did exist, and he had sworn to rid the seas of it. He was a kind of Knight of Rhodes, a second Dieudonné de Gozon, going to meet the serpent which desolated the island. Either Captain Farragut would kill the narwhal, or the narwhal would kill the captain. There was no third course.

The officers on board shared the opinion of their chief. They were ever chatting, discussing, and calculating the various chances of a meeting, watching narrowly the vast surface of the ocean. More than one took up his quarters voluntarily in the cross-trees, who would have cursed such a berth under any other circumstances. As long as the sun described its daily course, the rigging was crowded with sailors, whose feet were burnt to such an extent by the heat of the deck as to render it unbearable; still the *Abraham Lincoln* had not yet breasted the suspected waters of the Pacific. As to the ship's company, they desired nothing better than to meet the unicorn, to harpoon it, hoist it on board, and despatch it. They watched the sea with eager attention.

Besides, Captain Farragut had spoken of a certain sum of two thousand dollars, set apart for whoever should first sight the monster, were he cabin boy, common seaman, or officer.

I leave you to judge how eyes were used on board the *Abraham Lincoln.*

For my own part, I was not behind the others, and left to no

1. *for a hundred reasons* Verne could count on his audience's knowing that the Argus was, in ancient mythology, a monster with one hundred eyes. He never closed more than a few of his eyes to get some sleep while he kept watch with the others. When Hera discovered that her husband Zeus had changed the nymph Io into a heifer—the better to keep his relations with her secret—Hera ordered Argus to guard Io from Zeus's lust. Zeus enlisted the aid of Hermes, who played his flute until Argus, charmed, closed every eye in sleep. Hermes then cut off Argus's head and released Io. Hera placed Argus's one hundred eyes in the tail of the peacock.

2. *Ned Land was a Canadian* Verne probably chose Ned's last name to suggest *earthiness*. Verne was a great admirer of the French Canadians; his novel *Family without a Name* (1889) is based on their 1837 revolt against British rule.

3. *whale or . . . cachalot* Verne's French terms make it easier to· distinguish one kind of whale from another. Here he talks of *une baleine . . . ou un cachalot,* that is, *a baleen whale . . . or̩ a spermaceti whale.*

4. *cannon always . . . ready to fire* A Freudian must be delighted throughout the novel with Aronnax's unabashed use of phallic symbolism. Of course, when Aronnax met Ned Land, Freud was only twelve, and everyone was still free to revel in unconscious use of sexual symbols. As we shall see, Verne's usage is consistent and true: later it will be Land who suffers most from having no "targets" for his "cannon," while Aronnax will express, in symbolic terms, his sweet satisfaction with narcissism.

Perhaps a psychoanalyst would go further and say that Lewis's omission of this passage was caused by his unconscious embarrassment over its phallicism.

one my share of daily observations. The frigate might have been called the *Argus,* for a hundred reasons.**1** Only one amongst us, Conseil, seemed to protest by his indifference against the question which so interested us all, and seemed to be out of keeping with the general enthusiasm on board.

I have said that Captain Farragut had carefully provided his ship with every apparatus for catching the gigantic cetacean. No whaler had ever been better armed. We possessed every known engine, from the harpoon thrown by the hand to the barbed arrows of the blunderbuss, and the explosive balls of the duck-gun. On the forecastle lay the perfection of a breech-loading gun, very thick at the breech, and very narrow in the bore, the model of which had been in the Exhibition of 1867. This precious weapon of American origin could throw with ease a conical projectile of nine pounds to a mean distance of ten miles.

Thus the *Abraham Lincoln* wanted for no means of destruction; and, what was better still, she had on board Ned Land, the prince of harpooners.

Ned Land was a Canadian,**2** with an uncommon quickness of hand, and who knew no equal in his dangerous occupation. Skill, coolness, audacity, and cunning, he possessed in a superior degree, and it must be a cunning whale or a singularly "cute" cachalot **3** to escape the stroke of his harpoon.

Ned Land was about forty years of age; he was a tall man (more than six feet high), strong built, grave and taciturn, occasionally violent, and very passionate when contradicted. His person attracted attention, but above all the boldness of his look, which gave a singular expression to his face.

[I believe that Commander Farragut had acted wisely in engaging this man. He alone was worth as much as the rest of the crew, because of his eye and his arm. I can do no better than to compare him with a powerful telescope that could double as a cannon always loaded and ready to fire.**4**]

Who calls himself Canadian calls himself French; and little communicative as Ned Land was, I must admit that he took a certain liking for me. My nationality drew him to me, no doubt. It was an opportunity for him to talk, and for me to hear, that old language of Rabelais, which is still in use in some Canadian provinces. The harpooner's family was originally from Quebec, and was already a tribe of hardy fishermen when this town belonged to France.

Little by little, Ned Land acquired a taste for chátting, and I loved to hear the recital of his adventures in the polar seas. He related his fishing, and his combats, with natural poetry of ex-

American sailors at their mess table on the berth deck. Engraving from 1864 edition of William N. Brady's *The Kedge Anchor.*

pression; his recital took the form of an epic poem, and I seemed to be listening to a Canadian Homer singing the Iliad of the regions of the North.

I am portraying this hardy companion as I really knew him. We are old friends now, united in that unchangeable friendship which is born and cemented amidst extreme dangers. Ah, brave Ned! I ask no more than to live a hundred years longer, that I may have more time to dwell the longer on your memory.

Now, what was Ned Land's opinion upon the question of the marine monster? I must admit that he did not believe in the unicorn, and was the only one on board who did not share that universal conviction. He even avoided the subject, which I one day thought it my duty to press upon him. One magnificent evening, the 30th of July 5—that is to say, three weeks after our departure—the frigate was abreast of Cape Blanc, thirty miles to leeward of the coast of Patagonia. We had crossed the tropic of Capricorn, and the Straits of Magellan opened less than seven hundred miles to the south. Before eight days were over, the *Abraham Lincoln* would be ploughing the waters of the Pacific.

Seated on the poop, Ned Land and I were chatting of one thing and another as we looked at this mysterious sea, whose great depths had up to this time been inaccessible to the eye of man. I naturally led up the conversation to the giant unicorn, and examined the various chances of success or failure of the expedition. But seeing that Ned Land let me speak without saying too much himself, I pressed him more closely.

"Well, Ned," said I, "is it possible that you are not con-

5. *30th of July*   The context makes it clear that this magnificent evening had to be on or about *the 25th of June.* The confusion of dates ends in this chapter. The next chapter opens with an event that occurs on *the 30th of June,* and from there on the dating is consistent with the context.

American sailors "lashing up hammocks." Engraving from *The Kedge Anchor* (1864) by William N. Brady.

6. *whales, cetaceans, or sea-unicorns* Here Lewis is all fouled up. Sea unicorns *are* whales, and whales *are* cetaceans. A more accurate, fuller rendering of Verne's language here would be: *baleen whales, cachalots (sperm whales), or sea-unicorns (narwhals)*. Our distinctions are not pedantic. Verne is preparing us for some scenes in which knowledge of these differences enhances our understanding.

7. *its name indicates . . . softness* Aronnax is reminding Ned that the word *mollusc* is related to the French word *mollet*, soft. The French *mollusque* has the additional, figurative meaning of *weakling*.

Aronnax himself knows that our modern word for mollusk derives from New Latin *mollusca*, the soft ones, from classic Latin *mollis*, soft.

And the English reader, of course, thinks of *mollify*, that is, *to make soft*.

8. *resist their pressure* Aronnax is hampered here by the prevailing beliefs of his day. It is known now that many forms of life have adapted to the deepest strata of the ocean. Living tissue is largely composed of water, which is practically incompressible. Whales and other sea mammals have developed special skeletal structures, musculature, and thick fat to protect vulnerable areas like the

vinced of the existence of the cetacean that we are following? Have you any particular reason for being so incredulous?"

The harpooner looked at me fixedly for some moments before answering, struck his broad forehead with his hand (a habit of his), as if to collect himself, and said at last, "Perhaps I have, M. Aronnax."

"But, Ned, you, a whaler by profession, familiarised with all the great marine mammalia—you, whose imagination might easily accept the hypothesis of enormous cetaceans, *you* ought to be the last to doubt under such circumstances!"

"That is just what deceives you, Professor," replied Ned. "That the vulgar should believe in extraordinary comets traversing space, and in the existence of antediluvian monsters in the heart of the globe, may well be; but neither astronomer nor geologist believes in such chimeras. As a whaler I have followed many a cetacean, harpooned a great number, and killed several; but however strong or well-armed they have been, neither their tails nor their weapons would have been able even to scratch the iron plates of a steamer."

"But, Ned, they tell of ships which the teeth of the narwhal has pierced through and through."

"Wooden ships—that is possible," replied the Canadian; "but I have never seen it done; and, until further proof, I deny that whales, cetaceans, or sea-unicorns,**6** could ever produce the effect you describe."

["Listen to me, Ned—"

"No, Professor, no. Anything you want, except that. A giant octopus, even—"

"Even less likely, Ned. The octopus is only a mollusc, and

even its name indicates the relative softness **7** of its flesh. Even if an octopus were 500 feet long—and remember, it is not a vertebrate—it would be incapable of damaging ships like the *Scotia* or the *Abraham Lincoln*. We must reject fables about the prowess of kraken and other monsters of that species."

"So, *monsieur le naturaliste"*—Ned was slyly reminding me that I was a scientist—"you persist in affirming the existence of an enormous cetacean?"]

"Well, Ned, I repeat it with a conviction resting on the logic of facts. I believe in the existence of a mammal powerfully organised, belonging to the branch of vertebrata, like the whales, the cachalots, or the dolphins, and furnished with a horn of defence of great penetrating power."

"Hum!" said the harpooner, shaking his head with the air of a man who would not be convinced.

"Notice one thing, my worthy Canadian," I resumed. "If such an animal is in existence, if it inhabits the depths of the ocean, if it frequents the strata lying miles below the surface of the water, it must necessarily possess an organisation the strength of which would defy all comparison."

"And why this powerful organisation?" demanded Ned.

"Because it requires incalculable strength to keep one's self in these strata and resist their pressure." **8**

["Really?" Ned winked at me.

"Really, as a few figures will prove to you."

"Oh figures! Figures can lie!"

"That may be true in business,**9** Ned, but not in mathematics.] Listen to me. Let us admit that the pressure of the atmosphere is represented by the weight of a column of water thirty-two feet high. In reality the column of water would be shorter, as we are speaking of sea water, the density of which is greater than that of fresh water. Very well, when you dive, Ned, as many times thirty-two feet of water as there are above you, so many times does your body bear a pressure equal to that of the atmosphere, that is to say, 15 lbs. for each square inch of its surface. It follows then, that at 320 feet, this pressure = that of atmospheres, of 100 atmospheres at 3200 feet, and of 1000 atmospheres at 32,000 feet, that is, about 6 miles; which is equivalent to saying that, if you could attain this depth in the ocean, each square ⅜ of an inch of the surface of your body **10** would bear a pressure of 5600 lbs. Ah! my brave Ned, do you know how many square inches you carry on the surface of your body?"

"I have no idea, Mr. Aronnax."

"About 6500; **11** and, as in reality the atmosphere pressure

lung cavity. Whales also have the power to collapse the lung as they descend, to expand it as they rise, and to control the distribution of oxygen throughout their bodies. Thus they prevent the adverse chemical effects that most bodies can suffer if they compress and decompress rapidly.

9. *Figures can lie. . . . in business* This remark is especially interesting because Verne had been a businessman and had been trained in law before he became a student of science.

Verne's father, Pierre, an attorney for merchants, had hesitated to lend Jules the money to buy a seat on the stock exchange precisely because Pierre felt that speculation in money values was shady business. Verne's brother-in-law had made easy money in stocks, which Verne's father considered obscene.

Why did Lewis omit this passage? Later we shall see that Lewis may have cut certain passages for political reasons. Did ideological considerations figure here, too? Whatever Lewis's allergies, they have already—only one-tenth of the way through the novel—resulted in serious damage to Verne's narration and dialogue.

10. *each square ⅜ of an inch of the surface of your body* Verne says *each square centimeter,* which Lewis crudely equates into this unmanageable fraction. The most convenient conversion here would be: *each square inch of the surface of your body would bear a pressure of about 15,000 pounds.* A centimeter is .39371 inch. Three-eighths is .375. Lewis's conversions give the reader very little to work with.

11. *About 6500* That would magnify Ned Land into a Paul Bunyan. In the original, Aronnax credits Ned with the French equivalent of *2600 square inches of body surface.* Therefore his body is bearing, at this moment, *not 97,500 pounds* but only *39,000 pounds.* (No wonder Mercier Lewis omitted Ned's remark that figures can lie!)

is about 15 lbs. to the square inch, your 6500 square inches bear at this moment a pressure of 97,500 lbs."

"Without my perceiving it?"

"Without your perceiving it. And if you are not crushed by such a pressure, it is because the air penetrates the interior of your body with equal pressure. Hence perfect equilibrium between the interior and exterior pressure, which thus neutralise each other, and which allows you to bear it without inconvenience. But in the water it is another thing."

"Yes, I understand," replied Ned, becoming more attentive; "because the water surrounds me, but does not penetrate."

"Precisely, Ned; so that at 32 feet beneath the surface of the sea you would undergo a pressure of 97,500 lbs.; at 320 feet, ten times that pressure; at 3200 feet, a hundred times that pressure; lastly, at 32,000 feet, a thousand times that pressure would be 97,500,000 lbs.[12]—that is to say, that you would be flattened as if you had been drawn from the plates of a hydraulic machine!"

"The devil!" exclaimed Ned.

"Very well, my worthy harpooner, if some vertebrate, several hundred yards long, and large in proportion, can maintain itself in such depths—of those whose surface is represented by millions of square inches, that is, by tens of millions of pounds, we must estimate the pressure they undergo. Consider, then, what must be the resistance of their bony structure, and the strength of their organisation to withstand such pressure!"

"Why!" exclaimed Ned Land, "they must be made of iron plates eight inches thick, like the armoured frigates."

"As you say, Ned. And think what destruction such a mass would cause, if hurled with the speed of an express train against the hull of a vessel."

"Yes—certainly—perhaps," replied the Canadian, shaken by these figures, but not yet willing to give in.

"Well, have I convinced you?"

"You have convinced me of one thing, sir, which is that, if such animals do exist at the bottom of the seas, they must necessarily be as strong as you say."

"But if they do not exist, mine obstinate harpooner, how explain the accident to the *Scotia?*"

["It is just maybe—"

"Yes, go on—"

"Maybe it is because it is not true!" Without knowing it, the Canadian was reproducing a celebrated response of Arago.[13]

But this answer merely proved how stubborn Ned could be,

---

12. *that pressure would be 97,500,000 lbs.* Correcting for Lewis's original deviation, we get *39,000,000 pounds.*

13. *a celebrated response of Arago* Arago's "response" was so well known to Verne's audience that he had only to refer to it and they would recall its occasion. It seems that Dominique-François Arago (1786–1856), famous French astronomer and physicist, was once involved in a discussion of "lunacy." In those days, the word was still taken literally by many to mean mental illnesses caused by the phases and eclipses of the moon (*lunar* phenomena). Francis Bacon (1561–1626), for example, supposedly had lost consciousness during lunar eclipses. King Charles VI supposedly suffered six fits of madness in 1399, each of them during either the new moon or the full moon. The discussion finally reached the point where someone was attributing dizzy spells, sleepwalking, and attacks of malaria to the "influence of the moon."

"How come? Why?" Arago was asked.

"Why?" he said. "Maybe it's because it's not true."

In *From the Earth to the Moon* (1865) the dashing Frenchman Michel Ardan (the name is an anagram for *Nadar,* Verne's friend) tells this story in Baltimore to Americans who had not yet heard it. As a result, Verne's readers in all major Western languages were familiar with the anecdote by the time that *Twenty Thousand Leagues* appeared (1870).

nothing more. I did not press him any further that day. The damage to the *Scotia* was undeniable. The hole in her side had required patching. What better proof of the existence of a hole can you have? That puncture was the effect of a cause. Rocks beneath the surface had not been the cause. The hole had to be the work of an animal armed with a spear or a punch.

Hence, as I saw it, for all these reasons, the animal belonged to the vertebrates. Class: mammals; group: pisciforms; order: cetaceans. As to its family—was it baleen whale, cachalot, dolphin?—and its genus or species, that was a question that required more work.

To answer it, we would have to dissect the monster; to dissect it, catch it; to catch it, harpoon it, and—well, that was Ned Land's business. To harpoon it, we would have to sight it, and that was the crew's job. If we were to sight it, we would first have to cross its path—and *that* was a question of luck.]

Circular card of the mariner's compass. A needle is attached to the underside of the card with the fleur-de-lis resting on the north pole of the needle. An agate or a garnet cap is set in the middle of the needle so as to "receive" a sharp point, standing in the middle of the compass box, upon which the needle-and-card are balanced. The box, made of copper or brass, is usually hemispherical or cylindrical, and covered with glass. Engraving from *The American Cyclopaedia* (1873).

PART 1: CHAPTER V

At a Venture[1]

1. *At a Venture*   That is, *at random, by chance. At a venture* was the English equivalent in the 1870s of Verne's title for this chapter: *A l'aventure!* Notice how this phrase echoes the concluding thought of the last chapter: *l'affaire du hasard* or *a question of luck.*

2. *30th of June*   The mixup in dates ended in Chapter IV. From here on the dating is consistent.

Notice that Lewis omits Verne's phrase that would help the reader locate on his map the place where the *Monroe* incident occurs.

The voyage of the *Abraham Lincoln* was for a long time marked by no special incident. But one circumstance happened which showed the wonderful dexterity of Ned Land, and proved what confidence we might place in him.

The 30th of June,[2] [off the Falkland Islands,] the frigate spoke some American whalers, from whom we learned that they knew nothing about the narwhal. But one of them, the captain of the *Monroe,* knowing that Ned Land had shipped on board the *Abraham Lincoln,* begged for his help in chasing a whale they had in sight. Commander Farragut, desirous of seeing Ned Land at work, gave him permission to go on board the *Monroe.* And fate served our Canadian so well that, instead of one whale, he harpooned two with a double blow, striking one straight to the heart, and catching the other after some minutes' pursuit.

Decidedly, if the monster ever had to do with Ned Land's harpoon, I would not bet in its favour.

The frigate skirted the south-east coast of America with great rapidity. The 3d of July we were at the opening of the Straits of Magellan, level with Cape Vierges. But Commander Farragut would not take a tortuous passage, but doubled Cape Horn.

The ship's crew agreed with him. And certainly it was possible that they might meet the narwhal in this narrow pass. Many of the sailors affirmed that the monster could not pass there, "that he was too big for that!"

The 6th of July, about three o'clock in the afternoon, the *Abraham Lincoln,* at fifteen miles to the south, doubled the solitary island, this lost rock at the extremity of the American continent, to which some Dutch sailors gave the name of their

native town, Cape Horn. The course was taken towards the
north-west, and the next day the screw of the frigate was at
last beating the waters of the Pacific.

"Keep your eyes open!" called out the sailors.

And they were opened widely. Both eyes and glasses,'a little
dazzled, it is true, by the prospect of two thousand dollars, had
not an instant's repose. Day and night they watched the surface
of the ocean, and even nyctalopes, whose faculty of seeing in
the darkness multiplies their chances a hundredfold, would
have had enough to do to gain the prize.

I myself, for whom money had no charms, was not the least
attentive on board. Giving but few minutes to my meals, but a
few hours to sleep, indifferent to either rain or sunshine, I did
not leave the poop of the vessel. Now leaning on the netting
of the forecastle, now on the taffrail, I devoured with eagerness
the soft foam which whitened the sea as far as the eye could
reach; and how often have I shared the emotion of the majority
of the crew, when some capricious whale raised its black back

*. . . I devoured . . . the soft foam which whitened the sea
as far as the eye could reach. . . .* Engraving from the
original edition (1870). Verne himself posed for the artist
Riou, who had decided that Verne should model as the
professor. Notice the resemblance to Nadar's photograph
of Verne reproduced on page 61.

3. *If . . . you would not squint* In the original, Verne is still developing his "third-person" joke about Conseil, who here says:

"If monsieur would not strain his eyes so much, monsieur could see better."

4. *Land continued to affect . . . scepticism* Lewis's omission damages Verne's characterization of both men. Ned is a man of action, but he cannot get excited by a false mission. Verne uses the Navy personnel as a foil: they *are* capable of precisely that kind of blind morale, at least for a time. Verne also gives us here a necessary warning of Ned's coming depression, which will be the result of his repeated frustration in every area of manly endeavor. Meanwhile, Verne continues to detail the weaknesses in Aronnax's makeup. He sees Ned as someone who is wilfully *affecting* indifference, sulking because he is "passionate when contradicted." Ironically, it is Aronnax himself who is tenacious in his views.

above the waves! The poop of the vessel was crowded in a moment. The cabins poured forth a torrent of sailors and officers, each with heaving breast and troubled eye watching the course of the cetacean. I looked, and looked, till I was nearly blind, whilst Conseil, always phlegmatic, kept repeating in a calm voice:

"If, sir, you would not squint [3] so much, you would see better!"

But vain excitement! The *Abraham Lincoln* checked its speed and made for the animal signalled, a simple whale, or common cachalot, which soon disappeared amidst a storm of execration.

But the weather was good. The voyage was being accomplished under the most favourable auspices. It was then the bad season in Australia, the July of that zone corresponding to our January in Europe; but the sea was beautiful and easily scanned round a vast circumference.

[Ned Land continued to affect the greatest scepticism.[4] When he was off-duty he even refused to look at the ocean—unless somebody else had sighted a whale. His great vision would have proved helpful to us. But the stubborn Canadian spent eight hours out of twelve reading or sleeping in his cabin. A hundred times I chided him for his indifference.

"Bah," was his answer, "it is a lot of nonsense, M. Aronnax. Even if there were some animal out there, what chance would we have of sighting it? Granted, we were told that this elusive creature had been spotted in the Pacific, but that was two months ago. Judging by the temperament of your narwhal, he does not enjoy hanging around the same place. On the contrary, he has a great facility for getting around. Now Professor, you know even better than I that Nature does not violate good sense. She would not give an animal slow by nature the faculty of fast movement unless it had some need of that faculty. So, if your beast exists, it is far away from here by now!"

I did not know how to answer that. Obviously we *were* stabbing in the dark. But how else could we proceed? Granted, our chances were limited, to say the least. But the crew never doubted we would be successful. Not a sailor on board would have bet against our sighting the narwhal, and soon.]

The 20th of July, the tropic of Capricorn was cut by 105° of longitude, and the 27th of the same month we crossed the equator on the 110th meridian. This passed, the frigate took a more decided westerly direction, and scoured the central waters of the Pacific. Commander Farragut thought, and with reason, that it was better to remain in deep water, and keep clear of continents or islands, which the beast itself seemed to shun (perhaps because there was not enough water for him! suggested the greater part of the crew). The frigate passed at some distance from Marquesas and the Sandwich Islands, crossed the tropic of Cancer, and made for the China Seas. We were on the theatre of the last diversions of the monster; and to say truth, we no longer *lived* on board. Hearts palpitated, fearfully preparing themselves for future incurable aneurism. The entire ship's crew were undergoing a nervous excitement, of which I can give no idea: they could not eat, they could not sleep—twenty times a day, a misconception or an optical illusion of some sailor seated on the taffrail, would cause dreadful perspirations, and these emotions, twenty times repeated, kept us in a state of excitement so violent that a reaction was unavoidable.

And truly, reaction soon showed itself. For three months, during which a day seemed an age, the *Abraham Lincoln* furrowed all the waters of the Northern Pacific, running at whales, making sharp deviations from her course, veering suddenly from one tack to another, stopping suddenly, putting on steam, and backing ever and anon at the risk of deranging her machinery; and not one point of the Japanese or American coast was left unexplored. [And with no results! We saw nothing but an immense, deserted ocean! Nothing that resembled a gigantic narwhal, or a submerged island, or a floating wreck, or a shifting reef—nothing at all unusual!

And so the reaction set in. Discouragement led to disbelief. A new sentiment grew on board, three-tenths shame, seven-tenths fury. For the men felt embarrassed at having been led on a wild goose chase, and that infuriated them. The mountains of arguments that had been piled up in support of the expedition collapsed, and everybody wanted now to catch up on his eating and sleeping, to make up for the time he had sacrificed. With human fickleness, the crew's morale went from one extreme to the other.]

The warmest partisans of the enterprise now became its most ardent detractors. Reaction mounted from the crew to the captain himself, and certainly, had it not been for resolute determination on the part of Captain Farragut, the frigate would have headed due southward. This useless search could not last much longer. The *Abraham Lincoln* had nothing to reproach herself with, she had done her best to succeed. Never

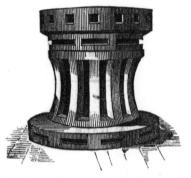

Type of capstan—or machine for moving heavy weights, like an anchor—probably used on the *Abraham Lincoln*. Under direction of a bo's'n, sailors insert bars into the sockets in the drumhead and rotate it to wind in the cable and the weight attached. Engraving from the 1864 edition of *The Kedge Anchor* by William N. Brady.

had an American ship's crew shown more zeal or patience; its failure could not be placed to their charge—there remained nothing but to return.

This was represented to the commander. The sailors could not hide their discontent, and the service suffered. I will not say there was a mutiny on board, but after a reasonable period of obstinacy, Captain Farragut (as Columbus did) asked for three days' patience. If in three days the monster did not appear, the man at the helm should give three turns of the wheel, and the *Abraham Lincoln* would make for the European seas.

This promise was made on the 2d of November. It had the effect of rallying the ship's crew. The ocean was watched with renewed attention. Each one wished for a last glance in which to sum up his remembrance. Glasses were used with feverish activity. It was a grand defiance given to the giant narwhal, and he could scarcely fail to answer the summons and "appear."

Two days passed, the steam was at half pressure; a thousand schemes were tried to attract the attention and stimulate the apathy of the animal in case it should be met in those parts. Large quantities of bacon were trailed in the wake of the ship, to the great satisfaction (I must say) of the sharks. Small craft radiated in all directions round the *Abraham Lincoln* as she lay to, and did not leave a spot of the sea unexplored. But the night of the 4th of November arrived without the unveiling of this submarine mystery.

The next day, the 5th of November, at twelve the delay would (morally speaking) expire; after that time, Commander Farragut, faithful to his promise, was to turn the course to the south-east and abandon for ever the northern regions of the Pacific.

The frigate was then in 31° 15′ north latitude and 136° 42′ east longitude. The coast of Japan still remained less than two hundred miles to leeward. Night was approaching. They had just struck eight bells; large clouds veiled the face of the moon, then in its first quarter. The sea undulated peaceably under the stern of the vessel.

At that moment I was leaning forward on the starboard netting. Conseil, standing near me, was looking straight before him. The crew, perched in the ratlines, examined the horizon, which contracted and darkened by degrees. Officers with their night glasses scoured the growing darkness; sometimes the ocean sparkled under the rays of the moon, which darted between two clouds, then all trace of light was lost in the darkness.

In looking at Conseil, I could see he was undergoing a little of the general influence. At least I thought so. Perhaps for the first time his nerves vibrated to a sentiment of curiosity.

"Come, Conseil," said I, "this is the last chance of pocketing the two thousand dollars."

"May I be permitted to say, sir," replied Conseil, "that I never reckoned on getting the prize; and, had the government of the Union offered a hundred thousand dollars, it would have been none the poorer."

"You are right, Conseil. It is a foolish affair after all, and one upon which we entered too lightly. What time lost, what useless emotions! We should have been back in France six months ago."

"In your little room, sir," [5] replied Conseil, "and in your museum, sir, and I should have already classed all your fossils, sir. And the Babiroussa would have been installed in its cage in the Jardin des Plantes, and have drawn all the curious people of the capital!"

"As you say, Conseil. I fancy we will run a fair chance of being laughed at for our pains."

"That's tolerably certain," replied Conseil, quietly; "I think they will make fun of you, sir. And, must I say it?"

"Go on, my good friend."

"Well, sir, you will only get your deserts."

"Indeed!"

"When one has the honor [6] of being a savant as you are, sir, one should not expose one's self to—"

Conseil had not time to finish his compliment. In the midst of general silence a voice had just been heard. It was the voice of Ned Land shouting—

"Look out there! the very thing we are looking for—on our weather beam!" [7]

5. *In your little room, sir* Verne had in mind nothing so crowded or intimate. He has Conseil say, *"Dans le petit appartement de monsieur"*; that is, *in monsieur's flat* or *little suite of rooms.*

6. *When one has the honor* In the original, this is one of the best examples of how Conseil expresses strong identification with Aronnax without dropping his third-person formality: *"When one has the honor of being a savant as monsieur is, one does not expose one's self to—."*

7. *"Look. . . . on our weather beam!"* The weather side would be the direction from which the wind is blowing: *to windward.* In French that is *au vent.* But here Verne says *sous le vent* or *to leeward,* the point toward which the wind is blowing.

A more accurate rendering of Ned's nautical language here would be: *"Ahoy! The thing itself! Abeam to leeward!"*

A flying fish as pictured in A.C.L.G. Günther's *An Introduction to the Study of Fishes* (1880).

PART 1: CHAPTER VI

At Full Steam

1. *monster emerged some fathoms from the water* Verne has not yet written *Master of the World* (1904), in which just such a monster will appear—one capable of emerging from underwater and ascending into the air.

Here Lewis has mistranslated Verne's word *immergé* as *emerged*. Actually Verne is saying that the monster is *immersed*, or *submerged*, *some fathoms below the surface*.

A *fathom* is officially given as a *distance of six feet*. In practice, it is the distance between a man's finger-tips when his arms are outstretched wide. A seaman finds this to be the maximum convenient length for gathering up the line used to sound the depths. And so he expresses his measurement of depth in fathoms. He is likely to measure horizontal distance in fathoms, too.

At this cry the whole ship's crew hurried towards the harpooner,—commander, officers, masters, sailors, cabin boys; even the engineers left their engines, and the stokers their furnaces.

The order to stop her had been given, and the frigate now simply went on by her own momentum. The darkness was then profound, and however good the Canadian's eyes were, I asked myself how he had managed to see, and what he had been able to see. My heart beat as if it would break. But Ned Land was not mistaken, and we all perceived the object he pointed to. At two cables' lengths from the *Abraham Lincoln,* on the starboard quarter, the sea seemed to be illuminated all over. It was not a mere phosphoric phenomenon. The monster emerged some fathoms from the water,1 and then threw out that very intense but inexplicable light mentioned in the report of several captains. This magnificent irradiation must have been produced by an agent of great *shining* power. The luminous part traced on the sea an immense oval, much elongated, the centre of which condensed a burning heat, whose overpowering brilliancy died out by successive gradations.

"It is only an agglomeration of phosphoric particles," cried one of the officers.

"No, sir, certainly not," I replied. "Never did pholades or salpae produce such a powerful light. That brightness is of an essentially electrical nature. Besides, see, see! It moves; it is moving forwards, backwards; it is darting towards us!"

A general cry rose from the frigate.

"Silence!" said the Captain; "up with the helm, reverse the engines."

[Sailors returned to their stations on deck, engineers to

their machinery.] The steam was shut off,**2** and the *Abraham Lincoln*, beating to port, described a semicircle.

"Right the helm, go ahead," cried the Captain.

These orders were executed, and the frigate moved rapidly from the burning light.

I was mistaken. She tried to sheer off, but the supernatural animal approached with a velocity double her own.

We gasped for breath. Stupefaction more than fear made us dumb and motionless. The animal gained on us, sporting with the waves. It made the round of the frigate, which was then making fourteen knots, and enveloped it with its electric rings like luminous dust. Then it moved away two or three miles, leaving a phosphorescent track, like those volumes of steam that the express trains leave behind. All at once from the dark line of the horizon whither it retired to gain its momentum, the monster rushed suddenly towards the *Abraham Lincoln* with alarming rapidity, stopped suddenly about twenty feet from the hull, and died out,—not diving under the water, for its brilliancy did not abate,—but suddenly, and as if the source of this brilliant emanation was exhausted. Then it reappeared on the other side of the vessel, as if it had turned and slid under the hull. Any moment a collision might have occurred which would have been fatal to us. However, I was astonished at the manoeuvres of the frigate. She fled and did not attack.

On the captain's face, generally so impassive, was an expression of unaccountable astonishment.

"Mr. Aronnax," he said, "I do not know with what formidable being I have to deal, and I will not imprudently risk my frigate in the midst of this darkness. Besides, how attack this unknown thing, how defend one's self from it? Wait for daylight, and the scene will change."

"You have no further doubt, captain, of the nature of the animal?"

"No, sir; it is evidently a gigantic narwhal, and an electric one."

"Perhaps," added I, "one can only approach it with a gymnotus or a torpedo." **3**

"Undoubtedly," replied the captain, "if it possesses such dreadful power,**4** it is the most terrible animal that ever was created. That is why, sir, I must be on my guard."

The crew were on their feet all night. No one thought of sleep. The *Abraham Lincoln,* not being able to struggle with such velocity, had moderated its pace, and sailed at half speed. For its part, the narwhal, imitating the frigate, let the waves rock it at will, and seemed decided not to leave the scene of the

2. *The steam was shut off* Verne says that *the engines were reversed,* as Farragut had ordered.

The electric gymnotus as pictured in A. E. Brehm's *Merveilles de la Nature* (1885).

3. *approach it with a gymnotus or a torpedo* That would be awkward, pointless, and not what Verne had in mind.

A gymnotus is an *electric eel.* A torpedo, in this context, means a *numbfish* or *crampfish,* one of the members of the genus torpedo who can produce strong electric discharge.

And what Aronnax is really saying, in the original, sounds something like this: *Maybe we can get no closer to it than we could to an electric eel or a numbfish.*

Incidentally, the military torpedo, originally an underwater mine that exploded on contact, was named after the torpedo fish.

4. *such dreadful power* . . . That is, the power to electrocute, like lightning, as Verne makes clear.

5. *you have the prize* Notice that for five hours after he sighted "the thing" under difficult conditions, Ned Land apparently has waited in vain for some reassurance about the prize. Ned is finally forced to remind the captain, whose late recognition of Ned's feat is offhand and stingy.

Such neglect of the morale of his men seems typical of Farragut's behavior under stress. His conduct now belies all we were led to expect of him early in Chapter IV. Such contrast between initial promise and later performance is one of Verne's motifs in characterization.

Verne was endlessly fascinated by the military personality. In *From the Earth to the Moon* (1865), for example, he satirizes the bloodthirsty militarist that he believed had emerged from the American Civil War. Verne distrusted even the psychological effects of military preparedness. In correspondence with his father in the late 1860s, he commented on new legislation that would beef up the French Army:

"We have a military law that carries us back to the time of the Huns and Visigoths. . . . We are faced with the prospects of stupid wars. . . . When will men learn to reason without rifles? . . . Will they never listen to any arguments. other than those of the professional military caste?"

Verne's impressions of the way some military men talk and act were gained largely from four people with whom he spent much time. He soaked up a rich diet of service anecdotes from his brother Paul, a career naval officer; his father-in-law, M. de Viane, a retired captain of cuirassiers; and Alexandre Lelong and Alfred Berlot, retired sailors who served as Verne's crew on his first yacht. Lelong had seen combat in the Crimean War.

While working on *Twenty Thousand Leagues*, Verne himself had not yet seen military service. Later, in the Franco-Prussian War, he would command a coast-guard unit that would patrol the Somme in his yacht, *Saint Michel*.

struggle. Towards midnight, however, it disappeared, or, to use a more appropriate term, it "died out" like a large glow-worm. Had it fled? One could only fear, not hope. But at seven minutes to one o'clock in the morning a deafening whistling was heard, like that produced by a body of water rushing with great violence.

The captain, Ned Land, and I, were then on the poop, eagerly peering through the profound darkness.

"Ned Land," asked the commander, "you have often heard the roaring of whales?"

"Often, sir; but never such whales the sight of which brought me in two thousand dollars."

["Of course, Mr. Land, you have the prize.**5** But now tell me, is that not the noise cetaceans make as they blow water out of their vents?"

"The same kind of noise, Captain, although this is incomparably louder. But there is no mistaking it. That is certainly a cetacean out there. With your permission," added the harpooner, "we will speak a few words with him when day breaks."

"If he is in a mood to listen to you, Master Land," I replied sceptically.]

"If I can only approach within four harpoon lengths of it!"

"But to approach it," said the commander, "I ought to put a whaler at your disposal?"

"Certainly, sir."

"That will be trifling with the lives of my men."

"And mine too," simply said the harpooner.

Towards two o'clock in the morning, the burning light reappeared, not less intense, about five miles to windward of the *Abraham Lincoln*. Notwithstanding the distance, and the noise of the wind and sea, one heard distinctly the loud strokes of the animal's tail, and even its panting breath. It seemed that, at the moment that the enormous narwhal had come to take breath at the surface of the water, the air was engulphed in its lungs, like the steam in the vast cylinders of a machine of two thousand horsepower.

"Hum!" thought I, "a whale with the strength of a cavalry regiment would be a pretty whale!"

We were on the *qui vive* till daylight, and prepared for the combat. The fishing implements were laid along the hammock nettings.**6** The second lieutenant loaded the blunderbusses, which could throw harpoons to a distance of a mile, and long duck-guns, with explosive bullets, which inflicted mortal wounds even to the most terrible animals. Ned Land contented himself with sharpening his harpoon—a terrible weapon in his hands.

At six o'clock day began to break; and with the first glimmer of light, the electric light of the narwhal disappeared. At seven o'clock the day was sufficiently advanced, but a very thick sea fog obscured our view, and the best spy-glasses could not pierce it. That caused disappointment and anger.

I climbed the mizzen-mast. Some officers were already perched on the mast heads. At eight o'clock the fog lay heavily on the waves, and its thick scrolls rose little by little. The horizon grew wider and clearer at the same time. Suddenly, just as on the day before, Ned Land's voice was heard:

"The thing itself on the port quarter!" cried the harpooner.

Every eye was turned towards the point indicated. There, a mile and a half from the frigate, a long blackish body emerged a yard above the waves. Its tail, violently agitated, produced a considerable eddy. Never did a caudal appendage beat the sea with such violence. An immense track, of a dazzling whiteness, marked the passage of the animal, and described a long curve.

The frigate approached the cetacean. I examined it thoroughly.

The reports of the *Shannon* and of the *Helvetia* had rather exaggerated its size, and I estimated its length at only two hundred and fifty feet. As to its dimensions, I could only conjecture them to be admirably proportioned. While I watched this phenomenon, two jets of steam and water were ejected from its vents, and rose to the height of 120 feet; thus I ascertained its way of breathing. I concluded definitely that it belonged to the vertebrate branch, class mammalia,[7] [subclass of monodelphians, group of pisciforms, order of cetaceans, family of . . . Here I was stumped. The order of cetaceans comprises three families: baleen whales, spermaceti whales or cachalots, and dolphins. Now the narwhals belong to the last family. Each family is divided into several genera, each genus into species, each species into varieties. So I had not yet established variety, species, genus, and family. But I did not doubt that with the aid of Providence and the Captain, I could complete my classification.]

The crew waited impatiently for their chief's orders. The latter, after having observed the animal attentively, called the engineer. The engineer ran to him.

"Sir," said the commander, "you have steam up?"

"Yes, sir," answered the engineer.

"Well, make up your fires and put on all steam."

Three hurrahs greeted this order. The time for the struggle

6. *along the hammock nettings* Verne says *le long des bastingages,* or *along the lockers on the bulwarks for stowing hammocks.* These lockers form a protection on deck against small-arms fire. The phrase can also be rendered as *along the rails.*

In the next sentence, the officer who is loading weapons is simply called, in the French, *the second in command.*

7. *vertebrate branch, class mammalia* This may satisfy Lewis as a definite conclusion, but not Aronnax, as we can see from our restoration.

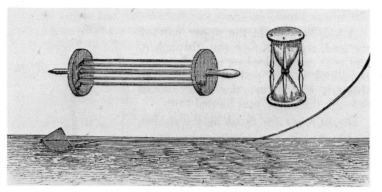

Log reel, log glass, and log line trailing the log, as pictured in the 1864 edition of William N. Brady's *The Kedge Anchor*.

8. *We heaved the log* The "log" is really a *chip of log* shaped like a big piece of pie. Its rim is loaded with lead so that once it is heaved into the sea, it will assume a vertical position. It is attached to a log line so tied as to hold the log square against the water. The log line is payed out from a reel at the stern.

So, when a seaman "heaves the log," the chip settles firmly in one spot on the surface of the sea and the ship moves away from it, paying out the line. This line is knotted at intervals of 47.25 feet. The number of knots that pay out in 28 seconds shows the speed of the ship, which is reported in "knots." Timing is done with a sandglass called the "log glass."

Measurements of the log line and of the time are based on this equation:

$$\frac{47.25 \text{ feet}}{6080 \text{ feet}} = \frac{28 \text{ seconds}}{3600 \text{ seconds}}$$

In other words, a knot is the same part of a sea mile (6080 feet) as 28 seconds is of an hour (3600 seconds).

had arrived. Some moments after, the two funnels of the frigate vomited torrents of black smoke, and the bridge quaked under the trembling of the boilers.

The *Abraham Lincoln,* propelled by her powerful screw, went straight at the animal. The latter allowed it to come within half a cable's length; then, as if disdaining to dive, it took a little turn, and stopped a short distance off.

This pursuit lasted nearly three-quarters of an hour, without the frigate gaining two yards on the cetacean. It was quite evident that at that rate we should never come up with it.

[Enraged, the Captain twisted the thick tuft of hair that bristled beneath his chin.

"Ned Land!" he shouted, and the Canadian reported at once.]

"Well, Mr. Land," asked the Captain, "do you advise me to put the boats out to sea?"

"No, sir," replied Ned Land; "because we shall not take that beast easily."

"What shall we do then?"

"Put on more steam if you can, sir. With your leave, I mean to post myself under the bowsprit, and if we get within har-pooning distance I shall throw my harpoon."

"Go, Ned," said the Captain. "Engineer, put on more pressure."

Ned Land went to his post. The fires were increased, the screw revolved forty-three times a minute, and the steam poured out of the valves. We heaved the log,**8** and calculated that the *Abraham Lincoln* was going at the rate of 18½ miles an hour.

But the accursed animal swam too at the rate of 18½ miles.

For a whole hour, the frigate kept up this pace, without gaining six feet. It was humiliating for one of the swiftest sailers in the American navy. A stubborn anger seized the crew; the sailors abused the monster, who, as before, disdained to answer them; the captain no longer contented himself with twisting his beard—he gnawed it.

The engineer was again called.

"You have turned full steam in?"

"Yes, sir," replied the engineer.

["And what is the pressure?"

"Six and a half atmospheres."

"Get it up to ten atmospheres."

A typical American command! The way it is done in those races on the Mississippi.**9**

"Conseil," I said to my faithful servant standing at my side, "you know, we will probably be blown up!"

"Whatever pleases monsieur," he answered. And I admit I *was* pleased to take this chance.

The valves were charged. More coal was flung into the furnaces, which were ventilated with torrents of air.]

The speed of the *Abraham Lincoln* increased. Its masts trembled down to their stepping holes, and the clouds of smoke could hardly find way out of the narrow funnels.

They heaved the log a second time.

"Well?" asked the captain of the man at the wheel.

"Nineteen miles and three-tenths, sir."

"Clap on more steam."

The engineer obeyed. The manometer showed ten degrees.

9. *races on the Mississippi* Captains of steamboats plying the Mississippi, Ohio, and Hudson rivers were notorious for the reckless way they raced each other. They sacrificed everything for speed. They would "make fast" the safety valves on their boilers so that, for example, a boiler made to work at 25 pounds pressure might work at 60. They would burn up all their coal and start stoking their furnaces with furniture from the state rooms. In one race, the captain of the Mississippi steamer *Pioneer* deliberately rammed his adversary, the *Ontario,* sinking her and killing a passenger.

The paying customers were continually protesting because—even without racing—boiler explosions were a common occurrence. Steamer after steamer burned herself up.

"Getting up" the steam pressure symbolized for Verne his deepest anxieties about the excesses of technology, especially American technology. In his first novel, *Five Weeks in a Balloon* (1863), Dick Kennedy, a big-game hunter, says:

"By dint of inventing machinery, men will end in being eaten up by it. I have always thought that the end of the earth will come when some enormous boiler, charged to three thousand millions of atmospheric pressure, will explode and blow up the world!"

Joe, a servant, adds:

"And I bet the Yankees will have a hand in it."

"Yes," Dr. Samuel Ferguson, leader of the balloon expedition, says, "they *are* great boiler-makers. . . ."

An American riverboat in a productive—and more typical—activity: "loading with cotton." Engraving from *Mitchell's School Geography* (1863).

American sailors at their gun station. Engraving from the 1864 edition of *The Kedge Anchor* by William N. Brady.

But the cetacean grew warm itself, no doubt; for without straining itself it made $19\frac{3}{10}$ miles.

What a pursuit! No, I cannot describe the emotion that vibrated through me. Ned Land kept his post, harpoon in hand. Several times the animal let us gain upon it.—"We shall catch it! We shall catch it!" cried the Canadian. But just as he was going to strike, the cetacean stole away with a rapidity that could not be estimated at less than thirty miles an hour, and even during our maximum speed, it bullied the frigate, going round and round it. A cry of fury broke from every one!

At noon we were no further advanced than at eight o'clock in the morning.

The captain then decided to take more direct means.

"Ah!" said he, "that animal goes quicker than the *Abraham Lincoln*. Very well! we will see whether it will escape these conical bullets. Send your men to the forecastle, sir."

The forecastle gun was immediately loaded and slewed round. But the shot passed some feet above the cetacean, which was half a mile off.

"Another more to the right," **10** cried the commander, "and five dollars to whoever will hit that infernal beast."

An old gunner with a grey beard—that I can see now—with steady eye and grave face, went up to the gun and took a long aim. A loud report was heard, with which were mingled the cheers of the crew.

The bullet did its work; it hit the animal, but not fatally, and sliding off the rounded surface, was lost in two miles depth **11** of sea.

["Oh, that . . . !" The old cannoneer was in a rage. "That thing must be covered with plates six inches thick!"

10. *Another more to the right*   No, in the original the captain is *not* calling for another shot more "to the right" (*à droite*). Rather he is calling for another gunner who is more *adroit* in his aim. Furthermore, the captain offers a prize not of *five dollars* but of *five hundred* dollars.

11. *two miles depth*   No, no, what's really going on, in Verne's French, is that the cannonball has bounced off the *beast* and plunged into the sea *two miles away*.

"Curses on it!" cried the Captain.]

The chase began again, and the Captain leaning towards me, said—

"I will pursue that beast till my frigate bursts up."

"Yes," answered I; "and you will be quite right to do it."

I wished the beast would exhaust itself, and not be insensible to fatigue like a steam engine! But it was of no use. Hours passed, without its showing any signs of exhaustion.

However, it must be said in praise of the *Abraham Lincoln,* that she struggled on indefatigably. I cannot reckon the distance she made under three hundred miles during this unlucky day, November the 6th. But night came on, and overshadowed the rough ocean.

Now I thought our expedition was at an end, and that we should never again see the extraordinary animal. I was mistaken. At ten minutes to eleven in the evening the electric light reappeared three miles to windward of the frigate, as pure, as intense as during the preceding night.

The narwhal seemed motionless; perhaps, tired with its day's work, it slept, letting itself float with the undulation of the waves. Now was the chance of which the captain resolved to take advantage.

He gave his orders. The *Abraham Lincoln* kept up half steam, and advanced cautiously so as not to awake its adversary. It is no rare thing to meet in the middle of the ocean whales so sound asleep that they can be successfully attacked, and Ned Land had harpooned more than one during its sleep. The Canadian went to take his place under the bowsprit.

The frigate approached noiselessly, stopped at two cables' lengths from the animal, and following its track. No one breathed; a deep silence reigned on the bridge. We were not a hundred feet from the burning focus, the light of which increased and dazzled our eyes.

At this moment, leaning on the forecastle bulwark, I saw below me Ned Land grappling the martingale in one hand,**12** brandishing his terrible harpoon in the other, scarcely twenty feet from the motionless animal. Suddenly his arm straightened, and the harpoon was thrown; I heard the sonorous stroke of the weapon, which seemed to have struck a hard body. The electric light went out suddenly, and two enormous waterspouts broke over the bridge of the frigate, rushing like a torrent from stem to stern, overthrowing men, and breaking the lashing of the spars. A fearful shock followed, and, thrown over the rail without having time to stop myself, I fell into the sea.

12. *grappling the martingale in one hand* As he promised, Ned has posted himself under the *bowsprit,* the thick spar that extends forward from the bow. From the bowsprit there extends downward a smaller spar, usually called the *dolphin striker* but sometimes the *martingale*. From this vertical spar, ropes extend in several directions. Two that stretch diagonally from the dolphin striker up to the bowsprit are also called *martingales*. Two that stretch from the striker back to either side of the bow are called *backropes*. Presumably Ned is standing with one foot on each backrope, grappling either a martingale rope or the dolphin striker with his left hand, and brandishing his harpoon with his right.

PART 1: CHAPTER VII

An Unknown Species of Whale

1. *to rival Byron or . . . Poe* The names of these great Romantics are associated with heroic swimming for different reasons. The poet Lord Byron had proved in public that he himself—like his heroes—was a master swimmer. He achieved fame as a daring athlete when he swam the Hellespont (the Dardanelles) in 1810. Thus he proved that a modern man could duplicate the feat of the legendary Leander, who swam nightly from Abydos to visit his lover, Hero, in Sestos. On a night of choppy seas, Leander drowned.

But Edgar Allan Poe's talents as a swimmer were manifest mainly in his fiction. In several of his magnificent stories—already famous in Europe in Aronnax's day—Poe's heroes perform prodigious feats in the water. One of these—"A Descent into the Maelström" (1841)—surely influenced Verne in his handling of a scene later in this novel.

Verne's essay *Edgar Poe et ses oeuvres* (*Edgar Poe and His Works*) had appeared in 1864, three years before the present action. While greatly admiring Poe, Verne pinpointed some of the American's errors in his fictional use of science.

2. *with much greater ease* In his last conversation with the professor,

This unexpected fall so stunned me that I have no clear recollection of my sensations at the time. I was at first drawn down to a depth of about twenty feet. I am a good swimmer (though without pretending to rival Byron or Edgar Poe,[1] who were masters of the art), and in that plunge I did not lose my presence of mind. Two vigorous strokes brought me to the surface of the water. My first care was to look for the frigate. Had the crew seen me disappear? Had the *Abraham Lincoln* veered round? Would the captain put out a boat? Might I hope to be saved?

The darkness was intense. I caught a glimpse of a black mass disappearing in the east, its beacon lights dying out in the distance. It was the frigate! I was lost.

"Help, Help!" I shouted, swimming towards the *Abraham Lincoln* in desperation.

My clothes encumbered me; they seemed glued to my body, and paralysed my movements.

I was sinking! I was suffocating!

"Help!"

This was my last cry. My mouth filled with water; I struggled against being drawn down the abyss. Suddenly my clothes were seized by a strong hand, and I felt myself drawn up to the surface of the sea; and I heard, yes, I heard these words pronounced in my ear—

"If master would be so good as to lean on my shoulder, master would swim with much greater ease." [2]

I seized with one hand my faithful Conseil's arm.

"Is it you?" said I, "you?"

"Myself," answered Conseil; "and waiting master's orders."

"That shock threw you as well as me into the sea?"

"No; but being in my master's service, I followed him."

The worthy fellow thought that was but natural.

"And the frigate?" I asked.

"The frigate?" replied Conseil, turning on his back; "I think that master had better not count too much on her."

"You think so?"

"I say that, at the time I threw myself into the sea, I heard the men at the wheel say, 'The screw and the rudder are broken.'"

"Broken?"

"Yes, broken by the monster's teeth. It is the only injury the *Abraham Lincoln* has sustained. But it is bad look out for us—she no longer answers her helm."

"Then we are lost!"

"Perhaps so," calmly answered Conseil. "However, we have still several hours before us, and one can do a good deal in some hours."

Conseil's imperturbable coolness set me up again. I swam more vigorously; but, cramped by my clothes, which stuck to me like a leaden weight, I felt great difficulty in bearing up. Conseil saw this.

"Will master let me make a slit?" said he; and slipping an open knife under my clothes, he ripped them up from top to bottom very rapidly. Then he cleverly slipped them off me, while I swam for both of us.

Then I did the same for Conseil, and we continued to swim near to each other.

Nevertheless, our situation was no less terrible. Perhaps our disappearance had not been noticed; and if it had been, the frigate could not tack, being without its helm. Conseil argued on this supposition, and laid his plans accordingly. This phlegmatic boy was perfectly self-possessed. We then decided that, as our only chance of safety was being picked up by the *Abraham Lincoln's* boats, we ought to manage so as to wait for them as long as possible. I resolved then to husband our strength, so that both should not be exhausted at the same time; and this is how we managed: while one of us lay on our back, quite still, with arms crossed, and legs stretched out, the other would swim and push the other on in front. This towing business [3] did not last more than ten minutes each; and relieving each other thus, we could swim on for some hours, perhaps till daybreak. Poor chance! but hope is so firmly rooted in the heart of man! Moreover, there were two of us.

Conseil addressed Aronnax in the second person as *"you."* Here Conseil speaks to/of Aronnax in the third person as *"master."* Such inconsistencies in the "standard translation" suggest that Mercier Lewis employed one or more assistants whose work he failed to correlate with his own.

3. *This towing business* Verne's French *Ce rôle de remorqueur* suggests the action of a tugboat which can *push* or *drag along* as well as tow.

Indeed I declare (though it may seem improbable) if I sought to destroy all hope—if I wished to despair, I could not.

The collision of the frigate with the cetacean had occurred about eleven o'clock the evening before. I reckoned then we should have eight hours to swim before sunrise, an operation quite practicable if we relieved each other. The sea, very calm, was in our favour. Sometimes I tried to pierce the intense darkness that was only dispelled by the phosphorescence caused by our movements. I watched the luminous waves that broke over my hand, whose mirror-like surface was spotted with silvery rings. One might have said that we were in a bath of quicksilver.

Near one o'clock in the morning, I was seized with dreadful fatigue. My limbs stiffened under the strain of violent cramp. Conseil was obliged to keep me up, and our preservation devolved on him alone. I heard the poor boy pant; his breathing became short and hurried. I found that he could not keep up much longer.

"Leave me! Leave me!" I said to him.

"Leave my master? Never!" replied he. "I would drown first."

Just then the moon appeared through the fringes of a thick cloud that the wind was driving to the east. The surface of the sea glittered with its rays. This kindly light reanimated us. My head got better again. I looked at all the points of the horizon. I saw the frigate! She was five miles from us, and looked like a dark mass, hardly discernible. But no boats!

I would have cried out. But what good would it have been at such a distance! My swollen lips could utter no sounds. Conseil could articulate some words, and I heard him repeat at intervals: "Help! Help!"

Our movements were suspended for an instant; we listened. It might be only a singing in the ear, but it seemed to me as if a cry answered the cry from Conseil.

"Did you hear?" I murmured.

"Yes! yes!"

And Conseil gave one more despairing call.

This time there was no mistake! A human voice responded to ours! Was it the voice of another unfortunate creature, abandoned in the middle of the ocean, some other victim of the shock sustained by the vessel? Or rather was it a boat from the frigate, that was hailing us in the darkness?

Conseil made a last effort, and leaning on my shoulder, while I struck out in a despairing effort, he raised himself half out of the water, then fell back exhausted.

"What did you see?"

"I saw"—murmured he; "I saw—but do not talk—reserve all your strength!"

What had he seen? Then, I know not why, the thought of the monster came into my head for the first time! But that voice? The time is past for Jonahs **4** to take refuge in whales' bellies! However, Conseil was towing me again. He raised his head sometimes, looked before us, and uttered a cry of recognition, which was responded to by a voice that came nearer and nearer. I scarcely heard it. My strength was exhausted; my fingers stiffened; my hand afforded me support no longer; my mouth, convulsively opening, filled with salt water. Cold crept over me. I raised my head for the last time, then I sank.

At this moment a hard body struck me. I clung to it: then I felt that I was being drawn up, that I was brought to the surface of the water, that my chest collapsed:—I fainted.

It is certain that I soon came to, thanks to the vigorous rubbings that I received. I half opened my eyes.

"Conseil!" I murmured.

"Does master call me?" **5** asked Conseil.

Just then, by the waning light of the moon, which was sinking down to the horizon, I saw a face which was not Conseil's and which I immediately recognised.

"Ned!" I cried.

"The same, sir, who is seeking his prize!" replied the Canadian.

"Were you thrown into the sea by the shock of the frigate?"

"Yes, Professor; but more fortunate than you, I was able to find a footing almost directly upon a floating island." **6**

"An island?"

"Or, more correctly speaking, on our gigantic narwhal."

"Explain yourself, Ned!"

"Only I soon found out why my harpoon had not entered its skin and was only blunted."

"Why, Ned, why?"

"Because, Professor, that beast is made of sheet iron."

The Canadian's last words produced a sudden revolution in my brain. I wriggled myself quickly to the top of the being, or object, half out of the water, which served us for a refuge. I kicked it. It was evidently a hard impenetrable body, and not the soft substance that forms the bodies of the great marine mammalia. But this hard body might be a bony carapace, like that of the antediluvian animals; and I should be free to class this monster among amphibious reptiles, such as tortoises or alligators.

4. *The time is past for Jonahs* But is the time past? Like many of the professor's reflections, this one will prove to be ironic. Students of mythopoesis regard Jonah's taking refuge in the whale as a descent into the self. He withdraws from life so that he can be cast forth "reborn." Jonah's time in the whale is thus equated with Dante's descent into Hell and Captain Marlow's trip into *The Heart of Darkness*. Notice that Jonah was already attempting such withdrawal when he sought refuge in the "belly" of the ship.

If Aronnax can think that *the time is past* for such epic journeys, it's only because he has not yet suffered his own great "identity crisis."

5. *Does master call me* In the original, this line is a pleasant joke because what Conseil really says is: *"Did monsieur ring for me?"*

6. *a floating island* From Aronnax and Land we have now heard enough about *a shifting reef* and a *submerged* or *floating island* to discuss the relation of this notion to Verne's own psychohistory.

As a child he lived on the Ile Feydeau, an island in the Loire River off Nantes. The Ile Feydeau was ship-shaped, pointed at one end, rounded at the other. In March the flood-swollen Loire smashed against the stone quays guarding Ile Feydeau and sometimes would even spill onto the island and pour through the streets and into the cellars.

Jules was afraid that the island would be torn from its anchorage and float out to sea.

Notice how much of the speculation in *Twenty Thousand Leagues* has been a reenactment of Jules's boyhood fantasy. There has been a dreamlike confusion over whether *this moving mass* is a ship, an animal large enough to be an island, or a stretch of rock let loose in the flood.

Verne's nightmare is most thoroughly explored in his novel *The Fur Country* (1873). The Hudson Bay

Fur Company has established an outpost at the edge of the Arctic Ocean. Unknown to its builders, this post actually rests upon a shelf of ice, converted by deposits of sand and earth into apparently solid ground "clothed with vegetation" and connected with the mainland. Then an earthquake separates this shelf of ice from the land, and Fort Hope, as Verne ironically dubbed it, with all its people, buildings, streets, and trees, becomes *a floating island.*

7. *like a huge fish of steel* To appreciate how this line would excite Verne's original readers, we must remember that up until 1870, some twenty-five known experiments with submersible boats had all led to dead ends. In 1620, a Dutchman, Cornelius van Drebbel, successfully operated a submarine in the Thames but various accounts disagreed as to the details. It was claimed that van Drebbel used a chemical to revive the atmosphere inside the craft—possibly a soda ash that absorbed the carbon dioxide. In 1720 an Englishman, John Day, built a "tub" in which he stayed under thirty feet of water for twelve hours. But on his second descent, in a larger vessel, he went down "into perpetual night," as one observer reported, and failed to return.

The first operational submarine was invented and built by Connecticut's David Bushnell. It was commissioned by General George Washington in 1776. The *Turtle* derived its name from the fact that it resembled two large turtle shells joined at the edges, with the long dimension—about nine feet—being the vertical one. Actually, from the side, the *Turtle* looked more like a lemon. An Army sergeant, Ezra Lee, was trained to serve as crew. Sitting on a bicycle-type seat, he worked a ballast pump with foot pedals. With his hands, he directed the rudder and cranked one propeller for horizontal movement, another for vertical. He could also operate a large screw that was designed to attach a timed explosive charge to the bottom of an enemy vessel.

Lee's first—and only—target was

We were lying upon the back of a sort of submarine boat, which appeared . . . like a huge fish of steel. Engraving from original edition (1870).

Well, no! The blackish back that supported me was smooth, polished, without scales. The blow produced a metallic sound; and incredible though it may be, it seemed, I might say, as if it was made of riveted plates.

There was no doubt about it! This monster, this natural phenomenon that had puzzled the learned world, and overthrown and misled the imagination of seamen of both hemispheres, was, it must be owned, a still more astonishing phenomenon, inasmuch as it was a simply human construction.

[To come upon the most fabulous, most mythical being could not have shocked me so much. It is quite simple to believe that prodigious things come from the hands of God. But suddenly to find the impossible, mysteriously shaped by human beings, that staggered the mind.]

We had no time to lose, however. We were lying upon the back of a sort of submarine boat, which appeared (as far as I could judge) like a huge fish of steel.**7** Ned Land's mind was made up on this point. Conseil and I could only agree with him.

["So then," I said, "this apparatus must have some means of locomotion inside it, and a crew to manoeuvre it. Do you agree?"

"Evidently," replied the harpooner. "Still, in the three hours I have inhabited this floating isle, it has shown no sign of life."

"You mean this boat has not moved?"

"No, Professor. It just rides the waves, but it does not move itself."

"But we know, beyond any doubt, that it is capable of great speed. Now, it needs machinery to develop that speed, and an engineer to control the machinery. And so I conclude that we are saved."

"Hummh," said Ned, in his sceptical voice.]

Just then, [as though to prove my point,] a bubbling began at the back of this strange thing (which was evidently propelled by a screw), and it began to move. We had only just time to seize hold of the upper part, which rose about seven feet out of the water,[8] and happily its speed was not great.

"As long as it sails horizontally," muttered Ned Land, "I do not mind; but if it takes a fancy to dive, I would not give two straws for my life."

The Canadian might have said still less. It became really necessary to communicate with the beings, whatever they were, shut up inside the machine. I searched all over the outside for an aperture, a panel or a man-hole, to use a technical expression; but the lines of the iron rivets, solidly driven into the joints of the iron plates, were clear and uniform. Besides, the moon disappeared then, and left us in total darkness.

[We were obliged to wait for daylight before we could find some means of getting inside this submarine boat.

Therefore our fate depended entirely on the whims of the mysterious helmsmen who manoeuvred this craft, for if they submerged, we were lost. But unless that happened, I did not doubt the possibility of making contact with them. As a matter of fact, if they did not produce their own air,[9] they would be forced to spend time on the surface in order to replenish their supply of oxygen. So, there just had to be some opening, some connection between the inside and the outside.

As for hoping to be saved by Commander Farragut, we had to forget all about that. We had drifted to the west, and I estimated that our speed was moderate, maybe twelve knots. The propeller was beating the water with mathematical regularity, protruding sometimes above the surface and throwing phosphorescent spray to great heights.

At about four o'clock in the morning, the craft increased its

the H.M.S. *Eagle,* the British flagship anchored off Governors Island in New York harbor. Although he succeeded, under cover of darkness, in maneuvering under the sixty-four-gun ship-of-the-line, he could not get the screw to bite into the hull. Perhaps the *Eagle* bottom was sheathed with copper for worm protection, or he had come up under the iron fittings for the rudder.

Bushnell continued his experiments for a quarter of a century. He was trying to interest the French government in them in 1800 when a competitor, Robert Fulton of Pennsylvania, arrived in Paris. Fulton obtained funds from Napoleon to build a 21-foot torpedolike submersible which he dubbed the *Nautilus.* A crew of two could submerge by admitting water into a hollow, cast-iron keel, and rise by pumping it out. They could propel the boat by cranking a bladed propeller. At a demonstration the *Nautilus,* completely submerged, approached a 40-foot sloop, drove a gunpowder mine into her side with a spike, withdrew to a safe distance before the target ship was blown to smithereens, surfaced, furled a sail, and returned to her dock. But because of political misunderstandings and his own fear of theft of his invention, Fulton destroyed the *Nautilus.* After he made a modest fortune from his steamboat *Clermont,* he built a new, 80-foot submarine in 1815, but he died before it could be tested.

Since the American Civil War fostered tremendous advances in technology, it is no surprise to find that it included the first successful attack on a warship by a submarine. The Confederate Army built, in addition to a series of semisubmersibles called "Davids" (designed to attack Union "Goliaths"), three genuine submarines. Most notable was the *H. L. Hunley,* named for its inventor. About 38 feet in length, the *Hunley* was powered by eight men cranking its propeller while its commander handled the details of submergence, maneuver, and attack. Five times the *Hunley* sank, with great loss of life

—including Hunley himself—before General Pierre Beauregard forbade further descents. Then Lieutenant George Dixon gained permission to use the *Hunley* as a semisubmersible. He rigged a 10-foot spar torpedo on the bow. On the night of February 17, 1864, the *Hunley* sailed out to attack the new Union sloop-of-war, the *Housatonic,* outside of Charleston. Her decks awash, the *Hunley* succeeded in sneaking up in the dark and placing her charge against the thirteen-gun warship. The *Hunley's* commander pulled the firing lanyard. The *Housatonic* sank slowly, but the *Hunley* broke up and went down with all hands.

That same year, the Union Navy began work on a handcranked experimental sub, *The Intelligent Whale* (it is now on exhibit at the Navy Shipyard in Washington). There was worldwide speculation that a "break through" in submarine science and art was imminent. It was typical of Verne's approach that he would choose a scientific subject at this stage of its development. Thus his immediate readers would live to see some of his prophecies borne out while later generations would still be waiting for others to be realized.

8. *rose about seven feet out of the water* Verne says that it was standing about 80 centimeters, or *less than three feet,* out of water.

9. *if they did not produce their own air* In this restored passage, is Aronnax really fighting down the uncanny thought that the submarines are able to seal themselves into a self-sufficient container for indefinite periods? If so, then Aronnax's uneasy hunch constitutes one of Verne's thousands of predictions. For the modern nuclear submarine is capable of staying under water for months at a time.

10. *harmony produced by distant words of command* Verne says *produced by the distant playing of musical chords.*

speed. We found it difficult to hang on, and the propellers were pounding furiously behind us. Happily, Ned managed to find a large mooring-ring, and we held on for dear life.]

At last this long night passed. My indistinct remembrance prevents my describing all the impressions it made. I can only recall one circumstance. During some lulls of the wind and sea, I fancied I heard several times vague sounds, a sort of fugitive harmony produced by distant words of command.**10** What was then the mystery of this submarine craft, of which the whole world vainly sought an explanation? What kind of beings existed in this strange boat? What mechanical agent caused its prodigious speed?

Daybreak appeared. The morning mists surrounded us, but they soon cleared off. I was about to examine the hull, which formed on deck a kind of horizontal platform, when I felt it gradually sinking.

"Oh! confound it!" cried Ned Land, kicking the resounding plate; "open, you inhospitable rascals!"

[But it was difficult to make ourselves heard above the noise of the propeller.] Happily the sinking movement ceased. Suddenly a noise, like iron works violently pushed aside, came from the interior of the boat. One iron plate was moved, a man appeared, uttered an odd cry, and disappeared immediately.

Some moments after, eight strong men, with masked faces, appeared noiselessly, and drew us down into their formidable machine.

A jelly-fish (*Rhyzostoma*), about one-fourth actual size, as pictured in *Animal Forms: A Textbook of Zoology* (1902) by D. S. Jordan and Harold Heath.

PART 1: CHAPTER VIII
Mobilis in Mobili[1]

This forcible abduction, so roughly carried out, was accomplished with the rapidity of lightning. [My companions and I had no time to collect ourselves. I do not know how they felt as we were being dragged down into that floating prison, but as for me,] I shivered all over. Whom had we to deal with? No doubt some new sort of pirates, who explored the sea in their own way.

Hardly had the narrow panel closed upon me, when I was enveloped in darkness. My eyes, dazzled with the outer light, could distinguish nothing. I felt my naked feet cling to the rungs of an iron ladder. Ned Land and Conseil, firmly seized, followed me. At the bottom of the ladder, a door opened, and shut after us immediately with a bang.

We were alone. Where, I could not say, hardly imagine. All was black, and such a dense black that, after some minutes, my eyes had not been able to discern even the faintest glimmer [such as one imagines he sees on the darkest of nights].

Meanwhile, Ned Land, furious at these proceedings, gave vent to his indignation.

"Confound it!" cried he, "here are people who come up to the Scotch for hospitality. They only just miss being cannibals. I shall not be surprised at it, but I declare that they shall not eat me without my protesting."

"Calm yourself, friend Ned, calm yourself," replied Conseil, quietly. "Do not cry out before you are hurt. We are not quite done for yet."

"Not quite," sharply replied the Canadian, "but pretty near,[2] at all events. Things look black. Happily, my bowie-knife[3] I have still, and I can always see well enough to use it. The first of these pirates who lays a hand on me——"

1. *Mobilis in Mobili* This Latin phrase means *mobile within the mobile element*. Helpful variations would be *flexible within flux* or *changing with change*.

2. *not quite done for. . . . but pretty near* In the French, Conseil and Ned are actually engaging in the running wordplay that makes the original dialogue such continual delight. Conseil says:
"We are not yet in the roasting pan."
And Ned retorts:
"In the roaster, no, but in the oven, yes."

3. *bowie-knife* In his original edition, Verne explained the phrase *bowie-knife*[1] to his French readers with this odd footnote:
[1] *Dagger with a large blade which an American always carries with him.*
The current French edition omits the *which* clause. Whether Verne intended to be facetious or factual, the note is a commentary on the American reputation for violence.
The bowie knife was a single-edged hunting knife, about fifteen inches long, with a hilt and a crosspiece. It was named after either Colonel James Bowie of the Texas army, who popularized it, or his brother, Rezin Bowie, who probably designed it.

4. *phormium* A strong fiber made from the leaves of New Zealand flax or hemp and used for cordage, twine, and matting. Notice how Aronnax is always the curious naturalist, identifying a great variety of natural materials even under the most distressing circumstances.

5. *prosopopeia, metonymy, and hyphallage* Aronnax, like his creator Verne, is a great lover of figures of speech and of classification. So it's no surprise to find the professor, in a passage of gentle self-mockery, trotting out three technical terms from classical rhetoric.

For a good example of *prosopopeia* we could go to one of Aronnax's favorite authors, Victor Hugo. In *The Toilers of the Sea,* he has this line: "The insolent sea was in a good humor." *Prosopopeia,* in short, is the figure of speech in which something inanimate or abstract is portrayed with human form or qualities.

Metonymy is the use of a suggestive word in place of the thing meant. Thus *the crown* can mean *the monarch* or *monarchy,* and *the bottle* can mean *alcohol.*

Hyphallage is the interchange in syntax between two terms. Thus Edmund Spenser speaks of "Sansfroy's dead dowry," meaning "dead Sansfroy's dowry."

6. *Gratiolet or Engel* Louis-Pierre Gratiolet (1815–1865), French physician and naturalist, and Josef Engel (1816–1874), Austrian anatomist, were physiognomists or "experts" in judging character from facial features.

"Do not excite yourself, Ned," I said to the harpooner, "and do not compromise us by useless violence. Who knows that they will not listen to us? Let us rather try to find out where we are."

I groped about. In five steps I came to an iron wall, made of plates bolted together. Then turning back I struck against a wooden table, near which were ranged several stools. The boards of this prison were concealed under a thick mat of phormium,**4** which deadened the noise of the feet. The bare walls revealed no trace of window or door. Conseil, going round the reverse way, met me, and we went back to the middle of the cabin, which measured about twenty feet by ten. As to its height, Ned Land, in spite of his own great height, could not measure it.

Half an hour had already passed without our situation being bettered, when the dense darkness suddenly gave way to extreme light. Our prison was suddenly lighted—that is to say, it became filled with a luminous matter, so strong that I could not bear it at first. In its whiteness and intensity I recognized that electric light which played round the submarine boat like a magnificent phenomenon of phosphorescence. After shutting my eyes involuntarily, I opened them and saw that this luminous agent came from a half globe, unpolished, placed in the roof of the cabin.

"At last one can see," cried Ned Land, who, knife in hand, stood on the defensive.

"Yes," said I, [risking the antithesis,] "but we are still in the dark about ourselves."

"Let master have patience," said the imperturbable Conseil.

The sudden lighting of the cabin enabled me to examine it minutely. It only contained a table and five stools. The invisible door might be hermetically sealed. No noise was heard. All seemed dead in the interior of this boat. Did it move, did it float on the surface of the ocean, or did it dive into its depths? I could not guess. [However, the luminous globe had not been turned on without good reason. And so I was expecting some members of the crew to appear. For if you want to forget people, consign them to oblivion, you do not light up their cell. And I was not mistaken.]

A noise of bolts was now heard, the door opened, and two men appeared.

One was short, very muscular, broad-shouldered, with robust limbs, strong head, an abundance of black hair, thick moustache, a quick penetrating look, and the vivacity which characterizes the population of Southern France. [Diderot has maintained, with great justification, that a man's gestures are metaphoric. This little man was certainly the living proof. One could sense that his everyday speech sparkled with prosopopeia, metonymy, and hypallage.5 But I was never able to verify this, because in my presence at least he always spoke a language I could not understand.]

The second stranger merits a more detailed description. A disciple of Gratiolet or Engel 6 would have read his face like an open book. I made out his prevailing qualities directly:— self-confidence,—because his head was well set on his shoulders, and his black eyes looked around with cold assurance; calmness,—for his skin, rather pale, showed his coolness of blood; energy,—evinced by the rapid contraction of his lofty brows; and courage,—because his deep breathing denoted great power of lungs.

[I sensed that this man was proud. I felt that his firm, calm gaze reflected thoughts of a lofty nature. The harmony of his facial expression and his physical attitude—if the physiognomists 7 are correct—indicated a man of great candour. I felt "involuntarily" reassured by his presence. I felt more optimistic about our confrontation.]

Whether this person was thirty-five or fifty years of age, I could not say. He was tall, had a large forehead, straight nose, a clearly cut mouth, beautiful teeth, with fine taper hands, [which, according to a term used by chirognomists,7 were] indicative of a highly nervous temperament. This man was certainly the most admirable specimen I had ever met. One particular feature was his eyes, rather far from each other, and which could take in nearly a quarter of the horizon at once.

This faculty—(I verified it later)—gave him a range of vision far superior to Ned Land's. When this stranger fixed upon an object his eyebrows met, his large eyelids closed around so as to contract the range of his vision, and he looked as if he magnified the objects lessened by distance, as if he pierced those sheets of water so opaque to our eyes, and as if he read the very depths of the seas.

The two strangers, with caps made from the fur of the sea otter, and shod with sea boots of seal's skin, were dressed in clothes of a particular texture, which allowed free movement of the limbs. The taller of the two, evidently the chief on board, examined us with great attention, without saying a word: then turning to his companion, talked with him in an unknown tongue. It was a sonorous, harmonious, and flexible dialect, the vowels seeming to admit of very varied accentuation.

The other replied by a shake of the head, and added two or

7. *physiognomists . . . chirognomists* In Aronnax's day, physiognomy, the science of judging character from the face, and chirognomy, the practice of reading personality from the hands, were taken quite seriously. And Verne uses these "vogues" to good artistic ends. They make it possible for him to provide more description of the two men than we could otherwise absorb at this point. Having Aronnax try out physiognomic theory makes the description more dynamic. Verne continually experiments with such contrapuntal techniques for advancing the action.

Early in his student days in Paris, Verne had met the chevalier d'Arpentigny, an expert on chirognomy. It was d'Arpentigny who introduced Verne to Alexandre Dumas, another enthusiastic believer in palmistry.

Physiognomy had intrigued no less a mind than Johann Wolfgang von Goethe (1749–1832), author of *Faust* and the most admired artist of his day. He collaborated in writing up the researches of Johann Kaspar Lavater (1741–1801), founder of physiognomics. Lavater believed that the interaction between mind and body would inevitably leave "traces of the spirit" on the features. Criminologists like Cesare Lombroso (1836–1909) attempted to identify criminal "types" by their appearance alone.

Most nineteenth-century typologies, such as Aronnax is using here, have been discredited. But new ones are proposed by every generation of psychologists. Ernst Kretschmer (1888–1964), for example, attempted to classify personalities according to their skeletal makeup. And Eric Berne offers yet another system for judging people by their looks in his *A Layman's Guide to Psychiatry and Psychoanalysis*. And of course, everyone from the most inarticulate layman to the most meticulous author, has his own secret, intuitive, infallible system of detecting character from the physique. Albert Camus, Nobel prize-winner, went so far as to justify such detection because "After forty, every man is responsible for his own face."

8. *violation of human rights* This passage, omitted by Lewis, is important for proper characterization of Ned and even for understanding some later remarks by the *chief on board*.

Ned is not simply a man of action and of common sense; he is also an idealist with a good understanding of civil rights. The principles he invokes here are Anglo-Saxon and North American; he is the only one of the threesome (French Aronnax, Belgian Conseil, Canadian Land) likely to raise these points. A later statement by the chief on board, as we shall see, will make full sense only if the reader has heard these significant charges by Ned.

9. *language of Arago . . . of Faraday* Aronnax's assumptions and inferences here are dramatic. To be chief on board of such a technological marvel as this underwater boat, the captain would presumably have to be familiar with the principles of physics. At that time, *French*—because of the writings of D. F. Arago (1786–1856)—and *English*—in which Michael Faraday (1791–, 1867) published—were the major languages in which these principles were to be found. If the chief on board *understood* neither of these tongues, then Aronnax is worried that the man's technology comes from some body of knowledge unknown to international science.

10. *What! You speak German?* With omission of this passage, the "standard translation" has now weakened the characterization of all five people in the scene.

It is a commonplace of Verne criticism in English that his characterization is shallow and based on types. Certainly, as we shall be better able to see later on, he does rely on types. But his typing is not so crude, nor his portrayal so shallow, as Mercier Lewis —the source used by critics working in English—made it appear.

In this scene alone Lewis has partly or entirely destroyed our chances of appreciating: the expressiveness of the second visitor's "body language"; the

three perfectly incomprehensible words. Then he seemed to question me by a look.

I replied in good French that I did not know his language; but he seemed not to understand me, and my situation became more embarrassing.

"If master were to tell our story," said Conseil, "perhaps these gentlemen may understand some words."

I began to tell our adventures, articulating each syllable clearly, and without omitting one single detail. I announced our names and rank, introducing in person Professor Aronnax, his servant Conseil, and master Ned Land, the harpooner.

The man with the soft calm eyes listened to me quietly, even politely, and with extreme attention; but nothing in his countenance indicated that he had understood my story. When I finished, he said not a word. There remained one resource, to speak English. Perhaps they would know this almost universal language. I knew it, as well as the German language,—well enough to read it fluently, but not to speak it correctly. But, anyhow, we must make ourselves understood.

"Go on in your turn," I said to the harpooner; "speak your best Anglo-Saxon, and try to do better than I."

Ned did not beg off, and recommenced our story. [I could follow what he was saying. His basic message was the same, but his manner was different. True to his nature, he spoke with great animation. He complained vigorously about being imprisoned in violation of human rights,[8] demanded to know the legal basis for his detention, invoked the principles of habeas corpus, threatened to take to court anyone who held him without due cause, ranted, gesticulated, shouted, and at last by a very expressive sign, indicated we were starving to death. Of course this was perfectly true, but we had almost forgotten it.]

To his great disgust, the harpooner did not seem to have made himself more intelligible than I had. Our visitors did not stir. They evidently understood neither the language of Arago nor of Faraday.[9]

Very much embarrassed, after having vainly exhausted our philological resources, I knew not what part to take, when Conseil said—

"If master will permit me, I will relate it in German."

["What! You speak German?" **10** I exclaimed.

"Like a Belgian. Does monsieur mind?"

"Not at all, to the contrary, go ahead, my boy."

And Conseil, in his tranquil voice, gave the third account of the various stages of our history.] But in spite of the elegant turns and good accent of the narrator, the German language had no success. At last, nonplussed, I tried to remember my first lessons, and to narrate our adventures in Latin. [Cicero would have shut his ears and sent me back to the kitchen. Nevertheless, I did manage to get to the end of our story.] But with no better success. This last attempt being of no avail, the two strangers exchanged some words in their unknown language, and retired [without so much as a reassuring nod in our direction, as might have been expected in any country in the world].

The door shut.

"It is an infamous shame," cried Ned Land, who broke out for the twentieth time; "we speak to those rogues in French, English, German, and Latin, and not one of them has the politeness to answer!"

"Calm yourself," I said to the impetuous Ned, "anger will do no good."

"But do you see, Professor," replied our irascible companion, "that we shall absolutely die of hunger in this iron cage?"

"Bah," said Conseil, philosophically; "we can hold out some time yet."

"My friends," I said, "we must not despair. We have been worse off than this. Do me the favour to wait a little before forming an opinion upon the commander and crew of this boat."

"My opinion is formed," replied Ned Land, sharply. "They are rascals."

"Good! And from what country?"

"From the land of rogues!"

"My brave Ned, that country is not clearly indicated on the map of the world; but I admit that the nationality of the two strangers is hard to determine. Neither English, French, nor German, that is quite certain. However, I am inclined to think that the commander and his companion were born in low latitudes. There is southern blood in them. But I cannot decide by their appearance whether they are Spaniards, Turks, Arabians, or Indians. As to their language, it is quite incomprehensible."

"There is the disadvantage of not knowing all languages," said Conseil, "or the disadvantage of not having one universal language." 11

["What good would that do?" said Ned. "These people have invented their own private language with which to torment people who are asking for food! In every country, does not moving your jaws up and down, clicking your teeth, smacking

"chief's" appearance of being frank, proud, at peace with himself; the wordplay the three companions love so much; the self-mocking pedantry of the professor (antithesis, hypallage!) and his eagerness to classify; Conseil's custom of revealing little about his abilities even to Aronnax; the fact that Ned is not only active but activist!

All of Verne's characters—even the walk-ons like the second officer in this scene—are more alive, more complicated, than readers of the standard translation could ever imagine.

11. *one universal language* Verne was a great believer in the need for an artificial international language. His young friend, Raoul Duval, Paris deputy, was one of the first speakers of Volapük, created in 1879. On a cruise on Verne's yacht, Duval made a passionate, impromptu speech in Volapük to the Pillars of Hercules! In 1887 Esperanto was invented, and in the 1890s Verne served as chairman of the Esperantist group of his region.

your lips, mean just one thing? Whether you are in Quebec or the Pomotou Islands, in Paris or the Antipodes, do you have to know their words for: 'Please feed me, I am hungry'?"

"Oh," Conseil said, "some people are just unintelligent by nature."]

As he said these words, the door opened. A steward entered. He brought us clothes, coats and trousers, made of a stuff I did not know. I hastened to dress myself, and my companions followed my example. During that time, the steward—dumb, perhaps deaf—had arranged the table, and laid three plates.

"This is something like," said Conseil.

"Bah," said the rancorous harpooner, "what do you suppose they eat here? Tortoise liver, filleted shark, and beefsteaks from sea-dogs."

"We shall see," said Conseil.

The dishes, of bell metal, were placed on the table, and we took our places. Undoubtedly we had to do with civilised people, and had it not been for the electric light which flooded us, I could have fancied I was in the dining-room of the Adelphi Hotel at Liverpool, or at the Grand Hotel in Paris. I must say, however, that there was neither bread nor wine. The water was fresh and clear, but it was water, and did not suit Ned Land's taste. Amongst the dishes which were brought to us, I recognized several fish delicately dressed; but of some, although excellent, I could give no opinion, neither could I tell to what kingdom they belonged, whether animal or vegetable. As to the dinner service, it was elegant, and in perfect taste. Each utensil, spoon, fork, knife, plate, had a letter engraved on it, with a motto above it, of which this is an exact facsimile:— **12**

MOBILIS IN MOBILI

N.

[*"Mobile within the mobile element!"* That motto was certainly appropriate for this submarine craft, so long as the preposition "in" was translated as "within" and not "on." **13**]

The letter N was no doubt the initial of the name of the enigmatical person, who commanded at the bottom of the sea.

Ned and Conseil did not reflect much. They devoured the food, and I did likewise. I was, besides, reassured as to our fate; and it seemed evident that our hosts would not let us die of want.

However, everything has an end, everything passes away, even the hunger of people who have not eaten for fifteen hours. Our appetites satisfied, we felt overcome with sleep. [This was

12. *this is an exact facsimile* The original French edition says that every implement *bore a letter encircled by a motto.*

13. *"within" and not "on"* With Aronnax's comment on the proper way to translate the Latin motto, Verne has succeeded in this chapter in characterizing the scientist as an accomplished student of linguistics. But notice that by omitting all of Aronnax's remarks about:
antithesis
prosopopeia
metonymy
hypallage
translation of the Latin word in Mercier Lewis has all but destroyed this dimension of the professor's character.

our natural reaction to having spent an interminable night
fighting against death.]

"Faith! I shall sleep well," said Conseil.

"So shall I," replied Ned Land.

My two companions stretched themselves on the cabin
carpet, and were soon sound asleep. For my own part, too
many thoughts crowded my brain; too many insoluble questions pressed upon me; too many fancies kept my eyes half
open. Where were we? What strange power carried us on? I
felt—or rather fancied I felt—the machine sinking down to
the lowest beds of the sea. Dreadful nightmares beset me; I
saw in these mysterious asylums a world of unknown animals,
amongst which this submarine boat seemed to be of the same
kind, living, moving, and formidable as they. Then my brain
grew calmer, my imagination wandered into vague unconsciousness, and I soon fell into a deep sleep.

*My two companions stretched themselves on the cabin
carpet. . . .* Engraving from the original French edition
(1870).

PART 1: CHAPTER IX

Ned Land's Tempers[1]

1. *Ned Land's Tempers* Ned's tantrums will seem, in the Mercier Lewis translation, to be quite arbitrary and sudden. This is because Lewis has omitted more than half the chapter. As our restoration will show, Verne was careful to build up Ned's mood gradually and realistically.

2. *oxygen . . . in . . . 176 pints of air* Verne says *cent litres d'air*, 100 liters of air, *3½ cubic feet*. The dimensions of the room were about $20 \times 10 \times 8$, which means the prisoners started out with no more than 1600 cubic feet of air. Three men have been consuming the oxygen in 10½ cubic feet every hour. As we shall see soon, they estimate that they have slept at least 24 hours. They might have already used up the oxygen in 252 cubic feet of their supply. As Aronnax says, this means that their atmosphere is now charged with *a nearly equal quantity* of carbon dioxide. Hence his terror at the thought of prolonged confinement. (Actually, his figures would be slightly lower if he considered that we consume less oxygen asleep than awake.) This scene is a brief foreshadowing of a longer ordeal of airlessness that awaits the characters later in the novel. Like a writer well trained in the theater, Verne makes good use of *foreshadowings and echoes*, as we have already seen in the obsession with a *floating island*.

How long we slept I do not know; but our sleep must have lasted long, for it rested us completely from our fatigues. I woke first. My companions had not moved, and were still stretched in their corner.

Hardly roused from my somewhat hard couch, I felt my brain freed, my mind clear. I then began an attentive examination of our cell. Nothing was changed inside. The prison was still a prison,—the prisoners, prisoners. However, the steward, during our sleep, had cleared the table. [So there was nothing to indicate that our situation would change, and I worried now whether we were destined to live forever in this cage. This prospect was so painful that, even though my mind was clear of the obsessions of the day before, still I felt a strange weight on my chest.]

I breathed with difficulty. The heavy air seemed to oppress my lungs. Although the cell was large, we had evidently consumed a great part of the oxygen that it contained. Indeed, each man consumes, in one hour, the oxygen contained in more than 176 pints of air,[2] and this air, charged (as then) with a nearly equal quantity of carbonic acid, becomes unbreathable.

It became necessary to renew the atmosphere of our prison, and no doubt the whole in the submarine boat. That gave rise to a question in my mind. How would the commander of this floating dwelling-place proceed? Would he obtain air by chemical means,[3] in getting by heat the oxygen contained in chlorate of potass, and in absorbing carbonic acid by caustic potash? [This would force him to make regular visits to shore to get the required chemicals. Or did he store compressed air in tanks, releasing it as the crew needed it?] Or, a more convenient, economical, and consequently more profitable alternative, would he be satisfied to rise and take breath at the surface of the water, like a cetacean, and so renew for twenty-four hours the atmospheric provision? [Whatever means he used, it seemed to me urgent to use it now.]

In fact, I was already obliged to increase my respirations to eke out of this cell the little oxygen it contained,[4] when suddenly I was refreshed by a current of pure air, and perfumed with saline emanations. It was an invigorating sea breeze, charged with iodine. I opened my mouth wide, and my lungs saturated themselves with fresh particles.

At the same time I felt the boat rolling. The ironplated monster had evidently just risen to the surface of the ocean to breathe, after the fashion of whales. I found out from that the mode of ventilating the boat.

When I had inhaled this air freely, I sought the conduit-pipe, which conveyed to us the beneficial whiff, and I was not long in finding it. Above the door was a ventilator, through which volumes of fresh air renewed the impoverished atmosphere of the cell.

I was making my observations, when Ned and Conseil awoke almost at the same time, under the influence of this reviving air. They rubbed their eyes, stretched themselves, and were on their feet in an instant.

"Did master sleep well?" asked Conseil, with his usual politeness.

"Very well, my brave boy. And you, Mr. Land?"

"Soundly, Professor. But I don't know if I am right or not; there seems to be a sea breeze!"

A seaman could not be mistaken, and I told the Canadian all that had passed during his sleep.

"Good!" said he; "that accounts for those roarings we heard, when the supposed narwhal sighted the *Abraham Lincoln*."

"Quite so, Master Land; it was taking breath."

"Only, Mr. Aronnax, I have no idea what o'clock it is, unless it is dinner-time."

"Dinner-time! my good fellow? Say rather breakfast-time, for we certainly have begun another day."

"So," said Conseil, "we have slept twenty-four hours?"

"That is my opinion."

"I will not contradict you," replied Ned Land. "But dinner or breakfast, the steward will be welcome, whichever he brings."

["Maybe both," said Conseil.

"Fine!" said Ned. "We deserve two meals, we could do justice to both."

3. *Would he obtain air by chemical means* Another characteristic of the professor—his tendency to rehearse all the possibilities—is also blurred by Lewis's savage cuts. In these scientific exercises that Aronnax sets for himself, Verne is educating his audience as to the extent of man's technical prowess. And in allowing Aronnax to consider possibilities like "visits to shore," Verne creates more suspense than Lewis cares to preserve.

4. *little oxygen it contained* The professor is getting so little oxygen that he's not thinking well. It would be better in this situation for him to be taking slow, shallow breaths. This is the well-established technique used by fakirs and stage magicians in "living burial" tests. In 1926 Houdini managed to stay in a coffin—submerged in a swimming pool—for ninety minutes by remaining motionless and using shallow breathing.

5. "*. . . dinner hour.*" In the original, Verne writes: *"Master Land," I replied, "we must conform to ship's regulations. I imagine that our stomachs are ahead of the cook's clock."*

6. *What good would complaining do* Lewis's omission of this 900-word passage did inestimable damage to our knowledge of the real Verne. This is one of those passages in which Verne can create moody drama in a seemingly static situation—three men locked in a room! Their full conversation, as restored here, shows how, in their despair, they turn on each other, try each other out, temporize. Notice that at one point the usually placid Conseil actually goads Ned into continuing, and that at another point the usually honest professor substitutes diplomacy for candor. Throughout their wretchedness, Verne impresses us with the way the men are coming to know—and respect—each other. Furthermore, once again Verne has used dialogue to create greater suspense: while waiting for something to happen, the men think of lots of things that *could* happen. Finally, in a masterful way, Verne creates an extraordinary sense of *time passing.*

One cannot help feeling that in scenes like this Verne is tapping his experiences in those hours aboard the first *Saint Michel* where, in tiny quarters, he and one or two intimates would talk all night—searchingly.

"But we must be patient," I cautioned. "It is clear these mysterious people do not intend to let us starve to death. Otherwise that last meal they fed us would make no sense."

"Suppose," responded Ned, "they are merely fattening us up?"

"Cut that out!" I admonished. "There is no reason to think we are in the hands of cannibals!"

"One occasion does not establish a custom," the Canadian observed. "Suppose these people have had to go for a long time without fresh meat. In that case, three healthy specimens like the professor, his servant, and me—"

"Banish such thoughts, Master Land," I told the harpooner. "Do not let such ideas make you angry at our hosts. That might only aggravate the situation."

"In any event," he said, "I am famished, and whether it be breakfast, lunch, or dinner, it is long overdue!"]

"Master Land, we must conform to the rules on board, and I suppose our appetites are in advance of the dinner hour." **5**

["In that case, we will have to adjust to the cook's schedule," Conseil said calmly.]

"That is just like you, friend Conseil," said Ned, impatiently. "You are never out of temper, always calm; you would return thanks before grace, and die of hunger rather than complain!"

["What good would complaining do?" **6** Conseil asked.

"Complaining does not have to *do* good, it *feels* good. And if these pirates—out of respect for the professor, I will not call them cannibals—think they can suffocate me in this cage without hearing my favorite curse-words, they are mistaken! Do you think they plan to keep us locked up in this iron box for long?"

"Truthfully, friend Land, I know only what you know, no more, no less."

"Yes, but what do you *think?*"

"I think that mere chance has made us privy to some important secret. And if this submarine crew wants to keep their secret *secret,* and if that is more important to them than the lives of three strangers, then I believe that our very existence has been compromised. If the opposite is true, then the monster that has swallowed us will take us back to the world of civilised people."

"Unless," said Conseil, "they impress us into the crew, and force us to serve—"

"Until," Ned continued, "a frigate that is faster and more manoeuvrable than the *Abraham Lincoln* captures these pirates and forces the whole crew—us included—to walk the plank." 7

"Well reasoned, Master Land," I replied. "But they have suggested nothing like that. There is no point talking about what we would do in that case. I repeat, we must be guided by developments, and not do anything until we see what is to be done."

"On the contrary, Professor." The harpooner could not imagine retreating. "We've got to do *something!*"

"Like what, Master Land?"

"Escape!"

"To escape from prison on land is difficult enough. To escape from a prison under water, that seems quite impossible."

"So, friend Ned," Conseil demanded. "How can you meet the professor's argument? I cannot believe that an American is at the end of his rope!" 8

Visibly embarrassed, the harpooner said nothing. To escape the trap in which we had fallen seemed out of the question. But a Canadian is half French, as Master Land demonstrated in his response.

"So, Professor Aronnax," he said after a few minutes' reflection, "you cannot imagine what men do when they cannot break out of their prison?"

"No, I cannot, my friend."

"It is really simple. They arrange things so they can *afford* to stay."

"Right!" said Conseil. "I would rather stay inside this boat than outside in the water!"

"But only after we jettison our jailers, turn-keys, and guards," Ned added.

"What! Ned, you're seriously thinking of taking command of the ship?"

"Yes, I am serious."

"Impossible."

"Why, Professor? If a good opportunity presents itself, why should we not profit by it? Suppose there are some twenty men in the crew, how can they hold back two Frenchmen and a Canadian!"

It seemed wiser at the moment to accept his plan than to discuss it. So I was content to say: "Let us be guided by circumstances, let us see what develops. But until something does develop, contain yourself. Our only chance is to invent some stratagem, and flying into a rage will not accomplish that. So promise me that you will accept the situation without going into a tantrum over it."

7. *to walk the plank* The notion that pirates forced their captives to walk the plank seems to be a "fabrication of later generations," according to Hugh F. Rankin, *The Golden Age of Piracy* (1969). "They had methods of dealing with undesirables that made walking the plank seem merciful. It has often been said that Stede Bonnet was the only pirate captain to force his prisoners to walk the plank, but the rather full account of his trial (in which many things of a far more sinister character are documented) makes no mention of his disposing of his victims in this fashion."

8. *at the end of his rope* Notice that Conseil calls the Canadian *an American*. Although many citizens of the United States think only of themselves as "Americans," all the rest of the world thinks of all persons born in North or South America as deserving that name.

"You have my promise." But he did not sound convincing. "Not a word of anger, no menacing gestures, even if they do not feed us properly!"

"Word of honor, Ned," I replied.

The conversation petered out. Each of us withdrew into his own thoughts. In spite of the harpooner's confidence, I entertained no illusions. I saw no chance at all of carrying out Ned's wild plans. Navigation of this submarine required a large crew. If it came to an all-out fight, we would be hopelessly outnumbered. Besides, you must be able to get at your enemy to fight, and we were immobilized in this iron cell. If the chief on board had some secret that he must maintain at all costs—and that seemed likely to me—then he would have to limit our movements on board. Would he dispose of us in some direct, violent way, or would he leave us stranded in some remote land? Too many unknowns. But one thing was certain. You had to be a harpooner to have any hope under these circumstances.

Ned was thinking things over too, and apparently getting madder by the minute. I could hear him muttering those favorite curse-words, and I saw him making menacing gestures. He prowled our cage like a wild beast, throwing himself at the walls.]

Time was getting on, and we were fearfully hungry; and this time the steward did not appear. It was rather too long to leave us, if they really had good intentions towards us. Ned Land, tormented by the cravings of hunger, got still more angry; and, notwithstanding his promise,[9] I dreaded an explosion when he found himself with one of the crew.

For two hours more Ned Land's temper increased; he cried, he shouted, but in vain. The walls were deaf. There was no sound to be heard in the boat: all was still as death. It did not move, for I should have felt the trembling motion of the hull under the influence of the screw. Plunged in the depths of the waters, it belonged no longer to earth:—this silence was dreadful.

[Abandoned, isolated, imprisoned. I had no idea how long this could go on. Hopes I had entertained after our interview with the Captain were fading bit by bit. His seeming gentleness, the generosity implied in his physiognomy, his noble bearing, all that was vanishing from my mind. I was forming a new impression of this enigmatic person. He was pitiless, cruel, outside of humanity, an implacable enemy of man, against whom he could well have sworn an oath of everlasting hatred. Could he really intend to let us starve, one by one,

9. *notwithstanding his promise*   Here the coverup fails. Lewis omitted the passage that produced the promise, but fails to omit this reference back to it. Yet four generations of editors, proofreaders, and publishers of the "standard translation" have seen nothing wrong with this puzzling nonreference. By the end of the ninth chapter, Lewis's vagueness has become, to the English reader, vintage Verne.

shut up like this, exposed to those awful temptations **10** induced by extreme hunger? I was becoming obsessed with this possibility.]

I felt terrified. Conseil was calm, Ned Land roared.

Just then a noise was heard outside. Steps sounded on the metal flags. The locks were turned, the door opened, and the steward appeared.

Before I could rush forward to stop him, the Canadian had thrown him down, and held him by the throat. The steward was choking under the grip of his powerful hand.

Conseil was already trying to unclasp the harpooner's hand from his half-suffocated victim, and I was going to fly to the rescue, when suddenly I was nailed to the spot by hearing these words in French—

"Be quiet, Master Land; and you, Professor, will be so good as to listen to me?"

10. *those awful temptations* This is typical of Verne's *echo* technique. Earlier, Ned had suggested that the crew might have cannibalistic designs on their prisoners. Now Aronnax worries that the prisoners might be driven so mad as to practice cannibalism among themselves. Again, this is foreshadowing of still another threat of barbarous death later in the story.

Before I could . . . stop him, the Canadian had thrown [the steward] down. . . . Engraving from the original edition (1870).

PART 1: CHAPTER X

The Man of the Seas

1. *with his arms folded* This was
Verne's own most characteristic posture. Two well-known representations
of him show him in this attitude.

In 1854 when Verne was twenty-
five and working as secretary of
Théâtre-Lyrique in Paris, his friend
Nadar photographed him. Verne is
caught in a three-quarter view, staring
quizzically into the distance, arms
folded loosely and low on his chest.
In 1869 Riou, illustrator for *Twenty
Thousand Leagues,* decided to have
Verne himself serve as the model for
Professor Aronnax. One etching, used
in Chapter V, shows the "professor"
staring off into the far sea with the
same head thrown back—the same
high forehead and curly hair—but
now in profile, the same strong arms
folded loosely over a much fuller mid-
riff.

That Verne should, in the text itself, picture Nemo as also standing
this way is no surprise. Apparently
Verne saw this as the natural posture
of the independent man: *aloof physi-*

It was the commander of the vessel who thus spoke. At these
words, Ned Land rose suddenly. The steward, nearly stran-
gled, tottered out on a sign from his master; but such was the
power of the commander on board, that not a gesture betrayed
the resentment which this man must have felt towards the
Canadian. Conseil, interested in spite of himself, I stupefied
awaited in silence the result of this scene.

The commander, leaning against a corner of the table with
his arms folded,**1** scanned us with profound attention. Did he
hesitate to speak? Did he regret the words which he had just
spoken in French? One might almost think so.

After some moments of silence, which not one of us
dreamed of breaking, "Gentlemen," said he, in a calm and
penetrating voice, "I speak French, English, German, and
Latin equally well. I could, therefore, have answered you at
our first interview, but I wished to know you first, then to reflect. The story told by each one, entirely agreeing in the main
points, convinced me of your identity. I know now that chance
has brought before me M. Pierre Aronnax, Professor of
Natural History at the Museum of Paris, entrusted with a
scientific mission abroad, Conseil his servant, and Ned Land,
of Canadian origin, harpooner on board the frigate *Abraham
Lincoln* of the navy of the United States of America."

I bowed assent. It was not a question that the commander
put to me. Therefore there was no answer to be made. This
man expressed himself with perfect ease, without any accent.
His sentences were well turned, his words clear, and his flu-
ency of speech remarkable. Yet, I did not recognise in him a
fellow-countryman.

He continued the conversation in these terms:

Jules Verne, aged twenty-five, as photographed by Nadar in 1854. Compare this photo with the engraving of Professor Aronnax, for which Verne himself modeled (Part 1: Chapter V).

cally but involved mentally. And of course, while Nemo and Aronnax are created out of two different sides of Verne's own nature, they also share some of Verne's qualities.

"You have doubtless thought, sir, that I have delayed long in paying you this second visit. The reason is that, your identity recognised, I wished to weigh maturely what part to act towards you. I have hesitated much. Most annoying circumstances have brought you into the presence of a man who has broken all the ties of humanity. You have come to trouble my existence."

"Unintentionally!" said I.

"Unintentionally?" replied the stranger, raising his voice a little; "was it unintentionally that the *Abraham Lincoln* pursued me all over the seas? Was it unintentionally that you took passage in this frigate? Was it unintentionally that your cannon balls rebounded off the plating of my vessel? Was it unintentionally that Mr. Ned Land struck me with his harpoon?"

I detected a restrained irritation in these words. But to these recriminations I had a very natural answer to make and I made it.

"Sir," said I, "no doubt you are ignorant of the discussions which have taken place concerning you in America and Europe. You do not know that divers accidents, caused by collisions with your submarine machine, have excited public feeling in the two continents. I omit the hypotheses without number by which it was sought to explain the inexplicable phenomenon of which you alone possess the secret. But you

2. *what you call a civilised man* In this crucial speech, Verne introduces a major motif of the novel and indeed of his oeuvre. First the captain, with his phrase "what you call a civilised man," challenges Aronnax's definition of civilization, raising the question of whether Aronnax's world *is* civilized. Then the captain clearly states the position of the Higher Conscience, the Great Refusal, in effect summarizing the message of H. D. Thoreau's *Civil Disobedience* (1849) and foreshadowing the worldwide "dropout" movement of the 1960s and 1970s.

3. *What cuirass, however thick* A *cuirass* was a piece of armor for protecting the breast and the back. A *cuirassier* was a horse soldier who wore a cuirass. By extension, the French word *cuirasse*—which Verne used here—came to mean armor generally. Verne likes to use the word figuratively. Since his father-in-law was an ex-captain of cuirassiers, the word was never far from Verne's mind.

4. *as . . . Oedipus regarded the Sphinx* The simile is perfect and provocative, as we can see by comparing Oedipus's situation with Aronnax's. Oedipus, warned by an oracle that he would kill his father and marry his mother, fled the home of the couple he thought were his parents. On the road to Thebes he quarreled with and killed an old man. Then he encountered a Sphinx that promised death to anyone who could not answer her riddle. And Thebes was promising its kingship to anyone who could free the city from the terror of the Sphinx. Her riddle was: "What is it that walks on four legs in the morning, on two at noon, on three in the evening?" Oedipus had the answer: "Man—as a babe he crawls on all fours, grown up he walks on two legs, in old age he needs a third—a walking stick." Oedipus won the kingship and married the queen (who would prove to be his real mother as the old man he killed would prove to have been his real father).

Aronnax has good reasons to iden-

must understand that, in pursuing you over the high seas of the Pacific, the *Abraham Lincoln* believed itself to be chasing some powerful sea-monster, of which it was necessary to rid the ocean at any price."

A half-smile curled the lips of the commander: then, in a calmer tone—

"M. Aronnax," he replied, "dare you affirm that your frigate would not as soon have pursued and cannonaded a submarine boat as a monster?"

This question embarrassed me, for certainly Captain Farragut might not have hesitated. He might have thought it his duty to destroy a contrivance of this kind, as he would a gigantic narwhal.

"You understand then, sir," continued the stranger, "that I have the right to treat you as enemies?"

I answered nothing, purposely. For what good would it be to discuss such a proposition, when force could destroy the best arguments?

"I have hesitated for some time," continued the commander; "nothing obliged me to show you hospitality. If I chose to separate myself from you, I should have no interest in seeing you again; I could place you upon the deck of this vessel which has served you as a refuge, I could sink beneath the waters, and forget that you had ever existed. Would not that be my right?"

"It might be the right of a savage," I answered, "but not that of a civilised man."

"Professor," replied the commander quickly, "I am not what you call a civilised man! **2** I have done with society entirely, for reasons which I alone have the right of appreciating. I do not therefore obey its laws, and I desire you never to allude to them before me again!"

This was said plainly. A flash of anger and disdain kindled in the eyes of the Unknown, and I had a glimpse of a terrible past in the life of this man. Not only had he put himself beyond the pale of human laws, but he had made himself independent of them, free in the strictest acceptation of the word, quite beyond their reach. Who then would dare to pursue him at the bottom of the sea, when, on its surface, he defied all attempts made against him? What vessel could resist the shock of his submarine monitor? What cuirass, however thick,**3** could withstand the blows of his spur? No man could demand from him an account of his actions; God, if he believed in one—his conscience, if he had one,—were the sole judges to whom he was answerable.

These reflections crossed my mind rapidly, whilst the

stranger personage was silent, absorbed, and as if wrapped up in himself. I regarded him with fear mingled with interest, as doubtless, Oedipus regarded the Sphinx.**4**

After rather a long silence, the commander resumed the conversation.

"I have hesitated," said he, "but I have thought that my interest might be reconciled with that pity to which every human being has a right. You will remain on board my vessel, since fate has cast you there. You will be free; and in exchange for this liberty, I shall only impose one single condition. Your word of honour to submit to it will suffice."

"Speak, sir," I answered. "I suppose this condition is one which a man of honour may accept?"

"Yes, sir; it is this. It is possible that certain events, unforeseen, may oblige me to consign you to your cabins for some hours or some days, as the case may be. As I desire never to use violence, I expect from you, more than all the others, a passive obedience. In thus acting, I take all the responsibility: I acquit you entirely, for I make it an impossibility for you to see what ought not to be seen. Do you accept this condition?"

Then things took place on board which, to say the least, were singular, and which ought not to be seen by people who were not placed beyond the pale of social laws. Amongst the surprises which the future was preparing for me, this might not be the least.

"We accept," **5** I answered; "only I will ask your permission, sir, to address one question to you—one only."

"Speak, sir."

"You said that we should be free on board."

"Entirely."

"I ask you, then, what you mean by this liberty?"

"Just the liberty to go, to come, to see, to observe even all that passes here,—save under rare circumstances,—the liberty, in short, which we enjoy ourselves, my companions and I."

It was evident that we did not understand one another.

"Pardon me, sir," I resumed, "but this liberty is only what every prisoner has of pacing his prison. It cannot suffice us."

"It must suffice you, however."

"What! We must renounce for ever seeing our country, our friends, our relations again?"

"Yes, sir. But to renounce that unendurably worldly yoke which men believe to be liberty, is not perhaps so painful as you think."

"Well," exclaimed Ned Land, "never will I give my word of honour not to try to escape."

tify with Oedipus at this moment. Like Oedipus, Aronnax must *fear* death in a crucial interview. Like Oedipus, Aronnax has more *interest* at stake than mere survival: both men have been thrust into an identity crisis. Oedipus was at a crossroads in his life, homeless, unsure who he really was. Aronnax is lost at sea. We have already noted the psychological implications of his thinking of Jonah and the whale's belly. He was contemplating a crucial descent into the self. Now he is *in* the whale's belly or, as he expresses it at this point, at the crossroads with Oedipus.

5. *We accept* Notice that without hesitation, Aronnax presumes to speak for all three men. A moment later the captain will make it clear to Ned that indeed he is not being consulted. Aronnax, with his nineteenth-century view of social hierarchy, sees himself as the natural leader here. Ned, on both whaling ships and on the *Abraham Lincoln,* has become accustomed to hierarchy, and Conseil yearns for it. Notice that later Aronnax will offer no protest when Ned and Conseil, *as social inferiors,* are not allowed to eat with the captain and his only guest, the professor.

"I did not ask you for your word of honour, Master Land," answered the commander, coldly.

"Sir," I replied, beginning to get angry in spite of myself, "you abuse your situation towards us; it is cruelty."

"No, sir, it is clemency. You are my prisoners of war. I keep you, when I could, by a word, plunge you into the depths of the ocean. You attacked me. You came to surprise a secret which no man in the world must penetrate,—the secret of my whole existence. And you think that I am going to send you back to that world which must know me no more? Never! In retaining you, it is not you whom I guard—it is myself."

These words indicated a resolution taken on the part of the commander, against which no arguments would prevail.

"So, sir," I rejoined, "you give us simply the choice between life and death?"

"Simply."

"My friends," said I, "to a question thus put, there is nothing to answer. But no word of honour binds us to the master of this vessel."

"None, sir," answered the Unknown.

Then, in a gentler tone, he continued—

"Now, permit me to finish what I have to say to you. I know you, M. Aronnax. You and your companions will not perhaps, have so much to complain of in the chance which has bound you to my fate. You will find amongst the books which are my favourite study the work which you have published on 'the depths of the sea.' I have often read it. You have carried your work as far as terrestrial science permitted you. But you do not know all—you have not seen all. Let me tell you then, Professor, that you will not regret the time passed on board my vessel. You are going to visit the land of marvels.

["Astonishment will probably become your normal **6** state of mind! It will not be possible for you to be bored at the endless spectacle I shall put before you. I am now planning another tour of the submarine world—who knows, it could be my last —visiting again everything I have ever studied on the floor of the sea. And you shall be my fellow student! From this day forward, you enter into a new element, you will be seeing what no man has seen before you—because my men and I no longer count—and our planet, thanks to me, will reveal its last secrets—to you.]"

These words of the commander had a great effect upon me. I cannot deny it. My weak point was touched; and I forgot, for a moment, that the contemplation of these sublime subjects was not worth the loss of liberty. Besides, I trusted to the

6. *Astonishment . . . normal* The climax of the captain's speech shows that he, like the professor, has been lonely. He is actually thrilled to have aboard someone who is his peer intellectually as well as socially. This passage also shows that the captain is concerned for the professor only. The inducements he offers are not likely to interest Ned and, anyhow, the captain welcomes only one fellow student. Finally, this passage, like the next one omitted by Lewis, adds tremendously to the emotional resonance of the scene.

future to decide this grave question. So I contented myself with saying—

["Monsieur, even though you have broken with humanity, I still cannot believe you have rejected all human sentiment. We are survivors of a shipwreck, charitably taken aboard by you, and we cannot easily forget that. And I must admit that, if my interest in science could cancel out my love of freedom, this promised voyage would offer me tremendous compensations."

I thought he would extend his hand, so that we could shake as a sign of understanding. He did nothing. I regretted that.

"One final question," I said, when this inexplicable being seemed ready to go.

"Speak, Professor."]

"By what name ought I to address you?"

"Sir," replied the commander, "I am nothing to you but Captain Nemo; 7 and you and your companions are nothing to me but the passengers of the *Nautilus*." 8

Captain Nemo called. A steward appeared. The captain gave him his orders in that strange language which I did not understand. Then, turning towards the Canadian and Conseil—

"A repast awaits you in your cabin," said he. "Be so good as to follow this man."

["I will not refuse!" said the harpooner. And so Conseil and Ned finally left the cell where they had been confined for more than thirty hours.]

"And now, M. Aronnax, our breakfast is ready.9 Permit me to lead the way."

"I am at your service, Captain."

I followed Captain Nemo; and as soon as I had passed through the door, I found myself in a kind of passage lighted by electricity, similar to the waist of a ship. After we had proceeded a dozen yards, a second door opened before me.

I then entered a dining-room, decorated and furnished in severe taste.10 High oaken sideboards, inlaid with ebony, stood at the two extremities of the room, and upon their shelves glittered china, porcelain, and glass of inestimable value. The plate on the table sparkled in the rays which the luminous ceiling shed around, while the light was tempered and softened by exquisite paintings.

In the centre of the room was a table richly laid out. Captain Nemo indicated the place I was to occupy.

["Sit down and enjoy a good meal," he said. "You must be famished."]

7. *nothing . . . but Captain Nemo* The captain has chosen an extraordinary name for himself. In Latin, Nemo means *no man, nobody*. And this is the name that Odysseus assumed when the Cyclops Polyphemus demanded to know his identity. Hence when other Cyclopes heard Polyphemus screaming, they shouted: "Who is hurting you?" and when he answered, "No Man is hurting me," they went away.

So the captain's name recalls the wiles of Odysseus, the man of the seas. His name also reflects his withdrawal from society: he is the romantic outcast, the "nameless one." Of course, it is an ironic name. For he is *not* a *nobody,* as we shall soon discover.

8. *the Nautilus* The captain has been equally artistic in naming his submarine. He has commemorated the submersible *Nautilus* built by Robert Fulton in 1801, and, like Fulton, Nemo has honored one of the world's most extraordinary creatures.

Fulton's boat was named after a spiral-shelled mollusk whose genus has survived for hundreds of millions of years. It ascends to reefs or descends to the depths by adjusting the amount of gas in its chambers. Thus jet-propelled, it swings in the water, like a pendulum.

The U.S. Navy presumably has honored Verne as well as Fulton and the living-fossil mollusk by giving the name *Nautilus* to a submarine in World War II and later to the first atomic submarine to sail across the North Pole by traveling under the ice pack.

9. *our breakfast is ready* Verne says *déjeuner*, which could mean *lunch*.

10. *furnished in severe taste* Verne's words *avec un goût sévère* mean *with austere, correct, pure taste.*

The breakfast consisted of a certain number of dishes, the contents of which were furnished by the sea alone; and I was ignorant of the nature and mode of preparation of some of them. I acknowledged that they were good, but they had a peculiar flavour, which I easily became accustomed to. These different aliments appeared to me to be rich in phosphorus, and I thought they must have a marine origin.

Captain Nemo looked at me. I asked him no questions, but he guessed my thoughts, and answered of his own accord the questions which I was burning to address to him.

"The greater part of these dishes are unknown to you," he said to me. "However, you may partake of them without fear. They are wholesome and nourishing. For a long time I have renounced the food of the earth, and am never ill now. My crew, who are healthy, are fed on the same food."

"So," said I, "all these eatables are the produce of the sea?"

"Yes, Professor, the sea supplies all my wants. Sometimes I cast my nets in tow, and I draw them in ready to break. Sometimes I hunt in the midst of this element, which appears to be inaccessible to man, and quarry the game which dwells in my submarine forests. My flocks, like those of Neptune's old shepherds,11 graze fearlessly in the immense prairies of the ocean. I have a vast property there, which I cultivate myself, and which is always sown by the hand of the Creator of all things."

"I can understand perfectly, sir, that your nets furnish excellent fish for your table; I can understand also that you hunt aquatic game in your submarine forests; but I cannot understand at all how a particle of meat, no matter how small, can figure in your bill of fare."

["No, monsieur," the Captain rejoined. "I never eat of the flesh of land animals."

"Then what is this?" I pointed to a dish containing what appeared to be slices of filleted meat.]

"This, which you believe to be meat, Professor, is nothing else than fillet of turtle. Here are also some dolphins' livers, which you take to be ragout of pork. My cook is a clever fellow, who excels in dressing these various products of the ocean. Taste all these dishes. Here is a preserve of holothuria,12 which a Malay would declare to be unrivalled in the world; here is a cream, of which the milk has been furnished by the cetacea, and the sugar by the great fucus of the North Sea; 13 and lastly, permit me to offer you some preserve of anemones, which is equal to that of the most delicious fruits."

11. *Neptune's old shepherds* Sea gods, like Proteus in the *Odyssey,* are often represented as herding flocks of seals.

"This . . . is nothing else than fillet of turtle. . . ." Drawing of a green turtle that appeared in *Mitchell's School Geography* (1863).

12. *preserve of holothuria* The holothuria could be any one of various wormlike aquatic animals, for example, a sea cucumber.

13. *the great fucus of the North Sea* A fucus is a brown alga; the word derives from the Greek for *seaweed.*

I tasted more from curiosity than as a connoisseur, whilst Captain Nemo enchanted me with his extraordinary stories.

["But this ocean, M. Aronnax, this inexhaustible great provider, does more than just feed me. She clothes me as well. Those materials you are wearing are woven from the fibres of certain shell-fish. They have been dyed with the purple of the ancients and shaded with violet that I extract from the Mediterranean sea hare. The perfumes that you will find on your bureau in your cabin I make by distilling sea plants. Your mattress is made from the softest sea-grass. You will find a pen made from whale-bone, and ink that is juice secreted by the squid. I get everything from the sea, just as the sea will someday claim me."]

"You like the sea, Captain?"

"Yes; I love it! The sea is everything. It covers seven-tenths of the terrestrial globe. Its breath is pure and healthy. It is an immense desert, where man is never lonely, for he feels life stirring on all sides. The sea is only the embodiment of a supernatural and wonderful existence. It is nothing but love and emotion; it is the 'Living Infinite,' as one of your. poets has said. In fact, Professor, Nature manifests herself in it by her three kingdoms, mineral, vegetable, and animal. [The animal kingdom is represented by the four groups of zoophytes, three classes of articulates, five classes of vertebrates, mammals, reptiles, myriad legions of fish, an infinite order of animals comprising more than 13,000 species, only one-tenth of which also belong to fresh water.]

"The sea is the vast reservoir of Nature. The globe began with sea, so to speak; and who knows if it will not end with it? In it is supreme tranquillity. The sea does not belong to despots. Upon its surface men can still exercise unjust laws, fight, tear one another to pieces, and be carried away with terrestrial horrors. But at thirty feet below its level, their reign ceases, their influence is quenched, and their power disappears. Ah! sir, live—live in the bosom of the waters! There only is independence! There I recognise no masters! There I am free!"

Captain Nemo suddenly became silent in the midst of this enthusiasm, by which he was quite carried away. For a few moments he paced up and down, much agitated. Then he became more calm, regained his accustomed coldness of expression, and turning towards me—

"Now, Professor," said he, "if you wish to go over the *Nautilus,* I am at your service." **14**

14. *I am at your service* And here, with his good sense of theater, Verne ends the chapter. For some strange reason, Lewis ignored this chapter break and lumped Chapter XI into Chapter X.

[PART 1: CHAPTER XI

The *Nautilus*]¹⁵

15. [*Chapter XI: The Nautilus*] Lewis's omission of this chapter break disturbs the natural rhythm of Verne's narrative. Ironically, it also omits a key phrase from the table of contents: the *Nautilus*.

16. *men no longer think or write* Here, and in his later remark that *"Masters have no age,"* Nemo voices a desire for total regression to a Garden of Eden—a timelessness, stasis, immortality, in which all history is simultaneous. This wish to escape time is a denial of his basic suffering. But, as we shall see, he is the prisoner of a traumatic experience that simply will not let him get outside history.

17. *took up by chance* To Aronnax the classifier, it is *strange* that Nemo does not have his library systematized. It's almost as if Aronnax does not know the pleasure of meandering, *indiscriminately* picking his reading as it were almost by free association. The professor is revealing as much of himself as of Nemo. Verne uses the most casual bit of action not only to reflect character but to effect contrasts.

18. *Madame Sand* Verne's inclusion of her works in Captain Nemo's collection of *masterpieces* suggests that Nemo admires freedom and independence not only in speech but in practice, not for men alone but also for women.

Captain Nemo rose. I followed him. A double door, contrived at the back of the dining-room, opened, and I entered a room equal in dimensions to that which I had just quitted.

It was a library. High pieces of furniture, of black violet ebony inlaid with brass, supported upon their wide shelves a great number of books uniformly bound. They followed the shape of the room, terminating at the lower part in huge divans, covered with brown leather, which were curved, to afford the greatest comfort. Light movable desks, made to slide in and out at will, allowed one to rest one's book while reading. In the centre stood an immense table, covered with pamphlets, amongst which were some newspapers, already of old date. The electric light flooded everything; it was shed from four unpolished globes half sunk in the volutes of the ceiling. I looked with real admiration at this room, so ingeniously fitted up, and I could scarcely believe my eyes.

"Captain Nemo," said I to my host, who had just thrown himself on one of the divans, "this is a library which would do honour to more than one of the continental palaces, and I am absolutely astounded when I consider that it can follow you to the bottom of the seas."

"Where could one find greater solitude or silence, Professor?" replied Captain Nemo. "Did your study in the Museum afford you such perfect quiet?"

"No, sir; and I must confess that it is a very poor one after yours. You must have six or seven thousand volumes here."

"Twelve thousand, M. Aronnax. These are the only ties which bind me to the earth. But I had done with the world on the day when my *Nautilus* plunged for the first time beneath the waters. That day I bought my last volumes, my last pamphlets, my last papers, and from that time I wish to think that men no longer think or write.**16** These books, Professor, are at your service besides, and you can make use of them freely."

I thanked Captain Nemo and went up to the shelves of the library. Works on science, morals, and literature abounded in every language; but I did not see one single work on political economy; that subject appeared to be strictly proscribed. Strange to say, all these books were irregularly arranged, in whatever language they were written; and this medley proved that the Captain of the *Nautilus* must have read indiscriminately the books which he took up by chance.**17**

[Amongst these books I found masterpieces both ancient and modern, everything worthwhile in history, poetry, fiction, and science, from Homer to Victor Hugo, from Xenophon to Michelet, from Rabelais to Madame Sand.**18** But science predominated in this library. Books on mechanics, ballistics, hydrography, meteorology, geography, geology, etc., held a place no less important than the works of natural history. I realised that these were the Captain's principal studies. I found all of Humboldt, all of Arago, the works of Foucault, Henry Sainte-Claire Deville, Chasles, Milne-Edwards, Quatrefages, Tyndall, Faraday, Berthelot, the Abbé Secchi, Petermann. Commander Maury,**19** Agassiz, and others, publications of the Academy of Sciences, bulletins of geographical societies, and—in a position of prominence—the two volumes that probably won me such a welcome from Captain Nemo.

Amongst the works of Joseph Bertrand, his book *The Founders of Astronomy* gave me a key date. Since I knew it had appeared in 1865, I now realised that the *Nautilus* could not have been launched before that. So, Captain Nemo had been at sea for no more than three years. Maybe more recent works would enable me to pinpoint the time more exactly. But I could check on that later. Right now I wanted to make an overall inspection of the marvels of the *Nautilus*.]

"Sir," said I to the Captain, "I thank you for having placed this library at my disposal. It contains treasures of science, and I shall profit by them."

"This room is not only a library," said Captain Nemo, "it is also a smoking-room."

"A smoking-room!" I cried. "Then one may smoke on board?"

"Certainly."

"Then, sir, I am forced to believe that you have kept up a communication with Havannah."

George Sand (pseudonym of Aurore Dupin, Baronne du Dudevant, 1804–1876) was a French romantic novelist. She took an active part in the Revolution of 1848, writing a series of appeals to the people. She was notorious for her succession of love affairs, and must be counted as one of the earliest successful advocates of total sexual freedom.

At the time Aronnax is staring at her books, she is regarded as one of the literary greats, a friend of Gustave Flaubert and Alexandre Dumas. Her two contemporaries that Aronnax chooses to represent the modern age were also her friends, also in their advanced years: Jules Michelet (1798–1874), French historian, and Victor Hugo (1802–1885), novelist, playwright, poet, "lord of language," giant of French romanticism.

Hugo especially, and Michelet and Sand as well, were out of favor with Emperor Louis Napoleon. Verne's emphasis on their greatness then is not only a literary but also a political judgment.

19. *Commander Maury* Maury is the one author in Nemo's library whose works would surely be found in every captain's cabin in 1868. As a matter of fact, he was probably the scientist best known even to laymen.

Navy Lieutenant Matthew Fontaine Maury (1806–1873), a Virginian, was lamed in a carriage accident in 1839. Disqualified for further sea duty, he was appointed officer in charge of the depot of charts and instruments. As he reviewed the routine observations on winds and currents that naval vessels submitted, he realized the value of correlating these data. Soon he was publishing his first "Wind and Current Charts," which made available to a navigator the combined experience "of a thousand vessels that had preceded him on the same voyage."

The first charts were an immediate boon to captains, helping them to choose speedier and safer routes. And so Maury had no trouble drawing their attention to the "blank spaces" still to be filled in. He promised that all captains who would send logs of their voyages to Washington would receive, free of charge, the improved charts and sailing directions that could thus be compiled and shared.

In his own words, he now had "more than a thousand navigators engaged day and night, in all parts of the ocean, in making and recording observations according to a uniform plan."

Maury organized the International Maritime Conference, held at Brussels in 1853, at which his work won enthusiastic support from the other major sea powers. In 1854 the president of the British Association estimated that Maury's *Explanations and Sailing Directions to Accompany the Wind and Current Charts* had cut passage from Britain to Australia by 20 days and to California by 30 days. Maury himself reported that passage from New York to California had been shortened by 48 days.

Meanwhile Maury had supervised development of a new depth-sounding machine. With data obtained with this apparatus, he prepared the first depth map of the North Atlantic, down to 4000 fathoms (24,000 feet). Thus he paved the way for the laying of the Atlantic Cable, a fact that provides Verne with some of his best material later in the novel.

In 1855 Maury published his classic *The Physical Geography of the Sea and Its Meteorology.* Although there is an odd legend that Maury never rose above the rank of lieutenant, Verne is right—that same year Maury was made a commander.

Nemo and Aronnax will often, in the course of their 20,000-league association, engage in one of the favorite intellectual pastimes of that period: discussing the theories and accomplishments of Commander Maury. As we shall see later, his theoretical efforts remain controversial. But no one has ever disputed the massive benefit of his practical methods and data to world shipping.

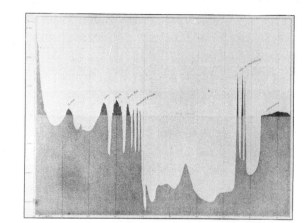

Matthew Maury's "Vertical Section—North Atlantic," which he described as "showing the contrasts of its bottom with the sea-level in a line from Mexico across Yucatan, Cuba, San Domingo, and the Cape de Verds, to the coast of Africa. . . ."

"Not any," answered the Captain. "Accept this cigar, M. Aronnax; and though it does not come from Havannah, you will be pleased with it, if you are a connoisseur."

I took the cigar which was offered me; its shape recalled the London ones, but it seemed to be made of leaves of gold. I lighted it at a little brazier, which was supported upon an elegant bronze stem, and drew the first whiffs with the delight of a lover of smoking who has not smoked for two days.

"It is excellent," said I, "but it is not tobacco."

"No!" answered the Captain, "this tobacco comes neither from Havannah nor from the East. It is a kind of sea-weed, rich in nicotine, with which the sea provides me, but somewhat sparingly." [In a moment he asked, "Now do you think you will miss your Havannahs?"

"From this day on," I replied, "I shall despise them."

"Well, smoke these as you will. And do not worry about their origin. They may not bear an official excise-stamp, but they are none the worse for that, I imagine."

"On the contrary."]

At that moment Captain Nemo opened a door which stood opposite to that by which I had entered the library, and I passed into an immense drawing-room splendidly lighted.

It was a vast four-sided room, thirty feet long, eighteen wide, and fifteen high. A luminous ceiling, decorated with light arabesques, shed a soft clear light over all the marvels accumulated in this museum. For it was in fact a museum, in which an intelligent and prodigal hand had gathered all the treasures of nature and art, with the artistic confusion which distinguishes a painter's studio.

Thirty first-rate pictures, uniformly framed, separated by bright drapery, ornamented the walls, which were hung with tapestry of severe design. I saw works of great value, the greater part of which I had admired in the special collections of Europe, and in the exhibitions of paintings. The several schools of the old masters were represented by a Madonna of Raphael, a Virgin of Leonardo da Vinci, a nymph of Corregio, a woman of Titian, an Adoration of Veronese, an Assumption of Murillo, a portrait of Holbein, a monk of Velasquez, a martyr of Ribera, a fair of Rubens, two Flemish landscapes of Teniers, three little "genre" pictures of Gerard Dow, Metsu, and Paul Potter, two specimens of Géricault and Prudhon, and some sea-pieces of Backhuysen and Vernet. Amongst the works of modern painters were pictures with the signatures of Delacroix, Ingres, Decamps, Troyon, Meissonier, Daubigny, etc.; and some admirable statues in marble and bronze, after the finest antique models, stood upon pedestals in the corners of this magnificent museum. Amazement, as the Captain of the *Nautilus* had predicted, had already begun to take possession of me.

"Professor," said this strange man, "you must excuse the unceremonious way in which I receive you, and the disorder of this room."

"Sir," I answered, "without seeking to know who you are, I recognise in you an artist."

"An amateur, nothing more, sir. Formerly I loved to collect these beautiful works created by the hand of man. I sought them greedily, and ferreted them out indefatigably, and I have been able to bring together some objects of great value. These are my last souvenirs of that world which is dead to me. In my eyes, your modern artists are already old; they have two or three thousand years of existence; I confound them in my own mind. Masters have no age."

"And these musicians?" said I, pointing out some works of Weber, Rossini, Mozart, Beethoven, Haydn, Meyerbeer, Hérold, Wagner, Auber, Gounod, and a number of others, scattered over a large model piano-organ which occupied one of the panels of the drawing-room.

"These musicians," replied Captain Nemo, "are the contemporaries of Orpheus; for in the memory of the dead all chronological differences are effaced; and I am dead, Professor; as much dead as those of your friends who are sleeping six feet under the earth!"

Captain Nemo was silent, and seemed lost in a profound reverie. I contemplated him with deep interest, analysing in

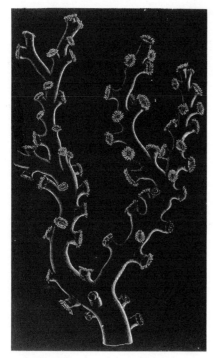

Nemo's *whole series of madrepores* would include the *Dendrophyllia nigrescens,* pictured in James D. Dana's *Corals and Coral Islands* (1872).

20. *my master Milne Edwards* Does Aronnax mean that the great Milne-Edwards was his teacher or his "chief," his director? Either or both could be the case. Henri Milne-Edwards (1800–1885), born in Belgium of British parents, took his medical degree in Paris in 1823, taught natural history in the *lycée* Henri IV in Paris, and in 1844 became professor of zoology and comparative physiology at the Museum of Natural History. He was the author of numerous standard works, some of which the professor has already spotted on Nemo's shelves. Milne-Edwards was a leading anti-Darwinist, believing that zoological distribution could be explained by special creation in different areas.

If Aronnax was forty in Chapter III, then he was born in 1827 and could have studied under Milne-Edwards at the *lycée.* In any event, it is certain that Aronnax knew Milne-Edwards at the museum where they both worked and where Milne-Edwards would have been the senior man.

silence the strange expression of his countenance. Leaning on his elbow against an angle of a costly mosaic table, he no longer saw me,—he had forgotten my presence.

I did not disturb this reverie, and continued my observation of the curiosities which enriched this drawing-room. [Next to the works of art, natural rarities predominated. These consisted principally of plants, shells, and other marine products, which the Captain must have collected himself. In the middle of the room, a jet of water, lighted by electricity, poured into a large bowl made from a single giant clam. This shell had come from the largest of the acephalous molluscs. Its rim was delicately scalloped and measured about twenty feet in circumference. It was larger than those beautiful giant shells given to François I by the Venetian Republic and made into two huge holy-water basins for the church of Saint-Sulpice in Paris.]

Under elegant glass cases, fixed by copper rivets, were classed and labelled the most precious productions of the sea which had ever been presented to the eye of a naturalist. My delight as a professor may be conceived.

The division containing the zoophytes presented the most curious specimens of the two groups of polypi and echinodermes. In the first group, the tubipores, were gorgones arranged like a fan, soft sponges of Syria, ises of the Moluccas, pennatules, an admirable virgularia of the Norwegian seas, variegated unbellulairae, alcyonariae, a whole series of madrepores, which my master Milne Edwards **20** has so cleverly classified, amongst which I remarked some wonderful flabellinae oculinae of the Island of Bourbon, the "Neptune's car" of the Antilles, superb varieties of corals—in short, every species of those curious polypi of which entire islands are formed, which will one day become continents. Of the echinodermes, remarkable for their coating of spines, asteri, sea-stars, pantacrinae, comatules, astérophons, echini, holothuri, etc., represented individually a complete collection of this group.

A somewhat nervous conchyliologist would certainly have fainted before other more numerous cases, in which were classified the specimens of molluscs. It was a collection of inestimable value, which time fails me to describe minutely. Amongst these specimens I will quote from memory only the elegant royal hammer-fish of the Indian Ocean, whose regular white spots stood out brightly on a red and brown ground, an imperial spondyle, bright-coloured, bristling with spines, a rare specimen in the European museums—(I estimated its

value at not less than £1000); a common hammer-fish of the seas of New Holland, which is only procured with difficulty; exotic buccardia of Senegal; fragile white bivalve shells, which a breath might shatter like a soap-bubble; several varieties of the aspirgillum of Java, a kind of calcareous tube, edged with leafy folds, and much debated by amateurs; **21** a whole series of trochi, some a greenish-yellow, found in the American seas, others a reddish-brown, natives of Australian waters; others from the Gulf of Mexico, remarkable for their imbricated shell; stellari found in the Southern Seas; and the rarest of all, the magnificent spur of New Zealand.

[Also there were remarkable sulphurized tellins, precious specimens of cytherean and venus shells, the trellised sundial from Tranquebar waters, the marble turban conch with its pearly gleam, the green parrot-shell from the China Seas, the rare conical shell of the genus *Coenodueli,* all varieties of the polished cowries that are used as money in India and Africa, "the glory of the sea," the most precious East Indian shell, and finally, littorinidae, "delphiniums," turritellidae, janthinidae, ovulidae, miter shells, helmet shells, purpurae, whelks, harpae, murices, tritons, cerithidae, spindles, strombidae, wing-shells, limpets, hyalines, cleodores.] And every description of delicate and fragile shells to which science has given appropriate names.

Apart, in separate compartments, were spread out chaplets of pearls of the greatest beauty, which reflected the electric light in little sparks of fire; pink pearls, torn from the pinna-marina of the Red Sea; green pearls of the haliotyde iris; yellow, blue and black pearls, the curious productions of the divers molluscs of every ocean, and certain mussels of the watercourses of the North; lastly, several specimens of inestimable value which had been gathered from the rarest pintadines. Some of these pearls were larger than a pigeon's egg, and were worth as much, and more than that which the traveller Tavernier **22** sold to the Shah of Persia for three millions, and surpassed the one in the possession of the Imaum of Muscat, which I believed to be unrivalled in the world.

Therefore to estimate the value of this collection was simply impossible. Captain Nemo must have expended millions in the acquirement of these various specimens, and I was thinking what source he could have drawn from, to have been able thus to gratify his fancy for collecting, when I was interrupted by these words—

"You are examining my shells, Professor? Unquestionably

21. *much debated by amateurs* Aronnax is not using the word *amateur* in a pejorative sense. He simply means *much discussed, much sought after, by collectors* or *enthusiasts.*

In French the word *amateur,* more so in Verne's day, retains some of its original meaning: someone who is a *lover* of a certain pursuit. He may be anyone from a successful *connoisseur* to a hopeless *dilettante,* so long as he feels *amatory* toward the subject.

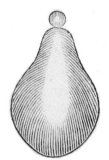

Some of these pearls were larger . . . than that which the traveller Tavernier sold to the Shah of Persia. . . . Tavernier's pearl was pear-shaped, .6 inch in diameter at its widest, 1.5 inches long. The engraving above, which appeared in *Chambers's Miscellany* (1870), is a copy of Tavernier's own sketch of the famous gem.

22. *the traveller Tavernier* This casual reference sufficed in Verne's day, when "the traveller Tavernier" was still as popular a legendary figure as "the traveller Marco Polo" is today. Jean-Baptiste Tavernier (1605–1689) was born into a family of Parisian geographers. He made six long journeys to such exotic lands as Turkey, Persia, India, Java, Russia. He socialized with the greatest princes of the East, inspected their fabulous treasures, diamond mines, and pearl fisheries, and traded jewels with them. He is especially remembered as a pioneer in European trade with India and as author of three books about his travels.

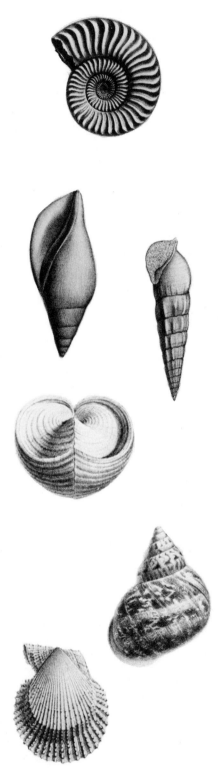

A somewhat nervous conchyliologist would . . . have fainted before . . . cases, in which were classified the specimens of molluscs. Engravings from the *Journal de Conchyliologie,* Paris, various issues from 1853 to 1870.

they must be interesting to a naturalist; but for me they have a far greater charm, for I have collected them all with my own hand, and there is not a sea on the face of the globe which has escaped my researches."

"I can understand, Captain, the delight of wandering about in the midst of such riches. You are one of those who have collected their treasures themselves. No museum in Europe possesses such a collection of the produce of the ocean. But if I exhaust all my admiration upon it, I shall have none left for the vessel which carries it. I do not wish to pry into your secrets; but I must confess that this *Nautilus,* with the motive power which is confined to it, the contrivances which enable it to be worked, the powerful agent which propels it, all excite my curiosity to the highest pitch. I see suspended on the walls of this room instruments of whose use I am ignorant. [May I presume to ask . . . ?"

"M. Aronnax," the Captain answered, "I have told you, you have complete liberty aboard my ship. Therefore no part of the *Nautilus* is forbidden to you. You may inspect it in detail. It would please me to serve as your guide."

"I do not know how to thank you, monsieur, and I don't want to abuse the privilege. But would you mind telling me something about these instruments, what they are for, how you use them?]"

"You will find these same instruments in my own room, Professor, where I shall have much pleasure in explaining their use to you. But first come and inspect the cabin which is set apart for your own use. You must see how you will be accommodated on board the *Nautilus."*

I followed Captain Nemo, who, by one of the doors opening from each panel of the drawing-room, regained the waist. He conducted me towards the bow, and there I found, not a cabin, but an elegant room, with a bed, dressing-table, and several other pieces of furniture.

I could only thank my host.

"Your room adjoins mine," said he, opening a door, "and mine opens into the drawing-room that we have just quitted."

I entered the Captain's room: it had a severe, almost a monkish, aspect. A small iron bedstead, a table, some articles for the toilet; the whole lighted by a skylight. No comforts, the strictest necessaries only.

Captain Nemo pointed to a seat.

"Be so good as to sit down," he said. I seated myself, and he began thus:

PART 1: CHAPTER XI[1]
All by Electricity[2]

"Sir," said Captain Nemo, showing me the instruments hanging on the walls of his room, "here are the contrivances required for the navigation of the *Nautilus*. Here, as in the drawing-room, I have them always under my eyes, and they indicate my position and exact direction in the middle of the ocean. Some are known to you, such as the thermometer, which gives the internal temperature of the *Nautilus;* the barometer, which indicates the weight of the air and foretells the changes of the weather; the hygrometer, which marks the dryness of the atmosphere; the storm-glass, the contents of which, by decomposing, announce the approach of tempests; the compass, which guides my course; the sextant, which shows the latitude by the altitude of the sun; chronometers, by which I calculate the longitude; and glasses for day and night, which I use to examine the points of the horizon, when the *Nautilus* rises to the surface of the waves."

"These are the usual nautical instruments," I replied, "and I know the use of them. But these others, no doubt, answer to the particular requirements of the *Nautilus*. This dial with the movable needle is a manometer, is it not?"

"It is actually a manometer. But by communication with the water, whose external pressure it indicates, it gives our depth at the same time."

"And these other instruments, the use of which I cannot guess?"

"Here, Professor, I ought to give you some explanations. Will you be kind enough to listen to me?"

He was silent for a few moments, then he said—

"There is a powerful agent, obedient, rapid, easy, which conforms to every use, and reigns supreme on board my ves-

1. *Chapter XI* All the remaining chapters of Part I are misnumbered by one digit. After skipping the chapter heading for "Chapter XI: The *Nautilus*" (see page 68), Mercier Lewis followed suit and renumbered Chapters XII to XXIV as XI to XXIII, respectively. And so this is really Chapter XII.

2. *All By Electricity* When this novel appeared in 1870, Verne's typical readers—both European and American—knew of electricity only as a curiosity at carnivals and World's Fairs. They might, for example, have seen the first practical dynamos demonstrated at the Paris Exhibition of 1867. But not until 1878 would Parisians be able to boast that "electric candles" lighted their way to the Opera. A few thousand New Yorkers would be able to buy electricity for domestic lighting by 1882. Citizens of Buffalo could claim by 1886 that their city was the first to be "electrified." And for visitors to the Paris Exhibition of 1889, the main attraction in the American Pavilion would be—a giant Edison incandescent lamp!

So, with electricity for street and house lighting still only a promise in 1870, readers of early editions of *Twenty Thousand Leagues* were fascinated to discover that Captain Nemo had gone beyond lighting. Nemo uses electricity for motive power, heating, cooking, ventilation—even security.

This would always be one of Verne's main appeals in his own lifetime. He undertook to tell his readers how imminent developments would affect them in ten or twenty years.

sel. Everything is done by means of it. It lights it, warms it, and is the soul of my mechanical apparatus. This agent is electricity."

"Electricity?" I cried in surprise.

"Yes, sir."

"Nevertheless, Captain, you possess an extreme rapidity of movement, which does not agree with the power of electricity. Until now, its dynamic force has remained under restraint, and has only been able to produce a small amount of power."

"Professor," said Captain Nemo, "my electricity is not everybody's. [That is all I can say at the moment."

"All right, monsieur, I will not press you. Suffice it to say, I am astonished at the results you get. But there is one other question I would like to ask, if you do not mind. The material you use to produce this marvellous power must be consumed so quickly. For example, how can you replenish your supply of zinc, since you have foresworn all contact with the land?"

"That question I shall answer," Captain Nemo said. "First, consider that in the ocean floor there are not only zinc mines, but also iron, silver, and gold mines that I could easily exploit. But I do not want to use the same metals that land-people use. I want to take my electricity from the sea!"

"The sea?"

"Of course, Professor. Such means are not lacking. I could even establish a circuit between wires at different depths, getting electricity by means of the reaction to different temperatures 'sensed' by those wires. But I prefer a more practical method."

"And what method is that?"]

"You know what sea-water is composed of. In a thousand grammes are found 96½ per cent. of water, and about 2⅔ per cent. of chloride of sodium; then, in a smaller quantity, chlorides of magnesium and of potassium, bromide of magnesium, sulphate of magnesia, sulphate and carbonate of lime. You see, then, that chloride of sodium forms a large part of it. So it is this sodium that I extract from sea-water, and of which I compose my ingredients."

["Sodium?"

"Yes, Professor. Mixed with mercury, sodium forms an amalgam which can take the place of zinc in Bunsen batteries. The mercury is never consumed, only the sodium is used up, and that is supplied from sea-water. Moreover, sodium batteries [3] are the most powerful, since their motive force is twice that of zinc batteries."

"I can see how sodium serves your needs. And there is

3. *sodium batteries* By omitting this crucial passage, Mercier Lewis made Verne vulnerable to sneering attacks on his integrity as a science-fiction writer. For example, Theodore L. Thomas, in his influential article "The Watery Wonders of Captain Nemo" (*Galaxy,* December 1961), charged that Verne had failed to provide adequate descriptions of "the storage batteries used aboard the *Nautilus.* There are none," he said flatly.

Oddly enough, Thomas preferred to accuse Verne rather than suspect the translator. As you can see for yourself, (1) Verne *did* provide adequate descriptions of Nemo's batteries and (2) Verne has been the innocent victim of literary mayhem.

plenty of it in sea-water. But you have to manufacture it, to extract it. How? You could use your batteries to extract it, but, it seems to me, you would need more sodium for such equipment than it would be extracting. I mean, would you not consume more than you would produce?"

"No, I do not use batteries, at least not for the extraction process. I use heat generated by coal."

"Coal?" I pressed him for an answer. "Coal!"

"Let us call it *sea*-coal."

"You mean you mine coal from the ocean floor?"

"Some day you will see how we do it, Professor. I ask you to be patient. And you will have enough time for patience. Just remember one thing:] I owe all to the ocean; it produces electricity, and electricity gives heat, light, motion, and, in a word, life to the *Nautilus*."

"But not the air you breathe?"

"Oh! I could manufacture the air necessary for my consumption, but it is useless, because I go up to the surface of the water when I please. However, if electricity does not furnish me with air to breathe, it works at least the powerful pumps that are stored in spacious reservoirs, and which enable me to prolong at need, and as long as I will, my stay in the depths of the sea."

["Captain," I replied, "I admire you. You are the first to discover what someday other men must also realise: the motive power of electricity."

"I don't know whether *they* will ever realise it," he answered coldly. "In any event, now you at least understand this first use that *I* have made of this precious power.] It gives a uniform and unintermittent light, which the sun does not. Now look at this clock; it is electrical, and goes with a regularity that defies the best chronometers. I have divided it into twenty-four hours, like the Italian clocks, because for me there is neither night nor day, sun or moon, but only that factitious light that I take with me to the bottom of the sea. Look! Just now, it is ten o'clock in the morning."

"Exactly."

"Another application of electricity. This dial hanging in front of us indicates the speed of the *Nautilus*. An electric thread **4** puts it in communication with the screw, and the needle indicates the real speed. Look! Now we are spinning along with a uniform speed of fifteen miles an hour."

"It is marvellous! And I see, Captain, you were right to make use of this agent that takes the place of wind, water, and steam."

4. *An electric thread* The French word *fil* can mean either *thread* or *wire*. In this context, Nemo is obviously talking about a wire.

5. *the exact division* Verne gives all of Aronnax's figures as *meters.* Lewis roughly converts these into *yards.* But a meter is 39.37 inches, while a yard is only 36 inches. And so, if Aronnax sees 35 meters in the forward part of the ship, Lewis is off by more than 10 feet in his total length. That is, 35 yards indeed are 105 feet, but 35 meters are more than 115 feet.

6. *starting from the ship's head* Verne says, in effect, *going from amidships to the bow.*

7. *india-rubber instruments* Read: *rubber seals* or *gaskets.*

8. *I exclaimed, in surprise* Aronnax's surprise seems out of all proportion to the facts (what big ship wouldn't have a dinghy?) until we realize that he's covering up for his spontaneous delight in discovering that a means of escape does exist. Surely Nemo understands that this is what really had crossed Aronnax's mind. Still, Nemo proceeds to tell the professor exactly how to use the boat. This adds to the humor and suspense, for it clearly indicates Nemo is certain his prisoners will never get away.

9. *An electric thread* Again, read *an electric wire.*

10. *streams . . . furnaces . . . sponges* For *streams, furnaces,* and *sponges* read *wires, stoves,* and *platinum plates.*

11. *berthroom . . . sixteen feet long* Conseil and Ned are eating in a cabin 2 meters (80 inches) long, and the crewmen share a berth room 5 meters (16 feet) long. Compare this to Nemo's own private dining room, 5 meters long, and private drawing room, 10 meters (33 feet) long, which he enjoys in addition to his private cabin.

Nemo is the typical nineteenth-century liberal who believed in freedom but not necessarily in equality. Aronnax also believes in freedom within hierarchy, as is evident in his complete unquestioning acceptance of the

"We have not finished, M. Aronnax," said Captain Nemo, rising; "if you will follow me, we will examine the stern of the *Nautilus.*"

Really, I knew already the anterior part of this submarine boat, of which this is the exact division,**5** starting from the ship's head **6**:—the dining-room, five yards long, separated from the library by a water-tight partition; the library, five yards long; the large drawing-room, ten yards long, separated from the Captain's room by a second water-tight partition; the said room, five yards in length; mine, two and a half yards; and lastly, a reservoir of air, seven and a half yards, that extended to the bows. Total lengths thirty-five yards, or one hundred and five feet. The partitions had doors that were shut hermetically by means of india-rubber instruments,**7** and they ensured the safety of the *Nautilus* in case of a leak.

I followed Captain Nemo through the waist, and arrived at the centre of the boat. There was a sort of well that opened between two partitions. An iron ladder, fastened with an iron hook to the partition, led to the upper end. I asked the Captain what the ladder was used for.

"It leads to the small boat," he said.

"What! Have you a boat?" I exclaimed, in surprise.**8**

"Of course; an excellent vessel, light and insubmersible, that serves either as a fishing or as a pleasure boat."

"But then, when you wish to embark, you are obliged to come to the surface of the water?"

"Not at all. This boat is attached to the upper part of the hull of the *Nautilus,* and occupies a cavity made for it. It is decked, quite water-tight, and held together by solid bolts. This ladder leads to a man-hole made in the hull of the *Nautilus,* that corresponds with a similar hole made in the side of the boat. By this double opening I get into the small vessel. They shut the one belonging to the *Nautilus,* I shut the other by means of screw pressure. I undo the bolts, and the little boat goes up to the surface of the sea with prodigious rapidity. I then open the panel of the bridge, carefully shut till then; I mast it, hoist my sail, take my oars, and I'm off."

"But how do you get back on board?"

"I do not come back, M. Aronnax; the *Nautilus* comes to me."

"By your orders?"

"By my orders. An electric thread **9** connects us. I telegraph to it, and that is enough."

"Really," I said, astonished at these marvels, "nothing can be more simple."

After having passed by the cage of the staircase that led to the platform, I saw a cabin six feet long, in which Conseil and Ned Land, enchanted with their repast, were devouring it with avidity. Then a door opened into a kitchen nine feet long, situated between the large storerooms. There electricity, better than gas itself, did all the cooking. The streams under the furnaces gave out to the sponges **10** of platina a heat which was regularly kept up and distributed. They also heated a distilling apparatus, which, by evaporation, furnished excellent drinkable water. Near this kitchen was a bathroom comfortably furnished, with hot and cold water taps.

Next to the kitchen was the berthroom of the vessel, sixteen feet long.**11** But the door was shut, and I could not see the management of it, which might have given me an idea of the number of men employed on board the *Nautilus*.

At-the bottom **12** was a fourth partition that separated this office from the engine-room. A door opened, and I found myself in the compartment where Captain Nemo—certainly an engineer of a very high order—had arranged his locomotive machinery. This engine-room, clearly lighted, did not measure less than sixty-five feet in length. It was divided into two parts; the first contained the materials for producing electricity, and the second the machinery that connected it with the screw.

[I was surprised to sniff a strange odour in this compartment. Captain Nemo noticed my concern.

"That is a gas produced by the use of sodium. It is only a slight inconvenience. Anyhow, we surface every morning to ventilate the ship."]

I examined everything with great interest, in order to understand the machinery of the *Nautilus*.

"You see," said the Captain, "I use Bunsen's contrivances, not Ruhmkorff's.**13** Those would not have been powerful enough. Bunsen's are fewer in number, but strong and large, which experience proves to be the best. The electricity produced passes forward,**14** where it works, by electro-magnets of great size, on a system of levers and cog-wheels that transmit the movement to the axle of the screw. This one, the diameter of which is nineteen feet, and the thread twenty-three feet, performs about a hundred and twenty revolutions in a second."

"And you get then?"

"A speed of fifty miles an hour."

[There was still a mystery there, but I did not insist on exploring it. How could electricity produce such power? **15** What source of energy was he tapping? Had he developed a

segregation of Conseil and Ned. Verne himself subscribed to these bourgeois values. In his novel *The Mysterious Island,* Captain Hardy's servant, a Negro named Neb, and the captain's dog, Top, are both admired for a virtue they have in common: total willingness to die for the captain. We recall, of course, Conseil's voluntary plunge into the sea after Aronnax's involuntary fall.

12. *At the bottom*   Verne says *in the back part, at the far end.*

13. *Bunsen's contrivances, not Ruhmkorff's*   At the time that Nemo and Aronnax are chatting, Robert Wilhelm Bunsen (1811–1899) is professor of chemistry at Heidelberg. His Bunsen cell, which has been on the market since 1842, has a longer life and produces a higher voltage than other cells available.

Heinrich Daniel Rühmkorff (1803–1877), a German instrument maker living in Paris, is—in Nemo's time—famous mainly for the Rühmkorff induction coil. This is a type of transformer that can generate high-tension discharges.

Nemo's comparison seems to suggest to Aronnax (as we shall see in a moment in a restored passage) that maybe Nemo has developed a new kind of coil that produces a very high voltage—that is, higher than Rühmkorff's.

14. *The electricity . . . passes forward*   That would be ridiculous. The propeller is at the rear of the boat. In Verne's original, Nemo says: *"The electricity produced is conducted aft. . . ."*

15. *How could electricity produce such power*   Aronnax is doubtless thinking of early experiments in electromotion which all seemed to lead nowhere. In 1834 Thomas Davenport, a Vermont blacksmith, had built a small battery-powered motor and used it to run a small railroad car on a short section of tracks. In 1838 Robert Davidson, of Aberdeen, Scotland, built a five-ton electric locomotive which propelled itself on an experimental run on the Edinburgh-Glasgow line. But a group of drivers and stokers, fearing loss of their jobs on steam locomotives, destroyed the Davidson machine at Perth. And in 1851 Charles G. Page operated a small electric car from Washington, D.C., to Bladensburg, Maryland, attaining speeds up to 19 miles per hour. But there were many mishaps that discouraged his backers in Congress. The biggest drawback in all such experiments was that they relied on storage batteries that were very expensive.

new kind of high voltage? Had he developed a new transmission system, a secret system of levers, that could step up the power? * I could not figure it out.]

"I have seen the *Nautilus* manoeuvre before the *Abraham Lincoln,* and I have my own ideas as to its speed. But this is not enough. We must see where we go. We must be able to direct it to the right, to the left, above, below. How do you get to the great depths, where you find an increasing resistance, which is rated by hundreds of atmospheres? How do you return to the surface of the ocean? And how do you maintain yourselves in the requisite medium? Am I asking too much?"

"Not at all, Professor," replied the Captain, with some hesitation; "since you may never leave this submarine boat. Come into the saloon, it is our usual study, and there you will learn all you want to know about the *Nautilus.*"

[* And indeed there has been talk recently of invention of a new type of lever-system that produces considerable power. Is it possible that the inventor has known Captain Nemo?—J. V.]

This engine-room, clearly lighted, did not measure less than sixty-five feet in length. Engraving from the original edition (1870).

PART 1: CHAPTER XII[1]
Some Figures

A moment after we were seated on a divan in the saloon smoking. The Captain showed me a sketch that gave the plan, section, and elevation of the *Nautilus*. Then he began his description in these words:—

"Here, M. Aronnax, are the several dimensions of the boat you are in. It is an elongated cylinder with conical ends. It is very like a cigar in shape, a shape already adopted in London in several constructions of the same sort. The length of this cylinder, from stem to stern, is exactly 232 feet,[2] and its maximum breadth is twenty-six feet. It is not built quite like your long-voyage steamers, [which are built in the ratio of ten-to-one,] but its lines are sufficiently long, and its curves prolonged enough, to allow the water to slide off easily, and oppose no obstacle to its passage. These two dimensions enable you to obtain by a simple calculation the surface and cubic contents [3] of the *Nautilus*. Its area measures 6032 feet; and its contents about 1500 cubic yards—that is to say, when completely immersed it displaces 50,000 feet of water, or weighs 1500 tons.

"When I made the plans for this submarine vessel, I meant that nine-tenths should be submerged: consequently, it ought only to displace nine-tenths of its bulk—that is to say, only to weigh that number of tons.[4] I ought not, therefore, to have exceeded that weight, constructing it on the aforesaid dimensions.

"The *Nautilus* is composed of two hulls, one inside, the other outside, joined by T-shaped irons, which render it very strong. Indeed, owing to this cellular arrangement it resists like a block, as if it were solid. Its sides cannot yield; it coheres spontaneously, and not by the closeness of its rivets; and the homogeneity of its construction, due to the perfect union of the materials, enables it to defy the roughest seas.

"These two hulls are composed of steel plates, whose density

1. *Chapter XII* In the Verne text, this is Chapter XIII.

2. *length . . . is exactly 232 feet* In the French, Nemo says the length is *exactly 70 meters* (228.9 feet) and the breadth *8 meters* (26.16 feet). Nemo's metric figures prove to be much easier to work with. And so, in addition to correcting Lewis's faulty conversions and restoring passages he omitted, we shall supply Nemo's metric figures throughout. The reader need only keep in mind that the meter is 39.37 inches, or about 1.1 yards.

3. *surface and cubic contents* In the French, Verne says that its surface area is 1011.45 square meters (10,885 square feet), and its contents 1500.2 cubic meters (52,980 cubic feet). When entirely submerged, then, the *Nautilus* displaces 1500.2 cubic meters or 1500.2 metric tons.

4. *that number of tons* In the French, Nemo gives "that number" as 1356.48 metric tons.

5. *whose density is from .7 to .8 that of water* Mercier Lewis's figure for Nemo's steel—"whose density is .7 to .8 that of water"—is nonsensical. It would mean that Nemo's steel is lighter than water and therefore could float. Lewis's carelessness here provided the author of the famous *Galaxy* attack on Verne with further "proof" that "Verne can get away with almost anything, and he does." Verne, he claims, "has grossly understated [the] density of steel. . . ." Not bothering to check the original French, working only with Lewis, the *Galaxy* writer smugly notes that Verne "also states the weight and dimension of the outer shell, so it is pretty easy to calculate the density of his steel for ourselves. It works out to be the normal heavy steel we are used to, and not the light stuff he says it is."

But Verne neither said nor implied that "his steel" was "light stuff." He knew what every schoolboy knows: the specific gravity of iron is 7.8. Hence, in the original, Verne has Captain Nemo say: *"Ces deux coques sont fabriquées en tôle d'acier dont la densité rapport à l'eau est de sept-huit dixièmes . . ."* A sympathetic English rendering would be: *"The two hulls are made of steel plates whose density is 7.8 that of water."*

6. *The first . . . and. . . . the second envelope* Lewis's slapdash work here, never corrected in dozens of editions, certainly compromises Verne's meticulous arithmetic and exposition. What Verne actually says is:

The first hull . . . weighs 394.96 metric tons. The second includes the keel, which is 20 inches high and 10 thick and alone weighs 62 tons; the machinery; the ballast; the accessories and instruments; the bulkheads, braces, and so on—all this adds up to another 961.62 tons.

7. *reservoirs . . . holding 150 tons* In the French, Nemo says *150.72 metric tons.*

8. *every thirty feet of water* Earlier, in Chapter IV, when explaining the

is from .7 to .8 that of water.[5] The first is not less than two inches and a half thick, and weighs 394 tons. The second envelope,[6] the keel, twenty inches high and ten thick, weighs alone sixty-two tons. The engine, the ballast, the several accessories and apparatus appendages, the partitions and bulkheads, weigh 961.62 tons. [This, added to 394.96, comes to 1356.58 metric tons or just about the weight desired.] Do you follow all this?"

"I do."

"Then, when the *Nautilus* is afloat under these circumstances, one-tenth is out of the water. Now, if I have made reservoirs of a size equal to this tenth, or capable of holding 150 tons,[7] and if I fill them with water, the boat, weighing then 1507 tons, will be completely immersed. That would happen, Professor. These reservoirs are in the lower parts of the *Nautilus.* I turn on taps and they fill, and the vessel sinks that had just been level with the surface."

"Well, Captain, but now we come to the real difficulty. I can understand your rising to the surface; but diving below the surface, does not your submarine contrivance encounter a pressure, and consequently undergo an upward thrust of one atmosphere for every thirty feet of water,[8] just about fifteen pounds per square inch?"

"Just so, sir."

"Then, unless you quite fill the *Nautilus,* I do not see how you can draw it down to those depths."

"Professor, you must not confound statics with dynamics, or you will be exposed to grave errors. There is very little labour spent in attaining the lower regions of the ocean, for all bodies have a tendency to sink. [Let me continue."

"Very well, Captain."]

"When I wanted to find out the necessary increase of weight to sink the *Nautilus,* I had only to calculate the reduction of volume that sea-water acquires according to the depth."

"That is evident."

"Now, if water is not absolutely incompressible, it is at least capable of very slight compression. Indeed, after the most recent calculations this reduction is only .0000436 of an atmosphere for each thirty feet of depth. If we want to sink 3000 feet, I should keep account of the reduction of bulk under a pressure equal to that of a column of water of a thousand feet.[9] [That is to say, a pressure of 100 atmospheres. This reduction would be, then, .00436. So I would increase the weight from 1507.2 to 1513.77 metric tons. The increase would be only 6.57 metric tons."

"That is all?"

"That is all, M. Aronnax.] The calculation is easily verified. Now, I have supplementary reservoirs capable of holding a hundred tons. Therefore I can sink to a considerable depth. When I wish to rise to the level of the sea, I only let off the water, and empty all the reservoirs if I want the *Nautilus* to emerge from the tenth part of her total capacity."

I had nothing to object to these reasonings.

"I admit your calculations, Captain," I replied; "I should be wrong to dispute them since daily experience confirms them; but I foresee a real difficulty in the way."

"What, sir?"

"When you are about 1000 feet deep,**10** the walls of the *Nautilus* bear a pressure of 100 atmospheres. If, then, just now you were to empty the supplementary reservoirs, to lighten the vessel, and to go up to the surface, the pumps must overcome the pressure of 100 atmospheres, which is 1500 pounds per square inch. From that a power——"

"That electricity alone can give," said the Captain, hastily. "I repeat, sir, that the dynamic power of my engines is almost infinite. The pumps of the *Nautilus* have an enormous power, as you must have observed when their jets of water burst like a torrent upon the *Abraham Lincoln*. Besides I use subsidiary reservoirs only to attain a mean depth of 750 to 1000 fathoms, and that with a view of managing my machines.**11** Also, when I have a mind to visit the depths of the ocean five or six miles below the surface, I make use of slower but not less infallible means."

"What are they, Captain?"

"That involves my telling you how the *Nautilus* is worked."

"I am impatient to learn."

"To steer this boat to starboard or port, to turn—in a word, following a horizontal plane, I use an ordinary rudder fixed on the back of the stern-post, and with one wheel and some tackle to steer by. But I can also make the *Nautilus* rise and sink, and sink and rise, by a vertical movement by means of two inclined planes fastened to its sides, opposite the centre of flotation, planes that move in every direction, and that are worked by powerful levers from the interior. If the planes are kept parallel with the boat, it moves horizontally. If slanted, the *Nautilus,* according to this inclination, and under the influence of the screw, either sinks diagonally or rises diagonally as it suits me. And even if I wish to rise more quickly to the surface, I ship the screw,**12** and the pressure of the water causes the *Nautilus* to rise vertically like a balloon filled with hydrogen."

concept of *an atmosphere* to Ned, the professor talked in terms of a column of water 32 feet high. Here he rounds the figure out to 30 feet; sometimes he will round it to 33 feet. The English figure of 15 pounds per square inch is also a convenient round figure commonly used in general discussion.

9. *sink 3000 feet . . . thousand feet* Another mess-up. In the French, Nemo says 1000 meters both times, of course. In the same sentence, Lewis converts it first to 3000 feet and then to 1000 feet, and omits the further clarification of *100 atmospheres.*

10. *When you are about 1000 feet deep* Verne says *1000 meters deep.*

11. *managing my machines* The meaning here is *saving,* or *sparing, my engines.*

12. *ship the screw* That is, *disengage the propeller.*

13. *glazed box . . . furnished with lenses* The helmsman works in a glass dome, or a pilot house, raised above the deck. In the glass walls there are biconvex lenses. The dome can be lowered inside the boat.

14. *the boarding* Read: *the collision.*

"Bravo, Captain! But how can the steersman follow the route in the middle of the waters?"

"The steersman is placed in a glazed box, that is raised above the hull of the *Nautilus,* and furnished with lenses."13

"Are these lenses capable of resisting such pressure?"

"Perfectly. Glass, which breaks at a blow, is, nevertheless, capable of offering considerable resistance. During some experiments of fishing by electric light in 1864 in the Northern Seas, we saw plates less than a third of an inch thick resist a pressure of sixteen atmospheres. [At the same time, they admitted heat rays that broke up unevenly on their surface.] Now, the glass that I use is not less than thirty times thicker."

"Granted. But, after all, in order to see, the light must exceed the darkness, and in the midst of the darkness in the water, how can you see?"

"Behind the steersman's cage is placed a powerful electric reflector, the rays from which light up the sea for half a mile in front."

"Ah! bravo, bravo, Captain! Now I can account for this phosphorescence in the supposed narwhal that puzzled us so. I now ask you if the boarding 14 of the *Nautilus* and of the *Scotia,* that has made such a noise, has been the result of a chance rencontre?"

"Quite accidental, sir. I was sailing only one fathom below the surface of the water, when the shock came. It had no bad result."

"None, sir. But now, about your rencontre with the *Abraham Lincoln?*"

"Professor, I am sorry for one of the best vessels in the American navy; but they attacked me, and I was bound to defend myself. I contented myself, however, with putting the frigate *hors de combat;* she will not have any difficulty in getting repaired at the next port."

"Ah, Commander! Your *Nautilus* is certainly a marvellous boat."

"Yes, Professor; and I love it as if it were part of myself. If danger threatens one of your vessels on the ocean, the first impression is the feeling of an abyss above and below. On the *Nautilus* men's hearts never fail them. No defects to be afraid of, for the double shell is as firm as iron; no rigging to attend to; no sails for the wind to carry away; no boilers to burst; no fire to fear, for the vessel is made of iron, not of wood; no coal to run short, for electricity is the only mechanical agent; no collision to fear, for it alone swims in deep water; no tempest to brave, for when it dives below the water, it reaches absolute tranquillity. There, sir! that is the perfection of vessels! And if it is true that the engineer has more confidence in the vessel than the builder, and the builder than the captain himself, you understand the trust I repose in my *Nautilus;* for I am at once captain, builder, and engineer.".

[Captain Nemo spoke with winning eloquence. The fire in his eyes, the passion of his gestures, made him seem like a different man. Yes, he loved his ship as a father loves his child. But there was one question, indiscreet perhaps, that I could not help asking.

"So then you are an engineer by profession?"

"Yes, Professor, I studied in London, Paris, and New York, back in those days when I still belonged to the land."]

"But how could you construct this wonderful *Nautilus* in secret?"

"Each separate portion, M. Aronnax, was brought from different parts of the globe. The keel was forged at Creusot [in France], the shaft of the screw at Penn & Co.'s, London, the iron plates of the hull at Laird's of Liverpool, the screw itself at Scott's at Glasgow. The reservoirs were made by Cail & Co. at Paris, the engine by Krupp in Prussia, its beak **15** in Motala's workshop in Sweden, its mathematical instruments by Hart Brothers, of New York, etc.; and each of these people had my orders under different names."

"But these parts had to be put together and arranged?"

"Professor, I had set up my workshops upon a desert island in the ocean. There my workmen, that is to say, the brave men that I instructed and educated, and myself have put together our *Nautilus*. Then when the work was finished, fire destroyed all trace of our proceedings on this island, that I could have jumped over **16** if I had liked."

"Then the cost of this vessel is great?"

"M. Aronnax, an iron vessel costs £45 per ton. Now the *Nautilus* weighed 1500. It came therefore to £67,500, and £80,000 more for fitting it up, and about £200,000 with the works of art and the collections it contains."

"One last question, Captain Nemo."

"Ask it, Professor."

"You are rich?"

"Immensely rich, sir; and I could, without missing it, pay the national debt of France." **17**

I stared at the singular person who spoke thus. Was he playing upon my credulity? The future would decide that.

15. *its beak* That is, its *spur* or *ram.* Even in the ancient world, ships of war were built with beaks aimed to do the utmost damage. It was known that spurs that ran just below the surface were most dangerous. Nemo, of course, is able to decide in each case *just how much below* to aim his beak.

16. *this island . . . I could have jumped over* Verne uses the French word *sauter,* which can mean either *jump* or *blow up.* Of course, the translator made the wrong choice. What Nemo means, then, is that he destroyed by fire all trace of their work, and *if he had been able, he would have blown up the island as well.*

17. *national debt of France* In writing this "punch line" in 1868, Verne had in mind only the debts that Emperor Louis Napoleon had already piled up. But by 1872, when this novel was gaining its first wide audience, France also owed Germany huge indemnities for the 1870–71 war. And so Nemo's words about paying off "the national debt of France" took on a special prophetic and patriotic meaning. Verne's readers, his niece tells us, "thrilled with emotion" over this passage. He "suddenly acquired an unlooked-for prestige. In this fictitious disguise, his popularity grew so rapidly that at last the Academy . . . granted him one of its highest awards."

In the French original, Nemo specifies the prewar debt: *les douze milliards de dettes de la France.* That would be 12 thousand million francs, or, as Americans reckon billions, 12 billion francs, or 3 billion American dollars of that period.

What Lewis rendered as £200,000 for the total worth of the *Nautilus* is, in the original, 4 to 5 million francs or more than 1 million American dollars at that time.

PART 1: CHAPTER XIII

The Black River[1]

1. *Chapter XIII: The Black River* A better translation would be *The Black Stream,* today usually called *The Kuroshio Current.* And in Verne's text, this is of course Chapter XIV.

2. *eighty millions of acres* How Verne's detractors have laughed at this! Yet in his original Verne provided the proper figures for an easy conversion into *148 million square miles* or *94 billion acres.*

3. *igneous period succeeded to the aqueous* Again, Verne is made the object of ridicule by his translator. What Verne really said, of course, was that *the period of fire was succeeded by the period of water.*

4. *ocean . . . prevailed everywhere* Aronnax is here espousing the theory of the German geologist A. G. Werner (1750–1817). Werner maintained that originally there was a "universal ocean" and that nearly all rocks were formed as precipitates from its waters, which held in solution great quantities of mineral matter. Werner's followers, who popularized his theories for decades, were known as Neptunists. Geologists in the opposing school—who recognized the part taken by subterranean heat in composing the earth's crust—were known as Vulcanists or Plutonists. Today scientists believe that the origi-

The portion of the terrestrial globe which is covered by water is estimated at upwards of eighty millions of acres.[2] This fluid mass comprises two billions two hundred and fifty millions of cubic miles, forming a spherical body of a diameter of sixty leagues, the weight of which would be three quintillions of tons. To comprehend the meaning of these figures, it is necessary to observe that a quintillion is to a billion as a billion is to unity; in other words, there are as many billions in a quintillion as there are units in a billion. This mass of fluid is equal to about the quantity of water which would be discharged by all the rivers of the earth in forty thousand years.

During the geological epochs, the igneous period succeeded to the aqueous.[3] The ocean originally prevailed everywhere.[4] Then by degrees, in the silurian period, the tops of the mountains began to appear, the islands emerged, then disappeared in partial deluges, reappeared, became settled, formed continents, till at length the earth became geographically arranged, as we see in the present day. The solid had wrested from the liquid thirty-seven million six hundred and fifty-seven square miles, equal to twelve billion nine hundred and sixty millions of acres.[5]

The shape of continents allows us to divide the waters into five great portions: the Arctic or Frozen Ocean, the Antarctic or Frozen Ocean, the Indian, the Atlantic, and the Pacific Oceans.

The Pacific Ocean extends from north to south between the two polar circles, and from east to west between Asia and America, over an extent of 145 degrees of longitude. It is the quietest of seas; [6] its currents are broad and slow, it has medium tides, and abundant rain. Such was the ocean that my fate destined me first to travel over under these strange conditions.

"Sir," said Captain Nemo, "we will, if you please, take our bearings and fix the starting-point of this voyage. It is a quarter to twelve, I will go up again to the surface."

The Captain pressed an electric clock three times.7 The pumps began to drive the water from the tanks; the needle of the manometer marked by a different pressure the ascent of the *Nautilus,* then it stopped.

"We have arrived," said the Captain.

I went to the central staircase which opened on to the platform, clambered up the iron steps, and found myself on the upper part of the *Nautilus.*

The platform was only three feet out of water. The front and back of the *Nautilus* was of that spindle-shape which caused it justly to be compared to a cigar. I noticed that its iron plates, slightly overlaying each other, resembled the shell which clothes the bodies of our large terrestrial reptiles. It explained to me how natural it was, in spite of all glasses, that this boat should have been taken for a marine animal.

Towards the middle of the platform the long-boat, half buried in the hull of the vessel, formed a slight excrescence. Fore and aft rose two cages of medium height with inclined sides, and partly closed by thick lenticular glasses; one destined for the steersman who directed the *Nautilus,* the other containing a brilliant lantern to give light on the road.

The sea was beautiful, the sky pure. Scarcely could the long vehicle feel the broad undulations of the ocean. A light breeze from the east rippled the surface of the waters. The horizon, free from fog, made observation easy. Nothing was in sight. Not a quicksand, not an island. [No sign of the *Abraham Lincoln*.] A vast desert.

Captain Nemo, by the help of his sextant, took the altitude of the sun, which ought also to give the latitude. He waited for some moments till its disc touched the horizon. Whilst taking observations not a muscle moved, the instrument could not have been more motionless in a hand of marble.

"Twelve o'clock, sir," said he. "When you like——"

I cast a look upon the sea, slightly yellowed by the Japanese coast,8 and descended to the saloon. [Here, the Captain calculated our longitude 9 by the chronometer and checked it against his previous observations.

"M. Aronnax, we are at 137° 15′ west. . . ."

"Of which meridian?" I asked eagerly, hoping that his answer would give me some clue to his nationality.

nal oceans were small and increased gradually to their present size.

5. *twelve billion . . . acres* Verne says *not* acres but *hectares.* A hectare is a metric unit of area equal to 2.471 acres.

6. *It is the quietest of seas* It was because of its serene, tranquil nature that the Pacific was so named: *pacific* means peaceful.

7. *electric clock three times* No, Nemo presses a button that rings a bell.

8. *yellowed by the Japanese coast* Verne simply means that the sea seems slightly *yellowish near* the Japanese coast. The *Nautilus* is east of the Yellow Sea, which is named for its sediment-laden waters, the muddy discharge of the great rivers of China.

9. *calculated our longitude* In this clever passage, omitted in the "standard translation," Verne gives his readers their rightful chance to follow the voyagers on the map and he uses the discussion of longitude for some nice psychological fencing. We see now why Verne established the fact, early in the novel, that calculating longitude from Greenwich is just one possibility. This is Verne at his best, with every interchange of mere information a potential source of subtle interplay between characters.

10. *"frustrated genuises," . . . like
. . . Maury* Maury had never suffered the kind of overt persecution
experienced by Galileo Galilei (1564–
1642). The Italian was forced by the
religious authorities to retract his
teachings that the sun (not the earth)
was the center of the universe. Galileo
spent his last years under house arrest.

But Maury always did suffer the
petty miseries that bureaucracy provides for the genius. He was appalled
at the Navy's crude methods of training officers. His official protests having little effect, he took to publishing
pseudonymous articles attacking Navy
policies. His "superiors" apparently
tried at least once to cashier him.
Even when he became world-re-
nowned (by 1855, as we have seen in
an earlier note), the Navy still be-
grudged him the rank he deserved. In
1861, nineteen years after he had
taken over the Depot of Charts and
Instruments, he was still only a commander.

Aronnax thinks that it was the Civil
War that blighted Maury's career, but
that might be a simplification. Maury
resigned his position in order to serve
the Confederacy, a move that in some
respects gave his genius new outlets.
He was put in command of coastal,
harbor, and river defenses, and invented an electric torpedo (harbor
mine) that certainly wrought havoc
on Northern warships. But again he
got in trouble with the hierarchy, who
apparently sent him on a mere pur-
chasing mission to England with the
ulterior motive of getting rid of him.

After the war he diffused his ener-
gies in various abortive schemes, like
trying to plant a colony of Virginians
in Mexico, but by 1868 he settled
down as professor of meteorology at
the Virginia Military Institute. His last
five years were relatively satisfying as
he saw his textbooks widely adopted
in American schools.

11. *The sea has its . . . rivers* Here
Aronnax echoes a famous sentence in
Maury's *Physical Geography of the
Sea and Its Meteorology.* Maury, a

"I have chronometers set by the meridians of Paris, Greenwich, and Washington. But in your honour, I am using the
Paris chronometer."

I bowed. I had learned nothing.

"Longitude 137° 15′ west of the Paris meridian, latitude
30° 7′ north, which is to say, about 300 miles off the coast of
Japan. At midday, November 8th, we begin our exploration
of the submarine world!"

"May God preserve us!" I said.]

"And now, sir, I leave you to your studies," added the Captain; "our course is E.N.E., our depth is twenty-six fathoms.
Here are maps on a large scale by which you may follow it.
The saloon is at your disposal, and with your permission I will
retire." Captain Nemo bowed, and I remained alone, lost in
thoughts all bearing on the commander of the *Nautilus.*

[Would I ever be able to discover the nationality of this
strange person who boasted that he had none? What had
provoked his hatred for humanity, a hatred that perhaps was
seeking some awful vengeance? Was he one of those unrecognized savants, one of those "frustrated geniuses," as Conseil
had put it; a modern Galileo, or one of those scientists like
the American Maury,[10] whose career had been shattered by a
political revolution? I could not yet say. As for me, chance had
put me aboard his ship, my fate was in his hands, he had received me coldly but hospitably. He had never shaken hands
with me when I extended mine, and he had never extended
his.]

For a whole hour was I deep in these reflections, seeking to
pierce this mystery so interesting to me. Then my eyes fell
upon the vast planisphere spread upon the table, and I placed
my finger on the very spot where the given latitude and
longitude crossed.

The sea has its large rivers [11] like the continents. They are
special currents known by their temperature and their colour.
The most remarkable of these is known by the name of the
Gulf Stream. Science has decided on the globe the direction of
five principal currents: one in the North Atlantic, a second in
the South, a third in the North Pacific, a fourth in the South,
and a fifth in the Southern Indian Ocean. It is even probable
that a sixth current existed at one time or another in the
Northern Indian Ocean, when the Caspian and the Aral seas
formed but one vast sheet of water.

At this point indicated on the planisphere one of these
currents was rolling, the Kuro-Sivo of the Japanese, the Black

River **12** which, leaving the Gulf of Bengal where it is warmed by the perpendicular rays of a tropical sun, crosses the Straits of Malacca along the coast of Asia, turns into the North Pacific to the Aleutian Islands, carrying with it trunks of camphor-trees and other indigenous productions, and edging the waves of the ocean with the pure indigo of its warm water. It was this current that the *Nautilus* was to follow. I followed it with my eye; saw it lose itself in the vastness of the Pacific, and felt myself drawn with it, when Ned Land and Conseil appeared at the door of the saloon.

My two brave companions remained petrified at the sight of the wonders spread before them.

"Where are we, where are we?" exclaimed the Canadian. "In the museum at Quebec?"

["If it pleases monsieur," said Conseil, "it seems more like the Hôtel du Sommerard." **13**]

"My friends," I answered, making a sign for them to enter, "you are not in Canada [or France], but on board the *Nautilus* fifty yards below the level of the sea."

["It must be so, if monsieur says so," Conseil replied, "but frankly, this room is enough to astonish even a Fleming like me."

"You ought to be astonished, my friend. For a classifier of your calibre, there is plenty of work here."

There was no need to urge him on. Bending over the glass cases, he was already murmuring, in the language of naturalists, "Class of Gastropods, family of buccinoids, genus of porcelains, species of *Cypraea Madagascariensis*. . . ."

Meanwhile Ned, not much of a conchyliologist, queried me about my interview with Nemo. Had I learned who he was, where he came from, where he was going, to what depths he was taking us, and a thousand questions I could not answer. I told him all I knew, or rather all I did not know, and asked him whether he had learned or seen anything himself.

"Nothing learned, nothing seen," the Canadian said. "Not even a sign of the crew. You do not think that they run by electricity too, do you?" **14**

"Electrical sailors!"

"I swear, I am ready to think so.]

"But, M. Aronnax," said Ned Land, "can you tell me how many men there are on board? Ten, twenty, fifty, a hundred?"

"I cannot answer you, Mr. Land; it is better to abandon for a time all idea of seizing the *Nautilus* or escaping from it. This ship is a masterpiece of modern industry, and I should be sorry

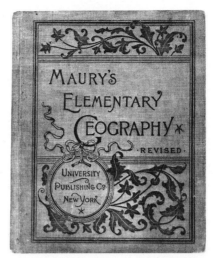

As late as 1901, *Maury's Revised Elementary Geography* was still used in "primary and intermediate" classes in the United States. The title page said it was "Revised and Abridged from the *First Lessons* and *World We Live In* of M. F. Maury, LL.D."

superb phrasemaker, dramatically opens his second chapter, "The Gulf Stream," with these words:

"There is a river in the ocean. . . ."

12. *the Kuro-Sivo . . . the Black River* We know it today as the Kuroshio Current, or the Japan Current. It comes up from the South China Sea and it (allegedly) warms southeastern Japan just as the Gulf Stream (allegedly) warms the British Isles. We shall come back to that "alleged" warming in Verne's Chapter XIX (Part 2): *The Gulf Stream.*

13. *like the Hôtel du Sommerard* Alexandre du Sommerard (1779–1842) was a French archaeologist who made extensive studies of ancient monuments in France and Italy. His collections were exhibited both in the Sommerard Palace and in the Hôtel de Cluny in Paris.

14. *by electricity too, do you?* Ned's notion that maybe Nemo's crew are also run by electricity is an excellent commentary on the sailors' robotlike quality.

"*. . . Type: . . . perch.*"
"*Good to eat!*" *pronounced Ned.*
Illustration from *Fishes, Living and Fossil* (1895) by Bashford Dean.

15. *hypothesis of Ehrenberg* At this moment that Aronnax is thinking of him, the German biologist Christian Gottfried Ehrenberg (1795–1876) is one of the most internationally honored of European scientists. For his work on microorganisms he has been elected to the Berlin Academy of Sciences in 1827, the Royal Society of England in 1837, and the Institut de France in 1860.

not to have seen it. Many people would accept the situation forced upon us, if only to move amongst such wonders. So be quiet and let us try and see what passes around us."

"See!" exclaimed the harpooner, "but we can see nothing in this iron prison! We are walking—we are sailing—blindly."

Ned Land had scarcely pronounced these words when all was suddenly darkness. The luminous ceiling was gone, and so rapidly that my eyes received a painful impression.

We remained mute, not stirring, and not knowing what surprise awaited us, whether agreeable or disagreeable. A sliding noise was heard: one would have said that panels were working at the sides of the *Nautilus*.

"It is the end of the end!" said Ned Land.

["Order of hydromedusa," Conseil was murmuring.]

Suddenly light broke at each side of the saloon, through two oblong openings. The liquid mass appeared vividly lit up by the electric gleam. Two crystal plates separated us from the sea. At first I trembled at the thought that this frail partition might break, but strong bands of copper bound them, giving an almost infinite power of resistance.

The sea was distinctly visible for a mile all round the *Nautilus*. What a spectacle! What pen can describe it? Who could paint the effects of the light through those transparent sheets of water, and the softness of the successive graduations from the lower to the superior strata of the ocean?

We know the transparency of the sea, and that its clearness is far beyond that of rock water. The mineral and organic substances which it holds in suspension heightens its transparency. In certain parts of the ocean at the Antilles, under seventy-five fathoms of water, can be seen with surprising clearness a bed of sand. The penetrating power of the solar rays does not seem to cease for a depth of one hundred and fifty fathoms. But in this middle fluid travelled over by the *Nautilus,* the electric brightness was produced even in the bosom of the waves. It was no longer luminous water, but liquid light. [If we accept the hypothesis of Ehrenberg **15** that there is phosphorescent illumination of the submarine depths —then surely Nature has reserved for the denizens of the deep one of her most prodigious spectacles. But now I was also privileged to enjoy the endless variations of this phenomenon.]

On each side a window opened into this unexplored abyss. The obscurity of the saloon showed to advantage the brightness outside, and we looked out as if this pure crystal had been the glass of an immense aquarium. [The *Nautilus* seemed to be standing still, because there was nothing nearby to serve as a point of reference.**16** But every once in a while, the water, parted by the ship's bow, would swirl by in eddies, indicating that we were moving at great speed. Astonished, we leaned against the windows, and no one broke that silence of stupefaction until Conseil said:]

"You wished to see, friend Ned; well, you see now."

"Curious! curious!" muttered the Canadian, who, forgetting his ill-temper, seemed to submit to some irresistible attraction; "and one would come further than this to admire such a sight!"

"Ah!" thought I to myself, "I understand the life of this man; he has made a world apart for himself, in which he treasures all his greatest wonders."

["But where are the fish?" Ned suddenly realized: "I have not seen any fish!"

"What can that matter to you?" Conseil teased. "You could not classify them anyhow."

"Me? Are you crazy, I am a fisherman!"

And so began a strange argument **17** between the two friends. They were both familiar with fish, but in entirely different ways.

All the world knows that fish constitute the fourth and last class of the subdivision of vertebrates. They are defined as "vertebrates with a double circulatory system and cold blood, breathing through gills and destined to live only in the water." There are two distinct series: bony fish, whose spinal column is made of bony vertebrae, and cartilaginous fish, whose spine is made of cartilaginous vertebrae.

Now Ned was probably aware of this gross distinction, but Conseil could carry the classification down to the finest detail. And since Ned was now a friend of his, Conseil was ready to share his specialised knowledge with the harpooner.

"Ned, you are a fisherman by vocation. You have caught great numbers of these interesting creatures, but I bet you do not know how to *classify* them."

"I sure can," the harpooner replied in all seriousness. "There are two classes: those you can eat, those you cannot eat."

"That is the way the gourmand thinks of fish. But can you tell me the essential differences between the bony fish and the cartilaginous?"

"Sure I could, Conseil."

"And the subdivisions of these two major groups?"

"Well, you see, now—"

"So listen, Ned! Bony fish are subdivided into six orders. First, the acanthopterygians. Their upper jaw is complete and mobile, their gills are shaped like a comb. This order comprises

16. *a point of reference* Here Verne seems to have a fine (pre-Einstein) appreciation of relativity.

17. *a strange argument* Verne has devised a clever way to introduce his reader to the scientific problem of classifying fish. Hereafter the reader can refer back to this little skit whenever the professor gets technical. This is Verne at his best as a popularizer of science, actually developing information useful to the reader while advancing the characterization. What a pity Mercier Lewis didn't bother to translate it.

". . . Types: carp and pike."
"Pee-yew!"
Illustration of carp (above) is from *The American Cyclopaedia* (1873) and illustration of pike (below) is from *An Introduction to the Study of Fishes* (1800) by A. C. L. G. Günther.

fifteen families, three-fourths of all the known fish. Type: the common perch."

"Good to eat!" pronounced Ned.

"The second order are the abdominals. Their ventral fins are underneath the abdomen, behind the pectorals, but not attached to the shoulder bone. There are five families, including most fresh-water fish. Types: carp and pike."

"Pee-yew!" Ned said scornfully. "Fresh-water types!"

"Third," said Conseil, "the subbrachians. Their ventral fins are beneath the pectorals and attached to the shoulder bone. There are four families in this order. Types: plaice, dab, brill, sole, etc."

"Superb! Superb!" cried Ned, still classifying fish according to their food value.

"Fourth," Conseil persisted, "the apods. They have elongated bodies and no ventral fins. They are covered with thick —often sticky—skin. Just one family in this order. Types: the common eel and the electric eel."

"Mediocre," Ned groaned, "just plain mediocre."

"Fifth, the lophobranchiates. Their jaws are complete and mobile, their gills arranged in tufts. Again, only one family. Types: sea-horse and pipe-fish."

"Awful, just awful."

"Sixth and last, the plectognathians. Their upper jaw is attached to the skull, making it immobile. They have no true ventral fins. There are two families. Types: globe-fish and moon-fish."

"I would not soil a bucket with those!"

"Do you understand?" Conseil asked in his most pedagogical manner.

"Not at all. But go right ahead, it sounds impressive."

The imperturbable Conseil went right on. "There are only three orders of cartilaginous fish."

"Good news."

"First, the cyclostomes. They have round mouths, and gills with a large number of openings. There is just one family. Type: the lamprey."

"To know him is to love him."

"Second, the selachians. Their gills are like the cyclostomes, but they have mobile lower jaws. This order, which is the most important in its class, comprises two families. Types: the ray and the shark."

"What! Rays and sharks in the same order! Well, friend *Conseil,* on behalf of the rays, I would not *counsel* you to put them in the same tank!"

"*. . . Sole, etc.*"
"*Superb! Superb!*"
Picture of common sole is from *The American Cyclopaedia* (1873).

"*. . . The common eel . . .*"
"*Mediocre. . . .*"
Picture from *A Guide to the Study of Fishes* (1905) by D. S. Jordan.

"Third, the sturionians. Usually, their gills are formed of one opening with a gill-cover. There are four genera in this order. Type: the sturgeon."

"Ah, friend Conseil, you have saved the best for last. It is the last, I hope?"

"Well, when you have mastered what I have already recited, you have made a good start. But then, these families are divided into genera, genera into subgenera, subgenera into species, species into varieties. . . ."

"Good, Conseil," Ned exclaimed, leaning against the glass. "Here come all your varieties!"

"Fish!" Conseil was amazed. "Like in the aquarium!"

"No," I joined in. "An aquarium is like a cage, and those fish are as free as birds in the open air." **18**

"What are you waiting for, Conseil?" Ned said, "Go ahead and *classify*."

"Me! I cannot actually *recognise* them, Ned. The professor does that!"

And that was the situation. Conseil was a fanatic classifier but not a working naturalist, and I do not believe he could have distinguished a tuna from a bonito. And Ned was the opposite: he could identify each fish but could not classify them scientifically.

"A trigger-fish," I said.

"And a *Chinese* trigger-fish," Ned said.

"Genus: balistes, family: sclerodermi, order: plectognathi," Conseil murmured.

Decidedly, Ned and Conseil together could make one distinguished naturalist.

The Canadian was not mistaken. Frolicking around the *Nautilus* was a school of trigger-fish, with flat bodies, grainy skin, a spike on the dorsal fin, and four rows on each side of of the tail. Their bodies were admirable: grey on the bottom, white on top, with touches of gold scintillating in the sombre waters. Among the trigger-fish, some rays were undulating like sheets in the wind. I was delighted by a Chinese ray, yellow on top, pink underneath, with three spikes behind his eye. This is a rare species whose real existence was still in doubt in Lacepédè's day. He knew of it only from Japanese drawings.]

For two whole hours an aquatic army escorted the *Nautilus*. During their games, their bounds, while rivaling each other in beauty, brightness, and velocity, I distinguished the green labre; the banded mullet, marked by a double line of black; the round-tailed goby, of a white colour, with violet spots on the back; the Japanese scombrus, a beautiful mackerel of those

18. *free as birds in the open air* Verne's neat language play here reminds the reader that it is Aronnax, Ned, and Conseil who are in the cage.

"*. . . Types: sea-horse and pipe-fish.*"
"*Awful, just awful.*"
Illustrations: sea horse from *A Guide to the Study of Fishes* (1905) by D. S. Jordan; pipefish from *Fishes, Living and Fossil* (1895) by Bashford Dean.

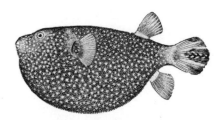

"*. . . Globe-fish. . . .*"
"*I would not soil a bucket with those!*"
Picture from *A Guide to the Study of Fishes* (1905) by D. S. Jordan.

seas, with a blue body and silvery head; the brilliant azurors, whose name alone defies description; some banded spares, with variegated fins of blue and yellow; some aclostones, the woodcocks of the seas, some specimens of which attain a yard in length; Japanese salamanders, spider lampreys, serpents six feet long, with eyes small and lively, and a huge mouth bristling with teeth; with many other species.

Our imagination was kept at its height, interjections followed quickly on each other. Ned named the fish, and Conseil classed them. I was in ecstasies with the vivacity of their movements and the beauty of their forms. Never had it been given to me to surprise these animals, alive and at liberty, in their natural element. I will not mention all the varieties which passed before my dazzled eyes, all the collection of the seas of China and Japan. These fish, more numerous than the birds of the air, came, attracted, no doubt, by the brilliant focus of the electric light.

Suddenly there was daylight in the saloon, the iron panels closed again, and the enchanting vision disappeared. But for a long time I dreamt on till my eyes fell on the instruments hanging on the partition. The compass still showed the course to be N.N.E., the manometer indicated a pressure of five atmospheres, equivalent to a depth of twenty-five fathoms, and the electric log gave a speed of fifteen miles an hour. I expected Captain Nemo, but he did not appear. The clock marked the hour of five.

Ned Land and Conseil returned to their cabin, and I retired to my chamber. My dinner was ready. It was composed of turtle soup made of the most delicate hawkbills, of a surmullet served with puff paste (the liver of which, prepared by itself, was most delicious), and fillets of the emperor-holocanthus, the savour of which seemed to me superior even to salmon.

I passed the evening reading, writing, and thinking. Then sleep overpowered me, and I stretched myself on my couch of zostera, and slept profoundly, whilst the *Nautilus* was gliding rapidly through the current of the Black River.

"*. . . Type: the lamprey.*"
"*To know him is to love him.*"
Lampreys as pictured in *Animal Forms: A Text-Book of Zoology* (1902) by D. S. Jordan and Harold Heath.

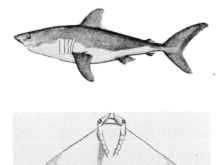

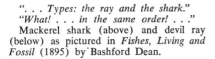

"*. . . Types: the ray and the shark.*"
"*What! . . . in the same order! . . .*"
Mackerel shark (above) and devil ray (below) as pictured in *Fishes, Living and Fossil* (1895) by Bashford Dean.

PART 1: CHAPTER XIV [1]
A Note of Invitation

The next day was the 9th of November. I awoke after a long sleep of twelve hours. Conseil came, according to custom, to know "how I had passed the night," and to offer his services. He had left his friend the Canadian sleeping like a man who had never done anything else all his life. I let the worthy fellow chatter as he pleased, without caring to answer him. I was pre-occupied by the absence of the Captain during our sitting of the day before, and hoping to see him to-day.

[I put on my garments, all made of byssus. This fabric had excited the curiosity of Conseil. I told him that it was made from the glossy, silken threads with which certain bivalve molluscs—quite common on the Mediterranean coast—attach themselves to rocks. In olden days, these silken filaments were woven into a soft, warm cloth from which beautiful gloves and stockings were made. Since the crew of the *Nautilus* had ready access to this byssus, they did not have to depend on sheep, silkworm, or cotton plant for their clothing.]

As soon as I was dressed I went into the saloon. It was deserted.

I plunged into the study of the conchological treasures hidden behind the glasses. I revelled also in great herbals filled with the rarest marine plants, which, although dried up, retained their lovely colours. Amongst these precious hydrophytes I remarked some vorticellae, pavonariae, delicate ceramies with scarlet tints, some fan-shaped agari, and some natabuli like flat mushrooms, which at one time used to be classed as zoophytes; in short, a perfect series of algae.

The whole day passed without my being honoured by a visit from Captain Nemo. The panels of the saloon did not

1. *Chapter XIV* In the Verne text, this is Chapter XV.

I was admiring this joyous rising of the sun . . . when I heard steps approaching the platform. Engraving from the original edition (1870).

2. *zostera marina* A marine plant with very long, narrow leaves, *zostera marina* is found in abundance along the North Atlantic coast, where it is called *eelgrass* or *grass wrack*.

3. *the pinnace* The little dinghy that excited the professor so much when he first heard about it from Nemo.

4. *mare's tails* White, filmy (cirrus) clouds, with a long, slender, flowing shape. Verne's phrase is *"langues de chat"* (*finger biscuits*) and he footnotes it: *Little white clouds with indented edges.*

5. *Nautron respoc lorni virch* Apparently Aronnax is so distracted by so many new circumstances that he cannot analyze this sentence right away. But he has all the background for the task and need only relax into it. He has a working knowledge of English, German, and Latin, in addi-

open. Perhaps they did not wish us to tire of these beautiful things.

The course of the *Nautilus* was E.N.E., her speed twelve knots, the depth below the surface between twenty-five and thirty fathoms.

The next day, 10th of November, the same desertion, the same solitude. I did not see one of the ship's crew: Ned and Conseil spent the greater part of the day with me. They were astonished at the inexplicable absence of the Captain. Was this singular man ill?—had he altered his intentions with regard to us?

After all, as Conseil said, we enjoyed perfect liberty, we were delicately and abundantly fed. Our host kept to his terms of the treaty. We could not complain, and, indeed, the singularity of our fate reserved such wonderful compensation for us, that we had no right to accuse it as yet.

That day I commenced the journal of these adventures which has enabled me to relate them with more scrupulous exactitude and minute detail. I wrote it on paper made from the zostera marina.**2**

11th November, early in the morning. The fresh air spreading over the interior of the *Nautilus* told me that we had come to the surface of the ocean to renew our supply of oxygen. I directed my steps to the central staircase, and mounted the platform.

It was six o'clock, the weather was cloudy, the sea grey but calm. Scarcely a billow. Captain Nemo, whom I hoped to meet, would he be there? I saw no one but the steersman imprisoned in his glass cage. Seated upon the projection formed by the hull of the pinnace,**3** I inhaled the salt breeze with delight.

By degrees the fog disappeared under the action of the sun's rays, the radiant orb rose from behind the eastern horizon. The sea flamed under its glance like a train of gunpowder. The clouds scattered in the heights were coloured with lively tints of beautiful shades, and numerous "mare's tails," **4** which betokened wind for that day. But what was wind to this *Nautilus* which tempests could not frighten!

I was admiring this joyous rising of the sun, so gay, and so lifegiving, when I heard steps approaching the platform. I was prepared to salute Captain Nemo, but it was his second (whom I had already seen on the Captain's first visit) who appeared. He advanced on the platform not seeming to see me. With his powerful glass to his eye he scanned every point of the horizon with great attention. This examination over, he approached the panel and pronounced a sentence in exactly these terms. I have remembered it, for every morning it was repeated under exactly the same conditions. It was thus worded—

"Nautron respoc lorni virch." 5

What it meant I could not say.

These words pronounced, the second descended. I thought that the *Nautilus* was about to return to its submarine navigation. I regained the panel and returned to my chamber.

Five days sped thus, without any change in our situation. Every morning I mounted the platform. The same phrase was pronounced by the same individual. But Captain Nemo did not appear.

I had made up my mind that I should never see him again, when, on the 16th November, on returning to my room with Ned and Conseil, I found upon my table a note addressed to me. I opened it impatiently. It was written in a bold, clear hand, the characters rather pointed, recalling the German type. The note was worded as follows:—

"16th of *November,* 1867.

To Professor Aronnax, on board the *Nautilus.*

"Captain Nemo invites Professor Aronnax to a hunting-party, which will take place to-morrow morning in the forests of the island of Crespo. He hopes that nothing will prevent the Professor from being present, and he will with pleasure see him joined by his companions.

"Captain Nemo, Commander of the *Nautilus.*"

"A hunt!" exclaimed Ned.

"And in the forests of the island of Crespo!" added Conseil.

"Oh! then the gentleman is going on *terra firma?*" replied Ned Land.

"That seems to me to be clearly indicated," said I, reading the letter once more.

"Well, we must accept," said the Canadian. "But once more on dry ground, we shall know what to do. Indeed, I shall not be sorry to eat a piece of fresh venison."

Without seeking to reconcile what was contradictory between Captain Nemo's manifest aversion to islands and continents, and his invitation to hunt in a forest, I contented myself with replying—

"Let us first see where the island of Crespo is."

I consulted the planisphere, and in 32° 40' north lat., and 157° 50' west long.,6 I found a small island, recognised in

tion to an exquisite sensitivit[y] native tongue. He is aware of ety[mol]ogy—remember his remark on *mo[l]lusc?* It will be interesting, then, to observe how gradually Aronnax comes to sense the meaning of this four-word sentence.

Nautron should be easy for him. It should suggest the French word *nautique* and its English cognate, *nautical.* This should remind him of the classical roots in Greek *naus,* ship, and *nautes,* sailor, as well as in Latin *navis,* ship. It must soon occur to Aronnax that *nautron* has something to do with ships!

Respoc might take more reflection, but the classical prefix *re-,* meaning *back* or *again,* should also suggest to Aronnax that the language used on board the *Nautilus* is in the Indo-European family. Ultimately he should see here *spoko-,* an ancient form of the root *spec-,* to observe, which he uses in scores of French words like *spectateur,* spectator.

And *lorni* echoes English words like *lorn,* bereft of, *forlorn,* deserted, and German words like *verloren,* lost.

And so, when he begins to digest and assimilate all his new experiences, Aronnax will surely begin to sense that maybe *Nautron respoc lorni virch* means something like *The vista is devoid of ships,* or, *Not a ship in sight!*

The larger question, of course, is what language is this? And that might well be why the professor will take until November 18, nine days, to catch the meaning of these four words. Because he tends to think deductively, from the broad, general, larger question down to the immediate, specific question. If he could figure out what language it is, he could figure out its meaning so much faster! All of which leads to future notes.

6. *157° 50' west long* Verne says 167° 50'. On Verne's own map, published in the French editions, *I. Crespo* is northwest of the Sandwich Islands, the name originally given to the Hawaiian Islands by Captain James Cook.

1801 by Captain Crespo, and marked in the ancient Spanish maps as Rocca de la Plata, the meaning of which is "The Silver Rock." We were then about eighteen hundred miles from our starting point, and the course of the *Nautilus,* a little changed, was bringing it back towards the south-east.

I showed this little rock lost in the midst of the North Pacific to my companions.

"If Captain Nemo does sometimes go on dry ground," said I, "he at least chooses desert islands."

Ned Land shrugged his shoulders without speaking, and Conseil and he left me.

After supper, which was served by the steward mute and impassive, I went to bed, not without some anxiety.

The next morning, the 17th of November, on awakening I felt that the *Nautilus* was perfectly still. I dressed quickly and entered the saloon.

Captain Nemo was there, waiting for me. He rose, bowed, and asked me if it was convenient for me to accompany him. As he made no allusion to his absence during the last eight days, I did not mention it, and simply answered that my companions and myself were ready to follow him.

["But monsieur," I added, "permit me to pose one question."

"Go ahead, M. Aronnax. If I am able to answer, I shall."

"Well, Captain, how is it that you, who have severed all ties with the land, can still own forests on the island of Crespo?"

"Professor, the forests I possess do not depend on the sun for either light or heat. Neither lions nor tigers nor panthers nor any other quadrupeds frequent my forests. They are known only to me, they grow only for me. They are not terrestrial forests, they are submarine forests."

"Submarine forests!" I cried.

"Yes, Professor."

"And you intend to take me there!"

"Certainly."

"On foot?"

"Yes, and without getting your feet wet!"

"And we will hunt?"

"We will hunt."

"Gun in hand?"

"Gun in hand."

I glanced at the commander of the *Nautilus* in a way that must have seemed unflattering.

"Surely he is touched with madness," I thought. "He has

7. *the Rouquayrol apparatus* In the original, Verne specifies *"Rouquayrol-Denayrouze apparatus"* because it was jointly developed by Benoît Rouquayrol, mining engineer, and Auguste Denayrouze, naval officer. This is what Nemo means by his mention of Aronnax's *"two . . . countrymen."*

Development of the Rouquayrol-Denayrouze apparatus was not possible until scientists understood the problem of equalizing the pressure. As a diver descends, the water pressure on his chest increases. When he is more than a few feet below the surface, he does not have the strength to expand his chest against the outer (water) pressure if his lungs are filled with air at normal pressure. Hence he cannot breathe even if he is supplied with normal surface air through a hose. This was why early diving helmets with surface hoses attached were ineffective. The great breakthrough came when scientists realized that the diver must have compressed air in his lungs the pressure of which equals the pressure of the surrounding water.

had a bad attack, it has lasted all week, and he is not over it yet. Pity! I liked him better eccentric than insane!" These apprehensions must have shown clearly on my face, but Captain Nemo invited me to follow him, and I did, prepared for almost anything.]

We entered the dining-room, where breakfast was served.

"M. Aronnax," said the Captain, "pray share my breakfast without ceremony; we will chat as we eat. For though I promised you a walk in the forest, I did not undertake to find hotels there. So breakfast as a man who will most likely not have his dinner till very late."

I did honour to the repast. It was composed of several kinds of fish, and slices of holothuridae (excellent zoophytes), and different sorts of sea-weed. Our drink consisted of pure water, to which the Captain added some drops of a fermented liquor, extracted by the Kamschatcha method from a sea-weed known under the name of *Rhodomenia palmata*. Captain Nemo ate at first without saying a word. Then he began—

"Sir, when I proposed to you to hunt in my submarine forest of Crespo, you evidently thought me mad. Sir, you should never judge lightly of any man."

"But, Captain, believe me—"

"Be kind enough to listen, and you will then see whether you have any cause to accuse me of folly and contradiction."

"I listen."

"You know as well as I do, Professor, that man can live under water, providing he carries with him a sufficient supply of breathable air. In submarine works, the workman, clad in an impervious dress, with his head in a metal helmet, receives air from above by means of forcing pumps and regulators."

"That is a diving apparatus," said I.

"Just so, but under these conditions the man is not at liberty; he is attached to the pump which sends him air through an india-rubber tube, and if we were obliged to be thus held to the *Nautilus,* we could not go far."

"And the means of getting free?" I asked.

"It is to use the Rouquayrol apparatus,[7] invented by two of your own countrymen, which I have brought to perfection for my own use, and which will allow you to risk yourself under these new physiological conditions, without any organ whatever suffering. It consists of a reservoir of thick iron plates, in which I store the air under a pressure of fifty atmospheres. This reservoir is fixed on the back by means of braces, like a soldier's knapsack. Its upper part forms a box

Rouquayrol and Denayrouze designed their tank with a "demand valve," which automatically supplies air at the pressure required. Presumably this is what Nemo means when he says *"the air . . . cannot escape unless at its normal tension,"* that is, at the proper pressure for the particular depth the diver is at.

As this early scuba gear was used about 1865 on, it worked like this: The cylinder tank on the diver's back was connected by a long hose to a compressor on the surface. When his cylinder was fully charged, the diver could unplug the hose and walk about freely underwater until his air supply diminished. Then he could return to the hose and plug in for a fresh supply.

One of Nemo's improvements, then, is that he is able to charge his tank with air so highly compressed that the diver need not return to the vicinity of the compressor for many hours. Another modification Nemo has made is that he combines the Rouquayrol-Denayrouze apparatus with a *"ball of copper,"* a version of the closed helmet developed by Augustus Siebe in the late 1830s. But here an odd question intrudes. Since 1840, Siebe's helmet had been equipped with check valves. These made it unnecessary for the diver to use his tongue to control incoming and outgoing air. Why then does Nemo continue to use the old-fashioned tongue control?

Now Verne himself—an avid reader of technical journals—surely knew about Siebe's check valves. Furthermore, brother Paul Verne, a naval officer, was reading the manuscript for technical accuracy and could have raised the question. We can assume then that Verne had some story angle in mind that made him prefer to have Nemo use the old-fashioned method. But this proved to be a mistake. As we shall see, it led to one of Verne's worst bloopers, a classic instance of that weakness that *The New Yorker* treats under the heading of "Our Forgetful Authors." Continued, of course, in another note.

in which the air is kept by means of a bellows, and therefore cannot escape unless at its normal tension. In the Rouquayrol apparatus such as we use, two india-rubber pipes leave this box and join a sort of tent which holds the nose and mouth; one is to introduce fresh air, the other to let out the foul, and the tongue closes one or the other according to the wants of the respirator. But I, in encountering great pressures at the bottom of the sea, was obliged to shut my head, like that of a diver, in a ball of copper; and it is to this ball of copper that the two pipes, the inspirator and the expirator, open."

"Perfectly, Captain Nemo; but the air that you carry with you must soon be used; when it only contains fifteen per cent. of oxygen, it is no longer fit to breathe."

"Right! but I told you, M. Aronnax, that the pumps of the *Nautilus* allow me to store the air under considerable pressure, and on these conditions, the reservoir of the apparatus can furnish breathable air for nine or ten hours."

"I have no further objections to make," I answered; "I will only ask you one thing, Captain—how can you light your road at the bottom of the sea?"

"With the Ruhmkorff apparatus, M. Aronnax; one is carried on the back, the other is fastened to the waist. It is composed of a Bunsen pile, which I do not work with bichromate of potash, but with sodium. A wire is introduced which collects the electricity produced, and directs it towards a particularly made lantern. In this lantern is a spiral glass which contains a small quantity of carbonic gas. When the apparatus is at work this gas becomes luminous, giving out a white and continuous light. Thus provided, I can breathe and I can see."

"Captain Nemo, to all my objections you make such crushing answers, that I dare no longer doubt. But if I am forced to admit the Rouquayrol and Ruhmkorff apparatus, I must be allowed some reservations with regard to the gun I am to carry."

"But it is not a gun for powder," answered the Captain.

"Then it is an air-gun."

"Doubtless! How would you have me manufacture gunpowder on board, without either saltpetre, sulphur or charcoal?"

"Besides," I added, "to fire under water in a medium eight hundred and fifty-five times denser than the air, we must conquer very considerable resistance."

"That would be no difficulty. There exist guns, according to Fulton, perfected in England by Philip Coles and Burley, in France by Furcy, and in Italy by Landi, which are furnished with a peculiar system of closing,**8** which can fire under these conditions. But I repeat, having no powder, I use air under great pressure, which the pumps of the *Nautilus* furnish abundantly."

"But this air must be rapidly used?"

"Well, have I not my Rouquayrol reservoir, which can furnish it at need? A tap is all that is required. Besides, M. Aronnax, you must see yourself that, during our submarine hunt, we can spend but little air and but few balls."

"But it seems to me that in this twilight, and in the midst of this fluid, which is very dense compared with the atmosphere, shots could not go far, nor easily prove mortal."

"Sir, on the contrary, with this gun every blow is mortal; and however lightly the animal is touched, it falls as if struck by a thunderbolt."

"Why?"

"Because the balls sent by this gun are not ordinary balls, but little cases of glass (invented by Leniebroek, an Austrian chemist), of which I have a large supply.**9** These glass cases are covered with a case of steel, and weighted with a pellet of lead; they are real Leyden bottles, into which the electricity is forced to a very high tension. With the slightest shock they are discharged, and the animal, however strong it may be, falls dead. I must tell you that these cases are size number four, and that the charge for an ordinary gun would be ten." **10**

"I will argue no longer," I replied, rising from the table; "I have nothing left me but to take my gun. At all events, I will go where you go."

Captain Nemo then led me aft; and in passing before Conseil's cabin, I called my two companions, who followed immediately. We then came to a kind of cell near the machinery-room, in which we were to put on our walking-dress.

8. *a peculiar system of closing* That is, they are watertight.

9. *of which I have a large supply* In Verne's *The Mysterious Island* (1875), we learn how these Leniebroek bullets affect a human target. Captain Cyrus Harding, leader of the castaways on the island, has found five dead pirates stretched out on the bank of a stream:

". . . The bodies bore no obvious trace of any wound. Only after carefully examining them did Pencroft find—on the forehead of one, the chest of another, the shoulder of that one—a little red spot, a sort of scarcely visible bruise, the cause of which it was impossible to imagine.

" 'Yes, that's where they have been struck,' said Harding.

" 'But with what weapon?' cried the reporter.

" 'A weapon lightning-like in its impact, a weapon of which we do not have the secret!' "

On his deathbed, Nemo tells the castaways it was he who killed the pirates *with the electric balls of which he possessed the secret.*

10. *charge . . . would be ten* That is, these glass capsules are size-four shot, and an ordinary gun could be loaded with ten of them.

The shark *Carcharias Glaucus* as pictured in A. E. Brehm's *Merveilles de la Nature* (1885).

PART 1: CHAPTER XV[1]

A Walk on the Bottom of the Sea

1. *Chapter XV* To Verne himself, this was Chapter XVI.

This cell was, to speak correctly, the arsenal and wardrobe of the *Nautilus*. A dozen diving apparatuses hung from the partition, waiting our use. Ned Land, on seeing them, showed evident repugnance to dress himself in one.

"But my worthy Ned, the forests of the Island of Crespo are nothing but submarine forests."

"Good!" said the disappointed harpooner, who saw his dreams of fresh meat fade away. "And you, M. Aronnax, are you going to dress yourself in those clothes?"

"There is no alternative, Master Ned."

"As you please, sir," replied the harpooner, shrugging his shoulders; "but as for me, unless I am forced, I will never get into one."

"No one will force you, Master Ned," said Captain Nemo.

"Is Conseil going to risk it?" asked Ned.

"I follow my master wherever he goes," replied Conseil.

At the Captain's call two of the ship's crew came to help us to dress in these heavy and impervious clothes, made of india-rubber without seam, and constructed expressly to resist considerable pressure. One would have thought it a suit of armour, both supple and resisting. This formed trousers and waistcoat. The trousers were finished off with thick boots, weighted with heavy leaden soles. The texture of the waistcoat was held together by bands of copper, which crossed the chest, protecting it from the great pressure of the water, and leaving the lungs free to act; the sleeves ended in gloves, which in no way restrained the movement of the hands. There was a vast difference noticeable between these consummate apparatuses and the old cork breastplates,

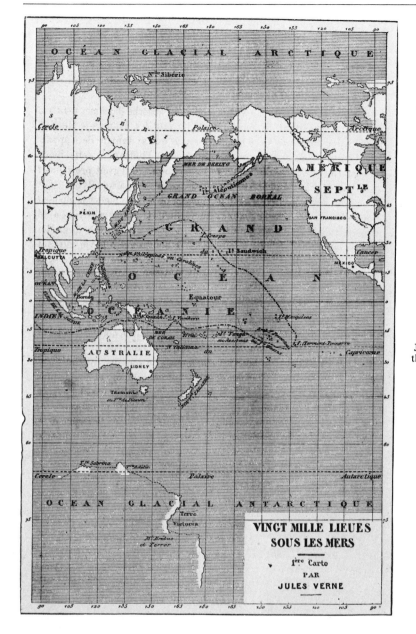

Jules Verne's own map of the first part of the 20,000-league journey under the sea.

jackets, and other contrivances in vogue during the eighteenth century.

Captain Nemo and one of his companions (a sort of Hercules, who must have possessed great strength), Conseil, and myself, were soon enveloped in the dresses. There remained nothing more to be done but enclose our heads in the metal box. But before proceeding to this operation, I asked the Captain's permission to examine the guns we were to carry.

One of the *Nautilus* men gave me a simple gun, the butt end of which, made of steel, hollow in the centre, was rather large. It served as a reservoir for compressed air, which a valve, worked by a spring, allowed to escape into a metal

2. *escape into a metal tube* That is, the chamber.

tube.[2] A box of projectiles, in a groove in the thickness of the butt end, contained about twenty of these electric balls, which, by means of a spring, were forced into the barrel of the gun. As soon as one shot was fired, another was ready.

"Captain Nemo," said I, "this arm is perfect, and easily handled; I only ask to be allowed to try it. But how shall we gain the bottom of the sea?"

"At this moment, Professor, the *Nautilus* is stranded in five fathoms, and we have nothing to do but to start."

"But how shall we get off?"

"You shall see."

Captain Nemo thrust his head into the helmet, Conseil and I did the same, not without hearing an ironical "Good sport!" from the Canadian. The upper part of our dress terminated in a copper collar, upon which was screwed the metal helmet. Three holes, protected by thick glass, allowed us to see in all directions, by simply turning our head in the interior of the head-dress. As soon as it was in position, the Rouquayrol apparatus on our backs began to act; and, for my part, I could breathe with ease.

With the Ruhmkorff lamp hanging from my belt, and the gun in my hand, I was ready to set out. But to speak the truth, imprisoned in these heavy garments, and glued to the deck by my leaden soles, it was impossible for me to take a step.

But this state of things was provided for. I felt myself being pushed into a little room contiguous to the wardrobe-room. My companions followed, towed along in the same way. I heard a water-tight door, furnished with stopper plates, close upon us, and we were wrapped in profound darkness.

After some minutes, a loud hissing was heard. I felt the cold mount from my feet to my chest. Evidently from some part of the vessel they had, by means of a tap, given entrance to the water, which was invading us, and with which the room was soon filled. A second door cut in the side of the *Nautilus* then opened. We saw a faint light. In another instant our feet trod the bottom of the sea.

And now, how can I retrace the impression left upon me by that walk under the waters? Words are impotent to relate such wonders! [When the painter himself is incapable of reproducing the precise qualities of the liquid element, how can one hope to achieve it with the pen?] Captain Nemo walked in front, his companion followed some steps behind. Conseil and I remained near each other, as if an exchange of words had been possible through our metallic cases. I no longer felt the weight of my clothing, or of my shoes, of my reservoir of air, or my thick helmet, in the midst of which my head rattled like an almond in its shell. [All these objects, once immersed in water, lost a portion of their weight equal to the weight of the water they displaced. I was profitting now from this law of physics discovered by Archimedes. I was no longer an inert mass. I had relatively great freedom of movement.]

The light, which lit the soil thirty feet below the surface of the ocean, astonished me by its power. The solar rays shone through the watery mass easily, and dissipated all colour, and I clearly distinguished objects at a distance of a hundred and fifty yards. Beyond that the tints darkened into fine gradations of ultramarine, and faded into vague obscurity.3 Truly this water which surrounded me was but another air denser than the terrestrial atmosphere, but almost as transparent. Above me was the calm surface of the sea.

We were walking on fine even sand, not wrinkled, as on a flat shore, which retains the impression of the billows. This dazzling carpet, really a reflector, repelled the rays of the sun with wonderful intensity, which accounted for the vibration which penetrated every atom of liquid. Shall I be believed when I say that, at the depth of thirty feet, I could see as if I was in broad daylight?

For a quarter of an hour I trod on this sand, sown with the impalpable dust of shells. The hull of the *Nautilus,* resembling a long shoal, disappeared by degrees; but its lantern, when darkness should overtake us in the waters, would help to guide us on board by its distinct rays. [This effect is difficult to imagine if one has seen search-light rays only on land. There, the dust suspended in the air gives these rays the appearance of a luminous fog. But on the water and under the water, electric rays are transmitted with incomparable purity.4

We continued walking. The vast sandy plain seemed endless. My hands seemed to be parting liquid curtains, they closed quietly behind me, and my footsteps were quickly washed away under the pressure of the water.]

Soon forms of objects outlined in the distance were discernible. I recognized magnificent rocks, hung with a tapestry of zoophytes of the most beautiful kind, and I was at first struck by the peculiar effect of this medium.

It was then ten in the morning; the rays of the sun struck the surface of the waves at rather an oblique angle, and at

3. *ultramarine . . . faded into vague obscurity* Here Aronnax is contemplating one of the mysteries of the sea—how its colors are determined. Scientists once believed they could explain the sea's color entirely as the result of the scattering of light from minute particles suspended in the water. But today they also take into account the relative absorption of solar-energy spectrums by the water molecules themselves. Light visible to man is composed of rays that range from the longer wavelengths of red through orange, yellow, and green, to the shorter wavelengths of blue, indigo, and violet. Water does not absorb every wavelength at the same rate; it absorbs the longer wavelengths like red and orange most rapidly. As James B. Rucker of the U.S. Naval Oceanographic Office reports, at a depth of fifteen feet the red portion of the visible spectrum is reduced to 2 percent of its surface intensity. The remaining wavelengths penetrate further; the blues of the shortest wavelengths are the last to be extinguished.

Hence Aronnax is correct in reporting that at a depth of thirty feet, the solar rays *dissipated all colour* and *the tints darkened into fine gradations of ultramarine*—the longer, redder waves have been absorbed first. And today skin divers report that at lower depths, red blood from fish seems to be green.

4. *rays . . . with incomparable purity* This entire passage indicates that Aronnax is walking in an exceptionally clear part of the ocean. In some inshore areas, for example, half the light is extinguished after passing through 6 feet of water. Ninety-nine percent of the light is lost 26 feet down at Woods Hole, Massachusetts; 105 feet down in the Gulf of Maine; and 490 feet down in the Sargasso Sea and in some Mediterranean waters.

the touch of their light, decomposed by refraction as through a prism, flowers, rocks, plants, shells, and polypi were shaded at the edges of the seven solar colours. It was marvellous, a feast for the eyes, this complication of coloured tints, a perfect kaleidoscope of green, yellow, orange, violet, indigo, and blue; in one word, the whole palette of an enthusiastic colourist! Why could I not communicate to Conseil the lively sensations which were mounting to my brain, and rival him in expressions of admiration? For aught I knew, Captain Nemo and his companion might be able to exchange thoughts by means of signs previously agreed upon. So, for want of better, I talked to myself; I declaimed in the copper box, which covered my head, thereby expending more air in vain words than was perhaps expedient.

[In the midst of that splendid spectacle, Conseil had also stopped. Evidently that fine boy, in the presence of so many zoophytes and molluscs, was classifying, always classifying! Polyps and echinoderms covered the sea-floor.] Various kinds of isis, clusters of pure tuft-coral, prickly fungi, and anemones, formed a brilliant garden of flowers, enamelled with porphitae, decked with their collarettes of blue tentacles, sea-stars studding the sandy bottom, together with asterophytons like fine lace embroidered by the hands of naïads, whose festoons were waved by the gentle undulations caused by our walk. It was a real grief to me to crush under my feet the brilliant specimens of molluscs which strewed the ground by thousands, of hammer-heads, donaciae, (veritable bounding shells), of staircases, and red helmet-shells, angel-wings, and many others produced by this inexhaustible ocean. But we were bound to walk, so we went on, whilst above our heads waved shoals of physalides leaving their tentacles to float in their train, medusae whose umbrellas of opal or rose-pink, escalloped with a band of blue, sheltered us from the rays of the sun and fiery pelagiae, which, in the darkness, would have strewn our path with phosphorescent light.

All these wonders I saw in the space of a quarter of a mile, scarcely stopping, and following Captain Nemo, who beckoned me on by signs. Soon the nature of the soil changed; to the sandy plain succeeded an extent of slimy mud, which the Americans call "ooze," composed of equal parts of silicious and calcareous shells. We then travelled over a plain sea-weed of wild and luxuriant vegetation. This sward was of close texture, and soft to the feet, and rivalled the softest carpet woven by the hand of man. But whilst verdure was spread at our feet, it did not abandon our heads. A light network of marine plants, of that inexhaustible family of sea-weeds of which more than two thousand kinds are known, grew on the surface of the water. I saw long ribbons of fucus floating, some globular, others tuberous; laurenciae and cladostephi of most delicate foliage, and some rhodomeniae palmatae, resembling the fan of a cactus. I noticed that the green plants kept nearer the top of the sea, whilst the red were at a greater depth, leaving to the black or brown hydrophytes the care of forming gardens and parterres in the remote beds of the ocean.[5]

[These algae are truly a prodigy of creation, one of the marvels of world flora. This family produces, at the same time, both the smallest and the biggest plants on earth. At one extreme, we can count hundreds of thousands of microscopic plants in a cubic inch of water; at the other, we can find sea-wrack up to 1600 feet in length.]

We had quitted the *Nautilus* about an hour and a half. It was near noon; I knew by the perpendicularity of the sun's rays, which were no longer refracted. The magical colours disappeared by degrees and the shades of emerald and sapphire were effaced. We walked with a regular step, which rang upon the ground with astonishing intensity; the slightest noise was transmitted with a quickness to which the ear is unaccustomed on the earth; indeed, water is a better conductor of sound than air, in the ratio of four to one. At this period the earth sloped downwards; the light took a uniform tint. We were at a depth of a hundred and five yards and twenty inches, undergoing a pressure of six atmospheres.[6]

[My diver's suit was so well designed that I was not affected by this pressure. At first I had felt some difficulty in moving my fingers, but even this discomfort had disappeared. I would have expected to be fatigued by walking in such harness, but after two hours I still felt no sign of weariness. On the contrary, aided by the bouyancy of the water, I could move with surprising ease.]

At this depth I could still see the rays of the sun, though feebly; to their intense brilliancy had succeeded a reddish twilight, the lowest state between day and night; but we could still see well enough; it was not necessary to resort to the Ruhmkorff apparatus as yet. At this moment Captain Nemo stopped; he waited till I joined him, and then pointed to an obscure mass, looming in the shadow, at a short distance.

"It is the forest of the Island of Crespo," thought I;—and I was not mistaken.

5. *remote beds of the ocean* Of course Aronnax was not aware that these color differences might have been the effect of light absorption. Plants of the same color could appear to be different colors at different depths.

6. *a pressure of six atmospheres* At this depth—one hundred meters—*the pressure is ten atmospheres.* And that's exactly what Verne says. But Mercier Lewis often confuses the French *dix* (*ten*) with *six* (*six*). Needless to say, Verne's detractors have put the blame for such careless reckoning not on his translator but on him.

PART 1: CHAPTER XVI[1]
A Submarine Forest

1. *Chapter XVI* If you're checking Verne in the original, remember, this is really his Chapter XVII.

We had at last arrived on the borders of this forest, doubtless one of the finest of Captain Nemo's immense domains. He looked upon it as his own, and considered he had the same right over it that the first men had in the first days of the world. And, indeed, who would have disputed with him the possession of this submarine property? What other hardier pioneer would come, hatchet in hand, to cut down the dark copses?

This forest was composed of large tree-plants; and the moment we penetrated under its vast arcades, I was struck by the singular position of their branches—a position I had not yet observed.

Not a herb which carpeted the ground, not a branch which clothed the trees, was either broken or bent, nor did they extend horizontally; all stretched up to the surface of the ocean. Not a filament, not a ribbon, however thin they might be, but kept as straight as a rod of iron. The fuci and llianas grew in rigid perpendicular lines, due to the density of the element which had produced them. Motionless, yet when bent to one side by the hand, they directly resumed their former position. Truly it was the region of perpendicularity!

I soon accustomed myself to this fantastic position, as well as to the comparative darkness which surrounded us. The soil of the forest seemed covered with sharp blocks, difficult to avoid. The submarine flora struck me as being very perfect, and richer even than it would have been in the arctic or tropical zones, where these productions are not so plentiful. But for some minutes I involuntarily confounded the genera, taking zoophytes for hydrophytes, animals for plants; and who would not have been mistaken? The fauna and the flora are too closely allied in this submarine world.

[I observed that all these specimens of the vegetable kingdom have only the slightest foundation in the earth. Devoid of roots, they seem to require no nourishment from sand, soil, or pebble. All they require is a point of support.]

These plants are self-propagated, and the principle of their existence is in the water, which upholds and nourishes them. The greater number, instead of leaves, shot forth blades of capricious shapes, comprised within a scale of colours,— pink, carmine, green, olive, fawn, and brown. I saw there (but not dried up, as our specimens of the *Nautilus* are) pavonari spread like a fan, as if to catch the breeze; scarlet ceramies, whose laminaries extended their edible shoots of fern-shaped nereocysti, which grow to a height of fifteen feet; 2 clusters of acetabuli, whose stems increase in size upwards; and numbers of other marine plants, all devoid of flowers!

"Curious anomaly, fantastic element!" said an ingenious naturalist, "in which the animal kingdom blossoms, and the vegetable does not!"

Under these numerous shrubs (as large as trees of the temperate zone), and under their damp shadow, were massed together real bushes of living flowers, hedges of zoophytes, on which blossomed some zebrameandrines, with crooked grooves, some yellow caryophylliae; and, to complete the allusion, the fish-flies flew from branch to branch like a swarm of hummingbirds, whilst yellow lepisacomthi, with bristling jaws, dactylopteri, and monocentrides rose at our feet like a flight of snipes.

In about an hour Captain Nemo gave the signal to halt. I, for my part, was not sorry, and we stretched ourselves under an arbour of alariae, the long thin blades of which stood up like arrows.

This short rest seemed delicious to me; there was nothing wanting but the charm of conversation; but, impossible to speak, impossible to answer, I only put my great copper head to Conseil's. I saw the worthy fellow's eyes glistening with delight, and to show his satisfaction, he shook himself in his breastplate of air in the most comical way in the world.

After four hours of this walking I was surprised not to find myself dreadfully hungry. How to account for this state of the stomach I could not tell. But instead I felt an insurmountable desire to sleep, which happens to all divers. And my eyes soon closed behind the thick glasses, and I fell into a heavy

2. *a height of fifteen feet*   Verne says *a height of fifteen meters,* closer to *fifty feet.*

3. *fell into a heavy slumber* Here, alas, is where Verne fell into the ghastly trap we already mentioned in our note on *the Rouquayrol apparatus* (note 7, chapter XIV). In all fairness to T. L. Thomas, we hasten to say that here at least he *is* justified in his attack on Verne (*Galaxy,* December 1961). For this error *is* Verne's own, not the translator's. And so let us see how Thomas handles it.

"Things have been happening so fast and furiously," says Thomas, "that both Verne and the reader alike forget that Verne's SCUBA gear demands that the tongue alternately pop into and out of the two breathing tubes, a good trick when one is asleep."

Now this blooper occurred, Thomas believes, because "Verne simply did not bother to get out of his chair and check" on the details of the Siebe diving helmet, which was equipped with check valves. For *with* check valves, Nemo's party truly could have slept under water. And *without* check valves, they had to stay awake to maintain tongue control, or die.

Blaming this on Verne's alleged "laziness" makes sense if, like Thomas, you feel you have "discovered" that Verne has "lazily" failed to describe Nemo's batteries and "lazily" tried to palm off a steel "lighter than water." But if you are aware—as our annotations have surely proved—that these last two errors were not Verne's but his translator's, then you can entertain an alternative hypothesis.

When storytellers are functioning well, they think of many more developments than they can possibly use. At one point in his planning, Verne must have imagined some story development that would require that Nemo's diving helmet employ tongue control. Later he saw a development that required check valves. *He used only one of these—the underwater sleep that required check valves—and then he forgot to go back and change Nemo's description in Chapter XV to suit the subsequent action.*

Anyone familiar with the process of fiction writing knows how this kind of

slumber,**3** which the movement alone had prevented before. Captain Nemo and his robust companion, stretched in the clear crystal, set us the example.

How long I remained buried in this drowsiness I cannot judge; but, when I woke, the sun seemed sinking towards the horizon. Captain Nemo had already risen, and I was beginning to stretch my limbs, when an unexpected apparition brought me briskly to my feet.

A few steps off, a monstrous sea-spider, about thirty-eight inches high, was watching me with squinting eyes, ready to spring upon me. Though my diver's dress was thick enough to defend me from the bite of this animal, I could not help shuddering with horror. Conseil and the sailor of the *Nautilus* awoke at this moment. Captain Nemo pointed out the hideous crustacean, which a blow from the butt end of the gun knocked over, and I saw the horrible claws of the monster writhe in terrible convulsions. This accident reminded me that other animals more to be feared might haunt these obscure depths, against whose attacks my diving-dress would not protect me. I had never thought of it before, but I now resolved to be upon my guard. Indeed, I thought that this halt would mark the termination of our walk; but I was mistaken, for, instead of returning to the *Nautilus,* Captain Nemo continued his bold excursion. The ground was still on the incline, its declivity seemed to be getting greater, and to be leading us to greater depths. It must have been about three o'clock when we reached a narrow valley, between high perpendicular walls, situated about seventy-five fathoms deep. Thanks to the perfection of our apparatus, we were forty-five fathoms below the limit which nature seems to have imposed on man as to his submarine excursions.**4**

I say seventy-five fathoms, though I had no instrument by which to judge the distance. But I knew that even in the clearest waters the solar rays could not penetrate further. And accordingly the darkness deepened. At ten paces not an object was visible. I was groping my way, when I suddenly saw a brilliant white light. Captain Nemo had just put his electric apparatus into use; his companion did the same, and Conseil and I followed their example. By turning a screw I established a communication between the wire and the spiral glass, and the sea, lit by our four lanterns, was illuminated for a circle of thirty-six yards.**5**

Captain Nemo was still plunging into the dark depths of the forest, whose trees were getting scarcer at every step. I noticed that vegetable life disappeared sooner than animal life. The medusae had already abandoned the arid soil, from which a great number of animals, zoophytes, articulata, molluscs, and fishes, still obtained sustenance.

As we walked, I thought the light of our Ruhmkorff apparatus could not fail to draw some inhabitant from its dark couch. But if they did approach us, they at least kept at a respectful distance from the hunters. Several times I saw Captain Nemo stop, put his gun to his shoulder, and after some moments drop it and walk on. At last, after about four hours,[6] this marvellous excursion came to an end. A wall of superb rocks, in an imposing mass, rose before us, a heap of gigantic blocks, an enormous steep granite shore, forming dark grottos, but which presented no practicable slope; it was the prop of the Island of Crespo. It was the earth! Captain Nemo stopped suddenly. A gesture of his brought us all to a halt, and however desirous I might be to scale the wall, I was obliged to stop. Here ended Captain Nemo's domains. And he would not go beyond them. Further on was a portion of the globe he might not trample upon.

The return began. Captain Nemo had returned to the head of his little band, directing their course without hesitation. I thought we were not following the same road to return to the *Nautilus*. The new road was very steep, and consequently very painful. We approached the surface of the sea rapidly. But this return to the upper strata was not so sudden as to cause relief from the pressure too rapidly, which might have produced serious disorder in our organisation, and brought on internal lesions, so fatal to divers.[7] Very soon light reappeared and grew, and the sun being low on the horizon, the refraction edged the different objects with a spectral ring. At ten yards and a half deep, we walked amidst a shoal of little fishes of all kinds, more numerous than the birds of the air, and also more agile; but no aquatic game worthy of a shot had as yet met our gaze, when at that moment I saw the Captain shoulder his gun quickly, and follow a moving object into the shrubs. He fired;—I heard a slight hissing, and a creature fell stunned at some distance from us. It was a magnificent sea-otter, an enhydrus, the only exclusively marine quadruped. This otter was five feet long, and must have been very valuable. Its skin, chestnut-brown above, and silvery underneath, would have made one of those beautiful furs so sought after in the Russian and Chinese markets; the fineness and the lustre of its coat would certainly fetch £80. I admired this curious mammal, with its rounded head ornamented with short ears, its round eyes and white whiskers like

mistake can occur. *The New Yorker* has been able to sustain a regular feature, "Our Forgetful Authors," with examples galore. A classic occurs in Act IV, scene iii of *Julius Caesar*. First Brutus tells Cassius that Portia (Brutus's wife) is dead. *A few minutes later, Brutus tells Messala he has had no news about Portia.* Some Shakespeare scholars believe that the bard had canceled out one of these two passages but the printer overlooked the cancellation. Or Shakespeare could have "cut" one of these passages in production but forgotten to delete it in the manuscript.

4. *limit . . . submarine excursions* Actually, at 75 fathoms (450 feet), they are considerably below the limits now recommended for amateur divers using modern scuba equipment. The U.S. Divers Corporation's basic rule number 12 is: "Although record dives have been made to 300 feet, amateur divers should not exceed 130 feet."

5. *thirty-six yards* Verne says *25 meters,* closer to *27.5 yards.*

6. *after about four hours* Verne says *at about four o'clock.* They had already been walking for four hours *before* they took their nap.

7. *so fatal to divers* This *serious disorder,* known in Verne's day as "caisson disease," is now called "the bends." It is caused by formation of minute nitrogen bubbles in the joints, muscles, and nerve control centers. The bends can cripple or even kill a diver.

He can go down to 30 feet without trouble. But as he dives deeper, the increased pressure forces larger amounts of atmospheric gases into solution in his blood plasma. The most abundant gas is nitrogen, which constitutes about 79 percent of the atmosphere.

As the diver descends from 100 to 300 feet, enough nitrogen could dissolve into his blood to interfere with his brain and nervous system. He may experience mental imbalance, euphoria, poor coordination, maybe even

. . . Curious mammal, with its rounded head ornamented with short ears, its round eyes and white whiskers like those of a cat, with webbed feet and nails, and tufted tail. The sea otter as pictured in The American Cyclopaedia *(1873).*

unconsciousness—all symptoms of nitrogen narcosis ("rapture of the deep"). Some persons are more susceptible than others. Even a veteran diver, wearing "hard hat" gear, might experience trouble below 400 feet. His ability to concentrate on the simplest tasks might be reduced to almost zero.

As the diver begins his return to the surface, excessive amounts of dissolved nitrogen in his system could get him into serious difficulties. If he ascends too fast, reducing pressure too quickly, his blood and body fluids might suddenly effervesce like champagne. If these gas bubbles lodge in his joints, he suffers the painful "bends." If they block the smaller vessels in his brain, lungs, or heart, he may never dive again.

How credible, then, is the *Nautilus* party's promenade on the sea floor? First we have to accept as a given the ability of Nemo's tanks to supply air for ten hours. At the start, the men are strolling at a safe depth of 30 feet. They do descend gradually over many hours. They are *about seventy-five fathoms deep* (450 feet) by three o'clock. But Aronnax admits this is a guess. So Verne has given himself this margin for error: Aronnax could easily have overestimated the depth by 10 or 15 fathoms. Now maybe Nemo and the Herculean sailor could have developed the ruggedness required at a depth of 360 feet, but surely Aronnax and Conseil would have been very hard-pressed.

those of a cat, with webbed feet and nails, and tufted tail. This precious animal, hunted and tracked by fishermen, has now become very rare, and taken refuge chiefly in the northern parts of the Pacific, or probably its race would soon become extinct.[8]

Captain Nemo's companion took the beast, threw it over his shoulder, and we continued our journey. For one hour a plain of sand lay stretched before us. Sometimes it rose to within two yards and some inches of the surface of the water. I then saw our image clearly reflected, drawn inversely, and above us appeared an identical group reflecting our movements and our actions; in a word, like us in every point, except that they walked with their heads downward and their feet in the air.

Another effect I noticed, which was the passage of thick clouds which formed and vanished rapidly; but on reflection I understood that these seeming clouds were due to the varying thickness of the reeds at the bottom, and I could even see the fleecy foam which their broken tops multiplied on the water, and the shadows of large birds passing above our heads, whose rapid flight I could discern on the surface of the sea.

On this occasion, I was witness to one of the finest gunshots which ever made the nerves of a hunter thrill. A large bird of great breadth of wing, clearly visible, approached, hovering over us. Captain Nemo's companion shouldered his gun and fired, when it was only a few yards above the waves.[9] The creature fell stunned, and the force of its fall brought it within the reach of the dexterous hunter's grasp. It was an albatross of the finest kind.

Our march had not been interrupted by this incident. For two hours we followed these sandy plains, then fields of algae very disagreeable to cross. Candidly, I could do no more when I saw a glimmer of light, which, for a half mile, broke the darkness of the waters. It was the lantern of the *Nautilus.* Before twenty minutes were over we should be on board, and I should be able to breathe with ease, for it seemed that my reservoir supplied air very deficient in oxygen. But I did not reckon on an accidental meeting, which delayed our arrival for some time.

I had remained some steps behind, when I presently saw Captain Nemo coming hurriedly towards me. With his strong hand he bent me to the ground, his companion doing the same to Conseil. At first I knew not what to think of this sudden attack, but I was soon reassured by seeing the Captain lie down beside me, and remain immovable.

I was stretched on the ground, just under shelter of a bush of algae, when, raising my head, I saw some enormous mass, casting phosphorescent gleams, pass blusteringly by.

My blood froze in my veins as I recognized two formidable sharks which threatened us. It was a couple of tintoreas, terrible creatures, with enormous tails and a dull glassy stare, the phosphorescent matter ejected from holes pierced around the muzzle. Monstrous brutes! which would crush a whole man in their iron jaws. I did not know whether Conseil stopped to classify them; for my part, I noticed their silver bellies, and their huge mouths bristling with teeth, from a very unscientific point of view, and more as a possible victim than as a naturalist.

Happily the voracious creatures do not see well. They passed without seeing us, brushing us with their brownish fins, and we escaped by a miracle from a danger certainly greater than meeting a tiger full-face in the forest. Half an hour after, guided by the electric light, we reached the *Nautilus*. The outside door had been left open, and Captain Nemo closed it as soon as we had entered the first cell. He then pressed a knob. I heard the pumps working in the midst of the vessel, I felt the water sinking from around me, and in a few moments the cell was entirely empty. The inside door then opened, and we entered the vestry.

There our diving-dress was taken off, not without some trouble; and, fairly worn out from want of food and sleep, I returned to my room, in great wonder at this surprising excursion at the bottom of the sea.

A large bird of great breadth of wing . . . approached, hovering over us. The albatross as pictured in *The American Cyclopaedia* (1873).

Their return seems a bit more realistic: *The new road was very steep, and consequently very painful*— probably in the knees and ankles especially. Still, their ascent is much too fast for safety. The U.S. Navy standard decompression tables say that for 150 minutes at 300 feet (the lowest the tables will consider), a diver needs 1165 minutes of ascent time. So Verne was really pressing the limits in this escapade. Probably he would have written it differently after 1875, when Paul Bert won a 20,000-franc prize from the French Academy of Sciences for his research into proper rates of ascent.

8. *its race would soon become extinct* Indeed, by 1900 it was believed that the sea otter *had* become extinct. Since its luxurious coat could then command as much as two thousand dollars on the fur market, hunters had all but wiped out the species. And since sea otters were competing with man for the meat of abalones, fishermen had helped destroy these webfooted members of the weasel family.

But it developed that a precious few sea otters had managed to survive. Through efforts of conservationists, the species was placed under strict protection and is now making a comeback. Sea otters are now sighted from the Aleutians to north California.

They live in dense kelp beds. A full-grown specimen, like the one Nemo has shot, can weigh eighty pounds. The sea otter is one of the few animals who can use tools. He can balance a flat stone on his chest and use it as an anvil on which to break shellfish. He plays games with stones! And he wraps kelp around his waist at night to anchor himself to his home coast!

9. *yards above the waves* One reason this was such a remarkable shot is that the bird was in one medium (air) and the marksman in another (water). In taking aim, the marksman had to compensate for the fact that light bends as it passes from one medium to another.

PART 1: CHAPTER XVII[1]

Four Thousand Leagues under the Pacific

1. *Chapter XVII* If you plan to consult the French text, remember, this is really Chapter XVIII.

2. *the second lieutenant* In the French, Aronnax simply says *the second in command.*

3. *a number of the sailors* Verne says *some twenty sailors.* This is the first clue we have as to the size of the crew. The international character of the crew will prove to be increasingly symbolic. (By *Candiote* Verne means a *Cretan:* Candia is the largest city on the island of Crete. And *Sclaves* is obsolete English for *Slavs.*) Verne describes the crewmen as *sobres de paroles.* Lewis renders this as *civil* but the meaning is that they are *men of few words.* We must see their restrained behavior as extraordinary, accustomed as we are to thinking of nineteenth-century sailors singing sea chanteys while working. As we watch Nemo's silent myrmidons at their tasks throughout the novel, we must wonder about the reasons behind their grim taciturnity. Remember Ned's suspicion that they, too, are *"run by electricity"*—in short, robots run by Nemo?

4. *They . . . used that odd language* Verne is building up suspense about

The next morning, the 18th of November, I had quite recovered from my fatigues of the day before, and I went up on to the platform, just as the second lieutenant [2] was uttering his daily phrase.

[It occurred to me that this expression either referred to the weather conditions or meant something like "There is nothing in sight." And truly, the ocean was deserted. Not a sail on the horizon. The heights of the Island of Crespo had disappeared. The sea, absorbing all colours of the spectrum except blue, reflected them in all directions and was itself tinted a beautiful indigo. A broad, wavy pattern seemed to be printed on a silken surface.]

I was admiring the magnificent aspect of the ocean when Captain Nemo appeared. He did not seem to be aware of my presence, and began a series of astronomical observations. Then, when he had finished, he went and leant on the cage of the watch-light, and gazed abstractedly on the ocean. In the meantime, a number of the sailors [3] of the *Nautilus,* all strong and healthy men, had come up on to the platform. They came to draw up the nets that had been laid all night. These sailors were evidently of different nations, although the European type was visible in all of them. I recognised some unmistakable Irishmen, Frenchmen, some Sclaves, and a Greek or a Candiote. They were civil, and only used that odd language [4] among themselves, the origin of which I could not guess, neither could I question them.

The nets were hauled in. They were a large kind of "chaluts," [5] like those on the Normandy coasts, great pockets that the waves and a chain fixed in the smaller meshes, kept open. These pockets, drawn by iron poles, swept through the water, and gathered in everything in its way. That day they brought up curious specimens from those productive coasts,—fishing-frogs that, from their comical movements, have acquired the name of buffoons; black commersons, furnished with antennae; trigger-fish, encircled with red bands; orthragorisci, with very subtle venom; some olive-coloured lampreys; macrorhynci, covered with silvery scales; trichiuri, the electric power of which is equal to that of the gymnotus and cramp-fish; scaly notoperi, with transverse brown bands; greenish cod; several varieties of gobies, etc.; also some larger fish; a caranx with a prominent head a yard long; several fine bonitos, streaked with blue and silver; and three splendid tunnies, which, spite of the swiftness of their motion, had not escaped the net.

I reckoned that the haul had brought in more than nine hundred weight of fish. It was a fine haul, but not to be wondered at. Indeed, the nets are let down for several hours, and enclose in their meshes an infinite variety. We had no lack of excellent food, and the rapidity of the *Nautilus* and the attraction of the electric light could always renew our supply. These several productions of the sea were immediately lowered through the panel to the steward's room, some to be eaten fresh, and others pickled.

The fishing ended, the provision of air renewed, I thought that the *Nautilus* was about to continue its submarine excursion, and was preparing to return to my room, when, without further preamble, the Captain turned to me, saying—

"Professor, is not this ocean gifted with real life? It has its tempers and its gentle moods. Yesterday it slept as we did, and now it has woke after a quiet night. Look!" he continued, "it wakes under the caresses of the sun. It is going to renew its diurnal existence. It is an interesting study to watch the play of its organisation. It has a pulse, arteries, spasms; and I agree with the learned Maury, who discovered in it a circulation as real as the circulation of blood in animals."

[I sensed that the Captain was not expecting me to answer. It seemed pointless to punctuate his remarks with "of course," "certainly," and "I agree." He seemed to be thinking aloud, pausing after each idea.]

"Yes, the ocean has indeed circulation, and to promote it, the Creator has caused things to multiply in it—caloric, salt, and animalculae. [Changes in temperature cause variations in density, thus creating currents and counter-currents.6

it. Is it an *artificial* language? Developing such a deliberately constructed language was one of Verne's pet ideas. Is *that odd language* Nemo's own invention? This could have been Nemo's answer to the communications problems posed by the international makeup of his crew. Or is it the language (or dialect) of Nemo's homeland, taught to those of his crew from other countries as their international medium, much as English and French often serve as auxiliary tongues?

Our earlier analysis of *nautron, respoc,* and *lorni* becomes relevant here, too. Some theorists, in Verne's time and our own, have constructed artificial languages out of classical Indo-European roots. Thus, since the roots *nau-, lorn-, spec-* figure in many "real" languages, we can expect they will be used as building blocks in artificial tongues. So Nemo's *odd language* could well be that kind of artificial patchwork. But Verne has cleverly kept open the other possibility, too. *Nautron respoc lorni virch* could well be from one of those many "real" Indo-European languages, dead or alive, that are unknown to Aronnax and to most of Verne's readers. For example, how can Aronnax, and the average reader, be certain, at this point, that this sentence is *not* from Old Persian? Or modern Assamese?

5. *chaluts* Dragnets, used in trawling.

6. *currents and counter-currents* Omission of this passage deprives the reader of Verne's careful foreshadowing (*"the pole!"*) and of more evidence of Nemo's passionate belief in the doctrines of Maury.

Maury has figured prominently in the centuries-long debate over the causes of ocean currents. Benjamin Franklin (the first to chart the Gulf Stream) had said that frictional drag of the winds over the surface causes currents. But Maury believed that "winds have little to do with the general system of aqueous circulation in the ocean." Instead Maury theorized that deep ocean currents circulate so as to replace the water moving in the surface layer. The principal driving force of ocean currents, as he saw it, is the difference in density between equatorial waters and polar waters. Because of greater warming of equatorial waters by the sun, those waters expand, stand "higher," and then move "downhill" from the equator toward the poles.

James Croll, Scots geologist, opposed Maury on this and revived the Franklin hypothesis. Croll believed that the force of gravity acting on a "slope" of the sea's surface was not enough to create the vast system of circulation of currents. He emphasized the coincidence of wind and sea-current systems at the interface of sea and air, a coincidence Maury discounted.

But twentieth-century studies have shown that while the subject is far more complex than either Franklin, Maury, or Croll could have imagined, both the Franklin-Croll and the Maury views are reflected in the total explanation. The Norwegian physicist Vilhelm Bjerknes (1862–1951) has shown that variations in the density of sea water *do* cause pressure differences and these *do* indeed initiate and sustain fluid motion.

And Swedish oceanographer Vagn Walfrid Ekman (1874–1954) has shown that while wind-drag does indeed cause currents, the direction of the currents is affected by the rotation of the earth. This rotational force is known as the Coriolis effect. Thus, a steady wind plus Coriolis force will drive the surface layer at a 45° angle to the *right* of wind direction in the northern hemisphere (to the left in the southern). This surface movement induces successively deeper currents, which are offset at increasingly greater angles to the wind direction because of the Coriolis effect. At a certain depth (200 to 500 feet), the current will actually flow in a direction exactly opposite to that of the wind. In addition to the shift in flow direction at each lower level, there has been a gradual loss of velocity. At a depth somewhere between 200 and 500 feet, the velocity of the countercurrent might be as little as 4 percent that of the surface current.

Evaporation, which is non-existent in the extreme north but active in the equatorial zones, brings about a perpetual interchange of polar and tropical waters. Moreover, I have come upon currents going from top to bottom and from bottom to top, which constitute the true respiration of the ocean. I have seen a molecule of ocean water, heated at the surface, drop into the depths, attain its maximum density at two degrees below zero Centigrade, then cool further, become lighter, and rise again. At the pole you will observe the consequence of this phenomenon. You will see why, through this law of provident Nature, water freezes only at the surface." [7]

As he spoke this sentence, I thought: *"The pole!* Does this audacious character intend to take us there?" [8] After a moment of silence, in which he surveyed that element that was to him a subject of deep and endless study, he resumed:

"As you know, Professor, salts are abundant in the sea. If you extracted all the salts in the sea, you would have a mass equal to four and a half million cubic leagues! Spread out all over the earth, that mass would form a layer more than ten metres high. Do not think now that the presence of these salts is a caprice of Nature. No. They render the waters less evaporable, so that winds cannot pick up too much vapour which, when condensed, would submerge the temperate zones! They play a major role, the role of regulating the general ecology of the globe!"

Again he paused, took a few steps on the deck and returned: "And the infusiorians, those billions of microscopic organisms, millions of them in a drop of water, 800,000 of them needed to make one milligram of weight—their role is no less important. They absorb marine salts, absorb the solid elements in the water, they make corals and madrepores, and so they build calcareous continents. Thus the drop of water, lighter when deprived of its mineral element, ascends to the surface again, absorbs the salts left by evaporation, becomes heavier, descends to bring the infusorians new materials to absorb. We have then a double current, ascending and descending, continuous movement, perpetual life. Marine life is more intense than land life, more exuberant, more infinite, spread throughout the sea. The sea has been called the element of death for man, the element of life for myriads of animals—and so it is for me!"]

When Captain Nemo spoke thus, he seemed altogether changed, and aroused an extraordinary emotion in me.

"Also," he added, "true existence is there; and I can imagine the foundations of nautical towns, clusters of submarine houses, which, like the *Nautilus,* would ascend every morning to breathe at the surface of the water, free towns, independent cities. Yet who knows whether some despot——"

Captain Nemo finished his sentence with a violent gesture. Then, addressing me as if to chase away some sorrowful thought—

"M. Aronnax," he asked, "do you know the depth of the ocean?"

"I only know, Captain, what the principal soundings have taught us."

"Could you tell me them, so that I can suit them to my purpose?"

"These are some," I replied, "that I remember. If I am not mistaken, a depth of 8000 yards has been found in the North Atlantic, and 2500 yards in the Mediterranean. The most remarkable soundings have been made in the South Atlantic, near the 35th parallel, and they gave 12,000 yards, 14,000 yards, and 15,000 yards. So sum up all, it is reckoned that if the bottom of the sea were levelled, its mean depth would be about one and three-quarter leagues." **9**

"Well, Professor," replied the Captain, "we shall show you better than that, I hope. As to the mean depth of this part of the Pacific, I tell you it is only 4000 yards."

Having said this, Captain Nemo went towards the panel, and disappeared down the ladder. I followed him, and went into the large drawing-room. The screw was immediately put in motion, and the log gave twenty miles an hour.

During the days and weeks that passed, Captain Nemo was very sparing of his visits. I seldom saw him. The lieutenant pricked the ship's course regularly on the chart, so I could always tell exactly the route of the *Nautilus.* [But Conseil and Ned did spend many hours with me. Conseil had told Ned about the marvels of our under-water promenade, and the Canadian was sorry he had not gone along with us. I felt, however, that he would surely have another chance to visit the oceanic forests.]

Nearly every day, for some time, the panels of the drawing-room were opened, and we were never tired of penetrating the mysteries of the submarine world.

The general direction of the *Nautilus* was southeast, and it kept between 100 and 150 yards of depth. One day, however, I do not know why, being drawn diagonally by means of the inclined planes, it touched the bed of the sea.**10** The thermometer indicated a temperature of 4.25 (cent.); a temperature that at this depth seemed common to all latitudes.

7. *water freezes only at the surface* "This law of provident Nature" is crucial to the existence of life. Notice that Nemo says, casually, that as water will *"cool further"* it will "become lighter." This seems contrary to the general rule that as substances cool, they contract and become denser and heavier. Water (like silver and bismuth) is a partial exception. It does contract as it cools, but at a certain point ($-2°$ C in the case of sea water) it begins to expand again and to become lighter. Hence when Nemo's *"molecule of ocean water"* freezes, it will "rise again" and float as ice. Because it floats, the sun can melt it. If ice didn't expand, rise, and float—that is, if it formed in the oceans from the bottom up—the seas would soon freeze solid. Even more likely, the oceans would not have been able to develop at all. Either way, there wouldn't be any life on Earth, because life began in the water.

"This phenomenon," as Nemo terms it, is due to the peculiar molecular structure of water.

8. *take us there* Aronnax is astonished because in 1868, no explorer has gotten any closer to the South Pole than the 78th parallel, 800 miles away, reached by Captain James Ross on February 22, 1842.

9. *one and three-quarter leagues* In this discussion of *"principal soundings,"* wherever Mercier Lewis says *yards,* read *meters.* Aronnax's *"most remarkable soundings"*—up to 15,000 meters or 49,000 feet—actually had been reported but they were based on faulty procedures. After Commander Maury instituted more accurate sounding practices, such figures were no longer reported. Today's "most remarkable soundings" include several of more than 34,000 feet, the deepest being the Challenger Deep, near Guam: 35,600 feet. Where Aronnax gives his *"mean depth,"* read *seven kilometers,* about 4 miles. Today's oceanographers give the average depth of the world's oceans as 2 miles.

10. *touched the bed of the sea* Verne

says they reached a depth of 2,000 meters, or about 6500 feet. The thermometer reading would be 39.65° Fahrenheit.

. . . The Nautilus. *. . . sighted the Sandwich Islands, . . .* where, according to *Mitchell's School Geography* (1863), the natives were probably "burning an Idol."

11. *the Sandwich Islands, where Cook died* Captain James Cook (1728–1779) is important to Aronnax especially because Cook's voyages were the first genuine scientific expeditions. When Cook's *Endeavour* sailed from England in 1768, it was the first ship to carry a team of scientists and also the first to be completely equipped for modern navigation. Cook's first voyage, three years long, took him around the Horn to the Cape of Good Hope. His second (1772–1775) led him toward the South Pole and around the world. On his third voyage (1776–1779) he discovered the Sandwich Islands (now called the Hawaiian Islands), where he was killed in a fight with natives.

Cook left to science its first overall survey of the Pacific, which he had explored from the Bering Straits to the Antarctic. He recorded extensive data on winds, currents, temperature, and ocean depth, which he sounded to 200 fathoms. Both Aronnax and Nemo will speak reverently of him on several occasions.

At three o'clock in the morning of the 26th of November, the *Nautilus* crossed the tropic of Cancer at 172° longitude. On the 27th instant it sighted the Sandwich Islands, where Cook died,**11** February 14, 1779. We had then gone 4860 leagues from our starting-point. In the morning, when I went on the platform, I saw, two miles to windward, Hawaii, the largest of the seven islands that form the group. I saw clearly the cultivated ranges, and the several mountain chains that run parallel with the side, and the volcanoes that overtop Mouna-Rea, which rise 5000 yards above the level of the sea. Besides other things the nets brought up, were several flabellariae and graceful polypi, that are peculiar to that part of the ocean. The direction of the *Nautilus* was still to the south-east. It crossed the equator December 1, in 142° longitude; and on the 4th of the same month, after crossing rapidly and without anything particular occurring, we sighted the Marquesas group. I saw, three miles off, at 8° 57′ latitude south, and 139° 32′ west longitude, Martin's peak in Nouka-Hiva, the largest of the group that belongs to France. I only saw the woody mountains against the horizon, because Captain Nemo did not wish to bring the ship to the wind. There the nets brought up beautiful specimens of fish; choryphenes, with azure fins and tails like gold, the flesh of which is unrivalled; hologymnoses, nearly destitute of scales, but of exquisite flavour; ostorhyncs, with bony jaws, and yellow-tinged thasards, as good as bonitos; all fish that would be of use to us. After leaving these charming islands protected by the French flag, from the 4th to the 11th of December the *Nautilus* sailed over about 2000 miles. This navigation was remarkable for the meeting with an immense shoal of calmars, near neighbors to the cuttle. The French fishermen call them *hornets;* **12** they belong to the cephalopod class, and to the dibranchial family, that comprehends the cuttles and the argonauts. These animals were particularly studied by students of antiquity, and they furnished numerous metaphors to the popular orators, as well as excellent dishes for the tables of the rich citizens, if one can believe Athenaeus, a Greek doctor, who lived before Galen. It was during the night of the 9th or 10th of December that the *Nautilus* came across this shoal of molluscs, that are peculiarly nocturnal. One could count them by millions. They emigrate from the temperate to the warmer zones, following the track of herrings and sardines. We watched them through the thick crystal panes, swimming down the wind with great rapidity, moving by means of their locomotive tube, pursuing fish and molluscs, eating the little ones, eaten by the big ones, and tossing about in indescribable confusion the ten arms that nature has placed on their heads like a crest of pneumatic serpents. The *Nautilus,* in spite of its speed, sailed for several hours in the midst of these animals, and its nets brought in an enormous quantity, among which I recognized the nine species that D'Orbigny **13** classed for the Pacific. One saw, while crossing, that the sea displays the most wonderful sights. They were in endless variety. The scene changed continually, and we were called upon not only to contemplate the works of the Creator in the midst of the liquid element, but to penetrate the awful mysteries of the ocean.

During the daytime of the 11th of December, I was busy reading in the large drawing-room. Ned Land and Conseil watched the luminous water through the half-open panels. The *Nautilus* was immovable. While its reservoirs were filled, it kept at a depth of 1000 yards, a region rarely visited in the ocean, and in which large fish were seldom seen.

I was then reading a charming book by Jean Macé,**14** "The Slaves of the Stomach," and I was learning some valuable lessons from it, when Conseil interrupted me.

"Will master come here for a moment?" he said, in a curious voice.

"What is the matter, Conseil?"

"I want master to look."

I rose, went and leaned on my elbows before the panes and watched.

In a full electric light, an enormous black mass, quite immovable, was suspended in the midst of the waters. I watched

12. *French fishermen call them hornets* Mercier Lewis, or maybe his printer, shies away from Verne's naughty joke in this passage. In the original, Aronnax says that French fishermen give these calamaries the name of *encornets,* that is, *squid* or *cuttlefish.* But the name is also a pun on *encorné* (*horned*) and *encorner* (*to cuckold*). Thus Aronnax prepares us for his tongue-in-cheek remark that these animals furnished *metaphors* to the orators of antiquity.

Lewis is still flustered when he gets to Aronnax's description of the calamaries' movement. Aronnax does not say they swim *down the wind,* he says they swim *backward.*

13. *species that D'Orbigny* Like Pierre Aronnax himself, Alcide d'Orbigny (1802–1857) had been a traveling naturalist for the Museum of Natural History at Paris. He became the museum's professor of paleontology in 1853. He is credited with laying the foundations of cephalopod systematics. Doubtless Aronnax has read d'Orbigny's monograph *Histoire Naturelle, générale et particulaire, des Céphalopodes actéabulifères,* which is considered to be a landmark in modern zoology. It's probably in Nemo's library.

14. *Jean Macé* Jean Macé was, along with Jules Verne, a codirector of Pierre Hetzel's review for young people, *Magasin d'Education et de Récréation.* A man of republican sympathies, Macé also founded the League of Education.

it attentively, seeking to find out the nature of this gigantic cetacean. But a sudden thought crossed my mind. "A vessel!" I said, half aloud.

"Yes," replied the Canadian, "a disabled ship that has sunk perpendicularly."

Ned Land was right; we were close to a vessel of which the tattered shrouds still hung from their chains. The keel seemed to be in good order, and it had been wrecked at most some few hours. Three stumps of masts, broken off about two feet above the bridge, showed that the vessel had had to sacrifice its masts. But, lying on its side, it had filled, and it was heeling over to port. This skeleton of what it had once been, was a sad spectacle as it lay lost under the waves, but sadder still was the sight of the bridge, where some corpses, bound with ropes, were still lying. I counted five—four men, one of whom was standing at the helm, and a woman standing by the poop, holding an infant in her arms. She was quite young. I could distinguish her features, which the water had not decomposed, by the brilliant light from the *Nautilus*. In one despairing effort, she had raised her infant above her head, poor little thing! whose arms encircled its mother's neck. The attitude of the four sailors was frightful, distorted as they were by their convulsive movements, whilst making a last effort to free themselves from the cords that bound them to the vessel. The steersman alone, calm, with a grave, clear face, his grey hair glued to his forehead, and his hand clutching the wheel of the helm, seemed even then to be guiding the three broken masts through the depths of the ocean.

What a scene! We were dumb; our hearts beat fast before this shipwreck, taken as it were from life, and photographed in its last moments. And I saw already, coming towards it with hungry eyes, enormous sharks, attracted by the human flesh.

However, the *Nautilus,* turning, went round the submerged vessel, and in one instant I read on the stern—*"The Florida, Sunderland."*

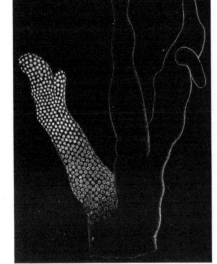

Illustration of *Porites levis,* found in the Pacific by James D. Dana, appeared in his book *Corals and Coral Islands* (1872).

PART 1: CHAPTER XVIII[1]
Vanikoro

This terrible spectacle was the forerunner of the series of maritime catastrophes that the *Nautilus* was destined to meet with in its route. As long as it went through more frequented waters, we often saw the hulls of shipwrecked vessels that were rotting in the depths, and deeper down, cannons, bullets, anchors, chains, and a thousand other iron materials eaten up by rust. However, on the 11th of December, we sighted the Pomotu Islands, the old "dangerous group" of Bougainville,[2] that extend over a space of 500 leagues at E.S.E., to W.N.W., [between 13° 30′ and 23° 50′ south latitude, and 125° 30′ and 151° 30′ west longitude,] from the Island Ducie to that of Lazareff. This group covers an area of 370 square leagues, and it is formed of sixty groups of islands, among which the Gambier group is remarkable, over which France exercises sway. These are coral islands, slowly raised, but continuous, created by the daily work of polypi [which may someday connect them]. Then this new island will be joined later on to the neighboring groups, and a fifth continent will stretch from New Zealand and New Caledonia, and from thence to the Marquesas.

One day, when I was suggesting this theory to Captain Nemo, he replied coldly—

"The earth does not want new continents, but new men."

Chance had conducted the *Nautilus* towards the Island of Clermont-Tonnere, one of the most curious of the group, that was discovered in 1822 by Captain Bell of the *Minerva*. I could study now the madreporal system, to which are due the islands in this ocean.

Madrepores (which must not be mistaken for corals) have a tissue lined with a calcareous crust, and the modifications

1. *Chapter XVIII* Verne's Chapter XIX of Part 1.

2. *"dangerous group" of Bougainville* Another famous explorer whose exploits were well known to .Verne's readers was the Frenchman Louis de Bougainville (1729–1811). The archipelago that he named the "dangerous group" is now known as the Tuamotu or "Low" Archipelago, French Polynesia.

3. *madrepores known as . . . madrepores . . . astreas* Verne gives the four names as *millepores, porites, meandrines, and astraeas.*

4. *Darwin's theory . . . of the atolls* Although Darwin had formulated his theory of the atolls as early as 1837, it could not be proved until 1952.

In his book *The Structure and Distribution of Coral Reefs* (1842), Darwin argued that the atoll forms in this manner:

A coral reef develops around the edges of a volcanic isle. Then the volcano subsides slowly into the sea. The "various minute and tender animals," he wrote, continue to build the surface of the reef upward. They keep pace with the subsidence, which occurs at a rate that lets them continue their housebuilding at their normal depth: the top 150 to 180 feet of tropical water. For coral can only grow in depths illuminated by strong light. Eventually the central peak of the volcano disappears. Nothing re-

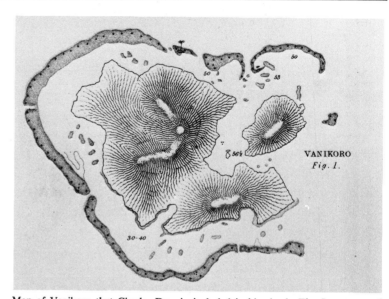

Map of Vanikoro that Charles Darwin included in his classic *The Structure and Distribution of Coral Reefs* (1842). The larger island is about twelve miles long, its summit 3,032 feet. Numbers (e.g., "30–40") represent depths in fathoms.

Charles Darwin's sketch of Whitsunday Island, an atoll, from his book *The Structure and Distribution of Coral Reefs* (1842).

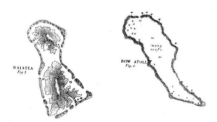

Two maps that Charles Darwin used to support his theory of atoll formation. In the Raiatea Islands (left), the volcanic mountains are surrounded by *a barrier reef.* In the Bow Atoll (right), the mountains have subsided, leaving *an atoll.* It was Darwin's argument that a *barrier reef* and *an atoll* are simply different stages in the same process; as the mountains subsided, "the coral continued to grow upwards." Raiatea is thirty miles long; Bow is thirty-five.

of its structure have induced M. Milne Edwards, my worthy master, to class them into five sections. The animalculae that the marine polypus secretes live by millions at the bottom of their cells. Their calcareous deposits become rocks, reefs, and large and small islands. Here they form a ring, surrounding a little inland lake, that communicates with the sea by means of gaps. There they make barriers of reefs like those on the coasts of New Caledonia and the various Pomotou islands. In other places, like those at Reunion and at Maurice, they raise fringed reefs, high, straight walls, near which the depth of the ocean is considerable.

Some cable-lengths off the shores of the Island of Clermont I admired the gigantic work accomplished by these microscopical workers. These walls are specially the work of those madrepores known as milleporas, porites, madrepores, and astraeas.[3] These polypi are found particularly in the rough beds of the sea, near the surface; and consequently it is from the upper part that they begin their operations, in which they bury themselves by degrees with the debris of the secretions that support them. Such is, at least, Darwin's theory, who thus explains the formation of the *atolls*,[4] a superior theory (to my mind) to that given of the foundation of the madreporical works, summits of mountains or volcanoes, that are submerged some feet below the level of the sea.[5]

I could observe closely these curious walls, for perpendicularly they were more than 300 yards deep, and our electric sheets lighted up this calcareous matter brilliantly. Replying to a question Conseil asked me as to the time these colossal barriers took to be raised, I astonished him much by telling him that learned men reckoned it about the eighth of an inch in a hundred years.

["So, to build these walls," he said, "must have taken . . ."

"One hundred and ninety-two thousand years,6 my boy. That means we have to see those 'days' referred to in the Bible 7 as really longer periods of time. In addition, the formation of coal—the mineralisation of forests submerged by floods, and the cooling down of basaltic rocks—also required a much longer time. So, you see, the 'days' referred to in the Bible must represent epochs, and not literally the time between sunrise and sunrise. As a matter of fact, the Bible itself does not date the sun from the first day of Creation."

When the *Nautilus* surfaced again, I was able to visualise the history of the island of Clermont-Tonnerre, which was low and covered with woods. Its madreporal rocks had evidently ·been fertilised by waterspouts and storms. Then a seed, carried by some hurricane from nearby land, fell on these limestone deposits, mixed with the decomposing refuse of marine plants and animals, and formed a vegetable humus. Maybe a cocoa-nut, floating in on the waves, was left on this coast and germinated. The tree that grew prevented water from evaporating and so a stream developed. Vegetation

mains but the reef enclosing a lagoon —what we call an atoll.

These atolls are commonly called "coral" but most of them, strictly speaking, are *algal* in nature.

In 1881, shortly before he died, Darwin was quite impatient to establish final proof of this hypothesis. He wrote to the American zoologist Alexander Agassiz (1835–1910) saying he wished some "rich millionaire" would have borings made in some atolls and bring back cores from "500 or 600 feet." But not until 1952 were the necessary borings made. U.S. scientists drove two shafts down through the coral at Eniwetok Atoll. At 4158 feet on one end of the atoll, at 4610 feet at the other end, they hit volcanic rock. And most of the limestone resting on the volcano contained the remains of organisms that could live only in shallow water!

Thus Darwin's theory was proved. Seismic studies have also confirmed the theory. So if Darwin had never done anything else (like promulgate a theory of evolution), his theory of atolls alone would have given him some measure of fame.

5. *submerged . . . below the level of the sea* Before Darwin's theory of atoll formation was published, the best explanation offered was that atolls were all supported on submarine mountain summits. The trouble with that hypothesis, Darwin said, was that it "implies the existence of submarine chains of mountains of almost the same height, extending over areas of many thousand square miles." The alternative, he wrote in his book *Coral Reefs,* is to believe in "the prolonged subsidence of the foundations on which the atolls were primarily based, together with the upward growth of the reef-constructing corals." *Coral Reefs*—especially the introduction, Chapter V, and the "Recapitulation" in Chapter VI—is a masterpiece of reasoning and technical exposition.

6. *ninety-two thousand years* If you're having trouble getting the same results, it's partly that Aronnax really says the walls are *more than 300*

These walls are specially the work of . . . madrepores known as milleporas. . . . Illustration of *Millepora alicornis,* found in the Pacific by Yale Professor James D. Dana, appeared in his book *Corals and Coral Islands* (1872). Professor Dana was himself studying Pacific corals in 1842 at the very time that Darwin's work appeared. Dana recalls in his preface that, "I was afterward enabled to speak of [Darwin's] theory as established with more positiveness than he himself, in his philosophic caution, had been ready to adopt."

meters deep (thus not 900 but almost 1000 feet) and mainly that Aronnax is way off in his computation. If the walls were raised at the rate of one eighth of an inch every century, then it *"must have taken"* 9,600,000 years. Or, if the walls really took 192,000 years, then they rose at the rate of one foot every 192 years.

7. *those 'days' referred to in the Bible* Aronnax is offering Conseil an early hypothesis that makes it possible to reconcile Darwin's theory of evolution with the teachings of the Book of Genesis. The idea rests upon the assumption that the six "days" of Creation are simply metaphors for six major epochs of geological time.

Notice that this passage on the Creation was deleted by Mercier Lewis. He was a practicing clergyman.

8. *a sea-serpent called munirophis* Verne says *un serpent de mer nommé murénophis:* a sea snake, one of the moray eels.

9. *Then came Cook* But not in 1714, even though the French editions continue to print this error. As we have already detailed it in an earlier note, Cook made all his voyages between 1768 and 1779. And Verne himself will soon tell us that Cook named the New Hebrides in 1773.

gradually flourished. Some animalcules, worms, insects, living in tree trunks on other islands, were swept here by the wind. Turtles came and laid their eggs. Birds made their nests in the young trees. Thus animal life developed. Man was then attracted here by the green vegetation, the fertility of the soil. That is how this island came to be, through the great work of microscopic organisms.]

Towards evening Clermont-Tonnerre was lost in the distance, and the route of the *Nautilus* was sensibly changed. After having crossed the tropic of Capricorn in 135° longitude, it sailed W.N.W., making again for the tropical zone. Although the summer sun was very strong, we did not suffer from heat, for at fifteen or twenty fathoms below the surface, the temperature did not rise above from ten to twelve degrees.

On December 15, we left to the east the bewitching group of the Societies and the graceful Tahiti, queen of the Pacific. I saw in the morning, some miles to the windward, the elevated summits of the island. These waters furnished our table with excellent fish, mackerel, bonitos, and albicores, and some varities of a sea-serpent called munirophis.[8]

[The *Nautilus* had travelled 8100 miles. And we had logged 9720 miles as we passed through the archipelago of Tonga-Tabou, where the crews of the *Argo,* the *Port-au-Prince,* and the *Duke of Portland* had perished, and the archipelago of Navigators, where Captain Langle, friend of La Pérouse, was killed. Then we sighted the archipelago of Viti, where savages had massacred both the crew of the *Union* and Captain Bureau, of Nantes, commander of the *Amiable Josephine.*

This archipelago extends over hundreds of leagues from north to south and ninety leagues from east to west. It lies between 6° and 2° south latitude and 174° and 179° west longitude. It consists of the islands of Viti-Levu, Vanoua-Levu, Kandubon, and other isles and reefs.

Tasman discovered this archipelago in 1643, the same year when Torricelli invented the barometer and Louis XIV ascended the throne. The reader may decide for himself which of these events benefitted humanity most. Then came Cook [9] in 1714, d'Entrecasteaux in 1793, and Dumont d'Urville in 1827, who unravelled the geography of this archipelago. The *Nautilus* moved in to the Bay of Wailea, where Captain Dillon, the first to throw light on the mystery of the La Pérouse wreck, had met with terrible adventures.

We dragged our nets across the bay repeatedly, collecting a large number of superb oysters. As Seneca had advised, we opened them at the table, and stuffed ourselves. These molluscs were from the species known as ostrea lamellosa, quite common in Corsican waters. The Wailea oyster beds must have been extensive. If they had not been controlled by various natural checks, these shell-fish would have filled the bay, since each oyster can produce up to 2,000,000 eggs.

If Ned suffered no gastric disturbances on that occasion, it was only because oysters are the only food that never causes indigestion. Indeed, a man would have to eat sixteen dozen of these acephalous molluscs in order to gain the 315 grammes of nitrogen he requires daily.]

On the 25th of December the *Nautilus* sailed into the midst of the New Hebrides, discovered by Quiros in 1606, and that Bougainville explored in 1768, and to which Cook gave its present name in 1773. This group is composed principally of nine large islands, that form a band of 120 leagues N.N.S. to S.S.W.,[10] between 15° and 2° south latitude, and 164° and 168° longitude. We passed tolerably near to the island of Aurou, that at noon looked like a mass of green woods, surmounted by a peak of great height.

That day being Christmas Day, Ned Land seemed to regret sorely the non-celebration of "Christmas," the family fête of which Protestants are so fond. I had not seen Captain Nemo for a week, when, on the morning of the 27th, he came into the large drawing-room, always seeming as if he had seen you five minutes before. I was busily tracing the route of the *Nautilus* on the planisphere. The Captain came up to me, put his finger on one spot on the chart and said this single word—

"Vanikoro."

The effect was magical! It was the name of the islands on which La Perouse had been lost! I rose suddenly.

"The *Nautilus* has brought us to Vanikoro?" I asked.

"Yes, Professor," said the Captain.

"And I can visit the celebrated island where the *Boussole* and the *Astrolabe* struck?"

"If you like, Professor."

"When shall we be there?"

"We are there now."

Followed by Captain Nemo, I went up on to the platform, and greedily scanned the horizon.

To the N.E. two volcanic islands emerged of unequal size, surrounded by a coral reef that measured forty miles in circumference. We were close to Vanikoro, really the one to which Dumont d'Urville gave the name of Isle de la Recherche, and exactly facing the little harbour of Vanou, situated

10. *N.N.S. to S.S.W.* Verne says *N.N.W. to S.S.E.*

11. *Mount Kapogo, 476 feet high*
Verne says *476 fathoms high,* or
2,856 feet.

12. *these two sloops* Verne says
corvettes, which can be translated as
corvettes or *sloops-of-war.* The difference is important in English. A corvette is rated as smaller than a frigate,
a sloop-of-war as larger than a gun-
boat.

in 16° 4′ south latitude, and 164° 32′ east longitude. The
earth seemed covered with verdure from the shore to the
summits in the interior, that were crowned by Mount Kapogo,
476 feet high.**11** The *Nautilus,* having passed the outer belt
of rocks by a narrow strait, found itself among breakers
where the sea was from thirty to forty fathoms deep. Under
the verdant shade of some mangroves I perceived some
savages, who appeared surprised at our approach. In the
long black body, moving between wind and water, did they
not see some formidable cetacean that they regarded with
suspicion?

Just then Captain Nemo asked me what I knew about the
wreck of La Perouse.

"Only what every one knows, Captain," I replied.

"And could you tell me what every one knows about it?" he
inquired, ironically.

"Easily."

I related to him all the last works of Dumont d'Urville had
made known—works from which the following is a brief
account.

La Perouse, and his second, Captain de Langle, were sent
by Louis XVI, in 1785, on a voyage of circumnavigation.
They embarked in the corvettes the *Boussole* and the
Astrolabe, neither of which were again heard of. In 1791,
the French Government, justly uneasy as to the fate of these
two sloops,**12** manned two large merchantmen, the *Recherche*
and the *Espérance,* which left Brest the 28th of September
under the command of Bruni d'Entrecasteaux.

Two months after, they learned from Bowen, commander
of the *Albemarle,* that the debris of shipwrecked vessels had
been seen on the coasts of New Georgia. But D'Entrecasteaux,
ignoring this communication—rather uncertain, besides—directed his course towards the Admiralty Isles, mentioned
in a report of Captain Hunter's as being the place where
La Perouse was wrecked.

They sought in vain. The *Espérance* and the *Recherche*
passed before Vanikoro without stopping there, and in fact,
this voyage was most disastrous, as it cost D'Entrecasteaux
his life, and those of two of his lieutenants, besides several of
his crew.

Captain Dillon, a shrewd old Pacific sailor, was the first to
find unmistakable traces of the wrecks. On the 15th of May,
1824, his vessel, the *St. Patrick,* passed close to Tikopia, one
of the New Hebrides. There a Lascar came alongside in a
canoe, sold him the handle of a sword in silver, that bore the

print of characters engraved on the hilt. The Lascar pretended that six years before, during a stay at Vanikoro, he had seen two Europeans that belonged to some vessels that had run aground on the reefs some years ago.

Dillon guessed that he meant La Perouse, whose disappearance had troubled the whole world. He tried to get on to Vanikoro, where, according to the Lascar, he would find numerous debris of the wreck, but winds and tide prevented him.

Dillon returned to Calcutta. There he interested the Asiatic Society and the Indian Company in his discovery. A vessel, to which was given the name of the *Recherche,* was put at his disposal, and he set out, January 23, 1827, accompanied by a French agent.

The *Recherche,* after touching at several points in the Pacific, cast anchor before Vanikoro, July 7, 1827, in that same harbour of Vanou where the *Nautilus* was at this time.

There it collected numerous relics of the wreck—iron utensils, anchors, pulley-strops, swivel-guns, an 18 lb.-shot, fragments of astronomical instruments, a piece of crownwork, and a bronze clock, bearing this inscription—*"Bazin m'a fait,"* 13 the mark of the foundry of the arsenal at Brest about 1785. There could be no further doubt.

Dillon, having made all inquiries, stayed in the unlucky place till October. Then he quitted Vanikoro, and directed his course towards New Zealand; put into Calcutta, April 7, 1828, and returned to France, where he was warmly welcomed by Charles X.

But at the same time, without knowing Dillon's movements, Dumont d'Urville had already set out to find the scene of the wreck. And they had learned from a whaler that some medals and a cross of St. Louis had been found in the hands of some savages of Louisiade and New Caledonia. Dumont d'Urville, commander of the *Astrolabe,* had then sailed, and two months after Dillon had left Vanikoro, he put into Hobart Town. There he learned the results of Dillon's inquiries, and found that a certain James Hobbs, second lieutenant of the *Union* of Calcutta, after landing on an island situated 8° 18′ south latitude, and 156° 30′ east longitude, had seen some iron bars and red stuffs 14 used by the natives of these parts. Dumont d'Urville, much perplexed, and not knowing how to credit the reports of low-class journals, decided to follow Dillon's track.

On the 10th of February, 1828, the *Astrolabe* appeared off Tikopia, and took as guide and interpreter a deserter found

13. *"Bazin m'a fait"* "Bazin made me."

14. *red stuffs* The natives were wearing red cloth.

on the island; made his way to Vanikoro, sighted it on the 12th inst., lay among the reefs until the 14th, and not until the 20th did he cast anchor within the barrier in the harbour of Vanou.

On the 23rd, several officers went round the island, and brought back some unimportant trifles. The natives, adopting a system of denials and evasions, refused to take them to the unlucky place. This ambiguous conduct led them to believe that the natives had ill-treated the castaways, and indeed they seemed to fear that Dumont d'Urville had come to avenge La Perouse and his unfortunate crew.

However, on the 26th, appeased by some presents, and understanding that they had no reprisals to fear, they led M. Jacquireot to the scene of the wreck.

There, in three or four fathoms of water, between the reefs of Pacou and Vanou, lay anchors, cannons, pigs of lead and iron, embedded in the limy concretions. The large boat and the whaler belonging to the *Astrolabe* were sent to this place, and, not without some difficulty, their crews hauled up an anchor weighing 1800 lbs., a brass gun, some pigs of iron and two copper swivel-guns.

Dumont d'Urville, questioning the natives, learned, too, that La Perouse, after losing both his vessels on the reefs of this island, had constructed a smaller boat, only to be lost a second time. Where?—no one knew.

[The Captain of the *Astrolabe* then built a memorial to the famous La Pérouse and his crew. This was a simple four-sided pyramid, set on a coral base, with no metal fittings to tempt the natives. Now Dumont d'Urville was all set to leave. But fever had undermined the health of the crew, and sick himself, he was not able to depart until March 17.]

But the French Government, fearing that Dumont d'Urville was not acquainted with Dillon's movements, had sent the sloop *Bayonnaise*,15 commanded by Legoarant de Tromelin, to Vanikoro, which had been stationed on the west coast of America. The *Bayonnaise* cast her anchor before Vanikoro some months after the departure of the *Astrolabe,* but found no new document; but stated that the savages had respected the monument to La Perouse. That is the substance of what I told to Captain Nemo.

"So," he said, "no one knows now where the third vessel perished that was constructed by the castaways on the island of Vanikoro?"

"No one knows."

Captain Nemo said nothing, but signed to me to follow

15. *the sloop Bayonnaise* Again, Verne calls it a *corvette.*

him into the large saloon. The *Nautilus* sank several yards below the waves, and the panels were opened.

I hastened to the aperture, and under the crustations of coral, covered with fungi, syphonules, alcyons, madrepores, through myriads of charming fish—girelles, glyphisidri, pompherides, diacopes, and holocentres—I recognised certain debris that the drags **16** had not been able to tear up—iron stirrups, anchors, cannons, bullets, capstan fittings, the stem of a ship, all objects clearly proving the wreck of some vessel, and now carpeted with living flowers. While I was looking on this desolate scene, Captain Nemo said, in a sad voice—

"Commander La Perouse set out December 7, 1785, with his vessels *La Boussole* and the *Astrolabe*. He first cast anchor at Botany Bay, visited the Friendly Isles, New Caledonia, then directed his course towards Santa Cruz, and put into Namouka, one of the Hapaï group. Then his vessels struck on the unknown reefs of Vanikoro. The *Boussole,* which went first, ran aground on the southerly coast. The *Astrolabe* went to its help, and ran aground too. The first vessel was destroyed almost immediately. The second, stranded under the wind, resisted some days. The natives made the castaways welcome. They installed themselves in the island, and constructed a smaller boat with the debris of the two large ones. Some sailors stayed willingly at Vanikoro; the others, weak and ill, set out with La Perouse. They directed their course towards the Solomon Isles, and there perished, with everything, on the westerly coast of the chief island of the group, between Capes Deception and Satisfaction."

"How do you know that?"

"By this, that I found on the spot where was the last wreck."

Captain Nemo showed me a tin-plate box, stamped with the French arms, and corroded by the salt water. He opened it, and I saw a bundle of papers, yellow but still readable.

They were the instructions of the naval minister to Commander La Perouse, annotated in the margin in Louis XVI.'s handwriting.

"Ah! it is a fine death for a sailor!" said Captain Nemo, at last. "A coral tomb makes a quiet grave; and I trust that I and my comrades will find no other."

16. *drags* The dredges that d'Urville had used.

Mollusk shells as pictured in the *Journal de Conchyliologie* (1853).

PART 1: CHAPTER XIX

Torres Straits[1]

1. *Chapter XIX: Torres Straits* Verne's title for this chapter (XX in his text) is typical of his ability to create suspense with a mere place name.

Since the 1600s, the phrase "Torres Strait" had, for the European mind, connoted the impenetrable mysteries of the South Pacific. Dutch explorers had tried in 1605–1606 to sail through these dangerous waters—between what we now call New Guinea and Australia—but the barrier reefs turned back many a navigator. In 1606 Luis Paz de Torres, in the only ship left of a fleet sent out by Philip III of Spain, discovered and named the Strait. He reported that the "desolate coasts" were inhabited by "wild, cruel, black savages" and that there were no commercial opportunities whatever in this region.

In 1644 Abel Janszoon Tasman, last in a series of Dutch East India Company captains to try these waters, actually reported that *there wasn't any Torres Strait*. It is no surprise then to read that Captain Cook is credited, in 1770, with the *re*discovery of the Torres Strait.

And so, for Verne's early readers, this chapter title promised dangerous adventure in exotic territory.

2. *1st of January, 1863* The *Nautilus* is not a time machine. How can Aronnax find himself back in 1863? The error is not Verne's—all French

During the night of the 27th or 28th of December, the *Nautilus* left the shores of Vanikoro with great speed. Her course was south-westerly, and in three days she had gone over the 750 leagues that separated it from La Perouse's group and the south-east point of Papua.

Early on the 1st of January, 1863,[2] Conseil joined me on the platform.

"Master, will you permit me to wish you a happy new year?"

"What! Conseil; exactly as if I were at Paris in my study at the Jardin des Plantes? Well, I accept your good wishes, and thank you for them. Only, I will ask you what you mean by a 'Happy new year,' under our circumstances? Do you mean the year that will bring us to the end of our imprisonment, or the year that sees us continue this strange voyage?"

"Really, I do not know how to answer, master. We are sure to see curious things, and for the last two months we have not had time for ennui. The last marvel is always the most astonishing; and if we continue this progression, I do not know how it will end. It is my opinion that we shall never again see the like."

["Never, Conseil."

"Furthermore, M. Nemo really does justice to his Latin name.[3] He could not trouble us less if he did not exist at all!"

"I agree, Conseil."]

"I think, then, with no offence to master, that a happy year would be one in which we could see everything."

["Seeing everything, Conseil, could take a long time. What does Master Land think of all this?"

"Ned Land thinks exactly the opposite of what I think.

He is a positive spirit with a demanding stomach. He is tired of looking at fish on his plate all the time. The lack of wine, bread, and meat does not suit the dignity of an Anglo-Saxon. He is accustomed to beefsteaks, brandy, and gin, in moderation, of course."

"And I, Conseil, find it easy to adjust to the diet on board."

"And so do I. I am as happy to stay on board as Master Land is to escape. If this new year is a bad one for me, it will be a good one for him, and vice-versa. No matter what happens, monsieur, someone will be pleased. But as for monsieur, I hope that *he* is the one who is pleased."

"Thank you, my boy. But a New Year's gift is impossible right now. A good handshake must suffice for this year! That is all I have to give!"

"Monsieur has never been more generous," Conseil said. And then he left me.]

On January 2, we had made 11,340 miles, or 5250 French leagues,[4] since our starting-point in the Japan Seas. Before the ship's head stretched the dangerous shores of the coral sea,[5] on the north-east coast of Australia. Our boat lay along some miles from the redoubtable bank on which Cook's vessel was lost,[6] June 10, 1770. The boat in which Cook was struck on a rock, and if it did not sink, it was owing to a piece of the coral that was broken by the shock, and fixed itself in the broken keel.[7]

I had wished to visit the reef, 360 leagues long, against which the sea, always rough, broke with great violence, with a noise like thunder. But just then the inclined planes drew the *Nautilus* down to a great depth, and I could see nothing of the high coral walls. I had to content myself with the different specimens of fish brought up by the nets. I remarked, among others, some germons, a species of mackerel as large as a tunny, with bluish sides, and striped with transverse bands, that disappeared with the animal's life.

These fish followed us in shoals, and furnished us with very delicate food. We took also a large number of giltheads, about one and a half inches long, tasting like dorys; and flying pyrapeds like submarine swallows, which, in dark nights, light alternately the air and water with their phosphorescent light. Among the molluscs and zoophytes, I found in the meshes of the net several species of alcyonarians, echini, hammers, spurs, dials, cerites, and hyalleae. The flora was represented by beautiful floating sea-weeds, laminariae, and macrocystes, impregnated with the mucilage that transudes through their pores; and among which I gathered an admirable *Nemastoma*

editions say 1868—and all "standard" English editions say 1863. The translator must himself have suffered a New Year's hangover the day he translated this passage, as witness the following:

(1) Verne speaks of the *night from the* 27th *to the* 28th; (2) he says that 750 leagues separate La Pérouse's group from southeast Papua; and (3) he says that Conseil asks his master's permission to wish *him* (not *you*) a happy new year in (4) 1868. The third point is important for reasons we stressed in Chapter III.

Now Lewis proceeds to omit a passage that sharpens the characterization of Conseil and Ned.

3. *his Latin name* The name Nemo has given himself means "no one" or "nobody." We discussed the Byronic significance of this name on page 65.

4. *or 5250 French leagues* Here we can see that Verne is reckoning a league as 2.16 miles.

5. *coral sea* Verne says *la mer de Corail,* the Coral Sea.

6. *Cook's vessel was lost* Verne says *almost* lost, and Verne is right; Cook eventually made his way back to England in this ship, the *Endeavour,* having circumnavigated the globe.

7. *fixed itself in the broken keel* On that memorable night of June 10, 1770, Captain Cook dumped six cannons overboard in a successful effort to lighten his ship.

On the memorable day of January 10, 1969, an expedition from the Philadelphia Academy of Natural Sciences recovered Cook's cannons. Virgil Kauffman and others flew a helicopter dragging a magnetometer through the area where they knew Cook had jettisoned the guns. When the magnetometer indicated the presence of metal, divers went down. They found the cannons, encrusted in coral, in sixty feet of water.

At least ten scientific expeditions of record had searched for them before Kauffman's crew arrived.

Geliniarois, that was classed among the natural curiosities of the museum.

Two days after crossing the coral sea, January 4, we sighted the Papuan coasts. On this occasion, Captain Nemo informed me that his intention was to get into the Indian Ocean by the Strait of Torres. His communication ended there. [Ned was pleased. This route would take him closer to European waters!

The Strait of Torres is regarded as dangerous not only because of its reefs but also because of the savages who live on its coasts. It separates New Holland from the large island of Papua, known also as New Guinea.8 Papua is 400 leagues long, 130 leagues wide, with a surface of 40,000 leagues. It lies between 0° 19′ and 10° 2′ south latitude, and between 128° 23′ and 146° 15′ east longitude. At midday, when the second in command was shooting the sun, I noticed the peaks of the Arfalx Mountains. They are very pointed and stand out prominently, one behind the other, at different levels.

This land was discovered in 1511 by the Portuguese Francisco Serrano. It was visited successively by Don José de Meneses in 1526, by Grijalva in 1527, by the Spanish general, Alvar de Saavedra in 1528, by Juigo Artez in 1545, by the Dutchman Shouten in 1616, by Nicolas Sruic in 1753, by Tasman, Dampier, Fumel, Carteret, Edwards, Bougain-

8. *New Holland from . . . New Guinea* That portion of Australia lying south of the Torres Strait was known originally to Europeans as New Holland. Papua lies to the north of the strait. The western half of Papua belongs to Indonesia. The eastern half, which had been held by Australia since 1906, became the independent nation of Papua New Guinea on September 16, 1975.

The *Zygaena malleus*, or hammerhead shark, should be easy for Conseil to classify. He will see it in nearly all deep warm seas, from the East Indies to the Mediterranean. Engraving from *The American Cyclopaedia* (1873).

ville, Cook, Forrest, MacClure, and d'Entrecasteaux in 1792, by Duperrey in 1823, and by Dumont d'Urville in 1827.

"This is the very heartland of the blacks who occupy the Malay Archipelago," M. de Rienzi has said. I did not doubt that this hazardous passage would bring me face to face with the redoubtable Andaman.

In short, the *Nautilus* was set to enter the world's most dangerous strait, one that even the most courageous navigators rarely attempt. Luis Paz de Torres braved it on his return to Melanesia from the South Seas. Dumont d'Urville nearly lost his battered corvettes there in 1840. And now the *Nautilus*, superior in facing all hazards of navigation, would negotiate these dreaded reefs.]

The Torres Straits are nearly thirty-four leagues wide; but they are obstructed by an innumerable quantity of islands, islets, breakers, and rocks, that make its navigation almost impracticable; so that Captain Nemo took all needful precautions to cross them. The *Nautilus*, floating betwixt wind and water, went at a moderate pace. Her screw, like a cetacean's tail, beat the waves slowly.

Profiting by this, I and my two companions went up on to the deserted platform. Before us was the steersman's cage, and I expected that Captain Nemo was there directing the course of the *Nautilus*. I had before me the excellent charts of the Strait of Torres made out by the hydrographical engineer Vincendon Dumoulin [and by Ensign Coupvent-Desbois, now an admiral]. These and Captain King's are the best charts that clear the intricacies of this strait, and I consulted them attentively. Round the *Nautilus* the sea dashed furiously. The course of the waves, that went from south-east to north-west at the rate of two and a half miles, broke on the coral that showed itself here and there.

"This is a bad sea!" remarked Ned Land.

"Detestable indeed, and one that does not suit a boat like the *Nautilus*."

"The captain must be very sure of his route, for I see there pieces of coral that would do for its keep if it only touched them slightly."

Indeed the situation was dangerous, but the *Nautilus* seemed to slide like magic off these rocks. It did not follow the routes of the *Astrolabe* and the *Zélée* exactly, for they proved fatal to Dumont d'Urville.[9] It bore more northwards, coasted the Island of Murray, and came back to the south-west towards Cumberland Passage. I thought it was going to pass it by, when, going back to the north-west, it went through

9. *fatal to Dumont d'Urville* Verne's word *fatal* was not meant to be taken literally here. His original readers knew well that Verne meant *disastrous*. Dumont's ships were badly damaged and almost destroyed in the Torres Strait, but they were able to return to France, arriving in Toulon on November 6, 1841. As Verne's audience was well aware, what proved to be literally fatal to Dumont was a railway accident half a year after his return.

10. *Island Sound . . . Canal Mauvais*
Of course there were no canals in that
part of the world. The French word
canal can mean *channel, irrigation
ditch, canal, strait,* or *duct;* context
provides the immediate sense. And
here context tells us that *le Canal
Mauvais* means *the Bad* or *Evil Channel.* The first island in question is
Tound Island.

Mercier Lewis's error here foreshadows a similar mistake that has
figured in science *non*fiction. In 1877
an Italian astronomer, G. V. Schia-
parelli, observed a network of lines
or *grooves* on the surface of Mars.
He reported them as *canali,* meaning,
in this context, *channels.* His word
was mistranslated as *canals.* The
English-speaking world, assuming canals could be made only by creatures
resembling human engineers, became
excited about "intelligent life on
Mars." Photographs sent back by
space probes suggest that the *canali*
are some sort of natural feature, perhaps rock faults.

11. *Island of Gilboa* The island
that Lewis calls *Gilboa* is actually
Gueboroar in the original.

12. *that I still saw* What Aronnax
says, in the French, is that *he can
still recall the appearance of the island
because of its remarkable fringe of
pandanus or screw-pines.*

13. *how it will be reinflated* The
Nautilus is no more a balloon than it
is a time machine. Read: *how it will
be refloated.*

a large quantity of islands and islets little known, towards
the Island Sound and Canal Mauvais.**10**

I wondered if Captain Nemo, foolishly imprudent, would
steer his vessel into that pass where Dumont d'Urville's two
corvettes touched; when, swerving again, and cutting straight
through to the west, he steered for the Island of Gilboa.**11**

It was then three in the afternoon. The tide began to re-
cede, being quite full. The *Nautilus* approached the island,
that I still saw,**12** with its remarkable border of screw-pines.
He stood off it at about two miles distant. Suddenly a shock
overthrew me. The *Nautilus* just touched a rock, and stayed
immovable, laying lightly to port side.

When I rose, I perceived Captain Nemo and his lieutenant
on the platform. They were examining the situation of the
vessel, and exchanging words in their incomprehensible
dialect.

She was situated thus:—Two miles, on the starboard side,
appeared Gilboa, stretching from north to west like an immense arm. Towards the south and east some coral showed
itself, left by the ebb. We had run aground, and in one of
those seas where the tides are middling,—a sorry matter for
the floating of the *Nautilus*. However, the vessel had not suffered, for her keel was solidly joined. But if she could neither
glide off nor move, she ran the risk of going for ever fastened
to these rocks, and then Captain Nemo's submarine vessel
would be done for.

I was reflecting thus, when the Captain, cool and calm,
always master of himself, approached me.

"An accident?" I asked.

"No; an incident."

"But an incident that will oblige you perhaps to become
an inhabitant of this land from which you flee?"

Captain Nemo looked at me curiously, and made a negative gesture, as much as to say that nothing would force him
to set foot on *terra firma* again. Then he said—

"Besides, M. Aronnax, the *Nautilus* is not lost; it will carry
you yet into the midst of the marvels of the ocean. Our voyage
is only begun, and I do not wish to be deprived so soon of
the honour of your company."

"However, Captain Nemo," I replied, without noticing the
ironical turn of his phrase, "the *Nautilus* ran aground in open
sea. Now the tides are not strong in the Pacific; and if you
cannot lighten the *Nautilus,* I do not see how it will be
reinflated." **13**

"The tides are not strong in the Pacific; you are right there,

Professor; but in Torres Straits, one finds still a difference of a yard and a half between the level of high and low seas. To-day is January 4, and in five days the moon will be full. Now, I shall be very much astonished if that complaisant satellite does not raise these masses of water sufficiently, and render me a service that I should be indebted for."

Having said this, Captain Nemo, followed by his lieutenant, re-descended to the interior of the *Nautilus*. As to the vessel, it moved not, and was immovable, as if the coralline polypi had already walled it up with their indestructible cement.

"Well, sir?" said Ned Land, who came up to me after the departure of the Captain.

"Well, friend Ned, we will wait patiently for the tide on the 9th instant; for it appears that the moon will have the goodness to put it off again."

"Really?"

"Really."

"And this Captain is not going to cast anchor **14** at all since the tide will suffice?" said Conseil, simply.

The Canadian looked at Conseil, then shrugged his shoulders.

"Sir, you may believe me when I tell you that this piece of iron will navigate neither on nor under the sea again; it is only fit to be sold for its weight. I think, therefore, that the time has come to part company with Captain Nemo."

"Friend Ned, I do not despair of this stout *Nautilus,* as you do; and in four days we shall know what to hold to on the Pacific tides. Besides, flight might be possible if we were in sight of the English or Provençal coasts; but on the Papuan shores, it is another thing; and it will be time enough to come to that extremity if the *Nautilus* does not recover itself again, which I look upon as a grave event."

"But do they know, at least, how to act circumspectly? **15** There is an island; on that island there are trees; under those trees, terrestrial animals, bearers of cutlets and roast-beef, to which I would willingly give a trial."

"In this, friend Ned is right," said Conseil, "and I agree with him. Could not master obtain permission from his friend Captain Nemo to put us on land, if only so as not to lose the habit of treading on the solid parts of our planet?"

"I can ask him, but he will refuse."

"Will master risk it?" asked Conseil, "and we shall know how to rely upon the Captain's amiability."

To my great surprise Captain Nemo gave me the permission I asked for, and he gave it very agreeably, without even

"*. . . This Captain is not going to cast anchor . . . ?*" The common wrought-iron anchor of the 1870s, as it was pictured in *The American Cyclopaedia* (1873): "It is evident from the direction of the strain that any forward movement will cause the lower fluke and arm to be buried still deeper in the earth." The fluke is the triangular blade at the end of the curved arm.

14. *not going to cast anchor* In the original, Ned says: *"And the Captain isn't going to put down his anchors, connect the chains to his engines, and try to pull himself off the reef?"*

In other words, Ned, drawing on his own sea experience, wants to know why Nemo doesn't use a simple system of winches. And Conseil answers:

"Why go to all that trouble, if the tide will get us off?"

15. *how to act circumspectly* What Ned says, in the original, is: *"But can't we at least get the lay of the land?"*

exacting from me a promise to return to the vessel; but flight across New Guinea might be very perilous, and I should not have counselled Ned Land to attempt it. Better to be a prisoner on board the *Nautilus* than to fall into the hands of the natives. [The dinghy was put at our disposal for the following morning. I did not ask whether Captain Nemo would go along. I imagined that none of the crew would be assigned to us, but that Ned Land would be put in charge. The island was only two miles away. It would be an easy task for the Canadian to steer the dinghy between reefs so fatal to larger vessels. The next day, January 5, the dinghy was detached from the platform and launched into the sea. Two men sufficed for this operation. The oars were in the boat. We had only to take our seats.]

At eight o'clock, armed with guns and hatchets, we got off the *Nautilus*. The sea was pretty calm; a slight breeze blew on land. Conseil and I rowing, we sped along quickly, and Ned steered in the straight passage that the breakers left between them. The boat was well handled, and moving rapidly.

Ned Land could not restrain his joy. He was like a prisoner that had escaped from prison, and knew not that it was necessary to re-enter it.

"Meat! We are going to eat some meat; and what meat!" he replied. "Real game! No, bread, indeed. **16**

"I do not say that fish is not good; we must not abuse it; but a piece of fresh venison, grilled on live coals, will agreeably vary our ordinary course."

"Gourmand!" said Conseil, "he makes my mouth water."

"It remains to be seen," I said, "if these forests are full of game, and if the game is not such as will hunt the hunter himself."

"Well said, M. Aronnax," replied the Canadian, whose teeth seemed sharpened like the edge of a hatchet; "but I will eat tiger—loin of tiger—if there is no other quadruped on this island."

"Friend Ned is [making me] uneasy about it," said Conseil.

"Whatever it may be," continued Ned Land, "every animal with four paws without feathers, or with two paws without feathers, will be saluted by my first shot." **17**

"Very well! Master Land's imprudences are beginning."

"Never fear, M. Aronnax," replied the Canadian; "I do not want twenty-five minutes to offer you a dish of my sort."

At half-past eight the *Nautilus* boat ran softly aground, on a heavy sand, after having happily passed the coral reef that surrounds the Island of Gilboa.

16. *No, bread, indeed*   Ned's meaning, in the original, is: *"Still no bread, though."*

17. *by my first shot*   Of course, what Ned really says is: *". . . any animal with four legs and without feathers, or with two legs and with feathers. . . ."*

PART 1: CHAPTER XX[1]
A Few Days on Land

I was much impressed on touching land. Ned Land tried the soil with his feet, as if to take possession of it. However, it was only two months before that we had become, according to Captain Nemo, "passengers on board the *Nautilus*," but in reality, prisoners of its commander.

In a few minutes we were within musket-shot of the coast.[2] The soil was almost entirely madreporical, but certain beds of dried-up torrents, strewn with debris of granite, showed that this island was of the primary formation.[3] The whole horizon was hidden behind a beautiful curtain of forests. Enormous trees, the trunks of which attained a height of 200 feet, were tied to each other by garlands of bindweed, real natural hammocks, which a light breeze rocked. They were mimosas, ficuses, casuarinae, teks,[4] hibisci, and palm-trees, mingled together in profusion; and under the shelter of their verdant vault grew orchids, leguminous plants, and ferns.

But without noticing all these beautiful specimens of Papuan flora, the Canadian abandoned the agreeable for the useful. He discovered a cocoa-tree, beat down some of the fruit, broke them, and we drunk the milk and ate the nut, with a satisfaction that protested against the ordinary food on the *Nautilus*.

"Excellent!" said Ned Land.

"Exquisite!" replied Conseil.

"And I do not think," said the Canadian, "that he would object to our introducing a cargo of cocoa-nuts on board."

"I do not think he would, but he would not taste them."

"So much the worse for him," said Conseil.

"And so much the better for us," replied Ned Land. "There will be more for us."

"One word only, Master Land," I said to the harpooner,

1. *Chapter XX* In Mercier Lewis's numbers game, read *Chapter XXI*.

2. *within musket-shot of the coast* They have moved inland so fast that they are already a gunshot away from the shore!

3. *primary formation* Aronnax establishes the fact that the island is of the *primordial* (not "primary") formation.

.4. *ficuses . . . teks* The *ficuses* are the kind of "rubber plant" so popular as house plants, not the kind from which we get commercial rubber. *Teks*—as the word appears in most editions of the "standard translation" —is French for *teaks*.

Chance rewarded our search for eatable vegetables, and one of the most useful products of the tropical zones furnished us with precious food that we missed on board. The breadfruit tree as pictured in The American Cyclopaedia *(1873).*

5. bread-fruit . . . cultivated with success The *Artocarpus altilis* tree has played a dramatic role in world history and in popular literature.

After Captain James Cook saw the breadfruit tree in the Pacific Islands, he recommended that it be transplanted to the New World to supply foodstuff for Negro slaves. The task fell to Captain William Bligh and his 220-ton H.M.S. *Bounty.* But, as readers of sea lore know by heart, after the *Bounty* had sailed from Tahiti as far as the Friendly Islands, on April 28, 1789, part of the crew mutinied. Bligh and eighteen others were set adrift in an open boat. In one of the great sagas of the sea, they actually managed to travel 4000 miles to safety in Timor. Bligh made a second voyage to Tahiti in 1792 and this time successfully transplanted the breadfruit to the West Indies. The tree failed to live up to its expectations as slave fodder because the Negroes preferred bananas and plantains.

Nevertheless, *Artocarpus* has flourished from Mexico to Brazil, where it grows in dooryards and where its "fruit" sells in the markets.

As Verne's description makes clear, breadfruit is not "fruit" in the usual

who was beginning to ravage another cocoa-nut tree. "Cocoa-nuts are good things, but before filling the canoe with them it would be wise to reconnoitre and see if the island does not produce some substance not less useful. Fresh vegetables would be welcome on board the *Nautilus.*"

"Master is right," replied Conseil; "and I propose to reserve three places in our vessel, one for fruits, the other for vegetables, and the third for venison, of which I have not yet seen the smallest specimen."

"Conseil, we must not despair," said the Canadian.

"Let us continue," I returned, "and lie in wait. Although the island seems uninhabited, it might still contain some individuals that would be less hard than we on the nature of game."

"Ho! ho!" said Ned Land, moving his jaws significantly.

"Well, Ned!" cried Conseil.

"My word!" returned the Canadian, "I begin to understand the charms of anthropophagy."

"Ned! Ned! what are you saying? You, a man-eater, I should not feel safe with you, especially as I share your cabin. I might perhaps wake one day to find myself half devoured."

"Friend Conseil, I like you much, but not enough to eat you unnecessarily."

"I would not trust you," replied Conseil. "But enough. We must absolutely bring down some game to satisfy this cannibal, or else one of these fine mornings, master will find only pieces of his servant to serve him."

While we were talking thus, we were penetrating the sombre arches of the forest, and for two hours we surveyed it in all directions.

Chance rewarded our search for eatable vegetables, and one of the most useful products of the tropical zones furnished us with precious food that we missed on board. I would speak of the bread-fruit **5** tree, very abundant in the Island of Gilboa; and I remarked chiefly the variety destitute of seeds, which bears in Malaya the name of "rima." [This tree was distinguished by its straight trunk and its height, about forty feet. Its top was rounded gracefully and composed of large, multi-lobed leaves. This made it easy for the naturalist to identify it as the artocarpus, which has been cultivated with success **5** in the Mascarene Islands in the Indian Ocean. Big globe-shaped fruit, about four inches across, with hexagonal wrinkles on the outside rind, hung down from heavy foliage. This useful vegetable has been a godsend in areas that lack wheat, for without requiring any special attention, it provides fruit for eight months out of twelve.]

Ned Land knew these fruits well. He had already eaten many during his numerous voyages, and he knew how to prepare the eatable substance. Moreover, the sight of them excited him, and he could contain himself no longer.

"Master," he said, "I shall die if I do not taste a little of this bread-fruit pie."

"Taste it, friend Ned—taste it as you want. We are here to make experiments—make them."

"It won't take long," said the Canadian.

And provided with a lentil, he lighted a fire **6** of dead wood, that crackled joyously. During this time, Conseil and I chose the best fruits of the artocarpus. Some had not then attained a sufficient degree of maturity; and their thick skin covered a white but rather fibrous pulp. Others, the greater number yellow and gelatinous, waited only to be picked.

These fruits enclosed no kernel. Conseil brought a dozen to Ned Land, who placed them on a coal-fire, after having cut them in thick slices, and while doing this repeating—

"You will see, master, how good this bread is. More so when one has been deprived of it so long. It is not even bread," added he, "but a delicate pastry. You have eaten one, master?"

"No, Ned."

"Very well, prepare yourself for a juicy thing. If you do not come for more, I am no longer the king of harpooners."

After some minutes, the part of the fruits that was exposed to the fire was completely roasted. The interior looked like a white pastry, a sort of soft crumb, the flavour of which was like that of an artichoke.

It must be confessed this bread was excellent, and I ate of it with great relish.

["Too bad," I said, "bread-fruit will not keep. So there is not much point in taking a supply back on board."

"What!" said Ned incredulously. "You are talking like a naturalist. But I am going to act like a baker. Conseil, let us collect some of this fruit and we will pick it up on our way back."

"And how are you going to preserve them?" I asked.

"From the pulp I can ferment a paste that will keep indefinitely," Ned said. "When I get a yen for some, I will cook it in the galley. It will have a slightly acid taste, but I like it."

"And this food makes a dish all by itself?"

sense of the word. It must be cooked —boiled or baked. It is tasteless by itself, but served with butter, salt, or gravy it is palatable. It is a staple food in the South Pacific. Its inner bark provides a fiber from which cloth can be made; its wood is used for canoes and furniture, and the viscous milky juice that can be tapped out of the living trunk can serve as glue and caulking material.

6. *with a lentil, he lighted a fire* Verne means a *lens,* of course. In Latin the word *lens* originally meant a *lentil,* an annual plant with a seed that is round and flattened. With development of the double-convex glass used as a "magnifying glass" or a "burning glass," the new instrument was called a *lens* because its shape resembles the *lentil.* The French word *lentille* is used for both meanings.

"*. . . You have to eat it with real fruit, or at least with vegetables.*" Breadfruit as pictured in *The American Cyclopaedia* (1873).

7. *impressed with Ned's ability* Verne's early readers in English were deprived of many passages—like these we have restored—in which Verne glorifies man's ingenuity in the face of nature. And so English and American readers have not had a true picture of Ned's worth. He emerges now as a man who does more than crave meat and liquor. He exults in his ability to combine brainwork with brawn. He is happiest when facing situations that challenge the total unified man. He is amused when Aronnax talks *only* like a *naturalist,* while he, Ned, can serve as harpooner and baker and cook and quartermaster and woodsman *and!* Verne and his readers had great admiration for this kind of person. Ned is a zesty version of Daniel Defoe's Robinson Crusoe and of characters in numerous works like Johann David Wyss's *The Swiss Family Robinson.* Verne tells the Crusoe story over and over again, not only in scenes like *A Few Days on Land* but in whole novels like *The Mysterious Island.*

"No, you have to eat it with real fruit, or at least with vegetables."

When we had collected a supply of bread-fruit, we set out to find other foods. And not in vain. By noon we had picked an ample supply of bananas. These delicious products of the torrid zones ripen all year long. Malaysians call them "pisant" and eat them uncooked. We also picked some big jack-fruit, which has a strong taste, juicy mangoes, and huge pine-apples. This took time but we didn't regret that a bit.

Conseil kept his eye on Ned. The harpooner led the way, selecting the fruits he needed to complete his menu.

"Well," Conseil asked, "is this not enough?"

"Hum!" said the Canadian.

"What! You can still complain!"

"These vegetables do not make a meal. They are just the trimmings. We need soup and a roast!"

"Ned did promise us some cutlets," I recalled, "but I do not think we will find them."

"Professor," Ned said, "the hunt cannot be over when it has not even begun. We are sure to run across some flesh or fowl some place."

"If not today, then tomorrow," Conseil added. "But we must not go too far. I think we should get back to the boat."

"Why? So soon!" Ned cried.

"We should get back before nightfall," I said.]

"What time is it now?" asked the Canadian.

"Two o'clock at least," replied Conseil.

"How time flies on firm ground!" sighed Ned Land.

"Let us be off," replied Conseil.

We returned through the forest, and completed our collection by a raid upon the cabbage-palms, that we gathered from the tops of the trees, little beans that I recognized as the "abrou" of the Malays, and yams of a superior quality.

We were loaded when we reached the boat. But Ned Land did not find his provision sufficient. Fate, however, favoured us. Just as we were pushing off, he perceived several trees, from twenty-five to thirty feet high, a species of palm-tree. These trees, as valuable as the artocarpus, justly are reckoned among the most useful products of Malaya. [Called sago-palms, they grow wild. Like blackberry bushes, they multiply by means of sprouts and berries.

I was impressed with Ned's ability **7** to work with trees. Wielding his axe with great vigour, he felled two or three of these sago-palms. I could tell their maturity from the white dust on their leaves.

More as a naturalist than as a hungry man, I watched him at work. He was stripping bands of bark off each trunk. This bark was about an inch thick, and was covered with long fibres which were knotted and held together by a kind of glutenous flour. This was the sago flour, a common food among Malayans.

Ned was content for the moment to cut the trunks into small logs, as though he were collecting firewood. But later he would extract the flour and sift it through cloth to separate it from its fibres. Then he would dry it in the sun, letting it harden into little balls.]

At last, at five o'clock in the evening, loaded with our riches, we quitted the shore, and half an hour after we hailed the *Nautilus*. No one appeared on our arrival. The enormous ironplated cylinder seemed deserted. The provisions embarked, I descended to my chamber, and after supper slept soundly.

. . . Reckoned among the most useful products of Malaya. Called sago palms, they grow wild. . . . Engraving from *The American Cyclopaedia* (1873).

The next day, January 6, nothing new on board. Not a sound inside, not a sign of life. The boat rested along the edge, in the same place in which we had left it. We resolved to return to the island. Ned Land hoped to be more fortunate than on the day before with regard to the hunt, and wished to visit another part of the forest.

At dawn we set off. The boat, carried on by the waves that flowed to shore, reached the island in a few minutes.

We landed, and thinking that it was better to give in to the Canadian, we followed Ned Land, whose long limbs threatened to distance us. He wound up the coast towards the west: then, fording some torrents, he gained the high plain that was bordered with admirable forests. Some kingfishers were rambling along the water-courses, but they would not let themselves be approached. Their circumspection proved to me that these birds knew what to expect from bipeds of our species, and I concluded that, if the island was not inhabited, at least human beings occasionally frequented it.

After crossing a rather large prairie, we arrived at the skirts of a little wood that was enlivened by the songs and flight of a large number of birds.

"There are only birds," said Conseil.

"But they are eatable," replied the harpooner.

"I do not agree with you, friend Ned, for I see only parrots there."

"Friend Conseil," said Ned, gravely, "the parrot is like pheasant to those who have nothing else."

"And," I added, "this bird, suitably prepared, is worth knife and fork."

Indeed, under the thick foliage of this wood, a world of parrots were flying from branch to branch, only needing a careful education to speak the human language. For the moment, they were chattering with parrots **8** of all colours, and grave cockatoos, who seemed to meditate upon some philosophical problem, whilst brilliant red lories passed like a piece of bunting carried away by the breezes; papuans, with the finest azure colours, and in all a variety of winged things most charming to behold, but few eatable.

However, a bird peculiar to these lands, and which has never passed the limits of the Arrow and Papuan islands, was wanting in this collection. But fortune reserved it for me before long.

After passing through a moderately thick copse, we found a plain obstructed with bushes. I saw then those magnificent birds, the disposition of whose long feathers obliges them to fly against the wind. Their undulating flight, graceful aerial curves, and the shading of their colours, attracted and charmed one's looks. I had no trouble in recognising them.

"Birds of paradise!" I exclaimed.

["Order of sparrows, section of clystomores," Conseil added.

"Family of partridges?" inquired Ned.

"I do not believe so," I said. "But Master Land, I am counting on you to get one of these charming products of the tropics!"

"I will try, Professor. But I am really better with harpoons than with guns."]

The Malays, who carry on a great trade in these birds with the Chinese, have several means that we could not employ for taking them. Sometimes they put snares at the top of high trees that the birds of paradise prefer to frequent. Sometimes they catch them with a viscous birdlime that paralyses their movements. They even go so far as to poison the fountains that the birds generally drink from. But we were obliged to fire at them during flight, which gave us few chances to bring them down; and indeed, we vainly exhausted one half of our ammunition.

About eleven o'clock in the morning, the first range of mountains that form the centre of the island was traversed, and we had killed nothing. Hunger drove us on. The hunters had relied on the products of the chase, and they were wrong. Happily Conseil, to his great surprise, made a double shot and

8. *chattering with parrots* Verne's sense here is that the *parrots* were chattering with *parakeets*.

The Greater Paradise Bird—described by Aronnax as one of *those magnificent birds, the disposition of whose long feathers obliges them to fly against the wind*—as pictured in *The American Cyclopaedia* (1873).

secured breakfast. He brought down a white pigeon and a wood-pigeon, which, cleverly plucked and suspended from a skewer, was roasted before a red fire of dead wood. Whilst these interesting birds were cooking, Ned prepared the fruit of the artocarpus. Then the wood-pigeons were devoured to the bones, and declared excellent. The nutmeg, with which they are in the habit of stuffing their crops, flavours their flesh and renders it delicious eating.

["As delicious as if they had been stuffed with truffles," remarked Conseil.]

"Now, Ned, what do you miss now?"

"Some four-footed game, M. Aronnax. All these pigeons are only side-dishes, and trifles; and until I have killed an animal with cutlets, I shall not be content."

"Nor I, Ned, if I do not catch a bird of paradise."

"Let us continue hunting," replied Conseil. "Let us go towards the sea. We have arrived at the first declivities of the mountains, and I think we had better regain the region of forests."

That was sensible advice, and was followed out. After walking for one hour, we had attained a forest of sago-trees. Some inoffensive serpents glided away from us. The birds of paradise fled at our approach, and truly I despaired of getting near one, when Conseil, who was walking in front, suddenly bent down, uttered a triumphal cry, and came back to me bringing a magnificent specimen.

"Ah! bravo, Conseil!"

"Master is very good."

"No, my boy; you have made an excellent stroke. Take one of these living birds, and carry it in your hand."

"If master will examine it, he will see that I have not deserved great merit."

"Why, Conseil?"

"Because this bird is as drunk as a quail."

"Drunk!"

"Yes, sir; drunk with the nutmegs that it devoured under the nutmeg-tree, under which I found it. See, friend Ned, see the awful effects of intemperance!"

"By Jove!" exclaimed the Canadian, "because I have drunk gin 9 for two months, you must needs reproach me!"

However, I examined the curious bird. Conseil was right. The bird, drunk with the juice, was quite powerless. It could not fly; it could hardly walk.

This bird belonged to the most beautiful of the eight species that are found in Papua and in the neighbouring islands. It

9. *because I have drunk gin* In the original, Ned's retort is much more ironic, for of course on board the *Nautilus* he has been unable to get any gin at all. A better rendering would be:

"The devil! You surely have good grounds for reproaching me, considering all the gin I've consumed these past two months."

was the "large emerald bird, the most rare kind." It measured three feet in length. Its head was comparatively small, its eyes placed near the opening of the beak, and also small. But the shades of colour were beautiful, having a yellow beak, brown feet and claws, nut-coloured wings with purple tips, pale yellow at the back of the neck and head, and emerald colour at the throat, chestnut on the breast and belly. Two horned downy nets rose from below the tail, that prolonged the long feathers of admirable fineness, and they completed the whole of this marvellous bird, that the natives have poetically named the "bird of the sun."

[I regretted not being able to take this bird back to the Paris Museum, which did not have a single live specimen.

"Are they so rare?" Ned spoke as a hunter who does not think of game from the aesthetic point of view.

"Very rare, Ned, and hard to capture alive. But even dead they command a good price on the market. Natives often make fake ones, just as people make fake pearls or diamonds."

"What, they make fake birds of paradise!" exclaimed Conseil. "Does monsieur know how they do it?"

"Yes. During the monsoon season, birds of paradise lose these magnificent feathers around their tails—we naturalists call them *plumes subalaires*. A counterfeiter will pick up these feathers, kill a partridge, attach these feathers to the partridge, sew up the wounds, varnish the end product, and sell it to a European museum or collector."

"Well," said easy-going Ned, "if the museum does not get the whole bird, at least they get the real genuine feathers!"]

The bird, drunk with the juice, . . . could not fly; it could hardly walk. Engraving from the original edition (1870).

But if my wishes were satisfied by the possession of the bird of paradise, the Canadian's were not yet. Happily about two o'clock Ned Land brought down a magnificent hog, from the brood of those the natives call "barioutang." The animal came in time for us to procure real quadruped meat, and he was well received. Ned Land was very proud of his shot. The hog, hit by the electric ball, fell stone dead. The Canadian skinned and cleaned it properly, after having taken half-a-dozen cutlets, destined to furnish us with a grilled repast in the evening. Then the hunt was resumed, which was still more marked by Ned and Conseil's exploits.

Indeed, the two friends, beating the bushes, roused a herd of kangaroos, that fled and bounded along on their elastic paws. But these animals did not take flight so rapidly but what the electric capsule could stop their course.

"Ah, Professor!" cried Ned Land, who was carried away by the delights of the chase, "what excellent game, and stewed too! What a supply for the *Nautilus!* two! three! five down! And to think that we shall eat that flesh, and that the idiots on board shall not have a crumb!"

I think that, in the excess of his joy, the Canadian, if he had not talked so much, would have killed them all. But he contented himself with a single dozen of these interesting marsupians, ["which," Conseil noted, "constitute the first order of aplacental mammals"]. These animals were small. They were a species of those "kangaroo rabbits" that live habitually in the hollows of trees, and whose speed is extreme; but they are moderately fat, and furnish, at least, estimable food. We were very satisfied with the results of the hunt. Happily Ned proposed to return to this enchanting island the next day, for he wished to depopulate it of all the eatable quadrupeds. But he reckoned without his host.

At six o'clock in the evening we had regained the shore, our boat was moored to the usual place. The *Nautilus,* like a long rock, emerged from the waves two miles from the beach. Ned Land, without waiting, occupied himself about the important dinner business. He understood all about cooking well. The "barioutang," grilled on the coals, soon scented the air with a delicious odour.

[Was I catching the contagious enthusiasm of this Canadian? Was I truly euphoric at the sight of fresh-grilled pork? May I be forgiven, as I forgave Ned Land, and for the same reasons!]

Indeed, the dinner was excellent. Two wood-pigeons completed this extraordinary *menu.* The sago pasty, the artocarpus bread, some mangoes, half-a-dozen pine-apples, and the liquor fermented from some cocoa-nuts, overjoyed us. I even think that my worthy companions' ideas had not all the plainness desirable.

"Suppose we do not return to the *Nautilus* this evening?" said Conseil.

"Suppose we never return?" added Ned Land.

Just then a stone fell at our feet, and cut short the harpooner's proposition.

Mollusk shells as pictured in the *Journal de Conchyliologie* (1853).

PART 1: CHAPTER XXI[1]

Captain Nemo's Thunderbolt

1. *Chapter XXI* As Verne conceived it, Chapter XXII.

2. *the name of aerolites* *Aërolite* and *aërolith* were names commonly used in Verne's day for *stony meteorites*. And *aerolithology* is the science that deals with meteorites.

3. *apes? . . . Very nearly—they are savages* This chapter's dialogue perfectly sums up Verne's contradictory feelings about the colored peoples. Here Conseil says in effect that *these savages are close to the apes.* But in the next scene, Nemo will have the best answer to that kind of racism:

> *"Where does one not meet savages? And in any case, are these people whom you call savages any worse than those in any other land?"*

Verne's ambivalence about these questions is beautifully treated in Jean Chesneaux's *The Political and Social Ideas of Jules Verne* (1971). Chesneaux says that, at one extreme, Verne's writings "naively reflect the racist, ethnocentric prejudices that provided easy rationalization for colonial expansion and pillage of colonial lands." At the other extreme, Chesneaux finds Verne's novels "redolent of 18th-century idealist views about the superiority of a 'state of nature'" with its "noble savage."

Verne's self-contradictions begin in

We looked at the edge of the forest without rising, my hand stopping in the action of putting it to my mouth, Ned Land's completing its office.

"Stones do not fall from the sky," remarked Conseil, "or they would merit the name of aerolites." [2]

A second stone, carefully aimed, that made a savoury pigeon's leg fall from Conseil's hand, gave still more weight to his observation. We all three arose, shouldered our guns, and were ready to reply to any attack.

"Are they apes?" cried Ned Land.

"Very nearly—they are savages." [3]

"To the boat!" I said, hurrying to the sea.

It was indeed necessary to beat a retreat, for about twenty natives armed with bows and slings, appeared on the skirts of a copse that masked the horizon to the right, hardly a hundred steps from us.

Our boat was moored about sixty feet from us. The savages approached us, not running, but making hostile demonstrations. Stones and arrows fell thickly.

Ned Land had not wished to leave his provisions; and, in spite of his imminent danger, his pig on one side, and kangaroos on the other, he went tolerably fast. In two minutes we were on the shore. To load the boat with provisions and arms, to push it out to sea, and ship the oars, was the work of an instant. We had not gone two cable lengths, when a hundred savages, howling and gesticulating, entered the water up to their waists. I watched to see if their apparition would attract some men from the *Nautilus* on to the platform. But no. The enormous machine, lying off, was absolutely deserted.

Twenty minutes later we were on board. The panels were open. After making the boat fast, we entered into the interior of the *Nautilus*.

I descended to the drawing-room, from whence I heard some chords. Captain Nemo was there, bending over his organ, and plunged in a musical ecstasy.

"Captain!"

He did not hear me.

"Captain!" I said again, touching his hand.

He shuddered, and turning round, said, "Ah! it is you, Professor? Well, have you had a good hunt, have you botanised successfully?"

"Yes, Captain; but we have unfortunately brought a troop of bipeds, whose vicinity troubles me."

"What bipeds?"

"Savages."

"Savages!" he echoed, ironically. "So you are astonished, Professor, at having set foot on a strange land and finding savages? Savages! where are there not any? Besides, are they worse than others, these whom you call savages?"

"But, Captain——"

["All I can say, Professor, is that savages are to be found everywhere."]

"But Captain, unless you wish to entertain them on the *Nautilus,* you had better take some precautionary measures."

"Relax, M. Aronnax, there is nothing to worry about."

"But they are so numerous!"]

"How many have you counted?"

"A hundred at least."

"M. Aronnax," replied Captain Nemo, placing his fingers on the organ stops, "when all the natives of Papua are assembled on this shore, the *Nautilus* will have nothing to fear from their attacks."

The Captain's fingers were then running over the keys of the instrument, and I remarked that he touched only the black keys, which gave to his melodies an essentially Scotch character. Soon he had forgotten my presence, and had plunged into a reverie that I did not disturb. I went up again on to the platform:—night had already fallen; for, in this low latitude, the sun sets rapidly and without twilight. I could only see the island indistinctly; but the numerous fires, lighted on the beach, showed that the natives did not think of leaving it. I was alone for several hours, sometimes thinking of the natives, —but without any dread of them, for the imperturbable confidence of the Captain was catching,—sometimes forgetting

his very first novel, *Five Weeks in a Balloon* (1863). In one passage "a whole collection of blacks" is described as being "as naturally imitative as monkeys." In still other passages, some Africans are viewed as noble and proud, while Dr. Samuel Ferguson, the hero, says:

"Who knows that this country may not some day become the center of civilization!"

Often Verne's scorn for African and Pacific natives seems directed mainly at their ruling classes. In *Propeller Island* (1895), for example, he describes the Polynesian notion of *taboo* as "laws invented by the strong for use against the weak, by the rich against the poor. . . ."

Verne's basic conflict was painful; but, with benefit of hindsight, it is easy for us to comprehend it. He was on the side of "progress" which in his day meant exploitation of nature by scientific technology for the good of all mankind. He saw nonindustrialized lands as "progressive" to the extent that they welcomed the white man's technology and commerce. And so wherever "primitive" peoples clung to their own way of life, Verne would be likely to see them as willfully standing in the way of progress.

The more we read Verne, the more we see him tiptoeing around the problem. In *Around the World in 80 Days* (1873), he scorns the backwardness of the Sioux Indians. In *The Mysterious Island* (1875), he pities the people of India for their "ignorance and superstition" which led them to "rebel against their English rulers who had brought them out of anarchy and misery." Yet in *César Cascabel* (1890), Verne can admire the Eskimos for "the most perfect equality that prevails among them."

them to admire the splendours of the night in the tropics. My remembrances went to France, in the train of those zodiacal stars that would shine in some hours' time. The moon shone in the midst of the constellations of the zenith.

[Then I remembered that the day after to-morrow this helpful satellite would reappear, raise these waters, and extricate the *Nautilus* from this coral reef. At midnight all seemed calm beneath the trees on shore and on the dusky surface of the sea. I went to my cabin and fell into a deep sleep.]

The night slipped away without any mischance, the islanders frightened no doubt at the sight of a monster aground in the bay. The panels were open, and would have offered an easy access to the interior of the *Nautilus*.

At six o'clock in the morning of the 8th of January, I went up on to the platform. The dawn was breaking. The island soon showed itself through the dissipating fogs, first the shore, then the summits.

The natives were there, more numerous than on the day before—500 or 600 perhaps—some of them, profiting by the low water, had come on to the coral, at less than two cable lengths from the *Nautilus*. I distinguished them easily; they were true Papuans, with athletic figures, men of good race, large high foreheads, large, but not broad and flat, and white teeth. Their woolly hair, with a reddish tinge, showed off on their black shining bodies like those of the Nubians. From the lobes of their ears, cut and distended, hung chaplets of bones. Most of these savages were naked. Amongst them, I remarked some women, dressed from the hips to knees in quite a crinoline of herbs, that sustained a vegetable waistband. Some chiefs had ornamented their necks with a crescent and collars of glass beads, red and white; nearly all were armed with bows, arrows, and shields, and carried on their shoulders a sort of net containing those round stones which they cast from their slings with great skill. One of these chiefs, rather near to the *Nautilus*, examined it attentively. He was, perhaps, a "mado" of high rank, for he was draped in a mat of banana leaves, notched round the edges, and set off with brilliant colours.

I could easily have knocked down this native, who was within a short length; but I thought it was better to wait for real hostile demonstrations. Between Europeans and savages, it is proper for the Europeans to parry sharply, not to attack.[4]

During low water the natives roamed about near the *Nautilus*, but were not troublesome; I heard them frequently repeat

4. *parry sharply, not to attack* Here Verne gives us a good example of the sanctimonious European attitudes so prevalent in his day. For a European like Aronnax to say, at this point, that he will be noble and *only parry, not attack* is hypocritical. As the natives see it, the very presence of Europeans on the natives' land is already an aggression. The colonialist view, of course, is that as soon as the native counterattacks, it is he who has commenced hostilities. The white man will be the victim justified in protecting himself—in a land he has invaded.

. . . Some of them, profiting by the low water, had come on to the coral. . . . Engraving from the original edition (1870).

the word "Assai," and by their gestures I understood that they invited me to go on land, an invitation that I declined.

So that, on that day, the boat did not push off, to the great displeasure of Master Land, who could not complete his provisions.

This adroit Canadian employed his time in preparing the viands and meat that he had brought off the island. As for the savages, they returned to the shore about eleven o'clock in the morning, as soon as the coral tops began to disappear under the rising tide; but I saw their numbers had increased considerably on the shore. Probably they came from the neighbouring islands, or very likely from Papua. However, I had not seen a single native canoe. Having nothing better to do, I thought of dragging these beautiful limpid waters, under which I saw a profusion of shells, zoophytes, and marine plants. Moreover, it was the last day that the *Nautilus* would pass in these parts, if it float in open sea the next day, according to Captain Nemo's promise.

I therefore called Conseil, who brought me a little light drag, very like those for the oyster fishery.

["How about those savages?" Conseil asked. "If it does not displease monsieur, I would say they do not look very menacing."

"They are still cannibals, my boy."

"But one can be a cannibal and still be honourable," Conseil declared, "just as one can be a glutton and still be honest. One does not exclude the other."

"Good, Conseil! I agree that there are honest cannibals, and that they devour their prisoners with a sense of decency. Even so, since I do not wish to be devoured, even with decorum, I shall be on my guard, especially since the Captain does not seem to be taking any precautions."]

Now to work! For two hours we fished unceasingly, but without bringing up any rarities. The drag was filled with midas-ears, harps, melames, and particularly the most beautiful hammers I have ever seen. We also brought up some holothurias, pearl-oysters, and a dozen little turtles, that were reserved for the pantry on board.

But just when I expected it least, I put my hand on a wonder, I might say a natural deformity, very rarely met with. Conseil was just dragging, and his net came up filled with divers ordinary shells, when, all at once, he saw me plunge my arm quickly into the net, to draw out a shell, and heard me utter a conchological cry, that is to say, the most piercing cry that human throat can utter.

"What is the matter, sir?" he asked, in surprise; "has master been bitten?"

"No, my boy; but I would willingly have given my finger for my discovery."

"What discovery?"

"This shell," I said, holding up the object of my triumph.

"It is simply an olive porphyry, genus olive, order of the pectinibranchidae, class of gasteropods, sub class of mollusca."

"Yes, Conseil; but instead of being rolled from right to left, this olive turns from left to right."

"Is it possible?"

"Yes, my boy; it is a left shell."

["A left-handed shell!" Conseil said excitedly.

"Look at the spiral."

"Ah, believe me, monsieur"—he was taking the shell with a trembling hand—"this is such a thrilling moment!"

Indeed, it was something to get excited about. As naturalists will tell you, dextrality—or right-handedness—seems to be a law of nature. Stars and their satellite bodies, rotating about the heavens, revolve from right to left. Man is typically right-handed rather than left-handed, and so the things he creates, his instruments and apparatus, like his staircases, locks, watch springs, are designed to operate from right to left. Nature usually follows the same law in spiralling her shells.]

Shells are all right-handed with rare exceptions; and, when by chance their spiral is left, amateurs are ready to pay their weight in gold.[5]

Conseil and I were absorbed in the contemplation of our treasure, and I was promising myself to enrich the museum with it, when a stone unfortunately thrown by a native, struck against, and broke the precious object in Conseil's hand. I uttered a cry of despair! Conseil took up his gun, and aimed at a savage who was poising his sling at ten yards from him. I would have stopped him, but his blow took effect, and broke the bracelet of amulets which encircled the arm of the savage.

"Conseil!" cried I; "Conseil!"

"Well, sir! do you not see that the cannibal has commenced the attack."

"A shell is not worth the life of a man," said I.

"Ah! the scoundrel!" cried Conseil; "I would rather he had broken my shoulder!"

Conseil was in earnest, but I was not of his opinion. However the situation had changed some minutes before, and we were not perceived.[6] A score of canoes surrounded the *Nautilus*. These canoes, scooped out of the trunk of a tree, long, narrow, well adapted for speed, were balanced by means of a long bamboo pole, which floated on the water. They were managed by skilful half-naked paddlers and I watched their advance with some uneasiness. It was evident that these Papuans had already had dealings with the Europeans, and knew their ships. But this long iron cylinder anchored in the bay, without masts or chimney, what could they think of it? Nothing good, for at first they kept at a respectful distance. However, seeing it motionless, by degrees they took courage, and sought to familiarise themselves with it. Now, this familiarity was precisely what it was necessary to avoid. Our arms, which were noiseless, could only produce a moderate effect on the savages, who have little respect for aught but blustering things. The thunderbolt without the reverberations of thunder would frighten man but little, though the danger lies in the lightning, not in the noise.

At this moment the canoes approached the *Nautilus,* and a shower of arrows alighted on her.

5. *amateurs . . . pay their weight in gold* That is, collectors, enthusiasts, buffs, those who feel *amatory* about this pursuit!

6. *we were not perceived* Aronnax really says, of course, *and we had not perceived it.*

7. *calculations of x and other quantities* You can imagine how Verne's American detractors have laughed at *that!* Thomas, in his *Galaxy* article, says condescendingly:

"Now, nobody with even a smattering of mathematics would put it that way. People don't sit around calculating '*x* and other quantities' as an end in itself. Such a remark could only be made by a man with no mathematical background whatsoever."

But of course, it wasn't Verne who "put it that way." It was a master of arts from Oxford University. The way Verne himself put it was this:

. . . *Je trouvai le capitaine Nemo plongé dans un calcul ou les X et autres signes algébriques ne manquaient pas.*

That is: . . . *I found Captain Nemo deep in calculation in which X and other algebraic signs were not wanting.*

X was not a *quantity* to Verne but a *sign*. And the whole remark is cast in Aronnax's characteristic humor. Here is his nervous denial of the gravity of the situation, his recognition of its irony, its absurdity. The *Nautilus* is surrounded by real, "primitive" warriors, using spears and arrows in the known world, while the intellectual captain is immersed in abstractions, using algebra to explore the unknown.

Verne was so compulsive about his mathematics that he always checked passages like this with his cousin, Henri Garcet, a mathematics professor at the *lycée* Henri IV in Paris. Garcet was the author of several textbooks, including *Elements of Mechanics.* It was Garcet who helped Verne not only with his equations but with the proper language for discussing them. Thus, in *The Mysterious Island,* Cyrus Harding gives teenager Herbert a lesson in the practical use of *x* (as the unknown) in solving a trigonometric problem. And in *From the Earth to the Moon,* Verne's mathematical problems were so gracefully expounded that the rumor spread that Sir John Herschel himself had collaborated with Verne!

["The devil, it is hailing!" said Conseil. "And maybe the hailstones are poisoned!"

"I have got to inform Captain Nemo," I said.]

I went down to the saloon, but found no one there. I ventured to knock at the door that opened into the Captain's room. "Come in," was the answer.

I entered, and found Captain Nemo deep in algebraical calculations of *x* and other quantities.[7]

"I am disturbing you," said I, for courtesy sake.

"That is true, M. Aronnax," replied the Captain; "but I think you have serious reasons for wishing to see me?"

"Very grave ones; the natives are surrounding us in their canoes, and in a few minutes we shall certainly be attacked by many hundreds of savages."

"Ah!" said Captain Nemo, quietly, "they are come with their canoes?"

"Yes, sir."

"Well, sir, we must close the hatches."

"Exactly, and I came to say, to you——"

"Nothing can be more simple," said Captain Nemo. And pressing an electric button, he transmitted an order to the ship's crew.

"It is all done, sir," said he, after some moments. "The pinnace is ready,[8] and the hatches are closed. You do not fear, I imagine, that these gentlemen could stave in walls on which the balls of your frigate have had no effect?"

"No, Captain; but a danger still exists."

"What is that, sir?"

"It is that to-morrow, at about this hour, we must open the hatches to renew the air of the *Nautilus.*"

["Indeed, monsieur, our ship must come up for air, like the cetaceans."]

"Now, if, at this moment, the Papuans should occupy the platform, I do not see how you could prevent them from entering."

"Then, sir, you suppose that they will board us?"

"I am certain of it."

"Well, sir, let them come. I see no reason for hindering them. After all, these Papuans are poor creatures, and I am unwilling that my visit to the Island of Gueberoan should cost the life of a single one of these wretches."

Upon that I was going away; but Captain Nemo detained me, and asked me to sit down by him. He questioned me with interest about our excursions on shore, and our hunting; and seemed not to understand the craving for meat that possessed the Canadian. Then the conversation turned on various subjects, and without being more communicative, Captain Nemo showed himself more amiable.

Amongst other things, we happened to speak of the situation of the *Nautilus,* run aground in exactly the same spot in this strait where Dumont d'Urville was nearly lost. Apropos of this—

"This D'Urville was one of your great sailors," said the Captain, to me, "one of your most intelligent navigators. He is the Captain Cook of you Frenchmen. Unfortunate man of science, after having braved the icebergs of the south pole, the coral reefs of Oceania, the cannibals of the Pacific, to perish miserably in a railway train! If this energetic man could have reflected during the last moments of his life, what must have been uppermost in his last thoughts, do you suppose?"

So speaking Captain Nemo seemed moved, and his emotion gave me a better opinion of him. Then, chart in hand, we reviewed the travels of the French navigator, his voyage of circumnavigation, his double detention at the south pole,**9** which led to the discovery of Adelaide and Louis Philippe, and fixing the hydrographical bearings of the principal islands of Oceania.

"That which your D'Urville has done on the surface of the seas," said Captain Nemo, "that have I done under them, and more easily, more completely than he. The *Astrolabe* and the *Zelia,* incessantly tossed about by the hurricanes, could not be worth the *Nautilus,* quiet repository of labour that she is,**10** truly motionless in the midst of the waters."

["Nevertheless, Captain, there is still one point of resemblance between Dumont d'Urville's corvettes and the *Nautilus.*"

"Yes?"

"The *Nautilus* has also run aground."

"Professor," Nemo responded coldly, "the *Nautilus* has not run aground. The *Nautilus* is built so as to be able to lie on the sea-floor. I have no recourse to the painful work and manoeuvres forced on Dumont d'Urville. The *Astrolabe* and the *Zélée* almost sank, but the *Nautilus* is in no danger. Tomorrow, the appointed day, and at the appointed hour, she will rise with the tide and she will resume her voyage."

"I do not doubt that—"]

"To-morrow," added the Captain, rising, "to-morrow, at twenty minutes to three P.M., the *Nautilus* shall float, and leave the Strait of Torres uninjured."

Having curtly pronounced these words, Captain Nemo

8. *The pinnace is ready* That is, it has been secured.

9. *double detention at the south pole* Verne says *sa double tentative: his double attempt.*

10. *quiet repository of labour that she is* In the French, Nemo dubs her *tranquille cabinet de travail,* that is, a quiet study, a peaceful place to work, a laboratory. Verne used similar language in talking about his own boat, the *Saint Michel,* on which he wrote most of this novel.

bowed slightly. This was to dismiss me, and I went back to my room.

There I found Conseil, who wished to know the result of my interview with the Captain.

"My boy," said I, "when I feigned to believe that his *Nautilus* was threatened by the natives of Papua, the Captain answered me very sarcastically. I have but one thing to say to you: Have confidence in him, and go to sleep in peace."

"Have you no need of my services, sir?"

"No, my friend. What is Ned Land doing?"

"If you will excuse me, sir," answered Conseil, "friend Ned is busy making a kangaroo-pie, which will be a marvel."

I remained alone, and went to bed, but slept indifferently. I heard the noise of the savages, who stamped on the platform uttering deafening cries. The night passed thus, without disturbing the ordinary repose of the crew. The presence of these cannibals affected them no more than the soldiers of a masked battery care for the ants that crawl over its front.

At six in the morning I rose. The hatches had not been opened. The inner air was not renewed, but the reservoirs, filled ready for any emergency, were now resorted to, and discharged several cubic feet of oxygen **11** into the exhausted atmosphere of the *Nautilus*.

I worked in my room till noon, without having seen Captain Nemo, even for an instant. On board no preparations for departure were visible.

I waited still some time, then went into the large saloon. The clock marked half-past two. In ten minutes it would be high-tide; and, if Captain Nemo had not made a rash promise, the *Nautilus* would be immediately detached. If not, many months would pass ere she could leave her bed of coral.

However, some warning vibrations began to be felt in the vessel. I heard the keel grating against the rough calcareous bottom of the coral reef.

At five-and-twenty minutes to three, Captain Nemo appeared in the saloon.

"We are going to start," said he.

"Ah!" replied I.

"I have given the order to open the hatches."

"And the Papuans?"

"The Papuans?" answered Captain Nemo, slightly shrugging his shoulders.

"Will they not come inside the *Nautilus?*"

"How?"

"Only by leaping over the hatches you have opened."

11. *cubic feet of oxygen* In the French, Aronnax declares that several cubic *meters* of oxygen were released into the air.

"M. Aronnax," quietly answered Captain Nemo, "they will not enter the hatches of the *Nautilus* in that way, even if they were open."

I looked at the Captain.

"You do not understand?" said he.

"Hardly."

"Well, come and you will see."

I directed my steps towards the central staircase. There Ned Land and Conseil were slyly watching some of the ship's crew, who were opening the hatches, while cries of rage and fearful vociferations re-sounded outside.

The port lids were pulled down outside.**12** Twenty horrible faces appeared. But the first native who placed his hand on the stair-rail, struck from behind by some invisible force, I know not what, fled, uttering the most fearful cries, and making the wildest contortions.

Ten of his companions followed him. They met with the same fate.

Conseil was in ecstasy. Ned Land, carried away by his violent instincts, rushed on to the staircase. But the moment he seized the rail with both hands, he, in his turn, was overthrown.

"I am struck by a thunderbolt," cried he, with an oath.

This explained all. It was no rail, but a metallic cable, charged with electricity from the deck,**13** communicating with the platform. Whoever touched it felt a powerful shock—and this shock would have been mortal, if Captain Nemo had discharged into the conductor the whole force of the current. It might truly be said that between his assailants and himself he had stretched a network of electricity which none could pass with impunity.

Meanwhile, the exasperated Papuans had beaten a retreat, paralysed with terror. As for us, half laughing, we consoled and rubbed the unfortunate Ned Land, who swore like one possessed.

But, at this moment, the *Nautilus,* raised by the last waves of the tide, quitted her coral bed exactly at the fortieth minute fixed by the Captain.**14** Her screw swept the waters slowly and majestically. Her speed increased gradually, and sailing on the surface of the ocean, she quitted safe and sound the dangerous passes of the Straits of Torres.

12. *pulled down outside*   No, Verne says: *The hatches were opened outward.*

13. *electricity from the deck*   The rail, Verne really says, is an electric cable extending *up to the deck.*

14. *the . . . minute fixed by the Captain*   Such perfect timing is reminiscent of Verne's father Pierre, with his telescope trained on the town clock, and his knowledge of the precise number of steps he had to take from house to office.

PART 1: CHAPTER XXII

"Aegri Somnia"[1]

1. *Chapter XXII: "Ægri Somnia"* The title is Latin for "bitter dreams." And the chapter number is really XXIII.

2. *The reefs were . . . more equalised* That is, not so close together; more spaced out.

3. *sons of crocodiles* Here we have a good example of Verne's scorn for primitive beliefs as it seems to be directed at rulers who profit by these beliefs. Aronnax emphasizes the cruelty to women in such societies. In Verne's time, of course, should any European woman question the propriety of European takeover of such places, she would be silenced with arguments about the white man's duty to save "young maidens" and beautiful women from "crocodiles" and slavery.

The following day, 10th January, the *Nautilus* continued her course between two seas, but with such remarkable speed that I could not estimate it at less than thirty-five miles an hour. The rapidity of her screw was such that I could neither follow nor count its revolutions. When I reflected that this marvellous electric agent, after having afforded motion, heat, and light to the *Nautilus,* still protected her from outward attack, and transformed her into an ark of safety, which no profane hand might touch without being thunderstricken, my admiration was unbounded, and from the structure it extended to the engineer who had called it into existence.

Our course was directed to the west, and on 11th January we doubled Cape Wessel, situated in 135° longitude, and 10° north latitude, which forms the east point of the Gulf of Carpentaria. The reefs were still numerous, but more equalised,[2] and marked on the chart with extreme precision. The *Nautilus* easily avoided the breakers of Money to port, and the Victoria reefs to starboard, placed at 130° longitude, and on the tenth parallel which we strictly followed.

On the 13th January, Captain Nemo arrived in the Sea of Timor, and recognised the island of that name in 122° longitude. [Timor, with an area of 1625 square leagues, is ruled by rajahs. These princes are said to be the sons of crocodiles,[3] reputedly the highest lineage that a human being can claim. The rajahs' scaly ancestors swarm in all the rivers and are especially venerated. They are protected, pampered, adulated, nourished. Young maidens are served to them as food, and woe to the stranger who raises a finger against these sacred lizards.

But the *Nautilus* had no quarrel with these animals. The

island of Timor was visible just briefly, at midday, when the second charted her position. I caught only a glimpse of the little island of Rotti, part of the same archipelago, whose women have a reputation for beauty on the Malayan markets.]

From this point, the direction of the *Nautilus* inclined towards the south-west. Her head was set for the Indian Ocean. Where would the fancy of Captain Nemo carry us next? Would he return to the coast of Asia? or would he approach again the shores of Europe? Improbable conjectures both, for a man who fled from inhabited continents. Then, would he descend to the south? Was he going to double the Cape of Good Hope, then Cape Horn, and finally go as far as the antarctic pole? Would he come back at last to the Pacific, where his *Nautilus* could sail free and independently? Time would show.

After having skirted the sands of Cartier, of Hibernia, Seringapatam, and Scott, last efforts of the solid against the liquid element, on the 14th January we lost sight of land altogether. The speed of the *Nautilus* was considerably abated, and, with irregular course, she sometimes swam in the bosom of the waters, sometimes floated on their surface.

During this period of the voyage, Captain Nemo made some interesting experiments on the varied temperature of the sea, in different beds. Under ordinary conditions, these observations are made by means of rather complicated instruments, and with somewhat doubtful results, by means of thermometrical sounding-leads, the glasses often breaking under the pressure of the water, or an apparatus grounded on the variations of the resistance of metals to the electric currents. Results so obtained could not be correctly calculated. On the contrary, Captain Nemo went himself to test the temperature in the depths of the sea, and his thermometer, placed in communication with the different sheets of water, gave him the required degree immediately and accurately.

It was thus that, either by overloading her reservoirs, or by descending obliquely by means of her inclined planes, the *Nautilus* successively attained the depth of three, four, five, seven, nine, and ten thousand yards, and the definite result of this experience was, that the sea preserved an average temperature of four degrees and a half [centigrade], at a depth of five thousand fathoms, under all latitudes.[4]

[I followed these observations with great interest. Nemo threw himself into such work with a passion. And so I could not help wondering *why*. Was it for the benefit of his fellow mortals? That did not seem likely, since, one day or another, his labours would perish with him beneath some unknown

4. *fathoms, under all latitudes* In this passage, Verne gives all depths in *meters*. Lewis begins by converting roughly into *yards* and ends by converting wildly into *fathoms*. And so, where Aronnax says Nemo found a uniform temperature of 4.5° C (40° F), read: *at a depth of 1000 meters under all latitudes.*

5. *secret discoveries . . . not shared*
Verne is here preoccupied with the concept of *Faustian man versus Baconian man.* These two opposing attitudes toward science have played significant roles in modern history. Faust was medieval in the sense that his discoveries were not shared, they were his secrets, they increased his personal power and would die with him. We think here of the alchemist's search for the secret of transmutation of base metals into gold. We think of the astrologist's for-sale knowledge of individual destinies. But in *New Atlantis,* Francis Bacon (1561–1626) promulgated the modern doctrine: If scientists publish and thus share their results, they will all profit by each other's work and humanity will advance that much faster. This new approach was adopted by the Royal Society and other national academies when they were founded later in the century. And so, for example, Benjamin Franklin's kite experiment—in which he proved that lightning is electricity—could soon be repeated and discussed all over Europe.

Hence we see that Aronnax is implicitly accusing Nemo of being a Doctor Faustus when he could instead become a famous Baconian.

The newer, Baconian approach, even when it has thrived, has not completely eliminated the Faustian. Fulton, as we have seen, destroyed his submarine boat in order to keep personal control over its secrets. The Wright brothers tried to keep secret the details of their flying machine while they were dickering with the military. Of course, both the military and many sectors of industry remain Faustian. And the Baconian pooling of scientific knowledge that Aronnax is so proud of declined sharply during and after World War II. Physics journals have ceased to publish all new findings in nuclear physics, and master's and doctor's dissertations have all too often been stamped TOP SECRET. Whereas Maury had rushed all his findings into print, for all the world to use, one cannot be sure today that even oceanography is still

sea! Unless he intended to pass on his results to me. But that would be like saying that my voyage with him would someday end, and so far there was no sign it ever would.

In any event, the Captain shared with me the data he had obtained on the relative densities of water in the principal seas. From this communication, I learned something of personal benefit that had nothing to do with science.

It happened on the morning of the 15th of January. We were walking on the platform. The Captain inquired whether I knew the different densities of the ocean waters. I answered that I did not, because we had not yet conducted rigorous enough scientific observations of these phenomena.

"I have conducted such observations," he told me, "and I can vouch for their reliability."

"Oh fine," I answered, "but the *Nautilus* exists in a world apart. The secret discoveries of its scientists are not shared **5** with the rest of the world."

He was silent and then said, "You are right, Professor, the *Nautilus* is a separate world. It is as foreign to the earth as are the other planets. We shall never know what scientists on Saturn and Jupiter have discovered. But, since chance has brought you and me together, I can share my data with you."

"I am all ears, Captain."

"As you know, Professor, sea-water is denser than fresh-water, but not uniformly so. If I represent the density of fresh-water as 1.000, then I can tell you I find a density of 1.028 in Atlantic waters, 1.026 in Pacific waters, and 1.030 in the Mediterranean—"

Ha Hah, I thought, so he does **6** venture into the Mediterranean!

"—and 1.1018 in Ionian Sea waters, and 1.029 in Adriatic waters."

Decidedly, then, the *Nautilus* did not avoid the frequented seas of Europe, and I inferred he would take us—soon, maybe—towards our own civilisation. This would be such good news to share with Ned Land!

For several days more, we studied the salinity of water at various depths, its electric qualities, colouring, transparency. All through these observations, Nemo's ingenuity was equalled only by his graciousness towards me. Then suddenly he would disappear and I would work again all alone.]

On the 16th January, the *Nautilus* seemed becalmed, only a few yards beneath the surface of the waves. Her electric apparatus remained inactive, and her motionless screw left her to drift at the mercy of the currents. I supposed that the crew was occupied with interior repairs, rendered necessary by the violence of the mechanical movements of the machine.

My companions and I then witnessed a curious spectacle. The hatches of the saloon were open,7 and as the beacon-light of the *Nautilus* was not in action, a dim obscurity reigned in the midst of the waters. [Stormy skies, obscured with thick clouds, darkened the upper layers of the sea.] I observed the state of the sea under these conditions, and the largest fish appeared to me no more than scarcely defined shadows, when the *Nautilus* found herself suddenly transported into full light. I thought at first that the beacon had been lighted, and was casting its electric radiance into the liquid mass. I was mistaken, and after a rapid survey, perceived my error.

The *Nautilus* floated in the midst of a phosphorescent bed, which, in this obscurity, became quite dazzling. It was produced by myriads of luminous animalculae, whose brilliancy was increased as they glided over the metallic hull of the vessel. I was surprised by lightning in the midst of these luminous sheets, as though they had been rivulets of lead melted in an ardent furnace, or metallic masses brought to a white heat, so that, by force of contrast, certain portions of light appeared to cast a shade in the midst of the general ignition, from which all shade seemed banished. No; this was not the calm irradiation of our ordinary lightning. There was unusual life and vigour; this was truly living light!

In reality, it was an infinite agglomeration of coloured infusoria, of veritable globules of diaphanous jelly, provided with a thread-like tentacle, and of which as many as twenty-five thousand have been counted in less than two cubic half-inches of water; 8 and their light was increased by the glimmering peculiar to the medusae, starfish, aurelia, and other phosphorescent zoophytes, impregnated by the grease of the organic matter decomposed by the sea, and, perhaps, the mucus secreted by the fish.

During several hours the *Nautilus* floated in these brilliant waves, and our admiration increased as we watched the marine monsters disporting themselves like salamanders. I saw there, in the midst of this fire that burns not, the swift and elegant porpoise (the indefatigable clown of the ocean), and some swordfish, ten feet long, those prophetic heralds of the hurricane, whose formidable sword would now and then strike the glass of the saloon. Then appeared the smaller fish, the variegated balista,9 the leaping mackerel, wolf-thorntails, and a hundred others which striped the luminous atmosphere as they swam. This dazzling spectacle was enchanting! Perhaps some

Baconian. Professor J. Z. Young of the University of London says, for example, that whales "can locate objects so readily under water that their methods have attracted much attention from naval researchers. Much of the information is probably still kept secret by the navies of the world. . . ."

6. *Ha Hah . . . so he does* Masterfully, Verne now achieves an *ironic reversal*. It is now Nemo who is sharing his data with a fellow scientist, and Aronnax who is putting that information to secret personal use! Alas, the English-speaking reader who has relied on the "standard translation" has no idea that Verne is capable of such contrapuntal play with both themes and characters.

7. *the hatches of the saloon were open* This would be disastrous. Verne says that those sliding *panels* are open.

8. *two cubic half-inches of water* Verne says *30 cubic centimeters of water,* which converts neatly into *one ounce.*

9. *variegated balista* The triggerfish that Aronnax is always so delighted to see.

atmospheric condition increased the intensity of this phenomenon. Perhaps some storm agitated the surface of the waves.
But, at this depth of some yards, the *Nautilus* was unmoved by
its fury, and reposed peacefully in still water.

So we progressed, incessantly charmed by some new marvel.
Conseil arranged and classed his zoophytes, his articulata, his
molluscs, his fishes. The days passed rapidly away, and I took
no account of them. Ned, according to habit, tried to vary the
diet on board. Like snails, we were fixed to our shells, and I
declare it is easy to lead a snail's life.

Thus, this life seemed easy and natural, and we thought no
longer of the life we led on land; but something happened to
recall us to the strangeness of our situation.

On the 18th of January, the *Nautilus* was in 105° longitude
and 15° south latitude.**10** The weather was threatening, the sea
rough and rolling. There was a strong east wind. The barometer, which had been going down for some days, foreboded a
coming storm. I went up on to the platform just as the second
lieutenant was taking the measure of the horary angles,**11** and
waited, according to habit, till the daily phrase was said. But,
on this day, it was exchanged for another phrase not less incomprehensible. Almost directly, I saw Captain Nemo appear,
with a glass, looking toward the horizon.

For some minutes he was immovable, without taking his eye
off the point of observation. Then he lowered his glass, and
exchanged a few words with his lieutenant. The latter seemed
to be a victim to some emotion that he tried in vain to repress.
Captain Nemo, having more command over himself, was cool.
He seemed, too, to be making some objections, to which the
lieutenant replied by formal assurances. At least I concluded
so by the difference of their tones and gestures. For myself I
had looked carefully in the direction indicated without seeing
anything. The sky and water were lost in the clear line of the
horizon.

However, Captain Nemo walked from one end of the platform to the other, without looking at me, perhaps without seeing me. His step was firm, but less regular than usual. He
stopped sometimes, crossed his arms, and observed the sea.
What could he be looking for on that immense expanse?
The *Nautilus* was then some hundreds of miles from the
nearest coast.

The lieutenant had taken up the glass, and examined the
horizon steadfastly, going and coming, stamping his foot and
showing more nervous agitation than his superior officer. Besides, this mystery must necessarily be solved, and before long;

10. *105° longitude and 15° south
latitude*   The *Nautilus* is now out in
the Indian Ocean, roughly 800 miles
from the west coast of Australia, 500
miles south of Java.

11. *second . . . measure of the horary angles*   That is, the *hourly* angles. The second in command (*not*
the second lieutenant) measures the
angle of the sun's altitude and then
consults hourly tables and his chronometer to determine his position.

for, upon an order from Captain Nemo, the engine increasing its propelling power, made the screw turn more rapidly.

Just then, the lieutenant drew the Captain's attention again. The latter stopped walking and directed his glass towards the place indicated. He looked long. I felt very much puzzled, and descended to the drawing-room, and took out an excellent telescope that I generally used. Then leaning on the edge of the watch-light, that jutted out from the front of the platform, set myself to look over all the line of the sky and sea.

But my eye was no sooner applied to the glass, than it was quickly snatched out of my hands.

I turned round. Captain Nemo was before me, but I did not know him. His face was transfigured. His eyes flashed sullenly; his teeth were set; his stiff body, clenched fists, and head shrunk between his shoulders, betrayed the violent agitation that pervaded his whole frame. He did not move. My glass, fallen from his hands, had rolled at his feet.

Had I unwittingly provoked this fit of anger? Did this incomprehensible person imagine that I had discovered some forbidden secret? No; I was not the object of his hatred, for he was not looking at me, his eye was steadily fixed upon the impenetrable point of the horizon. At last Captain Nemo recovered himself. His agitation subsided. He addressed some words in a foreign language to his lieutenant, then turned to me. "M. Aronnax," he said, in rather an imperious tone, "I require you to keep one of the conditions that bind you to me."

A swordfish in action, as represented in A. E. Brehm's *Merveilles de la Nature* (1885).

"What is it, Captain?"

"You must be confined, with your companions, until I think fit to release you."

"You are the master," I replied, looking steadily at him. "But may I ask you one question?"

"None, sir."

There was no resisting this imperious command, it would have been useless. I went down to the cabin occupied by Ned Land and Conseil, and told them the Captain's determination. You may judge how this communication was received by the Canadian.

But there was no time for altercation. Four of the crew waited at the door, and conducted us to that cell where we had passed our first night on board the *Nautilus*.

Ned Land would have remonstrated, but the door was shut upon him.

"Will master tell me what this means?" asked Conseil.

I told my companions what had passed. They were as much

astonished as I, and equally at a loss how to account for it.

Meanwhile, I was absorbed in my own reflections, and could think of nothing but the strange fear depicted in the Captain's countenance. I was utterly at a loss to account for it, when my cogitations were disturbed by these words from Ned Land—

"Hallo! Breakfast is ready." 12

And indeed the table was laid. Evidently Captain Nemo had given this order at the same time that he had hastened the speed of the *Nautilus*.

"Will master permit me to make a recommendation?" asked Conseil.

"Yes, my boy."

"Well, it is that master breakfasts. It is prudent, for we do not know what may happen."

"You are right, Conseil."

"Unfortunately," said Ned Land, "they have only given us the ship's fare."

"Friend Ned," asked Conseil, "what would you have said if the breakfast had been entirely forgotten?"

This argument cut short the harpooner's recriminations.

We sat down to table. The meal was eaten in silence. [I could not eat much. Conseil "forced himself" because it was "prudent," and Ned Land did not miss a bite. The meal over, each of us retired to a corner.]

Just then, the luminous globe that lighted the cell went out, and left us in total darkness. Ned Land was soon asleep, and what astonished me was that Conseil went off into a heavy sleep. I was thinking what could have caused his irresistible drowsiness, when I felt my brain becoming stupefied. In spite of my efforts to keep my eyes open, they would close. A painful suspicion seized me. Evidently soporific substances had been mixed with the food we had just taken. Imprisonment was not enough to conceal Captain Nemo's projects from us, sleep was more necessary.

I then heard the panels shut.13 The undulations of the sea, which caused a slight rolling motion, ceased. Had the *Nautilus* quitted the surface of the ocean? Had it gone back to the motionless bed of water? I tried to resist sleep. It was impossible. My breathing grew weak. I felt a mortal cold freeze my stiffened and half-paralysed limbs. My eyelids, like leaden caps, fell over my eyes. I could not raise them; a morbid sleep, full of hallucinations, bereft me of my being. Then the visions disappeared, and left me in complete insensibility.

12. *Breakfast is ready* In the original, Ned says *"le déjeuner est servi."* In this context, the best translation seems to be *"Lunch is ready."*

13. *the panels shut* No, this time it's the *hatches* that are being closed.

PART 1: CHAPTER XXIII[1]
The Coral Kingdom

The next day I woke with my head singularly clear. To my great surprise I was in my own room. My companions, no doubt, had been reinstated in their cabin, without having perceived it any more than I. Of what had passed during the night they were as ignorant as I was, and to penetrate this mystery I only reckoned upon the chances of the future.

I then thought of quitting my room. Was I free again or a prisoner? Quite free. I opened the door, went to the half-deck, went up the central stairs. The panels, shut the evening before, were open. I went on to the platform.

Ned Land and Conseil waited there for me. I questioned them; they knew nothing. Lost in a heavy sleep in which they had been totally unconscious, they had been astonished at finding themselves in their cabin.

As for the *Nautilus*, it seemed quiet and mysterious as ever. It floated on the surface of the waves at a moderate pace. Nothing seemed changed on board.

[Ned Land, with his penetrating vision, scanned the sea. It was deserted. The Canadian saw nothing on the horizon, no sail, no land. A brisk wind blew from the west and long waves, whipped up by the breeze, made the ship roll. The *Nautilus* renewed her air supply, submerged, and sailed at an average depth of fifteen metres, apparently so she could surface quickly. And she did surface repeatedly that day—January 19th—which was unusual.]

The second lieutenant then came on to the platform and gave the usual order [which could be heard] below.

As for Captain Nemo, he did not appear.

Of the people on board, I only saw the impassive steward, who served me with his usual dumb regularity.

1. *Chapter XXIII* Really Chapter XXIV. This is the last chapter number to be affected by Lewis's omission of Verne's heading for Chapter XI: The *Nautilus*.

2. *colleagues have studied medicine*
The anxiety in Nemo's inquiry stems
from the fact that in Aronnax's day, a
naturalist might or might not have had
medical training. As we have seen in
our notes on Gratiolet and Milne-
Edwards, medical studies could serve
as one route to a career in natural history, zoology, paleontology, comparative anatomy, and related fields. But
Aronnax could have entered natural
history directly by studying under
specialists like Milne-Edwards and
d'Orbigny.

3. *my heart beat* What Aronnax
really says here could be rendered
better as: *I admit my heart was
pounding.*

About two o'clock, I was in the drawing-room, busied in arranging my notes, when the Captain opened the door and appeared. I bowed. He made a slight inclination in return, without speaking. I resumed my work, hoping that he would perhaps give me some explanation of the events of the preceding night. He made none. I looked at him. He seemed fatigued; his heavy eyes had not been refreshed by sleep; his face looked very sorrowful. He walked to and fro, sat down and got up again, took up a chance book, put it down, consulted his instruments without taking his habitual notes, and seemed restless and uneasy. At last, he came up to me, and said—

"Are you a doctor, M. Aronnax?"

I so little expected such a question, that I stared some time at him without answering.

"Are you a doctor?" he repeated. "Several of your colleagues have studied medicine [2] [—Gratiolet, Moquin-Tandon, and others]."

"Well," said I, "I am a doctor and resident surgeon to the hospital. I practised several years before entering the museum."

"Very well, sir."

My answer had evidently satisfied the Captain. But not knowing what he would say next, I waited for other questions, reserving my answers according to circumstances.

"M. Aronnax, will you consent to prescribe for one of my men?" he asked.

"Is he ill?"

"Yes."

"I am ready to follow you."

"Come, then."

I own my heart beat,[3] I do not know why. I saw a certain connection between the illness of one of the crew and the events of the day before; and this mystery interested me at least as much as the sick man.

Captain Nemo conducted me to the poop of the *Nautilus*, and took me into a cabin situated near the sailors' quarters.

There, on a bed, lay a man about forty years of age, with a resolute expression of countenance, a true type of an Anglo-Saxon.

I leant over him. He was not only ill, he was wounded. His head, swathed in bandages covered with blood, lay on a pillow. I undid the bandages, and the wounded man looked at me with his large eyes and gave no sign of pain as I did it. It was a horrible wound. The skull, shattered by some deadly weapon, left the brain exposed, which was much injured. Clots of blood had formed in the bruised and broken mass, in colour like the dregs of wine.

There was both contusion and suffusion of the brain.**4** His breathing was slow, and some spasmodic movements of the muscles agitated his face. I felt his pulse. It was intermittent. The extremities of the body were growing cold already, and I saw death must inevitably ensue. After dressing the unfortunate man's wounds, I readjusted the bandages on his head, and turned to Captain Nemo.

"What caused this wound?" I asked.

"What does it signify?" he replied, evasively. "A shock has broken one of the levers of the engine, which struck myself. [The second-in-command was at this man's side. This man flung himself forward to receive the blow.**5** It is that simple— a brother sacrifices himself for a brother, a friend for a friend —that is the law for all on board the *Nautilus*.**6**] But your opinion as to his state?"

I hesitated before giving it.

"You may speak," said the Captain. "This man does not understand French."

I gave a last look at the wounded man.

"He will be dead in two hours."

"Can nothing save him?"

"Nothing."

Captain Nemo's hand contracted, and some tears glistened in his eyes, which I thought incapable of shedding any.

For some moments I still watched the dying man, whose life ebbed slowly. His pallor increased under the electric light that was shed over his death-bed. I looked at his intelligent forehead, furrowed with premature wrinkles, produced probably by misfortune and sorrow. I tried to learn the secret of his life from the last words that escaped his lips.

"You can go now, M. Aronnax," said the Captain.

I left him in the dying man's cabin, and returned to my room much affected by this scene. During the whole day, I was haunted by uncomfortable suspicions, and at night I slept badly, and, between my broken dreams, I fancied I heard distant sighs like the notes of a funeral psalm. Were they the prayers of the dead, murmured in that language that I could not understand?

The next morning I went on the bridge. Captain Nemo was there before me. As soon as he perceived me he came to me.

"Professor, will it be convenient to you to make a submarine excursion to-day?"

"With my companions?" I asked.

4. *both contusion and suffusion of the brain* Verne says *both contusion and concussion.*

5. *to receive the blow* In the original, Nemo says that the *shock of a collision broke a lever and it struck* (not Nemo but) *this man.* As our restoration indicates, it struck *this man* because he had flung himself between the flying lever and the second-in-command, who otherwise would have taken the blow.

6. *law for . . . the Nautilus* This scene contrasts strongly with earlier scenes in which Aronnax has led us to see Nemo's crewmen as robotlike. Here, as Aronnax is able to look closely at one of them, hurt and needing help, he seems more human. He has voluntarily suffered to save another from suffering, and Aronnax learns that such altruism is *"the law"* on board. Maybe there is more esprit, more comradeship among Nemo's men than Aronnax has had a chance to observe. The rigid class distinction (Nemo and Aronnax on a level above all the others), the segregation of the "prisoners of war" from Nemo's crewmen, and the latter's use of an "artificial language" all make it difficult for Aronnax to learn how the crewmen do behave among themselves. Even at this point, our best information is that the crewmen are depressed, melancholy, grim men.

7. *put on your cork-jackets* In Chapter XV (Verne's XVI), Aronnax said about Nemo's rubber diving suits:

There was a vast difference . . . between these consummate apparatuses and the old cork . . . jackets . . . in vogue during the eighteenth century.

Yet now, when Nemo tells the three friends to don their *scaphandres* (diving suits), Mercier Lewis translates the word as *cork-jackets.* This is one of the several inconsistencies in Lewis's terminology suggesting that perhaps he farmed out portions of the translation job to collaborators and then failed to coordinate their work. On the title page of his 1874 translation of *From the Earth to the Moon,* as we have noted earlier, he did give credit to a cotranslator, Eleanor E. King.

The very next sentence—*It was not a question of dead or dying*—is also a mistranslation. In the original, Aronnax says: *There was no mention of the man who was dead or dying.*

8. *in the alcyon class . . . corollariae* Verne says: *in the class of alycyonarians* and in *the group of coralliae.*

. . . And the bush changed into a block of stony knobs. Engraving of branching coral, from *The American Cyclopaedia* (1873).

"If they like."

"We obey your orders, Captain."

"Will you be so good then as to put on your cork-jackets?" **7**

It was not a question of dead or dying. I rejoined Ned Land and Conseil, and told them of Captain Nemo's proposition. Conseil hastened to accept it, and this time the Canadian seemed quite willing to follow our example.

It was eight o'clock in the morning. At half-past eight we were equipped for this new excursion, and provided with two contrivances for light and breathing. The double door was open; and accompanied by Captain Nemo, who was followed by a dozen of the crew, we set foot, at a depth of about thirty feet, on the solid bottom on which the *Nautilus* rested.

A slight declivity ended in an uneven bottom, at fifteen fathoms depth. This bottom differed entirely from the one I had visited on my first excursion under the waters of the Pacific Ocean. Here, there was no fine sand, no submarine prairies, no sea-forest. I immediately recognised that marvellous region in which, on that day, the Captain did the honours to us. It was the coral kingdom. In the zoophyte branch and in the alcyon class I noticed the gorgoneae, the isidiae, and the corollariae.**8**

[That last group includes coral, curious substance that has at different times been classified as belonging to the mineral, vegetable, and animal kingdom! Medicine to the ancients, jewelry to the moderns, it was not definitively classified within the animal kingdom until 1694, by Peysonnel of Marseilles.

Coral is a colony of animalcules, assembled on a brittle, rock-like polypary. These polyps reproduce by a continuous budding process. Each creature has its individuality, yet all participate in the life of the community. It is a sort of natural socialism. I was familiar with the most recent research on this curious zoophyte, which is mineralised as it ramifies. Nothing could have interested me more than visiting one of the petrified forests that Nature has planted on the floor of the sea. We switched on our Ruhmkorff apparatus and followed a bank of coral which was in the process of formation and which will some day shut off this portion of the Indian Ocean!

Our route was bordered with tangled bushes, intertwining shrubbery covered with star-like flowers. But unlike plants that grow on land, these arborisations, fixed in the rocks, were growing downwards.]

The light produced a thousand charming varieties, playing in the midst of the branches that were so vividly coloured. I seemed to see the membraneous and cylindrical tubes tremble beneath the undulation of the waters. I was tempted to gather their fresh petals, ornamented with delicate tentacules, some just blown, the others budding, while small fish, swimming swiftly, touched them slightly, like flights of birds. But if my hand approached these living flowers, these animated sensitive plants, the whole colony took alarm. The white petals re-entered their red cases, the flowers faded as I looked, and the bush changed into a block of stony knobs.

Chance had thrown me just by the most precious specimens of this zoophyte. This coral was more valuable than that found in the Mediterranean, on the coasts of France, Italy, and Barbary. Its tints justified the poetical names of "Flower of Blood," and "Froth of Blood," that trade has given to its most beautiful productions. Coral is sold for £20 per ounce; and in this place, the watery beds would make the fortunes of a company of coral-divers. This precious matter, often confused with other polypi, formed then the inextricable plots called "macciota," and on which I noticed several beautiful specimens of pink coral.

But soon the bushes contract,9 and the arborisations increase. Real petrified thickets, long joists of fantastic architecture, were disclosed before us. Captain Nemo placed himself under a dark gallery, where by a slight declivity we reached a depth of 100 yards. The light from our lamps produced sometimes magical effects, following the rough outlines of the natural arches, and pendants disposed like lustres, that were tipped with points of fire. Between the coralline shrubs I noticed other polypi not less curious, melites, and irises with articulated ramifications, also some tufts of coral, some green, others red, like seaweed encrusted in their calcareous salts, that naturalists, after long discussion, have definitely classed in the vegetable kingdom. But following the remarks of a thinking man, "there is perhaps the real point where life rises obscurely from the sleep of a stone, without detaching itself from the rough point of departure."

At last, after walking two hours, we had attained a depth of about 300 yards, that is to say, the extreme limit on which coral begins to form. But there was no isolated bush, nor modest brushwood, at the bottom of lofty trees. It was an immense forest of large mineral vegetations, enormous petrified trees, united by garlands of elegant plumarias, sea-bindweed, all adorned with clouds and reflections. We passed freely under their high branches, lost in the shade of the waves, while at our feet, tubipores, mandrines, stars, fungi, and caryophyllidae formed a carpet of flowers sown with dazzling gems. What an indescribable spectacle!

9. *soon the bushes contract* That is, they grow closer together, they thicken, while the treelike formations grow taller.

10. *Why could we not share the life of the fish* Verne almost seems here to be suggesting that Aronnax has reached the euphoric—even hallucinatory—stage of nitrogen narcosis, discussed in an earlier note.

11. *I understood all* You must be heaving a sigh that finally the professor has put it all together. But here we have to connive at *a literary convention.* If an author is telling his story through the eyes of one character who serves as *narrator,* then it's best that that character be rather slow. For if he saw everything instantly, that would kill the suspense and deprive *you the reader* of your chance to make any connections all by yourself. Then, remember that the professor, being not so bright as the captain, sometimes not even so bright as the harpooner, therefore asks all the dumb questions that get *you* the answers. Would Sherlock Holmes ever get a chance to explain it all if Doctor Watson weren't a bit dense?

12. *the fires on board appeared* That is, the searchlight on the platform and the lights visible through the open panels of the saloon.

[If only we had been able to communicate our feelings! Why were we imprisoned in our masks of copper and glass! Why prevented from talking with each other! Why could we not share the life of the fish **10** that populate the liquid element, or better yet, the life of the amphibians who, for hours on end, can live on land or at sea, as their whim determines.]

Captain Nemo had stopped. I and my companions halted, and turning round, I saw his men were forming a semicircle round their chief. Watching attentively, I observed that four of them carried on their shoulders an object of an oblong shape.

We occupied, in this place, the centre of a vast glade surrounded by the lofty foliage of the submarine forest. Our lamps threw over this place a sort of clear twilight that singularly elongated the shadows on the ground. At the end of the glade the darkness increased, and was only relieved by little sparks reflected by the points of coral.

Ned Land and Conseil were near me. We watched, and I thought I was going to witness a strange scene. On observing the ground, I saw that it was raised in certain places by slight excrescences encrusted with limy deposits, and disposed with a regularity that betrayed the hand of man.

In the midst of the glade, on a pedestal of rocks roughly piled up, stood a cross of coral, that extended its long arms that one might have thought were made of petrified blood.

Upon a sign from Captain Nemo, one of the men advanced; and at some feet from the cross, he began to dig a hole with a pickaxe that he took from his belt. I understood all! **11** This glade was a cemetery, this hole a tomb, this oblong object the body of the man who had died in the night! The Captain and his men had come to bury their companion in this general resting-place, at the bottom of this inaccessible ocean! [Never had my mind been so excited! Never had such staggering impressions invaded my brain! I did not want to see what my eyes were looking at!]

The grave was being dug slowly; the fish fled on all sides while their retreat was being thus disturbed; I heard the strokes of the pickaxe, which sparkled when it hit upon some flint lost at the bottom of the waters. The hole was soon large and deep enough to receive the body. Then the bearers approached; the body, enveloped in a tissue of white byssus, was lowered into the damp grave. Captain Nemo, with his arms crossed on his breast, and all the friends of him who had loved them, knelt in prayer.

The grave was then filled in with the rubbish taken from

Captain Nemo, with his arms crossed on his breast, and all the friends of him who had loved them, knelt in prayer. Engraving from the original edition (1870).

the ground, which formed a slight mound. When this was done, Captain Nemo and his men rose; then, approaching the grave, they knelt again, and all extended their hands in a sign of a last adieu. Then the funeral procession returned to the *Nautilus,* passing under the arches of the forest, in the midst of thickets, along the coral bushes, and still on the ascent. At last the fires on board appeared,**12** and their luminous track guided us to the *Nautilus.* At one o'clock we had returned.

As soon as I had changed my clothes, I went up on to the platform, and, a prey to conflicting emotions, I sat down near the binnacle. Captain Nemo joined me. I rose and said to him—

"So, as I said he would, this man died in the night?"

"Yes, M. Aronnax."

"And he rests now, near his companions, in the coral cemetery?"

"Yes, forgotten by all else, but not by us. We dug the grave, and the polypi undertake to seal our dead for eternity." And burying his face quickly in his hands, he tried in vain to suppress a sob. Then he added—"Our peaceful cemetery is there, some hundred feet below the surface of the waves."

"Your dead sleep quietly, at least, Captain, out of the reach of sharks."

"Yes, sir, of sharks and *men,"* gravely replied the Captain.

PART 2: CHAPTER I

The Indian Ocean

1. *deep impression on my mind*
After the violent, tragic climax of
Part 1, Verne opens Part 2 with quiet,
meditative, almost static narrative.
Such contrast in mood and pacing is
of course a standard storyteller's trick.
But equally important, it perfectly
serves Verne's need to develop one of
his major themes: the submarine can
be more valuable to mankind when it
is used not for combat but for research and exploration.

2. *I dreaded it* When critics praise
Verne's gift of prophecy, they invariably think only of his predictions of
scientific advances. They rarely appreciate Verne's talent for anticipating
the social and psychological problems
arising out of a scientific endeavor.
Here is a perfect instance of that talent. Verne portrays Aronnax as torn
between his needs as a scientist and
his needs as a humanitarian. He has
the ideal technical conditions for making unprecedented progress in his
field. But he must work under the
most dubious auspices. Numerous
twentieth-century developments of this
conflict come to mind.

We think of nuclear physicists who
for at least two decades could get
proper facilities for their research only
by working under the military. Kurt
Vonnegut, Jr., expressed their conflict
in his 1969 speech to the American
Physical Society. He defined virtuous
physicists as those who "don't . . .
work on the development of new

We now come to the second part of our journey under the
sea. The first ended with the moving scene in the coral
cemetery, which left such a deep impression on my mind.**1**
Thus, in the midst of this great sea, Captain Nemo's life was
passing even to his grave, which he had prepared in one of its
deepest abysses. There, not one of the ocean's monsters could
trouble the last sleep of the crew of the *Nautilus,* of those
friends riveted to each other in death as in life. "Nor any man
either," had added the Captain. Still the same fierce, implacable defiance towards human society!

I could no longer content myself with the hypothesis which
satisfied Conseil.

That worthy fellow persisted in seeing in the commander of
the *Nautilus* one of those unknown savants who return mankind contempt for indifference. For him, he was a misunderstood genius, who, tired of earth's deceptions, had taken refuge
in this inaccessible medium, where he might follow his instincts freely. To my mind, this hypothesis explained but one
side of Captain Nemo's character.

Indeed, the mystery of that last night, during which we had
been chained in prison, the sleep, and the precaution so violently taken by the Captain of snatching from my eyes the
glass I had raised to sweep the horizon, the mortal wound of
the man, due to an unaccountable shock of the *Nautilus,* all
put me on a new track. No; Captain Nemo was not satisfied
with shunning man. His formidable apparatus not only suited
his instinct of freedom, but, perhaps, also the design of some
terrible retaliation.

At this moment, nothing is clear to me; I catch but a glimpse
of light amidst all the darkness, and I must confine myself to
writing as events shall dictate.

[Captain Nemo knew that we could not easily escape from the *Nautilus*. But we were not honour-bound to remain on board. We were simply captives, prisoners disguised as guests for the sake of courtesy. Certainly Ned Land, for one, had never given up hope of regaining his freedom. Certainly he would seize the first opportunity to escape. And so would I. But I would not escape without some regrets, for Captain Nemo had generously allowed us to share the mysteries of the *Nautilus*. Should we hate or admire that man? Was he a victim or a villain? To be perfectly truthful, I did not want to leave him forever until we had finished this submarine journey around the world. I wanted to see all those marvels he had promised, which no man had ever seen before, even if I might have to pay for this curiosity with my life. What had I learned so far? Nothing, relatively speaking, since we had so far travelled only six thousand leagues across the Pacific.

I could see that the *Nautilus* was approaching inhabited lands. If opportunities for escaping should present themselves, it would be cruel to sacrifice my companions to my quest for knowledge. I would have no choice except to follow them, maybe to lead them. Would such opportunities ever arise? As a man deprived of his freedom, I longed for such an occasion. As a scientist lusting for knowledge, I dreaded it! **2**]

That day, the 24th of January,**3** 1868, at noon, the second officer came to take the altitude of the sun. I mounted the platform, lit a cigar, and watched the operation. It seemed to me that the man did not understand French; for several times I made remarks in a loud voice, which must have drawn from him some involuntary sign of attention, if he had understood them; but he remained undisturbed and dumb.

As he was taking observations with the sextant, one of the sailors of the *Nautilus* (the strong man who had accompanied us on our first submarine excursion to the Island of Crespo) came to clean the glasses of the lantern. I examined the fittings of the apparatus, the strength of which was increased a hundred-fold by lenticular rings, placed similar to those in a lighthouse, and which projected their brilliance in a horizontal plane. The electric lamp was combined in such a way as to give its most powerful light. Indeed, it was produced in *vacuo* which insured both its steadiness and its intensity. This vacuum economised the graphite points between which the luminous arc was developed—an important point of economy for Captain Nemo, who could not easily have replaced them; and under these conditions their waste was imperceptible. When the *Nautilus* was ready to continue its submarine journey, I

weapons. . . . They don't work for corporations that pollute water or atmosphere or raid the public treasury." He added that some "physicists . . . are so virtuous that they don't go into physics at all."

Again, when Auguste Piccard and his son Jacques had difficulty getting funds for submarine research in the late 1950s, they welcomed the support of the U.S. Navy. They paid heavily for this compromise. For example, Jacques Piccard worked for years planning to dive in his *Trieste* down into the Challenger Deep. But at the last moment he heard that he had been scratched from the two-man crew. Navy orders. He had to fight the brass to get back into his own project. As E. H. Shenton writes in his superb book *Diving for Science* (1972), scientists working for Piccard became "angry when the uniformed military officers made a majority of the dives for training and were not as excited about the phenomena of the deep sea" as the scientists were.

Through Aronnax's conflicts, Verne foreshadowed one of the greatest psychological problems faced in our time by physicists, oceanographers, meteorologists, and even cetologists.

3. *the 24th of January* Verne says, *On the 21st of January, the second-in-command came. . . .*

went down to the saloon. The panels were closed, and the course marked direct west.

We were furrowing the waters of the Indian Ocean, a vast liquid plain, with a surface of 1,200,000,000 of acres, and whose waters are so clear and transparent, that any one leaning over them would turn giddy. The *Nautilus* usually floated between fifty and a hundred fathoms deep. We went on so for some days. To any one but myself, who had a great love for the sea, the hours would have seemed long and monotonous; but the daily walks on the platform, when I steeped myself in the reviving air of the ocean, the sight of the rich waters through the windows of the saloon, the books in the library, the compiling of my memoirs, took up all my time, and left me not a moment of ennui or weariness.

[We all managed to stay in perfect health. Ship's fare was good for us. So far as I was concerned, I could easily have done without those "variations in diet" that Ned Land, in a spirit of protest, managed to provide. And because of the even temperature on board, we were less liable to catch colds. Besides, we had a good supply of Madreporaria dendrophyllia, which they call "sea-fennel" in Provençal. We could have made a good cough syrup from the juicy flesh of its polyps.]

For some days we saw a great number of aquatic birds, sea-mews or gulls. Some were cleverly killed, and, prepared in a certain way, made very acceptable water-game. Amongst large winged birds, carried a long distance from all lands, and resting upon the waves from the fatigue of their flight, I saw some magnificent albatrosses, uttering discordant cries like the braying of an ass, and birds belonging to the family of the longipennates. The family of the totipalmates was represented by the sea-swallows, which caught the fish from the surface, and by numerous phaetons, or lepturi; amongst others, the phaeton with red lines, as large as a pigeon, whose white plumage, tinted with pink, shows off to advantage the blackness of its wings.

[The nets cast by the *Nautilus* brought in several kinds of sea-turtles, mainly hawkbills with their dome-shaped back and valuable shells. These reptiles can dive readily and stay under a long time simply by closing a fleshy valve in the external orifice of their nasal passage. Some of them were sleeping inside their shells when we took them. That is how they manage to sleep and still protect themselves from attack by other sea-animals. Their meat was nothing to rave about, but their eggs made an exquisite dish.]

As to the fish, they always provoked our admiration when

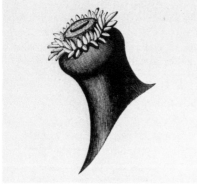

. . . We had a good supply of Madreporaria dendrophyllia which they call "sea-fennel" in Provençal. We could have made a good cough syrup from the juicy flesh of its polyps. Picture of one variety of *dendrophyllia* polyp from James D. Dana's *Corals and Coral Islands* (1872).

we surprised the secrets of their aquatic life through the open panels. I saw many kinds which I never before had a chance of observing.

I shall notice chiefly ostracions peculiar to the Red Sea, the Indian Ocean, and that part which washes the coast of tropical America. These fishes, like the tortoise, the armadillo, the sea-hedgehog, and the crustacea, are protected by a breastplate which is neither chalky nor stony, but real bone. In some it takes the form of a solid triangle, in others of a solid quadrangle. Amongst the triangular I saw some an inch and a half in length, with wholesome flesh and a delicious flavour; they are brown at the tail, and yellow at the fins, and I recommend their introduction into fresh water, to which a certain number of sea-fish easily accustom themselves. I would also mention quadrangular ostracions, having on the back four large tubercles; some dotted over with white spots on the lower part of the body, and which may be tamed like birds; trigons provided with spikes formed by the lengthening of their bony shell, and which, from their strange gruntings, are called "sea-pigs"; also dromedaries with large humps in the shape of a cone, whose flesh is very tough and leathery.

I now borrow from the daily notes of Master Conseil. "Certain fish of the genus petrodon **4** peculiar to those seas, with red backs and white chests, which are distinguished by three rows of longitudinal filaments; and some electrical, seven inches long, decked in the liveliest colours. Then, as specimens of other kinds, some ovoides, resembling an egg of a dark brown colour, marked with white bands, and without tails; diodons, real sea-porcupines, furnished with spikes, and capa-

A species of Tetrodon common to Indo-Pacific waters, as represented in A. C. L. G. Günther's *An Introduction to the Study of Fishes* (1880).

4. *genus petrodon*   Verne says *genre tétrodons,* or the genus Tetraodon.

These reptiles can . . . stay under a long time simply by closing a fleshy valve in the external orifice of their nasal passage. The hawkbill turtle as pictured in *Animal Forms: A Text-Book of Zoology* (1902) by D. S. Jordan and Harold Heath.

ble of swelling in such a way as to look like cushions bristling with darts; hippocampi, common to every ocean; some pegasi with lengthened snouts, which their pectoral fins, being much elongated and formed in the shape of wings, allow, if not to fly, at least to shoot into the air; pigeon spatulae, with tails covered with many rings of shell; macrognathi with long jaws, an excellent fish, nine inches long, and bright with most agreeable colours; pale-coloured calliomores, with rugged heads; [whole schools of jumping blennies, with black stripes and long pectoral fins, gliding speedily along the surface; delicious velifera, who raise their fins like sails to catch the current; splendid kurtidae, coloured yellow, sky-blue, silver, gold; trichoptera with wings formed of filaments; bullheads, with lemon-coloured spots, making hissing sounds; gurnards, whose liver is reputed to be dangerous to eat; greenlings, with flaps over their eyes;] and plenty of chaetodons, with long and tubular muzzles, which kill insects by shooting them, as from an air-gun, with a single drop of water. These we may call the fly-catchers of the seas. [Neither Chassepot nor Remington could have conceived of such a weapon!]

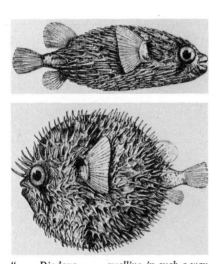

". . . Diodons, . . . swelling in such a way as to look like cushions bristling with darts. . . ." A diodon before and after inflation, as pictured in A. C. L. G. Günther's *An Introduction to the Study of Fishes* (1880).

"In the eighty-ninth genus of fishes, classed by Lacépède, belonging to the second lower class of bony, characterised by opercules and bronchial membranes, I remarked the scorpaena, the head of which is furnished with spikes, and which has but one dorsal fin; these creatures are covered, or not, with little shells, according to the sub-class to which they belong. The second sub-class gives us specimens of didactyles fourteen or fifteen inches in length, with yellow rays, and heads of a most fantastic appearance. As to the first sub-class, it gives several specimens of that singular-looking fish appropriately called a 'sea-frog,' with large head, sometimes pierced with holes, sometimes swollen with protuberances, bristling with spikes, and covered with tubercles; it has irregular and hideous horns; its body and tail are covered with callosities; its sting makes a dangerous wound; it is both repugnant and horrible to look at."

5. *twenty-two miles an hour* At that time the fastest steamers were lucky to average fifteen or sixteen miles per hour.

6. *Keeling Island* This is one of twenty-seven coral islets known as the Cocos Islands or Keeling Islands, about 1400 miles southeast of Sri Lanka (Ceylon). Discovered in 1609 by Captain William Keeling of the East India Company, they were settled by the British in the early nineteenth century and are now administered by Australia.

From the 21st to the 23d of January the *Nautilus* went at the rate of two hundred and fifty leagues in twenty-four hours, being five hundred and forty miles, or twenty-two miles an hour.**5** If we recognised so many different varieties of fish, it was because, attracted by the electric light, they tried to follow us; the greater part, however, were soon distanced by our speed, though some kept their place in the waters of the *Nautilus* for a time. The morning of the 24th, in 12° 5′ south latitude, and 94° 33′ longitude, we observed Keeling Island,**6** a madrepore formation, planted with magnificent cocoas, and which had been visited by Mr. Darwin and Captain Fitzroy.**7** The *Nautilus* skirted the shores of this desert island for a little distance. Its nets brought up numerous specimens of polypi, and curious shells of mollusca. Some precious productions of the species of delphinulae enriched the treasures of Captain Nemo, to which I added an astraea punctifera, a kind of parasite polypus often found fixed to a shell. Soon Keeling Island disappeared from the horizon, and our course was directed to the north-west in the direction of the Indian Peninsula.

["Civilised countries!" Ned exclaimed. "Better than those Papuan isles, where you run across more savages than deer! In India, Professor, there are roads and railroads, and English, French, and Hindu towns. We would not walk five miles without meeting a fellow countryman. Hey now, has not the time come to bid farewell to Captain Nemo?"

"Oh no, Ned," I said emphatically. "Let things ride, as you sailors say. The *Nautilus* is heading towards populated places, towards Europe. Let her take us there. And once we reach home waters, then we can decide what is best. But I cannot imagine that Captain Nemo will let us hunt on the coasts of Malabar or Coromandel as he did in the jungles of New Guinea."

"But, Professor, can we not act on our own, without his permission?"

Since I did not want an argument, I did not answer. Deep down, I wanted most to take full advantage of the fact that fate had put me on board the *Nautilus*.]

7. *Mr. Darwin and Captain Fitzroy* The fame of Charles Darwin (1809–1882) overshadows that of Robert Fitzroy (1805–1865), who in his own field and time was also a man of outstanding accomplishments. Verne, in his continuous effort to educate us in the history of science, gives Fitzroy due mention.

Captain Fitzroy assumed command of H.M.S. *Beagle,* a brig of 240 tons, in 1828, when she was engaged in surveying the coasts of Patagonia and Tierra del Fuego. He took her back to England in 1830 and then, with Darwin aboard, embarked on December 27, 1831 on their famous circumnavigation. Darwin, an unpaid naturalist (a "supernumerary"), lived in a "wretched little cabin" and endured "agonies of seasickness." The five-year voyage permanently ruined his health. But it provided him with the materials he needed for his theories of coral formation, natural selection, and organic evolution.

They visited Cape Verde, the South American coasts, Tahiti, New Zealand, Australia, Tasmania, Keeling Island, the Maldives, Mauritius, St. Helena, Ascension, and numerous other places. They returned on October 2, 1836.

Darwin settled down to write his classics: *The Structure and Distribution of Coral Reefs* (1842), *On the Origin of Species* (1859), *The Descent of Man* (1871). Fitzroy published a two-volume narrative of his scientific voyages with a third volume by Darwin (1839). Retiring as a vice-admiral, Fitzroy devoted his last ten years to practical meteorology. His *Weather Book* (1863) expressed views far in advance of his day.

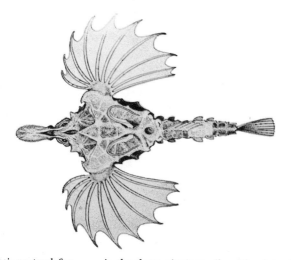

". . . *Their pectoral fins,* . . . *in the shape of wings, allow* [them] *to shoot into the air.* . . ." A pegasus, or sea moth, as pictured in D. S. Jordan's *A Guide to the Study of Fishes* (1905).

From Keeling Island our course was slower and more variable, often taking us into great depths. Several times they made use of the inclined planes, which certain internal levers placed obliquely to the water-line. In that way we went about two miles, but without ever obtaining the greatest depths of the Indian Sea, which soundings of seven thousand fathoms have never reached. As to the temperature of the lower strata, the thermometer invariably indicated 4° above zero. I only observed that, in the upper regions, the water was always colder in the high levels than at the surface of the sea.[8]

On the 25th of January, the ocean was entirely deserted; the *Nautilus* passed the day on the surface, beating the waves with its powerful screw, and making them rebound to a great height. Who under such circumstances would not have taken it for a gigantic cetacean? Three parts of this day I spent on the platform. I watched the sea. Nothing on the horizon, till about four o'clock a steamer running west on our counter. Her masts were visible for an instant, but she could not see the *Nautilus,* being too low in the water. I fancied this steamboat belonged to the P. O. Company,[9] which runs from Ceylon to Sydney, touching at King George's Point and Melbourne.

At five o'clock in the evening, before that fleeting twilight which binds night to day in tropical zones, Conseil and I were astonished by a curious spectacle.

[There is a charming animal which—according to the ancients—presages good luck if one happens to meet it. Aristotle, Athenaeus, Pliny, Oppianus studied its habits and wrote poetically about it in Greek and Latin. They called it the *nautilus* and *pompylius.* But modern science has not adopted these names. This mollusc is known now as the *argonaut.*

If anyone had asked Conseil, that boy would have explained that the molluscs comprise five classes. The first class, the cephalopods, which are sometimes naked and sometimes covered with a shell, comprises two families: the dibranchiata and the tetrabranchiata, which are distinguished by the number of their gills. The family of dibranchiata comprises three genera: the argonaut, the squid, and the cuttle-fish. The family of tetrabranchiata consists of only one genus, the nautilus.

Now, after hearing Conseil's classification, it would be unforgivable for the listener to confuse the argonaut, which is *acetabuliferous,* or equipped with siphons, with the nautilus, which is *tentaculiferous,* or equipped with tentacles.]

It was a shoal of argonauts travelling along on the surface of the ocean. We could count several hundreds. They be-

8. *at the surface of the sea*   Aronnax's point is that, according to his observations, the upper strata of shallow seas are always colder than the upper strata of the open seas.

9. *P. O. Company*   Verne says *la ligne Péninsulaire et Orientale,* the Peninsular and Oriental line of Great Britain, popularly known in English as the "P. and O. Line."

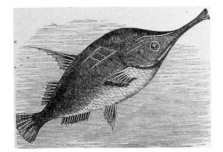

The bellows fish, which, as Aronnax says, can *kill insects by shooting them, as from an air-gun, with a single drop of water.* Only, in the original, Aronnax calls them *soufflets,* which means *bellows,* and he adds that *Neither Chassepot nor Remington could have conceived of such a weapon!* The picture above is from *The American Cyclopaedia* (1873).

longed to the tubercle kind which are peculiar to the Indian seas.

These graceful molluscs moved backwards by means of their locomotive tube, through which they propelled the water already drawn in. Of their eight tentacles, six were elongated, and stretching out floating on the water, whilst the other two, rolled up flat, were spread to the wind like a light sail. I saw their spiral-shaped and fluted shells, which Cuvier justly compares to an elegant skiff. A boat indeed! It bears the creature which secretes it without its adhering to it.

["The argonaut," I told Conseil, "is free to quit its shell if it wants to. But it never does." **10**

"Like Captain Nemo," Conseil said sagely. "He should have named his ship the *Argonaut*."]

For nearly an hour the *Nautilus* floated in the midst of this shoal of molluscs. Then I know not what sudden fright took them. But as if at a signal every sail was furled, the arms folded, the body drawn in, the shells turned over, changing their centre of gravity, and the whole fleet disappeared under the waves. Never did the ships of a squadron manoeuvre with more unity.

At that moment night fell suddenly, and the reeds, scarcely raised by the breeze, lay peaceably under the sides of the *Nautilus*.**11**

The next day, 26th of January, we cut the equator at the eighty-second meridian, and entered the northern hemisphere. During the day, a formidable troop of sharks accompanied us, terrible creatures, which multiply in these seas, and make them very dangerous. They were [—some of them—] "cestracio philippi" sharks, with brown backs and whitish bellies, armed with eleven rows of teeth—[and others were] eyed sharks—their throat being marked with a large black spot surrounded with white like an eye. There were also some Isabella sharks, with rounded snouts marked with dark spots. These powerful creatures often hurled themselves at the windows of the saloon with such violence as to make us feel very insecure. At such times Ned Land was no longer master of himself. He wanted to go to the surface and harpoon the monsters, particularly certain smooth-hound sharks, whose mouth is studded with teeth like a mosaic; and large tiger-sharks nearly six yards long, the last named of which seemed to excite him more particularly. But the *Nautilus*, accelerating her speed, easily left the most rapid of them behind.

The 27th of January, at the entrance of the vast Bay of Bengal, we met repeatedly a forbidding spectacle, dead bodies

10. *But it never does* Here we have a good example of the way biologists have overhauled their knowledge of marine life since Aronnax's day. Biologists now know that the argonaut does not spread two arms in the air *like a light sail*. Rather she uses these expanded arms to clasp her shell. We say "she" because we know today that only the female argonaut inhabits the *elegant skiff*. She uses it as an egg case. Finally, she is not only free to come and go, she does both.

11. *and the reeds . . . Nautilus* In the original, Aronnax says that it was *les lames*, the waves, that were scarcely raised by the breeze.

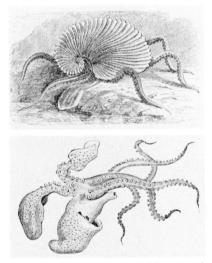

An argonaut within the shell (above) and without the shell (below), as pictured in *The American Cyclopaedia* (1873).

floating on the surface of the water. They were the dead of the Indian villages, carried by the Ganges to the level of the sea, and which the vultures, the only undertakers of the country, had not been able to devour. But the sharks did not fail to help them at their funereal work.

About seven o'clock in the evening, the *Nautilus,* half immersed, was sailing in a sea of milk. At first sight the ocean seemed lactified. Was it the effect of the lunar rays? No; for the moon, scarcely two days old, was still lying hidden under the horizon in the rays of the sun. The whole sky, though lit by the sidereal rays, seemed black by contrast with the whiteness of the waters.

Conseil could not believe his eyes, and questioned me as to the cause of this strange phenomenon. Happily I was able to answer him.

"It is called a milk sea," I explained, "a large extent of white wavelets often to be seen on the coasts of Amboyna, and in these parts of the sea."

"But, sir," said Conseil, "can you tell me what causes such an effect? for I suppose the water is not really turned into milk."

"No, my boy; and the whiteness which surprises you is caused only by the presence of myriads of infusoria, a sort of luminous little worm, gelatinous and without colour, of the thickness of a hair, and whose length is not more than 7/1000 of an inch. These insects **12** adhere to one another sometimes for several leagues."

"Several leagues!" exclaimed Conseil.

"Yes, my boy; and you need not try to compute the number of these infusoria. You will not be able; for, if I am not mistaken, ships have floated on these milk seas for more than forty miles."

[I cannot be sure he took my advice. He seemed to be deep in thought, maybe trying to calculate how many 7/1000s of an inch can be contained in an area forty miles square. I continued to observe these phenomena as the *Nautilus* cruised for several hours through milky seas. I noticed that it glided through these foamy waves quietly, as though floating in one of those frothy eddies that develop in bays when currents and counter-currents converge.]

Towards midnight the sea suddenly resumed its usual colour; but behind us, even to the limits of the horizon, the sky reflected the whitened waves, and for a long time seemed impregnated with the vague glimmerings of an aurora borealis.

12. *These insects* Verne says *bestioles,* little animals. He gives the length of one of them as no more than a fifth of a millimeter. For the sake of consistency, we shall use Mercier Lewis's *7/1000s of an inch* in our restoration.

PART 2: CHAPTER II[1]

A Novel Proposal of Captain Nemo's

On the 28th of February, when at noon the *Nautilus* came to the surface of the sea, in 9° 4′ north latitude, there was land in sight about eight miles to westward. The first thing I noticed was a range of mountains about two thousand feet high, the shapes of which were most capricious. On taking the bearings, I knew that we were nearing the Island of Ceylon, the pearl which hangs from the lobe of the Indian Peninsula.

[I went down into the library to search for a book on this island, which is one of the most fertile in the world. I came upon a volume by H. C. Sirr, *Ceylan and the Cingalese*.[2] Returning to the saloon, I read some basic facts about Ceylon, which has through the ages been known by so many different names.[3] It is situated between 5° 55′ and 9° 49′ north latitude, and between 79° 42′ and 82° 4′ longitude east of the Greenwich meridian. Its length is 275 miles. Its maximum width is 150 miles; its circumference 900 miles; its area 24,448 square miles, that is to say, somewhat less than the area of Ireland.]

Captain Nemo and his second appeared at this moment. The Captain glanced at the map. Then, turning to me, said—

"The Island of Ceylon, noted for its pearl-fisheries. Would you like to visit one of them, M. Aronnax?"

"Certainly, Captain."

"Well, the thing is easy. Though if we see the fisheries, we shall not see the fishermen. The annual exportation [4] has not yet begun. Never mind, I will give orders to make for the Gulf of Manaar, where we shall arrive in the night."

1. *Chapter II* In this chapter the little brackets ([ ]) tell a gruesome tale. They show how Lewis's ruthless cuts weakened Verne's attack on colonialism, his admiration for technique, and his humor. These excisions also messed up Verne's *pacing*. As we have noted, Verne composed a quiet Chapter I. Now in this chapter he creates suspense for new action in Chapter III. But Lewis, casting out about four pages of the best dialogue, completely reshaped the chapter. The result was a botch that made Verne look, to English-speaking critics, like a slapdash scribbler.

2. *Ceylan and the Cingalese* Verne gives the title in English, reminding us that the professor and the captain read in several languages. The spellings in Sirr's title (which today might be *Ceylon and the Singhalese*) reflect the difficulties in transliterating the *many different names* by which the island and its peoples have been known.

3. *so many different names* Ceylon was known in ancient times as *Taprobane*. The island has also been called *Sri Lanka* or *Sinhala*, as well as *Tamil Ilam* or *Ilanka*, after the two principal language groups, the Singhalese and the Ceylon Tamil. Other groups in-

clude Ceylon Moors, descendants of Arab merchants; Malays; Burghers, or descendants of Dutch sailors and Portuguese colonists; Eurasians; Tamil Indians.

Ceylon's name was officially changed to *Sri Lanka* in 1948 when it became an independent republic within the British Commonwealth of Nations. Sinhala is the official language and Tamil the secondary language.

One of Verne's successors in the field of science fiction, Arthur C. Clarke, lives on Sri Lanka. A scuba diver, Clarke was involved in one of the earliest marine-archaeology discoveries in the Pacific. In 1961 his friend Mike Wilson found a wreck of an eighteenth-century ship, with masses of 1702 Mogul rupees and a small cannon, on Ceylon's Great Basses Reef. In 1962 Clarke helped Wilson locate another gun and more coins. They believe the ship was loaded with silver to purchase silk in China.

4. *annual exportation* Verne's phrase *L'exploitation annuelle* connotes *annual harvest* and *exploitation* as well as *exportation*.

5. *mentions a Kaffir* Originally the Mohammedans gave this name to a South African Bantu people who were *Kafir,* that is, infidels or non-Muslims. European colonists picked up the word as a term of contempt to distinguish "colored" people from "whites." *Kaffir* in English and *Cafre* in French are instances of widespread influence on European languages by the medieval Arabic traders, soldiers, and explorers.

6. *can last 87 seconds* Nemo seems to be underestimating the stamina of the pearl divers. Captain Edward L. Beach, Naval War College expert on underwater activities, says that a five-minute dive "appears to be a reasonable maximum." The divers' secret is "hyperventilating." They take many deep diaphragmatic breaths before each dive.

The Captain said something to his second, who immediately went out. Soon the *Nautilus* returned to her native element, and the manometer showed that she was about thirty feet deep.

[On the chart I looked for the Gulf of Manaar. I found it at the 9th parallel, on the north-west coast of Ceylon. It is bounded on the north by the elongated little island of Manaar. In order to reach our goal, we would have to sail up the west coast of Ceylon.

"Monsieur le professeur," Captain Nemo said, "there are pearl-fisheries in the Bay of Bengal; the Indian Ocean; the Chinese, Japanese, and South American seas; the Gulf of Panama; and the Gulf of California. But the finest pearls of all are obtained in Ceylon. It is really too early to visit there, since the fishermen will not arrive in Manaar until March. With their 300 or so boats, they will spend about thirty days in very lucrative reaping of the ocean's treasure. Each boat will be manned by ten oarsmen and ten fishermen. The fishermen will take turns diving down to about 40 feet. They descend by holding a heavy stone between their feet. It is tied to their boat by a long rope."

"You mean," I asked, "that they actually use such primitive methods?"

"Yes, they still do," he replied, "although the Manaar fisheries belong to the world's most industrialised people, the English. They took possession in 1802 by the Treaty of Amiens."

"But would not diving equipment like yours prove useful in the fisheries?"

"It certainly would, because these poor fishermen cannot stay down very long. The Englishman Percival, in his account of his journey to Ceylon, mentions a Kaffir [5] who stayed down for five minutes without coming up for air. I find that hard to believe. But I do know some divers who can last as long as 57 seconds, and some very skilful ones can last 87 seconds.[6] Still such men are rare, and when these unfortunates do come back up on board, they are bleeding from their ears and noses. I believe that the average time for pearl-fishermen is 30 seconds. During that half-minute they hastily stuff a small net with all the pearl oysters they can gather. They do not live very long. Their vision gets weak, they develop ulcers on their eyes and sores on their bodies. Sometimes they are seized with apoplexy and die right in the water." [7]

"A grim occupation," I said, "and it serves only the whims

of fashion. Do you happen to know how many oysters a boat can gather, say, in one day?"

"Forty or fifty thousand. They say that in 1814, when the British sent down some of their own divers, they collected 76,000,000 oysters in twenty days."

"But are these fishermen well paid, at least?"

"Hardly, Professor. At Panama they make a dollar a week. In most places, they get one sou, maybe one penny, for each oyster that contains a pearl. And how many oysters contain no pearl at all!"

"A penny for these poor people who make their masters rich! That is appalling." **8]**

"Well, sir," said Captain Nemo, "you and your companions shall visit the Bank of Manaar, and if by chance some fisherman should be there, we shall see him at work."

"Agreed, Captain!"

"By the by, M. Aronnax, you are not afraid of sharks?"

"Sharks!" exclaimed I.

This question seemed a very hard one.

"Well?" continued Captain Nemo.

"I admit, Captain, that I am not yet very familiar with that kind of fish."

"*We* are accustomed to them," replied Captain Nemo, "and in time you will be too. However, we shall be armed, and on the road we may be able to hunt some of the tribe. It is interesting. So, till to-morrow, sir, and early."

This said in a careless tone, Captain Nemo left the saloon. Now, if you were invited to hunt the bear in the mountains of Switzerland, what would you say? "Very well! to-morrow we will go and hunt the bear." If you were asked to hunt the lion in the plains of Atlas, or the tiger in the Indian jungles, what would you say? "Ha! ha! It seems we are going to hunt the tiger or the lion!" But when you are invited to hunt the shark in its natural element, you would perhaps reflect before accepting the invitation. As for myself, I passed my hand over my forehead, on which stood large drops of cold perspiration. "Let us reflect," said I, "and take our time. Hunting otters in submarine forests, as we did in the Island of Crespo, will pass; but going up and down at the bottom of the sea, where one is almost certain to meet sharks, is quite another thing! I know well that in certain countries, particularly in the Andaman Islands, the negroes never hesitate to attack them with a dagger in one hand and a running noose in the other; but I also know that few who affront these creatures ever return alive.

7. *apoplexy . . . in the water* It is interesting here to compare Verne's information with the results of detailed studies of "The Diving Women of Korea and Japan" reported in the May 1967 *Scientific American* by Suk Ki Hong and Herman Rahn. These divers, called *ama,* stay down only a minute or two but they make up to 60 dives per hour when they work in depths of 15 to 20 feet. In such cases, as Verne says, the average-length dive is 30 seconds, with a 30-second rest between dives. But what Verne says about the life span of such divers does not apply to the female *ama.* They seem better suited physiologically for this work than the males. The females continue diving until they are 65, with no real breaks, even for pregnancy. Male pearl divers of the South Pacific, who go deeper than the women, do suffer effects similar to those that Verne describes. But it is not *"apoplexy"* that kills them. It's the bends. "When these divers come to the surface," Hong and Rahn say, "they are sometimes stricken by fatal attacks, which they call *taravana."*

8. *That is appalling* Aronnax's horror at this ruthless exploitation is probably the reason Mercier Lewis cut the whole passage. Here we have another example of Verne's conflict over colonialism. Generally his sympathies are for *"the world's most industrialised people,"* who stand for progress in Verne's system of values. But as a humanitarian, Verne cannot close his eyes to victimization of colonial peoples by their *"masters."*

Unfortunately, "progress" is not so simple as Verne imagined, or as Aronnax thought when he said, "*. . . would not diving equipment like yours prove useful in the fisheries?"* In the *Scientific American* (May 1967), Suk Ki Hong and Herman Rahn wrote: "By adopting scuba gear and other modern underwater equipment the divers could greatly increase their production; the present harvest could be obtained by not much more than a tenth of the present number of divers. This would raise havoc, however, with employment and the economy in the hundreds of small villages whose women daily go forth to seek their families' existence on the sea bottom. For that reason innovations are fiercely resisted. Indeed, many villages in Japan have outlawed the foam-rubber suit for divers to prevent too easy and too rapid harvesting of the local waters."

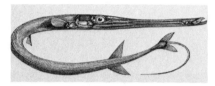

This serrated pipefish—common along the shores of the Indian Ocean—attains to a length of four to six feet. Engraving from *The American Cyclopaedia* (1873).

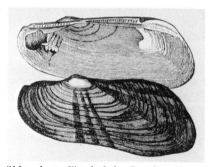

"Mussels, too?" asked the Canadian. Drawing of a pearl mussel shell from *Chamber's Miscellany* (1870).

9. *or the incidents* Verne's meaning, of course, is the *incidentals,* the *attendant circumstances.*

However, I am not a negro, and, if I were, I think a little hesitation in this case would not be ill-timed."

[There I was, dreaming of sharks, jaws bristling with rows of teeth that can cut a man in half. I could already feel pains in my back. And I was disturbed, too, by the casual way the Captain had issued that deplorable invitation. As if we were going fox-hunting!

"Well," I thought, "we shall see. Certainly Conseil will not want to go, and that will give me an easy way out." As for Ned Land, I could not count on him. The greater the danger, the more he would want to go. I picked up Sirr's book, but soon I realised I was turning the pages mechanically. I was staring not at the meaning of the print but into the open jaws of sharks!]

At this moment, Conseil and the Canadian entered, quite composed, and even joyous. They knew not what awaited them.

"Faith, sir," said Ned Land, "your Captain Nemo—the devil take him!—has just made us a very pleasant offer."

"Ah!" said I, "you know?"

"If agreeable to you, sir," interrupted Conseil, "the Commander of the *Nautilus* has invited us to visit the magnificent Ceylon fisheries to-morrow, in your company; he did it kindly, and behaved like a real gentleman."

"He said nothing more?"

"Nothing more, sir, except that he had already spoken to you of this little walk."

["He had indeed," I said. "But did he give *you* any details about . . ."

"None at all, *monsieur le naturaliste.* But you will be coming with us, I hope?

"I? Oh, surely, yes, of course. I can see that you are looking forward to this, Master Land."

"Definitely. It sounds great."

"It could be dangerous," I hinted.

"Dangerous?" Ned was scornful. "A trip to an oyster bed!"

Apparently Nemo had decided not to plant the idea of sharks in *their* heads. I looked a bit anxiously at them. They each still had four limbs. Should I not warn them? But how?]

"Sir," said Conseil, "would you give us some details of the pearl-fishery?"

"As to the fishing itself," I asked, "or the incidents,9 which?"

"On the fishing," replied the Canadian; "before entering upon the ground, it is as well to know something about it."

"Very well; sit down, my friends, and I will teach you. [I will tell you what I have just learned from the English writer, H. C. Sirr.]"

Ned and Conseil seated themselves on an ottoman, and the first thing the Canadian asked was—

"Sir, what is a pearl?"

"My worthy Ned," I answered, "to the poet, a pearl is a tear of the sea; to the Orientals, it is a drop of dew solidified; to the ladies, it is a jewel of an oblong shape, of a brilliancy of mother-of-pearl substance, which they wear on their fingers, their necks, or their ears; for the chemist, it is a mixture of phosphate and carbonate of lime, with a little gelatine; and lastly, for naturalists, it is simply a morbid secretion of the organ that produces the mother-of-pearl amongst certain bivalves."

"Branch of mollusca," said Conseil, "class of acephali, order of testacea."

"Precisely so, my learned Conseil; and, amongst these testacea, the earshell, the tridacnae, the turbots **10**—in a word, all those which secrete mother-of-pearl; that is, the blue, bluish, violet, or white substance which lines the interior of their shells, are capable of producing pearls."

"Mussels, too?" asked the Canadian.

"Yes, mussels of certain waters in Scotland, Wales, Ireland, Saxony, Bohemia, and France."

"Good! For the future I shall pay attention," replied the Canadian.

"But," I continued, "the particular mollusc which secretes the pearl is the *pearl-oyster,* the *meleagrina margaritifera,***11** that precious pintadine. The pearl is nothing but a nacreous formation, deposited in a globular form, either adhering to the oyster-shell, or buried in the folds of the creature. On the shell it is fast; in the flesh it is loose; but always [it] has for a kernel a small hard substance, may be a barren egg, may be a grain of sand,**12** around which the pearly matter deposits itself year after year successively, and by thin concentric layers."

"Are many pearls found in the oyster?" asked Conseil.

"Yes, my boy. There are some pintadines a perfect casket. One oyster has been mentioned, though I allow myself to doubt it, as having contained no less than a hundred and fifty sharks."

"A hundred and fifty sharks!" exclaimed Ned Land.

"Did I say sharks?" said I, hurriedly. "I meant to say a hundred and fifty pearls. Sharks would not be sense." **13**

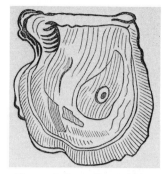

"*. . . The particular mollusc which secretes the pearl is . . . the* meleagrina margaritifera. *. . .*" Drawing of a pearl oyster shell from *Chambers's Miscellany* (1870).

10. *the turbots* This is indeed Verne's word—*les turbots.* But in English, the *turbot* is a *flatfish.* And *turbo* is the proper English term for that genus of marine snails that usually have a heavy *turbinate* (spiral) shell with a pearl lining. In the original, Verne also includes the abalones in Aronnax's listing.

11. *meleagrina margaritifera* Verne does not use this term; it's the translator's. *Meleagrina* was a genus of mollusks in some former systems of classification. The genus name today would be *Pinctada.*

12. *may be a grain of sand* Scientists who came after Aronnax thought that the main cause of pearl formation was the dead body of a minute parasite. Today scientists again see broader possibilities. *The New Columbia Encyclopedia* (1975) says that the nacreous material is "deposited in successive layers around an irritating object such as a parasite or a grain of sand that gets caught in the soft tissue" of the mollusk.

13. *Sharks would not be sense* Like most pre-Freudian authors, Verne was well aware of the superficial type of "slip" so neatly exploited here. But he was entirely unconscious of the real meaning of the profounder kind of association, such as Aronnax's "cannon" and "snail" metaphors (page 20 and 160).

14. *take the parenchyma* Parenchyma is the term used in anatomy
for the essential, characteristic tissue
of an organ, as distinguished from its
connective or supportive tissue.

15. *bright and diapered* Americans
now think only of their babies as being *bright and diapered.* Verne's word
is *diapré,* which means *dappled, variegated, mottled,* as indeed the pearl is
in its *whiteness.* And in English, too,
the word originally referred to a figured design, a repetitive diamond
shape, woven into rich textiles like
silk, later into linen. Hence linen
towels and table napkins were still
called *diapers* in nineteenth-century
England and America. So Mercier
Lewis's use of *diapered* correctly conveyed to our great-grandfathers the
idea of *dappled.* But today the English word mostly suggests the *baby's
loincloth,* which is likely to be uniformly white and made of paper. So
today we would have to translate
Aronnax's phrase as *bright and dappled.*

"Certainly not," said Conseil; "but will you tell us now by what means they extract these pearls?"

"They proceed in various ways. When they adhere to the shell, the fishermen often pull them off with pincers; but the most common way is to lay the pintadines on mats of the sea-weed which covers the banks. Thus they die in the open air; and at the end of ten days they are in a forward state of de-composition. They are then plunged into large reservoirs of sea-water; then they are opened and washed. Now begins the double work of the sorters. First they separate the layers of pearl, known in commerce by the name of bastard whites and bastard blacks, which are delivered in boxes of two hundred and fifty and three hundred pounds each. Then they take the parenchyma **14** of the oyster, boil it, and pass it through a sieve in order to extract the very smallest pearls."

"The price of these pearls varies according to their size?" asked Conseil.

"Not only according to their size," I answered, "but also according to their shape, their *water* (that is, their colour), and their lustre; that is, that bright and diapered **15** sparkle which makes them so charming to the eye. The most beautiful are called virgin pearls or paragons. They are formed alone in the tissue of the mollusc, are white, often opaque, and some-times have the transparency of an opal; they are generally round or oval. The round are made into bracelets, the oval into pendants; and, being more precious, are sold singly. Those adhering to the shell of the oyster are more irregular in shape, and are sold by weight. Lastly, in a lower order are classed those small pearls known under the name of seed-pearls; they are sold by measure, and are especially used in embroidery for church ornaments."

["But that must be tedious work," Ned said, "separating pearls according to size."

"No, my friend. They use a series of eleven sieves or strainers. Pearls that do not pass through a strainer with 20 to 80 holes are first-class. Those that do not pass through a strainer with 100 to 800 holes are second-class. Pearls for which they have to use a strainer with 900 to 1000 holes are called seed-pearls."

"Clever," Conseil said, "to classify pearls mechanically. Does monsieur know how much money they make from these oyster beds?"

"According to Mr. Sirr, they make three million sharks."

"Francs, monsieur," Conseil said. "Monsieur means *francs.*"

"Of course," I agreed, "three million *francs.* But I do not think these fisheries are yielding that much today. The American fisheries yielded four million—*francs* a year in the time of Charles V. Now they bring in maybe two-thirds that amount. The total proceeds from the entire pearl-fishing industry must now be about nine million francs."

"But monsieur," Conseil asked, "is it not true that some famous pearls have a very high value?"

"Yes, my boy, they do. Caesar is supposed to have offered Servilia **16** a pearl valued at one hundred and twenty thousand francs in today's money." **17**

"Was there not, in ancient times," Ned asked, "a lady who drank pearls in vinegar?"

"Cleopatra," **18** Conseil told him.

"Must have tasted terrible," Ned thought.

"A little glass of vinegar worth a million and a half francs is not to be shunned," Conseil pointed out.

"Too bad I did not marry that lady," Ned said rather distractedly.

"You marry Cleopatra?" Conseil joked.

"I was engaged to be married. It was not my fault that we broke it off. I even bought her—Kate Tender, my fiancée—a pearl necklace. But she went and married another man. And believe me, the pearls in that necklace would *not* have passed through that first-class sieve. And I got it for just one dollar and a half!"

"Oh Ned," I laughed, "those must have been artificial pearls. Hollow glass beads filled with a substance called *essence d'Orient.*"

"And is it expensive?"

"No, Ned, it is cheap. It is the substance we find on the silver scales of the bleak, a freshwater fish. It is preserved in ammonia. It has no commercial value." **19**

"No wonder she married someone else," Ned said philosophically.

"But," I said, "to get back to pearls of great value. I do not think any *sovereign* ever possessed a pearl more valuable than Captain Nemo's."

"Monsieur means that one." Conseil pointed to it in one of the glass cases.

"I am not far off in estimating its value at two million—"

"Francs!" Conseil cut in.

"Yes, two million francs. And all it cost Captain Nemo was the work of picking it up."

"And who knows!" cried Ned. "Maybe tomorrow we will find one just like it!"

16. *offered Servilia* She was the daughter of Quintus Servilius Caepio. She married Marcus Innius Brutus. Their son, Marcus Junius Brutus, was one of the principal assassins of Caesar in March of 44 B.C.

17. *francs in today's money* Suetonius (c. A.D. 69–140), in his *Lives of the Twelve Caesars,* says that this pearl was valued at six million sesterces. J. F. C. Fuller, in his 1964 biography of Julius Caesar, says this was the equivalent of 60,000 pounds sterling, about $150,000. Fuller adds that this gift was probably the reason that many Romans thought that Brutus was Caesar's natural son. And this is why Jorge Luis Borges, in his *ficción* "The Plot," has Caesar say not simply *Et tu!* but "You too, my son!"

18. *Cleopatra* Cleopatra and other heads of state possibly *"drank pearls in vinegar"* because powdered pearl was believed to be an antidote for poison. In the Orient, a dissolved pearl was part of the love potion. In Renaissance Italy, powdered pearl was thought to be a cure for epilepsy and hysteria.

19. *no commercial value* *"Artificial pearls"* such as Aronnax describes were first made in western Europe in 1680 by a Paris rosary-maker named Jacquin.

"Bah," said Conseil.

"Why not!"

"What good would a pearl worth millions do us on board the *Nautilus?*"

"On board, *no,* but on land, *yes.*"

"Oh, on land," Conseil shook his head.

"Ned is right," I said. "If we could take a pearl worth millions back to Europe—or to America—it would validate our story, and also set a high price on it!"

"I believe that," Ned agreed.]

"But," said Conseil, "is this pearl-fishery dangerous?"

"No," I answered, quickly; "particularly if certain precautions are taken."

"What does one risk in such a calling?" said Ned Land; "the swallowing of some mouthfuls of sea-water?"

"As you say, Ned. By the by," said I, trying to take Captain Nemo's careless tone, "are you afraid of sharks, brave Ned?"

"I!" replied the Canadian; "a harpooner by profession? It is my trade to make light of them."

"But," said I, "it is not a question of fishing for them with an iron swivel, hoisting them into the vessel, cutting off their tails with a blow of a chopper, ripping them up, and throwing their heart into the sea!"

"Then, it is a question of——"

"Precisely."

"In the water?"

"In the water."

"Faith, with a good harpoon! You know, sir, these sharks are ill-fashioned beasts. They must turn on their bellies to seize you, and in that time——"

Ned Land had a way of saying "seize," which made my blood run cold.

"Well, and you, Conseil, what do you think of sharks?"

"Me!" said Conseil. "I will be frank, sir."

"So much the better," thought I.

"If you, sir, mean to face the sharks, I do not see why your faithful servant should not face them with you."

Trochus abavus, Avellana cancellata, and *Cerithium rapum,* pictured in *Journal de Conchyliologie* (1870).

PART 2: CHAPTER III
A Pearl of Ten Millions

[N]ight fell. I went to bed. I slept badly. Sharks played a major role in my nightmares. I found it both just and unjust that the French word *requin* should be so close, etymologically speaking, to the word *requiem*.**1**]

The next morning at four o'clock I was awakened by the steward, whom Captain Nemo had placed at my service. I rose hurriedly, dressed, and went into the saloon.

Captain Nemo was awaiting me.

"M. Aronnax," said he, "are you ready to start?"

"I am ready."

"Then, please to follow me."

"And my companions, Captain?"

"They have been told, and are waiting."

"Are we not to put on our diver's dresses?" asked I.

"Not yet. I have not allowed the *Nautilus* to come too near this coast, and we are some distance from the Manaar Bank; but the boat is ready, and will take us to the exact point of disembarking, which will save us a long way. It carries our diving apparatus, which we will put on when we begin our submarine journey."

Captain Nemo conducted me to the central staircase, which led on to the platform. Ned and Conseil were already there, delighted at the idea of the "pleasure party" which was preparing. Five sailors from the *Nautilus,* with their oars, waited in the boat, which had been made fast against the side.

The night was still dark. Layers of clouds covered the sky, allowing but few stars to be seen. I looked on the side where the land lay, and saw nothing but a dark line enclosing three parts of the horizon, from south-west to north-west. The *Nautilus,* having returned during the night up the western coast of Ceylon, was now west of the bay, or rather gulf,

1. *requin . . . requiem* In English, too, the words are close. The *requin,* a voracious shark, is grimly known as the *requiem shark. Requiem* is the first word in the mass for the dead, which begins: *Requiem aeterna dona eis, Domine* (Grant them eternal rest, O Lord). In other words, Aronnax has lost a night's rest over fears that the requin will bring him eternal rest.

formed by the mainland and the Island of Manaar. There, under the dark waters, stretched the pintadine bank, an inexhaustible field of pearls, the length of which is more than twenty miles.

Captain Nemo, Ned Land, Conseil, and I, took our places in the stern of the boat. The master went to the tiller; his four companions leaned on their oars, the painter was cast off, and we sheered off.[2]

The boat went towards the south; the oarsmen did not hurry. I noticed that their strokes, strong in the water, only followed each other every ten seconds, according to the method generally adopted in the navy. Whilst the craft was running by its own velocity,[3] the liquid drops struck the dark depths of the waves crisply like spats of melted lead. A little billow, spreading wide, gave a slight roll to the boat, and some samphire reeds [4] flapped before it.

We were silent. What was Captain Nemo thinking of? Perhaps of the land he was approaching, and which he found too near to him, contrary to the Canadian's opinion, who thought it too far off. As to Conseil, he was merely there from curiosity.

About half-past five, the first tints on the horizon showed the upper line of coast more distinctly. Flat enough in the east, it rose a little to the south. Five miles still lay between us, and it was indistinct owing to the mist on the water. [Between us and the land, the sea was deserted. Not a boat, not a diver. Only a deep silence prevailed in this meeting-place of pearl-fishermen. Just as Captain Nemo had said: we had arrived a month too early.] At six o'clock it became suddenly daylight, with that rapidity peculiar to tropical regions, which know neither dawn nor twilight. The solar rays pierced the curtain of clouds, piled up on the eastern horizon, and the radiant orb rose rapidly. I saw land distinctly, with a few trees scattered here and there. The boat neared Manaar Island, which was rounded to the south. Captain Nemo rose from his seat and watched the sea.

At a sign from him the anchor was dropped, but the chain scarcely ran, for it was little more than a yard deep, and this spot was one of the highest points of the bank of pintadines.

"Here we are, M. Aronnax," said Captain Nemo. "You see that enclosed bay? Here, in a month, will be assembled the numerous fishing-boats of the exporters, and these are the waters their divers will ransack so boldly. Happily, this bay is well situated for that kind of fishing. It is sheltered from the strongest winds; the sea is never very rough here, which makes

2. *we sheered off*   Here the *master* is the mate or coxswain in charge of the dinghy. The *painter* is the rope used for securing the dinghy to the ship or to a dock.

3. *running by its own velocity*   That is, when the oars were in the air and the dinghy was moving on its own momentum.

4. *some samphire reeds*   Verne says *some wave crests*.

it favourable for the diver's work. We will now put on our dresses, and begin our walk."

I did not answer, and while watching the suspected waves, began with the help of the sailors to put on my heavy sea-dress. Captain Nemo and my companions were also dressing. None of the *Nautilus* men were to accompany us on this new excursion.

Soon we were enveloped to the throat in india-rubber clothing; the air apparatus fixed to our backs by braces. As to the Ruhmkorff apparatus, there was no necessity for it. Before putting my head into the copper cap, I had asked the question of the Captain.

"They would be useless," he replied. "We are going to no great depth, and the solar rays will be enough to light our walk. Besides, it would not be prudent to carry the electric light in these waters; its brilliancy might attract some of the dangerous inhabitants of the coast most inopportunely."

As Captain Nemo pronounced these words, I turned to Conseil and Ned Land. But my two friends had already encased their heads in the metal cap, and they could neither hear nor answer.

One last question remained to ask of Captain Nemo.

"And our arms?" asked I; "our guns?"

"Guns? What for? Do not mountaineers attack the bear with a dagger in their hands, and is not steel surer than lead? Here is a strong blade, put it in your belt, and we start."

I looked at my companions; they were armed like us, and, more than that, Ned Land was brandishing an enormous harpoon, which he had placed in the boat before leaving the *Nautilus*.

Then, following the Captain's example, I allowed myself to be dressed in the heavy copper helmet, and our reservoirs of air were at once in activity. An instant after we were landed, one after the other, in about two yards of water upon an even sand. Captain Nemo made a sign with his hand, and we followed him by a gentle declivity till we disappeared under the waves.

[Once I was in the water, all my fears vanished. I became serenely calm, much to my surprise. The ease with which I could move gave me new confidence, I suppose, and the strangeness of the spectacle captured my imagination. The sun's rays penetrated the water and I could see even the smallest objects with absolute clarity. After walking for ten minutes, we reached a depth of five metres, and the terrain flattened out.]

Over our feet, like coveys of snipe in a bog, rose shoals of fish, of the genus monoptera, which have no other fins but their tail. I recognized the Javanese, a real serpent two and a half feet long, of a livid colour underneath, and which might easily be mistaken for a conger eel if it were not for the golden stripes on its side. In the genus stromateus, whose bodies are very flat and oval, I saw some of the most brilliant colours, carrying their dorsal fin like a scythe; an excellent eating fish, which, dried and pickled, is known by the name of *Karawade;* then some tranquebars, belonging to the genus apsiphoroides, whose body is covered with a shell cuirass of eight longitudinal plates.

The heightening sun lit the mass of waters more and more. The soil changed by degrees. To the fine sand succeeded a perfect causeway of boulders, covered with a carpet of molluscs and zoophytes. Amongst the specimens of these branches I noticed some plancenae, with thin unequal shells, a kind of ostracion peculiar to the Red Sea and the Indian Ocean; some orange lucinae with rounded shells; [the awl-shaped terrebellum; some of those Persian purpura which provided the *Nautilus* with its marvellous dye;] rockfish three feet and a half long,[5] which raised themselves under the waves like hands ready to seize one. There were also some [cornigerous turbinellae, bristling with spines; lingulae hyantes; anatinae, molluscs that are sold in the food-markets of Hindustan;] panopyres, slightly luminous; and lastly, some oculines, like magnificent fans, forming one of the richest vegetations of these seas.

In the midst of these living plants, and under the arbours of the hydrophytes, were layers of clumsy articulates, particularly some raninae, whose carapace formed a slightly rounded triangle; and some horrible looking parthenopes.

[Another hideous animal that I met was the giant crab mentioned by Darwin. Nature has given this creature the instinct and strength to climb a cocoa-nut tree that grows on the coast and knock down its cocoa-nuts! They break open when they hit the ground. Then the giant crab eats the insides. Beneath these clear waves, I could see one moving with unbelievable speed. Errant turtles of a species found on the Malabar coast clambered around slowly among the rocks.]

At about seven o'clock we found ourselves at last surveying the oyster-banks, on which the pearl-oysters are reproduced by millions. [These precious molluscs were attached to the rocks by their brown byssus, which prevents them from moving. In this sense these oysters are inferior to mussels, which

5. *rockfish three feet and a half long* Verne says *horned murices fifteen centimeters* (six inches) *long.*

According to *The American Cyclopaedia* (*1873*), the cocoanut palm "attains a height of from 60 to 100 feet." According to Aronnax, the giant crab that he met underwater near Ceylon could climb a cocoanut tree and knock down its fruit.

enjoy some slight freedom of movement. The pearl-oyster, whose valves are about equal in size, has a thick, rounded shell with a gnarled exterior. Some of these were spotted and streaked with green, radiating from the top down. These were young oysters. Others, ten years old or more, had a rugged black shell. They measured up to six inches in diameter.]

Captain Nemo pointed with his hand to the enormous heap of oysters; and I could well understand that this mine was inexhaustible, for Nature's creative power is far beyond man's instinct of destruction. Ned Land, faithful to his instinct, hastened to fill a net which he carried by his side with some of the finest specimens. But we could not stop. We must follow the Captain, who seemed to guide himself by paths known only to himself. The ground was sensibly rising, and sometimes, on holding up my arm, it was above the surface of the sea. Then the level of the bank would sink capriciously. Often we rounded high rocks scarped into pyramids. In their dark fractures huge crustacea, perched upon their high claws like some war machines, watched us with fixed eyes, and under our feet crawled [myrianidae, ariciae, and] various kinds of annelides [which extended their long antennae and tentacles].

At this moment there opened before us a large grotto, dug in a picturesque heap of rocks, and carpeted with all the thick warp of the submarine flora. At first it seemed very dark to me. The solar rays seemed to be extinguished by successive gradations, until its vague transparency became nothing more than drowned light. Captain Nemo entered; we followed. My eyes soon accustomed themselves to this relative state of darkness. I could distinguish the arches springing capriciously from natural pillars, standing broad upon their granite base, like the heavy columns of Tuscan architecture. Why had our incomprehensible guide led us to the bottom of this submarine crypt? I was soon to know. After descending a rather sharp declivity, our feet trod the bottom of a kind of circular pit. There Captain Nemo stopped and with his hand indicated an object I had not yet perceived. It was an oyster of extraordinary dimensions, a gigantic tridacne, a goblet which could have contained a whole lake of holy water, a basin the breadth of which was more than two yards and a half, and consequently larger than that ornamenting the saloon of the *Nautilus*. I approached this extraordinary mollusc. It adhered by its byssus to a table of granite, and there, isolated, it developed itself in the calm waters of the grotto. I estimated the weight of this tridacne at 600 pounds. Such an oyster would contain thirty pounds of meat; and one must have the stomach of a

Gargantua to demolish some dozens of them.

Captain Nemo was evidently acquainted with the existence of this bivalve, and [I thought he had taken us there just to show us some curiosity of Nature. But I was wrong, for he] seemed to have a particular motive in verifying the actual state of this tridacne. The shells were a little open; the Captain came near and put his dagger between to prevent them from closing; then with his hand he raised the membrane with its fringed edges, which formed a cloak for the creature. There, between the folded plaits, I saw a loose pearl, whose size equalled that of a cocoa-nut.6 Its globular shape, perfect clearness, and admirable lustre made it altogether a jewel of inestimable value. Carried away by my curiosity I stretched out my hand to seize it, weigh it, and touch it; but the Captain stopped me, made a sign of refusal, and quickly withdrew his dagger, and the two shells closed suddenly. I then understood Captain Nemo's intention. In leaving this pearl hidden in the mantle of the tridacne, he was allowing it to grow slowly. Each year the secretions of the mollusc would add new concentric circles. [And only he knew of this grotto where this "fruit" was ripening. He was cultivating it so that someday he could add it to his collection. Perhaps, like the Chinese 7 and Indians, he had deliberately bred his own pearl by placing a piece of glass under the flesh of that creature. I compared it with others already in the Captain's collection.] I estimated its value at £500,000 at least. [But this was strictly a curiosity of Nature, not a piece of jewelry to dangle from a woman's ear! It was much too heavy for that.

Our visit to this rich tridacne clam came to its end. Captain Nemo was leaving the grotto. We climbed back to the oyster banks. The clear waters were still undisturbed by pearl divers.

We each wandered on his own, stopping, strolling. I was no longer obsessed with that ridiculous fear. Now the sea bottom was rising towards the surface. Soon I was wading with my head out of water. Conseil walked over to me and, resting his helmet against mine, he lifted his eyes in greeting. The high plateau lasted for only a short trek, and then we descended into deeper water.]

After ten minutes Captain Nemo stopped suddenly. I thought he had halted previous to returning. No; by a gesture he bade us crouch beside him in a deep fracture of the rock, his hand pointed to one part of the liquid mass, which I watched attentively.

About five yards from me a shadow appeared, and sank to the ground. The disquieting idea of sharks shot through my

6. *size . . . of a cocoa-nut* By contrast, the largest pearl on record is the Hope pearl, which has a maximum circumference of 4½ inches and weighs about three ounces.

7. *like the Chinese* Credited with being the first Chinese to "breed his own pearl" was Ye-jin-yang of Hoochow in the thirteenth century. He placed not a bit of glass, as Aronnax says, but pellets of mud, or bits of bone, wood, or brass under the flesh of river mussels. Some Chinese, by using molded lead or tin, even grew pearls in the shape of seated Buddhas.

mind, but I was mistaken; and once again it was not a monster of the ocean that we had anything to do with.

It was a man, a living man, an Indian, a fisherman, a poor devil who, I suppose, had come to glean before the harvest. I could see the bottom of his canoe anchored some feet above his head. He dived and went up successively. A stone held between his feet, cut in the shape of a sugar loaf, whilst a rope fastened him to his boat, helped him to descend more rapidly. This was all his apparatus. Reaching the bottom about five yards deep, he went on his knees and filled his bag with oysters picked up at random. Then he went up, emptied it, pulled up his stone, and began the operation once more, which lasted thirty seconds.

The diver did not see us. The shadow of the rock hid us from sight. And how should this poor Indian ever dream that men, beings like himself, should be there under the water watching his movements, and losing no detail of the fishing? Several times he went up in this way, and dived again. He did not carry away more than ten at each plunge, for he was obliged to pull them from the bank to which they adhered by means of their strong byssus. And how many of those oysters for which he risked his life had no pearl in them! I watched him closely, his manoeuvres were regular; and, for the space of half an hour, no danger appeared to threaten him.

I was beginning to accustom myself to the sight of this interesting fishing, when suddenly, as the Indian was on the ground, I saw him make a gesture of terror, rise, and make a spring to return to the surface of the sea.

I understood his dread. A gigantic shadow appeared just above the unfortunate diver. It was a shark of enormous size advancing diagonally, his eyes on fire, and his jaws open. I was mute with horror, and unable to move.

The voracious creature shot towards the Indian, who threw himself on one side in order to avoid the shark's fins; but not its tail, for it struck his chest, and stretched him on the ground.

This scene lasted but a few seconds: the shark returned, and, turning on his back, prepared himself for cutting the Indian in two, when I saw Captain Nemo rise suddenly, and then, dagger in hand, walk straight to the monster, ready to fight face to face with him. The very moment the shark was going to snap the unhappy fisherman in two, he perceived his new adversary, and turning over, made straight towards him.

I can still see Captain Nemo's position. Holding himself well together, he waited for the shark with admirable coolness,

Captain Nemo . . . waited for the shark with admirable coolness . . . burying his dagger deep into its side. Engraving from the original edition (1870).

and when it rushed at him, threw himself on one side with wonderful quickness, avoiding the shock and burying his dagger deep into its side. But it was not all over. A terrible combat ensued.

The shark had seemed to roar, if I might say so. The blood rushed in torrents from its wound. The sea was dyed red, and through the opaque liquid I could distinguish nothing more. Nothing more until the moment when, like lightning, I saw the undaunted Captain hanging on to one of the creature's fins, struggling, as it were, hand to hand with the monster, and dealing successive blows at his enemy, yet still unable to give a decisive one.

The shark's struggles agitated the water with such fury that the rocking threatened to upset me.

I wanted to go to the Captain's assistance, but, nailed to the spot with horror, I could not stir.

I saw the haggard eye; I saw the different phases of the fight. The Captain fell to the earth, upset by the enormous mass which leant upon him. The shark's jaws opened wide, like a pair of factory shears, and it would have been all over with the Captain; but, quick as thought, harpoon in hand, Ned Land rushed towards the shark and struck it with its sharp point.

The waves were impregnated with a mass of blood. They rocked under the shark's movements, which beat them with indescribable fury. Ned Land had not missed his aim. It was the monster's death-rattle. Struck to the heart, it struggled in dreadful convulsions, the shock of which overthrew Conseil.

But Ned Land had disentangled the Captain, who, getting up without any wound, went straight to the Indian, quickly cut the cord which held him to his stone, took him in his arms, and, with a sharp blow of his heel, mounted to the surface.

We all three followed in a few seconds, saved by a miracle, and reached the fisherman's boat.

Captain Nemo's first care was to recall the unfortunate man to life again. I did not think he could succeed. I hoped so, for the poor creature's immersion was not long; but the blow from the shark's tail might have been his death-blow.

Happily, with the Captain's and Conseil's sharp friction, I saw consciousness return by degrees. He opened his eyes. What was his surprise, his terror even, at seeing four great copper heads leaning over him! And, above all, what must he have thought when Captain Nemo, drawing from the pocket of his dress a bag of pearls, placed it in his hand! This munificent charity from the man of the waters to the poor

Cingalese was accepted with a trembling hand. His wondering eyes showed that he knew not to what superhuman beings he owed both fortune and life.

At a sign from the Captain we regained the bank, and following the road already traversed, came in about half an hour to the anchor which held the canoe of the *Nautilus* to the earth.

Once on board, we each, with the help of the sailors, got rid of the heavy copper helmet.

Captain Nemo's first word was to the Canadian.

"Thank you, Master Land," said he.

"It was in revenge, Captain," **8** replied Ned Land. "I owed you that."

A ghastly smile **9** passed across the Captain's lips, and that was all.

"To the *Nautilus*," said he.

The boat flew over the waves. Some minutes after, we met the shark's dead body floating. By the black marking of the extremity of its fins, I recognised the terrible melanopteron of the Indian Seas of the species of shark properly so called. It was more than twenty-five feet long; its enormous mouth occupied one-third of its body. It was an adult, as was known by its six rows of teeth placed in an isosceles triangle in the upper jaw.

Conseil looked at it with scientific interest, and I am sure that he placed it, and not without reason, in the cartilaginous class, of the chondropterygian order, with fixed gills, of the selac[h]ian family, in the genus of the sharks.

Whilst I was contemplating this inert mass, a dozen of these voracious beasts appeared round the boat; and, without noticing us, threw themselves upon the dead body and fought with one another for the pieces.

At half-past eight we were again on board the *Nautilus*. There I reflected on the incidents which had taken place in our excursion to the Manaar Bank.

Two conclusions I must inevitably draw from it—one bearing upon the unparalleled courage of Captain Nemo, the other upon his devotion to a human being, a representative of that race from which he fled beneath the sea. Whatever he might say, this strange man had not yet succeeded in entirely crushing his heart.

When I made this observation to him, he answered in a slightly moved tone—

"That Indian, sir, is an inhabitant of an oppressed country; and I am still, and shall be, to my last breath, one of them!" **10**

8. *It was in revenge, Captain*   Verne has nothing so vicious in mind. In the French, Ned says: *C'est une revanche*. According to context, that can mean: *Now we're quits. I only paid off a debt. I returned a favor.* That would be revenge only if it were requital for an injury. Ned is in an expansive mood because Nemo has given him a chance to exercise his skill, strength, and courage.

9. *A ghastly smile*   Verne's phrase is better rendered as a *wan, pale,* or *vague smile.* This entire exchange between these two strong men has been badly mangled in the "standard version."

10. *last breath, one of them*   Maintaining suspense over Nemo's nationality, Verne is deftly ambiguous with this curtain line. This is even clearer in the French. Nemo says: *"That Indian . . . is an inhabitant of the land of the oppressed."* He adds that he is also, and always will be, *"of that land."*

Poetic ambiguity stems from the two possible meanings of *that land.* Is Nemo speaking *figuratively* of an imaginary land of the oppressed to which all victims of oppression belong? If so, then he has not yet revealed his own specific nationality. Or is he speaking *literally* of India as *the* land of the oppressed and hence of himself as an Indian? Or does he intend both meanings? The grand ambiguity suits Nemo's romantic character and adds to the suspense.

The second possibility (the *literal* one) would mean, of course, that Nemo's oppressor, the target of his hatred, is Great Britain. But Verne does not fully reveal Nemo's origin and history until the end of *The Mysterious Island.* Since Verne intended at this point to keep us in suspense, we shall not discuss that revelation until we near the end of the present novel.

PART 2: CHAPTER IV

The Red Sea

1. *labyrinth of canals* Verne says *channels,* of course. The nature of Nemo's navigation problems here will be explained by the islanders' original name for these coral isles: *laksha divi,* or "One Hundred Thousand Isles." This name applied to both the Maldives and the Laccadives. Navigators seem to prefer the Eight Degree Channel, the One and a Half Degree Channel, or the Equatorial Channel, but apparently Nemo has chosen a strait farther north.

2. *7500 (French) leagues* Here again we have Verne's own conversion ratio. He has been reckoning a league as 2.16 miles.

3. *N.N.E.* Verne says *nord-nord-ouest,* or *N.N.W.*

In the course of the day of the 29th of January, the Island of Ceylon disappeared under the horizon, and the *Nautilus,* at a speed of twenty miles an hour, slid into the labyrinth of canals **1** which separate the Maldives from the Laccadives. It coasted even the Island of Kiltan, a land originally madreporic, discovered by Vasco da Gama in 1499, and one of the nineteen principal islands of the Laccadive Archipelago, situated between 10° and 14° 30′ north latitude, and 69° 50′ 12″ east longitude.

We had made 16,220 miles, or 7500 (French) leagues **2** from our starting-point in the Japanese Seas.

The next day (30th January), when the *Nautilus* went to the surface of the ocean, there was no land in sight. Its course was N.N.E.,**3** in the direction of the Sea of Oman, between Arabia and the Indian Peninsula, which serves as an outlet to the Persian Gulf. It was evidently a block without any possible egress. Where was Captain Nemo taking us to? I could not say. This, however, did not satisfy the Canadian, who that day came to me asking where we were going.

"We are going where our Captain's fancy takes us, Master Ned."

"His fancy cannot take us far, then," said the Canadian. "The Persian Gulf has no outlet: and if we do go in, it will not be long before we are out again."

"Very well, then, we will come out again, Master Land; and if, after the Persian Gulf, the *Nautilus* would like to visit the Red Sea, the Straits of Bab-el-mandeb are there to give us entrance."

"I need not tell you, sir," said Ned Land, "that the Red Sea is as much closed as the Gulf, as the Isthmus of Suez is not yet cut; and if it was, a boat as mysterious as ours would not risk itself in a canal cut with sluices.4 And again, the Red Sea is not the road to take us back to Europe."

"But I never said we were going back to Europe."

"What do you suppose, then?"

"I suppose that, after visiting the curious coasts of Arabia and Egypt, the *Nautilus* will go down the Indian Ocean again, perhaps cross the Channel of Mozambique, perhaps off the Mascarenhas, so as to gain the Cape of Good Hope."

"And once at the Cape of Good Hope?" asked the Canadian, with peculiar emphasis.

"Well, we shall penetrate into that Atlantic which we do not yet know. Ah! friend Ned, you are getting tired of this journey under the sea; you are surfeited with the incessantly varying spectacle of submarine wonders. For my part, I shall be sorry to see the end of a voyage which it is given to so few men to make."

["But M. Aronnax, do you realise we have been prisoners on the *Nautilus* for nearly three months?"

"I did not realise that. But then I have not been counting the days and the hours."

"But this has got to end!"

"The end will come in due time, Ned. Meanwhile, what can we do? What is the point of arguing? My good Ned—if ever you can come to me and say, 'I see a good chance to escape,' I will discuss it with you. But that is not the case right now. And to speak frankly, I do not think Captain Nemo will venture into European seas." 5

This dialogue makes it clear that I had become fanatically attached to the *Nautilus* and its Captain.

Ned ended our talk, muttering, more to himself than to me, "That may all be true, but to my way of thinking, a man is not really alive unless he is free."]

For four days, till the 3d of February, the *Nautilus* scoured the Sea of Oman, at various speeds and at various depths. It seemed to go at random, as if hesitating as to which road it should follow, but we never passed the tropic of Cancer.

In quitting this sea we sighted Muscat for an instant, one of the most important towns of the country of Oman. I admired its strange aspect, surrounded by black rocks upon which its white houses and forts stood in relief. I saw the rounded domes of its mosques, the elegant points of its minarets, its fresh and verdant terraces. But it was only a vision! The *Nautilus* soon sank under the waves of that part of the sea.

4. *canal cut with sluices*   Today we would say in English not *sluices* but *locks*.

5. *do not think . . . European seas*   Aronnax is really equivocating here. Earlier, when he learned that Nemo *does venture into the Mediterranean*, he thought: *This would be good news to share with Ned Land!* This shift in loyalties is what's on Aronnax's conscience as he writes his next sentence.

Charles Darwin's map of the Maldives that he used in his book *The Structure and Distribution of Coral Reefs* (1842). This section of the "One Hundred Thousand Isles" is 480 miles long.

I saw the rounded domes of . . . mosques, the elegant points of . . . minarets, . . . fresh and verdant terraces. A Mohammedan mosque as represented in *Mitchell's School Geography* (1863).

6. *for a distance of six miles*   Read: *at* a distance of six miles.

7. *according to . . . Edrisi*   Here is colorful evidence of Verne's artistic use of his voracious reading. Idrisi's *Kitāb Rūjār* (*The Book of Roger*), completed in 1154, was translated into a two-volume French edition in 1836–1840. Verne, as this chapter will make clear, apparently devoured the work, along with thousands of other books, the contents of which reemerge as monologue by Aronnax and dialogue by him and Nemo.

Abu 'Abdullah Mohammed Ibn Mohammed Ash-Sharif al-Idrisi (1100–c.1166), Arab geographer, was hailed to the court of Roger II, Norman king of Sicily, who commissioned Idrisi to do an illustrated treatise on "the whole of the known world." Idrisi worked on his *Book of Roger* for fifteen years. He consulted ancient authorities like Ptolemy and Orosius, and Arabic experts, but he also drew on travelers' accounts of the day as well as on official court records of Roger's own dominions. Hence Idrisi's detailed description of twelfth-century Sicily has great historical value. His famous map of the Mediterranean and Near East is far superior to any European map of that period. Anyone as familiar with nautical affairs as Nemo would be well acquainted with Idrisi's comments on the Red Sea.

8. *richest commercial magazine*   The word *magazine* is oddly appropriate here, since Verne is going into Arabic

We passed along the Arabian coast of Mahrah and Hadramaut, for a distance of six miles,**6** its undulating line of mountains being occasionally relieved by some ancient ruin. The 5th of February we at last entered the Gulf of Aden, a perfect funnel introduced into the neck of Bab-el-mandeb, through which the Indian waters entered the Red Sea.

The 6th of February, the *Nautilus* floated in sight of Aden, perched upon a promontory which a narrow isthmus joins to the mainland, a kind of inaccessible Gibraltar, the fortifications of which were rebuilt by the English after taking possession in 1839. I caught a glimpse of the octagon minarets of this town, which was at one time, according to the historian Edrisi,**7** the richest commercial magazine **8** on the coast.

I certainly thought that Captain Nemo, arrived at this point, would back out again; but I was mistaken, for he did no such thing, much to my surprise.

The next day, the 7th of February, we entered the Straits of Bab-el-mandeb, the name of which, in the Arab tongue, means "The gate of tears."

To twenty miles in breadth, it is only thirty-two in length. And for the *Nautilus,* starting at full speed, the crossing was scarcely the work of an hour. But I saw nothing, not even the Island of Perim, with which the British Government has fortified the position of Aden. There were too many English or French steamers of the line of Suez to Bombay, Calcutta to Melbourne, and from Bourbon to the Mauritus, furrowing this narrow passage, for the *Nautilus* to venture to show itself. So it remained prudently below. At last, about noon, we were in the waters of the Red Sea.

[The Red Sea, famous in Biblical tradition, is replenished rarely by rain and never by any important river. Its evapouration is so continuously high that its water level is dropping by a metre and a half every year. Singular gulf! If it were locked in by land on all sides, like a lake, it would probably dry up entirely. It is inferior in that sense to the neighbouring Caspian and Dead Seas, whose levels remain constant: their evapouration equals the amount of water that flows into their basins.

The Red Sea is 1600 miles in length and averages 150 miles in width. In the days of the Egyptian Ptolemies and Roman emperors, it was the main commercial artery of the world. When the Suez Canal is completed,**9** the region will win back much of its prestige, a prestige that the Suez railroads have already partly regained.]

I would not even seek to understand the caprice which had

decided Captain Nemo upon entering the gulf. But I quite approved of the *Nautilus* entering it. Its speed was lessened; sometimes it kept on the surface, sometimes it dived to avoid a vessel, and thus I was able to observe the upper and lower parts of this curious sea.

The 8th of February, from the first dawn of day, Mocha came in sight, now a ruined town, whose walls would fall at a gunshot, yet which shelters here and there some verdant date-trees; once an important city, containing six public markets, and twenty-six mosques, and whose walls, defended by fourteen forts, formed a girdle of two miles in circumference.

The *Nautilus* then approached the African shore, where the depth of the sea was greater. There, between two waters clear as crystal, through the open panels we were allowed to contemplate the beautiful bushes of brilliant coral, and large blocks of rocks clothed with a splendid fur of green algae and fuci. What an indescribable spectacle, and what variety of sites and landscapes along these sandbanks and volcanic islands which bound the Libyan coast! But where these shrubs appeared in all their beauty was on the eastern coast, which the *Nautilus* soon gained. It was on the coast of Tehama, for there not only did this display of zoophytes flourish beneath the level of the sea, but they also formed picturesque interlacings which unfolded themselves about sixty feet above the surface, more capricious but less highly coloured than those whose freshness was kept up by the vital powers of the waters.

What charming hours I passed thus at the window of the

history. European forms of the word all derive from an Arabic word for *warehouse, depot, commercial center.* We still call a military storehouse a magazine. By extension, the word came to cover the chamber in a gun that contains a supply of bullets, and then a periodical that supplies readers with a miscellany of literary items. The French also use the word in both original and extended senses: they call the department store *le grand magasin* and the illustrated magazine *le magazine.*

9. *When the Suez Canal is completed* That will be in November 1869, twenty-one months after the present action, as we shall see in our note on Ferdinand de Lesseps.

There were too many English or French steamers . . . furrowing this narrow passage, for the Nautilus *to show itself.* A French steamer of the period as pictured in A. E. Brehm's *Merveilles de la Nature* (1885).

saloon! What new specimens of submarine flora and fauna did I admire under the brightness of our electric lantern!

[I saw mushroom-shaped fungoids; slate-coloured sea-anemones; the thalassianthus aster, among others; tubular pores, corals shaped like flutes, waiting for the great god Pan to put them to his lips; conches peculiar to these waters, spiralled at the base, living in the hollows in madreporic formations; and thousands of specimens of a polypary I had not yet seen—the common sponge.

The class of sponges, first of the group of polyps, gives us a strange and curious product whose utility is uncontestable. The sponge is not a plant, although some naturalists still insist it is; to me it is an animal of the lowest species, a polyp inferior to that of the coral. To me its animal nature is no longer in question; I cannot accept even the view of those ancient savants who regarded the sponge as intermediate between plant and animal. I will concede that naturalists are not all of one mind on the structure of the sponge. For some, it is a polyp. For Milne-Edwards and others, it is *sui generis,* in a class all by itself.

The class of sponges comprises about three hundred species that are found in many seas. Some of them are found in certain rivers: they have been called fluviatiles. But their favourite waters are those of the Mediterranean, of the Greek Archipelago, of the Syrian coast, and of the Red Sea. There we find sponges of the highest quality, which can command prices up to 150 francs, like the blond Syrian sponge and the hard Barbary sponge. But I could not hope to study these zoophytes in the seaports of the Levant, since we were separated by the Isthmus of Suez, so I had to be content with observing them in the Red Sea.

I called Conseil to my side while the *Nautilus* was sailing, at a depth of 25 to 30 feet, slowly past those beautiful rocks of the east coast.]

There grew sponges of all shapes, pediculated, foliated, globular, and digital. They certainly justified the names of baskets, cups, distaffs, elks'-horns, lions'-feet, peacocks'-tails, and Neptune's-gloves, which have been given to them by the fishermen, greater poets than the savants.**10**

[From their fibrous tissue, infused with a gelatinous substance, there issues a tiny trickle of water. This gives life to each cell, and then it is expelled by contracting movements. This gelatinous substance disappears when the polyp dies, but it releases ammonia as it decomposes. What finally re-

10. *greater poets than the savants* Here Aronnax the romanticist is happily at odds with Aronnax the scientist. Aronnax is proud that the names fishermen give to sponges, corals, and fishes are so beautiful and imaginative. And he often enjoys quoting scientists who do use metaphor; remember how he responded to Cuvier's description of the argonaut's shell as *an elegant skiff.* As a romanticist, Aronnax feels that the man close to nature will intuitively express that unity in metaphor. For a metaphor by definition expresses the similarity between dissimilar things.

But from the scientist's point of view, such popular nomenclature (*lion's-feet, Neptune's-gloves*) gets in the way of universal classification. We can pick that up in a book that A. C. L. G. Gunther is probably working on even while the *Nautilus* is negotiating the Red Sea; his *The Study of Fishes* will appear in 1880. Gunther gruntles that Aristotle's "ideas of specific distinction were as vague as those of the fishermen whose nomenclature he adopted; it never occurred to him that such popular names are subject to change, or may be entirely lost with time, . . . or that [different] popular names are often applied . . . to the same fish, or that different stages of growth are designated by distinct [popular] names." We can infer what Aronnax's answer will be if he ever reads Gunther: "By all means, identify the fish or the sponge with a distinctive Latin name. And then relax and enjoy life by adding to your account the name given by the fishermen, greater poets than the savants."

mains are just the horny or brownish-red fibres that we call the domestic sponge. This is put to various uses, depending on its elasticity and durability.

Conseil and I saw these polyps clinging to rocks, to mollusc shells, even to the stems of hydrophytes. They decorated every crevice of rock, some spreading out, others standing tall, others hanging like coral growths. I explained to Conseil that sponges are collected either by dredging or by diving. And diving is preferable because picking them by hand does not damage the polypary fibres and so guarantees better prices.]

Other zoophytes which multiply near the sponges consist principally of medusae of a most elegant kind. The molluscs were represented by varieties of the calmar (which, according to Orbigny, are peculiar to the Red Sea); and reptiles by the virgata turtle, of the genus of cheloniae, which furnished a wholesome and delicate food for our table.

As to the fish, they were abundant, and often remarkable. The following are those which the nets of the *Nautilus* brought more frequently on board:—

Rays of a red-brick colour, with bodies marked with blue spots, and easily recognisable by their double spikes; [specimens of arnacks, with silver backs; whip-tail sting-rays; bockats, two metres long, moving like overcoats in the water; aodons, toothless although related to the sharks; dromedary-ostracions whose hump ends in a curved spine a foot and a half long; ophidians that resemble morays, with silver tails, blue backs, brown pectoral fins tinted with grey; fiatolae, a species of stromateidae, striped with gold and decked with the three colours of the French flag; blennies more than a foot long;] some superb caranxes, marked with seven transverse bands of jet-black, blue and yellow fins, and gold and silver scales; mullets with yellow heads; gobies, and a thousand other species, common to the ocean which we had just traversed.

The 9th of February, the *Nautilus* floated in the broadest part of the Red Sea, which is comprised between Souakin, on the west coast, and Koomfidah, on the east coast, with a diameter of [one hundred and] ninety miles.11

That day at noon, after the bearings were taken, Captain Nemo mounted the platform where I happened to be, and I was determined not to let him go down again without at least pressing him regarding his ulterior projects. As soon as he saw me he approached, and graciously offered me a cigar.

"Well, sir, does this Red Sea please you? Have you suffi-

I saw . . . slate-coloured sea-anemones. . . . Sea anemones (top) and solitary coral polyps (below) as pictured in *Animal Forms: A Text-Book of Zoology* (1902) by D. S. Jordan and Harold Heath.

The sponge is not a plant, although some naturalists still insist it is. . . . One of the simplest sponges, with a portion of its wall removed to show the inside, as represented in D. S. Jordan and Harold Heath's *Animal Forms: A Text-Book of Zoology* (1902).

11. [*one hundred and*] *ninety miles* The Red Sea is "up to 225 miles . . . wide," according to *The New Columbia Encyclopedia* (1975).

12. *Strabo . . . Etesian winds* The ancient Greek Strabo boasts in his *Geography* (completed about 7 B.C.) that he has wandered "east to west from Armenia to Tuscany . . . , north to south from the Black Sea to the Ethiopian borders." Actually, he seems rarely to have wandered off the main highways of the Roman world. But his book is still valuable because it is the only ancient treatise on geography to survive. He gives us broad outlines of the historical and economic development of many countries, but fortunately concentrates on the picturesque. Thus he tells us how the Indians capture apes and elephants, how whales behave in the Persian Gulf, and how Arabs extract fresh water from the sea. And as Nemo remarks, Strabo tells us the effect on the Red Sea of *the Etesian winds.* They come from the north down across the Mediterranean. Strabo calls them Etesian ("annual," from Greek *etos,* "year") since they return every summer.

13. *Gulf of Colzoum* Here Nemo refers obliquely to one of the problems in reading Idrisi, whose *Book of Roger* we have discussed. It is often difficult to identify places Idrisi talks about because his terminology differs from that of the European tradition.

14. *covered with powdered resin* Maybe the first navigators of the Red Sea sailed in reed boats, with the "clinker" construction that Nemo describes coming later.

". . . *Steam seems to have killed all gratitude in the hearts of sailors.* . . ." Engraving from *Chambers's Miscellany* (1870).

ciently observed the wonders it covers, its fishes, its zoophytes, its parterres of sponges, and its forests of coral? Did you catch a glimpse of the towns on its borders?"

"Yes, Captain Nemo," I replied; "and the *Nautilus* is wonderfully fitted for such a study. Ah! it is an intelligent boat!"

"Yes, sir, intelligent and invulnerable. It fears neither the terrible tempests of the Red Sea, nor its currents, nor its sandbanks."

"Certainly," said I, "this sea is quoted as one of the worst, and in the time of the ancients, if I am not mistaken, its reputation was detestable."

"Detestable, M. Aronnax. The Greek and Latin historians do not speak favourably of it, and Strabo says it is very dangerous during the Etesian winds,**12** and in the rainy season. The Arabian Edrisi portrays it under the name of the Gulf of Colzoum,**13** and relates that vessels perished there in great numbers on the sandbanks, and that no one would risk sailing in the night. It is, he pretends, a sea subject to fearful hurricanes, strewn with inhospitable islands, and 'which offers nothing good either on its surface or in its depths.' Such, too, is the opinion of Arrian, Agatharcides, and Artemidorus."

"One may see," I replied, "that these historians never sailed on board the *Nautilus.*"

"Just so," replied the Captain, smiling; "and in that respect moderns are not more advanced than the ancients. It required many ages to find out the mechanical power of steam. Who knows if, in another hundred years, we may not see a second *Nautilus?* Progress is slow, M. Aronnax."

"It is true," I answered; "your boat is at least a century before its time, perhaps an era. What a misfortune that the secret of such an invention should die with its inventor!"

Captain Nemo did not reply. After some minutes' silence he continued—

"You were speaking of the opinions of ancient historians upon the dangerous navigation of the Red Sea."

"It is true," said I; "but were not their fears exaggerated?"

"Yes and no, M. Aronnax," replied Captain Nemo, who seemed to know the Red Sea by heart. "That which is no longer dangerous for a modern vessel, well rigged, strongly built, and master of its own course, thanks to obedient steam, offered all sorts of perils to the ships of the ancients. Picture to yourself those first navigators venturing in ships made of planks sewn with the cords of the palm-tree, saturated with the grease of the sea-dog, and covered with powdered resin! **14**

They had not even instruments wherewith to take their bearings, and they went by guess amongst currents of which they scarcely knew anything. Under such conditions shipwrecks were, and must have been, numerous. But in our time, steamers running between Suez and the South Seas have nothing more to fear from the fury of this gulf, in spite of contrary trade-winds. The captain and passengers do not prepare for their departure by offering propitiatory sacrifices: and, on their return, they no longer go ornamented with wreaths and gilt fillets to thank the gods in the neighbouring temple."

"I agree with you," said I; "and steam seems to have killed all gratitude in the hearts of sailors. But, Captain, since you seem to have especially studied this sea, can you tell me the origin of its name?"

"There exist several explanations on the subject, M. Aronnax. Would you like to know the opinion of a chronicler of the fourteenth century?"

"Willingly."

"This fanciful writer pretends that its name was given to it after the passage of the Israelites,15 when Pharaoh perished in the waves which closed at the voice of Moses.

> [To signalise that miracle,
> The sea turned red and vermilion.
> What name could one give it then
> Except the name of the Red Sea?]"

"A poet's explanation, Captain Nemo," I replied; "but I cannot content myself with that. I ask you for your personal opinion."

"Here it is, M. Aronnax. According to my idea, we must see in this appellation of the Red Sea a translation of the Hebrew word 'Edom'; and if the ancients gave it that name, it was on account of the particular colour of its waters."

"But up to this time I have seen nothing but transparent waves and without any particular colour."

"Very likely! but as we advance to the bottom of the gulf, you will see this singular appearance. I remember seeing the Bay of Tor entirely red, like a sea of blood."

"And you attribute this colour to the presence of a microscopic seaweed?"

"Yes; it is a mucilaginous purple matter, produced by the restless little plants known by the name of trichodesmia, and of which it requires 40,000 to occupy the space of a square .04 of an inch.16 Perhaps we shall meet some when we get to Tor." 17

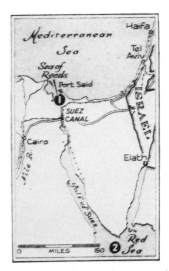

15. *passage of the Israelites* Modern biblical scholars say the Israelites crossed the Sea of Reeds (1) rather than the Red Sea (2). The Hebrew text, according to the Jewish Publication Society of America, gives the name of the area of the passage as *Yam Suf. Yam* means sea, *suf* means bulrushes or reeds. The area is now covered with sand, but when it was the Sea of Reeds it was a marshland with many pools of water. News of this new biblical interpretation, based on archaeological discoveries, made page one of *The New York Times* on October 12, 1962. (Map © 1962 by the New York Times Company. Reprinted by permission.)

16. *square .04 of an inch* That is, *one square millimeter.*

17. . . . *when we get to Tor* It sounds as if Nemo is describing here what is now called "the red tide." Parts of the Red Sea are rich in phytoplankton, minute floating plants. In a "plankton bloom," there may be forty million such cells in a quart of sea water. Because these plants contain red pigments, they can discolor the surface over wide areas.

An early record of a red tide appears in the Book of Exodus:

"Aaron . . . lifted up his staff and struck the water of the Nile . . . and all the water was changed into blood. The fish died and the river stank, and the Egyptians could not drink water from the Nile. But the Egyptian magicians did the same thing by their spells" (*The New English Bible*, 1970).

"So, Captain Nemo, it is not the first time you have overrun the Red Sea on board the *Nautilus?*"

"No, sir."

"As you spoke a while ago of the passage of the Israelites, and of the catastrophe to the Egyptians, I will ask whether you have met with traces under the water of this great historical fact?"

"No, sir; and for a very good reason."

"What is it?"

"It is, that the spot where Moses and his people passed is now so blocked up with sand, that the camels can barely bathe their legs there. You can well understand that there would not be water enough for my *Nautilus*."

"And the spot?" I asked.

"The spot is situated a little above the Isthmus of Suez, in the arm which formerly made a deep estuary, when the Red Sea extended to the Salt Lakes. Now, whether this passage were miraculous or not, the Israelites, nevertheless, crossed there to reach the Promised Land, and Pharaoh's army perished precisely on that spot; and I think that excavations made in the middle of the sand would bring to light a large number of arms and instruments of Egyptian origin."

"That is evident," I replied; "and for the sake of archaeologists let us hope that these excavations will be made sooner or later, when new towns are established on the isthmus, after the construction of the Suez Canal; a canal, however, very useless to a vessel like the *Nautilus*."

"Very likely; but useful to the whole world," said Captain Nemo. "The ancients well understood the utility of a communication between the Red Sea and the Mediterranean for their commercial affairs: but they did not think of digging a canal direct, and took the Nile as an intermediate. Very probably the canal which united the Nile to the Red Sea was begun by Sesostris, if we may believe tradition. One thing is certain, that in the year 615 before Jesus Christ, Necos undertook the works of an alimentary canal to the waters of the Nile, across the plain of Egypt, looking towards Arabia. It took four days to go up this canal, and it was so wide that two triremes could go abreast. It was carried on by Darius, the son of Hystaspes, and probably finished by Ptolemy II. Strabo saw it navigated; but its decline from the point of departure, near Bubastes, to the Red Sea was so slight, that it was only navigable for a few months in the year. This canal answered all commercial purposes to the age of Antoninus, when it was abandoned and blocked up with sand. Restored by order of the Caliph Omar, it was definitely destroyed in 761 or 762 by Caliph Al-Mansor, who wished to prevent the arrival of provisions to Mohammed-ben-Abdallah, who had revolted against him. During the expedition into Egypt, your General Bonaparte discovered traces of the works in the Desert of Suez; and surprised by the tide, he nearly perished before regaining Hadjaroth, at the very place where Moses had encamped three thousand years before him."

"Well, Captain, what the ancients dared not undertake, this junction between the two seas, which will shorten the road from Cadiz to India, M. [de] Lesseps has succeeded in doing; and before long he will have changed Africa into an immense island."

"Yes, M. Aronnax; you have the right to be proud of your countryman. Such a man brings more honour to a nation than great captains. He began, like so many others, with disgust and rebuffs; but he has triumphed, for he has the genius of will. And it is sad to think that a work like that, which ought to have been an international work, and which would have sufficed to make a reign illustrious, should have succeeded by the energy of one man. All honour to M. [de] Lesseps!" 18

"Yes, honour to the great citizen!" I replied, surprised by the manner in which Captain Nemo had just spoken.

"Unfortunately," he continued, "I cannot take you through the Suez Canal; but you will be able to see the long jetty of Port Said after to-morrow, when we shall be in the Mediterranean."

"The Mediterranean!" I exclaimed.

"Yes, sir; does that astonish you?"

"What astonishes me is to think that we shall be there the day after to-morrow."

"Indeed?"

"Yes, Captain, although by this time I ought to have accustomed myself to be surprised at nothing since I have been on board your boat."

"But the cause of this surprise?"

"Well, it is the fearful speed you will have to put on the *Nautilus,* if the day after to-morrow she is to be in the Mediterranean, having made the round of Africa, and doubled the Cape of Good Hope!"

"Who told you that she would make the round of Africa, and double the Cape of Good Hope, sir?"

"Well, unless the *Nautilus* sails on dry land, and passes above the isthmus—"

18. *All honour to M. [de] Lesseps* As Nemo and Aronnax are talking, Ferdinand de Lesseps is nearing the end of his Herculean labors on the Suez Canal, which will be opened officially on November 17, 1869. A sheik will utter a prayer, a priest will intone a *Te Deum,* and the Empress Eugénie will make a speech praising Lesseps. Returning home in triumph, Lesseps, a great admirer of Jules Verne, will nominate "the great romancer" for the Legion of Honor. The empress, in the absence of Napoleon III who will be at the front in 1870, will sign the decree granting Verne the decoration.

And so Verne will be one of those who will experience painful conflict when Lesseps (along with his son and the engineer Alexandre Eiffel) will be convicted of fraud in the Panama Canal scandal of 1893. As Kenneth Allott, Verne's biographer in English, summed it up, "Lesseps . . . suffered because the magnitude of his ideas drove him into underestimating expense and then into dishonesty to hide his difficulties."

Early in his career, Lesseps had said: "No operation, however difficult, is now regarded by modern art as impossible . . . it is merely a question of money. . . ."

"Or beneath it, M. Aronnax."

"Beneath it?"

"Certainly," replied Captain Nemo, quietly. "A long time ago Nature made under this tongue of land what man has this day made on its surface."

"What! such a passage exists?"

"Yes; a subterranean passage, which I have named the Arabian tunnel. It takes us beneath Suez, and opens into the Gulf of Pelusium."

"But this isthmus is composed of nothing but quicksands?"

"To a certain depth. But at fifty-five yards only, there is a solid layer of rock."

"Did you discover this passage by chance?" I asked, more and more surprised.

"Chance and reasoning, sir; and by reasoning even more than by chance."

["Captain, I can hardly believe my ears."

"Ah, monsieur, *Aures habent et non audient*—'They have ears but they hear not'—is an eternal truth.] Not only does this passage exist, but I have profited by it several times. Without that I should not have ventured this day into the impassable Red Sea."

["Would it be presumptuous on my part to ask how you found this tunnel?"

"Well, Professor, there can be no secrets between people who will never separate."

I ignored his basic premise, waiting for his story.

"Monsieur le professeur, the simple reasoning of the naturalist led me to discover my Arabian Tunnel.]

"I noticed that in the Red Sea and in the Mediterranean there existed a certain number of fishes of a kind perfectly identical—ophidia, fiatoles, [persegae, joels,] girelles, and exocoeti. Certain of that fact, I asked myself was it possible that there was no communication between the two seas? If there was, the subterranean current must necessarily run from the Red Sea to the Mediterranean, from the sole cause of difference of level. I caught a large number of fishes in the neighbourhood of Suez. I passed a copper ring through their tails, and threw them back into the sea. Some months later, on the coast of Syria, I caught some of my fish ornamented with the ring. Thus the communication between the two was proved.**19** I then sought for it with my *Nautilus;* I discovered it, ventured into it, and before long, sir, you too will have passed through my Arabian tunnel!"

19. *communication between the two was proved* Nemo's *"chance and reasoning"* foreshadows a similar twentieth-century experiment. Norbert Casteret—who in 1922 had discovered caves decorated with twenty-thousand-year-old art—cast bags of dye into waters running through caverns in southern France.

Later the dyes emerged in a stream in northern Spain. Casteret thus proved the existence of a natural tunnel that runs the entire width of the Pyrenees.

"It was Jules Verne," Casteret said, "who encouraged me to penetrate the great caves. . . ."

PART 2: CHAPTER V
The Arabian Tunnel[1]

[ater that day I reported to Conseil and Ned Land that part of my conversation with Nemo that I knew would interest them most. I explained that within two days we would be in Mediterranean waters. Conseil clapped his hands, but the Canadian shrugged his shoulders.

"An under-water tunnel," he cried, "a tunnel connecting two seas! Whoever heard of such nonsense!"

"Ned, whoever heard of the *Nautilus?*" Conseil asked. "Nobody. But it still exists! You should not be so willing to shrug off something just because you never heard of it."

"All right," Ned shook his head. "We will soon find out if it is true. After all, what could please me more than a tunnel if it gets us into European waters!"]

That same evening, in 20° 30′ north latitude,[2] the *Nautilus* floated on the surface of the sea, approaching the Arabian coast. I saw Djeddah, the most important counting-house of Egypt, Syria, Turkey, and India. I distinguished clearly enough its buildings, the vessels anchored at the quays, and those whose draught of water obliged them to anchor in the roads. The sun, rather low on the horizon, struck full on the houses of the town, bringing out their whiteness. Outside, some wooden cabins, and some made of reeds, showed the quarter inhabited by the Bedouins. Soon Djeddah was shut out from view by the shadows of night, and the *Nautilus* found herself under water slightly phosphorescent.

The next day, the 10th of February, we sighted several ships running to windward. The *Nautilus* returned to its submarine navigation; but at noon, when her bearings were taken, the sea being deserted, she rose again to her waterline.

Accompanied by Ned and Conseil, I seated myself on the

1. *The Arabian Tunnel* In 1863 Verne spent time with Charles Sainte-Claire Deville, a geographer who had explored the interior of volcanic craters from Teneriffe to Stromboli. Deville told Verne that many volcanoes "occur in well defined belts or chains." They discussed the possibility that volcanoes are connected by deep underground tunnels.

From such talks grew Verne's fictional obsession with natural tunnels. According to Kenneth Allott, Verne's English biographer, it didn't take much to trigger the obsession: Verne wanted to "return to the womb" and,

I saw Djeddah, the most important counting-house of Egypt, Syria, Turkey, and India. Engraving from *The American Cyclopaedia* (1873).

after all, "the first long words most boys learn are stalactite and stalagmite." But womb-returners are legion, and few ever produce novels like *A Journey to the Center of the Earth* (1864) or notions like Nemo's Arabian Tunnel.

After Verne's death it was discovered that underground passages created by natural forces are almost as common as he had imagined. One of the longest so far surveyed is the thirty-seven-mile Hölloch tunnel in Switzerland. The Casteret tunnel already discussed is probably longer.

Nature makes tunnels in several ways. Buckling of rock strata, now known to be intensified by the drift of the continental plates, opens many underground passageways. Water may enlarge the openings already created by rock faults. But flowing lava fashions the best tunnels of all. A lava stream may solidify on the surface while its deeper levels continue to flow. Then the fluid lava may drain away and leave a horizontal hollow tube, maybe tens of feet in diameter.

Recent researches on "continental drift" indicate that the Red Sea marks the boundary of two of the continental plates. This greatly increases the chances of there being undersea passages in that area, and it makes Verne's Arabian Tunnel all the more prophetic.

2. *20° 30′ north latitude* Verne says 21°, which is indeed closer to what is now known as Jiddah.

3. *fables about mermaids* One reason for the mermaid fables is that when she floats half upright, with a suckling baby under one flipper, the dugong does look like a "half woman, half fish," especially when the observer is not too close. It helps, of course, if the observer is a prurient sailor who has been too long between ports.

platform. The coast on the eastern side looked like a mass faintly printed upon a damp fog.

We were leaning on the sides of the pinnace, talking of one thing and another, when Ned Land, stretching out his hand towards a spot on the sea, said—

"Do you see anything there, sir?"

"No, Ned," I replied; "but I have not your eyes, you know."

"Look well," said Ned, "there, on the starboard beam, about the height of the lantern! Do you not see a mass which seems to move?"

"Certainly," said I, after close attention; "I see something like a long black body on the top of the water."

["Maybe another *Nautilus?*" suggested Conseil.

"No," answered the harpooner, "I could be wrong, but it looks like a sea animal."

"A whale in the Red Sea?" Conseil asked.

"Yes, my boy," I told him, "they are sometimes sighted in these waters."

"This is not a whale," Ned said, keeping his eyes on the black object. "Whales and I know each other. I cannot fail to recognise a whale."

"Patience," counseled Conseil. "The *Nautilus* is making right for it. We will soon know what it is."]

And certainly before long the black object was not more than a mile from us. It looked like a great sandbank deposited in the open sea.

["What could it be?" I wondered.

"It is moving!" Ned shouted. "It dived! It does not have the forked tail of a baleen whale or a sperm whale. And its fins look more like stumps."

"What could it be?" I repeated.

"Ha!" exclaimed Ned. "Now she is on her back with her teats in the air!"

"A siren! A genuine siren," Conseil said, "if I may be permitted to say so."

Conseil's word *siren* cinched it for me. I realised that this creature belonged to that order of sea-animals that inspired the ancients to create fables about mermaids [3]—half women, half fish.

"No," I told Conseil, "not a siren. But a strange creature, nonetheless. Only a few specimens remain in these waters. It is a dugong."

"Order of sirenians, group of pisciforms, subclass of monodelphians, class of mammals, branch of vertebrates," Conseil ran up the ladder. What more remained to be said?] It was a gigantic dugong!

Ned Land looked eagerly. His eyes shone with covetousness at the sight of the animal. His hand seemed ready to harpoon it. One would have thought he was awaiting the moment to throw himself into the sea, and attack it in its element.

["Oh monsieur," he said trembling with emotion. "I have never fought a creature like that." All his being was focussed on his word *that*.]

At this instant Captain Nemo appeared on the platform. He saw the dugong, understood the Canadian's attitude, and addressing him, said—

"If you held a harpoon just now, Master Land, would it not burn your hand?"

"Just so, sir."

"And you would not be sorry to go back, for one day, to your trade of a fisherman, and to add this cetacean to the list of those you have already killed?"

"I should not, sir."

"Well, you can try."

"Thank you, sir," said Ned Land, his eyes flaming.

"Only," continued the Captain, "I advise you for your own sake not to miss the creature."

"Is the dugong dangerous to attack?" I asked, in spite of the Canadian's shrug of the shoulders.

"Yes," replied the Captain; "sometimes the animal turns upon its assailants and overturns their boat. But for Master Land, this danger is not to be feared. His eye is prompt, his arm sure. [I am only urging that he not miss because the dugong's flesh is an esteemed delicacy. I know Master Land could not resist such an exquisite dish."

"I am delighted to hear that," exclaimed the Canadian.

"Yes, Master Land, in Malaya the flesh of the dugong is reserved for the table of the princes. And so an endless hunt is in progress for this animal. Like the manatee, its relative, the dugong is close to extinction." **4**

"In that case," Conseil said seriously, "this particular dugong could be the last of its race. Maybe it would be better to spare it, for the sake of science."

"Maybe it would be better to harpoon her, for the sake of cookery," said Ned.

"Go ahead," said Nemo.]

At this moment, seven men of the crew, mute and immovable as ever, mounted the platform. One carried a harpoon and a line similar to those employed in catching whales. The

"Is the dugong dangerous to attack?" The dugong as pictured in *The American Cyclopaedia* (1873).

4. *the dugong is close to extinction* Today the dugong is classed as an endangered species. One close relative of the dugong and the manatee —Steller's sea cow—became extinct in the eighteenth century. Since dugongs and manatees are vegetarians, they used to frequent coastal waters where vegetation is easier to find. But now, apparently in self-defense, they are venturing out into the high seas. If this stratagem proves successful, the dugong will evolve new characteristics. Such adaptations have already occurred in other mammals, like the polar bears, who have been driven further into a sea life. For example, the land bear still has its dished-in face while the polar bear has developed an aquiline nose better suited to fast distance swimming.

pinnace was lifted from the bridge, pulled from its socket, and let down into the sea. Six oarsmen took their seats, and the coxswain went to the tiller. Ned, Conseil, and I went to the back of the boat.

"You are not coming, Captain?" I asked.

"No, sir; but I wish you good sport."

The boat was put off, and lifted by the six rowers, drew rapidly towards the dugong, which floated about two miles from the *Nautilus*.

Arrived some cables' length from the cetacean, the speed slackened, and the oars dipped noiselessly into the quite waters. Ned Land, harpoon in hand, stood in the forepart of the boat. The harpoon used for striking the whale is generally attached to a very long cord, which runs out rapidly as the wounded creature draws it after him. But here the cord was not more than ten fathoms long, and the extremity was attached to a small barrel, which, by floating, was to show the course the dugong took under the water.

I stood, and carefully watched the Canadian's adversary. This dugong, which also bears the name of the halicore, closely resembled the manatee; its oblong body terminated in a lengthened tail, and its lateral fins in perfect fingers. Its difference from the manatee consisted in its upper jaw, which was armed with two long and pointed teeth, which formed on each side diverging tusks.[5]

This dugong, which Ned Land was preparing to attack, was of colossal dimensions; it was more than seven yards long.[6] It did not move, and seemed to be sleeping on the waves, which circumstance made it easier to capture.

The boat approached within six yards of the animal. The oars rested on the rowlocks. I half rose. Ned Land, his body thrown a little back, brandished the harpoon in his experienced hand.

Suddenly a hissing noise was heard, and the dugong disappeared. The harpoon, although thrown with great force, had apparently only struck the water.

"Curse it!" exclaimed the Canadian, furiously; "I have missed it!"

"No," said I; "the creature is wounded—look at the blood; but your weapon has not stuck in his body."

"My harpoon! my harpoon!" cried Ned Land.

The sailors rowed on, and the coxswain made for the floating barrel. The harpoon regained, we followed in pursuit of the animal.

The latter came now and then to the surface to breathe. Its

5. *diverging tusks* But only the male has these tusks visible in the upper jaw. So Ned could not have seen *"teats."* In Aronnax's day naturalists had not yet observed dugongs closely enough to supply the new profession of science fiction with all the facts it needed.

6. *colossal dimensions . . . seven yards long* This is truly colossal. Recent sightings of dugongs report their length as three yards on the average, with four yards considered exceptional.

wound had not weakened it, for it shot onwards with great rapidity.

The boat, rowed by strong arms, flew on its track. Several times it approached within some few yards, and the Canadian was ready to strike, but the dugong made off with a sudden plunge, and it was impossible to reach it.

Imagine the passion which excited impatient Ned Land! He hurled at the unfortunate creature the most energetic expletives in the English tongue. For my part, I was only vexed to see the dugong escape all our attacks.

We pursued it without relaxation for an hour, and I began to think it would prove difficult to capture, when the animal, possessed with the perverse idea of vengeance, of which he had cause to repent, turned upon the pinnace and assailed us in its turn.

This manoeuvre did not escape the Canadian.

"Look out!" he cried.

The coxswain said some words in his outlandish tongue, doubtless warning the men to keep on their guard.

The dugong came within twenty feet of the boat, stopped, sniffed the air briskly with its large nostrils (not pierced at the extremity, but in the upper part of its muzzle). Then taking a spring he threw himself upon us.

The pinnace could not avoid the shock, and half upset, shipped at least two tons of water, which had to be emptied; but thanks to the coxswain, we caught it sideways, not full front, so we were not quite overturned. While Ned Land, clinging to the bows, belaboured the gigantic animal with blows from his harpoon, the creature's teeth were buried in the gunwale, and it lifted the whole thing out of the water, as a lion does a roebuck. We were upset over one another, and I know not how the adventure would have ended if the Canadian, still enraged with the beast, had not struck it to the heart.

I heard its teeth grind on the iron plate, and the dugong disappeared, carrying the harpoon with him. But the barrel soon returned to the surface, and shortly after the body of the animal, turned on its back. The boat came up with it, took it in tow, and made straight for the *Nautilus*.

It required tackle of enormous strength to hoist the dugong on to the platform. It weighed 10,000 pounds. [It was quartered under Ned's supervision. He observed every detail of the operation. That night the steward served me some choice dugong cutlets, very skilfully prepared by the chef. I found dugong superior to veal, to say nothing of beef.]

The next day, February 11th, the larder of the *Nautilus* was enriched by some more delicate game. A flight of sea-swallows rested on the *Nautilus*. It was a species of the *Sterna nilotica*, peculiar to Egypt; its beak is black, head grey and pointed, the eye surrounded by white spots, the back, wings, and tail of a greyish colour, the belly and throat white, and claws red. They also took some dozen of Nile ducks, a wild bird of high flavour, its throat and upper part of the head white with black spots.

[Its flavour was excellent.

The *Nautilus* was cruising now at a moderate speed, casually. I noticed that Red Sea water was becoming less salty the closer we came to the Suez.]

About five o'clock in the evening we sighted to the north the Cape of Ras-Mohammed. This cape forms the extremity of Arabia Petraea, comprised between the Gulf of Suez and the Gulf of Acabah.

The *Nautilus* penetrated into the Straits of Jubal, which leads to the Gulf of Suez. I distinctly saw a high mountain, towering between the two gulfs of Ras-Mohammed. It was Mount Horeb, that Sinai at the top of which Moses saw God face to face. [In the imagination, this mountain is always crowned with lightning.]

At six o'clock the *Nautilus,* sometimes floating, sometimes immersed, passed some distance from Tor, situated at the end of the bay, the waters of which seemed tinted with red, an observation already made by Captain Nemo. Then night fell in the midst of a heavy silence, sometimes broken by the cries of the pelican and other night-birds, and the noise of the waves breaking upon the shore, chafing against the rocks, or the panting of some far-off steamer beating the waters of the gulf with its noisy paddles.

From eight to nine o'clock the *Nautilus* remained some fathoms under the water. According to my calculation we must have been very near Suez. Through the panel of the saloon I saw the bottom of the rocks brilliantly lit up by our electric lamp. We seemed to be leaving the straits behind us more and more.**7**

At a quarter-past nine, the vessel having returned to the surface, I mounted the platform. Most impatient to pass through Captain Nemo's tunnel, I could not stay in one place, so came to breathe the fresh night-air.

Soon in the shadow I saw a pale light, half discoloured by the fog, shining about a mile from us.

"A floating lighthouse!" said some one near me.

7. *behind us more and more*   In the original, Aronnax says it seemed to him that the gulf was getting narrower and narrower.

I turned, and saw the Captain.

"It is the floating light of Suez," he continued. "It will not be long before we gain the entrance of the tunnel."

"The entrance cannot be easy?"

"No, sir; and for that reason I am accustomed to go into the steersman's cage and myself direct our course. And now if you will go down, M. Aronnax, the *Nautilus* is going under the waves, and will not return to the surface until we have passed through the Arabian tunnel."

[I followed the Captain below. The panel was closed, the tanks were filled with water, the *Nautilus* dived to about thirty feet.

I was heading towards my room, but the Captain stopped me.

"Professor, would you not like to accompany me to the pilot's cage?"

"Oh yes! I did not presume to ask," I replied gratefully.

"Then come along. You will be able to see all that is to be seen in this trip through a subterranean—and submarine—passageway."]

Captain Nemo led me towards the central staircase; half-way down he opened a door, traversed the upper deck, and landed in the pilot's cage, which it may be remembered rose at the extremity of the platform. It was a cabin measuring six feet square, very much like that occupied by the pilot on the steamboats of the Mississippi or Hudson. In the midst worked a wheel, placed vertically, and caught to the tiller-rope, which ran to the back of the *Nautilus*. Four light-ports with lenticular glasses, let in a groove in the partition of the cabin, allowed the man at the wheel to see in all directions.8

This cabin was dark; but soon my eyes accustomed themselves to the obscurity, and I perceived the pilot, a strong man, with his hands resting on the spokes of the wheel. Outside, the sea appeared vividly lit up by the lantern, which shed its rays from the back of the cabin to the other extremity of the platform.

"Now," said Captain Nemo, "let us try to make our passage."

Electric wires connected the pilot's cage with the machinery room, and from there the Captain could communicate simultaneously to his *Nautilus* the direction and the speed. He pressed a metal knob, and at once the speed of the screw diminished.

I looked in silence at the high straight wall we were running by at this moment, the immovable base of a massive sandy

8. *man at the wheel to see in all directions* This is the second time that Aronnax thinks of making his point by invoking a comparison with the American riverboat. This shows us how familiar Europeans were with details of the romantic life on the Mississippi and Hudson rivers. And once again, Aronnax's analogy satisfies both technically and psychologically.

For the *Nautilus* pilothouse does resemble the riverboat's (which Mark Twain will soon describe as "fanciful . . . , all glass . ·. . , perched on the top of the . . . deck").

And Aronnax does in effect invite us to compare Nemo's attainments with the Mississippi pilot's. The American was famous for being able to float a tall boat "on a drop of morning dew." He had to take her out on a shallow river beset with snags, driftwood, and shoals just below the surface. Nemo, however, is taking a submarine boat into an underground tunnel that spills one sea into another!

9. *from the knob*　Actually, it's the compass that Nemo is watching.

10. *fucus . . . enormous claws . . . rock*　Fucus is seaweed, including some rockweeds, but what Verne is describing here—*and by name*—are *crustaceans,* apparently big crabs.

coast. We followed it thus for an hour only some few yards off.

Captain Nemo did not take his eye from the knob,**9** suspended by its two concentric circles in the cabin. At a simple gesture, the pilot modified the course of the *Nautilus* every instant.

I had placed myself at the port-scuttle, and saw some magnificent substructures of coral, zoophytes, seaweed, and fucus, agitating their enormous claws, which stretched out from the fissures of the rock.**10**

At a quarter past ten, the Captain himself took the helm. A large gallery, black and deep, opened before us. The *Nautilus* went boldly into it. A strange roaring was heard round its sides. It was the waters of the Red Sea, which the incline of the tunnel precipitated violently towards the Mediterranean. The *Nautilus* went with the torrent, rapid as an arrow, in spite of the efforts of the machinery, which, in order to offer more effective resistance, beat the waves with reversed screw.

On the walls of the narrow passage I could see nothing but brilliant rays, straight lines, furrows of fire, traced by the great speed, under the brilliant electric light. My heart beat fast.

At thirty-five minutes past ten, Captain Nemo quitted the helm; and, turning to me, said—

"The Mediterranean!"

In less than twenty minutes, the *Nautilus,* carried along by the torrent, had passed through the Isthmus of Suez.

. . . The Captain himself took the helm.
Engraving from the original edition (1870).

PART 2: CHAPTER VI

The Grecian Archipelago

The next day, the 12th of February, at the dawn of day, the *Nautilus* rose to the surface. I hastened on to the platform. Three miles to the south the dim outline of Pelusium was to be seen. A torrent had carried us from one sea to the other. [We had travelled downstream on that current, of course; it would be impossible to return upstream.] About seven o'clock Ned and Conseil joined me. [Those inseparable companions had slept so soundly they were totally unaware of the feat the *Nautilus* had accomplished.]

"Well, Sir Naturalist," said the Canadian, in a slightly jovial tone, "and the Mediterranean?"

"We are floating on its surface, friend Ned."

"What!" said Conseil, "this very night!"

"Yes, this very night; in a few minutes we have passed this impassable isthmus."

"I do not believe it," replied the Canadian.

"Then you are wrong, Master Land," I continued; "this low coast which rounds off to the south is the Egyptian coast."

["Professor, I am not that gullible."

"But if monsieur says it," Conseil protested, "then it must be true."

"Furthermore, Ned, the Captain did me the honour of letting me stand at his side while he steered us through that narrow tunnel.] And you, who have such good eyes, Ned, you can see the jetty of Port Said stretching into the sea."

The Canadian looked attentively.

"Certainly you are right, sir, and your Captain is a first-rate man. We are in the Mediterranean. Good! Now, if you please, let us talk of our own little affair, but so that no one hears us."

I saw what the Canadian wanted, and, in any case, I

1. *my book . . . in its very element* Verne's beautiful control of his plot mechanism is typified by his timing at this point. The *Nautilus*'s arrival in the Mediterranean offers Ned his best chance for escape. And it is inevitable by now that Aronnax would see that his book must be rewritten. Each man now has maximum motivation for resisting the other's needs.

Of course Verne himself knew all along that this undersea research would render Aronnax's "standard text" obsolete. But Verne saved that development for this crucial moment. *That's artistic storytelling.* All the more criminal, then, that Verne's pacing should have been tampered with to the extent of ten cuts in the preceding chapter, six in this one.

"The Greeks destroying a Turkish man-of-war" during the "bloody and protracted warfare" for Greek independence, according to *Mitchell's School Geography* (1863).

thought it better to let him talk, as he wished it; so we all three went and sat down near the lantern, where we were less exposed to the spray of the blades.

"Now, Ned, we listen; what have you to tell us?"

"What I have to tell you is very simple. We are in Europe; and before Captain Nemo's caprices drag us once more to the bottom of the Polar Seas, or lead us into Oceania, I ask to leave the *Nautilus.*"

I wished in no way to shackle the liberty of my companions, but I certainly felt no desire to leave Captain Nemo.

Thanks to him, and thanks to his apparatus, I was each day nearer the completion of my submarine studies; and I was rewriting my book of submarine depths in its very element.[1] Should I ever again have such an opportunity of observing the wonders of the ocean? No, certainly not! And I could not bring myself to the idea of abandoning the *Nautilus* before the cycle of investigation was accomplished.

"Friend Ned, answer me frankly, are you tired of being on board? Are you sorry that destiny has thrown us into Captain Nemo's hands?"

The Canadian remained some moments without answering. Then crossing his arms, he said—

"Frankly, I do not regret this journey under the seas. I shall be glad to have made it; but now that it is made, let us have done with it. That is my idea."

"It will come to an end, Ned."

"Where and when?"

"Where I do not know—when I cannot say; or rather, I suppose it will end when these seas have nothing more to teach us. [Everything that begins in this world must end."

"I agree," said Conseil. "It is highly likely that when Captain Nemo has completed this journey, he will end our captivity too."

"You mean end our lives!" cried the Canadian.

"Please, Ned," I said, "let us not exaggerate. I do not think we have anything like that to fear from the Captain. But I do not agree with Conseil either. We now know all the secrets of the *Nautilus.* The Captain could never accept the idea of letting us reveal those secrets to the world."]

"Then what do you hope for?" demanded the Canadian.

"That circumstances may occur as well six months hence as now by which we may and ought to profit."

"Oh!" said Ned Land, "and where shall we be in six months, if you please, Sir Naturalist?"

"Perhaps in China; you know the *Nautilus* is a rapid traveller. It goes through water as swallows through the air, or as an express on the land. It does not fear frequented seas: who can say that it may not beat the coasts of France, England, or America, on which flight may be attempted as advantageously as here."

"M. Aronnax," replied the Canadian, "your arguments are rotten at the foundation. You speak in the future, 'We shall be there! we shall be here!' I speak in the present, 'We are here, and we must profit by it.' "

Ned Land's logic pressed me hard, and I felt myself beaten on that ground. I knew not what argument would now tell in my favour.

"Sir," continued Ned, "let us suppose an impossibility; if Captain Nemo should this day offer you your liberty, would you accept it?"

"I do not know," I answered.

"And if," he added, "the offer he made you this day was never to be renewed, would you accept it?"

[I could not answer.

"And what do *you* have to say, my good friend?" Ned demanded of Conseil.

"Your good friend," Conseil said, "has nothing to say. Conseil is a bachelor—like his master, like his friend Ned. Conseil has no wife, no parents, no children waiting for his return. Conseil is in the service of monsieur. Conseil thinks and talks like monsieur. Conseil regrets he cannot be called upon to resolve this question. Only two people face each other in this matter: on the one side monsieur, on the other, Master Land. Conseil is here to listen, to keep score." 2

I could not help smiling at Conseil's self-annihilation. Surely Ned must be glad, I thought, that he did not have to contend with Conseil too.

"So, monsieur," Ned summed it up. "Since Conseil does not exist, it is up to you and me to settle this question. You know where I stand. What is your decision?"

I could not procrastinate much longer. I had to face the situation honestly.]

"Friend Ned, this is my answer. Your reasoning is against me. We must not rely on Captain Nemo's good-will. Common prudence forbids him to set us at liberty. On the other side, prudence bids us profit by the first opportunity to leave the *Nautilus.*"

"Well, M. Aronnax, that is wisely said."

"Only one observation—just one. The occasion must be serious, and our first attempt must succeed; if it fails, we shall never find another, and Captain Nemo will never forgive us."

"All that is true," replied the Canadian. "But your observa-

Arab family of the North African coast "removing," according to *Mitchell's School Geography* (1863).

2. *to keep score* This extraordinary speech typifies Verne's virtuosity in characterization. Conseil has now turned his third-person treatment on himself. This actually allows him to explore his condition objectively as well as obsequiously. His "unemotional" analysis also makes it clear that Conseil and Aronnax are content in their celibacy while it emphasizes the fact that Ned is frustrated. Finally, Conseil's clever use of the third person when talking about himself (as "he") does not preclude the possibility that he will still offer an opinion. For he need only return to talking of himself in the first person (as "I").

3. *nothing was to be seen but the pilot's cage* Why doesn't Nemo use a periscope? He must be running awash like this, with only the pilot-house a bit above water, so he can scan the surface with minimal risk of detection. This suggests that a military operation is under way.

Like most early submarine designers, Nemo apparently distrusted the periscope. Simon Lake did not include one in his designs until 1893, and John Philip Holland did not use one at all on his 1900 model. And while Nemo is way ahead of them in most aspects of submarine design, he seems comparatively uninterested in optics. After all, for Nemo's purposes, when no one is expecting a submarine, riding awash will do the trick! This proved true in the famous attack of the Confederate submersible *Hunley* on the Union ship *Housatonic*.

The periscope was distrusted because early models had proved almost worthless. In 1854 E. M. Marié-Davy, a Frenchman, designed a "submarine sight tube." It contained two mirrors, one above the other, facing in opposite directions. Each mirror was tilted at a 45° angle, so that the upper mirror caught horizontal rays "up there" and deflected them "down here" to the lower mirror, which deflected them horizontally to the user's eye.

Notice the shortcomings. To be of any value, the tube must be tall to allow the sub to operate well below the surface. But a long tube absorbs light, as do the mirrors themselves. Consider, too, the difficulty caused by the roll or pitch of the vessel and by the waves passing (if not covering) the upper mirror. Such a crude device would work well only under special conditions. For example, in the American Civil War, the Union monitor *Osage* ran aground and Confederate troops attacked her. The *Osage* crew had to retreat below deck. The captain, however, raised a short periscope through a hatch and could thus see the Grays and direct his own gunfire until his engineers could get him refloated. *His* periscope worked only because it was used to transmit a view from a *motionless*

tion applies equally to all attempts at flight, whether in two years' time, or in two days'. But the question is still this: If a favourable opportunity presents itself, it must be seized."

"Agreed! and now, Ned, will you tell me what you mean by a favourable opportunity?"

"It will be that which, on a dark night will bring the *Nautilus* a short distance from some European coast."

"And you will try and save yourself by swimming?"

"Yes, if we were near enough to the bank, and if the vessel was floating at that time. Not if the bank was far away, and the boat was under the water."

"And in that case?"

"In that case, I should seek to make myself master of the pinnace. I know how it is worked. We must get inside, and the bolts once drawn, we shall come to the surface of the water, without even the pilot, who is in the bows, perceiving our flight."

"Well, Ned, watch for the opportunity; but do not forget that a hitch will ruin us."

"I will not forget, sir."

"And now, Ned, would you like to know what I think of your project?"

"Certainly, M. Aronnax."

"Well, I think—I do not say I hope—I think that this favourable opportunity will never present itself."

"Why not?"

"Because Captain Nemo cannot hide from himself that we have not given up all hope of regaining our liberty, and he will be on his guard, above all, in the seas, and in the sight of European coasts."

"We shall see," replied Ned Land, shaking his head determinedly.

"And now, Ned Land," I added, "let us stop here. Not another word on the subject. The day that you are ready, come and let us know, and we will follow you. I rely entirely upon you."

Thus ended a conversation which, at no very distant time, led to such grave results. I must say here that facts seemed to confirm my foresight, to the Canadian's great despair. Did Captain Nemo distrust us in these frequented seas? or did he only wish to hide himself from the numerous vessels, of all nations, which ploughed the Mediterranean? I could not tell; but we were oftener between waters, and far from the coast. Or, if the *Nautilus* did emerge, nothing was to be seen but the pilot's cage; **3** and sometimes it went to great depths, for, between the Grecian Archipelago and Asia Minor, we could not touch the bottom by more than a thousand fathoms.**4**

Thus I only knew we were near the Island of Carpathos, one of the Sporades, by Captain Nemo reciting these lines from Virgil— **5**

> "Est in Carpathio Neptuni gurgite vates,
>   Cæruleus Proteus,"

as he pointed to a spot on the planisphere.

It was indeed the ancient abode of Proteus, the old shepherd of Neptune's flocks, now the Island of Scarpanto, situated between Rhodes and Crete.**6** I saw nothing but the granite base through the glass panels of the saloon.

The next day, the 14th of February, I resolved to employ some hours in studying the fishes of the Archipelago; but for some reason or other, the panels remained hermetically sealed. Upon taking the course of the *Nautilus* I found that we were going towards Candia, the ancient Isle of Crete. At the time I embarked on the *Abraham Lincoln,* the whole of this island had risen in insurrection against the despotism of the Turks. But how the insurgents had fared since that time I was absolutely ignorant, and it was not Captain Nemo, deprived of all land communications, who could tell me.

I made no allusion to this event when that night I found myself alone with him in the saloon. Besides, he seemed to be taciturn and preoccupied. Then, contrary to his custom, he ordered both panels to be opened, and going from one to the other, observed the mass of waters attentively. To what end I could not guess; so, on my side, I employed my time in studying the fish passing before my eyes.

Amongst others, I remarked some gobies, mentioned by Aristotle, and commonly known by the name of seabraches,**7** which are more particularly met with in the salt waters lying near the Delta of the Nile. Near them rolled some sea-bream, half phosphorescent, a kind of sparus, which the Egyptians ranked amongst their sacred animals, whose arrival in the waters of their river announced a fertile overflow, and was celebrated by religious ceremonies. I also noticed some cheilines about nine inches long, a bony fish with transparent shell, whose livid colour is mixed with red spots; they are great eaters of marine vegetation, which gives them an exquisite flavour. These cheilines were much sought after by the epicures of ancient Rome; the inside, dressed with the soft roe of the lamprey, peacocks' brains and tongues of the phenicoptera, composed that divine fish of which Vitellius was so enamoured.

Another inhabitant of these seas drew my attention, and led

deck to an observer just a few feet below.

By 1872 periscope designers were using prisms instead of mirrors. Prisms absorb less—and transmit more—light. But there were no really good telescopes until twentieth-century German physicists hit upon an ingenious combination of telescope *and* periscope. They improved that with a complicated use of *both* ends of the telescope (the magnifying and reducing ends). Ultimate perfection also involved a "tilting head prism" that automatically compensates for the pitch of the boat. But that's half a century ahead of our story.

4. *by more than a thousand fathoms* The idea is that they could not find bottom *even at* a depth of more than a thousand fathoms.

5. *these lines from Virgil   These lines* mean: *In Neptune's Carpathian Gulf there dwells a prophet / Cerulean Proteus. . . .*

In Latin, the word *caeruleus* not only denotes *sky blue* but can also connote *of the sea* as well as *of the sky.*

6. *between Rhodes and Crete   Of all* the references in literature to Carpathium (Scarpanto), why does Nemo think of one involving *Proteus?* The passage from Virgil's *Georgics* that Nemo quotes from gives us the answer. It shows how beautifully Verne could orchestrate his narrative.

Virgil retells the story of how Proteus, the Old Man of the Sea, can change his shape endlessly. It is from this myth that we get our word *protean,* meaning *capable of infinite variation.* Now Nemo knows well how many apparently stable conditions can undergo sudden, radical transformation. We are about to hear of *the map changing before our eyes,* of the cold sea *boiling,* of empires toppling in a day. And Proteus is never far from Nemo's mind: his napkins, his silverware, bear the motto *Mobilis in Mobili* (changing with change).

An interesting ironic contrast suggests itself here: Proteus means *all things,* Nemo means *no man, nothing.*

And incidentally, Verne's schoolteachers thought he was an indifferent student in Latin.

7. *name of seabraches* Verne says *loches de mer.* Probably Lewis rendered this as *sea loaches.* Maybe his handwriting misled the printer to set it as *seabraches.* In some editions some puzzled editor has changed it to *seabranches!* Anyhow, they really are *gobies.*

8. *the remora . . . on to the shark's belly* This little fish has a dorsal fin which has evolved into a suction cup. Whenever the remora so desires, it can attach itself to the belly of a shark or a mantra or a turtle, or even inside the gill chamber of the big sunfish. But the remora seems to prefer the shark.

One reason: The shark is a sloppy eater. As he gouges chunks of meat out of his prey, lots of scraps drift free. The remora detaches and feeds himself.

He earns the ride and the free picnic by cleaning crustaceans off the shark's skin. But he's all set to fend for himself if need be. Should the host shark be caught on a fisherman's hook, as soon as they are lifted out of the water, the guest remora departs.

Verne will make nice use of another kind of remora in Chapter XVII.

9. *the destiny of nations* Verne could count on his nineteenth-century readers to know that the one-day Battle of Actium had sharply changed the course of history.

For a while it had seemed, on September 2, 31 B.C., that the combined fleets of Antony and Cleopatra were going to win the day. But then something sudden and mysterious happened—some chain reaction that no one has ever reconstructed satisfactorily—and Cleopatra's sixty ships fled. In a panic, apparently, Antony deserted his men. They surrendered to Octavian.

Octavian became Augustus Caesar, undisputed master of the Roman

my mind back to recollections of antiquity. It was the remora, that fastens on to the shark's belly.**8** This little fish, according to the ancients, hooking on to the ship's bottom, could stop its movements; and one of them, by keeping back Antony's ship during the battle of Actium, helped Augustus to gain the victory. On how little hangs the destiny of nations! **9** I observed some fine anthiae, which belong to the order of lutjans, a fish held sacred by the Greeks, who attributed to them the power of hunting the marine monsters from waters they frequented. Their name signifies *flower,* and they justify their appellation by their shaded colours, their shades comprising the whole gamut of reds, from the paleness of the rose to the brightness of the ruby, and the fugitive tints that clouded their dorsal fin. My eyes could not leave these wonders of the sea, when they were suddenly struck by an unexpected apparition.

In the midst of the waters a man appeared, a diver carrying at his belt a leathern purse. It was not a body abandoned to the waves; it was a living man, swimming with a strong hand, disappearing occasionally to take breath at the surface.

I turned towards Captain Nemo, and in an agitated voice exclaimed—

"A man shipwrecked! He must be saved at any price!"

The Captain did not answer me, but came and leaned against the panel.

The man had approached, and with his face flattened against the glass, was looking at us.

To my great amazement, Captain Nemo signed to him. The diver answered with his hand, mounted immediately to the surface of the water, and did not appear again.

"Do not be uncomfortable," said Captain Nemo. "It is Nicholas of Cape Matapan, surnamed Pesca.**10** He is well known in all the Cyclades. A bold diver! Water is his element, and he lives more in it than on land, going continually from one island to another, even as far as Crete."

"You know him, Captain?"

"Why not, M. Aronnax?"

Saying which, Captain Nemo went towards a piece of furniture standing near the left panel of the saloon. Near this piece of furniture, I saw a chest with iron, on the cover of which was a copper plate, bearing the cypher of the *Nautilus* **11** with its device [*Mobilis in Mobili*].

At that moment, the Captain, without noticing my presence, opened the piece of furniture, a sort of strong box, which held a great many ingots.

They were ingots of gold. From whence came this precious

metal, which represented an enormous sum? Where did the Captain gather this gold from? And what was he going to do with it?

I did not say one word. I looked. Captain Nemo took the ingots one by one, and arranged them methodically in the chest, which he filled entirely. I estimated the contents at more than 4000 lbs. weight of gold, that is to say, nearly £200,000.[12]

The chest was securely fastened, and the Captain wrote an address on the lid, in characters which must have belonged to modern Greece.

This done, Captain Nemo pressed a knob, the wire of which communicated with the quarters of the crew. Four men appeared, and, not without some trouble, pushed the chest out of the saloon. Then I heard them hoisting it up the iron staircase by means of pulleys.

At that moment, Captain Nemo turned to me.

"And you were saying, sir?" said he.

"I was saying nothing, Captain."

"Then, sir, if you will allow me, I will wish you good-night."

Whereupon he turned and left the saloon.

I returned to my room much troubled, as one may believe. I vainly tried to sleep,—I sought the connecting link between the apparition of the diver and the chest filled with gold. Soon, I felt by certain movements of pitching and tossing, that the *Nautilus* was leaving the depths and returning to the surface.

Then I heard steps upon the platform! and I knew they were unfastening the pinnace, and launching it upon the waves. For one instant it struck the side of the *Nautilus,* then all noise ceased.

Two hours after, the same noise, the same going and coming was renewed; the boat was hoisted on board, replaced in its socket, and the *Nautilus* again plunged under the waves.

So these millions had been transported to their address. To what point of the Continent? Who was Captain Nemo's correspondent?

The next day, I related to Conseil and the Canadian the events of the night, which had excited my curiosity to the highest degree. My companions were not less surprised than myself.

"But where does he take his millions to?" asked Ned Land.

To that there was no possible answer. I returned to the saloon after having breakfast, and set to work. Till five o'clock in the evening, I employed myself in arranging my notes. At

world. Republican rule was swiftly changed to imperial control by one man. Cleopatra's government fell, and both she and Antony committed suicide.

In 31 B.C., Virgil might well have been revising the very passage that Nemo has recited. As Virgil and Nemo both knew, reality is protean. Verne will now dramatize that further on both the political and geological levels.

10. *surnamed Pesca* We would say, "nicknamed 'the Fish.'"

11. *the cypher of the Nautilus* In Mercier Lewis's day, a monogram, stamped or engraved on a plate, was often called a *cipher* and spelled *cypher.*

12. *nearly £200,000* Five million francs, or well over one million American dollars in 1868. In the original, Aronnax estimates the weight of the gold as more than 1000 kilograms or more than 2200 [not 4000] pounds.

"A man shipwrecked! He must be saved at any price!" Engraving from the original edition (1870).

13. *Forty-two degrees* Centigrade, of course. This is about 108° Fahrenheit.

14. *Island of Santorin* Santorin, which took its name from Saint Irene, protector of the island, has also been known as Stronghyli and, more recently, as Thira or Thera. This island figures mightily in recent geological and archaeological research.

Thera is associated with three smaller islands which all together form a ring about four miles in diameter. Research ships from the United States and Sweden have discovered that a volcano in this group erupted about 1500 B.C., or 3500 years ago. Recent studies show that the volume of lava, dust, vapors, and gases emitted was maybe four times that ejected by the famous Krakatoa eruption of 1883. "The cataclysm of Thera," said William R. Corliss in his book *Mysteries beneath the Seas* (1970), "was a true catastrophe of the first order." Thera was buried under 100 feet of ash; tidal waves 100 feet high probably swamped Crete, 70 miles away, and might have reached Egypt.

In 1966 James W. Mavor, Jr., took soundings around Thera which showed some geometrical resemblances to Plato's description of the mythic (?) city of Atlantis. Plato had described Atlantis as enclosed in a circular wall; the ring of four islets today could conceivably be remnants of an island-state so shaped. And so archaeologists (originally led by Spyridon Marinatos, who died in 1974) have been digging under the ash of Thera. They have found a city, roughly 3500 years old, with three-story houses, looms, pottery, lamps. They have found wall paintings that include some of the earliest known pictures of ships. But they have found few human remains. This could mean that the inhabitants, whose culture resembled that of Crete, had had enough warning to escape to other parts of the Mediterranean. "The parallelism between Thera and Atlantis," says Corliss, "becomes more and

that moment—(ought I to attribute it to some peculiar idiosyncrasy?),—I felt so great a heat that I was obliged to take off my coat of byssus! It was strange, for we were not under low latitudes; and even then, the *Nautilus,* submerged as it was, ought to experience no change of temperature. I looked at the manometer; it showed a depth of sixty feet, to which atmospheric heat could never attain.

I continued my work, but the temperature rose to such a pitch as to be intolerable.

"Could there be fire on board?" I asked myself.

I was leaving the saloon, when Captain Nemo entered; he approached the thermometer, consulted it, and turning to me, said—

"Forty-two degrees." **13**

"I have noticed it, Captain," I replied; "and if it gets much hotter we cannot bear it."

"Oh! sir, it will not get hotter if we do not wish it."

"You can reduce it as you please, then?"

"No; but I can go further from the stove which produces it."

"It is outward then!"

"Certainly; we are floating in a current of boiling water."

"Is it possible!" I exclaimed.

"Look."

The panels opened, and I saw the sea entirely white all round. A sulphurous smoke was curling amid the waves, which boiled like water in a copper. I placed my hand on one of the panes of glass, but the heat was so great that I quickly took it off again.

"Where are we?" I asked.

"Near the Island of Santorin, **14** sir," replied the Captain, "and just in the canal which separates **15** Nea Kamenni from Pali Kamenni. I wished to give you a sight of the curious spectacle of a submarine eruption."

"I thought," said I, "that the formation of these new islands was ended."

"Nothing is ever ended in the volcanic parts of the sea," replied Captain Nemo; "and the globe is always being worked by subterranean fires. Already, in the nineteenth year of our era, according to Cassiodorus and Pliny, a new island, Theia (the divine), appeared in the very place where these islets have recently been formed. Then they sank under the waves, to rise again in the year 69, when they again subsided. Since that time to our days, the Plutonian work has been suspended. But, on the 3rd of February, 1866, a new island, which they named George Island, emerged from the midst of the sulphurous vapour near Nea Kamenni, and settled again the 6th of the same month. Seven days after, the 13th of February, the Island of Aphroessa appeared, leaving between Nea Kamenni and itself a canal ten yards broad.**16** I was in these seas when the phenomenon occurred, and I was able therefore to observe all the different phases. The Island of Aphroessa, of round form, measured 300 feet in diameter, and thirty feet in height. It was composed of black and vitreous lava, mixed with fragments of felspar. And lately, on the 10th of March, a smaller island, called Reka, showed itself near Nea Kamenni, and since then, these three have joined together, forming but one and the same island."

"And the canal in which we are **17** at this moment?" I asked.

"Here it is," replied Captain Nemo, showing me a map of the Archipelago. "You see I have marked the new islands." **18**

["Will this channel be filled in, do you think?"

"Probably, Professor. Since 1866, eight isles have emerged from Port St. Nicholas of Palea Kaumene. Nea and Palea will be joined. If in the mid-Pacific we have microscopic organisms building continents, here we have volcanoes building islands. Just look, Professor, at the work going on out there."]

I returned to the glass. The *Nautilus* was no longer moving, the heat was becoming unbearable. The sea, which till now had been white, was red, owing to the presence of salts of iron. In spite of the ship's being hermetically sealed, an insupportable smell of sulphur filled the saloon, and the brilliancy of the electricity was entirely extinguished by bright scarlet flames. I was in a bath, I was choking, I was broiled.

"We can remain no longer in this boiling water," said I to the Captain.

"It would not be prudent," replied the impassive Captain Nemo.

An order was given; the *Nautilus* tacked about and left the furnace it could not brave with impunity. A quarter of an hour after we were breathing fresh air on the surface. The thought then struck me that, if Ned Land had chosen this part of the sea for our flight, we should never have come alive out of this sea of fire.

The next day, the 16th of February, we left the basin which, between Rhodes and Alexandria, is reckoned about 1500 fathoms in depth, and the *Nautilus,* passing some distance from Cerigo, quitted the Grecian Archipelago, after having doubled Cape Matapan.

more apparent: cataclysm, flood, people fleeing, cultural diffusion."

However, from Plato we can infer only that the Atlantis catastrophe occurred sometime—"centuries"—after 11,600 B.C. While the Thera cataclysm is certainly many centuries after that date, there were other geological events, earlier than the Thera upheaval, that must also be considered as possibly related to the Atlantis legend. But that is getting ahead of Verne's story and our notes.

15. *canal which separates* See note 17.

16. *canal ten yards broad* See note 17.

17. *And the canal in which we are* Throughout this dialogue, read *channel* whenever Lewis mistranslates the word as *canal.*

18. *You see . . . the new islands* In 1963 Icelandic fishermen also had a chance to *"observe all the different phases"* of the birth of new islands.

On November 14, sailing near the Westman Islands, they smelled sulphur and saw clouds of gas and volcanic fragments rising from the ocean. Their engineer took the ocean's temperature. It was 9° F higher than usual.

The night of November 15, a new island emerged. It was named Surtsey, after the mythical Norse giant who had brought fire to Iceland. By January 1964 the island was 670 feet high. Snow powdered the outer slopes of the still smoking volcano.

By May 1965 lava ceased flowing. Then a new island appeared nearby and disappeared. By mid-summer, the sea rocket, a green vesicular plant, took root on Surtsey.

As Aronnax would have explained, ocean currents had doubtless transported the seeds.

And Conseil would have murmured: *"Cakile edentula."*

PART 2: CHAPTER VII

The Mediterranean
in Forty-Eight Hours

1. *dispute the empire of the world*
From the beginning to the end of
this chapter, Aronnax's mind is still
awhirl with images of protean change.
Here he means that the sea god Neptune has to contend with eruptions
from the underworld god Pluto. Aronnax is continually preoccupied with
this "dispute." At the very beginning
of the journey, he noted (p. 86)
that the *solid had wrested from the
liquid* some 37,000,000 square miles.
It's appropriate that he expresses his
preoccupation in mythic terms. For
the early myths explained the apparent chaos in nature as endless
struggles between titanic gods who *are*
the natural forces. And again Verne
enjoys his flair for double meanings.
Just as *Neptune and Pluto still dispute the empire of the* [physical]
world so the Neptunists and Plutonists, or Vulcanists, were still disputing their theories in the scientific
world.

2. *says Michelet* Now Aronnax
thinks how man himself can be Proteus. Jules Michelet is one of those
great romanticists that Aronnax was
so happy to discover in Nemo's library. Michelet believed that man
makes his own history, but only in
continuous struggle against fatality.
He saw the emergence of the French
nation, for example, as a human victory over racial and geographical

The Mediterranean, the blue sea *par excellence,* "the great
sea" of the Hebrews, "the sea" of the Greeks, the "mare
nostrum" of the Romans, bordered by orange-trees, aloes,
cacti, and sea-pines; embalmed with the perfume of the
myrtle, surrounded by rude mountains, saturated with pure
and transparent air, but incessantly worked by underground
fires, a perfect battlefield in which Neptune and Pluto still
dispute the empire of the world! **1**

It is upon these banks, and on these waters, says Michelet,**2**
that man is renewed in one of the most powerful climates of
the globe. But, beautiful as it was, I could only take a rapid
glance at the basin whose superficial area is two million of
square yards.**3** Even Captain Nemo's knowledge was lost to
me, for this enigmatical person did not appear once during
our passage at full speed. I estimated the course which the
Nautilus took under the waves of the sea at about six hundred
leagues, and it was accomplished in forty-eight hours.**4** Starting on the morning of the 16th of February from the shores
of Greece, we had crossed the Straits of Gibraltar by sunrise
on the 18th.

It was plain to me that this Mediterranean, enclosed in the
midst of those countries which he wished to avoid, was distasteful to Captain Nemo. Those waves and those breezes
brought back too many remembrances, if not too many regrets. Here he had no longer that independence and that
liberty of gait which he had when in the open seas, and his
Nautilus felt itself cramped between the close shores of Africa
and Europe.

Our speed was now twenty-five miles an hour. It may be

well understood that Ned Land, to his great disgust, was obliged to renounce his intended flight. He could not launch the pinnace, going at the rate of twelve or thirteen yards every second. To quit the *Nautilus* under such conditions would be as bad as jumping from a train going at full speed—an imprudent thing, to say the least of it. Besides, our vessel only mounted to the surface of the waves at night to renew its stock of air; it was steered entirely by the compass and the log.5

I saw no more of the interior of this Mediterranean than a traveller by express train perceives of the landscape which flies before his eyes; that is to say, the distant horizon, and not the nearer objects which pass like a flash of lightning.

[Still, Conseil and I were able to observe some species of Mediterranean fish, especially those who could match the speed of the *Nautilus* long enough for us to identify them. We watched them through the panels and we took notes which will help me to describe, albeit briefly, the animal life of that sea.

Among the numerous species that swarm in those waters, I saw some very clearly, I could catch only a glimpse of others, and I must surely—given the speed of our boat— have missed the rest entirely. My classification therefore will be more impressionistic than scientific.]

In the midst of the mass of waters brightly lit up by the electric light, glided some of those lampreys, more than a yard long, common to almost every climate. Some of the oxyrhynchi, a kind of ray five feet broad, with white belly and grey spotted back, spread out like a large shawl carried along by the current. Other rays passed so quickly that I could not see if they deserved the name of eagles which was given to them by the ancient Greeks, or the qualification of rats, toads, and bats, with which modern fishermen have loaded them. A few milander sharks, twelve feet long, and much feared by divers, struggled amongst them. Sea-foxes eight feet long, endowed with wonderful fineness of scent, appeared like large blue shadows. Some dorades of the shark kind,6 some of which measured seven feet and a half, showed themselves in their dress of blue and silver, encircled by small bands which struck sharply against the sombre tints of their fins, a fish consecrated to Venus, the eyes of which are encased in a socket of gold, a precious species, friend of all waters, fresh or salt, an inhabitant of rivers, lakes, and oceans, living in all climates, and bearing all temperatures; a race belonging to the geological era of the earth, and which has

determinism. In his book *Le Peuple* (*The People;* 1846) he predicted the Revolution of 1848. When he refused to swear allegiance to Emperor Louis Napoleon, he lost his posts as government researcher and history professor. Verne's very mention of Michelet while Napoleon is still in power is itself a political act.

3. *two million of square yards* Ridiculous, as Verne's American detractors love to point out. Actually Verne says *two million square kilometers.* Apparently Mercier Lewis quickly misread that as *meters* and converted it into *yards!* A better conversion, then, would be *850,000 square miles.*

4. *accomplished in forty-eight hours* Perhaps Aronnax's emphasis on *speed* in this chapter was one of the reasons Mercier Lewis thought it best to jettison 1500 words of its text.

5. *by the compass and the log* This is the traditional "dead reckoning." Nemo is simply steering by compass, calculating the distance covered each day, and then finding his location on the map. What this gross estimating leaves out are deviations caused by winds and currents. In a closed body of water like the Mediterranean this is not so serious as it would be on the high seas, where use of the sextant and chronometer is imperative.

6. *dorades of the shark kind* Verne says *dorades du genre spare,* that is, *sparoids,* not sharks, and he says they measured about four feet.

preserved all the beauty of its first days. Magnificent sturgeons, nine or ten yards long, creatures of great speed, striking the panes of glass with their strong tails, displayed their bluish backs with small brown spots; they resemble the sharks, but are not equal to them in strength, and are to be met with in all seas. [In spring, they swim up large streams, struggling against the current in the Volga, the Po, the Rhine, the Loire, and the Oder, where they feed on herring, mackerel, salmon, and cod. Although they are cartilaginous fish, they are classed as delicacies! **7** They may be eaten fresh, dried, pickled, or salted. In ancient times sturgeon was considered fit for the table of Lucullus.**8**]

But of all the diverse inhabitants of the Mediterranean, those I observed to the greatest advantage, when the *Nautilus* approached the surface, belonged to the sixty-third genus of bony fish.**9** They were a kind of tunny, with bluish black backs, and silvery breastplates, whose dorsal fins threw out sparkles of gold. They are said to follow in the wake of vessels whose refreshing shade they seek from the fire of a tropical sky, and they did not belie the saying, for they accompanied the *Nautilus* as they did in former times the vessel of La Perouse. For many a long hour they struggled to keep up with our vessel. I was never tired of admiring these creatures really built for speed,—their small heads, their bodies lithe and cigar-shaped, which in some were more than three yards long, their pectoral fins and forked tail endowed with remarkable strength. They swam in a triangle, like certain flocks of birds, whose rapidity they equalled, and of which the ancients used to say that they understood geometry and strategy. But still they do not escape the pursuit of the Provençals, who esteem them as highly as the inhabitants of the Propontis **10** and of Italy used to do; and these precious, but blind and foolhardy creatures, perish by millions in the nets of the Marseillaise.

With regard to the species of fish common to the Atlantic and the Mediterranean, the giddy speed of the *Nautilus* prevented me from observing them with any degree of accuracy. [There were white gymnotes, sweeping past like vague mists; conger eels ten to thirteen feet long, vividly green, blue, and yellow; cod-fish a yard long, whose liver is a tasty morsel; coepolae-teniae, floating like sea-weed; gurnards, called lyre-fish by the poet and whistling-fish by the sailor—their snouts are provided with two triangular plates that look like Homer's lyre; flying swallows or flying gurnards, so-called because they can travel with the speed of birds; a red-headed perch whose dorsal fins are speckled with filaments; aloe, a variety of shad,

7. *they are classed as delicacies* Aronnax is reminding us that when Conseil was classifying fish for Ned, Ned found that the first two of the three orders of cartilaginous fish were inedible. But the sturgeons were in the third order, and Ned was glad Conseil had *"saved the best for last"*!

8. *table of Lucullus* Lucius Licinius Lucullus (c.114–57 B.C.) was born poor but after a successful career as a Roman general, he acquired great wealth and settled down to epicurean luxury. He is said to have introduced the cherry to Italy. His biography is included in Plutarch's *Lives*.

9. *sixty-third genus of bony fish* Verne calls them *scombres-thons* or *mackerel-tuna* (*tunny*).

10. *inhabitants of the Propontis* Propontis was the ancient name for the Sea of Marmora. Access to the Propontis might have been one of the war aims of the Greeks who attacked Troy.

A flying gurnard—which Aronnax says *can travel with the speed of birds*—as pictured in *The American Cyclopaedia* (1873).

its body flecked with black, grey, brown, blue, yellow, green, which is reported to be sensitive to the silver tones of little bells; splendid turbots, sea-pheasants, with a diamond-shaped body, brown and yellow spots, and yellow fins; and a school of red mullets, beautiful "birds of paradise" of the sea. Romans paid as much as 10,000 sesterces for the privilege of seeing a mullet die slowly, cruelly watching as it changed from deep vermilion to ghostly white.

Thanks to the dizzy speed with which the *Nautilus* plied those teeming seas, we were unable to identify any miralets, trigger-fish, tetradons, sea-horses, juans, bellows-fish, blennies, surmullets, wrasse, smelt, flying-fish, anchovies, sea-bream, boöps, orphes, or any specimens of the order of Pleuronectides, common to the Atlantic as well as the Mediterranean, like the dabs, plaice, flounder, and sole.]

As to marine mammals, I thought, in passing the entrance of the Adriatic, that I saw two or three cachalots,[11] furnished with one dorsal fin, of the genus physetera, some dolphins of the genus globicephali, peculiar to the Mediterranean, the back part of the head being marked like a zebra with small lines; also, a dozen of seals, with white bellies and black hair, known by the name of *monks,* and which really have the air of a Dominican; they are about three yards in length.

[Conseil thought he had spotted a sea-turtle six feet wide, with three ridges running down to its back. I was sorry to have missed this creature for, if Conseil was right, it was a luth, a leatherback, a rare creature. The only reptiles I could see were a few cacuans with elongated shells.]

As to zoophytes, for some instants I was able to admire a beautiful orange galeolaria, which had fastened itself to the port panel; it held on by a long filament, and was divided into an infinity of branches, terminated by the finest lace which could ever have been woven by the rivals of Arachne herself.[12] Unfortunately, I could not take this admirable specimen; and doubtless no other Mediterranean zoophyte would have offered itself to my observation, if, on the night of the 16th, the *Nautilus* had not, singularly enough, slackened its speed, under the following circumstances.

We were then passing between Sicily and the coast of Tunis. In the narrow space between Cape Bon and the Straits of Messina, the bottom of the sea rose almost suddenly. There was a perfect bank, on which there was not more than nine fathoms of water, whilst on either side the depth was ninety fathoms. The *Nautilus* had to manoeuvre very carefully so as not to strike against this submarine barrier.

11. *cachalots* Cachalots are sperm whales, the originals of Moby Dick. Ranging up to 60 feet in length and 33 tons in weight, they are the only large whales with teeth. Dr. Malcolm Clarke estimates that a cachalot eats at least 130 tons of squid alone each year. Marine ecologists say that in keeping the squid population down, the sperm whale performs a valuable function. But he has been so heavily hunted in the past 200 years that he is now an "endangered species." J. Z. Young, professor of anatomy at the University of London, warns that we must not "eliminate him for his pains."

12. *Arachne herself* Recent research suggests that the story of how Athene changed Arachne into a spider may reflect a historical situation.

According to the Greek myth, Arachne was a Lydian princess who was such a superb weaver that she felt confident enough to challenge the goddess Athene to a weaving contest. Arachne produced a fabric that infuriated Athene for two good reasons: Arachne's textile was flawless, and the weave depicted some of the more notorious amours of the gods. Athene tore the fabric and beat the weaver. Arachne hanged herself but Athene frustrated her in that, too. Athene changed the rope into a web and Arachne into a spider.

Robert Graves sees here a representation of commercial rivalry between Athens and Lydia, whose rulers were Cretans. Archaeologists have found in Crete seals with spider emblems which suggest that textile industries flourished there. Did the Cretans extend their spider-work to Lydia? Does the myth then show that Lydia (Arachne) was threatening Athens (Athene)? Is this why the spider was reputed to be the creature Athene hated most?

In any event, *arakhne* is Greek for *spider.* While mythology tells us the spider was named *after* Arachne and Athens *after* Athene, we know that often the reverse is true: the mythic figure may be invented to account for the word or name.

13. *Cape Boco* Now on our maps as Cape Bon.

14. *. . . were joined* Aronnax's mini-lecture on how *"in former times the continents . . . were joined"* foreshadows today's theories of "continental drift." It is now believed that the Mediterranean originated when the African plate swung away from the European plate. Belts of volcanoes around the world tend to fall along the meeting places of the great plates.

15. *years, my boy* Here Aronnax is projecting much too quick an end for planet Earth, if today's theories are any nearer correct than his.

I showed Conseil, on the map of the Mediterranean, the spot occupied by this reef.

"But if you please, sir," observed Conseil, "it is like a real isthmus joining Europe to Africa."

"Yes, my boy, it forms a perfect bar to the Straits of Libya, and the soundings of Smith have proved that in former times the continents between Cape Boco **13** and Cape Furina were joined." **14**

"I can well believe it," said Conseil.

"I will add," I continued, "that a similar barrier exists between Gibraltar and Ceuta, which in geological times formed the entire Mediterranean."

"What if some volcanic burst should one day raise these two barriers above the waves?"

"It is not probable, Conseil."

"Well, but allow me to finish, please, sir; if this phenomenon should take place, it will be troublesome for M. [de] Lesseps, who has taken so much pains to pierce the isthmus."

"I agree with you; but I repeat, Conseil, this phenomenon will never happen. The violence of subterranean force is ever diminishing. Volcanoes, so plentiful in the first days of the world, are being extinguished by degrees; the internal heat is weakened, the temperature of the lower strata of the globe is lowered by a perceptible quantity every century to the detriment of our globe, for its heat is its life."

"But the sun?"

"The sun is not sufficient, Conseil. Can it give heat to a dead body?"

"Not that I know of."

"Well, my friend, this earth will one day be that cold corpse; it will become uninhabitable and uninhabited like the moon, which has long since lost all its vital heat."

"In how many centuries?"

"In some hundreds of thousands of years, my boy." **15**

"Then," said Conseil, "we shall have time to finish our journey, that is, if Ned Land does not interfere with it."

And Conseil, reassured, returned to the study of the bank, which the *Nautilus* was skirting at a moderate speed.

There, beneath the rocky and volcanic bottom, lay outspread a living flora of sponges and reddish cydippes, which emitted a slight phosphorescent light, [beroes,] commonly known by the name of sea-cucumbers; and walking comatulae more than a yard long, the purple of which completely coloured the water around; [beautiful tree-like euryales, pavonaceae with long stalks; great numbers of edible sea-urchins of several species; and green sea-anemones almost hidden behind their olive-coloured tentacles.

Conseil had been busy identifying molluscs and articulata. While his list might make for dull reading, I ought not to do him the injustice of ignoring his observations.16

In the branch of the molluscs, he mentions numerous scallops; spondyli, spiny oysters stacked atop each other; triangular wedge-shells; trident-shaped hyalines with yellow fins and translucent shells; orange pleurobranchia, like eggs with green spots; aplysia, also called sea-hare; dolabellae; plump acerae; umbrella-shells peculiar to those waters; sea-ears which provide a good mother-of-pearl; reddish scallops; corrugated cockles, which the Languedoc people prefer to oysters; clovis, preferred in Marseilles; that species of clam found in such abundance off North America and so popular in New York; comb-shells of many colors; lithodes, in their holes, whose peppery taste I enjoy; furrowed venericardiae; cynthiae, covered with scarlet bumps; carniaria, turned up at each end like little gondolas; crowned feroles; spiral-shelled atlantes; grey thetys, speckled white and covered with fringe; aeolides that look like little slugs; cavoliniae creeping on their backs; and the oval-shaped auricula myosotis, the fawn-coloured scalaria, littoral periwinkles, ianthine, cinerariae, petricolae, lamellaria, cabochons, pandoras, and others.

In his notes, I find that Conseil properly grouped the articulata in six classes, three of which belong to the marine world: the crustaceans, the cirrhopoda, and the annelids.

The crustaceans are further divided into nine orders. The first comprises the decapods, animals with head and thorax usually joined, with mouths formed of several pairs of jaws, and with four, five, or six pairs of legs on the thorax.

Conseil followed our master, Milne-Edwards, who divided decapods into three sections: brachyura, macrura, and anomura. Although these names sound thoughtlessly barbarous, they are correct and precise.17 Among the brachyura, Conseil listed amathiae, with a head armed with a big horn on each side; the inachidae scorpion which—I cannot imagine why—the Greeks used as a symbol of wisdom; spider crabs, including one species that seemingly had wandered into these shallow seas: usually they frequent deeper waters; xanthi, pilumnae, rhomboides, granular calappae, which, Conseil notes, are easy to digest; toothless corystes; ebaliae; cymobolides; woolly dorripi, and so on.

Among macrura, subdivided into five families, there are ceriaceae; burrowers; astaci; palaemonidae; and ochyzopodes.

16. *ignoring his observations* Verne obviously expected that some readers would prefer to skip such passages. And so he often devises ingenious *detour signs* like this one. Aronnax's disclaimer sounds like the classic prototype in Sextus Julius Frontinus's report on the Roman aqueducts (c. A.D. 98):

"I know that such an enumeration will appear not only dry but also complicated. Still, I will make it . . . that nothing may be lacking to the data. . . . Those who are satisfied with knowing the totals may skip the details."

17. *they are correct and precise* That is, *brachyura* means short-tailed ones, with abdomen greatly reduced; *macrura* means long-tailed ones, with well-developed abdomens; *anomura* means irregular or unusual tails, with abdomen reduced and permanently flexed.

Conseil mentions the rock-lobster, the female of which is prized as food; scyllari, or squills, and other edible species. But he does not cite the astaci, including the lobster proper, because the spring-lobster is the only kind found in the Mediterranean. Among the anomura, he identified the drocinae, who make do inside whatever empty shells they can find; the homolae with spiny heads; and hermit-crabs, and porcelain crabs.

Here Conseil stopped. He did not have enough time to complete the crustaceans with any observation of stomatopods, amphipods, homopods, isopods, trilobites, branchiapods, ostrocodes, or entomostracae. And in order to complete his data on the marine articulata he would have had to mention the class of cirrhopoda, including the cyclopes and arguli, and the class of annelids, which he would have been careful to divide into the tubicoles and the dorsibranches. But time ran out.] The *Nautilus* having now passed the high bank in the Libyan Straits, returned to the deep waters and its accustomed speed.

From that time no more molluscs, no more articulates, no more zoophytes; barely a few large fish passing like shadows.

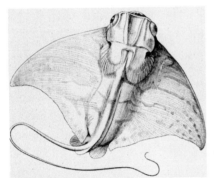

I could not see if they deserved the name of eagles . . . given to them by the ancient Greeks. . . . An eagle ray as pictured in T. W. Bridge's Fishes *(1904).*

During the night of the 16th and 17th February, we had entered the second Mediterranean basin, the greatest depth of which was 1450 fathoms. The *Nautilus,* by the action of its screw, slid down the inclined planes, and buried itself in the lowest depths of the sea.

[We saw no more natural marvels, but instead, terrible and moving spectacles. We were travelling that portion of the Mediterranean so fecund with tragedies. Between the Algerian and French coasts, how many ships had sunk to the bottom! The Mediterranean, compared to the vast stretches of the Pacific, is only a lake, but it is a capricious lake, one day favouring the fragile vessels that float between its blue waters and azure sky, the next day lashing them with winds, smashing the strongest ships with the powerful punch of its waves.

During our swift passage through its deeps, I saw disasters scattered everywhere. Some ships were already encrusted with coral, others were only rusted—anchors, guns, cannon-balls, chains, iron fittings, screws, cylinders, boilers, entire hulls, some upright in the water, others upside-down.

Some of these ships had been rammed in collisions, some had struck on granite reefs. Those that had dropped perpendicularly to the bottom, masts still in place and rigging tight, seemed to be anchored in one vast, eerie harbour, waiting for the order to cast off. As the *Nautilus* moved among them, with its lantern shining on them, I expected they would dip their flags in salute. But everything was motionless.

The number of wrecks increased sharply as we approached the Straits of Gibraltar. The African and European coasts come closer together, and collisions occur more frequently as ships converge here. I saw iron hulls, fantastic remains of steamers, some lying flat, some standing on end, like tall monsters.

One ship was ripped in the side, its funnel was bent, the paddle-wheels gone from their frame, the rudder parted from the stern but still held by a chain. Its rear name plate was corroded by sea-water. How many lives had been quenched in that wreck? Had any sailor survived to tell what had happened, or had the waves kept the secret?

I cannot explain it, but I thought this could be the *Atlas*. She had disappeared with all hands some twenty years before. What a grim history could be written about the Mediterranean depths, that vast boneyard, where such riches, so many victims, have gone down.

The *Nautilus* moved with rapidity and indifference among these ruins.] On the 18th of February, about three o'clock in the morning, we were at the entrance of the Straits of Gibraltar. There once existed two currents: **18** an upper one, long since recognised, which conveys the waters of the ocean into the basin of the Mediterranean; and a lower counter-current, which reasoning has now shown to exist. Indeed, the volume of water in the Mediterranean, incessantly added to by the waves of the Atlantic, and by rivers falling into it, would each year raise the level of this sea, for its evaporation is not sufficient to restore the equilibrium. As it is not so, we must necessarily admit the existence of an under-current, which empties into the basin of the Atlantic, through the Straits of Gibraltar, the surplus waters of the Mediterranean. A fact indeed; and it was this counter-current by which the *Nautilus* profited. It advanced rapidly by the narrow pass. For one instant I caught a glimpse of the beautiful ruins of the temple of Hercules, buried in the ground, according to Pliny [and Avienus],**19** and with the low island which supports it; and a few minutes later we were floating on the Atlantic.

18. *There once existed two currents* No, Verne says *there are two currents.*

19. *Pliny . . . Avienus* Pliny and Avienus were probably required reading when Aronnax was doing advanced studies in natural history. Pliny the Elder perished while taking notes on the eruption of Vesuvius in A.D. 79. He wrote voluminously, but only his *Naturalis Historia* survives.

Its thirty-seven books tell us much about the art, science, and superstition of his day that we would otherwise know nothing about.

Rufius Festus Avienus left us, in the fourth century, Latin translations of two Greek poems on geographical subjects.

PART 2: CHAPTER VIII
Vigo Bay[1]

1. *Vigo Bay* Again Verne uses a place name guaranteed to produce suspense and exotic complications. To European readers, at least, the words Vigo Bay conjure up images of a colorful port that has been a center of romance and heroism.

One of the most impressive of the Galician fjords, Vigo Bay extends inland for almost twenty miles. Sheltered by mountains, it provides a peaceful and spacious harbor.

Sir Francis Drake's English fleet attacked the town of Vigo in 1585 and again in 1589. And in 1702 the Bay was the scene of a naval battle in which the stakes were nothing less than a gargantuan treasure of precious metals.

The Atlantic! a vast sheet of water, whose superficial area covers twenty-five millions of square miles, the length of which is nine thousand miles, with a mean breadth of two thousand seven hundred. [A major sea practically unknown to the ancients, except perhaps to the Carthaginians who, in their commercial exploring, did sail the west coasts of Europe and Africa.] An ocean whose parallel winding shores embrace an immense circumference, watered by the largest rivers of the world, the St. Lawrence, the Mississippi, the Amazon, the Plata, the Orinoco, the Niger, the Senegal, the Elbe, the Loire and the Rhine, which carry water from the most civilised, as well as from the most savage countries! Magnificent field of water, incessantly ploughed by vessels of every nation, sheltered by the flags of every nation, and which terminates in those two terrible points so dreaded by mariners, Cape Horn, and the Cape of Tempests!

The *Nautilus* was piercing the water with its sharp spur, after having accomplished nearly ten thousand leagues in three months and a half, a distance greater than the great circle of the earth. Where were we going now? And what was reserved for the future? The *Nautilus,* leaving the Straits of Gibraltar, had gone far out. It returned to the surface of the waves, and our daily walks on the platform were restored to us.

I mounted at once, accompanied by Ned Land and Conseil. At a distance of about twelve miles, Cape St. Vincent was dimly to be seen, forming the south-western point of the Spanish peninsula. A strong southerly gale was blowing. The sea was swollen and billowy; it made the *Nautilus* rock violently. It was almost impossible to keep one's footing on the platform, which the heavy rolls of the sea beat over every instant. So we descended after inhaling some mouthfuls of fresh air.

I returned to my room, Conseil to his cabin; but the Canadian, with a preoccupied air, followed me. Our rapid passage across the Mediterranean had not allowed him to put his project into execution, and he could not help showing his disappointment. When the door of my room was shut, he sat down and looked at me silently.

"Friend Ned," said I, "I understand you; but you cannot reproach yourself. To have attempted to leave the *Nautilus* under the circumstances would have been folly."

Ned Land did not answer; his compressed lips, and frowning brow, showed with him the violent possession this fixed idea had taken of his mind.

"Let us see," I continued; "we need not despair yet. We are going up the coast of Portugal again; France and England are not far off, where we can easily find refuge. Now, if the *Nautilus,* on leaving the Straits of Gibraltar, had gone to the south, if it had carried us towards regions where there were no continents, I should share your uneasiness. But we know now that Captain Nemo does not fly from civilised seas, and in some days I think you can act with security."

Ned Land still looked at me fixedly, at length his fixed lips parted, and he said, "It is for to-night."

I drew myself up suddenly. I was, I admit, little prepared for this communication. I wanted to answer the Canadian, but words would not come.

"We agreed to wait for an opportunity," continued Ned Land, "and the opportunity has arrived. This night we shall be but a few miles from the Spanish coast. It is cloudy. The wind blows freely. I have your word, M. Aronnax, and I rely upon you."

As I was still silent, the Canadian approached me.

"To-night, at nine o'clock," said he. "I have warned Conseil. At that moment, Captain Nemo will be shut up in his room, probably in bed. Neither the engineers nor the ship's crew can see us. Conseil and I will gain the central staircase, and you, M. Aronnax, will remain in the library, two steps from us, waiting my signal. The oars, the mast, and the sail, are in the canoe. I have even succeeded in getting in some provisions. I have procured an English wrench,[2] to unfasten the bolts which attach it to the shell of the *Nautilus.* So all is ready, till to-night."

"The sea is bad."

"That I allow," replied the Canadian; "but we must risk

2. *an English wrench* We call it *a monkey wrench.* What Lewis has done is translate literally Verne's *une clef anglaise.* While the French regard it as an English tool, the English themselves have called it *a screw spanner.*

But the British can still use that name to get across the idea of *monkey business.* Where an American might be suspected of "throwing a monkey wrench into the works," an Englishman would be suspected of "throwing spanners."

3. *we may be a hundred leagues away*
That is, if we remain on the *Nautilus*
we may be a hundred leagues away.

that. Liberty is worth paying for; besides, the boat is strong, and a few miles with a fair wind to carry us, is no great thing. Who knows but by to-morrow we may be a hundred leagues away? **3** Let circumstances only favour us, and by ten or eleven o'clock we shall have landed on some spot of *terra firma,* alive or dead. But adieu now till to-night."

With these words, the Canadian withdrew, leaving me almost dumb. I had imagined that, the chance gone, I should have time to reflect and discuss the matter. My obstinate companion had given me no time; and, after all, what could I have said to him? Ned Land was perfectly right. There was almost the opportunity to profit by. Could I retract my word, and take upon myself the responsibility of compromising the future of my companions? To-morrow Captain Nemo might take us far from all land.

At that moment a rather loud hissing told me that the reservoirs were filling, and that the *Nautilus* was sinking under the waves of the Atlantic. [I remained in my room. I avoided the Captain because I was afraid that my deep feelings would betray me.]

A sad day I passed, between the desire of regaining my liberty of action, and of abandoning the wonderful *Nautilus,* and leaving my submarine studies incomplete. [How could I leave "my Atlantic," as I had come to call it, without having explored its greatest depths? It had its own mysteries comparable to those the Pacific and Indian Oceans had revealed to me. How could I end my "romance" in the middle of the story, how could I bear to be interrupted at this point in the dream?]

What dreadful hours I passed thus! sometimes seeing myself and companions safely landed, sometimes wishing, in spite of my reason, that some unforeseen circumstances would prevent the realisation of Ned Land's project.

Twice I went to the saloon. I wished to consult the compass. I wished to see if the direction the *Nautilus* was taking was bringing us nearer or taking us farther from the coast. But no; the *Nautilus* kept in Portuguese waters.

I must therefore take my part, and prepare for flight. My luggage was not heavy; my notes nothing more.

As to Captain Nemo, I asked myself what he would think of our escape; what trouble, what wrong it might cause him, and what he might do in case of its discovery or failure. Certainly I had no cause to complain of him; on the contrary, never was hospitality freer than his. In leaving him I could not be taxed with ingratitude. No oath bound us to him. It was on the

Flying fish (*Dactylopterus volitans*) as pictured in A. E. Brehm's *Merveilles de la Nature* (1885).

strength of circumstances he relied, and not upon our word, to fix us for ever.

I had not seen the Captain since our visit to the Island of Santorin. Would chance bring me to his presence before our departure? I wished it, and I feared it at the same time. I listened if I could hear him walking in the room contiguous to mine. No sound reached my ear. [His room must have been deserted.

Was this strange man still aboard? My ideas about him had changed since that night when the dinghy had left the *Nautilus* on its mysterious mission. I had come to think now that regardless of what he claimed, he still maintained some relations with the land. Did he himself ever leave the *Nautilus?* I could recall sometimes not seeing him for weeks on end. What did he do during those periods? Was he on some secret missions, the nature of which I could not imagine? Had I been wrong in seeing him as someone who frequented the seas in order to escape from man?

Such questions crowded my mind. Conjecture was unlimited in such strange circumstances as those that Ned and Conseil and I were in.] I felt an unbearable uneasiness. This day of waiting seemed eternal. Hours struck too slowly to keep pace with my impatience.

My dinner was served in my room as usual. I ate but little,

I was too preoccupied. I left the table at seven o'clock. A hundred and twenty minutes (I counted them) still separated me from the moment in which I was to join Ned Land. My agitation redoubled. My pulse beat violently. I could not remain quiet. I went and came, hoping to calm my troubled spirit by constant movement. The idea of failure in our bold enterprise was the least painful of my anxieties; but the thought of seeing our project discovered before leaving the *Nautilus,* of being brought before Captain Nemo, irritated, or (what was worse) saddened at my desertion, made my heart beat.

I wanted to see the saloon for the last time. I descended the stairs, and arrived in the museum where I had passed so many useful and agreeable hours. I looked at all its riches, all its treasures, like a man on the eve of an eternal exile, who was leaving never to return. These wonders of Nature, these masterpieces of Art, amongst which, for so many days, my life had been concentrated, I was going to abandon them for ever! I should like to have taken a last look through the windows of the saloon into the waters of the Atlantic: but the panels were hermetically closed, and a cloak of steel separated me from that ocean which I had not yet explored.

In passing through the saloon, I came near the door, let into the angle, which opened into the Captain's room. To my great surprise, this door stood ajar. I drew back, involuntarily. If Captain Nemo should be in his room, he could see me. But, hearing no noise, I drew nearer. The room was deserted. I pushed open the door, and took some steps forward. Still the same monk-like severity of aspect. [But then I saw something I had not noticed on my earlier visit—some etchings hanging on the wall. They were portraits of great men of history who had devoted their lives to a great human ideal. Kosciusko, the hero whose dying words had been *Finis Poloniae;* Botzaris, the Leonidas of modern Greece; O'Connell, the defender of Ireland; Washington, the founder of the American Union; Manin, the Italian Patriot; Lincoln, killed by a defender of slavery; and finally, that martyr to the emancipation of the black race, John Brown, hanging on the gallows, just as Victor Hugo had drawn him.

Now what spiritual tie did Captain Nemo feel with these heroes? Would these portraits help me unravel the mystery of his being? **4** Was he, like the heroes, himself a fighter for oppressed peoples, a liberator of oppressed races? Had he figured in the political and social uprisings of our century? Was he perhaps one of the heroes of that ghastly American

4. *unravel the mystery of his being* Indeed, these portraits are crucial to our understanding of Nemo's character and of the rationale behind his strange behavior.

Nemo's gallery of personal heroes includes men who have not hesitated to take up arms against established government when that government has proved to be evil. And what all these heroes had in common, rebels or not, was their absolute devotion to ideals of human freedom and civil rights.

Here we cannot avoid the conclusion that in omitting a passage very easy to translate, *Mercier Lewis was using his power to fight Verne's politics.*

Civil War, ghastly but glorious?]

Suddenly the clock struck eight. The first beat of the hammer on the bell awoke me from my dreams. I trembled as if an invisible eye had plunged into my most secret thoughts,5 and I hurried from the room.

There my eye fell upon the compass. Our course was still north. The log indicated moderate speed, the manometer a depth of about sixty feet.

I returned to my room, clothed myself warmly—sea boots, an otterskin cap, a great coat of byssus, lined with sealskin; I was ready, I was waiting. The vibration of the screw alone broke the deep silence which reigned on board. I listened attentively. Would no loud voice suddenly inform me that Ned Land had been surprised in his projected flight? A mortal dread hung over me, and I vainly tried to regain my accustomed coolness.

At a few minutes to nine, I put my ear to the Captain's door. No noise. I left my room and returned to the saloon, which was half in obscurity, but deserted.

I opened the door communicating with the library. The same insufficient light, the same solitude. I placed myself near the door leading to the central staircase, and there waited for Ned Land's signal.

At that moment the trembling of the screw sensibly diminished, then it stopped entirely. [Why had the *Nautilus* come to a halt? How would this affect Ned's plans? I could not know.] The silence was now only disturbed by the beatings of my own heart. Suddenly a slight shock was felt; and I knew that the *Nautilus* had stopped at the bottom of the ocean. My uneasiness increased. The Canadian's signal did not come. I felt inclined to join Ned Land and beg of him to put off his attempt. I felt that we were not sailing under our usual conditions.

At this moment the door of the large saloon opened, and Captain Nemo appeared. He saw me, and, without further preamble, began in an amiable tone of voice—

"Ah, sir! I have been looking for you. Do you know the history of Spain?"

Now, one might know the history of one's own country by heart; but in the condition I was at the time, with troubled mind and head quite lost, I could not have said a word of it.

"Well," continued Captain Nemo, "you heard my question? Do you know the history of Spain?"

"Very slightly," I answered.

"Well, here are learned men having to learn," said the Cap-

5. *invisible eye . . . my most secret thoughts* Aronnax's behavior here reveals a great deal about his psychology and even more about Verne's own psychohistory.

Aronnax worries that Nemo will be hurt by Aronnax's *desertion*. He worries whether he can be *taxed with ingratitude*. He fears he will be *caught and brought back before Nemo* in disgrace! He feels that he is being *watched by an invisible eye*. His feelings culminate in a dread of *eternal exile*. This is all the unmistakable language of the dependent son about to anger an Omnipotent Being.

Such situations in Verne's stories have led Marcel Moré, in two brilliant studies (see Bibliography), to declare that one major theme in Verne's work is *the search for the perfect father*. Moré believes that this search reenacts Verne's own search which ended in 1862. That was when the publisher Pierre Hetzel took over Verne's life. For the next forty years, Hetzel decided how many books Verne should write, how much he should be paid, and when he needed a vacation. Verne flourished under this benign paternalism. *Aronnax feels in this scene as Verne would if some personal crisis forced him to consider deserting Hetzel.*

Such father-son relations are not rare in literary history. Dr. Paul de Kruif, author of *Microbe Hunters* and our first great popularizer of science, said of his editor, Philip S. Rose: "I'm a bright kid, and Phil's my dad."

Aronnax's bout with his conscience also reenacts a crisis in Verne's life with his *real* father. One day, when he was eleven, Jules rose before dawn and tiptoed past his father's room and fled his parents' house. He signed on as a cabin boy on a ship bound for the West Indies. But a neighbor's *eye* had spotted Jules. As Jules's ship made its last stop in France, he was *caught* by his father and taken home *in disgrace*. He had to promise his parents that he would conduct all future journeys in his imagination.

6. *in the shadow* You may wonder why Nemo doesn't seem to notice that Aronnax is all dressed up for the cold out-of-doors. Even though Aronnax carefully sits *in the shadow,* Nemo can't miss that great coat and the skin cap the professor is wearing. Is it possible someone has seen Ned and Conseil heavily dressed, and that Nemo has surmised the escape plans? In any event, Nemo already had his present adventure under way, an adventure sure to thwart Ned's enterprise. And it suits Nemo's character as the mysteriously aloof, ironic, all-knowing genius that he would be content to frustrate Aronnax without saying a word about it.

tain. "Come, sit down, and I will tell you a curious episode in this history." [He sat down on a divan. Rather mechanically, I took my place next to him, in the shadow.**6**]

"Sir, listen well," said he; "this history will interest you on one side, for it will answer a question which doubtless you have not been able to solve."

"I listen, Captain," said I, not knowing what my interlocutor was driving at, and asking myself if this incident was bearing on our projected flight.

"Sir, if you have no objection, we will go back to 1702. You cannot be ignorant that your king, Louis XIV, thinking that the gesture of a potentate was sufficient to bring the Pyrenees under his yoke, had imposed the Duke of Anjou, his grandson, on the Spaniards. This prince reigned more or less badly under the name of Philip V, and had a strong party against him abroad. Indeed, the preceding year, the royal houses of Holland, Austria, and England, had concluded a treaty of alliance at The Hague, with the intention of plucking the crown of Spain from the head of Philip V, and placing it on that of an archduke to whom they prematurely gave the title of Charles III.

"Spain must resist this coalition; but she was almost entirely unprovided with either soldiers or sailors. However, money would not fail them, provided that their galleons, laden with gold and silver from America, once entered their ports. And about the end of 1702 they expected a rich convoy which France was escorting with a fleet of twenty-three vessels, commanded by Admiral Château-Renaud, for the ships of the coalition were already beating the Atlantic. This convoy was to go to Cadiz, but the Admiral, hearing that an English fleet was cruising in those waters, resolved to make for a French port.

"The Spanish commanders of the convoy objected to this decision. They wanted to be taken to a Spanish port, and if not to Cadiz, into Vigo Bay, situated on the northwest coast of Spain, and which was not blocked.

"Admiral Château-Renaud had the rashness to obey this injunction, and the galleons entered Vigo Bay.

"Unfortunately, it formed an open road which could not be defended in any way. They must therefore hasten to unload the galleons before the arrival of the combined fleet; and time would not have failed them had not a miserable question of rivalry suddenly arisen.

"You are following the chain of events?" asked Captain Nemo.

"Perfectly," said I, not knowing the end proposed by this historical lesson.

"I will continue. This is what passed. The merchants of Cadiz had a privilege by which they had the right of receiving all merchandise coming from the West Indies. Now, to disembark these ingots at the port of Vigo, was depriving them of their rights. They complained at Madrid, and obtained the consent of the weak-minded Philip that the convoy, without discharging its cargo, should remain sequestered in the roads of Vigo until the enemy had disappeared.

"But whilst coming to this decision, on the 22d of October, 1702, the English vessels arrived in Vigo Bay, when Admiral Château-Renaud, in spite of inferior forces, fought bravely. But seeing that the treasure must fall into the enemy's hands, he burnt and scuttled every galleon, which went to the bottom with their immense riches." **7**

Captain Nemo stopped. I admit I could not yet see why this history should interest me.

"Well?" I asked.

"Well, M. Aronnax," replied Captain Nemo, "we are in that Vigo Bay; and it rests with yourself whether you will penetrate its mysteries."

The captain rose, telling me to follow him. I had had time to recover. I obeyed. The saloon was dark, but through the transparent glass the waves were sparkling. I looked.

For half a mile around the *Nautilus,* the waters seemed bathed in electric light. The sandy bottom was clean and bright. Some of the ship's crew in their diving dresses were clearing away half rotten barrels and empty cases from the midst of the blackened wrecks. From these cases and from these barrels escaped ingots of gold and silver, cascades of piastres and jewels. The sand was heaped up with them. Laden with their precious booty the men returned to the *Nautilus,* disposed of their burden, and went back to this inexhaustible fishery of gold and silver.

I understood now. This was the scene of the battle of the 22d of October, 1702. Here on this very spot the galleons laden for the Spanish Government had sunk. Here Captain Nemo came, according to his wants, to pack up those millions with which he burdened the *Nautilus.* It was for him and him alone America had given up her precious metals. He was heir direct, without any one to share, in those treasures torn from the Incas and from the conquered of Ferdinand Cortez.

"Did you know, sir," he asked, smiling, "that the sea contained such riches?"

7. *to the bottom with their immense riches* But Admiral François Château-Renault did not succeed in sinking *all* the treasure. Admiral Sir George Rooke, commanding the combined British and Dutch fleet, captured about £1,000,000 worth of silver. This was only *part* of Renault's treasure!

Louis XIV did not hold Admiral Renault responsible for the great loss in Vigo Bay. In 1703 he made Renault a marshal of France, and in 1704, governor of Brittany.

8. *at two millions* Verne says that there are *two million tons of silver* in those waters.

"I knew," I answered, "that they value the money held in suspension in these waters at two millions." **8**

"Doubtless; but to extract this money the expense would be greater than the profit. Here, on the contrary, I have but to pick up what man has lost,—and not only in Vigo Bay, but in a thousand other spots where shipwrecks have happened, and which are marked on my submarine map. Can you understand now the source of the millions I am worth?"

"I understand, Captain. But allow me to tell you that in exploring Vigo Bay you have only been beforehand with a rival society."

"And which?"

"A society which has received from the Spanish Government the privilege of seeking these buried galleons. The shareholders are led on by the allurement of an enormous bounty, for they value these rich shipwrecks at five hundred millions."

"Five hundred millions they were," answered Captain Nemo, "but they are so no longer."

"Just so," said I; "and a warning to those shareholders would be an act of charity. But who knows if it would be well received? What gamblers usually regret above all is less the loss of their money, than of their foolish hopes. After all, I pity them less than the thousands of unfortunates to whom so much riches well-distributed would have been profitable, whilst for them they will be for ever barren."

I had no sooner expressed this regret, than I felt that it must have wounded Captain Nemo.

"Barren!" he exclaimed, with animation. "Do you think then, sir, that these riches are lost because I gather them? Is it for myself alone, according to your idea, that I take the trouble to collect these treasures? Who told you that I did not make a good use of it? Do you think I am ignorant that there are suffering beings and oppressed races on this earth, miserable creatures to console, victims to avenge? Do you not understand?"

Captain Nemo stopped at these last words, regretting perhaps that he had spoken so much. But I had guessed that whatever the motive which had forced him to seek independence under the sea, it had left him still a man, that his heart still beat for the sufferings of humanity, and that his immense charity was for oppressed races as well as individuals. And I then understood for whom those millions were destined, which were forwarded by Captain Nemo when the *Nautilus* was cruising in the waters of Crete.

PART 2: CHAPTER IX
A Vanished Continent

The next morning, the 19th of February, I saw the Canadian enter my room. I expected this visit. He looked very disappointed.

"Well, sir?" said he.

"Well, Ned, fortune was against us yesterday."

"Yes; that Captain must needs stop exactly at the hour we intended leaving his vessel."

"Yes, Ned, he had business at his banker's."

"His banker's!"

"Or rather his banking-house; by that I mean the ocean, where his riches are safer than in the chests of the State."

I then related to the Canadian the incidents of the preceding night, hoping to bring him back to the idea of not abandoning the Captain; but my recital had no other result than an energetically expressed regret from Ned, that he had not been able to take a walk on the battlefield of Vigo on his own account.

"However," said he, "all is not ended. It is only a blow of the harpoon lost. Another time we must succeed; and to-night, if necessary——"

"In what direction is the *Nautilus* going?" I asked.

"I do not know," replied Ned.

"Well, at noon we shall see the point." 1

The Canadian returned to Conseil. As soon as I was dressed, I went into the saloon. The compass was not reassuring. The course of the *Nautilus* was S.S.W. We were turning our backs on Europe.

I waited with some impatience till the ship's place was pricked on the chart. At about half-past eleven the reservoirs were emptied, and our vessel rose to the surface of the ocean.

1. *we shall see the point*   That is, *we shall get our bearings, establish our position.*

I rushed towards the platform. Ned Land had preceded me. No more land in sight. Nothing but an immense sea. Some sails on the horizon, doubtless those going to San Roque in search of favourable winds for doubling the Cape of Good Hope. The weather was cloudy. A gale of wind was preparing. Ned raved, and tried to pierce the cloudy horizon. He still hoped that behind all that fog stretched the land he so longed for.

At noon the sun showed itself for an instant. The second profited by this brightness to take its height. Then the sea becoming more billowy, we descended, and the panel closed.

An hour after, upon consulting the chart, I saw the position of the *Nautilus* was marked at 16° 17′ longitude, and 33° 22′ latitude, at 150 leagues from the nearest coast. There was no means of flight, and I leave you to imagine the rage of the Canadian, when I informed him of our situation.

For myself, I was not particularly sorry. I felt lightened of the load which had oppressed me, and was able to return with some degree of calmness to my accustomed work.

That night, about eleven o'clock, I received a most unexpected visit from Captain Nemo. He asked me very graciously if I felt fatigued from my watch of the preceding night. I answered in the negative.

"Then, M. Aronnax, I propose a curious excursion."

"Propose, Captain?"

"You have hitherto only visited the submarine depths by daylight, under the brightness of the sun. Would it suit you to see them in the darkness of the night?"

"Most willingly."

"I warn you, the way will be tiring. We shall have far to walk, and must climb a mountain. The roads are not well kept."

"What you say, Captain, only heightens my curiosity; I am ready to follow you."

"Come then, sir, we will put on our diving dresses."

Arrived at the robing-room, I saw that neither of my companions nor any of the ship's crew were to follow us on this excursion. Captain Nemo had not even proposed my taking with me either Ned or Conseil.

In a few moments we had put on our diving dresses; they placed on our backs the reservoirs, abundantly filled with air, but no electric lamps were prepared. I called the Captain's attention to the fact.

"They will be useless," he replied.

I thought I had not heard aright, but I could not repeat my

observation, for the Captain's head had already disappeared in its metal case. I finished harnessing myself, I felt them put an iron-pointed stick into my hand, and some minutes later, after going through the usual form, we set foot on the bottom of the Atlantic, at a depth of 150 fathoms. Midnight was near. The waters were profoundly dark, but Captain Nemo pointed out in the distance a reddish spot, a sort of large light shining brilliantly, about two miles from the *Nautilus*. What this fire might be, what could feed it, why and how it lit up the liquid mass, I could not say. In any case, it did light our way, vaguely, it is true, but I soon accustomed myself to the peculiar darkness, and I understood, under such circumstances, the uselessness of the Ruhmkorff apparatus. [Nemo and I walked side by side towards that glow. The sea-floor was rising imperceptibly. We took long strides and made good use of our pointed sticks.

Still, our progress was slow, for we kept sinking in a slimy mud mixed with sea-weed and flat stones.] As we advanced, I heard a kind of pattering above my head. The noise redoubling, sometimes producing a continual shower, I soon understood the cause. It was rain falling violently, and crisping the surface of the waves. Instinctively the thought flashed across my mind that I should be wet through! By the water! In the midst of the water! I could not help laughing at the odd idea. But, indeed, in the thick diving dress, the liquid element is no longer felt,2 and one only seems to be in an atmosphere somewhat denser than the terrestrial atmosphere. Nothing more.

After half an hour's walk the soil became stony. Medusae, microscopic crustacea, and pennatules lit it slightly with their phosphorescent gleam. I caught a glimpse of pieces of stone covered with millions of zoophytes, and masses of seaweed. My feet often slipped upon this viscous carpet of seaweed, and without my iron-tipped stick I should have fallen more than once. In turning round, I could still see the whitish lantern of the *Nautilus* beginning to pale in the distance.

[I realised that those pieces of stone were laid out on the ocean floor with inexplicable regularity. I noticed, too, huge furrows that trailed off into the distant darkness and whose length I could not even estimate. There were other details I found hard to explain. I had the sensation that my heavy lead soles were crushing bones that made a dry crackling sound. What was this strange plain that we were treading? I wanted to ask Nemo, but he had never taught me that sign language that he and his crew used on these sea-floor walks.]

2. *liquid element is no longer felt* Aronnax must mean that the *wetness* of the liquid element is no longer felt.

But the rosy light which guided us increased and lit up the horizon. The presence of this fire under water puzzled me in the highest degree. Was it some electric effulgence? Was I going towards a natural phenomenon as yet unknown to the savants of the earth? Or even (for this thought crossed my brain) had the hand of man aught to do with this conflagration? Had he fanned this flame? Was I to meet in these depths companions and friends of Captain Nemo whom he was going to visit, and who, like him, led this strange existence? Should I find down there a whole colony of exiles, who, weary of the miseries of this earth, had sought and found independence in the deep ocean? All these foolish and unreasonable ideas pursued me. And in this condition of mind, over-excited by the succession of wonders continually passing before my eyes, I should not have been surprised to meet at the bottom of the sea one of those submarine towns of which Captain Nemo dreamed.[3]

Our road grew lighter and lighter. The white glimmer came in rays from the summit of a mountain about 800 feet high. But what I saw was simply a reflection, developed by the clearness of the waters. The source of this inexplicable light was a fire on the opposite side of the mountain.

In the midst of this stony maze, furrowing the bottom of the Atlantic, Captain Nemo advanced without hesitation. He knew this dreary road. Doubtless he had often travelled over it, and could not lose himself. I followed him with unshaken confidence. He seemed to me like a genie of the sea; and, as he walked before me, I could not help admiring his stature, which was outlined in black on the luminous horizon.

It was one in the morning when we arrived at the first slopes of the mountain; but to gain access to them we must venture through the difficult paths of a vast copse.

Yes; a copse of dead trees, without leaves, without sap, trees petrified by the action of the water, and here and there overtopped by gigantic pines. It was like a coal pit, still standing, holding by the roots to the broken soil, and whose branches, like fine black paper cuttings, showed distinctly on the watery ceiling. Picture to yourself a forest in the Hartz, hanging on to the sides of the mountain, but a forest swallowed up. The paths were encumbered with seaweed and fucus, between which grovelled a whole world of crustacea. I went along, climbing the rocks, striding over extended trunks, breaking the sea bindweed, which hung from one tree to the other; and frightening the fishes, which flew from branch to branch. Pressing onward, I felt no fatigue. I fol-

---

3. *towns of which . . . Nemo dreamed* Nemo's "dream" is one of Verne's predictions about to come true in our time.

Early in 1969 a team of four scientist-aquanauts lived for two months at a depth of 50 feet off the island of St. John in the Virgin Islands. The following year ten different teams of five each—including one team of all women—stayed on the same ocean floor for 20 to 30 days at a time. They worked, cooked, and slept in submersible dwellings under a minimum pressure of one-and-a-half atmospheres, the first successful living under such sustained pressures. In the fall of 1971 a Soviet expedition lived underwater in the Baltic for 52 days before a storm terminated their experiment.

All the technology necessary has now been developed so that whole communities can dwell in submerged pressurized housing projects. When undersea dwellers want to step "out of doors" for a private stroll, they will simply strap on a pair of artificial "gills" and extract oxygen directly from the water as the true fish do. They will still be able to "surface for air" like any other mammal that has "returned to the sea." They will be the most adaptable of *Homo sapiens,* since they will still retain their power to live on land and soar into space.

lowed my guide, who was never tired. What a spectacle! How can I express it? How paint the aspect of those woods and rocks in this medium,—their under parts dark and wild, the upper coloured with red tints, by that light which the reflecting powers of the waters doubled? We climbed rocks, which fell directly after with gigantic bounds, and the low growling of an avalanche. To right and left ran long, dark galleries, where sight was lost. Here opened vast glades which the hand of man seemed to have worked; and I sometimes asked myself if some inhabitant of these submarine regions would not suddenly appear to me.

But Captain Nemo was still mounting. I could not stay behind. I followed boldly. My stick gave me good help. A false step would have been dangerous on the narrow passes sloping down to the sides of the gulfs; but I walked with firm step, without feeling any giddiness. Now I jumped a crevice the depth of which would have made me hesitate had it been among the glaciers on the land; now I ventured on the unsteady trunk of a tree, thrown across from one abyss to the other, without looking under my feet, having only eyes to admire the wild sites of this region.

There, monumental rocks, leaning on their regularly cut bases, seemed to defy all laws of equilibrium. From between their stony knees, trees sprang, like a jet under heavy pressure, and upheld others which upheld them. Natural towers, large scarps, cut perpendicularly, like a "curtain," inclined at an angle which the laws of gravitation could never have tolerated in terrestrial regions.

[I knew that these angles were possible because of the density of sea-water. That was the reason that I, in spite of my copper head-piece and lead soles, was scaling slopes of incredible steepness, and with the agility of a chamois, or a Pyrenee mountain-goat!

I know this account of my under-water stroll must sound incredible. But as a writer, I am bound to record what has actually happened, no matter how impossible it may seem. I was not dreaming. I saw, I felt what I am writing about!]

Two hours after quitting the *Nautilus,* we had crossed the line of trees, and a hundred feet above our heads rose the top of the mountain, which cast a shadow on the brilliant irradiation of the opposite slope. Some petrified shrubs ran fantastically here and there. Fishes got up under our feet like birds in the long grass. The massive rocks were rent with impenetrable fractures, deep grottoes and unfathomable holes, at the bottom of which formidable creatures might be heard

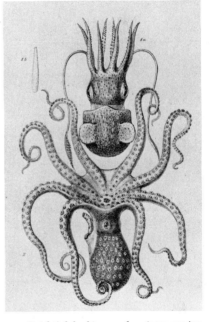

. . . Frightful looking poulps, interweaving their tentacles like a living nest of serpents. Plate from Edward Forbes, F. R. S., and Sylvanus Hanley's *A History of British Mollusca* (1853).

moving. My blood curdled when I saw enormous antennae blocking my road, or some frightful claw closing with a noise in the shadow of some cavity. Millions of luminous spots shone brightly in the midst of the darkness. They were the eyes of giant crustacea crouched in their holes; giant lobsters setting themselves up like halberdiers, and moving their claws with the clicking sound of pincers; titanic crabs, pointed like a gun on its carriage; and frightful looking poulps, interweaving their tentacles like a living nest of serpents.

[This truly was a world that even I as a naturalist did not know. To what order do these articulata belong, these who use rocks as a second shell? How has nature solved the problem of their nutrition? For how long have they lived on the sea-floor like this?

I could not pause to wonder. Nemo, well acquainted with these terrible creatures, was ignoring them.]

4. *on the first platform*   Verne says *à un premier plateau,* on a first plateau.

We had now arrived on the first platform,**4** where other surprises awaited me. Before us lay some picturesque ruins, which betrayed the hand of man, and not that of the Creator. There were vast heaps of stone, amongst which might be traced the vague and shadowy forms of castles and temples, clothed with a world of blossoming zoophytes, and over which, instead of ivy, sea-weed and fucus threw a thick vegetable mantle. But what was this portion of the globe which had been swallowed by cataclysms? Who had placed those rocks and stones like cromlechs of pre-historic times? Where was I? Whither had Captain Nemo's fancy hurried me?

I would fain have asked him; not being able to, I stopped him—I seized his arm. But shaking his head, and pointing to the highest point of the mountain, he seemed to say—

"Come, come along; come higher!"

I followed, and in a few minutes I had climbed to the top, which for a circle of ten yards commanded the whole mass of rock.

I looked down the side we had just climbed. The mountain did not rise more than seven or eight hundred feet above the level of the plain; but on the opposite side it commanded from twice that height the depths of this part of the Atlantic. My eyes ranged far over a large space lit by a violent fulguration. In fact, the mountain was a volcano.

5. *At fifty feet above . . . the liquid mass*   Verne says that the crater was 50 feet *below the peak.* The "standard translation" confuses *au-dessous* (below) with *au-dessus* (above).

At fifty feet above the peak, in the midst of a rain of stones and scoriae, a large crater was vomiting forth torrents of lava which fell in a cascade of fire into the bosom of the liquid mass.**5** Thus situated, this volcano lit the lower plain like an immense torch, even to the extreme limits of the horizon. I said that the submarine crater threw up lava, but no flames. Flames require the oxygen of the air to feed upon, and cannot be developed under water; but streams of lava, having in themselves the principles of their incandescence, can attain a white heat, fight vigorously against the liquid element, and turn it to vapour by contact.

Rapid currents bearing all these gases in diffusion, and torrents of lava, slid to the bottom of the mountain like an eruption of Vesuvius on another Torre del Greco.

There, indeed, under my eyes, ruined, destroyed, lay a town,—its roofs open to the sky, its temples fallen, its arches dislocated, its columns lying on the ground, from which one could still recognise the massive character of Tuscan architecture. Further on, some remains of a gigantic aqueduct; here the high base of an Acropolis, with the floating outline of a Parthenon; there traces of a quay, as if an ancient port had formerly abutted on the borders of the ocean, and disappeared with its merchant vessels and its war-galleys. Further on again, long lines of sunken walls and broad deserted streets—a perfect Pompeii escaped beneath the waters. Such was the sight that Captain Nemo brought before my eyes!

Where was I? Where was I? I must know, at any cost. I tried to speak, but Captain Nemo stopped me by a gesture, and picking up a piece of chalk stone, advanced to a rock of black basalt, and traced the one word—

ATLANTIS.

What a light shot through my mind! Atlantis, the ancient Meropis of Theopompus, the Atlantis of Plato, that continent denied by Origen, [Porphyry,] Jamblichus, D'Anville, Malte-Brun, and Humboldt, who placed its disappearance amongst the legendary tales admitted by Posidonius, Pliny, Ammianus, Marcellinus, Tertullian, Engel, [Sherer, Tournefort,] Buffon, and D'Avezac.6 I had it there now before my eyes, bearing upon it the unexceptionable testimony of its catastrophe. The region thus engulphed was beyond Europe, Asia, and Libya, beyond the columns of Hercules,7 where those powerful people, the Atlantides, lived, against whom the first wars of ancient Greece were waged.

[It was Plato who described the events of those ancient times. His dialogue between Timaeus and Critias had been inspired by Solon, the poet and law-giver.

One day Solon had been talking with the sages of Saïs, an ancient city then eight centuries old, as records engraved on their temple walls testified. One of the sages told the story

6. *Buffon, and D'Avezac* Here Verne lists a mere platoon of the many battalions of authors who have written about Atlantis. Marie-Armand-Pascal d'Avezac (1800–1875) was director of archives of the French Ministry of Marine. Georges Louis Leclerc, Comte de Buffon (1707–1788), was author of a thirty-six volume *Histoire naturelle*. Alexander von Humboldt (1769–1859) was a distinguished German explorer.

7. *the columns of Hercules* The Pillars of Hercules are two high points of rock projecting into the sea at the eastern end of the Straits of Gibraltar. These were regarded by many in the ancient world as marking the limits of navigation. Now the Phoenicians and Carthaginians probably fostered that belief. They themselves sailed beyond the Pillars and did a handsome trade with inhabitants of the west coasts of Europe and Africa. To keep the competition away, they even kept alive rumors of sea monsters in the western Mediterranean.

The Pillars got their name from the legend that Hercules, as one of his side feats late in his Twelve Labors, had put these two peaks of rock in place. The one on the European side is known as the Rock of Gibraltar; the other, on the African headland, is Mount Acho.

Gibraltar, one of the "Pillars of Hercules," as it appeared at about the time of Aronnax's journey. Engraving from *The American Cyclopaedia* (1873).

8. *larger than Africa and Asia combined* Two leading oceanographers have recently remarked that the legendary "lost Atlantis . . . existed . . . about where the Mid-Atlantic Ridge rises a mile or more from the ocean floor east of the Sargasso Sea." David B. Ericson and Goesta Wollin, in *The Ever-Changing Sea,* seem to feel that Atlantis may prove to be as great a spur to marine archaeology as Troy was to Heinrich Schliemann (1822–1890). They also invite consideration of the fact that in Plato's dialogues, Atlantis is reported to have planted colonies on another continent still farther west. During the Renaissance, it was rationalized that the new-found America was the colony of Atlantis that Plato had had in mind.

As Lewis Spence points out in *The History of Atlantis,* a book that Ericson and Wollin seem to respect, there were many similarities between Central American and Egyptian civilizations. Some writers believe these likenesses could be attributed to the Atlantides.

9. *historical memories* If we clarify some of Aronnax's *historical memories,* we can make some interesting connections with recent scientific discoveries.

of another city a thousand years older. This first Athenian city, nine hundred centuries old, had been invaded and partly destroyed by the Atlantides. These Atlantides, the sage said, inhabited a vast continent larger than Africa and Asia combined,**8** extending from 12° to 40° north latitude. Their dominions comprised even Egypt. They had tried to conquer Greece, but the Hellenes forced the Atlantides to withdraw.

Centuries passed and then suddenly a terrible cataclysm produced floods and earthquakes. One night and one day sufficed to destroy Atlantis, whose highest peaks—the Madeiras, Azores, Canaries, and Cape Verde Islands—still stand above the sea.

These were the historical memories **9** invoked for me by Captain Nemo's word in chalk.]

Thus, led by the strangest destiny, I was treading under foot the mountains of this continent, touching with my hand those ruins a thousand generations old, and contemporary with the geological epochs. I was walking on the very spot where the contemporaries of the first man had walked. [My leaden boots were crushing the skeletons of prehistoric creatures who had basked in the shade of these trees—now petrified.

Why did I have so little time! I would have liked to descend the steep slopes of this peak, explore this immense continent which probably joined Africa to America, and visit its antediluvian cities.**10** Perhaps before my eyes I would see war-like Makhimos and pious Eusebos, whose giants lived for centuries, who were so strong they could assemble these piles of stone that still resisted the action of the waves.

Some day some new volcanic eruption would return these ruins to the surface! Many submerged volcanoes have been reported in this area, many a ship's crew has reported tremors as they sailed over these tormented depths. Some have heard rumblings indicating some dispute between the elements, others have caught volcanic fragments thrown out of the sea. This entire area, as far as the equator, is still being worked over by Plutonian forces. Who knows, maybe in the remote future, because of successive eruptions of lava, these fiery mountain peaks may yet appear on the surface of the Atlantic!]

Whilst I was trying to fix in my mind every detail of this grand landscape, Captain Nemo remained motionless, as if petrified in mute ecstasy, leaning on a mossy stone. Was he dreaming of those generations long since disappeared? Was he asking them the secret of human destiny? Was it here this strange man came to steep himself in historical recollections, and live again this ancient life,—he who wanted no modern one? What would I not have given to know his thoughts, to share them, to understand them! We remained for an hour at this place, contemplating the vast plain under the brightness of the lava, which was sometimes wonderfully intense. Rapid tremblings ran along the mountains caused by internal bubblings, deep noises distinctly transmitted through the liquid medium were echoed with majestic grandeur. At this moment the moon appeared through the mass of waters, and threw her pale rays on the buried continent. It was but a gleam, but what an indescribable effect! The Captain rose, cast one last look on the immense plain, and then bade me follow him.

We descended the mountain rapidly, and the mineral forest once passed, I saw the lantern of the *Nautilus* shining like a star. The Captain walked straight to it, and we got on board as the first rays of light whitened the surface of the ocean.

Solon flourished about 600 B.C. Plato tells us in *Critias* that by Solon's time, 9000 years "had elapsed since the war . . . between those who dwelt outside the Pillars of Hercules and all who dwelt within." That would date the war, in modern terms, at about 9600 B.C. or about 11,600 years ago. Plato says that after the war, a "cataclysm" destroyed Atlantis. Ericson and Wollin remark the coincidence that "the last ice sheet of Europe began to waste away only about 11,000 years ago." And in 1975 University of Miami scientists reported finding evidence that torrents flowing down the Mississippi from a melting ice sheet some 11,600 years ago raised worldwide sea levels enough to explain many ancient stories of a great flood. Writing in *Science* (September 26, 1975), Dr. Cesare Emiliani and seven coauthors noted that this time coincides with that set by Plato for destruction of Atlantis by flooding.

10. *visit its antediluvian cities* In Jules Verne's posthumous tale *The Eternal Adam,* archaeologists of a future culture do find the ruins of Atlantis.

PART 2: CHAPTER X
The Submarine Coal-Mines

1. *Bailly . . . imaginative pages*
Jean Sylvain Bailly actually believed the Atlantides had lived at the North Pole, as Doctor Clawbonny tells the other characters in Verne's *Adventures of Captain Hatteras* (1866). Clawbonny admired the Atlantides for being a "well regulated people." Plato had used Atlantis as a kind of model for what he considered an ideal society. Some of this admiration has rubbed off on Aronnax, too. Normally pacifist, he now thinks of the conquering Atlantides as heroic.

Bailly was a French astronomer whose writing on science and the history of science was interrupted by the French Revolution. He was a Paris deputy to the Estates General, was elected President of the Third Estate in 1789, administered the famous Tennis Court Oath, served as acting mayor of Paris until 1791, and went to the guillotine in 1793.

2. *I followed him into ichthyology*
When we first met Conseil, he was able to classify fishes only in theory. But he could at that time identify shells. Apparently on this journey he has at last learned how to identify fishes as well.

3. *slightest whims of their mates*
This remark by the bachelor Aronnax is typical of dozens of passages in which Verne ridicules marriage. He himself had married for love but within a short time found himself tak-

The next day, the 20th of February, I awoke very late: the fatigues of the previous night had prolonged my sleep until eleven o'clock. I dressed quickly, and hastened to find the course the *Nautilus* was taking. The instruments showed it to be still towards the south, with a speed of twenty miles an hour, and a depth of fifty fathoms.

[When Conseil came in, I told him about our nocturnal expedition. The panels were open and he was able to get a glimpse of the lost continent. The *Nautilus* was cruising about five fathoms above the plains of Atlantis. I felt as if I were in a balloon floating over the prairies. But sitting in that saloon, we were more like passengers in a coach of an express-train.

We were looking out on chiselled rocks, forests of trees transformed from vegetables to minerals. Their silhouettes seemed to be grimacing beneath the waves. Masses of rocks were covered with a tapestry of axidies and anemones, bristling with long, vertical hydrophytes. Blocks of lava were strangely contorted in silent testimony to the violence of volcanic eruptions.

While we were staring at the eerie spectacle, lighted by our powerful lantern, I told Conseil the story of the Atlantides. I told him how they had inspired Bailly to write so many charming and imaginative pages.[1] I told him of the wars of these heroic people, speaking as one who could no longer doubt the existence of them and their continent. But soon I realised that Conseil was distracted. It was clear that he was indifferent to my discourse on ancient history.

Schools of fish were swimming by. Conseil, obsessed with the need to classify, was oblivious to me and Atlantis. Whenever he was in such a mood, I followed him into ichthyology.[2]]

The species of fishes here [in Atlantis] did not differ much from those already noticed. There were rays of giant size, five yards long, and endowed with great muscular strength, which enabled them to shoot above the waves; sharks of many kinds, amongst others, a glaucus of fifteen feet long, with triangular sharp teeth, and whose transparency rendered it almost invisible in the water; brown sagrae, humantins, prism-shaped, and clad with a tuberculous hide; sturgeons, resembling their congeners of the Mediterranean; trumpet syngnathes, a foot and a half long, furnished with greyish bladders, without teeth or tongue, and as supple as snakes.

Amongst bony fish, Conseil noticed some blackish makairas, about three yards long, armed at the upper jaw with a piercing sword; other bright coloured creatures, known in the time of Aristotle by the name of the sea-dragon, which are dangerous to capture on account of the spikes on their back; also some coryphaenes, with brown backs marked with little blue stripes, and surrounded with a gold border; some beautiful dorades; [moonfish that looked a bit like bluish dishes and, when sun-rays fell on them, they shimmered silver;] and swordfish four-and-twenty feet long, swimming in troops, fierce animals, but rather herbivorous than carnivorous. [Like hen-pecked husbands, they obey the slightest whims of their mates.3

While working with Conseil on classifying the marine life, I was still studying the broad plains of Atlantis. Capricious accidents in the terrain would sometimes force the *Nautilus* to slow down. Like a graceful cetacean, she would seek out a gap in the promontories. If this labyrinth seemed to block her way entirely, she would rise like a balloon to cross the obstacles, then descend to resume her course several fathoms above the sea-floor. This awesome, enchanting journey kept reminding me of a trip in a balloon,4 except of course that the *Nautilus* was much more controllable.]

About four o'clock, the soil, generally composed of a thick mud mixed with petrified wood, changed by degrees, and it became more stony, and seemed strewn with conglomerate and pieces of basalt, with a sprinkling of lava and sulphurous obsidian. I thought that a mountainous region was succeeding the long plains; and accordingly, after a few evolutions of the *Nautilus,* I saw the southerly horizon blocked by a high wall which seemed to close all exit. Its summit evidently passed the level of the ocean. It must be a continent, or at least an island,—one of the Canaries, or of the Cape Verde Islands. The bearings not being yet taken, perhaps designedly I was

ing long trips without his wife. Soon he was a stranger in most rooms of his own house except his library and workroom. He greatly admired the divorce laws in the United States but he himself resolved the problem of a boring marriage in the conventional European fashion. Apparently he found new romance with some "unique siren" and, when that ended —did she quit him or die? no one knows—he sank into private despair.

Madame Marguerite Allotte de la Fuÿe, wife of Verne's nephew and Verne's official biographer, reveals few of the family's well-kept secrets. She does suggest that a clue to Verne's private despair can be found in his *The Castle of the Carpathians* (1892). The story is about the strange effects of the death of a singer on two men who loved her.

Verne's adherence to the "European fashion" meant that in his official public statements in his own voice, he still recommended marriage, especially for ladies. For example, in an 1893 speech at a girls' school in Amiens, he told the girls not to "throw" themselves into "social struggles" or even into science, for "creation of a family home" was the "only true way in which a woman should make her influence felt in society."

For the record, then, he was pro-marriage and antifeminist. In his private life he devoured the daring books of Madame Sand. In his writing, it's a character like Nemo who admires Sand and one like Aronnax who sneers gently at uxorious creatures. The pattern holds true on most issues. As a citizen, Verne was bourgeois, conventional, conservative. In his writings, his greatest characters are nonconformists, outcasts, rebels. At the age of eleven, as we have seen, Verne had promised to leave the beaten path only in his imagination.

4. *a trip in a balloon* Verne's comparison is perfect and instructive. The submarine is buoyed in water as the balloon is buoyed in air. The principles regulating maneuvers in both media are so similar that Auguste Piccard insisted that in beginning with

In a balloon over Paris in 1858, Verne's friend Nadar took the first aerial photographs. This event was satirized by Honoré Daumier (1808–1879) who, unrecognized as a painter, was obliged to draw cartoons for the Paris weeklies.

balloons he had never really departed from his ambition to develop deep-water submersibles.

Early in his Paris days, young Verne became friends with Félix Tournachon who, under the name of Nadar, was famous as aeronaut, photographer, caricaturist, traveler, author. In 1858, in a balloon flight over Paris, Nadar took the first aerial photographs. Nadar helped Verne with most of the technical details that launched him on a new career with his *Five Weeks in a Balloon* (1863). While Verne was building that craft in fiction, Nadar was building his *Géant* in real life. This was a huge balloon with a two-story gondola that made a spectacular four-hundred-mile trip in October 1863. The *Géant* dragged through the country near Hanover, Germany, demolishing everything it hit and badly bruising its passengers.

Nadar became a hero in the Franco-Prussian War, making balloon trips in and out of beleaguered Paris.

While Verne keeps us reminded of balloon feats even in *Twenty Thousand Leagues under the Sea* and featured the balloon in novels like *The Mysterious Island* (1875), he cor-

ignorant of our exact position. In any case, such a wall seemed to me to mark the limits of that Atlantis, of which we had in reality passed over only the smallest part.

[Nightfall did not interrupt my observations. I was alone, for Conseil had returned to his cabin. Having reduced speed, the *Nautilus* now hovered over the confused masses of rock, then brushed the bottom as though seeking a place to rest, and sometimes unexpectedly surfaced. And so I caught sight of brilliant stars: those five or six that hang on the tail of Orion.]

Much longer should I have remained at the window, admiring the beauties of sea and sky, but the panels closed. At this moment the *Nautilus* arrived at the side of this high perpendicular wall. What it would do, I could not guess. I returned to my room; it no longer moved. I laid myself down with the full intention of waking after a few hours' sleep; but it was eight o'clock the next day when I entered the saloon. I looked at the manometer. It told me that the *Nautilus* was floating on the surface of the ocean. Besides, I heard steps on the platform. I went to the panel. It was open; but, instead of broad daylight, as I expected, I was surrounded by profound darkness. Where were we? Was I mistaken? Was it still night? No; not a star was shining, and night has not that utter darkness.

I knew not what to think, when a voice near me said—

"Is that you, Professor?"

"Ah! Captain," I answered, "where are we?"

"Under ground, sir."

"Under ground!" I exclaimed. "And the *Nautilus* floating still?"

"It always floats."

"But I do not understand."

"Wait a few minutes, our lantern will be lit, and if you like light places, you will be satisfied."

I stood on the platform and waited. The darkness was so complete that I could not even see Captain Nemo; but looking to the zenith, exactly above my head, I seemed to catch an undecided gleam, a kind of twilight filling a circular hole. At this instant the lantern was lit, and its vividness dispelled the faint light. I closed my dazzled eyes for an instant, and then looked again. The *Nautilus* was stationary, floating near a mountain which formed a sort of quay. The lake then supporting it was a lake imprisoned by a circle of walls, measuring two miles in diameter, and six in circumference. Its level (the manometer showed) could only be the same as the outside level, for there must necessarily be a communication between the lake and the sea. The high partitions, leaning forward on their base, grew into a vaulted roof bearing the shape of an immense funnel turned upside down, the height being about five or six hundred yards. At the summit was a circular orifice, by which I had caught the slight gleam of light, evidently daylight.

"Where are we?" I asked.

"In the very heart of an extinct volcano, the interior of which has been invaded by the sea, after some great convulsion of the earth. Whilst you were sleeping, Professor, the *Nautilus* penetrated to this lagoon by a natural canal, which opens about ten yards beneath the surface of the ocean. This is its harbour of refuge, a sure, commodious, and mysterious one, sheltered from all gales. Show me, if you can, on the coasts of any of your continents or islands, a road which can give such perfect refuge from all storms."

"Certainly," I replied, "you are in safety here, Captain Nemo. Who could reach you in the heart of a volcano? But did I not see an opening at its summit?"

rectly believed that the heavier-than-air ship would win out over the lighter-than-air craft. That's exactly what happens in *The Clipper in the Clouds* (1886).

Their balloon carries Dr. Samuel Ferguson, his servant Joe, and his friend Dick Kennedy across the Niger. Engraving from Verne's first novel, *Five Weeks in a Balloon* (1863).

5. *a simple sandbank* Verne says *simple écueil* and again Lewis translates Verne's *écueil* (reef, rock) as *sandbank*. Since this *simple écueil* is "about five or six hundred yards" in height (Verne says *mètres*), Lewis—with one stroke of his pen—created the greatest "sandbank" in world literature.

"Yes; its crater, formerly filled with lava, vapour, and flames, and which now gives entrance to the life-giving air we breathe."

"But what is this volcanic mountain?"

"It belongs to one of the numerous islands with which this sea is strewn,—to vessels a simple sandbank,— 5 to us an immense cavern. Chance led me to discover it, and chance served me well."

["Is it possible to pass through that crater up there?"

"No, monsieur. You can climb the lower walls of the crater, maybe up to a hundred feet. But above that, the walls lean too far inward, they overhang, they cannot be scaled."

"As always, Captain, Nature meets your needs. You are quite safe on this lake. You alone can visit here.] But of what use is this refuge, Captain? The *Nautilus* wants no port."

"No, sir; but it wants electricity to make it move, and the wherewithal to make the electricity—sodium to feed the elements, coal from which to get the sodium, and a coal-mine to supply the coal. And exactly on this spot the sea covers entire forests embedded during the geological periods, now mineralised, and transformed into coal; for me they are an inexhaustible mine."

"Your men follow the trade of miners here, then, Captain?"

"Exactly so. These mines extend under the waves like the mines of Newcastle. Here, in their diving dresses, pick-axe and shovel in hand, my men extract the coal, which I do not even ask from the mines of the earth. When I burn this combustible for the manufacture of sodium, the smoke, escaping from the crater of the mountain, gives it the appearance of a still active volcano."

"And we shall see your companions at work?"

"No; not this time at least; for I am in a hurry to continue our submarine tour of the earth. So I shall content myself with drawing from the reserve of sodium I already possess. The time for loading is one day only, and we continue our voyage. So if you wish to go over the cavern, and make the round of the lagoon, you must take advantage of to-day, M. Aronnax."

I thanked the Captain, and went to look for my companions, who had not yet left their cabin. I invited them to follow me without saying where we were. They mounted the platform. Conseil, who was astonished at nothing, seemed to look upon it as quite natural that he should wake under a mountain, after having fallen asleep under the waves. But Ned Land thought of nothing but finding whether the cavern had any exit. After breakfast, about ten o'clock, we went down on to the [shore near the] mountain.

"Here we are, once more on land," said Conseil.

"I do not call this land," said the Canadian. "And besides, we are not on it, but beneath it."

Between the walls of the mountain and the waters of the lake lay a sandy shore, which, at its greatest breadth, measured five hundred feet. On this soil one might easily make the tour of the lake. But the base of the high partitions was stony ground, with volcanic blocks and enormous pumice stones lying in picturesque heaps. All these detached masses, covered with enamel, polished by the action of the subterraneous fires, shone resplendent by the light of our electric lantern. The mica dust from the shore, rising under our feet, flew like a cloud of sparks. The bottom now rose sensibly, and we soon arrived at long circuitous slopes, or inclined planes, which took us higher by degrees; but we were obliged to walk carefully among these conglomerates, bound by no cement, the feet slipping on the glassy trachyte, composed of crystal, felspar, and quartz.

The volcanic nature of this enormous excavation was confirmed on all sides, and I pointed it out to my companions.

"Picture to yourselves," said I, "what this crater must have been when filled with boiling lava, and when the level of the incandescent liquid rose to the orifice of the mountain, as though melted on the top of a hot plate."

"I can picture it perfectly," said Conseil. "But, sir, will you tell me why the Great Architect has suspended operations, and how it is that the furnace is replaced by the quiet waters of the lake?"

"Most probably, Conseil, because some convulsion beneath the ocean produced that very opening which has served as a passage for the *Nautilus*. Then the waters of the Atlantic rushed into the interior of the mountain. There must have been a terrible struggle between the two elements, a struggle which ended in the victory of Neptune. But many ages have run out since then, and the submerged volcano is now a peaceable grotto."

"Very well," replied Ned Land; "I accept the explanation, sir; but, in our own interests, I regret that the opening of which you speak was not made above the level of the sea."

"But, friend Ned," said Conseil, "if the passage had not been under the sea, the *Nautilus* could not have gone through it. [And if the waters had not rushed in, this mountain would still be a volcano. So your regrets do not make much sense.]"

6. *sloping masses had to be turned* Read: *We had to work our way around protruding masses of rock.*

7. *height of about thirty-one feet* Verne says thirty meters, or about one hundred feet.

8. *bubbles . . . prisms* That is, the basalt masses in some places were honeycombed, in others, prism-shaped.

We continued ascending. The steps became more and more perpendicular and narrow. Deep excavations, which we were obliged to cross, cut them here and there; sloping masses had to be turned.**6** We slid upon our knees and crawled along. But Conseil's dexterity and the Canadian's strength surmounted all obstacles. At a height of about thirty-one feet,**7** the nature of the ground changed without becoming more practicable. To the conglomerate and trachyte succeeded black basalt, the first dispread in layers full of bubbles, the latter forming regular prisms,**8** placed like a colonnade supporting the spring of the immense vault, an admirable specimen of natural architecture. Between the blocks of basalt wound long streams of lava, long since grown cold, encrusted with bituminous rays; and in some places there were spread large carpets of sulphur. A more powerful light shone through the upper crater, shedding a vague glimmer over these volcanic depressions for ever buried in the bosom of this extinguished mountain. But our upward march was soon stopped at a height of about two hundred and fifty feet by impassable obstacles. There was a complete vaulted arch overhanging us, and our ascent was changed to a circular walk. At the last change vegetable life began to struggle with the mineral. Some shrubs, and even some trees, grew from the fractures of the walls. I recognised some euphorbias, with the caustic sugar coming from them; heliotropes, quite incapable of justifying their name, sadly drooped their clusters of flowers, both their colour and perfume half gone. Here and there some chrysanthemums grew timidly at the foot of an aloe with long sickly-looking leaves. But between the streams of lava, I saw some little violets still slightly perfumed, and I admit that I smelt them with delight. Perfume is the soul of the flower, and sea-flowers, those splendid hydrophytes, have no soul.

We had arrived at the foot of some sturdy dragon trees, which had pushed aside the rocks with their strong roots, when Ned Land exclaimed—

"Ah! sir, a hive! a hive!"

"A hive!" I replied, with a gesture of incredulity.

"Yes, a hive," repeated the Canadian, "and bees humming round it."

I approached, and was bound to believe my own eyes. There, at a hole bored in one of the dragon-trees, were some thousands of these ingenious insects, so common in all the Canaries, and whose produce is so much esteemed. Naturally enough, the Canadian wished to gather the honey, and I could not well oppose his wish. A quantity of dry leaves, mixed with sulphur, he lit with a spark from his flint, and he began to smoke out the bees. The humming ceased by degrees, and the hive eventually yielded several pounds of the sweetest honey, with which Ned Land filled his haversack.

"When I have mixed this honey with the paste of the artocarpus,"9 said he, "I shall be able to offer you a succulent cake."

"Upon my word," said Conseil, "it will be gingerbread."

"Never mind the gingerbread," said I; "let us continue our interesting walk."

At every turn of the path we were following, the lake appeared in all its length and breadth. The lantern lit up the whole of its peaceable surface which knew neither ripple nor wave. The *Nautilus* remained perfectly immovable. On the platform, and on the mountain, the ship's crew were working like black shadows clearly carved against the luminous atmosphere. We were now going round the highest crest of the first layers of rock which upheld the roof. I then saw that bees were not the only representatives of the animal kingdom in the interior of this volcano. Birds of prey hovered here and there in the shadows, or fled from their nests on the top of the rocks. There were sparrow-hawks with white breasts, and kestrels, and down the slopes scampered, with their long legs, several fine fat bustards. I leave any one to imagine the covetousness of the Canadian at the sight of this savoury game, and whether he did not regret having no gun. But he did his best to replace the lead by stones, and after several fruitless attempts, he succeeded in wounding a magnificent bird. To say that he risked his life twenty times before reaching it, is but the truth; but he managed so well, that the creature joined the honeycakes in his bag.

We were now obliged to descend towards the shore, the crest becoming impracticable. Above us the crater seemed to gape like the mouth of a well. From this place the sky could be clearly seen, and clouds, dissipated by the west wind, leaving behind them, even on the summit of the mountain, their misty remnants—certain proof that they were only moderately high, for the volcano did not rise more than eight hundred feet 10 above the level of the ocean.

Half an hour after the Canadian's last exploit we had regained the inner shore. Here the flora was represented by large carpets of marine crystal, a little umbelliferous plant very good to pickle, which also bears the name of piercestone, and sea-fennel. Conseil gathered some bundles of it.

9. *artocarpus* This is the breadfruit of which Ned gathered a good supply way back in the South Pacific.

10. *eight hundred feet* Earlier Aronnax estimated the volcano's height as five or six hundred yards, 1500 to 1800 feet. Either he is now correcting his earlier estimate or even Verne himself, like Homer, "sometimes nods."

11. *enclosed me in its bivalves* In spite of his disclaimer, Aronnax has now had his ultimate dream and one that is authentic, even though Freud is now only twelve years old.

Aronnax has talked of Jonah's taking refuge in whales' bellies. He has described his sheltered life on the *Nautilus* as resembling a snail's existence in its shell. And now, inside a cave, he makes the full return to the womb: he is an oyster inside its bivalves. He approaches the identity crisis from which he will emerge reborn.

His dream also fulfills Freud's description in its immediate function: it serves to let Aronnax continue sleeping, even while the water rises around him. The more Aronnax becomes mollusklike, the more he accepts water inside his shell and around his flesh.

12. *the hero of Walter Scott* When they were boys, Paul and Jules Verne heard Walter Scott from their father's lips; Pierre read novels aloud every night. As a young student in Paris on a tight budget, Jules often laid out his food money for still another volume of the great romantic novelist. At the age of thirty-one, preparing to take a trip to England and Scotland, Verne reread Scott's works. Verne's English biographer sums it up: "He knew the minutiae of Scott." As Kenneth Allott sees it, Verne loved Scott because Scott resembled Verne. Both writers would rather describe exotic country than deep passion, and "Real women . . . embarrassed" both of them. But while adventures in caves may abound in the works of both, it's only fair to Verne to say that he does not follow Scott at all in the older man's dogged reliance on murders, duels, combat, and torture.

As to the fauna, it might be counted by thousands of crustacea of all sorts, lobsters, crabs, palaemons, spider crabs, chameleon shrimps, and a large number of shells, rockfish and limpets.

[Then we discovered a magnificent cave. With great delight I stretched out on its sandy floor. Volcanic fire had enamelled the walls which glittered with mica dust. Ned Land was tapping the walls, testing their thickness. I could only smile. Talk turned inevitably to his plans for escape. I gave him some hope without gambling too much. I told him that Nemo had come south only to renew his sodium supply. I imagined now the *Nautilus* would skirt the coasts of Europe and America. That would give Ned some fair chance of success.

After we had rested there for an hour or so, the chatting grew desultory, and I let myself fall into a lazy nap. I dreamed —after all, one does not determine his own dreams—that I was slowly changing into a simple mollusc. This grotto was now the shell that enclosed me in its bivalves.[11]

Suddenly I was awakened by Conseil's voice.

"Monsieur! Monsieur!" he cried.

"What? What's wrong?"

"The water is rising! We will drown!"

I stood up at once. The sea was storming into our cave. Since we were not molluscs, we had to leave. In a few moments we had made it to higher ground, above the grotto.

"What is this, monsieur?" Conseil asked. "Some new phenomenon?"

"No, no, just the tide. The tide has surprised us as it did the hero of Walter Scott.[12] The ocean is rising outside this crater and so, following Nature's laws of equilibrium, the level of the lake is rising too. We escaped with just a little bath. Let us go change on the *Nautilus*."]

Three quarters of an hour later, we had finished our circuitous walk, and were on board. The crew had just finished loading the sodium, and the *Nautilus* could have left that instant. But Captain Nemo gave no order. Did he wish to wait until night, and leave the submarine passage secretly? Perhaps so. Whatever it might be, the next day, the *Nautilus,* having left its port, steered clear of all land at a few yards beneath the waves of the Atlantic.

PART 2: CHAPTER XI
The Sargasso Sea [1]

[The *Nautilus* did not change its direction. For the time being, at least, we had to abandon our hopes of returning to European waters. Captain Nemo held to his southern course. Where was he taking us? I dared not think about it.]

That day the *Nautilus* crossed a singular part of the Atlantic Ocean. No one can be ignorant of the existence of a current of warm water, known by the name of the Gulf Stream. After leaving the Gulf of Florida, we went in the direction of Spitzbergen.[2] But before entering the Gulf of Mexico, about the forty-fifth degree of north latitude, this current divides into two arms, the principal one going towards the coast of Ireland and Norway, whilst the second bends to the south about the height of the Azores; then, touching the African shore, and describing a lengthened oval, returns to the Antilles.[3] This second arm—it is rather a collar than an arm—surrounds with its circles of warm water that portion of the cold, quiet, immovable ocean called the Sàrgasso Sea, a perfect lake in the open Atlantic; it takes no less than three years for the great current to pass round it.

[The Sargasso Sea covers the submerged part of Atlantis. Some authors say that the numerous kinds of weeds in the Sargasso arise from the prairies of that lost continent. But it is more likely that these weeds, algae, and fucus have been brought to this area from European and American shores by the Gulf Stream. This was one of the reasons why Columbus assumed the existence of a New World. When the sailors of that hardy explorer arrived in the Sargasso, they had great difficulty getting through those weeds, which slowed them down. They spent three long weeks crossing the Sargasso! [4]]

Such was the region the *Nautilus* was now visiting, a perfect meadow, a close carpet of seaweed, fucus, and tropical ber-

1. *The Sargasso Sea* Again Verne uses a well-known place name as bait. The Sargasso Sea is the most famous mysterious region in the Atlantic. Only in recent years have some of its mysteries been solved, but—as we shall see—the legends linger on.

2. *we went in the direction of Spitzbergen* No, no, the *Gulf Stream* goes in the direction of Spitzbergen.

3. *returns to the Antilles* Twentieth-century studies indicate that the Gulf Stream really meanders. No reliable maps of its currents can be established. In early June 1950, for example, the principal current was making a big loop to the south between 65° and 60° west longitude. But from June 19 to June 22, the stream took a shortcut, eliminating the loop, which broke off as an eddy. As a result, subarctic waters were pushed into the subtropical Atlantic.

4. *three long weeks crossing the Sargasso* Columbus's men panicked in the Sargasso because they believed that these weeds signified that they were close to land and that they were in danger of cracking up on an unknown coast. But their soundings failed to reach bottom.

5. *beneath the surface of the waves*
Such has been the legend until our own time, namely that even big heavy vessels could become hopelessly entangled amid masses of sargassum weed. It was reported that crews trapped inside this current gyre of the Gulf Stream went mad from thirst and died of starvation. In 1855 Maury said that "the speed of vessels . . . is often much retarded." As late as 1897 a British magazine declared that not even a strong wind could push a sailing vessel through Sargasso. And in 1952 a French physician crossing the Atlantic on a raft carefully avoided the notorious weed-trap.

But modern ships often go right through the Sargasso. Ericson and Wollin have been "through the thick of it." They say it could "do nothing worse than perhaps slightly retard the progress of a sailing dinghy." And the *Reader's Digest* book *Secrets of the Seas* declares that the weeds occur in patches "no larger than a doormat." Scientists estimate that there are 7 to 10 million tons of weed in the Sargasso, but spread out over 2 million square miles.

6. *which signifies kelp* But it was the Portuguese sailors who gave this kelp its name. They noted the resemblance between the air-bladder floats of the weed and a small grape called *sarga* in Portugal.

7. *The Physical Geography of the Globe* The actual title of Maury's book—which everybody seemed to be reading except Verne's English translator—is *The Physical Geography of the Sea.*

8. *the floating bodies unite* Since Lewis did not quote Maury directly—but translated Verne's French translation back into English!—it will be helpful here to give this famous passage in the original:
". . . if bits of cork or chaff, or any floating substance, be put into a basin, and a circular motion be given to the water, all the light substances will be found crowding together near the centre of the pool, where there is the least motion. Just such a basin is

ries, so thick and so compact, that the stem of a vessel could hardly tear its way through it. And Captain Nemo, not wishing to entangle his screw in this herbaceous mass, kept some yards beneath the surface of the waves.**5** The name Sargasso comes from the Spanish word "sargazzo," which signifies kelp.**6** This kelp or varech, or berry-plant, is the principal formation of this immense bank. And this is the reason, according to the learned Maury, the author of "The Physical Geography of the Globe," **7** why these hydrophytes unite in the peaceful basin of the Atlantic. The only explanation which can be given, he says, seems to me to result from the experience known to all the world. Place in a vase some fragments of cork or other floating body, and give to the water in the vase a circular movement, the scattered fragments will unite in a group in the centre of the liquid surface, that is to say, in the part least agitated. In the phenomenon we are considering, the Atlantic is the vase, the Gulf Stream the circular current, and the Sargasso Sea the central point at which the floating bodies unite.**8**

I share Maury's opinion, and I was able to study the phenomenon in the very midst, where vessels rarely penetrate. Above us floated products of all kinds, heaped up among these brownish plants; trunks of trees torn from the Andes or the Rocky Mountains, and floated by the Amazon or the Mississippi; **9** numerous wrecks, remains of keels, or ships' bottoms, side planks stove in, and so weighted with shells and barnacles that they could not again rise to the surface. And time will one day justify Maury's other opinion, that these substances, thus accumulated for ages, will become petrified by the action of the water, and will then form inexhaustible coal-mines—a precious reserve prepared by far-seeing Nature for the moment when men shall have exhausted the mines of continents.

In the midst of this inextricable mass of plants and seaweed, I noticed some charming pink halcyons and actiniae, with their long tentacles trailing after them; medusae, green, red, and blue, and the great rhy[z]ostoms of Cuvier, the large umbrella of which was bordered and festooned with violet.

All the day of the 22d of February we passed in the Sargasso Sea, where such fish as are partial to marine plants and fuci find abundant nourishment.**10** The next, the ocean had returned to its accustomed aspect. From this time for nineteen days, from the 23d of February to the 12th of March, the *Nautilus* kept in the middle of the Atlantic, carrying us at a constant speed of a hundred leagues in twenty-four hours. Captain Nemo evidently intended accomplishing his submarine programme, and I imagined that he intended, after doubling Cape Horn, to return to the Australian seas of the Pacific. Ned Land had cause for fear. In the large seas, void of islands, we could not attempt to leave the boat. Nor had we any means of opposing Captain Nemo's will. Our only course was to submit; but what we could neither gain by force nor cunning, I liked to think might be obtained by persuasion. This voyage ended, would he not consent to restore our liberty, under an oath never to reveal his existence?—an oath of honour which we should have religiously kept. But we must consider that delicate question with the Captain. But was I free to claim this liberty? Had he not himself said from the beginning, in the firmest manner, that the secret of his life exacted from him our lasting imprisonment on board the *Nautilus?* And would not my four months' silence appear to him a tacit acceptance of our situation? And would not a return to the subject result in raising suspicions which might be hurtful to our projects, if at some future time a favourable opportunity offered to return to them?

[I was troubled by all these factors, and I discussed them with Conseil, who was in the same dilemma. Even though I am not easily discouraged, I began to fear that our chances of ever seeing our homeland again were growing dimmer by the day. Captain Nemo's course was taking us straight for the South Atlantic.]

During the nineteen days mentioned above, no incident of any note happened to signalise our voyage. I saw little of the Captain; he was at work. In the library I often found his books left open, especially those on Natural History. My work on submarine depths, conned over by him, was covered with marginal notes, often contradicting my theories and systems; **11** but the Captain contented himself with thus purging my work; it was very rare for him to discuss it with me. Sometimes I heard the melancholy tones of his organ; but only at night, in the midst of the deepest obscurity, when the *Nautilus* slept upon the deserted ocean. During this part of our voyage we sailed whole days on the surface of the waves. The sea seemed abandoned. A few sailing-vessels, on the road to India, were making for the Cape of Good Hope. One day we were followed by the boats of a whaler, who, no doubt, took us for some enormous whale of great price; but Captain Nemo did not wish the worthy fellows to lose their time and trouble, so ended the chase by plunging under the water.

[That incident seemed to affect Ned profoundly. I do not think I would be wrong in saying that the Canadian regretted that our steel cetacean could not be harpooned by those whalers.

the Atlantic Ocean to the Gulf Stream, and the Sargasso Sea is the centre of the whirl."

Maury's passage is a splendid example of that instructive device known in science writing as "the imaginary experiment." The *basin*—rather than a *vase*—makes visualization much easier, since the area being imagined should be seen as broader than it is deep.

9. *floated by the Amazon or the Mississippi* There is not much chance that many tree trunks could float from the Rocky Mountains to the Sargasso Sea. Tributaries of the Upper Missouri that start in the Rockies—and feed the Mississippi—are too small to carry trees except in floods. But they could carry green leaves on such a long trip.

Verne could have been led into this supposition because trees that grow in the Rockies are not identifiable as such: the same trees grow elsewhere along the path of the Mississippi.

10. *abundant nourishment* Aronnax could never have imagined that the creatures that *find abundant nourishment* in the Sargasso include the freshwater eels of American and European rivers. In Aronnax's day, the life cycle of the eel was a great mystery. It seemed to have no offspring: eggs and larvae were not found in the rivers where adult eels live. Aristotle had hypothesized that eels are generated out of mud. Other early naturalists thought horsehairs could change into eels. As late as 1905, the year of Verne's death, D. S. Jordan could only write that the common species migrate "to the sea in winter"—he could not say how far. "The young eels enter the streams two years after their parents drop down into the sea. It is doubtful whether eels breed in fresh water." No one had ever yet seen an eel egg.

Then in the 1920s Johannes Schmidt, the great Danish biologist, solved the mystery. On board the research vessel *Dana* he filtered huge quantities of Atlantic water and discovered that eel larvae are distributed according to a significant pattern.

Those closest to the mouths of European rivers were the largest; those farther west were smaller. Schmidt finally found their spawning place thousands of miles away in the western Atlantic—in the Sargasso Sea. The larvae take three years to drift back to their "natural" habitat in the rivers of Europe and America. During that time they change from a leaflike shape to the "silver eel" that ascends the rivers in enormous numbers.

11. *my theories and systems* That is, the professor's systems of classification. For example, Aronnax might classify a certain crustacean among the *anomura*. Nemo might disagree, placing it with the *macrura* or even in a special category intermediate between the *macrura* and *brachyura*. The problem is one of correctly charting the actual relationships by the *descent* of the various species.

12. *did not sing for us* The sciaenidae did not sing for Professor Aronnax, but the humpback whale has sung for Dr. Roger Payne of New York's Rockefeller University. Near Bermuda, Payne trailed hydrophones in the water to record the sounds made by humpbacks during their spring migration northward. He describes their calls as haunting, warbling notes, lower in pitch than those of birds. The humpback songs are true songs, like bird songs, in the sense that they are repeated. Unlike bird songs, they last for several minutes.

Since whales have no vocal cords, no one yet knows exactly how they sing. Evidently they can force air past valves and flaps in sacs beneath their blowholes. Differences in the way these structures vibrate might explain why these whales seem to have distinctive, individual "voices."

Fishes that Conseil and I observed during this time differed little from those we had noted in other latitudes. But we did see specimens of that terrible genus of cartilaginous fish that comprises three subgenera and thirty-two species: there were striped sharks, fifteen feet long, whose flat heads are bigger than their bodies, whose backs carry seven wide parallel stripes, and whose tail-fins are rounded. There were perlon sharks, cinder grey, with seven bronchial openings and a single dorsal fin in the middle of the body.

And we saw some large sea-dogs, voracious fish. Fishermen's stories are traditionally unbelievable, but for what they're worth, I will recall a few. In the body of one sea-dog, they found a buffalo head and a calf; in another, two tuna and a sailor in uniform; in a third, a horse and rider! These are apocryphal stories, but what is true is that no sea-dog ever allowed himself to be taken in our nets, and so I could neither prove nor disprove the legends.

Elegant dolphins, travelling in groups of five or six, accompanied us for days at a time, hunting in packs like wolves. These are just like sea-dogs in their voracity, if we can believe a Copenhagen professor who says he found thirteen porpoises and fifteen seals in a dolphin's stomach! Of course, it was a grampus, the biggest dolphin known, who can grow up to twenty-five feet in length. This family comprises ten genera; those I saw were delphinians. I could distinguish them by their very long and straight snout, four times as long as their skull. Ten feet in all, their bodies are black on top, pinkish-white below, often speckled.

In these waters we also saw some members of the order of acanthopterygians, family of sciaenidae. Some authors, more poetic perhaps than scientific, claim that these fish sing, that when they sing together they sometimes sound even better than a human choir. I can't say, for the sciaenidae did not sing for us.**12**

Finally, here Conseil got his chance to classify the flying fish. The dolphins chase them with unbelievable precision. No matter how far they flew, no matter what tangent they took, sometimes even when they leaped over the *Nautilus,* these flying fish always had the bad luck to land right in a dolphin's mouth. We also saw pirapedes, or flying gurnards, with luminous mouths. At night, after blazing a path in the air, they would plunge into the dark water like falling stars.]

Our navigation continued until the 13th of March; that day the *Nautilus* was employed in taking soundings, which greatly interested me. We had then made about 13,000 leagues since our departure from the high seas of the Pacific.

The bearings gave up 45° 37′ south latitude, and 37° 53′ west longitude. It was the same water in which Captain Denham of the *Herald* sounded 7000 fathoms without finding the bottom. There, too, Lieutenant Parker, of the American frigate *Congress,* could not touch the bottom with 15,140 fathoms.[13]

[Captain Nemo decided to check on Denham's and Parker's results. I was set to take notes on our experiment. The panels in the saloon were opened. We began the complex operation of diving to the remotest depths. It was not possible to do that by filling the reservoirs. That would not have added the great extra weight required. Besides, in order to surface again, we would have had to empty the tanks, and our pumps were not sufficiently powerful to overcome the outside pressure at such depths.]

Captain Nemo intended seeking the bottom of the ocean by a diagonal sufficiently lengthened by means of lateral planes placed at an angle of forty-five degrees with the water-line of the *Nautilus.* Then the screw set to work at its maximum speed, its four blades beating the waves with indescribable force. Under this powerful pressure the hull of the *Nautilus* quivered like a sonorous chord, and sank regularly under the water.

[Sitting in the saloon, we watched the needle of the manometer moving rapidly. Soon we had gone below the level where most fish can live. While some fish can live only in the upper strata or in the rivers, others live in profounder depths. Among these I now saw a hexanchus, resembling a sea-dog, with six gill-openings; a telescope-fish with huge eyes; an armoured malarmat, with grey lower fins, black upper fins, and red breasts protected with bony plates. And I saw the grenadier, at 4000 feet, who can live under a pressure of 120 atmospheres.

"Have you seen fish at lower depths than this?" I asked the Captain.

"Fish? Rarely. But in the present state of the science, what do we really know?"

"Well, Captain, we know that as we descend, vegetable life disappears sooner than animal life. We know that in some depths where we can still find life, we find not a single hydrophyte. We know that oysters and some scallops live at 6000 feet. McClintock, the hero of polar exploration, brought up a live star-fish from 8000 feet. And sailors on H.M.S. *Bulldog* fetched up a star-fish from more than 15,000 feet, in other words, more than a league down. So how can you say, 'What do we really know?' "

"True, monsieur, that was presumptuous of me. Still, may

13. *15,140 fathoms* Verne says 15,-140 *meters* or almost 50,000 feet. When such reports reached Maury's office, he suspected something was wrong. He overhauled the whole theory and practice of sounding.

It was originally believed that when the cannonball, or plummet, on the end of the sounding line touched bottom, there would be a discernible shock and the line would go slack. But Maury suspected that at great depths, the line would actually continue to pay out under its own weight. Maybe a crosscurrent acted as "a swigging force on the bight." So he promulgated his "Law of the Plummet's Descent." He ordered that the line be marked with bunting every 100 fathoms so that the speed of pay-out could be noted. When that speed suddenly diminished—even if the line still payed out—the fathom-marker at which the diminution had been noted was to be recorded as the depth of the bottom.

In 1852 Maury the perennial author published a chart giving depths along the proposed cable route between Britain and North America. And by 1855 he published a depth chart for the entire North Atlantic.

Elegant dolphins . . . accompanied us for days at a time. . . . The common dolphin as pictured in The American Cyclopaedia *(1873).*

I ask you, how can you account for the fact that animals can live at such depths?"

"I can explain it on two grounds. First of all, there are vertical currents produced by differences in density and salinity. They support the rudimentary life of the encrinidae and the starfish."

"Exactly," the Captain said.

"Secondly, with oxygen as the basic requirement, we know that the amount of oxygen dissolved in sea-water increases with the depth. The greater the depth, the more oxygen goes into solution."

"So! You do know that!" He seemed surprised. "Yes, I have also discovered that. I can tell you that the natatory bladders of fish hold more nitrogen than oxygen when caught in the upper strata, and more oxygen than nitrogen when caught in the lower strata. Which gives you more proof of your point. But let us resume our observations."

The manometer told us that we were now at a depth of 6000 meters or about 20,000 feet. We had been submerging for an hour, guided down by the inclined planes. The barren waters were admirably transparent, with a diaphaneity no painter could ever reproduce. An hour later, we had reached 13,000 meters—about 3¼ leagues—and there was still no sign of the bottom.]

At 7000 fathoms **14** I saw some blackish tops rising from the midst of the waters; but these summits might belong to high mountains like the Himalayas or Mount Blanc, even higher; and the depth of the abyss remained incalculable. The *Nautilus* descended still lower, in spite of the great pressure. I felt the steel plates tremble at the fastenings of the bolts; its bars bent, its partitions groaned; the windows of the saloon seemed to curve under the pressure of the waters. And this firm structure would doubtless have yielded, if, as its Captain had said, it had not been capable of resistance like a solid block. In skirting the declivity of these rocks, lost under water, I still saw some shells, some serpulae and spinorbes, still living, and some specimens of asteriads. But soon this last representative of animal life disappeared; and at the depth of more than three leagues, the *Nautilus* had passed the limits of submarine existence,**15** even as a balloon does when it rises above the respirable atmosphere. We had attained a depth of 16,000 yards (four leagues), and the sides of the *Nautilus* then bore a pressure of 1600 atmospheres, that is to say, 3200 pounds to each square two-fifths of an inch of its surface.**16**

"What a situation to be in!" I exclaimed. "To overrun these

14. *At 7000 fathoms* Verne says *14,000 meters,* or 46,200 feet.

15. *limits of submarine existence* On January 21, 1960, Jacques Piccard and Lieutenant Donald Walsh made their historic dive in the *Trieste* 35,-600 feet into the Challenger Deep. On the bottom they saw a shrimp, about one inch in diameter, and a sole about a foot long.

16. *each square two-fifths of an inch of its surface* Verne says 16,000 meters, which is about 52,800 feet. The normal conversion for 1600 atmospheres would be 23,520 pounds on each square inch of surface. This would make the *Nautilus* much stronger than the *Trieste,* which was built to withstand a pressure of 4000 pounds per square inch.

deep regions where man has never trod! Look, Captain, look at these magnificent rocks, these uninhabited grottoes, these lowest receptacles of the globe, where life is no longer possible! What unknown sights are here! Why should we be unable to preserve a remembrance of them?"

"Would you like to carry away more than the remembrance?" said Captain Nemo.

"What do you mean by those words?"

"I mean to say that nothing is easier than to take a photographic view of this submarine region."

I had not time to express my surprise at this new proposition, when, at Captain Nemo's call, an objective was brought into the saloon.**17** Through the widely opened panel, the liquid mass was bright with electricity, which was distributed with such uniformity, that not a shadow, not a gradation, was to be seen in our manufactured light. The *Nautilus* remained motionless, the force of its screw subdued by the inclination of its planes: the instrument was propped on the bottom of the oceanic site, and in a few seconds we had obtained a perfect negative. I here give the positive, from which may be seen those primitive rocks, which have never looked upon the light of heaven; that lowest granite which forms the foundation of the globe; those deep grottoes, woven in the stony mass whose outlines were of such sharpness, and the border lines of which marked in black, as if done by the brush of some Flemish artist. Beyond that again a horizon of mountains, an admirable undulating line, forming the prospective of the landscape. I cannot describe the effect of these smooth, black, polished rocks, without moss, without a spot, and of strange forms, standing solidly on the sandy carpet, which sparkled under the jets of our electric light.

But the operation being over, Captain Nemo said, "Let us go up; we must not abuse our position, nor expose the *Nautilus* too long to such great pressure."

"Go up again!" I exclaimed.

"Hold well on."

I had not time to understand why the Captain cautioned me thus, when I was thrown forward on to the carpet. At a signal from the Captain, its screw was shipped, and its blades raised vertically; the *Nautilus* shot into the air like a balloon, rising with stunning rapidity, and cutting the mass of waters with a sonorous agitation. Nothing was visible; and in four minutes it had shot through the four leagues which separated it from the ocean, and after emerging like a flying-fish, fell, making the waves rebound to an enormous height.

17. *an objective was brought into the saloon* A *camera,* of course. Objective was short for *objective glass,* the lens or combination of lenses that forms the image of the object.

I here give the positive. . . . Engraving from the original edition (1870).

PART 2: CHAPTER XII
Cachalots and Whales[1]

1. *Cachalots and Whales* In his original chapter title, Verne emphasizes the sharp distinction between *Sperm Whales and Baleen Whales,* a distinction easier to make in the French: *Cachalots et Baleines.* Action and motivation here both will hinge on essential differences between these two cetaceans.

During the nights of the 13th and 14th of March, the *Nautilus* returned to its southerly course. I fancied that, when on a level with Cape Horn, he would turn the helm westward, in order to beat the Pacific seas, and so complete the tour of the world. He did nothing of the kind, but continued on his way to the southern regions. Where was he going? To the pole? It was madness! I began to think that the Captain's temerity justified Ned Land's fears. For some time past the Canadian had not spoken to me of his projects of flight; he was less communicative, almost silent. I could see that this lengthened imprisonment was weighing upon him, and I felt that rage was burning within him. When he met the Captain, his eyes lit up with suppressed anger; and I feared that his natural violence would lead him into some extreme. That day, the 14th of March, Conseil and he came to me in my room. I inquired the cause of their visit.

"A simple question to ask you, sir," replied the Canadian.

"Speak, Ned."

"How many men are there on board the *Nautilus,* do you think?"

"I cannot tell, my friend."

"I should say that its working does not require a large crew."

"Certainly, under existing conditions, ten men, at the most, ought to be enough."

"Well, why should there be any more?"

"Why?" I replied, looking fixedly at Ned Land, whose meaning was easy to guess. "Because," I added, "if my surmises are correct, and if I have well understood the Captain's existence, the *Nautilus* is not only a vessel: it is also a place of refuge for those who, like its commander, have broken every tie upon earth."

"Perhaps so," said Conseil; "but, in any case, the *Nautilus* can only contain a certain number of men. Could not you, sir, estimate their maximum?"

"How, Conseil?"

"By calculation; given the size of the vessel, which you know, sir, and consequently the quantity of air it contains, knowing also how much each man expands at a breath, and comparing these results with the fact that the *Nautilus* is obliged to go to the surface every twenty-four hours."

Conseil had not finished the sentence before I saw what he was driving at.

"I understand," said I; "but that calculation, though simple enough, can give but a very uncertain result."

"Never mind," said Ned Land, urgently.

"Here it is, then," said I. "In one hour each man consumes the oxygen contained in twenty gallons of air; and in twenty-four, that contained in 480 gallons. We must, therefore, find how many times 480 gallons of air the *Nautilus* contains."

"Just so," said Conseil.

"Or," I continued, "the size of the *Nautilus* being 1500 tons; and one ton holding 200 gallons, it contains 300,000 gallons of air, which, divided by 480, gives a quotient of 625. Which means to say, strictly speaking, that the air contained in the *Nautilus* would suffice for 625 men for twenty-four hours."

"Six-hundred and twenty-five!" repeated Ned.

"But remember, that all of us, passengers, sailors, and officers included, would not form a tenth part of that number."

"Still too many for three men," murmured Conseil.[2]

["My poor Ned," I said, "I advise you simply to be patient."

"Maybe," said Conseil, "resignation is better than patience."

He had hit on the better word.

"After all," Conseil went on, "the Captain cannot head south forever! He must stop at some point. Maybe he will be stopped by an ice barrier. Then he will have to come back to the regular shipping lanes, and then we can think once more about Ned's plans for making a break."]

The Canadian shook his head, passed his hand across his forehead, and left the room without answering.

"Will you allow me to make one observation, sir?" said Conseil. "Poor Ned is longing for everything that he can't have. His past life is always present to him; everything that we are forbidden he regrets. His head is full of old recollections. And we must understand him. What has he to do here? Nothing; he is not learned like you, sir; and has not the same

2. " . . . *three men,*" murmured *Conseil* The life of Nemo's myrmidons is so subdued, and communication between them and Ned so lacking, that after living in the same boat with them for months, Ned still has no knowledge of their actual number. The professor is no help. He once saw as many as *some twenty* of them all on deck at once, and surely that tells him their *minimum* number. But was that the whole crew or just one watch? Nemo does not seem to post watches, but we can't be sure. He seems only to use a different detail of men for each project: one gun carrier on one hunt, a small crew for the dinghy on a few occasions, eight men to drag in the prisoners. How many were at the funeral? Ned was there and if he could be certain that everyone had attended those services, then he would have his answer.

Nemo's men are all in a state of chronic depression, apparently for reasons more connected with their previous lives than with their actual exile. The only signs we have had of any *esprit de corps* were (1) the self-sacrifice of one man to save another when a lever sprang loose and (2) the crew's tireless work to help finance the Cretan revolutionaries. Theirs seems to be a life of grim altruism.

The presence of so many men resigned to despair creates an atmosphere of horror in some ways unequaled in all the literature of horror. For this horror, unlike that of gothic tale and ghost story, seems to be a by-product of political and social injustice. At least that's what Nemo's remarks about *"civilization,"* freedom, the Cretans and Indians, and his picture gallery of heroes all seem to indicate. With this dimension of horror, Verne anticipates some of the terrors of modern life later to be explored in works like Eugene O'Neill's *The Hairy Ape* and Samuel Beckett's *Waiting for Godot*.

taste for the beauties of the sea that we have. He would risk everything to be able to go once more into a tavern in his own country."

Certainly the monotony on board must seem intolerable to the Canadian, accustomed as he was to a life of liberty and activity. Events were rare which could rouse him to any show of spirit; but that day an event did happen which recalled the bright days of the harpooner. About eleven in the morning, being on the surface of the ocean, the *Nautilus* fell in with a troop of whales—an encounter which did not astonish me, knowing that these creatures, hunted to the death, had taken refuge in high latitudes.

[Whales have played a major role in the history of navigation and exploration. It was the whale who led first the Basques, then the Asturians, English, and Dutch, to brave the dangers of the open sea and to seek both ends of the world. For whales frequent both Arctic and Antarctic waters. There are hoary legends that whales have led whalers to within seven leagues of the Pole! That may well be an exaggeration so far, but it could well foretell the future too.]

We were seated on the platform, with a quiet sea. The month of October in those latitudes gave us some lovely autumnal days. It was the Canadian—he could not be mistaken—who signalled a whale on the eastern horizon. Looking attentively one might see its black back rise and fall with the waves five miles from the *Nautilus*.

"Ah!" exclaimed Ned Land, "if I were on board a whaler now, such a meeting would give me pleasure. It is one of large size. See with what strength its blow-holes throw up columns of air and steam! Confound it, why am I bound to these steel plates?"

"What, Ned," said I, "you have not forgotten your old ideas of fishing?"

"Can a whale-fisher ever forget his old trade, sir? Can he ever tire of the emotions caused by such a chase?"

"You have never fished in these seas, Ned?"

"Never, sir; in the northern only, and as much in Behring as in Davis Straits."

"Then the southern whale is still unknown to you. It is the Greenland whale you have hunted up to this time, and that would not risk passing through the warm waters of the equator."

["Professor! What are you trying to tell me now!" Ned was incredulous.

"Only the truth, Ned."

It was the [right] whale who led first the Basques, then the Asturians, English, and Dutch, to . . . seek both ends of the world. The right whale as picture in *The American Cyclopaedia* (1873).

There are hoary legends that whales have led whalers to within seven leagues of the Pole! Great northern rorqual as pictured in *The American Cyclopaedia* (1873).

"Only nonsense! Just two-and-a-half years ago—in 1865—I brought in a whale near Greenland. And in its flesh I found a harpoon with the mark of a whaler from the Behring Sea.

"Now how could that whale be wounded in the *west* of America and come to be killed in the *east*, unless she had crossed the equator after rounding either Cape Horn or the Cape of Good Hope!"

"I agree with Ned," said Conseil. "I am interested in hearing what monsieur has to say to *that!*"

"Well, here is monsieur's answer.] Whales are localised, according to their kinds, in certain seas which they never leave. And if one of these creatures went from Behring to Davis Straits, it must be simply because there is a passage from one sea to the other, either on the American or the Asiatic side."

["You are serious," Ned winked with one eye.

"We must believe monsieur," Conseil insisted.]

"In that case, as I have never fished in these seas, I do not know the kind of whale frequenting them."

"I have told you, Ned."

"A greater reason for making their acquaintance," said Conseil.

"Look! look!" exclaimed the Canadian, "they approach; they aggravate me; they know that I cannot get at them!" 3

Ned stamped his feet. His hand trembled, as he grasped an imaginary harpoon.

"Are these cetacea as large as those of the northern seas?" asked he.

"Very nearly, Ned."

"Because I have seen large whales, sir, whales measuring a hundred feet. I have even been told that those of Hullamoch and Umgallick, of the Aleutian Islands, are sometimes a hundred and fifty feet long." 4

"That seems to me exaggeration. These creatures are only balaenopterons, provided with dorsal fins; and, like the cachalots, are generally much smaller than the Greenland whale."

"Ah!" exclaimed the Canadian, whose eyes had never left the ocean, "they are coming nearer; they are in the same water as the *Nautilus!*"

Then returning to the conversation, he said—

"You spoke of the cachalot as a small creature. I have heard of gigantic ones. They are intelligent cetacea. It is said of some that they cover themselves with seaweed and fucus, and then are taken for islands. People encamp upon them, and settle there; light a fire——"

"Can a whale-fisher ever forget his old trade, sir? Can he ever tire of the emotions caused by such a chase?" Ned's trade as illustrated in *Mitchell's School Geography* (1863).

3. *cannot get at them* This speech is even more poignant in the original. Actually Ned has so far sighted only *one* whale and says:

"She's coming closer! She's teasing me! She knows I can't get at her!"

The translator confused *she* (*elle*) and *they* (*elles*) in this scene, although context makes it clear in a later speech when Ned says: " . . . *it is not one whale.*"

4. *a hundred and fifty feet long* Today the largest whale—and apparently the largest creature that ever lived—is the baleen whale known as the blue whale. This species ranges up to 100 feet in length and 135 tons in weight.

"They say these sperm whales can circum-navigate the globe in fifteen days!" The sperm whale—or cachalot—as pictured in *The American Cyclopaedia* (1873).

5. *weigh a hundred thousand tons* Ned is really the winner in this game of irony. This is a sly dig at the professor's original hypothesis that *the enormous thing* was a gigantic cetacean.

6. *four metres per second* Sally Carrighar, naturalist, reports that a blue whale, "with his chest torn apart by a barbed harpoon, will drag a 500-ton boat, its engines reversed, many miles."

"And build houses," said Conseil.

"Yes, joker," said Ned Land. "And one fine day the creature plunges, carrying with it all the inhabitants to the bottom of the sea."

"Something like the travels of Sinbad the Sailor," I replied, laughing. ["Master Land, you are fond of tall tales. And they are amusing, I admit. But I hope you do not believe them yourself!"

"Monsieur le naturaliste," he answered in dead earnest, "in the case of whales, you had better believe everything you hear! Look at the fantastic speed of that one! See how she can hide herself! They say these sperm whales can circumnavigate the globe in fifteen days!"

"I would not doubt *that.*"

"What you probably do not know, M. Aronnax, is that at the beginning of the world whales could swim even faster than they can now."

"Now Ned! How can you say that?"

"Because in those days their tails were vertical, like fish-tails. They could swish the water right to left, left to right. When the Creator saw that they were swimming much too fast, he twisted their tales to a horizontal position. So now they have to beat the water up and down. So naturally they have lost some of their original speed."

"What are you trying to tell me now!" I mimicked Ned's own expression.

"Believe that," Ned said, "and I will tell you there are whales 300 feet long that weigh a hundred thousand tons." **5**

"That would be heavy," I agreed. "But some whales do grow to prodigious dimensions. Some of them give as much as one-hundred-and-twenty tons of whale-oil."

"I can vouch for that. I have seen them," Ned said.

"And I believe you. I can believe too that some whales attain the mass of one hundred elephants all rolled into one. Imagine the impact of such a mass launched at full speed ahead!"

"Does that mean," Conseil asked, "that they can really sink a ship?"

"A ship? No. But wait now. They say that in 1820—in these very seas—a whale collided with the *Essex* and pushed her backwards at a speed of four metres per second.**6** The stern was flooded and the *Essex* went down fast."

Ned looked askance at that.

"Well," he added, "I was once hit by a whale's tail. I was in a long boat, of course. We were thrown twenty feet in the air. But that was just a baby whale, compared to yours, Professor."

"Do they live long?" Conseil asked.

"A full thousand years," the Canadian said authoritatively.

"Ned, how do you know *that!*"

"That's what they say."

"Why do they say so?"

"I suppose they know," Ned answered.

"No, they do not know, and this is what I mean. When whalers first began hunting whales about four hundred years ago,[7] they were much bigger than they are now. That must be because in those days they were allowed to live a full life. Today they are not allowed to reach their old age. So it was natural for Buffon to estimate that they could and did live for a thousand years. You understand?"

He did not understand. He was not even listening. The whale was coming nearer, and Ned's attention was fixed exclusively on that.[8]

"Ah!" suddenly exclaimed Ned Land, "it is not one whale; there are ten,—there are twenty,—it is a whole troop! [9] And I not able to do anything! hands and feet tied!"

"But, friend Ned," said Conseil, "why do you not ask Captain Nemo's permission to chase them?"

Conseil had not finished his sentence when Ned Land had lowered himself through the panel to seek the Captain. A few minutes afterwards the two appeared together on the platform.

Captain Nemo watched the troop of cetacea playing on the waters about a mile from the *Nautilus*.

"They are southern whales," said he; "there goes the fortune of a whole fleet of whalers."

"Well, sir," asked the Canadian, "can I not chase them, if only to remind me of my old trade of harpooner?"

"And to what purpose?" replied Captain Nemo; "only to destroy! We have nothing to do with whale-oil on board."

"But, sir," continued the Canadian, "in the Red Sea you allowed us to follow the dugong."

"Then it was to procure fresh meat for my crew. Here it would be killing for killing's sake. I know that is a privilege reserved for man, but I do not approve of such murderous pastime. In destroying the southern whale (like the Greenland whale, an inoffensive creature), your traders do a culpable action, Master Land. They have already depopulated the whole of Baffin's Bay, and are annihilating a class of useful animals. Leave the unfortunate cetacea alone. They have

7. *about four hundred years ago* Historians would now say about one thousand years ago. Strange air-breathing sea monsters were being washed ashore on the beaches of the Bay of Biscay. The Basque peoples there found these right whales provided good meat and valuable oil. A new industry was born when some Basques took to the sea to capture whales in greater numbers.

Here, of course, Aronnox is talking of the origins of *European* whaling. The Eskimos had been hunting whales long before the Basques.

8. *fixed exclusively on that* Again Verne has given us one of those long, casual, man-to-man conversations that really establish the quality of a friendship. And again Mercier Lewis cut this one, just as he cut the leisurely, random talk the three had about pearls. Both conversations fill in many details about the personal lives and beliefs of these men, especially about Ned. And both passages are dramatically conceived so that casual talk runs parallel to some serious suspense: in the case of the pearls talk, the fear of sharks pervaded the atmosphere; and in this scene, their talk about whales mounts in excitement as they come closer to the real animals.

9. *it is a whole troop* True, in the French, Ned says *c'est un troupeau*. But in this context *troupeau* means a *gam*, that is, a *school of whales*. Whalers like Ned also used the word *gam* for a *social visit*, especially between whaling crews, but also for a *friendly conversation*, such as Ned has just had with Aronnax and Conseil.

plenty of natural enemies, cachalots, swordfish, and sawfish, without *your* troubling them."

[Ned's face showed his total lack of comprehension of Nemo's lecture. How could you expect a hunter to get the point Nemo was making? Ned gaped at the chief on board.]

The Captain was right. The barbarous and inconsiderate greed of these fishermen will one day cause the disappearance of the last whale in the ocean.**10** Ned Land whistled "Yankee-doodle" between his teeth, thrust his hands into his pockets, and turned his back upon us. But Captain Nemo watched the troop of cetacea, and addressing me, said—

"I was right in saying that whales had natural enemies enough, without counting man. These will have plenty to do before long. Do you see, M. Aronnax, about eight miles to leeward, those blackish moving points?"

"Yes, Captain," I replied.

"Those are cachalots,—terrible animals, which I have sometimes met in troops of two or three hundred. As to *those,* they are cruel, mischievous creatures; they would be right in exterminating them."

The Canadian turned quickly at the last words.

"Well, Captain," said he, "it is still time, in the interest of the whales." **11**

"It is useless to expose one's self, Professor. The *Nautilus* will disperse them. It is armed with a steel spur as good as Master Land's harpoon, I imagine."

The Canadian did not put himself out enough to shrug his shoulders. Attack cetacea with blows of a spur! Who had ever heard of such a thing?

"Wait, M. Aronnax," said Captain Nemo. "We will show you something you have never yet seen. We have no pity for these ferocious creatures. They are nothing but mouth and teeth."

Mouth and teeth! No one could better describe the macrocephalous cachalot, which is sometimes more than seventy-five feet long. Its enormous head occupies one-third of its entire body. Better armed than the [baleen] whale, whose upper jaw is furnished only with whale bone, it is supplied with twenty-five large tusks, about eight inches long, cylindrical and conical at the top, each weighing two pounds.**12** It is in the upper part of this enormous head, in great cavities divided by cartileges, that is to be found from six to eight hundred pounds of that precious oil called spermaceti. The cachalot is a disagreeable creature, more tadpole than fish, according to Fredol's description. It is badly

10. *one day . . . the last whale in the ocean* That day may well be upon us. Some whales—the Atlantic gray whale, the Korean gray whale, and the Greenland bowhead whale—may already have been destroyed. Other bowhead and gray whales are now hard to find. The blue and right whales are considered "an endangered species" and sperm and fin whales are now seriously threatened.

Extermination of whales could signal man's own suicide, according to David O. Hill. The more than half a million whales who once roamed the seas helped regulate the plankton economy. A major portion of the oxygen in our atmosphere is produced by this complicated ecosystem. Wiping out the whale could jeopardize the supply of oxygen that both marine and human life depend on.

11. *in the interest of the whales* Not Ned but the professor utters these words.

12. *each weighing two pounds* Here we have the essential distinction foreshadowed by Verne's chapter title.

The cachalot, or sperm whale, is the only large whale with teeth.

Where the cachalot has teeth, the baleen whale has *only . . . whale bone,* that is, rows of baleen plates that hang from the roof of its mouth. The baleen feeds on small organisms by filtering water through these plates.

formed, the whole of its left side being (if we may say it) a "failure," and being only able to see with its right eye. But the formidable troop was nearing us. They had seen the whales and were preparing to attack them. One could judge before-hand that the cachalots would be victorious, not only because they were better built for attack than their inoffensive ad-versaries, but also because they could remain longer under water without coming to the surface.

There was only just time to go to the help of the whales. The *Nautilus* went under water. Conseil, Ned Land, and I took our places before the window in the saloon, and Captain Nemo joined the pilot in his cage to work his apparatus as an engine of destruction. Soon I felt the beatings of the screw quicken, and our speed increased. The battle between the cachalots and the whales had already begun when the *Nautilus* arrived. [Nemo manoeuvred the *Nautilus* so as to divide the herd of cachalots.] They did not at first show any fear at the sight of this new monster joining in the conflict. But they soon had to guard against its blows. What a battle! [Even Ned was overwhelmed with excitement.]

The *Nautilus* was nothing but a formidable harpoon, brandished by the hand of its captain. It hurled itself against the fleshy mass, passing through from one part to the other, leaving behind it two quivering halves of the animal. It could not feel the formidable blows from their tails upon its sides, nor the shock which it produced itself, much more. One cachalot killed, it ran at the next, tacked on the spot that it might not miss its prey, going forwards and backwards, an-swering to its helm, plunging when the cetacean dived into the deep waters, coming up with it when it returned to the surface, striking it front or sideways, cutting or tearing in all directions, and at any pace, piercing it with its terrible spur. What carnage! What a noise on the surface of the waves! What sharp hissing, and what snorting peculiar to these en-raged animals. In the midst of these waters, generally so peaceful, their tails made perfect billows. For one hour this wholesale massacre 13 continued, from which the cachalots could not escape. Several times ten or twelve united tried to crush the *Nautilus* by their weight. From the window we could see their enormous mouths studded with tusks, and their for-midable eyes. Ned Land could not contain himself, he threatened and swore at them. We could feel them clinging to our vessel like dogs worrying a wild boar in a copse. But the *Nautilus,* working its screw, carried them here and there, or to the upper levels of the ocean, without caring for their

13. *this wholesale massacre* Verne aptly terms it *cet homérique massacre.* For the overall scene of slaughter does resemble those Homer describes in the *Iliad.* In addition, Verne uses the Homeric trick of coldly describing the actual dissection that one warrior per-forms on another. Thus the submarine *passes through* a *fleshly mass,* leaving behind *two quivering halves of the animal.*

enormous weight, nor the powerful strain on the vessel.

At length, the mass of cachalots broke up, the waves became quiet, and I felt that we were rising to the surface. The panel opened, and we hurried on to the platform. The sea was covered with mutilated bodies. A formidable explosion could not have divided and torn this fleshy mass with more violence. We were floating amid gigantic bodies, bluish on the back and white underneath, covered with enormous protuberances. Some terrified cachalots were flying towards the horizon. The waves were dyed red for several miles, and the *Nautilus* floated in a sea of blood. Captain Nemo joined us.

"Well, Master Land?" said he.

"Well, sir," replied the Canadian, whose enthusiasm had somewhat calmed; "it is a terrible spectacle, certainly. But I am not a butcher. I am a hunter, and I call this a butchery."

"It is a massacre of mischievous creatures," replied the Captain; "and the *Nautilus* is not a butcher's knife."

"I like my harpoon better," said the Canadian.

"Every one to his own," answered the Captain, looking fixedly at Ned Land.

I feared he would commit some act of violence, which would end in sad consequences. But his anger was turned by the sight of a whale which the *Nautilus* had just come up with. The creature had not quite escaped from the cachalot's teeth. I recognised the southern whale by its flat head, which is entirely black. Anatomically, it is distinguished from the white whale and the North Cape whale by the seven cervical vertebrae, and it has two more ribs than its congeners. The unfortunate cetacean was lying on its side, riddled with holes from the bites, and quite dead. From its mutilated fin still hung a young whale which it could not save from the massacre. Its open mouth let the water flow in and out, murmuring like the waves breaking on the shore. Captain Nemo steered close to the corpse of the creature. Two of his men mounted its side, and I saw, not without surprise, that they were drawing from its breasts all the milk which they contained, that is to say, about two or three tons. The Captain offered me a cup of the milk, which was still warm. I could not help showing my repugnance to the drink; but he assured me that it was excellent, and not to be distinguished from cow's milk.[14] I tasted it, and was of his opinion. It was a useful reserve to us, for in the shape of salt butter or cheese it would form an agreeable variety from our ordinary food. From that day I noticed with uneasiness that Ned Land's ill-will towards Captain Nemo increased, and I resolved to watch the Canadian's gestures closely.

14. *not to be distinguished from cow's milk* But whale's milk may contain ten times more butterfat than cow's milk. And Aronnax seems to be overestimating the amount of milk drawn from the whale's breast: one ton would be a more likely quantity.

PART 2: CHAPTER XIII
The Iceberg[1]

The *Nautilus* was steadily pursuing its southerly course, following the fiftieth meridian with considerable speed. Did he wish to reach the pole? I did not think so, for every attempt to reach that point had hitherto failed. Again the season was far advanced, for in the antarctic regions, the 13th of March corresponds with the 13th of September of northern regions, which begin at the equinoctial season. On the 14th of March I saw floating ice in latitude 55°, merely pale bits of debris from twenty to twenty-five feet long, forming banks over which the sea curled. The *Nautilus* remained on the surface of the ocean. Ned Land, who had fished in the arctic seas, was familiar with its icebergs; but Conseil and I admired them for the first time. In the atmosphere towards the southern horizon stretched a white dazzling band. English whalers have given it the name of "ice blink."[2] However thick the clouds may be, it is always visible, and announces the presence of an ice pack or bank. Accordingly, larger blocks soon appeared, whose brilliancy changed with the caprices of the fog. Some of these masses showed green veins, as if long undulating lines had been traced with sulphate of copper; others resembled enormous amethysts with the light shining through them. Some reflected the light of day upon a thousand crystal facets. Others shaded with vivid calcareous reflections resembled a perfect town of marble. The more we neared the south, the more these floating islands increased both in number and importance.

[Polar birds—petrels, damiers, puffins—were nesting on them by the thousands and their cries were deafening. Some of them seemed to mistake the *Nautilus* for a dead whale, and we could hear them pecking at our steel hull.

During our trip through the ice, Captain Nemo stayed a great deal of time on deck. As he studied these desolate areas,

1. *The Iceberg* Verne's title, *La Banquise,* means something closer to *The Ice Bank.* As the story develops, the ice formation in question will shape up more as *The Ice Shelf.*

2. *ice blink* Ice blink appears as a pillar in the sky over Antarctic sea ice. In some photographs it appears as a cross.

Optical phenomena have figured prominently in the history of polar exploration. A famous example has been revived in recent scientific discussions. In 1906 Robert E. Peary sighted a range of peaks above the ice-cap about 400 miles west of the northern tip of Greenland. He named these summits Crocker Land, and this land of peaks was actually noted on at least one map of the period. Then in 1913 Donald B. MacMillan led an expedition to Crocker Land. As his group approached 83° north, 103° west, the location given on their map, Commander MacMillan wrote: ". . . no doubt about it. Great Heavens, what a land! Hills, valleys, snow-capped peaks. . . ." Then, as they tramped 30 miles "inland" over the Arctic ice, the peaks began to disappear. By evening MacMillan knew there was nothing there but a vast plain of ice.

Crocker Land was a mirage of the most spectacular kind known as a *fata morgana* which means *Fairy Morgan* in Italian. Fairy Morgan was credited, in the legends of King Arthur, with the magical ability to create castles in thin air.

A meteorologist at Pennsylvania State University, Dr. Alistair B. Fraser, and his assistant, William H. Mach, have provided new, detailed explanations of such mirages. Under certain temperature and wind conditions, Doctor Fraser says, the atmosphere "behaves like a dime-store magnifying glass: it is astigmatic or unfocusing." The atmosphere tends to magnify distant objects vertically, causing a small boat, for example, to loom high as a tall lighthouse.

Doctor Fraser believes that mirages might explain such biblical phenomena as the parting of the Red Sea and Jesus' walking on the water. In the January 1976 issue of *Scientific American,* in which they reported their studies, Fraser and Mach present a photograph of a mirage of two boys "walking on the water" at Puget Sound. Actually they were trudging across a sand spit that had been uncovered at low tide. They were seen and photographed through a fluid medium, the air, that acted as a giant lens and distorted the light rays.

Fata morgana mirages, Doctor Fraser says, are most commonly seen on enclosed bodies of evenly illuminated water or ice. It is interesting to read Aronnax's descriptions of the polar regions with Fraser's findings in mind.

3. *two or three degrees below zero* Verne gives temperatures here according to the Centigrade scale. This reading of $-2°$ or $-3°$ Centigrade would be 28.4° to 26.6° Fahrenheit.

The Centigrade scale registers the *freezing point of fresh water* as 0°C and the *boiling point* as 100°C. This was the sensible scale proposed by Anders Celsius, Swedish astronomer (1701–1744). In his honor, the Centigrade scale, as it was known to Aronnax, is now called the Celsius.

The Fahrenheit is quite arbitrary, registering the freezing point as 32°F and boiling as 212°F. It is named after Gabriel Fahrenheit, German physicist living in Holland (1686–1736).

Conversion from one scale to the other is accomplished with this equa-

the placid expression on his face would change to one of animation. Was he thinking of these regions inaccessible to man as his true home, where he was supreme master? If so, he did not say so. He would stand motionless and would emerge from meditation only when the helmsman in him took over. Then he would steer with consummate ingenuity, dodging masses of ice, some of them miles long and up to 250 feet high. Sometimes they blocked out the horizon.]

At the sixtieth degree of latitude, every pass had disappeared. But seeking carefully, Captain Nemo soon found a narrow opening, through which he boldly slipped, knowing, however, that it would close behind him. Thus, guided by this clever hand, the *Nautilus* passed through all the [different masses of] ice [which are classified] with a precision which quite charmed Conseil; icebergs or mountains, ice-fields or smooth plains, seeming to have no limits, drift ice or floating ice packs, or plains broken up, called *palchs* when they are circular, and streams when they are made up of long strips. The temperature was very low; the thermometer exposed to the air marked two or three degrees below zero,[3] but we were warmly clad with fur, at the expense of the sea-bear and seal. The interior of the *Nautilus,* warmed regularly by its electric apparatus, defied the most intense cold. Besides, it would only have been necessary to go some yards beneath the waves to find a more bearable temperature. Two months earlier we should have had perpetual daylight in these latitudes; but already we had three or four hours night, and by and by there would be six months of darkness in these circumpolar regions. On the 15th of March we were in the latitude of New Shetland and South Orkney. The Captain told me that formerly numerous tribes of seals inhabited them; but that English and American whalers, in their rage for destruction, massacred both old and young; thus where there was once life and animation, they had left silence and death.

About eight o'clock on the morning of the 16th of March, the *Nautilus,* following the fifty-fifth meridian, cut the antarctic polar circle. Ice surrounded us on all sides, and closed the horizon. But Captain Nemo went from one opening to another, still going higher.

["Where is he heading?" I wondered.

"Straight ahead," said Conseil, "until he can go no farther."

"That does not make much sense," I said. But to be honest, I did admit to myself that I was delighted with this new adventure.]

I cannot express my astonishment at the beauties of these

new regions. The ice took most surprising forms. Here the grouping formed an oriental town, with innumerable mosques and minarets; there a fallen city thrown to the earth, as it were, by some convulsion of nature. The whole aspect was constantly changed by the oblique rays of the sun, or lost in the greyish fog amidst hurricanes of snow. Detonations and falls were heard on all sides, great overthrows of icebergs, which altered the whole landscape like a diorama.**4**

[When the *Nautilus* dived to avoid these cataclysms, great crashing noises echoed through the water. Whenever blocks of ice toppled into the sea, they made our boat roll and toss as though we were caught in a hurricane.]

Often seeing no exit, I thought we were definitely prisoners; but instinct guiding him at the slightest indication, Captain Nemo would discover a new pass. He was never mistaken when he saw the thin threads of bluish water trickling along the ice-fields; and I had no doubt that he had already ventured into the midst of these antarctic seas before. On the 16th of March, however, the ice-fields absolutely blocked our road. It was not the iceberg itself, as yet,**5** but vast fields cemented by the cold. But this obstacle could not stop Captain Nemo; he hurled himself against it with frightful violence. The *Nautilus* entered the brittle mass like a wedge, and split it with frightful cracklings. It was the battering ram of the ancients hurled by infinite strength. The ice, thrown high in the air, fell like hail around us. By its own power of impulsion our apparatus made a canal for itself; sometimes carried away by its own impetus it lodged on the ice-field, crushing it with its weight, and sometimes buried beneath it, dividing it by a simple pitching movement, producing large rents in it. Violent gales assailed us at this time, accompanied by thick fogs, through which, from one end of the platform to the other, we could see nothing. The wind blew sharply from all points of the compass, and the snow lay in such hard heaps that we had to break it with blows of a pickaxe. The temperature was always at five degrees below zero;**6** every outward part of the *Nautilus* was covered with ice. A rigged vessel could never have worked its way there, for all the rigging would have been entangled in the blocked-up gorges. A vessel without sails, with electricity for its motive power, and wanting no coal, could alone brave such high latitudes.

[Under these conditions, the barometer readings were very low. It even dropped to 73.5 centimetres.**7** And we could no longer rely on the compass. Its needle would move wildly in all directions as we approached the south magnetic pole,

tion: $F = 1.8C + 32$

If you're not familiar with freezing points, then you'll appreciate this tip for enjoying these passages: *sea water, because of its salt, has a freezing point two degrees lower than that of fresh water.* Thus when Aronnax says that *the thermometer exposed to the air marked two or three degrees below zero,* he is telling us that the *Nautilus* is in waters that could just be on the verge of freezing.

4. *like a diorama* To Verne's nineteenth-century reader, this comparison was dramatic and suggestive. Before the age of the cinema, *diorama* (like panorama and cyclorama) gave the visual artist and his audience golden opportunities to enjoy illusions and changing effects.

A simple diorama could be a three-dimensional scene with painted models standing in the foreground against an opaque painted background. *An elaborate diorama* could be painted on transparent hangings on which lights could be played to vary the effects. The audience would view a diorama either out in the open or through a peephole.

Early *peep-shows* certainly included dioramas, but credit for their development belongs to Louis Jacques Mandé Daguerre (1789–1851), French painter and physicist best known for his invention of the daguerreotype. In his Diorama, which opened in Paris in 1822 and later in London, he used translucent curtains and wings and he played with perspective as well as with lights.

Aronnax's simile—*altered the whole landscape like a diorama*—is therefore perfectly appropriate. He is talking of labyrinthine ice masses, some translucent, some mirrorlike, which refract and reflect daylight with great variety as the viewers on the *Nautilus* move by.

5. *not the iceberg itself, as yet* It was not yet the *ice shelf* or *ice cap*.

6. *five degrees below zero* Substituting this Centigrade reading for C in our formula for conversion—F =

1.8(−5) + 32—we find that the equivalent Fahrenheit reading is 23°.

7. *dropped to 73.5 centimeters* In the English system, this would be a barometer reading of 28.5. A standard seaman's guide of the nineteenth century gives that as the lowest reading: "28.5—Tempest."

But Maury makes it clear, in his *The Physical Geography of the Sea* (1855), that "a low barometer" was common in antarctic seas.

8. *"An iceberg!"* According to Verne, Ned said *"An icebank!"* And as we shall see when Nemo takes his bearings—*"as near as possible"*—they are probably facing what will later be known as the Filchner Ice Shelf.

which is not to be confused with the south pole itself. According to Hansten, the magnetic pole is located at approximately 70° latitude and 130° longitude, while Duperré locates it at 70° 30′ and 135°. We consequently took numerous compass readings in different parts of the ship and figured the average. Sometimes we could only use the roughest estimates in taking our bearings. This was not a satisfactory procedure, considering our zig-zag path through the ice-fields.]

At length, on the 18th of March, after many useless assaults, the *Nautilus* was positively blocked. It was no longer either streams, packs, or ice-fields, but an interminable and immovable barrier, formed by mountains soldered together.

"An iceberg!" said the Canadian **8** to me.

I knew that to Ned Land, as well as to all other navigators who had preceded us, this was an inevitable obstacle. The sun appearing for an instant at noon, Captain Nemo took an observation as near as possible, which gave our situation at 51° 30′ longitude and 67° 39′ of south latitude. We had advanced one degree more in this antarctic region. Of the liquid surface of the sea there was no longer a glimpse. Under the spur of the *Nautilus* lay stretched a vast plain, entangled with confused blocks. Here and there sharp points, and slender needles rising to a height of 200 feet; further on a steep shore, hewn as it were with an axe, and clothed with greyish tints; huge mirrors reflecting a few rays of sunshine, half drowned in the fog. And over this desolate face of Nature a stern silence reigned, scarcely broken by the flapping of wings of petrels and puffins. Everything was frozen—even the noise. The *Nautilus* was then obliged to stop in its adventurous course amid these fields of ice.

["Monsieur," Ned said, "if your Captain can get through this—"

"Yes?"

"Then he is truly superhuman!"

"Why, Ned?"

"Because nobody can break through this ice barrier. Maybe your Captain *is* superhuman, but by the Devil, he is not stronger than Nature herself. Where Nature puts up barriers, you had better stop."

"Maybe so, Ned. Still, I for one would like to see what is beyond that barrier. There is nothing more frustrating than a wall."

"Monsieur is right," Conseil said. "Walls were invented to frustrate scientists. There just should be no walls anywhere."

"Well," the Canadian said, "anyone can tell what is beyond that wall of ice."

"What?" I demanded.

"Ice! And beyond that, more ice!"

"You seem to be sure of your facts, Ned, but I am not. So I want to *see* what is there."

"You will have to renounce that ambition, Professor. You have arrived at the ice barrier, which in itself is something, but you will get no further. Nor will your Captain Nemo, nor his *Nautilus*. Willy-nilly, he is going to have to retrace his steps to the north—that is to say, to the land of sensible people!"

For the time being, I had to agree with Ned that until ships are built to travel over the ice, they are doomed to halt at the great ice barrier.] In spite of our efforts, in spite of the powerful means employed to break up the ice, the *Nautilus* remained immovable. Generally, when we can proceed no further, we have return still open to us; but here return was as impossible as advance, for every pass had closed behind us; and for the few moments when we were stationary, we were likely to be entirely blocked, which did, indeed, happen about two o'clock in the afternoon, the fresh ice forming around its sides with astonishing rapidity. I was obliged to admit that Captain Nemo was more than imprudent. I was on the platform at that moment. The Captain had been observing our situation for some time past, when he said to me—

"Well, sir, what do you think of this?"

"I think that we are caught, Captain."

["Caught! Whatever can you mean by that?"

"I mean we cannot go ahead, we cannot go back, we cannot go sideways, we are not free. That is the usual meaning of *caught,* at least in the populated areas of the world."]

"So, M. Aronnax, you really think that the *Nautilus* cannot disengage itself?"

"With difficulty, Captain; for the season is already too far advanced for you to reckon on the breaking up of the ice."

"Ah! sir," said Captain Nemo, in an ironical tone, "you will always be the same. You see nothing but difficulties and obstacles. I affirm that not only can the *Nautilus* disengage itself, but also that it can go further still."

"Further to the south?" I asked, looking at the Captain.

"Yes, sir; it shall go to the pole."

"To the pole!" I exclaimed, unable to repress a gesture of incredulity.

"Yes," replied the Captain, coldly, "to the antarctic pole,—

"An iceberg!" said the Canadian to me. I knew that to Ned Land, as well as to all . . . navigators who had preceded us, this was an inevitable obstacle. Engraving from the original edition (1870).

9. *but under it* Nemo is here antici-pating the precise way in which the U.S. nuclear submarines *Nautilus* and *Skate* will negotiate the Northwest Passage in 1958.

10. *four to one to that which is below* The professor has suddenly remem-bered that even if the surface is solid ice, the lower strata are *"free,"* that is, still fluid. The *"providential"* condi-tion he speaks of is an exceptional property of water that it shares with few other substances. As most sub-stances cool, they contract and their specific gravity increases. And so, too, with water, except that as it begins to freeze, it reverses this reaction: it be-gins to expand again.

This is what Aronnax means when he says that this *"law"* has *"placed the maximum of density of the waters of the ocean one degree higher than freezing point."* In the case of sea water, freezing point is $-2°C$, and it reaches its greatest specific gravity just before it hits that temperature. The heaviest water is that which is just about to freeze. And the heaviest water of course sinks to the lower strata, which remain fluid. Ice floats on the surface because, having ex-panded, it is now lighter than the fluid water underneath.

Since Aronnax and Nemo know the *"four to one"* ratio, they can estimate from the height of the ice above the surface just how far down the solid ice goes and where the *"free"* water begins.

to that unknown point from whence springs every meridian of the globe. *You* know whether I can do as I please with the *Nautilus!"*

Yes, I knew that. I knew that this man was bold, even to rashness. But to conquer those obstacles which bristled round the south pole, rendering it more inaccessible than the north, which had not yet been reached by the boldest navigators,— was it not a mad enterprise, one which only a maniac would have conceived? It then came into my head to ask Captain Nemo if he had ever discovered that pole which had never yet been trodden by a human creature.

"No, sir," he replied; "but we will discover it together. Where others have failed, *I* will not fail. I have never yet led my *Nautilus* so far into southern seas; but, I repeat, it shall go further yet."

"I can well believe you, Captain," said I, in a slightly iron-ical tone. "I believe you! Let us go ahead! There are no ob-stacles for us! Let us smash this iceberg! Let us blow it up; and if it resists, let us give the *Nautilus* wings to fly over it!"

"Over it, sir!" said Captain Nemo, quietly; "no, not *over* it, but *under* it!" **9**

"Under it!" I exclaimed, a sudden idea of the Captain's projects flashing upon my mind. I understood; the wonderful qualities of the *Nautilus* were going to serve us in this super-human enterprise.

"I see we are beginning to understand one another, sir," said the Captain, half smiling. "You begin to see the possi-bility—I should say the success—of this attempt. That which is impossible for an ordinary vessel, is easy to the *Nautilus*. If a continent lies before the pole, it must stop before the continent; but if, on the contrary, the pole is washed by open sea, it will go even to the pole."

"Certainly," said I, carried away by the Captain's reason-ing; "if the surface of the sea is solidified by the ice, the lower depths are free by the providential law which has placed the maximum of density of the waters of the ocean one de-gree higher than freezing point; and, if I am not mistaken, the portion of this iceberg which is above the water, is as four to one to that which is below." **10**

"Very nearly, sir; for one foot of iceberg above the sea there are three below it. If these ice mountains are not more than 300 feet above the surface, they are not more than 900 beneath. And what are 900 feet to the *Nautilus"*

"Nothing, sir."

"It could even seek at greater depths that uniform temperature of sea-water, and there brave with impunity the thirty or forty degrees of surface cold."

"Just so, sir—just so," I replied, getting animated.

"The only difficulty," continued Captain Nemo, "is that of remaining several days without renewing our provision of air."

"Is that all? The *Nautilus* has vast reservoirs; we can fill them, and they will supply us with all the oxygen we want."

"Well thought of, M. Aronnax," replied the Captain, smiling. "But not wishing you to accuse me of rashness, I will first give you all my objections."

"Have you any more to make?"

"Only one. It is possible, if the sea exists at the south pole, that it may be covered; and, consequently, we shall be unable to come to the surface."

"Good, sir! But do you forget that the *Nautilus* is armed with a powerful spur, and could we not send it diagonally against these fields of ice, which would open at the shock?"

"Ah! sir, you are full of ideas to-day."

"Besides, Captain," I added, enthusiastically, "why should we not find the sea open at the south pole as well as at the north? The frozen poles and the poles of the earth do not coincide, either in the southern or in the northern regions; and, until it is proved to the contrary, we may suppose either a continent or an ocean free from ice at these two points of the globe."

"I think so, too, M. Aronnax," replied Captain Nemo. "I only wish you to observe that, after having made so many objections to my project, you are now crushing me with arguments in its favour!"

[The Captain was right. I was now the one with greater audacity! Now it was *I* who was urging *him* to see that it was possible to go to the pole! I was pacing him. How could I have been so presumptuous! He had known all the answers in advance. He had been amusing himself, seeing me carried away by my plans for the impossible!

Meanwhile, he was losing no time. He was talking with his second in that incomprehensible language. Had the other man been briefed beforehand? Did he find the plan practicable? I could not know, except to see that he showed not the least surprise.

But Conseil outdid the second in his impassiveness. When I told him that our plans were to press on to the pole, he just uttered his usual:

"Whatever pleases monsieur."

But Ned lifted his shoulders more emphatically than ever.

"I pity you and your Captain," Ned said.

"But we *will* make it, Ned."

"Maybe you will *get* there. But you will never come back."
And to prevent himself from "doing something desperate," as
he put it, he went at once to his cabin.]

The preparations for this audacious attempt now began.
The powerful pumps of the *Nautilus* were working air into
the reservoirs and storing it at high pressure. About four
o'clock Captain Nemo announced the closing of the panels on
the platform. I threw one last look at the massive iceberg
which we were going to cross. The weather was clear, the atmosphere pure enough, the cold very great, being twelve degrees below zero; **11** but the wind having gone down, this
temperature was not so unbearable. About ten men mounted
the sides of the *Nautilus,* armed with pickaxes to break the
ice around the vessel, which was soon free. The operation was
quickly performed, for the fresh ice was still very thin. We
all went below. The usual reservoirs were filled with the newly
liberated water, and the *Nautilus* soon descended. I had taken
my place with Conseil in the saloon; through the open window
we could see the lower beds of the Southern Ocean. The
thermometer went up, the needle of the compass deviated on
the dial.**12** At about 900 feet, as Captain Nemo had fore-
seen, we were floating beneath the undulating bottom of the
iceberg. But the *Nautilus* went lower still—it went to the
depth of four hundred fathoms. The temperature of the water
at the surface showed twelve degrees, it was now only eleven;
we had gained two.**13** I need not say the temperature of the
Nautilus was raised by its heating apparatus to a much higher
degree; every manoeuvre was accomplished with wonderful
precision.

"We shall pass it, if you please, sir," said Conseil.

"I believe we shall," I said, in a tone of firm conviction.

In this open sea, the *Nautilus* had taken its course direct
to the pole, without leaving the fifty-second meridian. From
67° 30′ to 90°, twenty-two degrees and a half of latitude remained to travel; that is, about five hundred leagues.**14** The
Nautilus kept a mean speed of twenty-six miles an hour—the
speed of an express train. If that was kept up, in forty hours
we should reach the pole.

For a part of the night the novelty of the situation kept us
at the window. The sea was lit with the electric lantern; but
it was deserted; fishes did not sojourn in these imprisoned
waters: they only found there a passage to take them from the
antarctic ocean to the open polar sea. Our pace was rapid;

11. *twelve degrees below zero* Or,
10.4°F.

12. *needle of the compass deviated on
the dial* No, it was the needle of the
manometer that moved, showing that
they are descending.

13. *we had gained two* They are
"gaining" because the temperature has
risen from −12° to −11°.

14. *five hundred leagues* About
1080 miles.

we could feel it by the quivering of the long steel body. About two in the morning, I took some hours' repose, and Conseil did the same. In crossing the waist I did not meet Captain Nemo: I supposed him to be in the pilot's cage. The next morning, the 19th of March, I took my post once more in the saloon. The electric log told me that the speed of the *Nautilus* had been slackened. It was then going towards the surface; but prudently emptying its reservoirs very slowly. My heart beat fast. Were we going to emerge and regain the open polar atmosphere? No! A shock told me that the *Nautilus* had struck the bottom of the iceberg, still very thick, judging from the deadened sound. We had indeed "struck," to use a sea expression, but in an inverse sense, and at a thousand feet deep. This would give three thousand feet of ice above us; **15** one thousand being above the water-mark. The iceberg was then higher than at its borders—not a very reassuring fact. Several times that day the *Nautilus* tried again, and every time it struck the wall which lay like a ceiling above it. Sometimes it met with but 900 yards, [which meant 1200 yards of ice above us,] only 200 of which rose above the surface.**16** It was twice the height it was when the *Nautilus* had gone under the waves. I carefully noted the different depths, and thus obtained a submarine profile of the chain as it was developed under water. That night no change had taken place in our situation. Still ice between four and five hundred yards in depth! It was evidently diminishing, but still what a thickness between us and the surface of the ocean! It was then eight. According to the daily custom on board the *Nautilus,* its air should have been renewed four hours ago; but I did not suffer much, although Captain Nemo had not yet made any demand upon his reserve of oxygen. My sleep was painful that night; hope and fear besieged me by turns: I rose several times. The groping of the *Nautilus* continued. About three in the morning, I noticed that the lower surface of the iceberg was only about fifty feet deep.**17** One hundred and fifty feet now separated us from the surface of the waters. The iceberg was by degrees becoming an ice-field, the mountain a plain. My eyes never left the manometer. We were still rising diagonally to the surface, which sparkled under the electric rays. The iceberg was stretching both above and beneath into lengthening slopes; mile after mile it was getting thinner. At length, at six in the morning of that memorable day, the 19th of March, the door of the saloon opened, and Captain Nemo appeared.

"The sea is open!" was all he said.

15. *three thousand feet of ice above us* In the nineteenth-century French editions, Aronnax says they *"struck"* at a depth of *three thousand feet* (*trois mille pieds*), which meant they had *four thousand feet of ice* (*quatre mille pieds de glace*) above them. Here, as you can see from the French *pieds,* Verne himself used the English *feet.*

Most of the several French editions now in print follow the original faithfully. But there is one paperback edition that, oddly enough, gives only *one thousand feet* (*mille pied*s) of depth, with *two thousand feet* (*deux mille pieds*) of total thickness of the ice. So even if Mercier Lewis was working from an early version of *that* paperback, he was unfaithful to that one, too!

The fact that errors can occur even in the French reminds us how Verne's reliance on mathematics for much of his drama put great strain on his printers. Still, the error noted here in only *one* of several current French editions, plus the error in dating in Chapters II and IV of Part 1 in *all* editions, are the only egregious mistakes we can charge the French with in their production of this novel.

16. *only 200 of which arose above the surface* In the original, and in all current French editions, Aronnax says that *300 meters* rose above the surface. In this sentence Verne gave all three measurements in meters (900, 1200, 300). His ease in moving from feet to meters, *whichever would give him a round figure more readily,* prefigures the growth of that habit among today's scientists.

17. *only about fifty feet deep* No, here Aronnax says *fifty meters deep.* And then he himself uses the rough ratio in conversion, adding: *One hundred and fifty feet separated us from the surface.*

PART 2: CHAPTER XIV

The South Pole[1]

1. *The South Pole* When *Twenty Thousand Leagues* appears in 1870, both the North and South poles are still undiscovered—in real life. But Verne's hero in *The Adventures of Captain Hatteras* (1864) has gotten within yards of the North Pole, and the novel has helped keep alive the public's interest in polar exploration. Now Nemo's exploits will strengthen that interest during the four decades until Robert Peary reaches the North Pole in 1909 and Roald Amundsen the South Pole in 1911.

2. *three degrees centigrade above zero* Or 37.4°F—*comparatively spring*!

3. *A narrow canal* A *channel*, of course.

4. *circumference . . . at least, 2500 miles* Most of Maury's ideas that excite Aronnax here will prove to be true. Antarctica is a continent of more than 5,000,000 square miles and it is contained largely within the Antarctic Circle. It produces 90 percent of the earth's ice! Its ice shelves—ranging up to 10,000 feet in thickness—"calve" the giant icebergs that Nemo had been dodging in three dimensions.

I rushed on to the platform. Yes! the open sea, with but a few scattered pieces of ice and moving icebergs;—a long stretch of sea; a world of birds in the air, and myriads of fishes under those waters, which varied from intense blue to olive green, according to the bottom. The thermometer marked three degrees centigrade above zero.[2] It was comparatively spring, shut up as we were behind this iceberg, whose lengthened mass was dimly seen on our northern horizon.

"Are we at the pole?" I asked the Captain, with a beating heart.

"I do not know," he replied. "At noon I will take our bearings."

"But will the sun show himself through this fog?" said I, looking at the leaden sky.

"However little it shows, it will be enough," replied the Captain.

About ten miles south, a solitary island rose to a height of one hundred and four yards. We made for it, but carefully, for the sea might be strewn with banks. One hour afterwards we had reached it, two hours later we had made the round of it. It measured four or five miles in circumference. A narrow canal [3] separated it from a considerable stretch of land, perhaps a continent, for we could not see its limits. The existence of this land seemed to give some colour to Maury's hypothesis. The ingenious American has remarked, that between the south pole and the sixtieth parallel, the sea is covered with floating ice of enormous size, which is never met with in the North Atlantic. From this fact he has drawn the conclusion that the antarctic circle encloses considerable continents, as icebergs cannot form in open sea, but only on the coasts. According to these calculations, the mass of ice surrounding the southern pole forms a vast cap, the circumference of which must be, at least, 2500 miles.[4] But the *Nautilus,* for

fear of running aground, had stopped about three cables'
length from a strand over which reared a superb heap of
rocks. The boat was launched; the Captain, two of his men
bearing instruments, Conseil, and myself, were in it. It was
ten in the morning. I had not seen Ned Land. Doubtless the
Canadian did not wish to admit the presence of the south
pole. A few strokes of the oar brought us to the sand, where
we ran ashore. Conseil was going to jump on to the land,
when I held him back.

"Sir," said I to Captain Nemo, "to you belongs the honour
of first setting foot on this land."

"Yes, sir," said the Captain; "and if I do not hesitate to
tread this south pole, it is because, up to this time, no human
being has left a trace there."

Saying this he jumped lightly on to the sand. His heart
beat with emotion. He climbed a rock, sloping to a little
promontory, and there, with his arms crossed, mute and motionless, and with an eager look, he seemed to take possession
of these southern regions. After five minutes passed in this
ecstasy he turned to us.

"When you like, sir."

I landed, followed by Conseil, leaving the two men in the
boat. For a long way the soil was composed of a reddish,
sandy stone, something like crushed brick, scoriae, streams of
lava, and pumice stones. One could not mistake its volcanic
origin. In some parts, slight curls of smoke emitted a sulphurous smell, proving that the internal fires had lost nothing of
their expansive powers, though, having climbed a high ac-
clivity, I could see no volcano for a radius of several miles.
We know that in those antarctic countries, James Ross found
two craters, the Erebus and Terror, in full activity, on the
167th meridian, latitude 77° 32'.5 The vegetation of this
desolate continent seemed to me much restricted. Some lichens
of the species usnea melanoxantha lay upon the black rocks;
some microscopic plants, rudimentary diatomas, a kind of
cells, placed between two quartz shells; long purple and
scarlet fucus, supported on little swimming bladders, which
the breaking of the waves brought to the shore. These constituted the meagre flora of this region. The shore was strewn
with molluscs, little mussels, limpets, smooth bucards in the
shape of a heart,6 and particularly some clios, with oblong
membraneous bodies, the head of which was formed of two
rounded lobes. I also saw myriads of northern clios, one and a
quarter inches long, of which a whale would swallow a whole
world at a mouthful; 7 and some charming pteropods, perfect
sea-butterflies, animating the waters on the skirts of the shore.

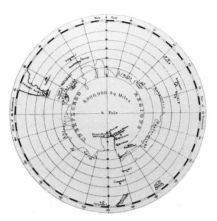

[Maury] has drawn the conclusion that the antarctic circle encloses considerable continents. . . . Of course, Aronnax has studied Maury's map of the South Pole area in his Physical Geography of the Sea (1855).

5. *latitude 77° 32'* James Clark Ross named these two volcanoes after his own ship, the *Erebus* (370 tons), and the *Terror* (340 tons), commanded by his second, F. R. M. Crozier. They discovered these volcanoes on Ross Island on January 28, 1841. Erebus is believed to be the only volcano still active in Antarctica today.

6. *bucards in the shape of a heart* Cockles.

7. *clios . . . mouthful* Today this whale food is called *krill*.

8. *little kingfishers* "Kingfishers" is a nickname given to *alcyons,* soft corals, because they resemble the nests made by those birds.

. . . Heavy and awkward . . . on the ground. . . . King penguin as pictured in *The American Cyclopaedia* (1873).

9. *ruffs' nests* Penguins' nests.

Amongst other zoophytes, there appeared on the high bottoms some coral shrubs, of that kind which, according to James Ross, live in the antarctic seas to the depth of more than 1000 yards. Then there were little kingfishers,[8] belonging to the species porcellaria pelagica, as well as a large number of asteriads, peculiar to these climates, and starfish studding the soil. But where life abounded most was in the air. There, thousands of birds fluttered and flew of all kinds, deafening us with their cries; others crowded the rocks, looking at us as we passed by without fear, and pressing familiarly close by our feet. There were penguins, so agile in the water, that they have been taken for the rapid bonitos, heavy and awkward as they are on the ground; they were uttering harsh cries, a large assembly, sober in gesture, but extravagant in clamour. Amongst the birds I noticed the chionis, of the long-legged family, as large as pigeons, white, with a short conical beak, and the eye framed in a red circle. Conseil laid in a stock of them, for these winged creatures, properly prepared, make an agreeable meat. Albatrosses passed in the air (the expanse of their wings being at least four yards and a half), and justly called the vultures of the ocean; some gigantic petrels, and some damiers, a kind of small duck, the under part of whose body is black and white; then there were a whole series of petrels, some whitish, with brown-bordered wings, others blue, peculiar to the antarctic seas, and so oily, as I told Conseil, that the inhabitants of the Ferroe Islands had nothing to do before lighting them, but to put a wick in.

"A little more," said Conseil, "and they would be perfect lamps! After that, we cannot expect Nature to have previously furnished them with wicks!"

About half a mile further on, the soil was riddled with ruffs' nests,[9] a sort of laying ground, out of which many birds were issuing. Captain Nemo had some hundreds hunted. They uttered a cry like the braying of an ass, were about the size of a goose, slate colour on the body, white beneath, with a yellow line round their throats; they allowed themselves to be killed with a stone, never trying to escape. But the fog did not lift, and at eleven the sun had not yet shown itself. Its absence made me uneasy. Without it no observations were possible. How, then, could we decide whether we had reached the pole? When I rejoined Captain Nemo, I found him leaning on a piece of rock, silently watching the sky. He seemed impatient and vexed. But what was to be done? This rash and powerful man could not command the sun as he did the sea. Noon arrived without the orb of day showing itself for an instant. We could not even tell its position behind the curtain of fog; and soon the fog turned to snow.

"Till to-morrow," said the Captain, quietly, and we returned to the *Nautilus* amid these atmospheric disturbances.

[There we found that the crew had cast out the nets, and I was interested in seeing what fishes they were hauling in. Antarctic waters constitute a refuge area for large numbers of migrants who flee the storms of other regions, only to be eaten by porpoises and seals. I noticed some southern sea-scorpions about four inches in length; a species of cartilaginous fish, white with livid stripes, covered with prickles; and Antarctic chimaerae, with a thin body a yard long, smooth silver-white skin, round head, three dorsal fins, and a hornlike snout that curves downward. I found chimaera flesh rather tasteless but Conseil liked it.]

The tempest of snow continued till the next day. It was impossible to remain on the platform. From the saloon, where I was taking notes of incidents happening during this excursion to the polar continent, I could hear the cries of petrels and albatrosses sporting in the midst of this violent storm. The *Nautilus* did not remain motionless, but skirted the coast, advancing ten miles more to the south in the half light left by the sun as it skirted the edge of the horizon. The next day, the 20th of March, the snow had ceased. The cold was a little greater, the thermometer showing two degrees below zero. The fog was rising, and I hoped that that day our observations might be taken. Captain Nemo not having yet appeared, the boat took Conseil and myself to land. The soil was still of the same volcanic nature; everywhere were traces of lava, scoriae, and basalt; but the crater which had vomited them I could not see. Here, as lower down, this continent was alive with myriads of birds. But their rule was now divided with large troops of sea-mammals, looking at us with their soft eyes. There were several kinds of seals, some stretched on the earth, some on flakes of ice, many going in and out of the sea. They did not flee at our approach, never having had anything to do with man; and I reckoned that there were provisions there for hundreds of vessels.

["It turns out to be a blessing that Ned did not come along," said Conseil.

"Why do you say that?"

"He would have killed every one of these creatures."

"Well, maybe not *every* one, but I agree, his harpoon would have been bloody. That would have upset Captain Nemo. He disapproves of unnecessary slaughter of harmless animals."

"He is right, monsieur."

"Yes, Conseil, but I am surprised. Are you not going to classify these superb specimens of marine fauna?"

"Monsieur knows I am not yet very knowledgeable in this field.] Sir," said Conseil, "will you tell me the names of these creatures?"

10. *seals and morses* *Morse* is the name first given to the *walrus*.

"They are seals and morses." **10**

["Two genera that belong to the family of pinnipeds," Conseil hastened to prove himself. "Order of carnivores, group of unguiculates, subclass of monodelphians, class of mammals, branch of the vertebrates."

"Excellent, Conseil. But the two genera of seals and walruses are divided into species, and if I am not wrong, we will now have a chance to see them. Shall we proceed?"]

It was now eight in the morning. Four hours remained to us before the sun could be observed with advantage. I directed our steps towards a vast bay cut in the steep granite shore. There, I can aver that earth and ice were lost to sight by the numbers of sea-mammals covering them, and I involuntarily sought for old Proteus, the mythological shepherd who watched these immense flocks of Neptune. There were more seals than anything else, forming distinct groups, male and female, the father watching over his family, the mother suckling her little ones, some already strong enough to go a few steps. When they wished to change their place, they took little jumps, made by the contraction of their bodies, and helped awkwardly enough by their imperfect fin, which, as with the lamantin, their congener, forms a perfect forearm. I should say that, in the water, which is their element—the spine of these creatures is flexible—with smooth and close skin, and webbed feet, they swim admirably. In resting on the earth they take the most graceful attitudes. Thus the ancients, observing their soft and expressive looks, which cannot be surpassed by the most beautiful look a woman can give, their clear voluptuous eyes, their charming positions, and the poetry of their manners, metamorphosed them, the male into a triton and the female into a mermaid. I made Conseil notice the considerable development of the lobes of the brain in these interesting cetaceans. No mammal, except

11. *such a quantity of cerebral matter* Aronnax is able to say this apparently because he has not yet been able to study the cerebral matter of the whale and the dolphin.

man, has such a quantity of cerebral matter; **11** they are also capable of receiving a certain amount of education, are easily domesticated, and I think, with other naturalists, that, if properly taught, they would be of great service as fishing-dogs. The greater part of them slept on the rocks or on the sand. Amongst these seals, properly so called, which have no external ears (in which they differ from the otter, whose ears are prominent), I noticed several varieties of stenorhynchi about three yards long, with a white coat, bulldog heads, armed with teeth in both jaws, four incisors at the top and four at the bottom, and two large canine teeth in the shape of a "fleur-de-lis." Amongst them glided sea-elephants, a kind of seal, with short flexible trunks. The giants of this species measured twenty feet round, and ten yards and a half in length; but they did not move as we approached.

"These creatures are not dangerous?" asked Conseil.

"No; not unless you attack them. When they have to defend their young, their rage is terrible, and it is not uncommon for them to break the fishing-boats to pieces."

"They are quite right," said Conseil.

"I do not say they are not."

Two miles further on we were stopped by the promontory which shelters the bay from the southerly winds. Beyond it we heard loud bellowings such as a troop of ruminants would produce.

"Good!" said Conseil; "a concert of bulls!"

"No; a concert of morses."

"They are fighting!"

"They are either fighting or playing."

["If it so pleases monsieur, I would like to see them."

"Of course."]

We now began to climb the blackish rocks, amid unforeseen stumbles, and over stones which the ice made slippery. More than once I rolled over at the expense of my loins.12 Conseil, more prudent or more steady, did not stumble, and helped me up, saying—

"If, sir, you would have the kindness to take wider steps, you would preserve your equilibrium better." 13

Arrived at the upper ridge of the promontory, I saw a vast white plain covered with morses. They were playing amongst themselves, and what we heard were bellowings of pleasure, not of anger.

[Walruses resemble seals in their bodies and limbs. But walruses have no lower canine teeth or incisors, and their upper canines are two tusks, sometimes thirty inches long and twelve in circumference at the base. These teeth are made of a very solid smooth ivory, which is harder even than elephant ivory and does not discolour easily. Needless to say, walrus ivory is in high demand, and so hunters slaughter them indiscriminately—babies and even pregnant females— at the rate of four thousand a year!]

As I passed near these curious animals, I could examine them leisurely, for they did not move. Their skins were thick and rugged, of a yellowish tint, approaching to red; their

12. *at the expense of my loins* A better translation would be: *hurting my back.*

13. *preserve your equilibrium better* Verne is still leading up to the climax of his third-person joke, and so here Conseil really says: *"If monsieur would just keep his feet farther apart, then monsieur could more easily keep his balance."*

hair was short and scant. Some of them were four yards and a quarter long. Quieter, and less timid than their congeners of the north, they did not, like them, place sentinels round the outskirts of their encampment. After examining this city of morses, I began to think of returning. It was eleven o'clock, and if Captain Nemo found the conditions favourable for observations, I wished to be present at the operation.14 [But I did not see much hope that the sun would shine. There were heavy clouds on the horizon. It seemed almost as if the sun were jealous, unwilling to let man discover the secrets of this part of the globe. Still, I turned back.]

We followed a narrow pathway running along the summit of the steep shore. At half-past eleven we had reached the place where we landed. The boat had run aground, bringing the Captain. I saw him standing on a block of basalt, his instruments near him, his eyes fixed on the northern horizon, near which the sun was then describing a lengthened curve.15 I took my place beside him, and waited without speaking. Noon arrived, and, as before, the sun did not appear. It was a fatality. Observations were still wanting. If not accomplished to-morrow, we must give up all idea of taking any. We were indeed exactly at the 20th of March. To-morrow, the 21st, would be the equinox; the sun would disappear behind the horizon for six months, and with its disappearance the long polar night would begin. Since the September equinox it had emerged from the northern horizon, rising by lengthened spirals up to the 21st of December. At this period, the summer solstice of the northern regions, it had begun to descend; and to-morrow was to shed its last rays upon them. I communicated my fears and observations to Captain Nemo.

"You are right, M. Aronnax," said he; "if to-morrow I cannot take the altitude of the sun, I shall not be able to do it for six months. But precisely because chance has led me into these seas on the 21st of March, my bearings will be easy to take, if at twelve we can see the sun."

"Why, Captain?"

"Because then the orb of day describes such lengthened curves, that it is difficult to measure exactly its height above the horizon, and grave errors may be made with instruments." 16

"What will you do then?"

"I shall only use my chronometer," replied Captain Nemo. "If to-morrow, the 21st of March, the disc of the sun, allowing for refraction, is exactly cut by the northern horizon, it will show that I am at the south pole."

"Just so," said I. "But this statement is not mathematically correct, because the equinox does not necessarily begin at noon."

14. *at the operation* Nemo must "shoot the sun" at noon probably because he is working from astronomical tables based on the position of the sun at that time of day. Probably these tables also time the March 21 equinox as occurring at noon.

15. *describing a lengthened curve* Aronnax only *knows* the sun is moving along the horizon in a long arc; because of the clouds, he cannot *see* it.

16. *made with instruments* The sun is traveling in a long arc close to the horizon and settling at the same time. By tomorrow, March 21, it will have settled so much further it will be below the horizon. Dr. David Woodruff of New York University has verified Verne's calculations in this passage. He reminds us that of course Nemo is working from standard astronomical tables.

"Very likely, sir; but the error will not be a hundred yards, and we do not want more. Till to-morrow then!"

Captain Nemo returned on board. Conseil and I remained to survey the shore, observing and studying until five o'clock. [I found no unusual objects except a large penguin egg. A collector would have offered a thousand francs for it. It was cream-coloured with markings like hieroglyphs. A rare find. I entrusted it to Conseil. That patient, sure-footed boy held it as though it were a piece of precious China and he delivered it intact to the *Nautilus*. There I put it into one of the show-cases. For supper, I had seal's liver, which tasted somewhat like pork.]

Then I went to bed, not, however, without invoking, like the Indian, the favour of the radiant orb. The next day, the 21st of March, at five in the morning, I mounted the platform. I found Captain Nemo there.

"The weather is lightening a little," said he. "I have some hope. After breakfast we will go on shore, and choose a post for observation."

That point settled, I sought Ned Land. I wanted to take him with me. But the obstinate Canadian refused, and I saw that his taciturnity and his bad humour grew day by day. After all I was not sorry for his obstinacy under the circumstances. Indeed, there were too many seals on shore, and we ought not to lay such temptations in this unreflecting fisherman's way. Breakfast over, we went on shore. The *Nautilus* had gone some miles further up in the night. It was a whole league from the coast, above which reared a sharp peak about five hundred yards high. The boat took with me Captain Nemo, two men of the crew, and the instruments, which consisted of a chronometer, a telescope, and a barometer. While crossing, I saw numerous whales belonging to the three kinds peculiar to the southern seas; the [true] whale, or the English "right whale," which has no dorsal fin; the "humpback," or balaenopteron, with reeved chest, and large whitish fins which, in spite of its name, do not form wings; and the finback, of a yellowish brown, the liveliest of all the cetacea. This powerful creature is heard a long way off when he throws to a great height columns of air and vapour, which look like whirlwinds of smoke. These different mammals were disporting themselves in troops in the quiet waters; and I could see that this basin of the antarctic pole served as a place of refuge to the cetacea too closely tracked by the hunters. I also noticed long whitish lines of salpae, a kind of gregarious mollusc, and large medusae floating between the reeds.

At nine we landed; the sky was brightening, the clouds

"Adieu, sun! . . . let a night of six months spread its shadows over my new domains!"
Engraving from the original edition (1870).

17. *seen only by reflection* No, only by *refraction*.

18. *At that moment Captain Nemo . . . said* At this moment, Lewis decides to omit 400 words of Verne. As the reader can see from our restoration, this gratuitous omission destroys two of Verne's intended effects:

(1) *Characterization.* Verne here characterizes Nemo as a man who knows by heart the history of polar exploration, can recount it with leisurely comments, and sees it all as one long build-up to his own inevitable triumph. Nemo's feat of memory is entirely credible, since by now he has been thoroughly characterized as a man who immerses himself in the literature of every enterprise he engages in. He sees maps and his own experience in terms of each other. Notice, too, that in a passage like this Verne is directly catering to his kind of audience. He knew well that his typical fan will check everything on the map or redo the arithmetic on the tablecloth.

(2) *Adult education.* Behind Nemo there is Verne the adult educator, the popularizer of science, giving his audience a capsule version of an important, persistent endeavor of the modern spirit.

19. *Cook . . . attained 71° 15'* James Cook was under orders to search for "the southern continent." Alexander Dalrymple, a noted geographer, had published a fanciful hypothesis about a South Land with fifty million inhabitants, all presumably waiting to be colonized. On January 17, 1773, Cook wrote jubilantly: ". . . we crossed the Antarctic Circle, and are undoubtedly the first and only ship that ever crossed that line." He crossed it twice more without finding any evidence to support Dalrymple's conjectures. He reported grumpily that if ever a South Land were to be discovered in those terrible regions, "the world will derive no benefit from it."

20. *Bellingshausen . . . 111° west longitude* Fabian von Bellingshausen sighted the first land ever seen inside

were flying to the south, and the fog seemed to be leaving the cold surface of the waters. Captain Nemo went towards the peak, which he doubtless meant to be his observatory. It was a painful ascent over the sharp lava and the pumice stones, in an atmosphere often impregnated with a sulphurous smell from the smoking cracks. For a man unaccustomed to walk on land, the Captain climbed the steep slopes with an agility I never saw equalled, and which a hunter would have envied. We were two hours getting to the summit of this peak, which was half porphyry and half basalt. From thence we looked upon a vast sea, which, towards the north, distinctly traced its boundary line upon the sky. At our feet lay fields of dazzling whiteness. Over our heads a pale azure, free from fog. To the north the disc of the sun seemed like a ball of fire, already horned by the cutting of the horizon. From the bosom of the water rose sheaves of liquid jets by hundreds. In the distance lay the *Nautilus* like a cetacean asleep on the water.

Behind us, to the south and east, an immense country, and a chaotic heap of rocks and ice, the limits of which were not visible. On arriving at the summit, Captain Nemo carefully took the mean height of the barometer, for he would have to consider that in taking his observations. At a quarter to twelve, the sun, then seen only by reflection,[17] looked like a golden disc shedding its last rays upon this deserted continent, and seas which never man had yet ploughed. Captain Nemo, furnished with a lenticular glass, which, by means of a mirror, corrected the refraction, watched the orb sinking below the horizon by degrees, following a lengthened diagonal. I held the chronometer. My heart beat fast. If the disappearance of the half-disc of the sun coincided with twelve o'clock on the chronometer, we were at the pole itself.

"Twelve!" I exclaimed.

"The South Pole!" replied Captain Nemo, in a grave voice, handing me the glass, which showed the orb cut in exactly equal parts by the horizon.

I looked at the last rays crowning the peak, and the shadows mounting by degrees up its slopes. At that moment Captain Nemo, resting with his hand on my shoulder, said— **18**

["Monsieur, in 1600, the Hollander Gheritk, driven by currents and tempests, reached 64° south latitude and discovered New Shetland.

"In 1773, the illustrious Cook, following the 38th meridian, reached 67° 30' south latitude; the following year, on the 109th meridian, he attained 71° 15'.**19**

"In 1819, the Russian Bellingshausen reached the 69th parallel and in 1821 got so far as the 76th at 111 ° west longitude.**20**

"In 1820, the Englishman Bransfield could not get past the 65th parallel. That same year, the American Morrel, whose records are questionable, reports that he went along the 42d meridian and found open sea at 70° 14′ latitude.

"In 1825, the Englishman Powell was stopped at the 62d parallel. That year also, a simple seal fisherman, an Englishman named Weddell, got so far as 72° 14′ south latitude, on the 35th meridian, and actually so far as 74° 15′ on the 36th.[21]

"In 1829, the Englishman Forster, Captain of the *Chanticleer,* took possession of the Antarctic Continent at 63° 26′ latitude and 66° 26′ longitude.

"On the 1st of February, 1831, the Englishman Briscoe discovered Enderby in latitude 68° 50′ south; on the 5th of February, 1832, he discovered Adelaide in 67° latitude, and on the 21st of February, Graham, in 64° 45′.

"In 1838, the Frenchman Dumont d'Urville was stopped by the Great Ice Barrier at 62° 57′ south, but he took the bearings of Louis-Philippe Land. Trying again, two years later on the 21st of January, he discovered Adélie Land at 66° 30′, and a week later, the Claire Coast at 64° 40′.

"Also in 1838, the Englishman Wilkes [22] advanced to the 69th parallel on the 100th meridian. In 1839, the Englishman Balleny discovered Sabina Land at the edge of the polar circle.

"And finally, on the 12th of January, 1842, James Ross, also English, commanding the *Erebus* and the *Terror,* discovered Victoria Land in latitude 76° 56′, 171° 7′ east longitude; on the 23d of the same month, he took his bearings at the 74th parallel, the farthest point reached up to that time; and on the 27th, he got so far as 76° 8′; on the 28th, 77° 32′, and on February 22d, 78° 4′! [23] But when he returned later that year, he was unable to get past the 71st parallel. And now—]

"I, Captain Nemo, on this 21st day of March, 1868, have reached the south pole on the ninetieth degree; and I take possession of this part of the globe, equal to one-sixth of the known continents."

"In whose name, Captain?" [24]

"In my own, sir!"

Saying which, Captain Nemo unfurled a black banner, bearing an N in gold quartered on its bunting. Then turning towards the orb of day, whose last rays lapped the horizon of the sea, he exclaimed—

"Adieu, sun! Disappear, thou radiant orb! Rest beneath this open sea, and let a night of six months spread its shadows over my new domains!" [25]

the Circle, a little island he named after Czar Peter I.

21. *Weddell . . . on the 36th* James Weddell sailed into the sea that now bears his name. But the Weddell Sea is in fact a huge bay. The Weddell seal, a large brown antarctic seal valued for its flesh and blubber, is also named after this English navigator.

22. *Englishman Wilkes* No, Charles Wilkes was an American, in command of the first exploring expedition launched by the U.S. Navy. One of his six ships reported having reached 70° south, 105° west.

23. *on February 22d, 78° 4′* And this was the record still standing in 1868 and the one Nemo had to beat. In real life, it remained the record until 1900, when explorers began to push further by crossing Antarctica on foot.

24. *In whose name, Captain* Aronnax was hoping that this moment would reveal Nemo's nationality. The classic formula for such a historic moment, of course, was: "I hereby take possession of this territory in the name of His Majesty . . . , the King of. . . ." Nemo's pointed abbreviation has already put the emphasis on the I, acting as agent for no one but *myself.*

25. *my new domains* Here Verne is the ultimate rebel, in fantasy. His Nemo becomes the Prince of Darkness, unfurling the black banner of defiance of international law, champion of the Shadow side of human nature.

PART 2: CHAPTER XV
Accident or Incident?

1. *the polar bear of antarctic regions* Verne says *polar star,* of course. Lewis's fuzzy associations here betray his contempt for worldly knowledge.

Since ancient times, the mariner has found north at night by locating Polaris, the last star in the handle of the Little Dipper, or Ursa Minor, the Lesser Bear. He may find it easier to locate Polaris by using the last two stars in the ladle of the Big Dipper—or Ursa Major, the Great Bear; they are called the Pointers because they line up with Polaris. Out of some vague familiarity with all that, Lewis has confused polar star with polar bear!

In the southern hemisphere, the traveler, like Aronnax, can use the constellation Crux, or the Southern Cross, to find his direction. He locates four of its stars that form the tips of an upright crucifix. The two center stars point to the south celestial pole.

2. *twelve degrees below zero* Or 10.4°F.

3. *the iceberg* By now, all the descriptions suggest that Aronnax is referring to what antarctic explorers of his day called the *great ice barrier.*

The next day, the 22d of March, at six in the morning, preparations for departure were begun. The last gleams of twilight were melting into night. The cold was great; the constellations shone with wonderful intensity. In the zenith glittered that wondrous Southern Cross—the polar bear of antarctic regions.[1] The thermometer showed twelve degrees below zero,[2] and when the wind freshened, it was most biting. Flakes of ice increased on the open water. The sea seemed everywhere alike. Numerous blackish patches spread on the surface, showing the formation of fresh ice. Evidently the southern basin, frozen during the six winter months, was absolutely inaccessible. What became of the whales in that time? Doubtless they went beneath the icebergs, seeking more practicable seas. As to the seals and morses, accustomed to live in a hard climate, they remained on these icy shores. These creatures have the instinct to break holes in the ice-fields, and to keep them open. To these holes they come for breath; when the birds, driven away by the cold, have emigrated to the north, these sea-mammals remain sole masters of the polar continent.

But the reservoirs were filling with water, and the *Nautilus* was slowly descending. At 1000 feet deep it stopped; its screw beat the waves, and it advanced straight towards the north, at a speed of fifteen miles an hour. Towards night it was already floating under the immense body of the iceberg.[3] [The panels in the saloon had been closed: after all, the *Nautilus* could be hit at any time by a block of submerged ice. So I spent the day fussing with my notes. But my mind kept returning to the south pole. We had actually reached that remote point without any strain or danger, just as if our craft had travelled on tracks! And now, would the return trip provide as many surprises?

During the five-and-a-half months that fate had kept us on the *Nautilus*, we had travelled fourteen thousand leagues. On this long voyage, longer than the circle of the earth at the equator, I had been fascinated by many adventures, some exotic; some dangerous: the hunting trip in the forests of Crespo; running aground in the Torres Straits; the funeral in the coral cemetery; the pearl fisheries of Ceylon; the Arabian tunnel; the fires of Santorin; the millions in Vigo Bay; Atlantis; the south pole!

During the night, I relived all these episodes, one by one, in fitful dreams.4]

At three in the morning I was awakened by a violent shock. I sat up in my bed and listened in the darkness, when I was thrown into the middle of the room. The *Nautilus*, after having struck, had rebounded violently. I groped along the partition, and by the staircase to the saloon, which was lit by the luminous ceiling. The furniture was upset. Fortunately the windows were firmly set, and had held fast. The pictures on the starboard-side, from being no longer vertical, were clinging to the paper,5 whilst those of the port-side were hanging at least a foot from the wall. The *Nautilus* was lying on its starboard side perfectly motionless. I heard footsteps, and a confusion of voices; but Captain Nemo did not appear. As I was leaving the saloon, Ned Land and Conseil entered.

"What is the matter?" said I, at once.

"I came to ask you, sir," replied Conseil.

"Confound it!" exclaimed the Canadian, "I know well enough! The *Nautilus* has struck; and judging by the way she lies, I do not think she will right herself as she did the first time in Torres Straits."

"But," I asked, "has she at least come to the surface of the sea?"

"We do not know," said Conseil.

"It is easy to decide," I answered. I consulted the manometer. To my great surprise it showed a depth of more than 180 fathoms. "What does that mean?" I exclaimed.

"We must ask Captain Nemo," said Conseil.

"But where shall we find him?" said Ned Land.

"Follow me," said I, to my companions.

We left the saloon. There was no one in the library. At the centre staircase, by the berths of the ship's crew, there was no one. I thought that Captain Nemo must be in the pilot's cage. It was best to wait. We all returned to the saloon.

4. *one by one, in fitful dreams* Here Verne has employed one of the strongest biconvex lenses in his toolbox. He has focused all our experience with the narrator into one day of suspense.

Aronnax's comparing his itinerary with the earth's girth makes it a global triumph: 14,000 leagues is 5,200 miles more than the distance around the equator. Our knowing from the book's title that the entire trip will total 20,000 leagues gives us a sense of mounting toward crescendo. Aronnax's ticking off of adventures he has survived makes us feel *but there can still be a price to pay*. And we know from the chapter's title—with its echo of an earlier crisis—that the pendulum *does* swing from incident to accident.

5. *clinging to the paper* Verne has a horror of wallpaper. In saying that Nemo's pictures were clinging *aux tapisseries*, Verne surely meant *to the tapestries*. Verne felt that wallpaper harbors disease. Presumably Nemo has his myrmidons cleaning the tapestries often enough to make them less a threat.

[I will pass over Ned's recriminations without comment. He needed this chance to blow off steam. I let him vent his foul humour without restraint or reply from me.]

For twenty minutes we remained thus, trying to hear the slightest noise which might be made on board the *Nautilus*, when Captain Nemo entered. He seemed not to see us; his face, generally so impassive, showed signs of uneasiness. He watched the compass silently, then the manometer; and going to the planisphere, placed his finger on a spot representing the southern seas. I would not interrupt him; but some minutes later, when he turned towards me, I said, using one of his own expressions in the Torres Straits—

"An incident, Captain?"

"No, sir; an accident this time."

"Serious?"

"Perhaps."

"Is the danger immediate?"

"No."

"The *Nautilus* has stranded?"

"Yes."

"And this has happened—how?"

"From a caprice of nature, not from the ignorance of man. Not a mistake has been made in the working. But we cannot prevent equilibrium from producing its effects. We may brave human laws, but we cannot resist natural ones."

Captain Nemo had chosen a strange moment for uttering this philosophical reflection. On the whole, his answer helped me little.

"May I ask, sir, the cause of this accident?"

"An enormous block of ice, a whole mountain, has turned over," he replied. "When icebergs are undermined at their base by warmer water or reiterated shocks, their centre of gravity rises, and the whole thing turns over. This is what has happened; one of these blocks, as it fell, struck the *Nautilus*, then, gliding under its hull, raised it with irresistible force, bringing it into beds which are not so thick, where it is lying on its side."

"But can we not get the *Nautilus* off by emptying its reservoirs, that it may regain its equilibrium?"

"That, sir, is being done at this moment. You can hear the pump working. Look at the needle of the manometer; it shows that the *Nautilus* is rising, but the block of ice is rising with it; and, until some obstacle stops its ascending motion, our position cannot be altered."

Indeed, the *Nautilus* still held the same position to star-

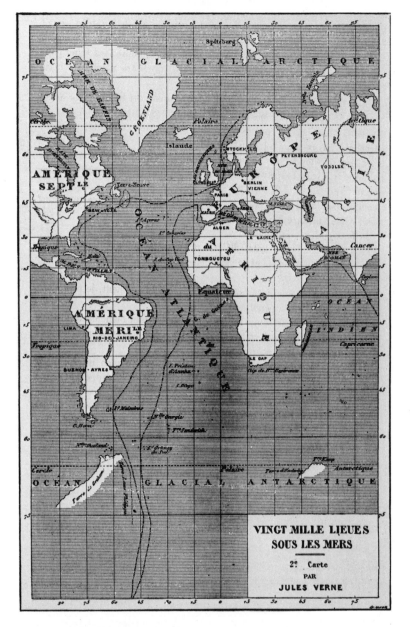

Jules Verne's own map for the second part of the 20,000-league journey under the sea.

board; doubtless it would right itself when the block stopped. But at this moment who knows if we may not be frightfully crushed between the two glassy surfaces? I reflected on all the consequences of our position.

Captain Nemo never took his eyes off the manometer. Since the fall of the iceberg, the *Nautilus* had risen about a hundred and fifty feet, but it still made the same angle with the perpendicular. Suddenly a slight movement was felt in the hold. Evidently it was righting a little. Things hanging in the saloon were sensibly returning to their normal position. The partitions were nearing the upright. No one spoke. With beating hearts we watched and felt the straightening. The boards became horizontal under our feet. Ten minutes passed.

"At last we have righted!" I exclaimed.

"Yes," said Captain Nemo, going to the door of the saloon.

"But are we floating?" I asked.

"Certainly," he replied; "since the reservoirs are not empty; and, when empty, the *Nautilus* must rise to the surface of the sea."

[The Captain left, and I soon understood that he had given orders to halt the ascent of the *Nautilus*. Had he not done that, we would have hit the underbelly of the upper ice mass. It was better to stay suspended in the water between the upper and lower blocks.

"Phew! A narrow escape," sighed Conseil.

"Yes, we could have been crushed between these two blocks, or at least closed in. Then, with no way to surface for air—Yes, a narrow escape."

"If we really did escape!" murmured Ned.

I was still avoiding argument with the Canadian. The panels opened, and light poured in through the windows.]

We were in open sea; but at a distance of about ten yards, on either side of the *Nautilus,* rose a dazzling wall of ice. Above and beneath the same wall. Above, because the lower surface of the iceberg stretched over us like an immense ceiling. Beneath, because the overturned block, having slid by degrees, had found a resting place on the lateral walls, which kept it in that position. The *Nautilus* was really imprisoned in a perfect tunnel of ice more than twenty yards in breadth, filled with quiet water. It was easy to get out of it by going either forward or backward, and then make a free passage under the iceberg, some hundreds of yards deeper.

The luminous ceiling had been extinguished, but the saloon was still resplendent with intense light. It was the powerful reflection from the glass partition sent violently back to the sheets of the lantern. I cannot describe the effect of the voltaic rays upon the great blocks so capriciously cut; upon every angle, every ridge, every facet was thrown a different light, according to the nature of the veins running through the ice; a dazzling mine of gems, particularly of sapphires, their blue rays crossing with the green of the emerald. Here and there were opal shades of wonderful softness, running through bright spots like diamonds of fire, the brilliancy of which the eye could not bear. The power of the lantern seemed increased a hundredfold, like a lamp through the lenticular plates of a first-class light-house.

"How beautiful! How beautiful!" cried Conseil.

"Yes," I said, "it is a wonderful sight. Is it not, Ned?"

"Yes, confound it! Yes," answered Ned Land, "it is superb! I am mad at being obliged to admit it. No one has ever seen anything like it; but the sight may cost us dear. And if I must say all, I think we are seeing here things which God never intended man to see."

Ned was right, it was too beautiful. Suddenly a cry from Conseil made me turn.

"What is it?" I asked.

"Shut your eyes, sir! Do not look, sir!" **6** Saying which, Conseil clapped his hands over his eyes.

"But what is the matter, my boy?"

"I am dazzled, blinded."

My eyes turned involuntarily towards the glass, but I could not stand the fire which seemed to devour them. I understood what had happened. The *Nautilus* had put on full speed. All the quiet lustre of the ice-walls was at once changed into flashes of lightning. The fire from these myriads of diamonds was blinding. It required some time to calm our troubled looks. At last the hands were taken down.

"Faith, I should never have believed it," said Conseil.

["I do not believe it yet," the Canadian grunted.

"When we get back on land," Conseil added, "we shall feel so sophisticated after seeing all these marvels of nature, we shall not be at all excited by the miserable creations of man! No, the inhabited world will be boring to us!"

Coming from a usually stolid Fleming, those words meant something. But the Canadian quenched that glow of enthusiasm fast.

"The world of man! Do not let that worry you, Conseil! You will never see that world again."]

It was then five in the morning; and at that moment a shock was felt at the bows of the *Nautilus*. I knew that its spur had struck a block of ice. It must have been a false manoeuvre, for this submarine tunnel, obstructed by blocks, was not very easy navigation. I thought that Captain Nemo, by changing his course, would turn these obstacles, or else follow the windings of the tunnel. In any case, the road before us could not be entirely blocked. But, contrary to my expectations, the *Nautilus* took a decided retrograde motion.

"We are going backwards?" said Conseil.

"Yes," I replied. "This end of the tunnel can have no egress."

"And then?"

6. *Shut your eyes. . . . Do not look, sir* That's what Aronnax *wishes* Conseil would say: *you, your.* Then Conseil's speech would be true to the strong psychological attraction between these two symbiotic lives. But in reality, in Verne's French, Conseil has said:

"Monsieur must close his eyes! Monsieur must not look!"

And then he follows his third-person speech with very first-personal action! Verne is building up to a moment when Conseil's own loneliness will force him to crash through this language wall—as Aronnax has wanted him to do ever since page 15.

7. *It will be a hindrance* That is, *This tactic will take longer, it will really be a setback.*

8. *your own book you are reading* As we near a moment when the professor will express his love for his servant with simple nonverbal directness, the servant is insulated in formality:

"It is monsieur's own book that monsieur is reading."

To adapt a famous line by Humphrey Bogart, directed at a butler in the movie *Sabrina:*

"Why, Conseil, you're a snob!"

"Then," said I, "the working is easy. We must go back again, and go out at the southern opening. That is all."

In speaking thus, I wished to appear more confident than I really was. But the retrograde motion of the *Nautilus* was increasing; and, reversing the screw it carried us at great speed.

"It will be a hindrance,"**7** said Ned.

"What does it matter, some hours more or less, provided we get out at last!"

"Yes," repeated Ned Land, "provided we do get out at last!"

For a short time I walked from the saloon to the library. My companions were silent. I soon threw myself on an ottoman, and took a book, which my eyes overran mechanically. A quarter of an hour after, Conseil, approaching me, said, "Is what you are reading very interesting, sir?"

"Very interesting!" I replied.

"I should think so, sir. It is your own book you are reading." **8**

"My book?"

And indeed I was holding in my hand the work on the "Great Submarine Depths." I did not even dream of it. I closed the book, and returned to my walk. Ned and Conseil rose to go.

"Stay here, my friends," said I, detaining them. "Let us remain together until we are out of this block."

"As you please, sir," Conseil replied.

Some hours passed. I often looked at the instruments hanging from the partition. The manometer showed that the *Nautilus* kept at a constant depth of more than three hundred yards; the compass still pointed to the south; the log indicated a speed of twenty miles an hour, which, in such cramped space, was very great. But Captain Nemo knew that he could not hasten too much, and that minutes were worth ages to us. At twenty-five minutes past eight a second shock took place, this time from behind. I turned pale. My companions were close by my side. I seized Conseil's hand. Our looks expressed our feelings better than words. At this moment the Captain entered the saloon. I went up to him.

"Our course is barred southward?" I asked.

"Yes, sir. The iceberg has shifted, and closed every outlet."

"We are blocked up, then?"

"Yes."

PART 2: CHAPTER XVI

Want of Air[1]

Thus, around the *Nautilus,* above and below, was an impenetrable wall of ice. We were prisoners to the iceberg. [The Canadian punched the table with his powerful fist. Conseil was quiet.] I watched the Captain. His countenance had resumed its habitual imperturbability. [His arms were folded across his chest. He stood meditating. The *Nautilus* was motionless.]

"Gentlemen," he said, calmly, "there are two ways of dying in the circumstances in which we are placed." (This inexplicable person had the air of a mathematical professor lecturing to his pupils.) "The first is to be crushed; the second is to die of suffocation. I do not speak of the possibility of dying of hunger, for the supply of provisions in the *Nautilus* will certainly last longer than we shall. Let us then calculate our chances."

"As to suffocation, Captain," I replied, "that is not to be feared, because our reservoirs are full."

"Just so; but they will only yield two days' supply of air. Now, for thirty-six hours we have been hidden under the water, and already the heavy atmosphere of the *Nautilus* requires renewal. In forty-eight hours our reserve will be exhausted."

"Well, Captain, can we be delivered before forty-eight hours?"

"We will attempt it, at least, by piercing the wall that surrounds us."

"On which side?"

"Sound will tell us.[2] I am going to run the *Nautilus* aground on the lower bank, and my men will attack the iceberg on the side that is least thick."

1. *Want of Air* This highly imaginative chapter is further distinguished, in the standard English version, by "want of cuts." Mercier Lewis & Co. deleted only 11 sentences, as our brackets ([]) will make clear. Why such restraint here? Two possibilities suggest themselves: (1) there are no strong political views or even implications in this chapter; and (2) there are no passages of sustained technical exposition. Of course, the translator has made mistakes that show the usual Lewis impatience with fine technical distinctions. But on the whole, we have here an idea of how Verne would have been passed on to readers of English if only he had been less concerned with science and social science.

2. *Sound will tell us* That is, *Depth soundings will tell us that.*

["May we have the panels open in the saloon?" I asked.

"No inconvenience there. We are no longer moving."]

Captain Nemo went out. Soon I discovered by a hissing noise that the water was entering the reservoirs. The *Nautilus* sank slowly, and rested on the ice at a depth of 350 yards, the depth at which the lower bank was immersed.

"My friends," I said, "our situation is serious, but I rely on your courage and energy."

"Sir," replied the Canadian, "I am ready to do anything for the general safety."

"Good! Ned," and I held out my hand to the Canadian.

"I will add," he continued, "that being as handy with the pickaxe as with the harpoon, if I can be useful to the Captain, he can command my services."

"He will not refuse your help. Come, Ned!"

I led him to the room where the crew of the *Nautilus* were putting on their cork-jackets.**3** I told the Captain of Ned's proposal, which he accepted. The Canadian put on his sea-costume, and was ready as soon as his companions. [Each of them had his Rouquayrol apparatus strapped to his back, with a large supply of pure air. This was a considerable, but necessary, drain on the ship's reserves. They did not take the Ruhmkorff lamps, since the surrounding waters were brilliantly lighted by the main lantern on deck.]

When Ned was dressed, I re-entered the drawing-room, where the panes of glass were open, and, posted near Conseil, I examined the ambient beds that supported the *Nautilus*. Some instants after, we saw a dozen of the crew set on foot on the bank of ice, and among them Ned Land, easily known by his stature. Captain Nemo was with them. Before proceeding to dig the walls, he took the soundings, to be sure of working in the right direction. Long sounding lines were sunk in the side walls, but after fifteen yards they were again stopped by the thick wall. It was useless to attack it on the ceiling-like surface, since the iceberg itself measured more than 400 yards in height. Captain Nemo then sounded the lower surface. There ten yards of wall separated us from the water, so great was the thickness of the ice-field. It was necessary, therefore, to cut from it a piece equal in extent to the waterline of the *Nautilus*.

There were about 6000 cubic yards to detach, so as to dig a hole by which we could descend [in] to the ice-field. Work was begun immediately, and carried on with indefatigable energy. Instead of digging round the *Nautilus,* which would have involved greater difficulty, Captain Nemo had an im-

3. *putting on their cork-jackets* No, as Nemo and Aronnax both have told us, the *Nautilus* people do not wear the *cork-jackets of the eighteenth century* but the latest-model *rubber-and-copper outfits of the nineteenth century.*

. . . I remarked that the side walls were gradually closing in. Engraving from the original edition (1870).

mense trench made at eight yards from the port quarter. Then the men set to work simultaneously with their screws, on several points of its circumference.[4] Presently the pickaxe attacked this compact matter vigorously, and large blocks were detached from the mass. By a curious effect of specific gravity, these blocks, lighter than water, fled, so to speak, to the vault of the tunnel, that increased in thickness at the top in proportion as it diminished at the base. But that mattered little, so long as the lower part grew thinner.

After two hours' hard work, Ned Land came in exhausted. He and his comrades were replaced by new workers, whom Conseil and I joined. The second lieutenant of the *Nautilus* superintended us. The water seemed singularly cold, but I soon got warm handling the pickaxe. My movements were free enough, although they were made under a pressure of thirty atmospheres. When I re-entered, after working two hours, to take some food and rest, I found a perceptible difference between the pure fluid with which the Rouquayrol engine supplied me, and the atmosphere of the *Nautilus,* already charged with carbonic acid.[5] The air had not been renewed for forty-eight hours, and its vivifying qualities were considerably enfeebled. However, after a lapse of twelve hours, we had only raised a block of ice one yard thick, on the marked surface, which was about 600 cubic yards![6] Reckoning that it took twelve hours to accomplish this much, it would take five nights and four days to bring this enterprise to a satisfactory conclusion. Five nights and four days! And we have only air enough for two days in the reservoirs? "Without taking into account," said Ned, "that, even if we get out of this infernal prison, we shall also be imprisoned under the iceberg, shut out from all possible communication with the atmosphere." True enough! Who could then foresee the minimum of time necessary for our deliverance? We might be suffocated before the *Nautilus* could regain the surface of the waves? Was it destined to perish in this ice-tomb, with all those it enclosed? The situation was terrible. But every one had looked the danger in the face, and each was determined to do his duty to the last.

As I expected, during the night a new block a yard square [7] was carried away, and still further sank the immense hollow. But in the morning when, dressed in my cork-jacket, I traversed the slushy mass at a temperature of six or seven degrees below zero, I remarked that the side walls were gradually closing in. The beds of water farthest from the trench, that were not warmed by the men's mere work, showed a tendency

4. *on several points of its circumference* Let's back up and get it right. Captain Nemo has his men *outline* the trench on the surface of the ice. Then they set to work with drills along the edges of the outlined mass. Now they have some openings in the ice through which they can start chipping away with their pickaxes. Verne has given the total mass to be "detached" as 6500 cubic meters.

5. *carbonic acid* We would be more likely today to call it *carbon dioxide.*

6. *a block of . . . 600 cubic yards* Actually, they have lifted out a *layer* one meter thick.

7. *a new block a yard square* Again, another *layer* a meter thick, so that now the men are working six or seven feet below the top of the trench. And they are now that much closer to the water beneath them.

to solidification. In presence of this new and imminent danger, what would become of our chances of safety, and how hinder the solidification of this liquid medium, that would burst the partitions of the *Nautilus* like glass?

I did not tell my companions of this new danger. What was the good of dampening the energy they displayed in the painful work of escape? But when I went on board again, I told Captain Nemo of this grave complication. **8**

"I know it," he said, in that calm tone which could counteract the most terrible apprehensions. "It is one danger more; but I see no way of escaping it; the only chance of safety is to go quicker than solidification. We must be beforehand with it, that is all."

[Be beforehand with it! Anticipate developments! Yes, I should have *anticipated* that he would say that!]

On this day for several hours I used my pickaxe vigorously. The work kept me up. Besides, to work was to quit the *Nautilus,* and breathe directly the pure air drawn from the reservoirs, and supplied by our apparatus, and to quit the impoverished and vitiated atmosphere. Towards evening the trench was dug one yard deeper. When I returned on board, I was nearly suffocated by the carbonic acid with which the air was filled—ah! if we had only the chemical means to drive away this deleterious gas. We had plenty of oxygen; all this water contained a considerable quantity, and by dissolving it with our powerful piles, it would restore the vivifying fluid. I had thought well over it; but of what good was that, since the carbonic acid produced by our respiration had invaded every part of the vessel? To absorb it, it was necessary to fill some jars with caustic potash, and to shake them incessantly. Now this substance was wanting on board and nothing could replace it. On that evening, Captain Nemo ought to open the taps of his reservoirs, and let some pure air into the interior of the *Nautilus;* without this precaution, we could not get rid of the sense of suffocation.

The next day, March 26th, I resumed my miner's work in beginning the fifth yard. The side walls and the lower surface of the iceberg thickened visibly. It was evident that they would meet before the *Nautilus* was able to disengage itself. Despair seized me for an instant, my pickaxe nearly fell from my hands. What was the good of digging if I must be suffocated, crushed by the water that was turning into stone?—a punishment that the ferocity of the savages even would not have invented! Just then Captain Nemo passed near me. I touched his hand and showed him the walls of our prison. The wall to port

8. *this grave complication* Here we have a passage suitable for illustrating the basic approach of the science-fiction author, an approach developed mainly by Verne. He puts his people into some novel danger that only their advanced technology could have exposed them to in the first place. Here, the world's only working submarine crew, attempting a dash under an ice field, gets caught between shifting slabs of ice. This means that now Verne himself must anticipate, step by step, each new natural development growing out of this hypothetical situation and counter it with all his (heroes') theoretical and practical ingenuity. Essentially the author, as much as his characters, is operating in unknown territory. Yet once he has set up the situation, his readers can also anticipate problems!

For example, at this point, some readers will begin to wonder, now that the crew has dug out seven feet of ice from beneath themselves: At what depth will they be hacking away at ice too thin to support all of them? At what point will the remaining ice layer break away from the supporting side walls?

Verne now has the option of raising the question at about the time it will occur to the reader, or of ignoring it so that the reader can be collaborating in building the suspense! Then Verne himself can resolve the chapter precisely by returning to the idea he seems to have overlooked.

had advanced to at least four yards from the hull of the *Nautilus*. The Captain understood me, and signed to me to follow him. We went on board. I took off my cork-jacket, and accompanied him into the drawing-room.

"M. Aronnax, we must attempt some desperate means, or we shall be sealed up in this solidified water as in cement."

"Yes, but what is to be done?"

"Ah! if my *Nautilus* were strong enough to bear this pressure without being crushed!"

"Well?" I asked, not catching the Captain's idea.

"Do you not understand," he replied, "that this congelation of water will help us? Do you not see that, by its solidification, it would burst through this field of ice that imprisons us, as, when it freezes, it bursts the hardest stones? Do you not perceive that it would be an agent of safety instead of destruction?"

"Yes, Captain, perhaps. But whatever resistance to crushing the *Nautilus* possesses, it could not support this terrible pressure, and would be flattened like an iron plate."

"I know it, sir. Therefore we must not reckon on the aid of nature, but on our own exertions. We must stop this solidification. Not only will the side walls be pressed together; but there is not ten feet of water before or behind the *Nautilus*. The congelation gains on us on all sides."

"How long will the air in the reservoirs last for us to breathe on board?"

The Captain looked in my face. "After tomorrow they will be empty!"

A cold sweat came over me. However, ought I to have been astonished at the answer? On March 22d the *Nautilus* was in the open polar seas. We were at 26°. **9** For five days we had lived on the reserve on board. And what was left of the respirable air must be kept for the workers. Even now, as I write, my recollection is still so vivid, that an involuntary terror seizes me, and my lungs seem to be without air. Meanwhile Captain Nemo reflected silently, and evidently an idea had struck him; but he seemed to reject it. At last, these words escaped his lips—

"Boiling water!" he muttered.

"Boiling water?" I cried.

"Yes, sir. We are enclosed in a space that is relatively confined. Would not jets of boiling water, constantly injected by the pumps, raise the temperature in this part, and stay the congelation?"

"Let us try it," I said, resolutely.

9. *We were at 26°* Meaningless, as the context makes clear. What Verne really wrote, of course, is: *Nous étions au 26,* that is, *We had now reached the 26th* [of March].

10. *at seven degrees outside* That's −7°C, or 19.4°F. But notice how much more satisfying it will be, in the coming action, to work only with Celsius (Centigrade). Qualitative changes (boiling, freezing) are reached at or around significant numerical changes: 100 and 0. But *the heat developed here is developed* not *by the troughs* (?!) but *by the batteries.*

11. *no more suffocation to fear* That doesn't make sense. What Nemo says, in the French, is that *"We have* only *suffocation to fear."*

12. *the dangers of solidification* What Aronnax really says is that he is reassured because *sea water will not freeze until it drops to* −2°C.

"Let us try, Professor."

The thermometer then stood at seven degrees outside. **10** Captain Nemo took me to the galleys, where the vast distillatory machines stood that furnished the drinkable water by evaporation. They filled these with water, and all the electric heat from the piles was thrown through the worms bathed in the liquid. In a few minutes this water reached a hundred degrees. It was directed towards the pumps, while fresh water replaced it in proportion. The heat developed by the troughs was such that cold water, drawn up from the sea, after only having gone through the machines, came boiling into the body of the pump. The injection was begun, and three hours after the thermometer marked six degrees below zero outside. One degree was gained. Two hours later, the thermometer only marked four degrees.

"We shall succeed," I said to the Captain, after having anxiously watched the result of the operation.

"I think," he answered, "that we shall not be crushed. We have no more suffocation to fear." **11**

During the night the temperature of the water rose to one degree below zero. The injections could not carry it to a higher point. But as the congelation of the sea-water produces at least two degrees, I was at last reassured against the dangers of solidification. **12**

The next day, March 27th, six yards of ice had been cleared, four yards only remaining to be cleared away. There was yet forty-eight hours' work. The air could not be renewed in the interior of the *Nautilus*. And this day would make it worse. An intolerable weight oppressed me. Towards three o'clock in the evening, this feeling rose to a violent degree. Yawns dislocated my jaws. My lungs panted as they inhaled this burning fluid, which became rarefied more and more. A moral torpor took hold of me. I was powerless, almost unconscious. My brave Conseil, though exhibiting the same symptoms and suffering in the same manner, never left me. He took my hand and encouraged me, and I heard him murmur, "Oh, if I could only not breathe, so as to leave more air for my master!"

Tears came into my eyes on hearing him speak thus. If our situation to all was intolerable in the interior, with what haste and gladness would we put on our cork-jackets to work in our turn! Pickaxes sounded on the frozen ice-beds. Our arms ached, the skin was torn off our hands. But what were these fatigues, what did the wounds matter? Vital air came to our lungs! we breathed! we breathed!

All this time, no one prolonged his voluntary task beyond the prescribed time. His task accomplished, each one handed in turn to his panting companions the apparatus that supplied him with life. Captain Nemo set the example, and submitted first to this severe discipline. When the time came, he gave up his apparatus to another, and returned to the vitiated air on board, calm, unflinching, unmurmuring.

On that day the ordinary work was accomplished with unusual vigour. Only two yards remained to be raised from the surface. Two yards only separated us from the open sea. But the reservoirs were nearly emptied of air. The little that remained ought to be kept for the workers; not a particle for the *Nautilus*. When I went back on board, I was half suffocated. What a night! I know not how to describe it. The next day my breathing was oppressed. Dizziness accompanied the pain in my head, and made me like a drunken man. My companions showed the same symptoms. Some of the crew had rattling in the throat.

On that day, the sixth of our imprisonment, Captain Nemo, finding the pickaxes work too slowly, resolved to crush the icebed that still separated us from the liquid sheet. This man's coolness and energy never forsook him. He subdued his physical pains by moral force.

By his orders the vessel was lightened, that is to say, raised from the ice-bed by a change of specific gravity. When it floated they towed it **13** so as to bring it above the immense trench made on the level of the water-line. Then filling his reservoirs of water, he descended and shut himself up in the hole.

Just then all the crew came on board, and the double door of communication was shut. The *Nautilus* then rested on the bed of ice, which was not one yard thick, and which the sounding leads had perforated in a thousand places. The taps of the reservoir were then opened, and a hundred cubic yards of water was let in, increasing the weight of the *Nautilus* 1800 tons. **14** We waited, we listened, forgetting our sufferings in hope. Our safety depended on this last chance. Notwithstanding the buzzing in my head, I soon heard the humming sound under the hull of the *Nautilus*. The ice cracked with a singular noise, like tearing paper, and the *Nautilus* sank.

"We are off!" murmured Conseil in my ear.

I could not answer him. I seized his hand, and pressed it convulsively. All at once, carried away by its frightful overcharge, the *Nautilus* sank like a bullet under the waters, that is to say, it fell as if it were in a vacuum. Then all the electric

13. *they towed it* This imaginative conception is Verne's version in three dimensions of a well-known naval maneuver executed in two dimensions. For example, on July 18, 1812, the U.S.S. *Constitution,* a frigate displacing 2000 tons and carrying fifty guns, was patrolling the coast of New Jersey. The British fleet approached and had the *Constitution* well within the range of their guns when the wind died down and the pride of the American Navy was about to take a drubbing from superior numbers.

But her crew took to five small boats and towed her out of British range.

14. *Nautilus 1800 tons* Verne gives it as *100 cubic meters,* adding 100,000 kilograms of ballast. Since a kilogram is about 2.2046 pounds, they are taking in 220,460 pounds or about 110 (*not* 1800) tons of water.

force was put on the pumps, that soon began to let the water out of the reservoirs. After some minutes, our fall was stopped. Soon, too, the manometer indicated an ascending movement. The screw, going at full speed, made the iron hull tremble to its very bolts, and drew us towards the north. But if this floating under the iceberg is to last another day before we reach the open sea, I shall be dead first.

Half stretched upon a divan in the library, I was suffocating. My face was purple, my lips blue, **15** my faculties suspended. I neither saw nor heard. All notion of time had gone from my mind. My muscles could not contract. I do not know how many hours passed thus, but I was conscious of the agony that was coming over me. I felt as if I was going to die. Suddenly I came to. Some breaths of air penetrated my lungs. Had we risen to the surface of the waves? Were we free of the iceberg? No; Ned and Conseil, my two brave friends, were sacrificing themselves to save me. Some particles of air still remained at the bottom of one apparatus. Instead of using it, they had kept it for me, and while they were being suffocated, they gave me life drop by drop. I wanted to push back the thing; they held my hands, and for some moments I breathed freely. I looked at the clock; it was eleven in the morning. It ought to be the 28th of March. The *Nautilus* went at a frightful pace, forty miles an hour. It literally tore through the water. Where was Captain Nemo? Had he succumbed? Were his companions dead with him? At the moment, the manometer indicated that we were not more than twenty feet from the surface. A mere plate of ice separated us from the atmosphere, could we not break it? Perhaps. In any case the *Nautilus* was going to attempt it. I felt that it was in an oblique position, lowering the stern, and raising the bows. The introduction of water had been the means of disturbing its equilibrium. Then, impelled by its powerful screw, it attacked the ice-field from beneath like a formidable battering-ram. It broke it by backing and then rushing forward against the field, which gradually gave way; and at last, dashing suddenly against it, shot forward on the icy field, that crushed beneath its weight. The panel was opened—one might say torn off—and the pure air came in in abundance to all parts of the *Nautilus*.

15. *My face was purple, my lips blue* How can Aronnax tell that his face is purple, his lips blue, when he's lying on a divan and not staring in a mirror?

Verne wrote in those benighted times before Henry James made both author and reader jumpy about "point of view." Still, Verne's less out of focus in these matters than his "beloved masters," Walter Scott and James Fenimore Cooper.

From Cape Horn
to the Amazon [1]

How I got on to the platform, I have no idea; perhaps the Canadian had carried me there. But I breathed, I inhaled the vivifying sea-air. My two companions were getting drunk with the fresh particles. The other unhappy men had been so long without food, that they could not with impunity indulge in the simplest aliments that were given them.[2] We, on the contrary, had no need to restrain ourselves; we could draw this air freely into our lungs, and it was the breeze, the breeze alone, that filled us with this keen enjoyment.

"Ah!" said Conseil, "how delightful this oxygen is! Master need not fear to breathe it. There is enough for everybody."

Ned Land did not speak, but he opened his jaws wide enough to frighten a shark. Our strength soon returned, and when I looked round me, I saw we were alone on the platform. The foreign seamen in the *Nautilus* were contented with the air that circulated in the interior; none of them had come to drink in the open air.[3]

The first words I spoke were words of gratitude and thankfulness to my two companions. Ned and Conseil had prolonged my life during the last hours of this long agony. All my gratitude could not repay such devotion.

["Oh, Professor, do not mention it!" Ned said. "How can you give us any credit for that? It was a matter of simple arithmetic. Your life is worth more than ours. We had to save you!"

"No, Ned, no person is superior to a man as noble and generous as you. And that is what you are."

"All right, if you say so." He was embarrassed.

1. *to the Amazon* Notice the basic biorhythm of Verne's science fiction. After his characters emerge from a major crisis, he uses the ensuing calm for some painless adult education.

2. *aliments that were given them* No one on the *Nautilus* has gone without food. What Aronnax says, in the original, is that *unfortunate people who have gone a long time without eating must be careful not to stuff themselves when rescued.*

3. *to drink in the open air* Here we have the most appalling evidence so far of the utter anomie of these *strange* (not *foreign*) seamen. The objective fact that fresh air will now circulate through the vessel is enough: They feel no need to break out on deck and breathe deep and see far. Or is it that they go on deck only when so ordered by Nemo? Still, they have chosen to serve on this boat. Outlaws all, they are presumably experienced enough in resistance and rebellion to endure only what they choose to endure. They toil in submarine mines, in ice traps, in combat with cachalots and other aggressors. Their only rewards seem to be quiet satisfaction in helping the victims of aggression and plentiful opportunity to meditate on the past.

"And Conseil, how you must have suffered."

"Not too much, if monsieur will permit me to say it. I was a bit out of breath, but I was expecting to get used to it. And when I saw monsieur in such distress, I lost all desire to breathe. It took the wind out of—"

Now he seemed embarrassed, confused perhaps by the unexpected pun in his banal phrase.]

"My friends," said I, "we are bound one to the other for ever, and I am under infinite obligations to you."

"Which I shall take advantage of," exclaimed the Canadian.

"What do you mean?" said Conseil.

"I mean that I shall take you with me when I leave this infernal *Nautilus.*"

"Well," said Conseil, "after all this, are we going right?"

"Yes," I replied, "for we are going the way of the sun, and here the sun is in the north."

"No doubt," said Ned Land; "but it remains to be seen whether he will bring the ship into the Pacific or the Atlantic Ocean, that is, into frequented or deserted seas."

I could not answer that question, and I feared that Captain Nemo would rather take us to the vast ocean that touches the coasts of Asia and America at the same time. He would thus complete the tour round the submarine world, and return to those waters in which the *Nautilus* could sail freely.

[But if we were to return to the Pacific, far from inhabited lands, what would come of Ned's plans for escape?] We ought, before long, to settle this important point. The *Nautilus* went at a rapid pace. The polar circle was soon passed, and the course shaped for Cape Horn. We were off the American point, March 31st, at seven o'clock in the evening. Then all our past sufferings were forgotten. The remembrance of that imprisonment in the ice was effaced from our minds. We only thought of the future. Captain Nemo did not appear again either in the drawing-room or on the platform. The point shown each day on the planisphere, and marked by the lieutenant, showed me the exact direction of the *Nautilus.* Now, on that evening, it was evident, to my great satisfaction, that we were going back to the north by the Atlantic. [And I passed on the good news to Ned and Conseil.

"Fine! But just where in the north are we going?" asked Ned.

"That I do not know yet."

"Maybe your Captain, having discovered the south pole, wants now to find the north pole and then get to the Pacific through the famous Northwest Passage!"

We were off the American point. . . . Then all our past sufferings were forgotten. Cape Horn as it was pictured in *The American Cyclopaedia* (1873).

"Do not *dare* him to do it," begged Conseil.

"Do not worry," the Canadian reassured him. "We will have left him before then."

"Nevertheless," Conseil added, "this Captain Nemo is one extraordinary man. We shall not regret having known him."

"No, not *after* we have left him," Ned agreed.]

The next day, April 1st, when the *Nautilus* ascended to the surface, some minutes before noon, we sighted land to the west. It was T[i]erra del Fuego, which the first navigators named thus from seeing the quantity of smoke that rose from the natives' huts.4 [Tierra del Fuego is a large island group, thirty leagues long and eighty leagues wide, situated between 53° and 56° south latitude, 67° 50′ and 77° 15′ west longitude.]

The coast seemed low to me, but in the distance rose high mountains. I even thought I had a glimpse of Mount Sarmiento, that rises 2070 yards above the level of the sea, with a very pointed summit, which, according as it is misty or clear, is a sign of fine or wet weather. [Or so Ned was telling me.

"Then it is a good barometer," I replied.

"Yes, monsieur, a natural barometer. And it served me well when I used to sail through the Straits of Magellan."]

At this moment, the peak was clearly defined against the sky. The *Nautilus,* diving again under the water, approached the coast, which was only some few miles off. From the glass windows in the drawing room, I saw long seaweeds, and gigantic fuci, and varech, of which the open polar sea contains so many specimens, with their sharp polished filaments; they measured about 300 yards in length,—real cables, thicker than one's thumb; and having great tenacity, they are often used as ropes for vessels. Another weed known as velp, with leaves four feet long, buried in the coral concretions, hung at the bottom. It served as nest and food for myriads of crustacea and molluscs, crabs and cuttle-fish. There seals and otters had splendid repasts, eating the flesh of fish with sea-vegetables, according to the English fashion. Over this fertile and luxuriant ground the *Nautilus* passed with great rapidity. Towards evening, it approached the Falkland group, the rough summits of which I recognised the following day. The depth of the sea was moderate.

[This confirmed my belief that these two islands, surrounded by many smaller isles, were once part of Patagonia. The Falklands were discovered by the famous John Davis, who called them the Davis Southland Islands. Later, Richard Hawkins named them the Maiden Islands, after the Virgin.

4. *rose from the natives' huts* Tierra del Fuego has played an unusual role in modern exploration, map-making, and colonial pillage.

In 1520 Ferdinand Magellan, in his *Victoria,* picked his way through the straits that now bear his name. One of his officers, Antonio Pigafetta, later published an account of *Magellan's Voyage around the World.* Pigafetta's map of Tierra del Fuego indicated he thought this land was the northern tip of a huge continent.

Even after William Cornelis Schouten proved, in 1616, that del Fuego was a separate archipelago, most European maps still represented it as part of a polar land mass. Alexander Dalrymple, as we have seen, as late as 1772 insisted that that land mass supported at least fifty million people. Tierra del Fuego was not thoroughly surveyed until Captain Fitzroy did the job on his famous *Beagle* voyage.

Ironically, the Ona, Yahgan, and Alacaluf Indians who fit simply but well into the marine ecology of del Fuego were soon all but wiped out by Europeans who discovered first the good pasture land and later the oil and the gold.

The fate of Tierra del Fuego under colonial aggression is dramatized by Verne in *The Survivors of the "Jonathan"* (posthumous; 1909). Early in the book the Magellan Straits are described as "belonging to no one," almost like the South Pole when Nemo takes possession. "It was not one of those well-ordered states where the police are interested in people's past lives and where it is impossible to remain unknown for long. Here, nobody was authorized to exercise authority, and a man could live in complete liberty, free of all constraint of law and custom." But when gold is found in del Fuego, the islands are overwhelmed by invaders from five continents and foreign control is firmly established.

The shores of Patagonia, as illustrated in *Mitchell's School Geography* (1863). Penguins presumably posing for the artist.

5. *tentacles drift in the water* The medusa is named after the Gorgon Medusa, a maiden who figures in Greek mythology. Medusa's hair was a nest of snakes, and she could *petrify* anyone who looked her in the face. The medusae that Aronnax talks about so often can *paralyze* their prey with stingers on their tentacles. Their tissues are 95 percent water. Since they weigh not much more than the water they displace, they can float or drift with ease.

6. *apparitions, that sink and evaporate* Verne says that they *dissolve* or *melt away and evaporate.*

7. *1600 miles* No, 16,000 *leagues.*

And at the beginning of the eighteenth century, fishermen from Saint Malo renamed them the Malouines. Finally the British, to whom they now belong, gave them the name of the Falklands.]

On the shores, our nets brought in beautiful specimens of seaweed, and particularly a certain fucus, the roots of which were filled with the best mussels in the world. Geese and ducks fell by dozens on the platform, and soon took their places in the pantry on board. With regard to fish, I observed especially specimens of the goby species, some two feet long, all over white and yellow spots. I admired also numerous medusae, and the finest of the sort, the chrysaora, peculiar to the sea about the Falkland Isles. [Sometimes they were shaped like a smooth semi-spherical umbrella, with red and brown stripes, and a fringe of twelve symmetrical tentacles. Sometimes they were like baskets out of which there trailed leaves on long red branches. They swam by moving their four arms and letting their tentacles drift in the water.**5**] I should have liked to preserve some specimens of these delicate zoophytes: but they are only like clouds, shadows, apparitions, that sink and evaporate **6** when out of their native element.

When the last heights of the Falklands had disappeared from the horizon, the *Nautilus* sank to between twenty and twenty-five yards, and followed the American coast. Captain Nemo did not show himself. Until the 3d of April we did not quit the shores of Patagonia, sometimes under the ocean, sometimes at the surface. The *Nautilus* passed beyond the large estuary formed by the mouth of the Plata, and was, on the 4th of April, fifty-six miles off Uruguay. Its direction was northwards, and followed the long windings of the coast of South America. We had then made 1600 miles **7** since our embarkation in the seas of Japan. About eleven o'clock in the morning the tropic of Capricorn was crossed on the thirty-seventh meridian, and we passed Cape Frio standing out to sea. Captain Nemo, to Ned Land's great displeasure, did not like the neighbourhood of the inhabited coasts of Brazil, for we went at a giddy speed. Not a fish, not a bird of the swiftest kind could follow us, and the natural curiosities of these seas escaped all observation.

This speed was kept up for several days, and in the evening of the 9th of April we sighted the most westerly point of South America that forms Cape San Roque. But then the *Nautilus* swerved again, and sought the lowest depth of a submarine valley which is between this cape and Sierra Leone on the African coast. This valley bifurcates to the parallel of the

Antilles, and terminates at the north by the enormous depression of 9000 yards. In this place, the geological basin of the ocean forms, as far as the Lesser Antilles, a cliff of three and a half miles perpendicular in height, and at the parallel of the Cape Verde Islands, another wall not less considerable, that encloses thus all the sunk continent of the Atlantic. The bottom of this immense valley is dotted with some mountains, that give to these submarine places a picturesque aspect. I speak, moreover, from the manuscript charts that were in the library of the *Nautilus*—charts evidently due to Captain Nemo's hand, and made after his personal observations.[8]

For two days the desert and deep waters were visited by means of the inclined planes. The *Nautilus* was furnished with long diagonal broadsides which carried it to all elevations. But, on the 11th of April, it rose suddenly, and land appeared at the mouth of the Amazon River, a vast estuary, the embouchure of which is so considerable that it freshens the seawater for the distance of several leagues.

The equator was crossed. Twenty miles to the west were the Guianas, a French territory, on which we could have found an easy refuge; but a stiff breeze was blowing, and the furious waves would not have allowed a single boat to face them. Ned Land understood that, no doubt, for he spoke not a word about it. For my part, I made no allusion to his schemes of flight, for I would not urge him to make an attempt that must inevitably fail. I made the time pass pleasantly by interesting studies. During the days of April 11th and 12th, the *Nautilus* did not leave the surface of the sea, and the net brought in a marvellous haul of zoophytes, fish and reptiles. Some zoophytes had been fished up by the chain of the nets; they were for the most part beautiful phyctallines, belonging to the actinidian family, and among other species the phyctalis protexta, peculiar to that part of the ocean, with a little cylindrical trunk, ornamented with vertical lines, speckled with red dots, crowning a marvellous blossoming of tentacles. As to the molluscs, they consisted of some I had already observed—turritellas, olive porphyras, with regular lines intercrossed, with red spots standing out plainly against the flesh; odd pteroceras, like petrified scorpions; translucid hyaleas, argonauts, cuttle-fish (excellent eating), and certain species of calmars that naturalists of antiquity have classed amongst the flying-fish, and that serve principally for bait for codfishing. I had now an opportunity of studying several species of fish on these shores. Amongst the cartilaginous ones, petromyzons-pricka, a sort of eel, fifteen inches long, with a green-

8. *charts . . . his personal observations* Nemo's observations of the *cliff* and the *wall* coincide roughly with what we now would call a portion of the Mid-Atlantic Ridge, one of the globe's most remarkable geologic features. It is now known to be part of the Mid-Ocean Ridge that runs continuously for 40,000 miles along the bottoms of the world's oceans. A peculiar feature of the ridge is the riftlike valley or trench that runs along its crest. This fissure averages 30 miles in width. The peaks of the ridge rise to 6000 feet on each side of the rift.

Much has been learned about parts of the underwater mountain range since Maury's time. But the pieces have been put together only in recent years. One epic account of the people and the problems involved is William Wertenbaker's classic of science writing, *The Floor of the Sea* (1974).

9. *tuberculated streaks* Here Verne's word *raies* means not rays of color but cartilaginous fishes called *rays*.

10. *somewhat dry perhaps* Aronnax the lover of wordplay is punning on his "wet" subject.

11. *twenty ounces* Mercier Lewis has been determined to ruin this joke ever since Verne first set it in motion way back on page 15. This rayfish—which would resemble a perfect disc *if* its tail were cut off—weighs some twenty-odd *kilograms,* or about *forty-five pounds.*

12. *not spoken to me in the third person* Yes, it's true that *in Verne, this is the first time.* But the "standard translation" has made this revelation meaningless by making it happen *numerous times.*

There are two reasons why we've been making such a fuss over it. First, this incident shows how carefully Verne planned his stories. In his third chapter (page 15), Verne had the professor say:

Conseil had one fault, he was ceremonious to a degree, and would never speak to me but in the third person, which was sometimes provoking.

Then Verne gave us example after example, including one just a few pages back where, even when he was almost blinded, Conseil would not drop his third-person reserve. All this time Verne was building up suspense: just what does it take to crash through. Conseil's ceremoniousness? So far as Verne was concerned, it took 38 chapters of careful plotting for this one element in his story line.

Second, far more important, is the way this long-in-the-works joke serves to characterize both Aronnax and Conseil. When he is half paralyzed, Conseil finally appeals to his boss, man-to-man, as "you," a luxury he has never admitted he needed. Moreover, Aronnax has yearned for the time when Conseil would take that step—without being told to! And now notice: the very first thing the professor thinks of when Conseil cries

ish head, violet fins, grey-blue back, brown belly, silvered and sown with bright spots, the pupil of the eye encircled with gold—a curious animal, that the current of the Amazon had drawn to the sea, for they inhabit fresh waters—tuberculated streaks,**9** with pointed snouts, and a long loose tail, armed with a long jagged sting; little sharks, a yard long, grey and whitish skin, and several rows of teeth, bent back, that are generally known by the name of pantouffles; vespertilios, a kind of red isosceles triangle, half a yard long, to which pectorals are attached by fleshy prolongations that make them look like bats, but that their horny appendage, situated near the nostrils, has given them the name of sea-unicorns; lastly, some species of balistae, the curassavian, whose spots were of a brilliant gold colour, and the capriscus of clear violet, and with varying shades like a pigeon's throat.

I end here this catalogue, which is somewhat dry perhaps,**10** but very exact, with a series of bony fish that I observed in passing belonging to the apteronotes, and whose snout is white as snow, the body of a beautiful black, marked with a very long loose fleshy strip; odontognathes, armed with spikes; sardines, nine inches long, glittering with a bright silver light; a species of mackerel provided with two anal fins; centronotes of a blackish tint, that are fished for with torches, long fish, two yards in length, with fat flesh, white and firm, which, when they are fresh, taste like eel, and when dry, like smoked salmon; labres, half red, covered with scales only at the bottom of the dorsal and anal fins; chrysoptera, on which gold and silver blend their brightness with that of the ruby and topaz; golden-tailed spares, the flesh of which is extremely delicate, and whose phosphorescent properties betray them in the midst of the waters; orange-coloured spares with long tongues; maigres, with gold caudal fins, dark thorntails, anableps of Surinam, etc.

Notwithstanding this "et cetera," I must not omit to mention fish that Conseil will long remember, and with good reason. One of our nets had hauled up a sort of very flat rayfish, which, with the tail cut off, formed a perfect disc, and weighed twenty ounces.**11** It was white underneath, red above, with large round spots of dark blue encircled with black, very glossy skin, terminating in a bilobed fin. Laid out on the platform, it struggled, tried to turn itself by convulsive movements, and made so many efforts, that one last turn had nearly sent it into the sea. But Conseil, not wishing to let the fish go, rushed to it, and, before I could prevent him, had seized it with both hands. In a moment he was overthrown, his legs in the air, and half his body paralysed, crying—

"Oh! Master, master! Come to me!"

It was the first time the poor boy had not spoken to me in the third person.[12] The Canadian and I took him up, and rubbed his contracted arms till he became sensible.

[Then that eternal classifier murmured, haltingly:

"Class of cartilaginous fishes, order of chondopterygians with fixed gills, suborder of selachians, family of rays, genus of torpedo fish!"

"Yes, my friend," I responded, "that was an electric ray that shocked you."

"Monsieur can believe me. I shall have my revenge on that animal."

"Just how?"

"In the eating of it!"

And that is just what he did, and purely for spite,[13] because frankly, that animal was tough as leather.]

The unfortunate Conseil had attacked a cramp-fish of the most dangerous kind, the cumana. This odd animal, in a medium conductor like water, strikes fish at several yards' distance, so great is the power of its electric organ, the two principal surfaces of which do not measure less than twenty-seven square feet. The next day, April 12th, the *Nautilus* approached the Dutch coast, near the mouth of the Maroni. There several groups of sea-cows herded together; they were manatees, that, like the dugong and the stellera,[14] belong to the sirenian order [and live in family groups]. These beautiful animals, peaceable and inoffensive, from eighteen to twenty-one feet in length, weigh at least sixteen hundredweight. I told Ned Land and Conseil that provident nature had assigned an important *rôle* to these mammalia. Indeed, they, like the seals, are designed to graze on the submarine prairies, and thus destroy the accumulation of weed that obstructs the tropical rivers.

"And do you know," I added, "what has been the result since men have almost entirely annihilated this useful race? That the putrefied weeds have poisoned the air, and the poisoned air causes the yellow fever, that desolates these beautiful countries. Enormous vegetations are multiplied under the torrid seas, and the evil is irresistibly developed from the mouth of the Rio de la Plata to Florida. If we are to believe Toussenel, this plague is nothing to what it would be if the seas were cleared of whales and seals. Then, infested with

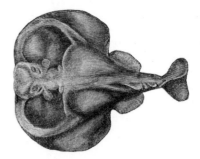

"Oh! Master, master! Come to me!" . . . Conseil had attacked a crampfish of the most dangerous kind. . . . The cramp-fish, or torpedo ray, as pictured in *The American Cyclopaedia* (1873).

out is that at last the gap has been closed.

13. *purely for spite* Now that Conseil has been massaged and nourished back to health, we can note that the torpedo ray doesn't come off so well even if he doesn't get eaten. Once he uses his electric charge—which is his main defensive and offensive mechanism—it takes him days to recharge his batteries.

14. *the stellera* This was Steller's sea cow, the last member of *the sirenian order* to be discovered, the first to be extinguished by the greed of man.

In 1741 Dr. Georg Steller, German naturalist on board the Russian ship *St. Peter,* saw—off an island in the Bering Straits—some huge humpbacked shapes moving in the water. Upon closer examination of one of these creatures, he realized he had discovered a previously unknown genus. He could see it was related to the manatee and the dugong but compared to them it was a giant, more than 25 feet in length. It was later named *Rhytina stelleri,* "Steller's wrinkled one," because its skin was not smooth, like other sirenians' skin, but corrugated.

Hunters who rushed to the Bering Islands after the *St. Peter's* voyage of discovery killed off most of the sea cows within thirty years. No more were reported after Aronnax's time.

"The animal's discovery was due in

the first place to man's perpetually questing spirit . . . , its destruction to the obverse side of this same human spirit," says Richard Carrigan in *Mermaids and Mastodons* (1957).

15. *infest the surface of the seas* While Aronnax's general *predictions* will prove valid, some of his specific *facts* will prove wrong.

Manatees have indeed been forced to move away from the big rivers of the world, and maybe that has caused an accumulation of vegetation where the rivers reach the sea. But yellow fever is not—as Aronnax thinks—produced by putrefaction of that uneaten vegetation. However, no one will suspect that yellow fever is caused by virus transmitted by mosquitoes until 1881. And no one will be able to prove it until 1900.

Talking of *"poulps"* and *"cuttle-fish,"* Aronnax doubtless means to include the squids. In the French, he talks of *poulpes* (*octopi, devilfish*) and *calmars* (*calamaries* or *giant squid*).

The squid population—as we noted earlier—was once controlled by sperm whales. Dr. Malcolm Clarke has estimated that a single eleven-ton sperm whale will eat 130 tons of squid a year. It has finally been demonstrated that *ambergris*—a mysterious substance found in sperm whales and once thought to be secreted by their own intestines—is actually an accumulation of the hard beaks of squid.

So Aronnax is right in predicting trouble when whales are wiped out. Marine ecologists are now concerned by a rise in squid since there are fewer sperm whales left to eat them.

This animal is . . . a living fishhook. . . . A species of sucking fish, the remora, pictured in D. S. Jordan's *A Guide to the Study of Fishes* (1905).

poulps, medusae, and cuttle-fish, they would become immense centres of infection, since their waves would not possess 'these vast stomachs that God had charged to infest the surface of the seas.' " **15**

However, without disputing these theories, the crew of the *Nautilus* took possession of half a dozen manatees. They provisioned the larders with excellent flesh, superior to beef and veal. This sport was not interesting. The manatees allowed themselves to be hit without defending themselves. Several thousand pounds of meat were stored up on board to be dried. On this day, a successful haul of fish increased the stores of the *Nautilus,* so full of game were these seas. [Some of these fish had heads that ended in an oval plaque or disc.] They were echeneides belonging to the third family of the malacopterygiens; their flattened discs were composed of transverse movable cartilaginous plates, by which the animal was enabled to create a vacuum, and so to adhere to any object like a cupping-glass. The remora that I had observed in the Mediterranean belongs to this species. But the one of which we are speaking was the echeneis osteochera, peculiar to this sea.

The fishing over, the *Nautilus* neared the coast. About here a number of sea-turtles were sleeping on the surface of the water. It would have been difficult to capture these precious reptiles, for the least noise awakens them, and their solid shell is proof against the harpoon. But the echeneis effects their capture with extraordinary precision and certainty. This animal is, indeed, a living fishhook, which would make the fortune of an inexperienced fisherman. The crew of the *Nautilus* tied a ring to the tail of these fish, so large as not to encumber their movements, and to this ring a long cord, lashed to the ship's side by the other end. The echeneids, thrown into the sea, directly began their game, and fixed themselves to the breast-plate of the turtles. Their tenacity was such, that they were [willing to be] torn rather than let go their hold. The men hauled them on board, and with them the turtles to which they adhered. They took also several cacouannes a yard long, which weighed 400 lbs. Their carapace covered with large horny plates, thin, transparent, brown, with white and yellow spots, fetch a good price in the market. Besides, they were excellent in an edible point of view, as well as the fresh turtles, which have an exquisite flavour. This day's fishing brought to a close our stay on the shores of the Amazon, and by nightfall the *Nautilus* had regained the high seas.

PART 2: CHAPTER XVIII

The Poulps

For several days the *Nautilus* kept off from the American coast. Evidently it did not wish to risk the tides of the Gulf of Mexico, or of the sea of the Antilles. [It was not a question of depth, for in those seas the average sounding is 1800 metres. It was more likely that the many islands and the many ships might have made Captain Nemo feel uncomfortable.]

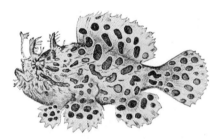

The frogfish of Caribbean seas, as pictured in D. S. Jordan's *A Guide to the Study of Fishes* (1905).

April 16th, we sighted Martinique and Guadaloupe from a distance of about thirty miles. I saw their tall peaks for an instant. The Canadian, who counted on carrying out his projects in the Gulf, by either landing, or hailing one of the numerous boats that coast from one island to another, was quite disheartened. Flight would have been quite practicable, if Ned Land had been able to take possession of the boat without the Captain's knowledge. But in the open sea it could not be thought of. The Canadian, Conseil, and I, had a long conversation on this subject. For six months we had been prisoners on board the *Nautilus*. We had travelled 17,000 leagues; and, as Ned Land said, there was no reason why it should not come to an end. [And now Ned made a proposal that was quite unexpected. He proposed that I ask the Captain, man-to-man, whether he really intended to keep us prisoners indefinitely. To me it seemed pointless to raise the question with Nemo.]

We could hope nothing from the Captain of the *Nautilus*, but only from ourselves. Besides, for some time past he had become graver, more retired, less sociable. He seemed to shun me. I met him rarely. Formerly, he was pleased to explain the submarine marvels to me; now, he left me to my studies, and came no more to the saloon. What change had come over him? For what cause? [I had done nothing to deserve this, and I could not blame myself. Was our presence on board beginning to be a burden or a nuisance to him? Even so, I held no illusions about his readiness to give us our freedom.

I asked Ned to let me think it over, because if we took such a step and we failed, it would certainly put the Captain on his guard. That would make our situation even more difficult, and it would make escaping impossible. Incidentally, I felt that I could not use our physical condition as an excuse. In spite of that awful ordeal under the ice barrier, all three of us were in good shape. Our nutritious diet, the salubrious sea air, the regularity of our routine, the even temperature in which we lived, all these circumstances kept us in good health.

Of course, it was Captain Nemo who profitted most from such a way of life. He had foresworn the life of the land, he was completely at home in the sea, it gave him all the elbow-room he needed, he could pursue that life of secrecy to which he seemed committed. But we had not foresworn humanity.]

For my part, I did not wish to bury with me my curious and novel studies. I had now the power to write the true book of the sea; and this book, sooner or later, I wished to see daylight. Then again, in the water by the Antilles, ten yards below the surface of the waters, by the open panels, what interesting products I had to enter on my daily notes! There were, among other zoophytes, those known under the name of physalis pelagica, a sort of large oblong bladder, with mother-of-pearl rays, holding out their membranes to the wind, and letting their blue tentacles float like threads of silk; charming medusae to the eye, real nettles to the touch, that distil a corrosive fluid.[1] There were also [among the articulata some] annelides, a yard and a half long, furnished with a pink horn, and with 1700 locomotive organs, that wind through the waters, and throw out in passing all the light of the solar spectrum. There were, in the fish category, some Malabar rays, enormous gristly things, ten feet long, weighing 600 pounds, the pectoral fin triangular in the midst of a slightly humped back, the eyes fixed in the extremities of the face, beyond the head, and which floated like weft,[2] and looked sometimes like an opaque shutter on our glass window. There were American balistae, which nature has only dressed in black and white; gobies, with yellow fins and prominent jaw; mackerel sixteen feet long, with short-pointed teeth, covered with small scales, belonging to the albicore species. Then, in swarms, appeared grey mullet, covered with stripes of gold from the head to the tail, beating their resplendent fins, like

1. *physalis pelagica . . . corrosive fluid* This animal is better known as the *Portuguese man-of-war*. It has a gas-filled float with a stiff central ridge that reaches above the surface and catches the wind. It really is not *an* animal but a whole *colony* of maybe 1000 creatures, none of which could live independently.

The tentacles of one such colony may extend 30 to 60 feet in the water: they are armed with stinging capsules. The venom these stingers eject—similar to the venom of the cobra—can kill a fish the size of an adult mackerel. The tentacles then contract and hoist the victim up to the many mouths of the colony.

Even a human being can be painfully injured by the Portuguese man-of-war. A swimmer entangled in the tentacles can react with shock and die in the water.

One little creature, as long as a finger, is immune to the venom. The Nomeus, or man-of-war fish, actually takes shelter among the tentacles.

2. *floated like weft* Verne says *like wreckage, like a stray*. And *weft* is archaic English for a *waif*.

masterpieces of jewellery, consecrated formerly to Diana, particularly sought after by rich Romans, and of which the proverb says, "Whoever takes them does not eat them." Lastly, pomacanthe dorees, ornamented with emerald bands, dressed in velvet and silk, passed before our eyes like Veronese lords; spurred spari passed with their pectoral fins; clupanodons fifteen inches long, enveloped in their phosphorescent light; mullet beat the sea with their large jagged tails; red vendaces seemed to mow the waves with their showy pectoral fins; and silvery selenes, worthy of their name, rose on the horizon of the waters like so many moons with whitish rays.

[My studies of new specimens of fish were ended as the *Nautilus* gradually dropped to the lower strata. The inclined planes took us down to 2000 and then 3500 metres. At such depths, the animal world was represented only by sea-lilies, starfish, charming pentacrines with medusa heads, their straight stalks holding a little chalice, some trochi, some "bleeding baby-teeth," and fissurellas, a huge species of coastal molluscs.]

April 20th, we had risen to a mean height of 1500 yards.[3] The land nearest us then was the archipelago of the Bahamas.. There rose high submarine cliffs, [walls formed by stones arranged like bricks, with many dark holes which our lantern beam could not penetrate. These rocks were] covered with large weeds, giant laminariae and fuci, a perfect espalier of hydrophytes worthy of a Titan world.

[Discussing these huge plants, Ned, Conseil, and I naturally talked about the giant animals of the sea, for whom this vegetation serves as food. But as I looked through the windows, the *Nautilus* being almost motionless, I could see amongst those tall plants only the main articulates of the division of the brachiourans: long-legged purple-blue crabs, and clios, the sea-butterflies of the Antilles.]

It was about eleven o'clock when Ned Land drew my attention to a formidable pricking, like the sting of an ant, which was produced by means of large sea-weeds.[4]

"Well," I said, "these are proper caverns for poulps, and I should not be astonished to see some of these monsters."

"What!" said Conseil; "cuttle-fish, real cuttle-fish, of the cephalopod class?"

"No," I said; "poulps of huge dimensions.[5] [But Ned might have been seeing things. There is nothing like that out there."

"Too bad," said Conseil. "I would like to come face to face with one of those poulps that can drag a ship down under. The ones called krak—"

. . . American balistae, which nature has only dressed in black and white. . . . Notice that Aronnax has now reported seeing triggerfish, or balistes, all the way from the Pacific to the Mediterranean and the Atlantic. The above picture of an American triggerfish is from D. S. Jordan's *A Guide to the Study of Fishes* (1905). "The first dorsal fin," says Jordan, "is composed of a short stout rough spine, with a smaller one behind it and usually a third so placed that by touching it the first spine may be set or released. This peculiarity gives the name of triggerfish as well as . . . *Balistes,* or crossbow shooter."

3. *mean height of 1500 yards* A mean *depth,* of course, and Verne says 1500 *meters* or about 1650 yards.

4. *by means of large sea-weeds* Oh, no! What Ned has noticed is a *formidable, swarming, wriggling movement out in those tall algae!* And the *sting of the ant* is Mercier Lewis's own strange contribution.

5. *poulps of huge dimensions* To Verne's original readers, this was an instant reminder of numerous appearances of giant squid that began in the 1860s.

6. *Krakens* As Ned's attitude indicates, these *krakens* were once thought to be products of the imagination. They were defined as "fabulous Scandinavian sea monsters" (the word *kraken* is Norwegian). But now, with the shrewdness of hindsight, we can see that the Scandinavian seafarers had actually spotted the kind of *giant sea squids* that would make some sixty or seventy documented appearances in the Atlantic and Mediterranean during Aronnax's lifetime.

"*Crock* will suffice," Ned cut in sarcastically.

"Krakens," **6** Conseil completed his sentence without regard to Ned's punning.]

"I will never believe that such animals exist," said Ned.

["Why not?" asked Conseil. "We believed in monsieur's narwhal!"

"And we were wrong!"

"But there are probably lots of people who still do believe in it!"

"Probably you are right," I agreed. "And I have learned my lesson. I will never believe in such monsters again until I have dissected them myself!"

"Does monsieur mean he does not believe in the existence of giant poulps?" Conseil asked.

"Who the devil ever did believe in them?" asked Ned.

"Many people, my friend."

"Not fishermen. Scientists, probably."

"Beg your pardon, Ned. Fishermen *and* scientists."]

"Well," said Conseil, with the most serious air in the world; "I remember perfectly to have seen a large vessel drawn under the waves by a cephalopod's arm."

"You saw that?" said the Canadian.

"Yes, Ned."

"With your own eyes?"

"With my own eyes."

"Where, pray, might that be?"

"At St. Malo," answered Conseil.

"In the port?" said Ned, ironically.

"No; in a church," replied Conseil.

"In a church!" cried the Canadian.

"Yes, friend Ned. In a picture representing the poulp in question."

"Good!" said Ned Land, bursting out laughing. ["Monsieur Conseil is putting one over on me."]

"He is quite right," I said. "I have heard of this picture; but the subject represented is taken from a legend, and you know what to think of legends in the matter of natural history. Besides, when it is a question of monsters, the imagination is apt to run wild. Not only is it supposed that these poulps can draw down vessels, but a certain Olaüs Magnus speaks of a cephalopod a mile long, that is more like an island than an animal. It is also said that the Bishop of Nidros was building an altar on an immense rock. Mass finished, the rock began to walk, and returned to the sea. The rock was a poulp."

["Is that all—I hope?" Ned said.]

"Another bishop, Pontoppidan, speaks also of a poulp on which a regiment of cavalry could manoeuvre."

["Bishops in those days," Ned explained, "knew some good yarns."]

"Lastly, the ancient naturalists speak of monsters whose mouths were like gulfs, and which were too large to pass through the Straits of Gibraltar."

["That story gets the prize," Ned said.]

"But how much is true of these stories?" asked Conseil.

"Nothing, my friends; at least of that which passes the limit of truth to get to fable or legend. Nevertheless, there must be some ground for the imagination of the storytellers. One cannot deny that poulps and cuttle-fish exist of a large species, inferior, however, to the cetaceans. Aristotle has stated the dimensions of a cuttle-fish as five cubits, or nine feet two inches. Our fishermen frequently see some that are more than four feet long. Some skeletons of poulps are preserved in the museums of Trieste and Montpelier, that measure two yards in length. Besides, according to the calculations of some naturalists, one of these animals, only six feet long, would have tentacles twenty-seven feet long. That would suffice to make a formidable monster."

"Do they fish for them in these days?" asked Ned.

"If they do not fish for them, sailors see them at least. One of my friends, Captain Paul Bos of Havre, has often affirmed that he met one of these monsters, of colossal dimensions, in the Indian seas. But the most astonishing fact, and which does not permit of the denial of the existence of these gigantic animals, happened some years ago, in 1861."

"What is the fact?" asked Ned Land.

"This is it. In 1861, to the north-east of Teneriffe, very nearly in the same latitude we are in now, the crew of the despatch-boat *Alector* perceived a monstrous cuttle-fish swimming in the waters. Captain Bouguer went near to the animal, and attacked it with harpoons and guns, without much success, for balls and harpoons glided over the soft flesh. After several fruitless attempts, the crew tried to pass a slip-knot round the body of the mollusc. The noose slipped as far as the caudal fins, and there stopped. They tried then to haul it on board, but its weight was so considerable that the tightness of the cord separated the tail from the body, and, deprived of this ornament, he disappeared under the water."

"Indeed! is that a fact?"

"An indisputable fact, my good Ned. They proposed to name this poulp 'Bouguer's cuttle-fish.' " 7

7. *this poulp 'Bouguer's cuttle-fish'* Bouguer's ship actually was the *Alecton,* named probably after Alecto, one of the Furies of Greek mythology. In the original, Aronnax notes that it was proposed to name this poulp *Bouguer's calmar,* that is, his *calamary* or *giant squid.*

What Aronnax does not tell his friends is that the *Alecton's* report was discredited by the French Academy. One Academician, Arthur Mangin, warned scientists against stories of creatures like "the giant squid, . . . existence of which would be some sort of contradiction of the great laws of harmony and equilibrium that rule over living nature. . . ." Mangin concluded that the *Alecton* crew had really grappled with a sea plant and had become victims of mass hysteria.

The Academy was soon proved guilty of carrying scientific skepticism too far. Just five years after Aronnax was telling this story, another calamary attacked some cod fishermen off Newfoundland. They chopped off one of its tentacles, which proved to be 19 feet long. Then in 1874 some herring fishermen caught an entire squid with a total length—trunk and tentacles—of 32 feet. Many fishermen reported similar sightings in those waters until about 1880. Then giant squid began making appearances in the Pacific. The biggest one has been found off New Zealand; total length, 57 feet.

"What length was it?" asked the Canadian.

"Did it not measure about six yards?" said Conseil, who, posted at the window, was examining again the irregular windings of the cliff.

"Precisely," I replied.

"Its head," rejoined Conseil, "was it not crowned with eight tentacles, that beat the water like a nest of serpents?"

"Precisely."

"Had not its eyes, placed at the back of its head, considerable development?"

"Yes, Conseil."

"And was not its mouth like a parrot's beak?"

"Exactly, Conseil."

"Very well! no offence to master," he replied, quietly; "if this is not Bouguer's cuttle-fish, it is, at least, one of its brothers."

I looked at Conseil. Ned hurried to the window.

"What a horrible beast!" he cried.

I looked in my turn, and could not repress a gesture of disgust. Before my eyes was a horrible monster, worthy to figure in the legends of the marvellous. It was an immense cuttle-fish, being eight yards long. It swam crossways in the direction of the *Nautilus* with great speed, watching us with its enormous staring green eyes. Its eight arms, or rather feet, fixed to its head, that have given the name of cephalopod to these animals, were twice as long as its body, and were twisted like the furies' hair. One could see the 250 air-holes on the inner side of the tentacles. [Some of these suckers, semi-discs, were sticking to the windows.] The monster's mouth, a horned beak like a parrot's, opened and shut vertically. Its tongue, a horned substance, furnished with several rows of pointed teeth, came out quivering from this veritable pair of shears. What a freak of nature, a bird's beak on a mollusc! Its spindle-like body formed a fleshy mass that might weigh 4000 to 5000 lbs.; the varying colour changing with great rapidity, according to the irritation of the animal, passed successively from livid grey to reddish brown. What irritated this mollusc? No doubt the presence of the *Nautilus,* more formidable than itself, and on which its suckers or its jaws had no hold.[8] Yet, what monsters these poulps are! What vitality the Creator has given them! What vigour in their movements! And they possess three hearts! Chance had brought us in presence of this cuttle-fish, and I did not wish to lose the opportunity of carefully studying this specimen of cephalopods. I overcame the horror that inspired me; and, taking a pencil, began to draw it.

8. *on which its suckers or its jaws had no hold* This is an acute observation, given the fact that so little was known about giant squid in Verne's day. Today it is common to find whales with numerous scars from these tooth-rimmed suckers. The *Nautilus,* the first steel cetacean they ever met, would surely irritate them. That, too—the fact that squid experience extreme emotions like irritation and fury—seems to be corroborated by Aronnax's successors.

It was an immense cuttle-fish. . . . Engraving from
the original edition (1870).

"Perhaps this is the same which the *Alector* saw," said
Conseil.

"No," replied the Canadian; "for this is whole, and the
other had lost its tail."

"That is no reason," I replied. "The arms and tails of these
animals are reformed by redintegration; **9** and, in seven years,
the tail of Bouguer's cuttle-fish has no doubt had time to
grow."

["Anyhow," Ned added, "if this one is not Bouguer's cuttle-
fish, then maybe it is one of those others."]

By this time other poulps appeared at the port light. I
counted seven. They formed a procession after the *Nautilus,*
and I heard their beaks gnashing against the iron hull. I
continued my work. These monsters kept in the water with
such precision, that they seemed immovable. [I could have
drawn their outline on the window. Of course, we were going
at a slow speed.**10**]

Suddenly the *Nautilus* stopped. A shock made it tremble in
every plate.

"Have we struck anything?" I asked.

"In any case," replied the Canadian, "we shall be free, for
we are floating."

9. *redintegration* The term now used
is *regeneration.*

10. *going at a slow speed* Again
Verne is working with remarkably
good information. Giant squid have
been "logged" at 12 knots, and Nemo
does seem to have been lazing all day
so far.

The *Nautilus* was floating, no doubt, but it did not move. A minute passed. Captain Nemo, followed by his lieutenant, entered the drawing-room. I had not seen him for some time. He seemed dull. Without noticing or speaking to us, he went to the panel, looked at the poulps, and said something to his lieutenant. The latter went out. Soon the panels were shut. The ceiling was lighted. I went towards the Captain.

"A curious collection of poulps?" I said. [Having put it that way, I felt like an amateur standing at the glass in the aquarium.]

"Yes, indeed, Mr. Naturalist," he replied; "and we are going to fight them, man to beast."

I looked at him. I thought I had not heard aright.

"Man to beast?" I repeated.

"Yes, sir. The screw is stopped. I think that the horny jaws of one of the cuttle-fish is entangled in the blades. That is what prevents our moving."

"What are you going to do?"

"Rise to the surface, and slaughter this vermin." **11**

"A difficult enterprise."

"Yes, indeed. The electric bullets are powerless against the soft flesh, where they do not find resistance enough to go off. But we shall attack them with the hatchet."

"And the harpoon, sir," said the Canadian, "if you do not refuse my help."

"I will accept it, Master Land."

"We will follow you," I said, and following Captain Nemo, we went towards the central staircase.

There, about ten men with boarding hatchets were ready for the attack. Conseil and I took two hatchets; Ned Land seized a harpoon. The *Nautilus* had then risen to the surface. One of the sailors, posted on the top ladder-step, unscrewed the bolts of the panels. But hardly were the screws loosed, when the panel rose with great violence, evidently drawn by the suckers of a poulp's arm. Immediately one of these arms slid like a serpent down the opening, and twenty others were above. With one blow of the axe, Captain Nemo cut this formidable tentacle, that slid wriggling down the ladder. Just as we were pressing one on the other to reach the platform, two other arms, lashing the air, came down on the seaman placed before Captain Nemo, and lifted him up with irresistible power. Captain Nemo uttered a cry, and rushed out. We hurried after him.

What a scene! The unhappy man, seized by the tentacle, and fixed to the suckers, was balanced in the air at the caprice

11. *slaughter this vermin* Nemo's emotional hatred for the giant squid seems odd for a man who is usually objective about natural phenomena. Perhaps these creatures, with their far-reaching tentacles, symbolize for him the power that the State has to interfere in the lives of its subjects.

12. *These words, spoken in French* This is the second time that a man on board the *Nautilus* has been put into such straits that he drops his guard and declares himself in language truer to his own nature.

of this enormous trunk. He rattled in his throat, he was stifled, he cried, "Help! help!" These words, *spoken in French,*12 startled me! I had a fellow-countryman on board, perhaps several! That heartrending cry! I shall hear it all my life. The unfortunate man was lost. Who could rescue him from that powerful pressure? However, Captain Nemo had rushed to the poulp, and with one blow of the axe had cut through one arm.13 His lieutenant struggled furiously against other monsters that crept on the flanks of the *Nautilus.* The crew fought with their axes. The Canadian, Conseil, and I, buried our weapons in the fleshy masses; a strong smell of musk penetrated the atmosphere. It was horrible!

For one instant, I thought the unhappy man, entangled with the poulp, would be torn from its powerful suction. Seven of the eight arms had been cut off. One only wriggled in the air, brandishing the victim like a feather. But just as Captain Nemo and his lieutenant threw themselves on it, the animal ejected a stream of black liquid [which these calamaries secrete in an abdominal sac]. We were blinded with it. When the cloud dispersed, the cuttle-fish had disappeared, and my unfortunate countryman with it. Ten or twelve poulps now invaded the platform and sides of the *Nautilus.* We rolled pell-mell into the midst of this nest of serpents, that wriggled on the platform in the waves of blood and ink.14 It seemed as though these slimy tentacles sprang up like the hydra's heads. Ned Land's harpoon, at each stroke, was plunged into the staring eyes of the cuttle-fish. But my bold companion was suddenly overturned by the tentacles of a monster he had not been able to avoid.

Ah! how my heart beat with emotion and horror! The formidable beak of a cuttle-fish was open over Ned Land. The unhappy man would be cut in two. I rushed to his succour. But Captain Nemo was before me; his axe disappeared between the two enormous jaws, and, miraculously saved, the Canadian, rising, plunged his harpoon deep into the triple heart of the poulp.15

"I owed myself this revenge!" 16 said the Captain to the Canadian.

Ned bowed without replying. The combat had lasted a quarter of an hour. The monsters, vanquished and mutilated, left us at last, and disappeared under the waves. Captain Nemo, covered with blood, nearly exhausted, [stood next to the deck lantern,] gazed upon the sea that had swallowed up one of his companions, and great tears gathered in his eyes.

In one emergency, Conseil was forced to abandon his language of formal distance, and now this unfortunate crewman forgets the artificial language of the *Nautilus* and appeals to his compatriots.

Verne did more than just plot carefully over a long distance: he developed *motifs* in a series of *echoes.*

13. *cut through one arm* The tentacles of these giant squid, it developed after Verne imagined this scene, can often grow to be the thickness of a man's thigh.

Verne's only serious technical error is that he gives the squid only eight tentacles. It's the *octo*pus that has eight; the squid is a *deca*pod, with two extra, somewhat longer tentacles, often with club-shaped ends. But when Verne was writing these lines, only one giant squid had been observed at all well—Bouguer's calamary—and the thrashing about reported in that episode was hardly conducive to accurate counting.

No, Bouguer's calamary could *not* have been an octopus. That creature seems to be a pacifist.

14. *waves of blood and ink* Verne calls it *India ink.* Artists in China and Japan have used it for centuries in their brush drawings. When it was introduced into Europe, it was called *sepia.* Aronnax, understandably, describes it as a *black liquid,* but under more objective circumstances, scientists like Ericson and Wollin say it is a "dark-brown fluid."

15. *the triple heart of the poulp* What Aronnax calls the triple heart is really three modified blood vessels; the squid does not have a heart in the true sense of the term.

16. *this revenge* Nemo does not mean *revenge* in our limited sense of the word. The French word *revanche* that Nemo and Ned have used on these occasions means, in their circumstances, *requital.*

"Now," Nemo is saying, *"I've paid you back."*

PART 2: CHAPTER XIX
The Gulf Stream [1]

1. *The Gulf Stream* Verne's early readers especially had a sentimental reaction to the very words "Gulf Stream." To them these words signified a miracle of nature that brought a wide "river" of warm water to heat northern Europe. Their awe was increased by Maury's lyric prose, which emphasizes divine purpose. Thus Europeans could bask in every reassurance that the entire globe was arranged for their benefit.

In this chapter, as throughout his *Twenty Thousand Leagues* journey, Aronnax is a disciple of Maury. And in the fringes of this chapter, we shall be obliged to indicate some severe modifications of the notion that it's the Stream that warms Europe.

2. *The Toilers of the Deep* How deftly Verne invokes the free association of his readers! When *Twenty Thousand Leagues* appeared, Verne's audience could see much more behind this casual allusion than now meets the eye.

Victor Hugo's *The Toilers of the Sea* (the usual English title) was published just three years before Aronnax's memoirs. It was still being hotly discussed for reasons both scientific and literary, both of which would now occur to Verne's audience:

(1) Hugo's plot depends partly on the existence of a giant *pieuvre* (octopus) lurking in an island cave in the English Channel. Zoologists, as Aron-

This terrible scene of the 20th of April none of us can ever forget. I have written it under the influence of violent emotion. Since then I have revised the recital; I have read it to Conseil and to the Canadian. They found it exact as to facts, but insufficient as to effect. To paint such pictures, one must have the pen of the most illustrious of our poets, the author of "The Toilers of the Deep." [2]

I have said that Captain Nemo wept while watching the waves; his grief was great. It was the second companion he had lost since our arrival on board, and what a death! That friend, crushed, stifled, bruised by the dreadful arms of a poulp, pounded by his iron jaws, would not rest with his comrades in the peaceful coral cemetery! In the midst of the struggle, it was the despairing cry uttered by the unfortunate man that had torn my heart. The poor Frenchman, forgetting his conventional language,[3] had taken to his own mother tongue, to utter a last appeal! Amongst the crew of the *Nautilus,* associated with the body and soul of the Captain, recoiling like him from all contact with men, I had a fellow countryman. Did he alone represent France in this mysterious association, evidently composed of individuals of divers nationalities? It was one of these insoluble problems that rose up unceasingly before my mind!

Captain Nemo entered his room, and I saw him no more for some time. But that he was sad and irresolute I could see by the vessel, of which he was the soul, and which received all his impressions. The *Nautilus* did not keep on in its settled course; it floated about like a corpse at the will of the waves. [The screw had been disentangled from the poulps. But the *Nautilus* rarely used its propeller.] It went at random. He could not tear himself away from the scene of the last struggle, from this sea that had devoured one of his men. Ten days passed thus. It was not till the 1st of May that the *Nautilus* resumed its northerly course, after having sighted the Bahamas at the mouth of the Bahama Channel. We were then following the current from the largest river to the sea, that has its banks, its fish, and its proper temperatures. I mean the Gulf Stream. It is really a river, that flows freely to the middle of the Atlantic, and whose waters do not mix with the ocean waters. It is a salt river, salt[i]er than the surrounding sea. Its mean depth is 1500 fathoms, its mean breadth ten miles.[4] In certain places the current flows with the speed of two miles and a half an hour. The body of its waters is more considerable than that of all the rivers in the globe.

[The true source of the Gulf Stream, as recognised by Commander Maury, its point of departure, so to speak, is located in the Bay of Biscay. There its waters, still lacking heat and colour, begin to take form. The Stream descends to the south along equatorial Africa, is warmed by the sun of the torrid zone, crosses the Atlantic, reaches Cape San Roque on the coast of Brazil, and divides into two branches, one of which is warmed still further by the Caribbean. Then the Stream—whose function it is to restore the balance between the extremes of temperature and to mix tropical with northern waters—takes on its stabilizing role. Attaining a "white

nax is well aware, had denied that such a giant mollusk could flourish there in modern times. Hugo's defenders actually had to explain his *pieuvre* as a kind of surrealist creature, to use today's term for it. The irony, of course, is that Aronnax has just rubbed elbows with a good dozen of these *pieuvres*. He has reminded his readers that Captain Bouguer's entire crew also square-danced with a *pieuvre* five years before Hugo "dreamed" one up.

(2) Hugo was also clobbered by critics for the density of his descriptions and his moralizing. Your present critic finds himself in that chorus. Having grown up in the time of Hemingway and Vonnegut, we have great love for the writer who *selects* and *suggests*. Hugo's prose sounds like a million afterthoughts, as though he had to restate every little notion in every possible way before he could advance his action one-half inch. But Verne, author of novels based on swift development of well-tuned plots, which he was obliged to turn out at the rate of two a year, admired and envied Hugo's leisurely approach.

And, of course, that part of the bourgeois Verne that could envy rebellion in others admired it in Hugo as in Nemo. Hugo wrote *The Toilers of the Sea,* a glorification of honest labor, while he was in self-imposed exile from the Second Empire.

3. *his conventional language* That is, the language the crewmen had agreed to use aboard the *Nautilus*. This artificial language was apparently Nemo's "scientific" version of the *lingua franca* that all maritime peoples know in the Mediterranean.

4. *mean breadth ten miles* Verne says its mean depth is *3,000 feet,* its mean breadth *sixty miles*. How much genius Verne had to have to shine through all that careless obfuscation!

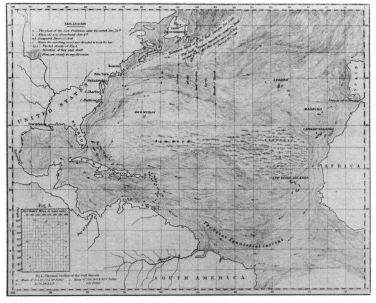

Maury's map of the "Gulf Stream and Drift" which appeared in his classic, *The Physical Geography of the Sea* (1855). To follow Aronnax's discussion of the Stream, start with the arrows north and west of Spain. As Aronnax is talking, the *Nautilus* is north of Cuba, where, as he says, the Stream *leaves the Gulf of Mexico.*

. . . mugilomores . . . shining with a soft light that Lacépède consecrated to . . . his wife. . . . Picture of striped mullet (*Mugil cephalus*) from D. S. Jordan's *A Guide to the Study of Fishes* (1905).

5. *beating the waters of the Atlantic* Maury was the first to try to explain the Atlantic currents as one vast regular system of circulation. Carrying on from Maury's great breakthrough, recent researchers see the system functioning differently.

D. B. Ericson and Goesta Wollin, of Lamont Geological Laboratory, say that the Gulf Stream is not so much a "broad river in the ocean" as it is a series of thin, swift currents overlapping each other "like shingles on a roof."

And Henry Stommel of Woods Hole Oceanographic Institution says the Stream is *not* an ocean river of warm water if by that is meant it flows between two bodies of cold water. He finds its temperature is *not* significantly higher than that of the water it passes to its right, the Sargasso Sea. He says the Gulf Stream is really a current along the junction of a mass of cold water to the left and a mass of warm water to the right. Finally, he says that it is not the Gulf Stream that gives Europe its mild climate. It is rather the westerly winds blowing across the hot Sargasso Sea that carry tropical warmth to the European land mass. He sums it all up by declaring that, in effect, the Gulf Stream and the Sargasso Sea are the same system.

6. *gristly . . . turbot* Verne says the most remarkable among the *cartilaginous* fish were these *rays*.

heat" in the Gulf of Mexico, it flows north along the American coast up to Newfoundland, is deflected by the cold current from the Davis Strait, and resumes its ocean route by following a rhumb line, a loxodromic curve. It divides into two arms in the area of the 43rd parallel. One, helped by the north-east trade winds, returns to the Bay of Biscay and the Azores. The other warms the seas of Ireland and Norway, meanders up to Spitzbergen, where its temperature drops to 4° Centigrade, and empties into the open polar sea.] It was on this ocean river that the *Nautilus* then sailed.

[Leaving the Bahama Channel, which is fourteen leagues wide and 350 metres deep, the Stream flows at about eight kilometres, or five miles, an hour. This speed tends to decrease as it heads north, a tendency that we hope will persist, for should its speed and direction be modified, the European climate would undergo changes of incalculable consequences.

Around noon, I was on the platform with Conseil. I was trying to acquaint him with all the pertinent facts about the Gulf Stream. When I had concluded my lecture, I invited him to put his hands into the current.

He did so, and was surprised to experience no sensation of either cold or heat.

"You see," I told him, "the temperature of the Stream, as it leaves the Gulf of Mexico, is just about the temperature of the human body. The Gulf Stream is a vast dispenser of warmth, making it possible for the European coasts to be decked with green. Maury puts it this way: If the heat of this current were fully utilized, it could keep a river of molten metal as big as the Amazon or the Missouri in a molten state."

Where we were, the current was running about seven feet per second. Its waters are so condensed that they rise higher than the surrounding ocean. There is a palpable difference between the Stream and the cold sea. Gulf Stream water is darker and saltier, its pure indigo standing out from the green water of the seas. The line of demarcation is so perceptible that when the *Nautilus* was off the Carolinas, her spur was in the Gulf Stream when her screw was still beating the waters of the Atlantic.5]

This current carried with it all kinds of living things. Argonauts, so common in the Mediterranean, were there in quantities. Of the gristly sort, the most remarkable were the turbot,6 whose slender tails form nearly the third part of the body, and that looked like large lozenges twenty-five feet long; also, small sharks a yard long, with large heads, short rounded muzzles, pointed teeth in several rows, and whose bodies seemed covered with scales. Among the bony fish I noticed some grey gobies, peculiar to these waters; black giltheads, whose iris shone like fire; sirenes a yard long, with large snouts thickly set with little teeth, that uttered little cries; blue coryphaenes, in gold and silver; parrots, like the rainbows of the ocean, that could rival in colour the most beautiful tropical birds; blennies with triangular heads; bluish rhombs destitute of scales; batrachoides covered with yellow transversal bands like a Greek τ; heaps of little gobies spotted with yellow; dipterodons with silvery heads and yellow tails; several specimens of salmon, mugilomores slender in shape, shining with a soft light that Lacépède consecrated to the service of his wife; and lastly, a beautiful fish, the American-knight,7 that, decorated with all the orders and ribbons, frequents the shores of this great nation, that esteems orders and ribbons so little.

I must add that, during the night, the phosphorescent waters of the Gulf Stream rivalled the electric power of our watch-light,8 especially in stormy weather that threatened us so frequently. May 8th, we were still crossing Cape Hatteras, at the height of North Carolina. The width of the Gulf Stream there is seventy-five miles, and its depth 210 yards. The *Nautilus* still went at random; all supervision seemed abandoned. I thought that, under these circumstances, escape would be possible. Indeed, the inhabited shores offered anywhere an easy refuge. The sea was incessantly ploughed by the steamers that ply between New York or Boston and the Gulf of Mexico, and overrun day and night by the little schooners coasting about the several parts of the American coast. We could hope to be picked up. It was a favourable opportunity, notwithstanding the thirty miles that separated the *Nautilus* from the coasts of the Union.

One unfortunate circumstance thwarted the Canadian's plans. The weather was very bad. We were nearing those shores where tempests are so frequent, that country of waterspouts and cyclones actually engendered by the current of the Gulf Stream. To tempt the sea in a frail boat was certain destruction. Ned Land owned this himself. He fretted, seized with nostalgia that flight only could cure.

"Master," he said that day to me, "this must come to an end. I must make a clean breast of it. This Nemo is leaving land and going up to the north. But I declare to you, I have had enough of the South Pole, and I will not follow him to the North."

"What is to be done, Ned, since flight is impracticable just now?"

7. *the American-knight* Aronnax must mean the *sea horse,* which looks like the knight on the chessboard. There are three species of sea horse common to the Atlantic waters that Aronnax is now describing. Possibly he has in mind here *the spotted sea horse.* With its coloring and its rings of bony plate, it could well suggest a bluff, horse-faced soldier bedecked with ribbons and medals.

8. *electric power of our watch-light* Ever since he was aboard the *Abraham Lincoln,* Aronnax has been fascinated with *phosphorescence,* and he has never exaggerated its *electric power.* Today's marine scientists say that in the deeps, *bioluminescence*—as they prefer to call it—can rival sunlight. Many different kinds of sea life collaborate to create this local illumination. They range from glowing microscopic organisms to luminescent fishes.

. . . *The American-knight* . . . A sea horse from the east coastal waters of the United States, as pictured in Bashford Dean's *Fishes, Living and Fossil* (1895).

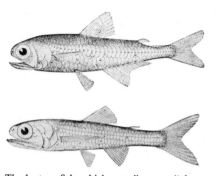

The lantern fish, which contributes to "phosphorescence" in the Gulf Stream. Its body
is covered with luminous dots. Engraving
from D. S. Jordan, *A Guide to the Study of
Fishes* (1905).

9. *perfect cold fish* Never in his
thirty-five years more of writing will
Verne surpass the complexity of characterization he achieves in this novel.
Here he sees human weakness and
human strength as partners.

Here Verne conceives of the liberal, open-minded professor as terrified by Ned's justified demands and
then taking it out on Conseil. In his
use of his servant as a scapegoat,
Aronnax goes so far as to picture
Conseil not as an individual but as a
vulgar type: the phlegmatic Fleming.
Notice how Verne will continue in
this chapter to portray Aronnax as a
man who can waver like a coward
and still be inspired by principle to
act with courage.

Aronnax will emerge as profoundly
human in this sense: the only courage
he has is the courage to beat down
his own cowardice.

"We must speak to the Captain," said he; "you said nothing
when we were in your native seas. I will speak, now we are in
mine. When I think that before long the *Nautilus* will be by
Nova Scotia, and that there near Newfoundland is a large bay,
and into that bay the St. Lawrence empties itself, and that the
St. Lawrence is my river, the river by Quebec my native town,
—when I think of this, I feel furious, it makes my hair stand
on end. Sir, I would rather throw myself into the sea! I will
not stay here! I am stifled!"

The Canadian was evidently losing all patience. His vigorous nature could not stand this prolonged imprisonment. His
face altered daily; his temper became more surly. I knew what
he must suffer, for I was seized with nostalgia myself. Nearly
seven months had passed without our having had any news
from land; Captain Nemo's isolation, his altered spirits,
especially since the fight with the poulps, his taciturnity, all
made me view things in a different light.

[No longer did I feel that enthusiasm I had had in those
early days on board. One had to be a Fleming like Conseil to
accept these circumstances, normally reserved for cetaceans
and other denizens of the deep. It was true, if that young man
had had gills in place of lungs, he would have made the
perfect cold fish! **9**]

"Well, sir?" said Ned, seeing I did not reply.

"Well, Ned! do you wish me to ask Captain Nemo his intentions concerning us?"

"Yes, sir."

"Although he has already made them known?"

"Yes; I wish it settled finally. Speak for me, in my name
only, if you like."

"But I so seldom meet him. He avoids me."

"That is all the more reason for you to go to see him."

["Well, I *will*, Ned."

"When?"

"When I see him."

"Professor, should I go and look for him?"

"No, Ned, I will do it. To-morrow I will—"

"To-day," Ned insisted.

"Well, to-day then." I did not want him to mess everything
up. Once he had left me I decided to compose myself, to ask
the Captain, to get it over with. I like to get things done rather
than have them hanging over my head.]

I went to my room. From thence I meant to go to Captain
Nemo's. It would not do to let this opportunity of meeting him
slip. I knocked at the door. No answer. I knocked again, then

turned the handle. The door opened, I went in. The Captain was there. Bending over his work-table, he had not heard me. Resolved not to go without having spoken, I approached him. He raised his head quickly, frowned, and said roughly, "You here! What do you want?"

"To speak to you, Captain."

"But I am busy, sir; I am working. I leave you at liberty to shut yourself up; cannot I be allowed the same?"

This reception was not encouraging; but I was determined to hear and answer everything.

"Sir," I said, coldly, "I have to speak to you on a matter that admits of no delay."

"What is that, sir?" he replied, ironically. "Have you discovered something that has escaped me, or has the sea delivered up any new secrets?"

We were at cross-purposes. But before I could reply, he showed me an open manuscript on his table, and said, in a more serious tone, "Here, M. Aronnax, is a manuscript written in several languages. It contains the sum of my studies of the sea; and, if it please God, it shall not perish with me. This manuscript, signed with my name, completed with the history of my life, will be shut up in a little insubmersible case. The last survivor of all of us on board the *Nautilus* will throw this case into the sea, and it will go whither it is borne by the waves."

This man's name! His history written by himself! His mystery would then be revealed some day.

"Captain," I said, "I can but approve of the idea that makes you act thus. The result of your studies must not be lost. But the means you employ seem to me to be primitive. Who knows where the winds will carry this case, and in whose hands it will fall? Could you not use some other means? Could not you, or one of yours——"

"Never, sir!" he said, hastily interrupting me.

"But I, and my companions are ready to keep this manuscript in store; and, if you will put us at liberty——"

"At liberty?" said the Captain, rising.

"Yes, sir; that is the subject on which I wish to question you. For seven months we have been here on board, and I ask you to-day, in the name of my companions, and in my own, if your intention is to keep us here always?"

"M. Aronnax, I will answer you today as I did seven months ago: Whoever enters the *Nautilus* must never quit it." 10

"You impose actual slavery on us!"

The barn-door skate, one of the largest of the skates, which Aronnax has seen in the western North Atlantic. It grows to nearly forty pounds in weight, more than two feet in length. Its wings are valuable for food. Engraving from Bashford Dean's *Fishes, Living and Fossil* (1895).

10. *must never quit it* Is this another reason for the despair of the myrmidons? Do they become galley slaves?

"Give it what name you please."

"But everywhere the slave has the right to regain his liberty."

"Who denies you this right? Have I ever tried to chain you with an oath?"

He looked at me with his arms crossed.

"Sir," I said, "to return a second time to this subject will be neither to your nor to my taste; but, as we have entered upon it, let us go through with it. I repeat, it is not only myself whom it concerns. Study is to me a relief, a diversion, a passion that could make me forget everything. Like you, I am willing to live obscure, in the frail hope of bequeathing one day, to future time, the result of my labours. [And I can admire you, sir, and I do. I can even follow in your path, willingly, at least in those areas of your life I can understand. And we have sometimes been touched by your suffering, sometimes inspired by your genius and courage. But at those times we had to stifle all expression of admiration that one naturally feels in the presence of someone noble and good: be he friend or foe. I guess it is that feeling—that we are really excluded from everything that is important to you—that feeling makes our situation unbearable. Even, recently, for me.]

"But it is otherwise with Ned Land. Every man, worthy of the name, deserves some consideration. Have you thought that love of liberty, hatred of slavery, can give rise to schemes of revenge in a nature like the Canadian's; that he could think, attempt, and try——"

I was silenced; Captain Nemo rose.

"Whatever Ned Land thinks of, attempts, or tries, what does it matter to me? I did not seek him! It is not for my pleasure that I keep him on board! As for you, M. Aronnax, you are one of those who can understand everything, even silence. I have nothing more to say to you. Let this first time you have come to treat of this subject be the last, for a second time I will not listen to you."

I retired. Our situation was critical. I related my conversation to my two companions.

"We know now," said Ned, "that we can expect nothing from this man. The *Nautilus* is nearing Long Island.**11** We will escape, whatever the weather may be."

But the sky became more and more threatening. Symptoms of a hurricane became manifest. The atmosphere was becoming white and misty. On the horizon fine streaks of cirrhous clouds were succeeded by masses of cumuli. Other low clouds passed swiftly by. The swollen sea rose in huge billows. The birds

11. *The Nautilus is nearing Long Island* The Nazis also picked the Long Island beaches as the best place to land men from a submarine.

disappeared, with the exception of the petrels, those friends of the storm. The barometer fell sensibly, and indicated an extreme tension of the vapours. The mixture of the storm glass was decomposed under the influence of the electricity that pervaded the atmosphere. The tempest burst on the 18th of May, just as the *Nautilus* was floating off Long Island, some miles from the port of New York. I can describe this strife of the elements for, instead of fleeing to the depths of the sea, Captain Nemo, by an unaccountable caprice, would brave it at the surface. The wind blew from the southwest at first. [It started at about 40 miles an hour and by three in the afternoon it was blowing at 50 miles an hour, the speed of a tempest.]

Captain Nemo, during the squalls, had taken his place on the platform. He made himself fast, to prevent being washed overboard by the monstrous waves. I had hoisted myself up, and made myself fast also, dividing my admiration between the tempest and this extraordinary man who was coping with it. The raging sea was swept by huge cloud-drifts, which were actually saturated with the waves. [No longer did I see any of those smaller waves that usually form in the spaces between the large ones. I could see only long murky undulations, so compact their crests never broke. They were coming taller and taller, pressing each other on.]

The *Nautilus,* sometimes lying on its side, sometimes standing up like a mast, rolled and pitched terribly. About five o'clock a torrent of rain fell, that lulled neither sea nor wind. The hurricane blew nearly forty leagues an hour. It is under these conditions that it overturns houses, breaks iron gates, displaces twenty-four pounders. However, the *Nautilus,* in the midst of the tempest, confirmed the words of a clever engineer, "There is no well-constructed hull that cannot defy the sea." This was not a resisting rock [which the storm could demolish; rather] it was a steel spindle, obedient and movable, without rigging or masts, that braved its fury with impunity. However, I watched these raging waves attentively. They measured fifteen feet in height, and 150 to 175 yards long, and their speed of propagation was thirty feet per second.[12] Their bulk and power increased with the depth of the water. [Here was proof of the role these waves play in Nature. They envelop air and carry it down to the bottom of the sea, where its oxygen nurtures life. It has been estimated that they can exert a pressure of three thousand kilogrammes, or about 6500 pounds, on every square foot of surface that they strike.] Such waves as these, at the Hebrides, have displaced a mass weighing

Oysters at different stages of growth, as pictured in *The American Cyclopaedia* (1873).

12. *thirty feet per second* Verne says these waves measured 15 *meters* or 50 feet in height, and their speed was 15 *meters* or 50 feet per second, *about half the speed of the wind.*

84,000 lbs. They are they which, in the tempest of December 23d, 1864, after destroying the town of Yeddo, in Japan, [travelled 450 miles per hour and] broke the same day on the shores of America.**13** The intensity of the tempest increased with the night. The barometer, as in 1860 at Reunion during a cyclone, fell seven-tenths at the close of day.**14** I saw a large vessel pass the horizon struggling painfully. She was trying to lie to under half steam, to keep up above the waves. It was probably one of the steamers of the line from New York to Liverpool, or Havre. It soon disappeared in the gloom. At ten o'clock in the evening the sky was on fire. The atmosphere was streaked with vivid lightning. I could not bear the brightness of it; while the Captain, looking at it, seemed to envy the spirit of the tempest. A terrible noise filled the air, a complex noise, made up of the howls of the crushed waves, the roaring of the wind, and the claps of thunder. The wind veered suddenly to all points of the horizon; and the cyclone, rising in the east, returned after passing by the north, west, and south, in the inverse course pursued by the circular storms of the southern hemisphere. Ah, that Gulf Stream! It deserves its name of the King of Tempests. It is that which causes those formidable cyclones, by the difference of temperature between its air and its currents. A shower of fire had succeeded the rain. The drops of water were changed to sharp spikes. One would have thought that Captain Nemo was courting a death worthy of himself, a death by lightning. As the *Nautilus,* pitching dreadfully, raised its steel spur in the air, it seemed to act as a conductor, and I saw long sparks burst from it. Crushed and without strength, I crawled to the panel, opened it, and descended to the saloon. The storm was then at its height. It was impossible to stand upright in the interior of the *Nautilus.* Captain Nemo came down about twelve. I heard the reservoirs filling by degrees, and the *Nautilus* sank slowly beneath the waves. Through the open windows in the saloon I saw large fish terrified, passing like phantoms in the water. Some were struck [dead by lightning] before my eyes. The *Nautilus* was still descending. I thought that at about eight fathoms deep we should find a calm. But no! the upper beds were too violently agitated for that. We had to seek repose at more than twenty-five fathoms in the bowels of the deep. But there, what quiet, what silence, what peace! Who could have told that such a hurricane had been let loose on the surface of that ocean? **15**

13. *broke the same day on the shores of America* The *tempest* Aronnax has in mind was really a *tsunami* or tidal wave sprung by an earthquake. And when it hit the United States, it helped some American scientists calculate the average depth of the Pacific.

The earthquake occurred in the morning of December 23 of 1854 (the error is the French printer's) near Jeddo, or Yeddo, now called Tokyo. Waves pounded Jeddo and the harbor for five hours, destroying most buildings, many ships, and many lives. Twelve hours later, seven waves smashed into San Francisco and San Diego.

The U.S. Coast and Geodetic Survey recorded them on tide gauges. A. D. Bache used a then-new law of physics that relates the speed of long waves to the depth of the water. He computed the average depth along the path of the tidal waves as 14,000 to 18,000 feet. Today's charts bear him out: they give the average depth as approximately 16,000 feet.

14. *seven-tenths at the close of day* The barometer dropped to 28 inches.

15. *hurricane . . . that ocean* This passage predicts an event that first occurred thirty years later. In 1898 two hundred ships were driven on to the coasts of Florida by a horrendous storm. Simon Lake, navigating the first submarine to operate successfully in the open sea, was caught in the same area. He submerged to calm and safety. When he reached port, he notified Jules Verne that the prediction in this passage had come true. Later, in his autobiography, Lake wrote: "Jules Verne was . . . the director-general of my life."

PART 2: CHAPTER XX

From Latitude 47° 24′
to Longitude[1] 17° 28′

In consequence of the storm, we had been thrown eastward once more. All hope of escape on the shores of New York or the St. Lawrence had faded away; and poor Ned, in despair, had isolated himself like Captain Nemo. Conseil and I, however, never left each other. I said that the *Nautilus* had gone aside to the east. I should have said (to be more exact) the north-east. For some days, it wandered first on the surface, and then beneath it, amid those fogs, so dreaded by sailors. [These fogs are generated by melting ice which saturates the air with vapour.] What accidents are due to these thick fogs! What shocks upon these reefs when the wind drowns the breaking of the waves! What collisions between vessels, in spite of their warning lights, whistles, and alarm bells! And the bottoms of these seas look like a field of battle, where still lie all the conquered of the ocean; some old and already encrusted, others fresh and reflecting from their iron bands and copper-plates the brilliancy of our lantern.

[Many of those vessels had gone down with all hands—including immigrants—around those places marked as dangerous on the navigation charts: Cape Race, St. Paul Island, Belle Island Strait, the estuary of the St. Lawrence! In the last few years alone, how many victims have been listed in the disaster records of the Royal Mail, of Inman,[2] of Montreal: the *Solway*, the *Isis*, the *Paramatta*, the *Hungarian*, the *Canadian*, the *Anglo-Saxon*, the *Humboldt*, the *United States*—all run aground; the *Arctic* and the *Lyonais*, sunk in collisons; the *President*, the *Pacific*, and the *City of Glasgow*, lost for reasons unknown. And now I saw all their dismal remains through the windows of the *Nautilus*.]

On the 15th of May we were at the extreme south of the Bank of Newfoundland. This bank consists of alluvia, or large

1. *From Latitude . . . to Longitude* A line of latitude crosses a line of longitude at just one place. You can't go *from* it *to* it! And so naturally Verne's original chapter title reads: *At Latitude 47° 24′ and Longitude 17° 28′.*

Mercier Lewis's error is almost as incredible as the fact that in many editions it still stands, in big capital letters at the head of the chapter, uncorrected! In some editions, it *has* been corrected, raising this question: Why didn't the discovery of *this* gigantic faux pas lead editors to suspect there might be others?

2. *Royal Mail, of Inman* These were magic names in the nineteenth cen-

William Inman (1825–1881), as pictured in *The Atlantic Ferry* (1893) by the British naval architect, A. J. Maginnis.

tury. The great Royal Mail Steam Packet Co. had started in 1838 in somewhat comic-opera style. All their officers were Royal Navy and they wore their swords on duty! The real name of the Inman Line was the Liverpool, New York, and Philadelphia Steamship Co. It was launched in 1850 by William Inman, who deliberately catered to the immigrant trade. He and his wife once traveled steerage just to see what the immigrants' lot on shipboard was like.

3. *or lump-fish . . . other fishes* Aronnax is so eager to get in his crack about the unusual sexual habits of the lumpfish that he overlooks another interesting characteristic of the *Cyclopterus lumpus.* Its two ventral fins are united to form a suction disk. Thus the lumpfish can attach itself to a rock and wait for the currents to bring its prey to it.

The crew . . . had trouble with this sea-scorpion. Illustration from *The American Cyclopaedia* (1873), which called the bull-head "the favorite food of the Greenlanders, though rarely if ever eaten by us."

4. *Eleven million* Actually it is Aronnax who is exaggerating, unwittingly.

Today naturalists say that a *large* female cod might produce as many as nine million eggs, but the *typical* female "only" about one million.

heaps of organic matter, brought either from the Equator by the Gulf Stream, or from the North Pole by the counter current of cold water which skirts the American coast. There also are heaped up those erratic blocks which are carried along by the broken ice; and close by, a vast charnel-house of molluscs or zoophytes, which perish here by millions. The depth of the sea is not great at Newfoundland—not more than some hundreds of fathoms; but towards the south is a depression of 1500 fathoms. There the Gulf Stream widens. It loses some of its speed and some of its temperature, but it becomes a sea.

[Among the fish that the *Nautilus* frightened as she passed through, I will mention the cyclopterus, or lump-fish, a metre long, with a black back, an orange belly, and a custom of marital fidelity seldom imitated by other fishes; **3** an unernack, an emerald moray, good to the palate; karracks, with big eyes and a dog's head; blennies, oviparous like the reptiles; black gobies or gudgeons about four inches long; silver grenadiers with long tails—fast fish that had ventured away from their northern habitat.

Our nets also dragged in a hardy, audacious fish, muscled and spiny, a veritable scorpion two or three metres long, the mortal enemy of blennies, cod-fish, and salmon. It was the bull-head of the north seas, with a brown, gnarled body and reddish fins. The crew of the *Nautilus* had trouble with this sea-scorpion. Thanks to the shape of its gill-covers, it can prevent its lungs from drying out in the air, and so it can live for some time out of water.

And for the record, I will cite too some bosquians, little fish that often trail after ships in the northern seas; sharp-snouted bleaks indigenous to the north Atlantic; hog-fish; and gadidae, represented by their main species, the cod, which I could now observe in their favourite waters, off the Grand Banks. Cod might well be called mountain-fish, for Newfoundland is actually a submarine mountain. As the *Nautilus* parted their thick ranks, Conseil exclaimed:

"What! Those are cod! I always thought cod were flat, like flounder or plaice!"

"Naive boy! You've seen cod only in the fish store where they have been opened and spread flat. In the sea, they have a spindle shape perfectly suited for swift movement."

"If monsieur says so, it is true. But what crowds!"

"Yes, and they would be even more numerous if it were not for hog-fish and men. Do you know how many eggs are found in one female?"

"I will exaggerate," Conseil said. "Five hundred thousand."

"Eleven million,**4** my friend."

"I cannot admit that until I have counted them myself."

"It would be easier for you to take my word for it. French, English, American, Danish, and Norwegian fishermen catch cod by the thousands. They are consumed in prodigious quantities. If it were not for their astonishing fecundity, the sea would soon be cleared of cod. In England and America alone, there are 5000 ships manned by 75,000 cod-fishermen. Each ship returns with about 40,000 fish, or twenty-five million cod. In Norway, it is a similar story."

"I will not count them, I will trust monsieur. But may I venture one observation?"

"Of course."

"If every egg hatched,[5] four cod could supply England, America, and Norway."

We were moving along the bottom of the Grand Banks. I could see the long lines, each one fitted with 200 fish-hooks, that each boat puts down by the dozens. Each line was held down by a small grappling anchor and was held up at the surface by a floating cork buoy. The *Nautilus* had to manoeuvre skilfully through that network! [6]

Soon we put those frequented waters behind us as we headed toward the 42d parallel, the latitude of St. John in Newfoundland and of Heart's Content, where the Atlantic Cable terminates. Now the *Nautilus* swung east, as if to follow the "telegraph plateau" on which the cable rests and where numerous depth-soundings had made it possible to map the floor with precision.]

It was on the 17th of May, about 500 miles from Heart's Content, at a depth of more than 1400 fathoms, that I saw the electric cable lying on the bottom. Conseil, to whom I had not mentioned it, thought at first that it was a gigantic sea-serpent. But I undeceived the worthy fellow, and by way of consolation related several particulars in the laying of this cable. The first one was laid in the years 1857 and 1858; but, after transmiting about 400 telegrams, would not act any longer. In 1863, the engineers constructed another one, measuring 2000 miles in length, and weighing 4500 tons, which was embarked on the *Great Eastern*.[7] This attempt also failed.

On the 25th of May the *Nautilus,* being at a depth of more than 1918 fathoms, was on the precise spot where the rupture occurred which ruined the enterprise. It was within 638 miles of the coast of Ireland; and at half-past two in the afternoon, they discovered that communication with Europe had ceased. The electricians on board resolved to cut the cable before fishing it up, and at eleven o'clock at night they had recovered the damaged part. They made another point and spliced it,

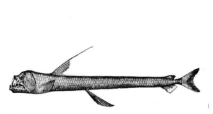

We were moving along the bottom of the Grand Banks, home of viper fishes like this one pictured in *A Guide to the Study of Fishes* (1905) by D. S. Jordan.

5. *If every egg hatched* Only one or two of a million cod eggs ever become adult fish.

6. *that network* Today steam trawlers use nets. As a result the cod population is on the decline.

7. *embarked on the Great Eastern* The *Great Eastern* was the only ship afloat big enough to lay all the cable in one trip. But she had to "fail" in the passenger service before she could be made available—for a fraction of her cost—for the cable-laying project.

She was 692 feet long, with a beam of 83 feet. She was equipped with *three modes of motive power:* a 24-foot propeller, two 258-foot paddle wheels, and 6500 square yards of canvas! She had six masts and five funnels. She was designed to accommodate 4000 passengers. She cost a fortune.

But she was dogged by bad luck and by that superstition that follows bad luck in maritime life. Her first of many accidents occurred during her launching. It took weeks to extricate her from that mishap. She was too big for most ports and denied entrance to many others. She rarely signed on more than 400 passengers. She changed owners as she drained each of them of their resources, and was then sold to Cyrus Field.

The ship Field had used in his 1857 and 1858 layings had been able to carry only half the cable, so the *Great Eastern* was a bonanza to him. He remodeled her, removing one mast and one funnel during the years that he owned her.

8. *goodwill towards men* After she had made history paying out the Atlantic cable, the *Great Eastern* was tried out again as a passenger steamer. And, by lovely coincidence, when Paul and Jules Verne boarded her in London in March 1867, they discovered that Cyrus West Field, *the bold promoter* and ex–paper salesman, was on the passenger list. During the two-week voyage to New York, Verne interviewed Field several times. When Field's men had grappled for the ends of the snapped cable—Verne asked— what kinds of marine life had they dredged up? Had they been surprised by any deep channels or submarine mountains not mentioned by Maury? How had currents affected their operations?

Verne was one of the earliest creative writers to use interviewing as part of literary research. He made friends with the sailors. He was not embarrassed to ask silly questions. Had whales ever attacked any ship they had served on? What was it like to fall overboard? Officers showed Verne through the two huge engine rooms—one for the propeller engines, one for the paddle engine. He filled a notebook with details about the giant ship and the open sea. For example, he stood on deck peering into a dense fog as the *Great Eastern* spent anxious hours edging past a field of icebergs. He studied a wrecked merchant ship drifting in the mid-Atlantic. He attended a sea burial of a sailor killed by a falling pulley (one of the *Great Eastern*'s continual mishaps!). He noted how "corpulent Americans" loved to sit on deck in rocking chairs. In short, that notebook became a major source for both *Twenty Thousand Leagues* (1870) and *A Floating City* (1871).

and it was once more submerged. But some days after it broke again, and in the depths of the ocean could not be recaptured. The Americans, however, were not discouraged. Cyrus Field, the bold promoter of the enterprise, as he had sunk all his own fortune, set a new subscription on foot, which was at once answered, and another cable was constructed on better principles. The bundles of conducting wires were each enveloped in gutta-percha, and protected by a wadding of hemp, contained in a metallic covering. The *Great Eastern* sailed on the 13th of July, 1866. The operation worked well. But one incident occurred. Several times in unrolling the cable they observed that nails had been recently forced into it, evidently with the motive of destroying it. Captain Anderson, the officers, and engineers, consulted together, and had it posted up that if the offender was surprised on board, he would be thrown without further trial into the sea. From that time the criminal attempt was never repeated.

On the 23d of July the *Great Eastern* was not more than 500 miles from Newfoundland, when they telegraphed from Ireland news of the armistice concluded between Prussia and Austria after Sadowa. On the 27th, in the midst of heavy fogs, they reached the port of Heart's Content. The enterprise was successfully terminated; and for its first despatch, young America addressed old Europe in these words of wisdom so rarely understood—"Glory to God in the highest, and on earth peace, goodwill towards men." **8**

I did not expect to find an electric cable in its primitive state, such as it was on leaving the manufactory. The long serpent, covered with the remains of shells, bristling with foraminiferae, was encrusted with a strong coating which served as a protection against all boring molluscs. It lay quietly sheltered from the motions of the sea, and under a favourable pressure for the transmission of the electric spark which passes from Europe to America in .32 of a second. Doubtless this cable will last for a great length of time, for they find that the gutta-percha covering is improved by the sea-water. Besides, on this level, so well chosen, the cable is never so deeply submerged as to cause it to break. The *Nautilus* followed it to the lowest depth, which was more than 2212 fathoms, and there it lay without any anchorage; and then we reached the spot where the accident had taken place in 1863. The bottom of the ocean then formed a valley about 100 miles broad, in which Mont Blanc might have been placed without its summit appearing above the waves. This valley is closed at the east by a perpendicular wall more than 2000 yards high. We arrived there on the 28th of May, and the *Nautilus* was then not more than 120 miles from Ireland.

Was Captain Nemo going to land on the British Isles? No. To my great surprise he made for the south, once more coming back towards European seas. In rounding the Emerald Isle, for one instant I caught sight of Cape Clear, and the light which guides the thousands of vessels leaving Glasgow or Liverpool. An important question then arose in my mind. Did the *Nautilus* dare entangle itself in the English Channel? Ned Land, who had reappeared since we had been nearing land, did not cease to question me. How could I answer? Captain Nemo remained invisible. After having shown the Canadian a glimpse of American shores, was he going to show me the coast of France?

But the *Nautilus* was still going southward. On the 30th of May, it passed in sight of the Land's End, between the extreme point of England and the Scilly Isles, which were left to starboard. If he wished to enter the English Channel he must go straight to the east. He did not do so.

During the whole of the 31st of May, the *Nautilus* described a series of circles on the water, which greatly interested me. It seemed to be seeking a spot it had some trouble in finding. At noon, Captain Nemo himself came to work the ship's log. He spoke no word to me, but seemed gloomier than ever. What could sadden him thus? Was it his proximity to European shores? Had he some recollections of his abandoned country? If not, what did he feel? Remorse or regret? For a long while this thought haunted my mind, and I had a kind of presentiment that before long chance would betray the Captain's secrets.

The next day, the 1st of June, the *Nautilus* continued the same process. It was evidently seeking some particular spot in the ocean. Captain Nemo took the sun's altitude as he had done the day before. The sea was beautiful, the sky clear. About eight miles to the east, a large vessel could be discerned on the horizon. No flag fluttered from its mast, and I could not discover its nationality. Some minutes before the sun passed the meridian, Captain Nemo took his sextant, and watched with great attention. The perfect rest of the water greatly helped the operation. The *Nautilus* was motionless; it neither rolled nor pitched.

I was on the platform when the altitude was taken, and the Captain pronounced these words—"It is here."

He turned and went below. Had he seen the vessel which was changing its course and seemed to be nearing us? I could

The *Great Eastern* as she was pictured in the original edition of Verne's *A Floating City* (1871). Was she unpopular among maritime peoples because she was not beautiful, as ships were expected to be?

9. *in Chesapeake Bay* Nemo's mere mention of the operation has more meaning for the Frenchman Aronnax than for the typical American reader because (1) in Europe this engagement is (justifiably) regarded as a major naval battle between England and France and (2) Frenchmen know world (and even American) history very, very well.

Admiral François Joseph Paul, comte de Grasse, commander of a French force of 28 ships-of-the-line and 3500 troops, had orders to co-operate with General Washington in a joint sea-land operation. De Grasse anchored in Chesapeake Bay before the British fleet arrived there on September 5, 1781. In a series of maneuvers over several days, de Grasse's fleet finally gained control of Virginia waters. Thus he helped decide the outcome of the land Battle of Yorktown and the American Revolution.

It was widely believed at the time that the overall campaign plan was Washington's, and so he gained world renown as a strategist. Actually the plan was the work of Jean Baptiste Donatien de Vimeur, comte de Rochambeau, who commanded 6000 French troops at Yorktown.

10. *Prair[i]al of the second year* Prairial was "the month of the pasture" (May 20 to June 18) or the ninth month in the French Revolutionary calendar. The "second year" was Year II in that calendar, or 1794. Nemo's knowing the Revolutionary calendar so well is another definite clue to his sympathies. As Nemo told Aronnax earlier, he had studied in Paris.

11. *Avenger! A good name* Here Nemo the romantic hero is setting the stage for a scene of vast symbolic proportions.

Of course, Nemo *has* seen what Aronnax called *the large vessel . . . on the horizon,* with no flag, *which was changing its course and seemed to be nearing* the submarine. So everything here takes on multiple significance. The *Avenger* fought in *two great revolutions:* the American and the French. But in both revolutions it fought *against the British.*

Notice, too, that Nemo says the French changed the name of the *Marseillais* but does not say what the new name was. And so Aronnax is forced to figure it out and to be the first to give voice to the phrase: "The *Avenger!"* Thus Nemo briefs Aronnax on the meanings of the coming action.

not tell. I returned to the saloon. The panels closed, I heard the hissing of the water in the reservoirs. The *Nautilus* began to sink, following a vertical line, for its screw communicated no motion to it. Some minutes later it stopped at a depth of more than 420 fathoms, resting on the ground. The luminous ceiling was darkened, then the panels were opened, and through the glass I saw the sea brilliantly illuminated by the rays of our lantern for at least half a mile round us.

I looked to the port side, and saw nothing but an immensity of quiet waters. But to starboard, on the bottom appeared a large protuberance, which at once attracted my attention. One would have thought it a ruin buried under a coating of white shells, much resembling a covering of snow. Upon examining the mass attentively, I could recognize the ever thickening form of a vessel bare of its masts, which must have sunk. It certainly belonged to past times. This wreck, to be thus encrusted with the lime of the water, must already be able to count many years passed at the bottom of the ocean.

What was this vessel? Why did the *Nautilus* visit its tomb? Could it have been aught but a shipwreck which had drawn it under the water? I knew not what to think, when near me in a slow voice I heard Captain Nemo say—

"At one time this ship was called the *Marseillais.* It carried seventy-four guns, and was launched in 1762. In 1778, the 13th of August, commanded by La Poype-Vertrieux, it fought boldly against the *Preston.* In 1779, on the 4th of July, it was at the taking of Granada, with the squadron of Admiral Estaing. In 1781, on the 5th of September, it took part in the battle of Comte de Grasse, in Chesapeake Bay.[9] In 1794, the French Republic changed its name. On the 16th of April, in the same year, it joined the squadron of Villaret Joyeuse, at Brest, being entrusted with the escort of a cargo of corn coming from America, under the command of Admiral Van Stabel. On the 11th and 12th Prair[i]al of the second year,[10] this squadron fell in with an English vessel. Sir, to-day is the 13th Prair[i]al, the 1st of June, 1868. It is now seventy-four years ago, day for day on this very spot, in latitude 47° 24', longitude 17° 28', that this vessel, after fighting heroically, losing its three masts, with the water in its hold, and the third of its crew disabled, preferred sinking with its 356 sailors to surrendering; and nailing its colours to the poop, disappeared under the waves to the cry of 'Long live the Republic!' "

"The *Avenger!"* I exclaimed.

"Yes, sir, the *Avenger!* A good name!" **11** muttered Captain Nemo, crossing his arms.

PART 2: CHAPTER XXI

A Hecatomb[1]

The way of describing this unlooked-for scene, the history of the patriotic ship, told at first so coldly, and the emotion with which this strange man pronounced the last words, the name of the *Avenger,* the significance of which could not escape me, all impressed itself deeply on my mind. My eyes did not leave the Captain; who, with his hand stretched out to sea, was watching with a glowing eye the glorious wreck. Perhaps I was never to know who he was, from whence he came, or where he was going to, but I saw the man moved, and apart from the savant. It was no common misanthropy which had shut Captain Nemo and his companions within the *Nautilus,* but a hatred, either monstrous or sublime, which time could never weaken. Did this hatred still seek for vengeance? The future would soon teach me that. But the *Nautilus* was rising slowly to the surface of the sea, and the form of the *Avenger* disappeared by degrees from my sight. Soon a slight rolling told me that we were in the open air. At that moment a dull boom was heard. I looked at the Captain. He did not move.

"Captain?" said I.

He did not answer. I left him and mounted the platform. Conseil and the Canadian were already there.

"Where did that sound come from?" I asked.

"It was a gunshot," replied Ned Land.

I looked in the direction of the vessel I had already seen. It was nearing the *Nautilus,* and we could see that it was putting on steam. It was within six miles of us.

"What is that ship, Ned?"

"By its rigging, and the height of its lower masts," said the Canadian, "I bet she is a ship of war. May it reach us; and, if necessary, sink this cursed *Nautilus.*"

1. *A Hecatomb* Again, Verne's chapter title is calculated to create suspense. In the ancient world a *hecatomb* was a *ritual sacrifice* of, say, a hundred or more oxen. By its very nature, it was a great, solemn occasion that could be staged only by an important leader. And to *sacrifice* meant to *make* [something] *sacred.* A community could make peace with the gods—after some great offense against the nature of things—by *sacrificing the criminals.*

We sense that Nemo is already involved in dramatic ritual because of the tableau he has just staged on the ocean floor. *Just what was the great offense against the nature of things? Who are the criminals to be sacrificed?*

Such are the questions that Verne's nineteenth-century readers—well versed in classical lore—would have in mind as they hit this page.

"Friend Ned," replied Conseil, "what harm can it do to the *Nautilus?* Can it attack it beneath the waves? Can it cannonade us at the bottom of the sea?"

"Tell me, Ned," said I, "can you recognize what country she belongs to?"

The Canadian knitted his eyebrows, dropped his eyelids, and screwed up the corners of his eyes, and for a few moments fixed a piercing look upon the vessel.

"No, sir," he replied; "I cannot tell what nation she belongs to, for she shows no colours. But I can declare she is a man-of-war, for a long pennant flutters from her main-mast."

For a quarter of an hour we watched the ship which was steaming towards us. I could not, however, believe that she could see the *Nautilus* from that distance; and still less, that she could know what this submarine engine was. Soon the Canadian informed me that she was a large armoured two-decker ram.[2] A thick black smoke was pouring from her two funnels. Her closely-furled sails were stopped to her yards. She hoisted no flag at her mizzen-peak. The distance prevented us from distinguishing the colours of her pennant, which floated like a thin ribbon. She advanced rapidly. If Captain Nemo allowed her to approach, there was a chance of salvation for us.

"Sir," said Ned Land, "if that vessel passes within a mile of us I shall throw myself into the sea, and I should advise you to do the same."

I did not reply to the Canadian's suggestion, but continued watching the ship. Whether English, French, American, or Russian, she would be sure to take us in if we could only reach her.

["Monsieur might well recall," Conseil said, "that we two have had some experience in swimming. He could rely on me to help him reach that ship. That is, if he decides to follow Ned."]

Presently a white smoke burst from the fore part of the vessel; some seconds after the water, agitated by the fall of a body, splashed the stern of the *Nautilus,* and shortly afterwards a loud explosion struck my ear.

"What! they are firing at us!" I exclaimed.

["More power to them," Ned murmured.]

"Well, they obviously do not see us as shipwrecked sailors clinging to wreckage and waiting to be rescued."

"If it does not displease monsieur—Oh my!" Conseil stopped to wipe away the water splashed on him by another shell.]

2. *a large armoured two-decker ram* The Union Navy has demonstrated, in the American Civil War, the value of the *ram* as a weapon. And so most large naval vessels are equipped with rams at the time that Aronnax is writing. His original audience would surely recall that in 1866, the Austrian Admiral Wilhelm von Tegetthof won the Battle of Vis by ramming the Italian flagship. Of course, we already know that the "beak" or spur is the only large offensive weapon that Nemo packs.

Most navies will abandon the ram by 1900. One good reason will be that in fleet maneuvers in 1875 and again in 1893 the Royal Navy will sink its own ships through accidental ramming!

"So please you, sir," said Ned, "they have recognised the unicorn, and they are firing at us." **3**

"But," I exclaimed, "surely they can see that there are men in the case?"

"It is, perhaps, because of that," replied Ned Land, looking at me.

A whole flood of light burst upon my mind. Doubtless they knew now how to believe the stories of the pretended monster. No doubt, on board the *Abraham Lincoln,* when the Canadian struck it with the harpoon, Commander Farragut had recognized in the supposed narwhal a submarine vessel, more dangerous than a supernatural cetacean. Yes, it must have been so; and on every sea they were now seeking this engine of destruction. Terrible indeed! if, as we supposed, Captain Nemo employed the *Nautilus* in works of vengeance. On the night when we were imprisoned in that cell, in the midst of the Indian Ocean, had he not attacked some vessel? The man buried in the coral cemetery, had he not been a victim to the shock caused by the *Nautilus?* Yes, I repeat it, it must be so. One part of the mysterious existence of Captain Nemo had been unveiled; and, if his identity had not been recognized, at least, the nations united against him were no longer hunting a chimerical creature, but a man who had vowed a deadly hatred against them. All the formidable past rose before me. Instead of meeting friends on board the approaching ship, we could only expect pitiless enemies. But the shot rattled above us. Some of them struck the sea and ricochetted, losing themselves in the distance. But none touched the *Nautilus.* The vessel was not more than three miles from us. In spite of the serious cannonade, Captain Nemo did not appear on the platform; but, if one of the conical projectiles had struck the shell of the *Nautilus,* it would have been fatal. The Canadian then said, "Sir, we must do all we can to get out of this dilemma. Let us signal them. They will then, perhaps, understand that we are honest folks."

Ned Land took his handkerchief to wave in the air; but he had scarcely displayed it, when he was struck down by an iron hand, and fell in spite of his strength, upon the deck.

"Fool!" exclaimed the Captain, "do you wish to be pierced by the spur of the *Nautilus* before it is hurled at this vessel?"

Captain Nemo was terrible to hear; he was still more terrible to see. His face was deadly pale, with a spasm at his heart. For an instant it must have ceased to beat. His pupils were fearfully contracted.**4** He did not *speak,* he *roared,* as, with his body thrown forward, he wrung the Canadian's shoul-

3. *they are firing at us* Verne wrote this speech for Conseil, who makes this un-Ned-like observation after wiping away the spray.

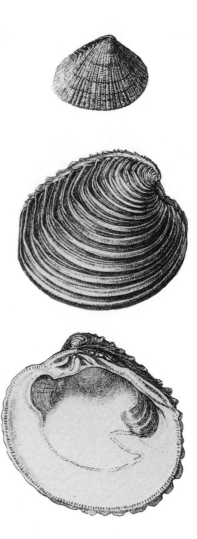

Engravings (here and on the following pages) from *A History of British Mollusca and their Shells* (1853) by Professor Edward Forbes, F.R.S., and Sylvanus Hanley.

4. *pupils were fearfully contracted* This is Aronnax the physician speaking.

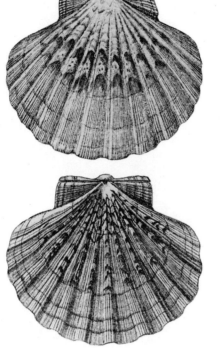

5. *hatred at the vessel nearing them* Not even a desperate need for fresh air can drive Nemo's men out on deck. But revenge will do it. Every detail in the Verne plot is calculated to add to characterization as well as to action.

6. *mingle with those of the Avenger* The romantic hero is quite accustomed to flinging speeches at people miles away or even at things or abstractions. Soon after this book becomes a best seller, Verne will take his yacht into the Mediterranean. On deck, one of his guests, the brilliant young deputy for Paris, Raoul Duval, will address a passionate speech to the Pillars of Hercules. Duval will utter his apostrophe in Volapük, an early artificial language.

Why doesn't Nemo use *his* artificial language in *his* apostrophes in this chapter? Apparently because his real audience is not his crew but Aronnax.

ders. Then, leaving him, and turning to the ship of war, whose shot was still raining around him, he exclaimed, with a powerful voice, "Ah, ship of an accursed nation, you know who I am! I do not want your colours to know you by! Look! And I will show you mine!"

And on the fore part of the platform Captain Nemo unfurled a black flag, similar to the one he had placed at the south pole. At that moment a shot struck the shell of the *Nautilus* obliquely, without piercing it; and, rebounding near the Captain, was lost in the sea. He shrugged his shoulders; and addressing me, said shortly, "Go down, you and your companions go down!"

"Sir," I exclaimed, "are you going to attack this vessel?"

"Sir, I am going to sink it."

"You will not do that?"

"I shall do it," he replied, coldly. "And I advise you not to judge me, sir. Fate has shown you what you ought not have seen. The attack has begun; go down."

"What is this vessel?"

"You do not know? Very well! So much the better! Its nationality to you, at least, will be a secret. Go down!"

We could but obey. About fifteen of the sailors surrounded the Captain, looking with implacable hatred at the vessel nearing them.**5** One could feel that the same desire of vengeance animated every soul. I went down at the moment another projectile struck the *Nautilus,* and I heard the Captain exclaim—

"Strike, mad vessel! Shower your useless shot! And then, you will not escape the spur of the *Nautilus*. But it is not here that you shall perish! I would not have your ruins mingle with those of the *Avenger!*" **6**

I reached my room. The Captain and his second had remained on the platform. The screw was set in motion, and the *Nautilus,* moving with speed, was soon beyond the reach of the ship's guns. But the pursuit continued, and Captain Nemo contented himself with keeping his distance.

About four in the afternoon, being no longer able to contain my impatience, I went to the central staircase. The panel was open, and I ventured on to the platform. The Captain was still walking up and down with an agitated step. He was looking at the ship, which was five or six miles to leeward.

He was going round it like a wild beast, and drawing it eastward, he allowed them to pursue. But he did not attack. Perhaps he still hesitated? I wished to mediate once more. But

I had scarcely spoken, when Captain Nemo imposed silence, saying—

"I am the law, and I am the judge! I am the oppressed, and there is the oppressor! Through him I have lost all that I loved, cherished, and venerated,—country, wife, children, father, and mother. I saw all perish! All that I hate is there! Say no more!" **7**

I cast a last look at the man-of-war, which was putting on steam, and rejoined Ned and Conseil.

"We will fly!" I exclaimed.

"Good!" said Ned. "What is this vessel?"

"I do not know; but whatever it is, it will be sunk before night. In any case, it is better to perish with it, than be made accomplices in a retaliation, the justice of which we cannot judge."

"That is my opinion too," said Ned Land, coolly. "Let us wait for night."

Night arrived. Deep silence reigned on board. The compass showed that the *Nautilus* had not altered its course. It was on the surface, rolling slightly. My companions and I resolved to fly when the vessel should be near enough either to hear us or to see us; for the moon, which would be full in two or three days, shone brightly. Once on board the ship, if we could not prevent the blow which threatened it, we could, at least we would, do all that circumstances would allow. Several times I thought the *Nautilus* was preparing for attack; but Captain Nemo contented himself with allowing his adversary to approach, and then fled once more before it.

Part of the night passed without any incident. We watched the opportunity for action. We spoke little, for we were too much moved. Ned Land would have thrown himself into the sea, but I forced him to wait. According to my idea, the *Nautilus* would attack the ship at her waterline,**8** and then it would not only be possible, but easy to fly.

At three in the morning, full of uneasiness, I mounted the platform. Captain Nemo had not left it. He was standing at the forepart near his flag, which a slight breeze displayed above his head. He did not take his eyes from the vessel. The intensity of his look seemed to attract, and fascinate, and draw it onward more purely than if he had been towing it. The moon was then passing the meridian. Jupiter was rising in the east. Amid this peaceful scene of nature, sky and ocean rivalled each other in tranquillity, the sea offering to the orbs of night the finest mirror they could ever have in which to

7. *Say no more* And Nemo need say no more. If he and his men have lost their country, then they are the victims of one of the conquering colonial powers. Their continued assaults on that power, terrible though they may be, at least make some sense now. *They are engaged in the kind of guerrilla warfare that the victims of foreign conquest—whether they be American Indians in 1843 or French* maquis *in 1943—consider justified.*

Now we can finally understand the statement by Jean Chesneaux that to Jules Verne, "heroism and nobility are to be found only in the ranks of anti-colonialism. . . ."

8. *at her waterline* In other words, at this point Aronnax assumes that the warship is armored only *above* the waterline.

reflect their image. As I thought of the deep calm of these elements, compared with all those passions brooding imperceptibly within the *Nautilus,* I shuddered.

The vessel was within two miles of us. It was ever nearing that phosphorescent light which showed the presence of the *Nautilus.* I could see its green and red lights, and its white lantern hanging from the large foremast. An indistinct vibration quivered through its rigging, showing that the furnaces were heated to the uttermost. Sheaves of sparks and red ashes flew from the funnels, shining in the atmosphere like stars.

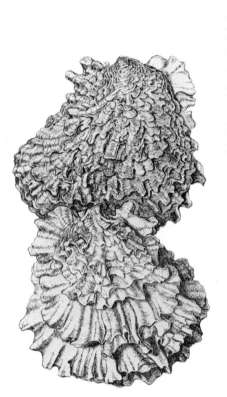

I remained thus until six in the morning, without Captain Nemo noticing me. The ship stood about a mile and a half from us, and with the first dawn of day the firing began afresh. The moment could not be far off when, the *Nautilus* attacking its adversary, my companions and myself should for ever leave this man. I was preparing to go down to remind them, when the second mounted the platform, accompanied by several sailors. Captain Nemo either did not, or would not, see them. Some steps were taken which might be called the signal for action. They were very simple. The iron balustrade around the platform was lowered, and the lantern and pilot cages were pushed within the shell until they were flush with the deck. The long surface of the steel cigar no longer offered a single point to check its manoeuvres. I returned to the saloon. The *Nautilus* still floated; some streaks of light were filtering through the liquid beds. With the undulations of the waves the windows were brightened by the red streaks of the rising sun, and this dreadful day of the 2d of June had dawned.

At five o'clock the log showed that the speed of the *Nautilus* was slackening, and I knew that it was allowing them to draw nearer. Besides, the reports were heard more distinctly, and the projectiles, labouring through the ambient water, were extinguished with a strange hissing noise.

"My friends," said I, "the moment is come. One grasp of the hand, and may God protect us!"

Ned Land was resolute, Conseil calm, myself so nervous that I knew not how to contain myself. We all passed into the library: but the moment I pushed the door opening on to the central staircase, I heard the upper panel close sharply. The Canadian rushed on to the stairs, but I stopped him. A well-known hissing noise told me that the water was running into the reservoirs, and in a few minutes the *Nautilus* was some yards beneath the surface of the waves. I understood the manoeuvre. It was too late to act. The *Nautilus* did not wish to strike at the impenetrable cuirass, but below the waterline, where the metallic covering no longer protected it.[9]

We were again imprisoned, unwilling witnesses of the dreadful drama that was preparing. We had scarcely time to reflect; taking refuge in my room, we looked at each other without speaking. A deep stupor had taken hold of my mind; thought seemed to stand still. I was in that painful state of expectation preceding a dreadful report. I waited, I listened, every sense was merged in that of hearing! The speed of the *Nautilus* was accelerated. It was preparing to rush. The whole ship trembled. Suddenly I screamed. I felt the shock, but comparatively light. I felt the penetrating power of the steel spur. I heard rattlings and scrapings. But the *Nautilus,* carried along by its propelling power, passed through the mass of the vessel, like a needle through sailcloth!

I could stand it no longer. Mad, out of my mind, I rushed from my room into the saloon. Captain Nemo was there, mute, gloomy, implacable; he was looking through the port panel. A large mass cast a shadow on the water; and that it might lose nothing of her agony, the *Nautilus* was going down into the abyss with her. Ten yards from me I saw the open shell through which the water was rushing with the noise of thunder, then the double line of guns and the netting. The bridge was covered with black agitated shadows.

The water was rising. The poor creatures were crowding the ratlines clinging to the masts, struggling under the water. It was a human ant-heap overtaken by the sea. Paralysed, stiffened with anguish, my hair standing on end, with eyes wide open, panting, without breath, and without voice, I too was watching! An irresistible attraction glued me to the glass! Suddenly an explosion took place. The compressed air blew up her decks, as if the magazines had caught fire. Then the unfortunate vessel sunk more rapidly. Her topmast, laden with victims, now appeared; then her spars, bending under the weight of men; and last of all, the top of her mainmast. Then the dark mass disappeared, and with it the dead crew, drawn down by the strong eddy.

I turned to Captain Nemo. That terrible avenger, a perfect archangel of hatred, was still looking. When all was over, he turned to his room, opened the door, and entered. I followed him with my eyes. On the end wall beneath his heroes,[10] I saw the portrait of a woman still young, and two little children. Captain Nemo looked at them for some moments, stretched his arms towards them, and kneeling down burst into deep sobs.

9. *no longer protected it* Nemo's diving *some yards* suggests that the warship is actually armored below the waterline as well. For example, in 1859 the British Admiralty had ordered two ironclads to be covered with armor 4½ inches thick and extending *6 feet below the waterline* and 21 feet above it. And that would serve as fair protection against surface boats equipped with rams. No warship was designed to meet a submarine ram.

10. *wall beneath his heroes* What heroes? Readers of the "standard translation" would never know, because Mercier Lewis cut the passage about Nemo's gallery of great nineteenth-century martyrs. Notice that Nemo includes his own family among those martyrs.

Why didn't Aronnax see the portrait of the woman and children earlier? Because at that time he was engaged in identifying pictures of people he could *recognize,* and in making an important generalization about their overall meaning. And it was perfectly in character for Aronnax to notice only the men.

PART 2: CHAPTER XXII

The Last Words of Captain Nemo

The panels had closed on this dreadful vision, but light had not returned to the saloon; all was silence and darkness within the *Nautilus*. At wonderful speed, a hundred feet beneath the water, it was leaving this desolate spot. Whither was it going? To the north or south? Where was the man flying to after such dreadful retaliation? I had returned to my room, where Ned and Conseil had remained silent enough. I felt an insurmountable horror for Captain Nemo. Whatever he had suffered at the hands of these men, he had no right to punish thus. He had made me, if not an accomplice, at least a witness of his vengeance. At eleven the electric light reappeared. I passed into the saloon. It was deserted. I consulted the different instruments. The *Nautilus* was flying northward at the rate of twenty-five miles an hour, now on the surface, and now thirty feet below it. On taking the bearings by the chart, I saw that we were passing the mouth of the Channel and that our course was hurrying us towards the northern seas at a frightful speed.

[And so I could catch only an occasional glimpse of the species at home in those waters. There were long-nosed sharks, hammer-head sharks, and spotted dog-fish; sea-horses that look like the knights on the chessboard; eels that writhe like the "serpents" in a fire-works display; armies of crabs moving sideways with pincers crossed on their shells; and schools of porpoises racing the *Nautilus*. But of course it was impossible to observe, study, and classify them.]

That night we had crossed two hundred leagues of the Atlantic. The shadows fell, and the sea was covered with darkness until the rising of the moon. I went to my room, but could not sleep. I was troubled with dreadful nightmares. The hor-

1. *the approach to the pole* As he heads toward the Pole, Aronnax naturally thinks of Poe's *fabulous* character. All France had thrilled to the polar adventures in *The Narrative of A. Gordon Pym* when it appeared in translation. Although Aronnax thinks of Poe's imagination as *overwrought* (not *foundered*), the fact is that Poe exerted a catalytic influence on European literature and a direct influence on Verne. We begin to get some idea of Verne's indebtedness to Poe when we look at Verne's works published in the years immediately before *Twenty Thousand Leagues*.

In his essay *Edgar Poe et ses oeuvres* (1864), Verne chooses to emphasize three themes in Poe's writing:

rible scene of destruction was continually before my eyes. From that day, who could tell into what part of the North Atlantic basin the *Nautilus* would take us? Still, with unaccountable speed. Still in the midst of these northern fogs. Would it touch at Spitzbergen, or on the shores of Nova Zembla? Should we explore those unknown seas, the White Sea, the Sea of Kara, the Gulf of Obi, the Archipelago of Liarrov, and the unknown coast of Asia? I could not say. I could no longer judge of the time that was passing. The clocks had been stopped on board. It seemed, as in polar countries, that night and day no longer followed their regular course. I felt myself being drawn into that strange region where the foundered imagination of Edgar Poe roamed at will. Like the fabulous Gordon Pym, at every moment I expected to see "That veiled human figure, of larger proportions than those of any inhabitant of the earth, thrown across the cataract which defends the approach to the pole." **1** I estimated (though, perhaps, I may be mistaken),—I estimated this adventurous course of the *Nautilus* to have lasted fifteen or twenty days. And I know not how much longer it might have lasted, had it not been for the catastrophe which ended this voyage. Of Captain Nemo I saw nothing whatever now, nor of his second. Not a man of the crew was visible for an instant. The *Nautilus* was almost incessantly under water. When we came to the surface to renew the air, the panels opened and shut mechanically. There were no more marks on the planisphere. I knew not where we were. And the Canadian, too, his strength and patience at an end, appeared no more. Conseil could not draw a word from him; and fearing that, in a dreadful fit of mad-

The hammerhead shark, specimens of which Aronnax "glimpsed" in the North Atlantic. Engraving from *Merveilles de la Nature* (1885) by A. E. Brehm.

the cryptographic, the lunar, the polar. These themes figure in the very novels Verne then has in the works: *Journey to the Center of the Earth* (1864), *From the Earth to the Moon* (1865), *The Adventures of Captain Hatteras* (1866). And Verne reveals a literary secret of Poe's which Verne has clearly adopted as his own. Pointing out that Poe uses "novel" situations, "out-of-the-way facts," and heroes with "strange personalities," Verne says: "And yet, throughout these impossibilities, there is an appearance of reality that makes everything credible to the reader." Verne has learned well from Poe that if you want to make a witch believable, mount her on an ordinary kitchen broom.

Poe figures like an offstage prompter in *Twenty Thousand Leagues*. Verne acknowledges his debt when he uses Poe as a reliable allusion to evoke desired effects. Aronnax mentions Poe in Part 1 to remind us of prodigious feats in swimming. And here he alludes to Poe not merely to suggest strange "impossibilities" in polar seas. He wants us to keep Poe in mind as we experience the outcome of the novel.

Verne will be obsessed by both Poe and Pym for decades to come. Poe ended *Pym* with these two sentences (why didn't Lewis go back to Poe's own English instead of retranslating Verne's French version?): "But there arose in our pathway a shrouded human figure, very far larger in its proportions than any dweller among men. And the hue of the skin of the figure was of the perfect whiteness of the snow."

Dissatisfied with his story, Poe left it unfinished at that point. Then later *Verne* becomes dissatisfied with what he considers to be unscientific aspects of Pym's adventures. Verne writes *The Sphinx of the Icefields* (1897) in which he completes Pym's narrative with natural explanations for all his Poe-ish adventures. For example, Poe's "shrouded human figure" turns out to be a great icy white mountain of magnetic ore which pulls all iron toward itself with irresistible force.

ness, he might kill himself, watched him with constant devotion. One morning (what date it was I could not say), I had fallen into a heavy sleep towards the early hours, a sleep both painful and unhealthy, when I suddenly awoke. Ned Land was leaning over me, saying, in a low voice, "We are going to fly."

I sat up.

"When shall we go?" I asked.

"To-morrow night.[2] All inspection on board the *Nautilus* seems to have ceased. All appear to be stupefied. You will be ready, sir?"

"Yes; where are we?"

"In sight of land. I took the reckoning this morning in the fog,—twenty miles to the east."

"What country is it?"

"I do not know; but whatever it is, we will take refuge there."

"Yes, Ned, yes. We will fly to-night, even if the sea should swallow us up."

"The sea is bad, the wind violent, but twenty miles in that light boat of the *Nautilus* does not frighten me. Unknown to the crew, I have been able to procure food and some bottles of water."

"I will follow you."

"But," continued the Canadian, "if I am surprised, I will defend myself; I will force them to kill me."

"We will die together, friend Ned."

I had made up my mind to all. The Canadian left me. I reached the platform, on which I could with difficulty support myself against the shock of the waves. The sky was threatening; but, as land was in those thick brown shadows, we must fly. I returned to the saloon, fearing and yet hoping to see Captain Nemo, wishing and yet not wishing to see him. What could I have said to him? Could I hide the involuntary horror with which he inspired me? No. It was better that I should not meet him face to face; better to forget him. And yet——. How long seemed that day, the last that I should pass in the *Nautilus*. I remained alone. Ned Land and Conseil avoided speaking, for fear of betraying themselves. At six I dined, but I was not hungry; I forced myself to eat in spite of my disgust, that I might not weaken myself. At half-past six Ned Land came to my room, saying, "We shall not see each other again before our departure. At ten the moon will not be risen. We will profit by the darkness. Come to the boat; Conseil and I will wait for you."

The Canadian went out without giving me time to answer.

2. *To-morrow night*   No, in the original, Ned says *"This very night."* Since Aronnax agrees by saying, just a moment later, *"We will fly tonight,"* why has this error stood uncorrected for over a century?

Conseil has now been able to practice classification of the great pipe-fish all the way across the Atlantic, and most of all in northern European waters. *Sygnathus acus* attains a length of eighteen inches, according to A. C. L. G. Günther in his *An Introduction to the Study of Fishes* (1880).

Wishing to verify the course of the *Nautilus,* I went to the saloon. We were running N.N.E. at frightful speed and more than fifty yards deep. I cast a last look on these wonders of nature, on the riches of art heaped up in this museum, upon the unrivalled collection destined to perish at the bottom of the sea, with him who had formed it. I wished to fix an indelible impression of it in my mind. I remained an hour thus, bathed in the light of that luminous ceiling, and passing in review those treasures shining under their glasses. Then I returned to my room.

I dressed myself in strong sea clothing. I collected my notes, placing them carefully about me. My heart beat loudly. I could not check its pulsations. Certainly my trouble and agitation would have betrayed me to Captain Nemo's eyes. What was he doing at this moment? I listened at the door of his room. I heard steps. Captain Nemo was there. He had not gone to rest. At every moment I expected to see him appear, and ask me why I wished to fly. I was constantly on the alert. My imagination magnified everything. The impression became at last so poignant, that I asked myself if it would not be better to go to the Captain's room, see him face to face and brave him with look and gesture.

It was the inspiration of a madman; fortunately I resisted the desire and stretched myself on my bed to quiet my bodily agitation. My nerves were somewhat calmer, but in my excited brain I saw over again all my existence on board the *Nautilus;* every incident either happy or unfortunate, which had happened since my disappearance from the *Abraham Lincoln;*—the submarine hunt, the Torres Straits, the savages of Papua, the running ashore, the coral cemetery, the passage of Suez, the Island of Santorin, the Cretan diver, Vigo Bay, Atlantis, the iceberg, the south pole, the imprisonment in the ice, the fight among the poulps, the storm in the Gulf Stream, the *Avenger,* and the horrible scene of the vessel sunk with all her crew. All these events passed before my eyes like scenes in a drama. Then Captain Nemo seemed to grow enormously, his features to assume superhuman proportions. He was no longer my equal, but a man of the waters, the genie of the sea.

It was then half-past nine. I held my head between my hands to keep it from bursting. I closed my eyes, I would not think any longer. There was another half hour to wait, another half hour of a nightmare, which might drive me mad.

At that moment I heard the distant strains of the organ, a sad harmony to an undefinable chaunt,[3] the wail of a soul longing to break these earthly bonds. I listened with every

3. *undefinable chaunt* Nemo is playing a simple, hymnlike, repetitive, deliberately monotonous melody of the kind used in liturgical chanting. *Chaunt* is archaic English for *chant.*

sense, scarcely breathing; plunged, like Captain Nemo, in that musical ecstasy, which was drawing him in spirit to the end of life.

Then a sudden thought terrified me. Captain Nemo had left his room. He was in the saloon, which I must cross to fly. There I should meet him for the last time. He would see me, perhaps speak to me. A gesture of his might destroy me, a single word chain me on board.

But ten was about to strike. The moment had come for me to leave my room, and join my companions.

I must not hesitate, even if Captain Nemo himself should rise before me. I opened my door carefully; and even then, as it turned on its hinges, it seemed to me to make a dreadful noise. Perhaps it only existed in my own imagination.

I crept along the dark stairs of the *Nautilus,* stopping at each step to check the beating of my heart. I reached the door of the saloon, and opened it gently. It was plunged in profound darkness. The strains of the organ sounded faintly. Captain Nemo was there. He did not see me. In the full light I do not think he would have noticed me, so entirely was he absorbed in the ecstasy.

I crept along the carpet, avoiding the slightest sound which might betray my presence. I was at least five minutes reaching the door, at the opposite side, opening into the library.

I was going to open it, when a sigh from Captain Nemo nailed me to the spot. I knew that he was rising. I could even see him, for the light from the library came through to the saloon. He came towards me silently, with his arms crossed, gliding like a spectre rather than walking. His breast was swelling with sobs; and I heard him murmur these words (the last which ever struck my ear)—

"Almighty God! Enough! Enough!"

Was it a confession of remorse which thus escaped from this man's conscience?

In desperation I rushed through the library, mounted the central staircase, and following the upper flight reached the boat. I crept through the opening, which had already admitted my two companions.

"Let us go! Let us go!" I exclaimed.

"Directly!" replied the Canadian.

The orifice in the plates of the *Nautilus* was first closed, and fastened down by means of a false key,**4** with which Ned Land had provided himself; the opening in the boat was also closed. The Canadian began to loosen the bolts which still held us to the submarine boat.

Suddenly a noise within was heard. Voices were answering

---

4. *a false key*   This is the same *mon-key wrench* that Ned spoke of earlier. Verne calls it, both times, *une clef anglaise,* an English wrench.

5. *The maëlstrom*   This *dreadful word* is the first ever uttered by the crew to be understood by Aronnax. One might wonder whether this means that once again, in a time of stress, the crew abandons its artificial language. On the other hand, it is characteristic of such languages that they adopt any word that has already attained international usage.

The word *maelstrom* is related to words meaning to *mill* or *grind,* and to the word for the product of the mill, the *meal.* And indeed the Maelstrom figures in Scandinavian folklore as "The Mill of the Sea." A legendary Danish king, Frodi, owned two huge magic millstones called Grotti. They ground out gold, peace, and good luck for him. But he became so greedy that the giant maids who turned the stones changed their spell and started grinding out warriors and bad luck. Their spell attracted a Viking named Mysinger. He slew Frodi, took the Grotti on his ship, each other loudly. What was the matter? Had they discovered our flight? I felt Ned Land slipping a dagger into my hand.

"Yes," I murmured, "we know how to die!"

The Canadian had stopped in his work. But one word many times repeated, a dreadful word, revealed the cause of the agitation spreading on board the *Nautilus*. It was not we the crew were looking after!

"The maëlstrom! **5** the maëlstrom!" I exclaimed.

The maëlstrom! Could a more dreadful word in a more dreadful situation have sounded in our ears! We were then upon the dangerous coast of Norway. Was the *Nautilus* being drawn into this gulf **6** at the moment our boat was going to leave its sides? We knew that at the tide the pent-up waters between the islands of Ferros and Loffoden rush with irresistible violence, forming a whirlpool from which no vessel ever escapes. From every point of the horizon enormous waves were meeting, forming a gulf justly called the "Navel of the Ocean," whose power of attraction extends to a distance of twelve miles. There, not only vessels, but whales are sacrificed, as well as white bears from the northern regions.**7**

It is thither that the *Nautilus,* voluntarily or involuntarily, had been run by the Captain.

It was describing a spiral, the circumference of which was lessening by degrees, and the boat, which was still fastened to its side, was carried along with giddy speed. I felt that sickly giddiness which arises from long-continued whirling round.

We were in dread. Our horror was at its height, circulation had stopped, all nervous influence was annihilated, and we were covered with cold sweat, like a sweat of agony! And what noise around our frail bark! What roarings repeated by the echo miles away! What an uproar was that of the waters broken on the sharp rocks at the bottom, where the hardest bodies are crushed, and trees worn away, "with all the fur rubbed off," according to the Norwegian phrase!

What a situation to be in! We rocked frightfully. The *Nautilus* defended itself like a human being. Its steel muscles cracked. Sometimes it seemed to stand upright, and we with it!

"We must hold on," said Ned, "and look after the bolts. We may still be saved if we stick to the *Nautilus*——"

He had not finished the words, when we heard a crashing noise, the bolts gave way, and the boat, torn from its groove, was hurled like a stone from a sling into the midst of the whirlpool.

My head struck on a piece of iron,**8** and with the violent shock, I lost all consciousness.

and ordered them to grind out salt, which was valuable in commerce. He, too, became greedy. The millstones ground out so much salt that his ship sank under the weight into the Norwegian Sea. The millstones made a deep hole in the sea floor.

It's the water rushing into that hole that creates the Maelstrom. And it's Mysinger's magic surplus of salt, dissolved in the water, that has made the seas salty.

6. *drawn into this gulf* Throughout Aronnax's discussions of the Maelstrom, whenever Mercier Lewis translates *gulf,* read *whirlpool.*

7. *bears from the northern regions* It has become fashionable to debunk the Maelstrom and we can only wonder how many more lives have been lost as a result. This strange contradiction figures even in the official *Sailing Directions for the Northwest and North Coasts of Norway.* Rumor, the *Directions* say, "has greatly exaggerated the importance of the Maelstrom."

But a few lines later there comes the warning that—as the strength of the tide increases, and as the sea becomes heavier between Mosken and Lofotodden—"no vessel should enter the Moskenstraumen."

Finally, there is the factual statement that in "the Saltström, boats and men have been drawn down by these vortices, and much loss of life has resulted."

Now we can see one additional reason why Verne reminded us of Poe earlier in this chapter. It does not damage Verne's credibility if the reader remembers Poe's "A Descent into the Maelstrom." For one thing, that tale dramatizes the terror those "vortices" hold for the fisherman and sailor. For another, Poe's story makes it clear that it is possible to escape death in the Maelstrom even if one's ship does go down.

8. *on a piece of iron* The entire dinghy is made of iron. In Verne, Aronnax says he hit his head on *une membrure de fer,* on one of the iron ribs.

PART 2: CHAPTER XXIII

Conclusion

1. *I cannot tell* However they escaped, the main factor in their luck is that the Maelstrom begins and ends with the tide.

The simplest explanation, then, would be that soon after they entered the Maelstrom, the tide changed and the whirlpools smoothed out. A second possibility is suggested in the *Sailing Directions* for the area: "Fishermen affirm that if they are aware of their approach" to one of the whirlpools and they "have time to throw an oar or other bulky body into it, they will get over it safely." For "when the continuity is broken and the whirling motion of the sea interrupted by something thrown into it, the water must rush in on all sides and fill up the cavity." Has the dinghy—flung suddenly into the whirlpool—served as the "bulky body"?

Verne's readers would think of a third possibility. The white-haired fisherman in Poe's "A Descent into the Maelstrom" claimed he had seen small objects going down more slowly than big ones: thus they might still be afloat when the whirlpool ceases. Aronnax & Co. were in a small dinghy.

2. *the history of his life* No, Aronnax is actually asking whether the sea will someday wash up on shore *Nemo's* manuscript, the one he was working on back on page 331. Aronnax's wondering whether we shall ever know Nemo's history is Verne's im-

Thus ends the voyage under the seas. What passed during that night—how the boat escaped from the eddies of the maëlstrom—how Ned Land, Conseil, and myself ever came out of the gulf, I cannot tell.**1**

But when I returned to consciousness, I was lying in a fisherman's hut, on the Loffoden Isles. My two companions, safe and sound, were near me holding my hands. We embraced each other heartily.

At that moment we could not think of returning to France. The means of communication between the north of Norway and the south are rare. And I am therefore obliged to wait for the steamboat running [twice] monthly from Cape North.

And among the worthy people who have so kindly received us, I revise my record of these adventures once more. Not a fact has been omitted, not a detail exaggerated. It is a faithful narrative of this incredible expedition in an element inaccessible to man, but to which Progress will one day open a road.

Shall I be believed? I do not know. And it matters little, after all. What I now affirm is, that I have a right to speak of these seas, under which, in less than ten months, I have crossed 20,000 leagues in that submarine tour of the world, which has revealed so many wonders [in the Pacific, the Indian Ocean, the Red Sea, the Mediterranean, the Atlantic, the antarctic and arctic seas].

But what has become of the *Nautilus?* Did it resist the pressure of the maëlstrom? Does Captain Nemo still live? And does he still follow under the ocean those frightful retaliations? Or, did he stop after that last hecatomb?

Will the waves one day carry to him this manuscript containing the history of his life? **2** Shall I ever know the name of this man? Will the missing vessel tell us by its nationality that of Captain Nemo? **3**

I hope so. And I also hope that his powerful vessel has conquered the sea at its most terrible gulf, and that the *Nautilus* has survived where so many other vessels have been lost! **4** If it be so—if Captain Nemo still inhabits the ocean, his adopted country, may hatred be appeased in that savage heart! May the contemplation of so many wonders extinguish for ever the spirit of vengeance! May the judge disappear, and the philosopher **5** continue the peaceful exploration of the sea! If his destiny be strange, it is also sublime. Have I not understood it myself? Have I not lived ten months of this unnatural life? And to the question asked by Ecclesiastes 3000 years ago,**6** "That which is far off and exceeding deep, who can find it out?" two men alone of all now living have the right to give an answer—

CAPTAIN NEMO AND MYSELF.

THE END

The death of Captain Nemo, at the age of sixty, as it was portrayed in the original edition of *The Mysterious Island* (1875). The scene is the saloon of the *Nautilus*. Standing nearest to Nemo is Captain Cyrus Harding, engineer of the Union Army. On his knees is the captain's servant, Neb. At the right are the other "colonists" in Harding's party. Escaping from their Confederate captors in a balloon, they had been driven to Nemo's isle by storms.

plicit promise to return to this question in a later book.

3. *nationality . . . of Captain Nemo* Verne and his publisher Hetzel corresponded for months about the possible political ties of Captain Nemo. Verne's letters make it clear that he himself thought of the "missing vessel" as British. But he did not assign a definite nationality to Nemo until late in *The Mysterious Island* (1875).

There the dying Nemo identifies himself as Prince Dakkar, son of the rajah of the Indian territory of Bundelkund. Dakkar served as a leader in the great Sepoy Revolt of 1857. He was "ten times wounded in twenty engagements," his family killed, the rebellion crushed, and "a price set upon his head" by the British Empire. He escaped with "some score of his most faithful followers" and took to the submarine life.

4. *vessels have been lost* Presumably the Maelstrom poses two dangers to a vessel: it might be sucked under and it might be dashed against the rocks. But the first of these was no problem to the *Nautilus*. So the panic of the crew must have been caused by their realizing that they were out of control on a treacherous coast.

5. *the judge . . . and the philosopher* Verne's symbolic end for Nemo is superb. In his despair, Nemo had fallen into a moral maelstrom and had to rouse himself to survive. As we learn in *The Mysterious Island*, he did extricate himself from the whirlpool and explored the seas for another thirteen years. Thus Verne makes his own use of the classical significance of the whirlpool as a metaphor for death and rebirth. To use Aronnax's terms, *the judge* did die and *the philosopher* was reborn.

6. *Ecclesiastes 3000 years ago* In the original, Aronnax says *6000 years ago,* reflecting the traditional belief about the date of the Bible. Mercier Lewis made this change apparently because he was aware of the new studies in biblical history.

AFTERWORD
Jules Verne, Rehabilitated

Now we can understand why adults on the Continent admire Verne and why Anglo-Americans disparage him as "fit merely for boys." Our reconstruction of Verne's masterpiece shows that European critics know precisely whereof they speak. As the German-born scientist Wernher von Braun puts it, Verne does do his scientific homework "so carefully." He is perfectly able to develop flesh-and-blood characters, although he may prefer to accent some of them as mythic archetypes. He is capable of creating mood and atmosphere, convincing motivation, and authentic dream states. He is mature in his ideological message, seeing science as intertwined with social and political circumstances. That is the real Verne, enjoyed by sea captains in Murmansk and social philosophers in Paris, and a perennial challenge to critics all over Europe.

The false "English" Verne proves to be a cynical creation of his early translators. One of those, the Reverend Lewis Page Mercier, master of arts from Oxford, working under the name of Mercier Lewis, cut 23 percent of Verne's text and committed hundreds of errors in translation. Many of his cuts seem ideologically motivated. Such tendentious carelessness has subjected a great man to generations of neglect by adult readers and to unmerited scorn by Anglo-American critics. Surely our reexamination here of just one of Verne's 65 volumes of fiction bears out Brian W. Aldiss's two hunches that "the poverty of English translations" has diminished Verne's chance of decent critical appraisal, and "a good translation . . . might effect a revaluation of his vast *oeuvre*."

Looking back over our restorations, corrections, and annotations, we see that Verne never failed to provide scientific underpinning for his story. T. L. Thomas to the contrary, Verne actually did meet head-on his responsibility for explaining how Nemo powered his *Nautilus*. Verne created an ingenious, humorous scene to teach the reader painlessly how scientists classify fishes. He explained the origin of pearls, the controversy over the nature of sponges, the basic assumptions of the modern scientific method, how life develops on an islet of naked rock, and the way scientists from Archimedes to Maury have shaped our views of Nature. But Anglo-American critics couldn't even begin to sense the scientific integrity in Verne because Lewis had cut all these passages and many others just as important. What he didn't cut he blurred, confusing bell with clock, manometer with compass, channel with canal, degree with date.

Again, our reconstituted story shows the mathematics in Verne's text to be accurate about 99 percent of the time. This was as much as an author of his day could hope for when herding hand-written technical materials into print. But almost every time that Verne's story swiveled on mathematics, or even on a single numerical value like the specific gravity of iron, Lewis muffed it. This gave rise to such sneering criticism as, "Verne can get away with almost anything, and he does."

Our restorations also enlarge our knowledge of Verne's gifts as prophet. He correctly predicted the modern technique of "driving" a submarine down deep with inclined planes, the development of submersible laboratories and even housing, the tactic of "crossing" the polar ice caps by sailing under them. He foresaw our need to obtain new foods from marine plants, and the ecological problems we would trigger by exterminating the manatee, the dugong, and the whale. He provided his characters with a special gun that anticipated both our modern compressed-air underwater guns and the electric "stun guns" developed in the 1970s.

But as a consequence of Mercier Lewis's cuts and blurs, a leading science-fiction magazine could run a diatribe against Verne that concluded with this ghastly canard about *Twenty Thousand Leagues:* ". . . there is not a single bit of valid speculation in it; none of its predictions has come true. The purported science in it is not semi-science or even pseudo-science. It is non-science."

So much in summary for the desecration of the science in Verne's science fiction. Now for the violation of the fiction.

Our restorations and corrections demonstrate that Verne was a master at plotting a story, creating suspense, and pacing his action. For example, he heightened the significance of the collision between the *Nautilus* and the *Scotia* by reviewing the safety record of the Cunard Line. By making Aronnax the kind of thinker who obsessively rehearses all the possibilities, Verne keeps us in a perpetual state of expectation. Regularly he plants ordinary seeds that later blossom into extraordinary circumstances; for example, Aronnax's early remark about his annoyance over Conseil's penchant for the third person. Mercier Lewis managed time and time again to botch Verne's artistry. For example, he emasculated the third-person joke; he cut the Cunard background; he omitted many of Aronnax's suspense-building hypotheses; he left out Aronnax's discovery of Nemo's gallery of heroes, so essential to understanding the captain's behavior. Lewis cut so much that the ebb and flow of the narrative—the very biorhythms of the fictional organism—are destroyed. As a consequence adult readers in English have regarded Verne's narration as "jerky," uneven, often amateurish.

Perhaps worst of all, Verne's characterization has been downgraded in translations like Lewis's. We simply cannot know the complexity of Aronnax's personality unless we are privy to his interior monologues about his shifting loyalties, his hypotheses about Nemo's intentions, his strategies to discover Nemo's nationality, and his fears of sharks and of Nemo's "madness." Yet Lewis considerably reduced or entirely omitted many such passages. We simply cannot feel as sympathetic toward Nemo as Verne was, if we do not know such crucial facts as who his heroes are and what the "law of the *Nautilus*" is. Lewis even cut the speech in which Nemo reveals the international character of his education.

Ned, too, is a much fuller person than most English readers could ever imagine. He is a passionate believer in civil rights and personal dignity; his behavior is powered equally by idealism and practical intelligence. Yet when Lewis is finished with Ned, the harpooner is all stomach and mouth, and there is little real motivation or build-up for his "tempers." In the reconstructed novel, we can see that while Conseil was intended only as a stock comic character, he is still a consistently successful one. In the original, for example, Conseil raises his head above the waves and asks the swimming Aronnax: "Did monsieur ring for me?" The grim parson translated that as "Did master call me?" Lewis either muffs or omits many of Conseil's jokes as well as the big joke that fate plays on Conseil when he is forced to call for help in the second person.

Our restorations and corrections make it clear that Verne knew well the separate artistic advantages of "developing" a character as opposed to using him as a type. With Conseil, for example, it is clear that Verne knew that some people want to be typed. They try hard to type themselves. Conseil deliberately takes refuge in the social stereotype of "the gentleman's gentleman." And Nemo, too, to the extent that he is a type, deliberately strikes the pose of the Romantic exile, the misunderstood Byronic hero fighting for Greek independence. Nemo serves also as the archetypal "perfect father" for the professor. Both Conseil and Nemo are further justified as types because they are seen as such through Aronnax's eyes, in both cases to satisfy his own psychological needs.

But Nemo also grows as a personality. He struggles with the contradictions between his love of absolute freedom and his passionate need for revenge. He actually binds himself to his ugly enemy by his need for retaliation, then yields to remorse, loses control, goes down in the moral maelstrom and, as Verne will show in *The Mysterious Island,* experiences the classic death-and-rebirth in the whirlpool. And Aronnax suffers through a full-blown identity crisis: He retreats like Jonah from world affairs into the whale's belly, switches loyalties from friend to friend's enemy, and finally tears himself away from the illusion of the "perfect father" to emerge as a stronger man.

Verne, at least in the reconstructed novel, proves to be talented in characterizing group mood and group behavior. Think of how little we would know of the three companions without their long man-to-man bull sessions over pearls and whales and that long scene in which, irritable and hungry, they probe each other's psyches. Mercier Lewis chose precisely those scenes for his biggest excisions. When Lewis finished, there was much less blood in Verne. I think this was why the critics could accuse Verne of "weak characterization," as Sam Moskowitz sums it up, and why Aldiss could say, "his characters are thin." Weakened and thinned, we now know, by translators like Mercier Lewis and Louis Mercier.

The restored novel shows that Verne's talent for metaphor and symbolism took him even into the realms of depth psychology. He describes Ned with exuberant phallic imagery: "powerful telescope that could double as a cannon always . . . ready to fire." He reveals Aronnax's perseveration about sharks through slips of the tongue. He explores Aronnax's unconscious desire to retreat to the womb in four separate analogies: his yearning to meet Jonah's whale, his happiness living like a snail in its shell, his happiness sleeping in a cave, and his dream of himself as a mollusk with now the cave as his shell. But alas, this dimension of Verne is almost entirely dynamited by Lewis who cut both the phallic imagery, the scene with the Freudian slips, and the cave scene with the dream. No wonder that Aldiss, unfamiliar with the full ebb and flow of Verne's action, his moody bull sessions, his dream symbolism, should say of Verne's writing, "His tone is flat."

Finally, the complete novel proves to be much richer in ideas than the "standard translation" had allowed us to think. Verne was not limited to expounding the concepts of Darwin and Maury. He was also concerned with such questions as the chance of reconciling Genesis with geological theory, the evils of imperialist treatment of aborigines, the nature of the so-called primitive peoples, and dishonesty in business. Mercier Lewis simply omitted most of Verne's crucial passages that explore these concerns.

In his other identity as the Reverend Lewis Page Mercier, the translator certainly expatiated on the text "By their fruits ye shall know them." By such logic we can reconstruct the translator himself. He was a humorless pastor and censor; he was contemptuous of science and technology; self-righteously he refused to consider any criticism of colonialism or commerce. Precisely not the person to be trusted with translating Verne.

But I promised that this would be an exposé with a happy ending. After a century of stultification in the Anglo-American world, Jules Verne now emerges vindicated. He should begin, with publication of *The Annotated Jules Verne,* to assume the stature among us that he enjoys among Continental readers.

WALTER JAMES MILLER

SELECTED BIBLIOGRAPHY

Listed here are selected writings—biographical, critical, historical, scientific, technical—likely to prove interesting to readers of *The Annotated Jules Verne*. Works from Verne's own period (1828–1905) show the state of knowledge in his day, the kinds of raw material out of which he fashioned his science fiction. Background works from our own day are helpful to us in judging the validity of Verne's predictions and in gaining new perspective on problems he tackled. Some writings listed are out of print and must be hunted down in libraries, antique shops, and rare-book stores. A few are not yet translated into English. Every one of these writings has figured in the shaping of *The Annotated Jules Verne*.

ALDISS, BRIAN W. *Billion Year Spree: The True History of Science Fiction.* Garden City, New York: Doubleday & Company, Inc., 1973.

ALLOTT, KENNETH. *Jules Verne.* New York: The Macmillan Company, 1941.

ALLOTTE DE LA FUŸE, MARGUERITE. *Jules Verne.* Translated by Erik de Mauny. New York: Coward-McCann, Inc., 1956.

BEACH, EDWARD L. "Man Beneath the Sea." Chapter 11 in C. P. Idyll, *Exploring the Ocean World* (see below).

BOWEN, FRANK C. *A Century of Atlantic Travel: 1830–1930.* Boston: Little, Brown, and Company, 1930.

———. *The Sea: Its History and Romance.* Four volumes. New York: Robert M. McBride and Company, 1927.

BRADY, WILLIAM N. *The Kedge-Anchor; or, Young Sailors' Assistant.* London: Sampson, Low, Son & Co., 1864.

CARRIER, RICK and BARBARA. *Dive: The Complete Book of Skin Diving.* Newly Revised by Charles Berlitz. New York: Funk & Wagnalls, 1973.

CARRIGHAR, SALLY. "Prince of the Sea." *The New York Times,* July 25, 1975.

CARRINGTON, RICHARD. *Mermaids and Mastodons: A Book of Natural and Unnatural History.* London: Chatto and Windus Ltd., 1957.

CARSON, RACHEL. *The Edge of the Sea.* Boston: Houghton Mifflin Company, 1955.

————. *The Sea Around Us*. Revised edition. New York: Oxford University Press, 1961.

CASTERET, NORBERT. *Ten Years under the Earth*. London: Thames and Hudson Limited, 1938.

CHESNEAUX, JEAN. *The Political and Social Ideas of Jules Verne*. Translated by Thomas Wikely. London: Thames and Hudson Limited, 1972.

CORLISS, WILLIAM R. *Mysteries Beneath the Sea*. New York: Thomas Y. Crowell Company, 1970.

COUSTEAU, JACQUES-YVES. *The Ocean World of Jacques Cousteau*. Twenty volumes. New York: The World Publishing Company, 1973.

CRITCHLOW, KEITH. *Into the Hidden Environment: The Oceans*. New York: The Viking Press, 1973.

CRONE, G. R., editor. *The Voyages of Discovery*. New York: G. P. Putnam's Sons, 1970.

DANA, JAMES D. *Corals and Coral Islands*. New York: Dodd & Mead, Publishers, 1872.

DARWIN, CHARLES. *The Structure and Distribution of Coral Reefs*. Third edition. New York: D. Appleton and Company, 1897.

DEAN, BASHFORD. *Fishes, Living and Fossil: An Outline of Their Forms and Probable Relationships*. New York: Macmillan and Co., 1895.

DIETZ, ROBERT S. "The Underwater Landscape." Chapter 2 in C. P. Idyll, *Exploring the Ocean World* (see below).

ERICSON, DAVID B., and GOESTA WOLLIN. *The Ever-Changing Sea*. New York: Alfred A. Knopf, Inc., 1970.

FORBES, EDWARD, and SYLVANUS HANLEY. *A History of British Mollusca, and Their Shells*. Four volumes. London: John Van Voorst, 1853.

FORBES, R. J., and E. J. DIJKSTERHUIS. *A History of Science and Technology*. Two volumes. Baltimore, Maryland: Penguin Books, Inc., 1963.

FRASER, ALISTAIR B., and WILLIAM H. MACH. "Mirages." *Scientific American,* January 1976.

FRONTINUS, SEXTUS JULIUS. "The Aqueducts of Rome." Chapter 3 in Walter James Miller, *Engineers as Writers* (see below).

GRAVES, ROBERT. *The Greek Myths*. Two volumes. Baltimore, Maryland: Penguin Books, Inc., 1955.

GÜNTHER, ALBERT C. L. G. *An Introduction to the Study of Fishes*. Edinburgh: Adam & Charles Black, 1880.

HUGO, VICTOR. *The Toilers of the Sea*. Translated by Isabel F. Hapgood. New York: The Heritage Press, 1961.

IDYLL, C. P., editor. *Exploring the Ocean World: A History of Oceanography*. Revised. New York: Thomas Y. Crowell Company, 1972.

JORDAN, DAVID STARR. *A Guide to the Study of Fishes*. Two volumes. New York: Henry Holt and Company, 1905.

————, and HAROLD HEATH. *Animal Forms: A Text-Book of Zoology*. New York: D. Appleton and Company, 1902.

KANE, JULIAN. "Surtsey: An Island Emerges." *Natural History,* March 1967.

LAKE, SIMON P. *The Autobiography of Simon Lake*. New York: Appleton-Century-Crofts, 1938.

LANE, CHARLES E. "Biology of the Sea." Chapter 3 in C. P. Idyll, *Exploring the Ocean World* (see above).

LOW, A. M. *The Submarine at War.* New York: Sheridan House, Inc., 1942.

MAGINNIS, ARTHUR J. *The Atlantic Ferry, Its Ships, Men, and Working.* London: Whittaker and Co., 1893.

MAURY, MATTHEW FONTAINE. *The Physical Geography of the Sea and Its Meteorology.* Edited by John Leighly. Cambridge, Massachusetts: The Belknap Press of Harvard University Press, 1963.

MILLER, WALTER JAMES. *Engineers as Writers.* New York: D. Van Nostrand Company, Inc., 1953. Freeport, New York: Books for Libraries Press, 1971.

MITCHELL, S. AUGUSTUS. *Mitchell's School Geography.* Revised edition. Philadelphia: Thomas, Cowperthwaite & Co., 1863.

MORÉ, MARCEL. *Nouvelles explorations de Jules Verne.* Paris: Gallimard, 1963.

————. *Le très curieux Jules Verne.* Paris: Gallimard, 1960.

MOSKOWITZ, SAM. *Explorers of the Infinite: Shapers of Science Fiction.* Cleveland and New York: The World Publishing Company, 1963.

PETERSON, MENDEL. "Underwater Archaeology." Chapter 9 in C. P. Idyll, *Exploring the Ocean World* (see above).

PICCARD, AUGUSTE. *Earth, Sky, and Sea.* New York: Oxford University Press, 1956.

PICCARD, JACQUES, and ROBERT S. DIETZ. *Seven Miles Down.* New York: G. P. Putnam's Sons, 1960.

RANKIN, HUGH F. *The Golden Age of Piracy.* New York: Holt, Rinehart, and Winston, 1969.

Reader's Digest. Secrets of the Seas. Pleasantville, New York: The Reader's Digest Association, Inc., 1972.

RUCKER, JAMES B. "Physics of the Sea." Chapter 4 in C. P. Idyll, *Exploring the Ocean World* (see above).

SCHLEE, SUSAN. *The Edge of an Unfamiliar World: A History of Oceanography.* New York: E. P. Dutton & Co., Inc., 1973.

SHENTON, EDWARD H. *Diving for Science: The Story of the Deep Submersible.* New York: W. W. Norton & Co., Inc., 1972.

SUK KI HONG and HERMAN RAHN. "The Diving Women of Korea and Japan." *Scientific American,* May 1967.

THOMAS, THEODORE L. "The Watery Wonders of Captain Nemo." *Galaxy Magazine,* December 1961.

TYLER, DAVID BUDLONG. *Steam Conquers the Atlantic.* New York: D. Appleton-Century Company, Incorporated, 1939.

WERTENBAKER, WILLIAM. *The Floor of the Sea.* Boston: Little, Brown, and Company, 1974.

WOLFE, GERARD R. *New York: A Guide to the Metropolis.* New York: New York University Press, 1975.

YOUNG, J. Z. "Save the Whales!" *The New York Review of Books,* July 17, 1975.

ZIM, HERBERT S. *Submarines: The Story of Undersea Boats.* New York: Harcourt, Brace and Company, 1942.